Preface

This Test Bank contains more than 3,800 questions carefully constructed to help you evaluate your students' understanding of *The Developing Person Through the Life Span,* Sixth Edition. Information about the format and features of the Test Bank follows.

1. Questions are organized by major chapter headings. The specific topic of each question and the text page where the answer is found precede each question. You will find it easy to select those questions that exactly match your reading assignments and the emphasis of your course. You can provide your students with a page reference to the textbook information that supports each answer. Note that items based on information presented in figures, tables, or boxes are clearly designated. Multiple questions are provided for the many key concepts, allowing instructors to create multiple versions of an exam or to test the same material on a midterm and a final.

2. Multiple choice items of a wide range of difficulty are included. Of course, the most reliable guide to the level of difficulty for test questions is the combination of your own experience in teaching the course and your awareness of your students' backgrounds. However, to provide general guidance, questions have been rated for difficulty by experienced teachers, including ourselves. Two factors have been taken into account: (1) the degree to which the text emphasizes the particular fact or concept, (2) whether the item can be answered by memorization of specific facts or numbers, or whether it requires careful reasoning. Items labeled as Easy tend to concentrate on direct recall of information, while items labeled as Moderate and Difficult tend to require a deeper understanding of the material and the ability to apply the concepts to real-world examples.

3. For those instructors who wish to vary their testing format, a selection of short-answer questions— true-or-false, fill-in-the-blanks—follow the multiple-choice section in each chapter. True-or-false questions are generally easier than multiple-choice questions for the student who has studied well, but they do require a logical turn of mind as well as knowledge of the material. Fill-in-the-blank questions require more active participation and accurate memory than the other testing formats and thus are more difficult. To make this type of test somewhat easier, many instructors provide students with a list that includes all the correct words and some distracters.

4. A selection of essay questions and applications completes each chapter of the Test Bank. (Answer guidelines for these questions are given at the back of this volume.) Essay questions require well-organized effort from students and thoughtful time-consuming evaluating by instructors. However, given the importance of helping students improve their writing and critical-thinking skills, essays are essential elements of a good education. You may want to assign "open book" questions so that students have an opportunity to do their best work. Because instructors' preferences for types of essay questions and topics covered vary greatly, the suggested questions at the end of each chapter of the Test Bank have been written so as to be useful resources for constructing your own questions.

5. A computerized version of the Text Bank is available for use on a Windows and Macintosh Dual-Platform CD-ROM. Created by Brownstone, the Diploma software guides professors step-by-step through the process of creating a test and allows them to add an unlimited number of questions, edit or scramble questions, format a test, and include pictures, equations, and multimedia links. The accompanying gradebook enables them to record students' grades throughout the course, and includes the capacity to sort student records, view detailed analyses of test items, curve tests, generate reports, add weights to grades, and more. The CD provides the access point for Diploma Online Testing, as well as for Blackboard- and WebCT-formatted versions of this Test Bank. For more information on Diploma, please visit Brownstone's Web site: http://www.brownstone.net/.

6. All questions have been written by teachers and by professionals with a particular interest in testing. In addition to the hundreds of new questions written by Robert R. Rainey and Jill L. Saxon, this edition contains the best questions from our previous Test Banks. For the original questions, we thank Karen Macrae, Clark E. Alexander, David Baskind, Carolyn J. Meyer, Diane Villwock, Joan Brown, Caroline Latham, Gary Ritchey, Anne Nowlin, James Eison, Katherine Van Giffen, Paul Kaplan, and Richard Scott. We hope that our work has resulted in a high-quality tool that will be of help to you in both testing and teaching.

We welcome your comments, or criticisms, and suggestions for improving the Test Bank.

Kathleen Stassen Berger
March 2004

Acknowledgments

The authors are deeply grateful to Worth Publishers for the opportunity to work on this endeavor. We wish to acknowledge the work of all previous contributors to earlier Test Banks to accompany Berger textbooks. For their support, encouragement, and editorial input, we would also like to thank Danielle Pucci, Eve Conte, and Jessica Bayne of Worth Publishers, as well as Stacey Alexander for her production expertise.

We hope instructors find this Test Bank valuable and are able to use it as an integral part of their student evaluation plan. We welcome any suggestions for improvement.

Robert R. Rainey
Jill L. Saxon
March 2004

TEST BANK

TEST BANK

to accompany

Kathleen Stassen Berger

The Developing Person Through the Life Span

Sixth Edition

Kathleen Stassen Berger

Bronx Community College
City University of New York

Robert R. Rainey

Florida Community College
at Jacksonville

Jill L. Saxon, Ph.D.

WORTH PUBLISHERS

TEST BANK
by Kathleen Stassen Berger, Robert R. Rainey, and Jill L. Saxon

to accompany

Berger: The Developing Person Through the Life Span, Sixth Edition

ISBN: 0-7167-0311-4 (EAN: 9780716703112)

First Printing, 2004

Worth Publishers
41 Madison Avenue
New York, NY 10010
www.worthpublishers.com

Contents

Testing Tips by Kathleen Stassen Berger

Ideally, your students read the text assignments regularly, pay close attention to lectures, participate in class discussions, and use tests to consolidate and evaluate their knowledge. You, in turn, use test results to adjust your teaching to better meet your students' needs. Experience has led me to use several strategies that help to accomplish these goals, and I offer these suggestions in the hope that they may help you, too.

1.   Frequent testing Reviewing course material on a regular schedule increases the likelihood that students will keep up with their work and decreases anxiety about any one test. Brief chapter quizzes designed to be easy for everyone who studied the chapter are effective in motivating students to read each assignment before the next class.

If the Study Guide is required, quiz and test questions can be taken directly from it—an added incentive for students to complete this part of their course work.

2.   Speedy feedback Grading tests in time to return them at the next class session increases the likelihood that students will learn from their mistakes and allows them to gain confidence as they move to new material.

3.   Review before a test A review of key ideas, followed by a practice test, can help students to focus their attention on the most important concepts and the supporting facts. An added benefit is that nervous students may relax a bit when they see that they are well prepared, while those who are too relaxed about their studies may realize it is time to develop better study skills.

4.   Review test answers in class Especially at the beginning of the term, it is important to allot class time to reviewing tests when you return them. Students often make mistakes that are unrelated to their knowledge of the material—in reading the questions, in reasoning about multiple-choice or true-or-false questions, or in organizing their answers to essay questions. Class time devoted to showing them how to read, write, and think more carefully will help to develop these skills. Handing out copies of some of the better essays, as well as some of the less adequate ones, and having students identify the differences between them, can help students to develop critical-thinking skills and keener judgment.

5.   Have students share their study tips After the first test you may ask students to tell about those study techniques that worked well for them and those that did not. This can be done in a class discussion or in small groups, or students can anonymously submit written descriptions of their study strategies, which can then be read to the class. Some students may confess that they did not read the textbook at all, yet still expected to do well. But others will describe their success in using good study techniques, such as SQ3R (see the Study Guide) or efficient scheduling of their time. Your class discussions can help students to discern the nature and importance of good study habits.

6.   "Tricky" questions Multiple-choice questions are often perceived as tricky, and, despite our best efforts, some of them are. There are several ways to deal with this problem. As you mark the tests, note any questions that more than half the class gets wrong. Then look closely at the question and answer; perhaps two answers could be considered correct, perhaps the question should be designated as "extra credit" (giving extra points to students who get the answer right but not deducting points from those who get it wrong). Perhaps the question covers material that has not been emphasized in the course or that students have not completely grasped because of its difficulty. You may decide that the question should not count at all. Your taking note of questions that pose particular difficulties and adjusting scores to compensate will make students realize that you pay attention to their work and do your best to be fair. In addition, such adjustments will help to avoid lengthy arguments about questions that many students get wrong.

7. Answer justification Some instructors have implemented a procedure called answer justification, abbreviated AJ. If students are confused by a multiple-choice question or its possible answers but believe they know the required information, they can write AJ beside the question and explain why they chose a particular answer on the back of the sheet. Instructors report that students are pleased with this option. Since the average student uses answer justification less than twice a term, and since the answer justified is often the correct one anyway, this process does not add excessively to the time required for grading. Of the incorrect answers justified, between one-eighth and one-third receive partial credit, depending on the instructor's criteria. For more information see:

Dodd, David K., and *Leal, Linda.* (1988). Answer justification: Removing the "trick" from multiple choice questions. *Teaching of Psychology, 15,* 37–38.

Nield, A. F., and *Wintre, M. G.* (1986). Multiple-choice questions with an option to comment: Student attitudes and use. *Teaching of Psychology, 13,* 196–199.

8. Curving grades Each institution and each department has norms for grading. If your grades tend to be much higher than those given by other instructors (because you want to encourage students, perhaps) or much lower (because you want to keep standards high), your students may feel less in control of their achievement, thus less motivated to study, with the result that they will learn less. Ideally, a department discusses grading philosophy, practice, and problems from time to time, and shared ideas result in a better, more consistent learning process for students.

Should you need to adjust your grades, the better methods include changing your scoring system, for example, by assigning each multiple-choice question a point value of either one or two, or by scoring the essays leniently or rigorously, or by designating some items as extra credit. These methods cause fewer problems than writing a test that is designed to be unusually difficult or easy (level of difficulty is not easy to predict) or curving the raw scores after tests have been corrected. (Students are suspicious if they score much lower than they expected and consider it an unearned gift if they score much higher.)

9. A final exam that is cumulative and includes essays These exams are demanding for students to take and for instructors to grade, but I am convinced that this type of examination can help to achieve the ultimate goal of the course—learning that is maintained after the term is over. I have found that much of the stress associated with a cumulative test can be reduced by class review, by study sheets that list terms and concepts likely to be covered, and by using essay questions drawn from a list of questions that the students know (and perhaps helped to write) in advance.

If, in the course of your teaching experience, you have developed effective testing techniques, I would be pleased to hear about them.

KSB

TEST BANK

CHAPTER 1 Introduction

MULTIPLE-CHOICE QUESTIONS

Studying the Life Span: Five Characteristics

Studying the Life Span: Five Characteristics, p. 3
Diff: M, Ans: e
1.   The study of human development involves examining which of the following?
   a.   *how* people change as they grow older
   b.   *how* people remain the same as they grow older
   c.   *why* people change as they grow older
   d.   *why* people remain the same as they grow older
   e.   all of the above

Studying the Life Span: Five Characteristics, p. 3
Diff: E, Ans: c
2.   Which of the following is the *best* description of what the study of human development attempts to understand?
   a.   how and why people who develop in different countries are different
   b.   how children learn to speak and understand language
   c.   how and why people change and stay the same across the lifespan
   d.   how humans and animals are similar and different

Studying the Life Span: Five Characteristics, pp. 3-4
Diff: E, Ans: c
3.   Which of the following is NOT a crucial element of the study of human development?
   a.   The focus is on both young and old people.
   b.   It is a science.
   c.   The focus is on middle-class American people.
   d.   It involves change over time.

Studying the Life Span: Five Characteristics, pp. 3-4
Diff: H, Ans: a
4.   Which of the following is true of the life-span perspective?
   a.   It examines the links between childhood and adulthood.
   b.   It is only concerned with adulthood and old age.
   c.   It is primarily concerned with characteristics of individuals that remain the same.
   d.   It is interested in universalities across people, not in their differences.

Studying the Life Span: Five Characteristics, p. 4
Diff: M, Ans: a 5

5. The study of human development begins at what point in humans' lives?
    a. conception
    b. birth
    c. childhood
    d. adulthood

Studying the Life Span: Five Characteristics, p. 4
Diff: E, Ans: b

6. A manner of studying human development that takes into account every moment of life is referred to as the:
    a. plastic nature of development.
    b. dynamic systems theory.
    c. life-span perspective.
    d. multicontextual effect.

Studying the Life Span: Five Characteristics, p. 4
Diff: M, Ans: b

7. Which of the following is an example of something that remains continuous, or stable, across the lifespan?
    a. physical size
    b. gender
    c. language skills
    d. all of the above

Studying the Life Span: Five Characteristics, p. 4
Diff: E, Ans: d

8. Which of the following is NOT a characteristic of human development emphasized by the life-span perspective?
    a. multicontextual
    b. multidisciplinary
    c. plasticity
    d. discontinuous

Multidirectional, p. 5
Diff: E, Ans: a

9. The notion that development involves gains and losses that do not always occur in a straight line refers to which characteristic of the life-span perspective?
    a. multidirectional
    b. multidisciplinary
    c. plasticity
    d. multicontextual

Multidirectional, p. 5 (Fig. 1.1)
Diff: H, Ans: d

10. Which of the following directions is an impossible direction for development to occur?
    a. erratic
    b. stable
    c. decline
    d. none of the above

Multidirectional, p. 5
Diff: M, Ans: b
11.   Which of the following refers to the process of change within each individual and social group, with each change connected to every other development in each individual and social group?
       a.   cohort
       b.   dynamic systems
       c.   life-span perspective
       d.   multicultural

Multidirectional, p. 5
Diff: H, Ans: e
12.   In which of the following domains is development linear?
       a.   parent-child attachment
       b.   physical growth
       c.   intellectual growth
       d.   all of the above
       e.   none of the above

Multidirectional, p. 5
Diff: H, Ans: d
13.   According to the view of development as a result of dynamic systems, which of the following could influence a child's physical development?
       a.   age
       b.   historical context
       c.   individual likes and dislikes
       d.   all of the above

Multidirectional, p. 6
Diff: E, Ans: a
14.   The notion that a small change has a large potential power is referred to as the:
       a.   butterfly effect.
       b.   dynamic systems approach.
       c.   life-span perspective.
       d.   scientific method.

Multidirectional, p. 6
Diff: H, Ans: c
15.   Which of the following is an application of the butterfly effect?
       a.   The death of her mother when Isabel was age 8 influenced her to experience depression at age 20.
       b.   Minerva's parents' divorce when she was an infant had less of an influence on Minerva's self-esteem than it did on her older sister's self-esteem.
       c.   A bully's one-time comment to nine-year-old Alex that he smelled dirty influenced Alex to be the first person in his family to finish high school and to pull himself out of poverty.
       d.   Living in Austria during the Holocaust influenced Martin to become charitable as an old man.

Multicontextual, p. 6
Diff: E, Ans: d
16.   Which of the following is NOT considered a major contextual influence on development?
       a.   culture
       b.   history
       c.   social class
       d.   genetics

Multicontextual, p. 7
Diff: E, Ans: b
17.   Cohort refers to a group of people who:
      a.   hold the same political beliefs.
      b.   are born within a few years of one another.
      c.   support each other in times of stress.
      d.   participate in a scientific experiment.

Multicontextual, p. 7
Diff: E, Ans: c
18.   When people belong to different cohorts, they differ in:
      a.   membership in community groups.
      b.   socioeconomic status.
      c.   age group or generation.
      d.   ethnic or racial groups.

Multicontextual, p. 7
Diff: M, Ans: d
19.   You and your high school classmates are part of the same:
      a.   social construction.
      b.   context.
      c.   socioeconomic status.
      d.   cohort.

Multicontextual, p. 7
Diff: M, Ans: a
20.   Which of the following groups is considered a cohort?
      a.   individuals born in the 1960s
      b.   individuals born in Asia
      c.   women who vote
      d.   men on welfare

Multicontextual, p. 7
Diff: M, Ans: c
21.   The concept of a cohort is important because individuals in the same cohort experience the same _____ circumstances.
      a.   educational
      b.   socioeconomic
      c.   historical
      d.   familial

Multicontextual, p. 7
Diff: H, Ans: b
22.   Which of the following is NOT true of the historical context?
      a.   Its impact varies with age.
      b.   It rarely affects individual development.
      c.   It involves economic circumstances.
      d.   It involves public events and popular trends.

Multicontextual, p. 7
Diff: M, Ans: c

23. Dora, who is 75 years old, disagrees completely with her teenage granddaughter about the proper role of women. Their arguments are most likely to arise from differences in which of the following contexts?
    a. cultural
    b. ethnic
    c. historical
    d. socioeconomic

Multicontextual, p. 7
Diff: M, Ans: b

24. Social constructions often vary by:
    a. family.
    b. cohort.
    c. physical health status.
    d. intelligence.

Multicontextual, p. 7
Diff: H, Ans: a

25. Many assumptions about how things "should be", such as that the husband should be the major wage earner in a married relationship, are:
    a. social constructions.
    b. cultural artifacts.
    c. universally accepted.
    d. objective reality.

Multicontextual, p. 7
Diff: M, Ans: d

26. Which of the following is NOT considered part of the historical context?
    a. political circumstances
    b. economic circumstances
    c. technological circumstances
    d. biological circumstances

Multicontextual, p. 9
Diff: E, Ans: c

27. Socioeconomic status refers to an individual's:
    a. culture.
    b. ethnicity.
    c. social class.
    d. race.

Multicontextual, p. 9
Diff: H, Ans: a

28. Which of the following is NOT included in an individual's socioeconomic status?
    a. ethnicity
    b. level of education
    c. neighborhood
    d. occupation

Multicontextual, p. 9
Diff: H, Ans: d

29. Which of the following is a true statement about collective efficacy?
    a. The collective efficacy in a neighborhood is a strong predictor of the emotional health of those living there.
    b. Religious institutions can enhance collective efficacy.
    c. Families benefit from neighborhoods with high levels of collective efficacy.
    d. All of the above are true statements about collective efficacy.

Multicontextual, p. 9
Diff: H, Ans: b

30. Which of the following is a true statement about the influence of the neighborhood context on families living in poverty?
    a. All individuals living in poverty are highly susceptible to severe problems, such as child abuse and drug addiction.
    b. The collective efficacy of a neighborhood group is a stronger predictor of individuals' emotional health than is average income.
    c. Religious institutions often enhance the poor effects of poverty on individuals.
    d. Raising resilient children in poverty is nearly impossible.

Multicontextual, p. 10
Diff: E, Ans: a

31. The values, assumptions, customs, clothing, technologies, and art that a group of people have developed over the years as a design for living are referred to as their:
    a. culture.
    b. cohort.
    c. ethnicity.
    d. environment.

Multicontextual, p. 10
Diff: M, Ans: c

32. Which of the following is NOT an example of a cultural phenomenon?
    a. Children in the United States begin formal school at age five.
    b. Most television viewing done by American adults occurs in the evening.
    c. American women tend to be shorter than American men.
    d. In American families, babies usually sleep in a crib in a room separate from their parents.

Multicontextual, p. 11
Diff: H, Ans: b

33. Differences among cultures in sleeping practices illustrate which of the following?
    a. Sleeping practices can heavily influence how successful children become as adults.
    b. Individuals are influenced by cultural values without even realizing it.
    c. Sleeping practices are similar in different cultures and therefore must be evolutionary.
    d. People in different cultures generally view other cultures' practices to be just as acceptable as their own.

Multicontextual, p. 11
Diff: M, Ans: c

34. Differences among cultures in sleeping practices generally reflect which of the following?
    a. cultural differences in parents' concern for their children
    b. genetic differences among ethnic groups
    c. differences in the values important in the cultures
    d. all of the above

Multicultural, p. 11
Diff: E, Ans: d

35. A researcher interested in making a multicultural comparison would be most likely to compare which of the following?
   a. males and females
   b. eight-year-olds and eighteen-year-olds
   c. computer users and non-users
   d. Australians and Canadians

Multicultural, p. 12
Diff: H, Ans: b

36. A multicultural study of the relation between women's income level and their marriage prospects indicated which of the following?
   a. Women of all income levels have similar marriage prospects in all cultures.
   b. Whether higher-income women were less likely to marry was dependent on cultural circumstances.
   c. All cultures demonstrated the link between high-income women and *decreased* marriage prospects.
   d. All cultures demonstrated the link between high-income women and *increased* marriage prospects.

Multicultural, p. 12
Diff: H, Ans: a

37. Which of the following groups of adolescents was NOT included in the study of the effect of sleeping in a Children's House on Israeli kibbutz-raised children's relations with their family members?
   a. American adolescents who slept in a family bed when they were children
   b. Israeli kibbutz-raised adolescents who had never slept in a Children's House
   c. Israeli kibbutz-raised adolescents who had slept in a Children's House only at a young age
   d. Israeli city-dwelling adolescents who had never lived on a kibbutz

Multicultural, p. 13
Diff: M, Ans: d

38. If a group of people have the same ancestors, religion, and language, they are said to be part of the same:
   a. nation.
   b. racial group.
   c. culture.
   d. ethnic group.

Multicultural, pp. 13-14
Diff: H, Ans: c

39. Ethnic categories are intended to have their basis in all of the following EXCEPT:
   a. sociology.
   b. psychology.
   c. biology.
   d. history.

Multicultural, p. 14
Diff: H, Ans: a

40. Which of the following is a true statement about the concept of race?
   a. In and of itself, it does not affect development.
   b. It is not intended to categorize people biologically.
   c. It includes a culture.
   d. It is more important to development than ethnicity.

Multicultural, p. 14
Diff: M, Ans: b
41.   Which of the following is intended to categorize people on the basis of genetic differences and differences in appearance?
      a.   ethnicity
      b.   race
      c.   SES
      d.   none of the above

Multidisciplinary, p. 14
Diff: E, Ans: a
42.   The study of human development is often divided into three domains:
      a.   biosocial, cognitive, and psychosocial.
      b.   racial, ethnic, and cultural.
      c.   family, neighborhood, and school.
      d.   prenatal period, childhood, and old age.

Plasticity, p. 15
Diff: E, Ans: d
43.   The notion of plasticity refers to the:
      a.   fact that many academic fields contribute data and insight to the science of development.
      b.   universals and specifics of human development in many cultural settings.
      c.   vast array of contexts in which development occurs.
      d.   ability of human traits to be altered during development.

In Person: My Nephew David, pp. 16-17
Diff: H, Ans: b
44.   The case study of the textbook author's nephew, David, illustrates which of the following?
      a.   how poverty can disrupt many facets of development
      b.   the plastic nature of human traits
      c.   how ethnic and cultural values can interrupt the normal course of development
      d.   the inevitable fate of some individuals who are born with severe disabilities

In Person: My Nephew David, pp. 16-17
Diff: M, Ans: c
45.   The case study of the textbook author's nephew, David, demonstrates that:
      a.   severely disabled children should always be cared for in special institutions.
      b.   retarded children should always be mainstreamed.
      c.   severely disabled children may live reasonably normal lives.
      d.   b and c

The Person Within the Context, p. 17
Diff: H, Ans: d
46.   Which of the following is a true statement about human development?
      a.   If you know an individual's ethnicity, family dynamics, and socioeconomic status, it is easy to predict how he or she will develop.
      b.   There are many people whose traits fit into the statistical average of an individual of their age.
      c.   Both a and b are true statements.
      d.   Neither a nor b is a true statement.

Developmental Study as a Science

The Scientific Method, pp. 18-19
Diff: M, Ans: c
47. The scientific method:
   a.   is used only for "hard" sciences, such as physics.
   b.   always involves conducting experiments.
   c.   requires systematical evaluation of hypotheses.
   d.   is not generally used in psychology, as it is quite susceptible to researcher bias.

The Scientific Method, p. 19
Diff: E, Ans: a
48. The first step in the scientific method involves:
   a.   forming a research question.
   b.   running an experiment.
   c.   selecting a group of participants.
   d.   asking people to participate in a research project.

The Scientific Method, p. 19
Diff: M, Ans: d
49. Within the scientific method, once a researcher has a research question, her next step is to:
   a.   draw conclusions.
   b.   run an experiment.
   c.   select a group of participants.
   d.   develop a hypothesis.

The Scientific Method, p. 19
Diff: M, Ans: b
50. John is about to test his idea that giving children a good breakfast helps them learn. John's idea is a(n):
   a.   theory.
   b.   hypothesis.
   c.   experiment.
   d.   research question.

The Scientific Method, p. 19
Diff: M, Ans: b
51. Which of the following is a hypothesis?
   a.   Do children miss more days of school in the winter or in the spring?
   b.   Children who like school miss fewer days than children who do not like school.
   c.   What factors are involved in keeping children from missing too much school?
   d.   Parents should make sure their kids do not miss too much school.

The Scientific Method, p. 19
Diff: H, Ans: a
52. Which of the following is a research question?
   a.   Do children miss more days of school in the winter or in the spring?
   b.   Children who like school miss fewer days than children who do not like school.
   c.   Should parents make sure their kids do not miss too much school?
   d.   none of the above

The Scientific Method, p. 19
Diff: E, Ans: d
53. Which of the following does NOT need to occur prior to drawing conclusions from a research study conducted in accordance with the scientific method?
    a. testing of the hypothesis
    b. development of a hypothesis
    c. formulation of a research question
    d. replication of the study

The Scientific Method, p. 19
Diff: H, Ans: b
54. A psychology professor publishes the results of her research in a professional journal. By doing so, she:
    a. is able to draw conclusions.
    b. allows other scientists to evaluate or build on her experiment.
    c. converts basic science into applied science.
    d. ensures that her findings will not be replicated.

The Scientific Method, p. 19
Diff: E, Ans: c
55. When we replicate a study, we:
    a. find ways of determining if our results are statistically significant.
    b. observe people in their natural environment.
    c. repeat a previous study to determine whether we will get similar results.
    d. learn a lot about one particular individual.

Research Methods, p. 19
Diff: H, Ans: b
56. If students complain that this exam does not really measure their understanding of Chapter One, they are complaining about the exam's:
    a. statistical significance.
    b. validity.
    c. generalizability.
    d. accuracy.

Research Methods, p. 19
Diff: H, Ans: b
57. A researcher is interested in children's levels of aggression at school. One of the study's participants is Roger, who often hits other children on the school playground. The laboratory measurement of aggression towards peers is NOT:
    a. using the scientific method.
    b. valid.
    c. accurate.
    d. generalizable.

Research Methods, p. 19
Diff: M, Ans: a
58. Which of the following is NOT an important aspect of research methods?
    a. simplicity
    b. generalizability
    c. accuracy
    d. validity

Research Methods, p. 19
Diff: E, Ans: a

59. Watching and recording others' behaviors in a systematic and objective manner is referred to as:
    a. scientific observation.
    b. a correlational design.
    c. cross-sectional research.
    d. a laboratory experiment.

Research Methods, p. 19
Diff: M, Ans: d

60. If a researcher watches one-week-old babies and records how many times they open and close their eyes while lying in their cribs, he is most likely using:
    a. the case-study method.
    b. a controlled experiment.
    c. cross-sectional research.
    d. scientific observation.

Research Methods, p. 19
Diff: M, Ans: d

61. If a scientist wanted to use naturalistic observation to see how frequently schoolchildren share food at lunch, she could:
    a. give half of them candy and see how many would share.
    b. mingle with the children and ask them about sharing.
    c. bring a small group into her laboratory and observe them eating.
    d. watch the children from an unobtrusive spot in the school lunchroom.
    e. do any of the above.

Research Methods, p. 19
Diff: E, Ans: a

62. Naturalistic observation permits:
    a. the study of individuals behaving as they normally do.
    b. determination of cause-and-effect relationships.
    c. precise control of the environment.
    d. systematic manipulation of variables.

Research Methods, p. 19
Diff: M, Ans: c

63. Which of the following is an example of naturalistic observation?
    a. asking employers about their employee's assertive behaviors at work
    b. asking teachers to rate children's activity levels in the classroom
    c. watching mother-child interactions at home
    d. bringing people to a laboratory to measure memory ability

Research Methods, p. 19
Diff: H, Ans: d

64. Naturalistic observation would probably be the best choice for a researcher interested in:
    a. beliefs of parents about the drinking behavior of their children.
    b. adolescents' risky sexual behavior.
    c. obtaining extensive information about a single adolescent's nutritional behavior.
    d. the frequency of bullying during school recess periods.

Research Methods, pp. 19-20
Diff: M, Ans: e
65.   Which of the following is a true statement about laboratory observations?
       a.   They are useful for studying internal thoughts and feelings.
       b.   They are helpful when a researcher wants to determine causation.
       c.   They are valid only for very young children.
       d.   all of the above
       e.   none of the above

Research Methods, p. 19
Diff: M, Ans: b
66.   The main disadvantage of observation is that it:
       a.   can only be done in a laboratory.
       b.   makes it difficult to determine the direct cause of a behavior.
       c.   is too controlled to be realistic.
       d.   takes years to collect the data.

Research Methods, p. 20
Diff: H, Ans: b
67.   Correlations do NOT tell:
       a.   how two variables are related.
       b.   about cause and effect.
       c.   how strong a relationship exists between two variables.
       d.   whether a relationship exists between two variables.

Research Methods, p. 20
Diff: M, Ans: a
68.   If you find a correlation between school grades and school attendance, you can conclude that:
       a.   high attendance and high grades tend to occur together.
       b.   high attendance causes high grades.
       c.   smart children often are sickly.
       d.   smart children enjoy school.

Research Methods, p. 20
Diff: E, Ans: d
69.   Experiments allow researchers to:
       a.   reflect the natural environment.
       b.   study the entire complexity and uniqueness of an individual.
       c.   inexpensively adhere to the scientific method.
       d.   determine a cause-and-effect relationship.

Research Methods, p. 20
Diff: M, Ans: c
70.   Which of the following can be used when a researcher is interested in the cause of a particular behavior?
       a.   case study
       b.   scientific observation
       c.   experiment
       d.   all of the above

Research Methods, p. 20
Diff: H, Ans: c
71.   Which of the following statements comparing experiments with observations is true?
       a.   Observations allow the researcher greater control over the test conditions.
       b.   Experiments provide opportunity to examine more possible explanations.
       c.   Experiments better enable the researcher to observe causes and effects.
       d.   Conclusions from experiments apply more accurately to the real world.

Research Methods, p. 20
Diff: M, Ans: a
72.   In an experiment, the dependent variable is:
   a.   the response.
   b.   any unmeasured factor that might affect the results.
   c.   what the researchers are manipulating.
   d.   the people receiving the treatment.

Research Methods, p. 20
Diff: M, Ans: c
73.   In an experiment, the independent variable is:
   a.   the response.
   b.   any unmeasured factor that might affect the results.
   c.   what the researchers are manipulating.
   d.   the people receiving the treatment.

Research Methods, p. 20
Diff: H, Ans: a
74.   Which of the following variables CANNOT be a dependent variable in an experiment?
   a.   gender
   b.   drinking behavior
   c.   school grades
   d.   level of depression

Research Methods, pp. 20-21
Diff: M, Ans: b
75.   Bandura (1973) was interested in whether watching violence affected children's behaviors. To examine this, he showed a violent film to one group of preschoolers and a nonviolent film to a second group of preschoolers. Following the films, the behaviors of the two groups were compared. This study was:
   a.   a naturalistic observation.
   b.   an experiment.
   c.   a case study.
   d.   longitudinal research.

Research Methods, pp. 20-21
Diff: H, Ans: a
76.   Bandura (1973) was interested in whether watching violence affected children's behaviors. To examine this, he showed a violent film to one group of preschoolers and a nonviolent film to a second group of preschoolers, and then he observed their aggression levels. In this study, the independent variable was the:
   a.   viewing of the violent film.
   b.   level of aggression displayed before the film.
   c.   level of aggression displayed following the film.
   d.   children's home environment.

Research Methods, pp. 20-21
Diff: M, Ans: b
77.   Bandura (1973) was interested in whether watching violence affected children's behaviors. To examine this, he showed a violent film to one group of preschoolers and a nonviolent film to a second group of preschoolers. Following the films, the behaviors of the two groups were compared. In this study, the comparison group was the:
   a.   children who watched the violent film.
   b.   children who watched the nonviolent film.
   c.   children whose behavior was the inspiration for the study.
   d.   none of the above

Research Methods, p. 21
Diff: E, Ans: c
78.   In an experiment, the group of participants who receive the imposed treatment or special condition is referred to as the _____ group.
      a.   independent
      b.   dependent
      c.   experimental
      d.   comparison

Research Methods, p. 21
Diff: E, Ans: d
79.   In an experiment, the group of participants who do NOT receive the imposed treatment or special condition is referred to as the _____ group.
      a.   independent
      b.   dependent
      c.   experimental
      d.   comparison

Research Methods, p. 21
Diff: H, Ans: d
80.   The text describes a study of Bosnian refugees, half of whom were given counseling to help them cope with their children's reactions to their wartime experiences. Which of the following was the purpose of the study?
      a.   to examine whether Bosnian mothers could benefit from counseling
      b.   to prove that Bosnian children did not need any help coping with their emotions
      c.   to investigate how Bosnian mothers talked to their children about the war
      d.   to explore the effects of maternal counseling on children's well-being

Research Methods, p. 21
Diff: M, Ans: a
81.   In the study of the Bosnian refugees, half of whom were given counseling to help them cope with their children's reactions to the wartime experiences, the counseling is considered the _____ variable.
      a.   independent
      b.   dependent
      c.   experimental
      d.   comparison

Research Methods, p. 21
Diff: E, Ans: b
82.   When differences between experimental and comparison groups are so small that they could have occurred by chance, they are considered to be:
      a.   significant.
      b.   insignificant.
      c.   effective.
      d.   ineffective.

Research Methods, p. 22
Diff: M, Ans: d
83.   Which of the following is a potential problem with experiments?
      a.   Research participants usually know they are involved in an experiment.
      b.   The situation may differ from those in normal, everyday life.
      c.   Research participants can try to produce results they think the researcher is trying to obtain.
      d.   all of the above

Research Methods, p. 22
Diff: M, Ans: d
84. The greatest disadvantage of experiments is that scientists are unable to:
    a. control the environment.
    b. determine which factor is the real cause.
    c. test a hypothesis scientifically.
    d. ensure that people's behaviors in the experiment are the same as they would be in normal life.

Research Methods, p. 22
Diff: H, Ans: c
85. The Israeli study of the impact of sleeping arrangements on children's relationships with their parents is best considered a:
    a. laboratory experiment.
    b. naturalistic observation.
    c. natural experiment.
    d. case study.

Research Methods, p. 22
Diff: H, Ans: a
86. Which of the following is considered to be the most accurate and ethical way to conduct developmental research on children?
    a. natural experiments
    b. case studies
    c. laboratory experiments
    d. surveys

Research Methods, p. 22
Diff: E, Ans: d
87. Which of the following is NOT an example of the survey method?
    a. personal interview
    b. phone interview
    c. written questionnaire
    d. school grades

Research Methods, p. 22
Diff: M, Ans: b
88. To study people's thoughts about aging, a researcher would most likely use:
    a. a laboratory experiment.
    b. a survey.
    c. naturalistic observation.
    d. the case-study method.

Research Methods, p. 22
Diff: M, Ans: d
89. Which of the following is a limitation of the survey method?
    a. The wording of particular questions can influence people's answers.
    b. Some people try to give answers that make themselves look "good."
    c. People may respond inaccurately.
    d. All of the above are limitations of the survey method.

Research Methods, p. 22
Diff: E, Ans: c

90.   A researcher has just completed a study of Princess Diana, including her family background, life history, and expressed opinions. This is an example of:
    a.   the survey method.
    b.   representative sampling.
    c.   the case-study method.
    d.   objective testing.

Research Methods, p. 22
Diff: M, Ans: c

91.   In a case study, it is important to:
    a.   find a large enough sample size.
    b.   get a representative sample.
    c.   intensively study one individual.
    d.   be able to draw conclusions about people in general.

Other Research Methods, p. 23
Diff: M, Ans: a

92.   Which of the following is true of the case study method?
    a.   It is a good starting point for researchers developing hypotheses.
    b.   It is an accurate way of examining the generalizabilities across individuals.
    c.   It is a quantitative method.
    d.   All of the above are true.

Research Methods, p. 22
Diff: H, Ans: a

93.   Which of the following is an example of collecting qualitative data?
    a.   talking with all of the each family members of a pair of conjoined twins
    b.   measuring the height of a large group of 4-year-olds
    c.   asking parents how much television their children watch in a given week
    d.   counting the aggressive behaviors displayed by a group of preschoolers

Research Methods, p. 22
Diff: M, Ans: c

94.   Quantitative information always involves:
    a.   a large number of subjects.
    b.   obtaining as much information as possible from research participants.
    c.   numerical data.
    d.   studying people over a period of time.

Research Methods, pp. 22-23
Diff: E, Ans: c

95.   Compared to other methods, the case study has a major limitation in that:
    a.   it is less intensive and thus less informative.
    b.   it does not provide sufficient detail on the individual.
    c.   its conclusions might not apply to anyone else.
    d.   it requires the consent of the individual being studied.

Studying Changes Over Time

Studying Changes Over Time, p. 23
Diff: E, Ans: b
96. For research to be truly developmental, developmental scientists need to include which of the following as a factor?
     a. surveys
     b. age
     c. in-depth analysis
     d. parent interviews

Studying Changes Over Time, p. 23
Diff: E, Ans: c
97. Which of the following is NOT an example of a research design that truly examines development?
     a. longitudinal
     b. cross-sequential
     c. base-sequential
     d. cross-sectional

Cross-Sectional Research, p. 23
Diff: E, Ans: d
98. Which of the following research designs compare groups of individuals who are of different ages?
     a. base-sequential
     b. case study
     c. longitudinal
     d. cross-sectional

Cross-Sectional Research, p. 23
Diff: M, Ans: a
99. The quickest way to study changes over the life span is with:
     a. cross-sectional research.
     b. the case study.
     c. cross-sequential studies.
     d. longitudinal research.

Cross-Sectional Research, p. 23
Diff: M, Ans: c
100. In cross-sectional research on development, each of the groups studied is of a different:
     a. sex.
     b. social class.
     c. age.
     d. political affiliation.

Cross-Sectional Research, p. 23
Diff: M, Ans: b
101. A researcher was interested in finding out whether children's ability to exhibit self-control when offered unhealthy food changed with age. He asked parents of three-year-old, six-year-old, and nine-year-old children to bring their children into the laboratory, where they were allowed to eat as much candy, cookies, and cake as they wanted. The researcher then compared the amount of food eaten by children of the three different ages. This is an example of:
     a. a naturalistic observation.
     b. cross-sectional research.
     c. longitudinal research.
     d. cross-sequential research.

Cross-Sectional Research, pp. 23-24
Diff: H, Ans: b

102. A researcher interested in how computer abilities change with age examines the computer skills of 14-year-olds and 20-year-olds. She finds that the computer skills of the 20-year-olds are better than those of the 14-year-olds. Which of the following is NOT a possible explanation for this result?
      a. increased computer abilities with age
      b. lack of a control group
      c. cohort differences
      d. differences in socioeconomic status

Cross-Sectional Research, p. 24
Diff: M, Ans: d

103. Which of the following is a problem with cross-sectional research?
      a. Participants may move far away during the course of the research.
      b. People may become more familiar with the materials with repeated exposure.
      c. It tends to be more time-consuming than longitudinal research.
      d. Differences may be due to cohort differences instead of age.

Cross-Sectional Research, p. 24
Diff: H, Ans: d

104. Research on people growing up in one historical time period might not apply to people growing up in another time because of:
      a. cultural differences.
      b. longitudinal sampling.
      c. cross-sequential discontinuities.
      d. cohort differences.

Longitudinal Research, p. 25
Diff: E, Ans: c

105. To study how members of a particular group change or remain the same as they grow older, the best method is:
      a. cross-sectional research.
      b. a survey at the end of the time period.
      c. longitudinal research.
      d. establishing an experimental group and a control group.

Longitudinal Research, p. 25
Diff: M, Ans: a

106. If a researcher wanted to study the development of handwriting ability in children, she could measure the handwriting of a group of second-graders and continue to take handwriting samples from these same children each year until sixth grade. This is an example of:
      a. longitudinal research.
      b. cross-sectional research.
      c. cross-dequential research.
      d. a replication study.

Longitudinal Research, p. 25
Diff: E, Ans: b

107. A researcher who tests the same individuals over thirty years, when they are 10, 20, 30, and 40-years-old, is conducting:
      a. cohort research.
      b. longitudinal research.
      c. continuous research.
      d. cross-sectional research.

Longitudinal Research, pp. 25-26
Diff: M, Ans: c

108. Longitudinal research:
    a. is relatively simple and inexpensive to conduct.
    b. has not produced any useful information regarding human development.
    c. can uncover not only change but the process of change.
    d. is never undertaken any more, since the computer provides quicker methods.

Longitudinal Research, p. 26
Diff: H, Ans: d

109. A researcher is interested in whether children who have more friends before they transition from elementary school to middle school get better grades in middle school. Which of the following research designs would best be able to answer this question?
    a. cross-sequential
    b. experimental
    c. cross-sectional
    d. longitudinal

Longitudinal Research, p. 27
Diff: E, Ans: a

110. Most developmental researchers consider longitudinal research to be:
    a. more revealing than cross-sectional studies.
    b. less time consuming than cross-sectional studies.
    c. more common than cross-sectional studies.
    d. not worth doing.

Cross-Sequential Research, p. 27
Diff: E, Ans: d

111. A cross-sequential design:
    a. examines a single group of people who are the same age at one point in time.
    b. examines two or more groups of people who are of different ages at one point in time.
    c. follows a single group of people over an extended period of time.
    d. follows two or more groups of people who are of different ages over a period of time.

Cross-Sequential Research, p. 27
Diff: M, Ans: a

112. Unlike other types of research, a cross-sequential design allows researchers to:
    a. disentangle differences due to development from differences related to historical period.
    b. study groups of individuals who are of different ages.
    c. reduce sample bias.
    d. conduct research over only a small time period.

The Ecological Systems Approach: A Synthesis, p. 27
Diff: M, Ans: c

113. Who recommended an ecological-systems approach to the study of human development?
    a. Jean Piaget
    b. Sigmund Freud
    c. Urie Bronfenbrenner
    d. Erik Erikson

The Ecological Systems Approach: A Synthesis, p. 27
Diff: E, Ans: d
114.   The ecological-systems approach to the study of human development maintains that in order to understand an individual's development, one needs to examine the:
a.   historical context.
b.   individual's family.
c.   schools and community.
d.   interplay between the individual and all of the above.

The Ecological Systems Approach: A Synthesis, p. 27
Diff: M, Ans: d
115.   On the playground, a father appears to be ignoring his crying 3-year-old. The ecological-systems approach suggests that which of the following is influencing this interaction?
a.   the father's beliefs about his child's behavior
b.   society's expectations about the roles of fathers
c.   the child's level of emotional maturity
d.   all of the above

The Ecological Systems Approach: A Synthesis, p. 27
Diff: M, Ans: b
116.   According to the ecological-systems perspective, the influence of David's family on his development is part of his:
a.   macrosystem.
b.   microsystem.
c.   exosysterm.
d.   mesosystem.

The Ecological Systems Approach: A Synthesis, p. 27
Diff: H, Ans: d
117.   Within the ecological-systems approach, the connections among the various microsystems are part of the:
a.   macrosystem.
b.   microsystem.
c.   exosysterm.
d.   mesosystem.

The Ecological Systems Approach: A Synthesis, p. 27
Diff: M, Ans: a
118.   Within the ecological-systems approach, the customs of the society, as well as the economic and political philosophies of the nation, are all a part of the:
a.   macrosystem.
b.   microsystem.
c.   exosysterm.
d.   mesosystem.

Ethics and Science

Ethics and Science, p. 29
Diff: M, Ans: a
119.   Which of the following is NOT a right of individuals who participate in research studies?
a.   payment for participation
b.   best possible protection from harm
c.   informed consent
d.   confidentiality

The Implications of Research, pp. 29-30
Diff: H, Ans: d

120.   Which of the following behaviors by a researcher would be considered unethical?
   a.   ignoring the possible ways in which the media might misinterpret the results of a study
   b.   changing the data to support the hypothesis
   c.   making hasty generalizations without fully explaining the results
   d.   doing all of the above

TRUE-FALSE QUESTIONS

Studying the Life Span: Five Characteristics

Ans: F, p. 4
1.   From the life-span perspective, the study of human development begins at birth.

Ans: T, p. 5 (Fig. 1.1)
2.   Development often involves declines or erratic changes.

Ans: F, p. 5
3.   Physical growth always occurs at a steady pace.

Ans: F, p. 6
4.   The butterfly effect refers to the idea that a large change can have a surprisingly small effect.

Ans: T, p. 7
5.   Individuals in the same cohort are exposed to the same historical context.

Ans: F, p. 7
6.   The term cohort refers only to individuals born in the same geographical region and within the same social class.

Ans: F, p. 9
7.   The socioeconomic status of a family primarily reflects only the household income.

Ans: F, p. 9
8.   People who share a common ancestry and language are all a part of the same socioeconomic status.

Ans: T, p. 9
9.   The level of collective efficacy in a neighborhood is a better measure of the emotional health of the individuals living there than is average income.

Ans: T, p. 10
10.   Quality of parenting is the single best predictor of a resilient child.

Ans: T, p. 10
11.   People are generally unaware of their culture until they are separated from it or it is challenged.

Ans: T, p. 11
12.   The extent to which independence is an important trait in a culture has an influence on sleeping practices in that culture.

Ans: F, p. 11
13.   Comparisons among cultures generally just get in the way of determining the impact of different practices.

Ans: T, pp. 13-14
14.   Members of an ethnic group might not all share the same racial identity.

Ans: F, p. 14
15.   There are clear-cut racial groups that are based in biology.

Ans: T, pp. 14-15
16.   Developmentalists often draw on other disciplines such as biology and sociology to gain insight into human development.

Ans: T, p. 15
17.   Plasticity refers both to how human traits can be molded into different forms and to how humans can maintain durability.

Developmental Study as a Science

Ans: F, pp. 18-19
18.   The purpose of the scientific method is to find ways to support researchers' hypotheses.

Ans: T, p. 19
19.   A research question becomes a hypothesis when it is restated as a prediction that can be tested.

Ans: T, p. 19
20.   Conclusions of a scientific study are based on whether the evidence supported the hypothesis.

Ans: F, p. 19
21.   The first step of the scientific method is to test the research question.

Ans: F, p. 19
22.   If the conclusions that can be drawn from a research study apply only to individuals who are similar to those involved in the study and not to other less similar groups of people, the study has poor validity.

Ans: T, p. 19
23.   A researcher who watches college students during an exam and counts how many students bite their nails is conducting a scientific observation.

Ans: F, p. 20
24.   The main advantage of observation is that the scientist can make determinations about cause and effect.

Ans: T, p. 20
25.   Correlations indicate that there is a connection between two variables, but they cannot indicate the reason for the connection.

Ans: F, p. 20
26.   If a change in one variable tends to go with change in another variable, it is clear that one variable causes the other variable to change.

Ans: F, p. 20
27.   If we were to find a correlation between level of education and verbal skills, we can then conclude that education causes increased verbal skills.

Ans: T, p. 20
28.   An advantage of the experimental method is that it has the ability to indicate cause and effect.

Ans: F, p. 21
29.   In an experiment, the group receiving the special treatment is referred to as the comparison group.

Ans: F, p. 21
30.   In an experiment, the comparison group often varies substantially from the experimental group on basic characteristics such as sex, age, and level of education.

Ans: T, p. 22
31.   One of the limitations of experiments is that researchers' control of variables may make the results of the experiment not applicable outside the artificial experimental setting.

Ans: F, p. 22
32.   Laboratory experiments are considered to be the most accurate and ethical way to conduct research on children.

Ans: T, p. 22
33.   A limitation of the interview or survey method is that people may give inaccurate or misleading information about themselves.

Ans: F, p. 22
34.   A survey enables the researcher to thoroughly study one individual.

Ans: F, p. 22
35.   A case study involves an intensive study of one person for the purpose of making generalizations about the larger population.

Ans: T, p. 22
36.   A case study is an example of qualitative research.

Studying Changes Over Time

Ans: T, p. 24
37.   One disadvantage of cross-sectional research is that differences could be due to cohort rather than development.

Ans: F, p. 25
38.   Longitudinal research allows a group of people of one age to be compared with groups of younger and older people of similar social class and educational background.

Ans: T, p. 25
39.   In longitudinal research, we measure the same people over a period of time.

Ans: T, p. 27
40.   Cross-sequential research is a combination of a cross-sectional design and a longitudinal design.

Ans: F, p. 27
41.   In the ecological-systems approach, the immediate family, peer groups, and classrooms are all parts of the macrosystem.

Ethics and Science

Ans: F, p. 29
42.   Researchers only need participants' informed consent when the researchers believe that harm may come to the participants during the study.

Ans: T, p. 29
43.   The possibility of harm to the participants in a research study varies according to the participant's age and condition.

Ans: F, pp. 29-30
44.   Researchers have little ethical responsibility for how media or politicians might interpret their research.

Ans: T, p. 30
45.   Researchers have an ethical responsibility to study topics that will help people.

FILL-IN-THE-BLANK QUESTIONS

Studying the Life Span: Five Characteristics

Ans: human development, p. 3
1.   The study of how and why people change over time and how and why they remain the same is the study of _____.

Ans: conception; death, p. 4
2.   The life-span perspective involves examining human development from _____ to _____.

Ans: dynamic, pp. 5-6
3.   The _____ systems approach points out that every change is part of a system.

Ans: cohort, p. 7
4.   A(n) _____ is a group of people born roughly at the same historical time.

Ans: construction, p. 7
5.   An idea built more on shared perceptions of the members of a society than on objective reality is a social _____.

Ans: socioeconomic status, p. 9
6.   When discussed in terms of development, "SES" refers to _____.

Ans: culture, p. 10
7.   The set of shared values, attitudes, customs, and physical objects that are maintained by people in a specific setting is known as _____.

Ans: race (or racial group), p. 14
8.   Social scientists have recently realized that _____ is a distorted concept and prefer to consider the impact of ethnicity and culture on development.

Ans: mainstreaming, p. 16
9.   The practice of educating children with special needs alongside normal children is called _____.

Developmental Study as a Science

Ans: question; hypothesis, p. 19
10.   After a researcher has formulated a research _____, he or she must reformulate it into a specific prediction called a(n) _____.

Ans: tested (or evaluated or examined), p. 19
11.   A hypothesis is a statement or prediction that can be _____ by various research methods.

Ans: replicate, p. 19

12.   Often the last step of the scientific method is to make the findings available so that other researchers can repeat, or _____, the research.

Ans: naturalistic, p. 19

13.   If a researcher observes a family at home, this is considered observation in a(n) _____ setting.

Ans: experiment, p. 20

14.   Researchers who want to establish a causal relationship between two variables should use a research design called a(n) _____.

Ans: experiment, p. 20

15.   In a(n) _____, the scientist deliberately changes one variable and measures the change in some other variable.

Ans: experimental; dependent, pp. 20-21

16.   A researcher is interested in examining whether a memory training program can improve the memory skills of elderly individuals. To examine this, the researcher splits a group of elderly individuals into two groups. The group of people who receive the memory training program is referred to as the _____ group. Memory skills at the end of the training are referred to as the _____ variable.

Ans: significant, p. 21

17.   When differences between the experimental group and the control group are so large that they could not have occurred simply by chance, they are considered to be _____.

Ans: survey, p. 22

18.   When obtaining information from large numbers of people from written questionnaires, one is using the _____ method.

Ans: case study, p. 22

19. .   A developmentalist who bases his conclusions on intensive study of one of his own children is using the _____ method.

Studying Changes Over Time

Ans: cross-sectional, p. 23

20.   Research that compares people of different ages who are similar in other important ways is called _____ research.

Ans: longitudinal, p. 25

21.   When a group of exceptionally gifted students are studied as the students go through elementary school, secondary school, and college, the research design is called _____ research.

Ans: cross-sectional; longitudinal, p. 27

22.   Cross-sequential research can be thought of as a mix between a _____ design and a _____ design.

Ans: ecological-systems, p.27

23.   Bronfenbrenner developed a(n) _____ approach to the study of development.

Ethics and Science

Ans: voluntary; confidential, p. 29

24.   Research subjects' participation must always be _____, and the information obtained from a particular subject must be kept _____.

Ans: ethics, p. 29

25.   Each academic discipline involved in research on human development has a code of _____.

ESSAY QUESTIONS

1.   Suppose you were curious about people's views about "instant messaging" and how it has impacted the lives of Americans. Would the age of the individuals whose opinions you asked matter? Thinking about the concept of a cohort, describe how "instant messaging" might tend to be viewed by individuals who are 12 years old, 30 years old, and 70 years old.

2.   Define the following three terms and describe how they are related to one another as well as how they are different: (a) race, (b) ethnic group, and (c) socioeconomic status.

3.   Imagine you hear the parent of a newborn make the following statement: "Development always occurs in a straight line. I can see my baby getting a little bit bigger, a little bit stronger, and a little bit more alert each day." Do you believe this parent is correct when he says that development is always linear? If so, explain why and provide two examples (besides those stated by the father) of linear development. If not, explain why not and provide two examples of development that is non-linear. For either answer, be sure to fully explain the direction of development and why it occurs in that direction.

4.   Think about a belief that you hold strongly but about which your parent (or grandparent or aunt or uncle) disagrees with you. This belief may concern marriage, education, drug and alcohol use, the roles of women and men, childrearing practices, or some other topic about which you feel strongly. Briefly describe your perspective on the topic, and then describe your parent's perspective. Describe how the historical context in which your parent grew up and the historical context in which you grew up could have influenced your differences on this issue.

5.   Explain why researchers interested in human development study different cultures. Give an example of a research question that would benefit from a multicultural comparison.

6.   Describe the five main steps involved in the scientific method.

7.   What is naturalistic observation? Give an example of a research question that could be addressed with this method. Describe one advantage and one limitation of this method.

8.   Define correlation and give an example. Can one determine cause and effect from correlations? Explain why or why not.

9.   What is an experiment? Give an example of a research question that could be addressed with this method. Describe one advantage and one limitation of this method.

10.   Describe two reasons why it is sometimes difficult to get valid data with a survey.

11.   What is a case study? Give an example of a research question that could be addressed with this method. Describe one advantage and one limitation of this research method.

12.   Imagine you are interested in the relationship between age and reading ability for children between 4- and 10-years-old. Briefly discuss how you could test this using a cross-sectional design.

13.   Give a brief description of longitudinal research and a brief description of cross-sequential research. Describe the differences between these two designs, and cite one advantage that each design has over the other.

14.   Think about your ideas on each of the following broad topics. Construct a hypothesis for two of these topics and suggest a way to test your hypothesis.
   a.   The effects of media violence on young children
   b.   The effects on children of having a mother who works outside the home
   c.   The extent to which teenagers reflect the values of their parents and relatives
   d.   The effects of a home computer on family relationships
   e.   The most important variables affecting the timing of a first pregnancy
   f.   The effects of aging on eye-hand coordination

15.   You are a developmental psychologist interested in the differences between the way parents treat their sons and daughters. Form a hypothesis, and describe the method you would use to test the hypothesis (e.g., experiment, observation, case study). Be sure to explain why you chose this particular method.

16.   Suppose you want to investigate how abuse in early childhood affects personality development in middle childhood, adolescence, and adulthood. What are the advantages and disadvantages using of cross-sectional and longitudinal research in exploring this topic?

17.   Using the ecological-systems approach, think about the impact of poverty on a child's cognitive development. Give an example of an influence within each of the following four contexts: family, school/peers, neighborhood/community, and cultural values/economic policies.

18.   What are some of the basic rights of children involved in research?

19.   Suppose you are on an advisory committee whose purpose it is to ensure that experiments involving young children are conducted in an ethical manner. Give an example of an experiment that you would consider ethical, one you would consider unethical, and one that would be difficult to evaluate. Explain your reasons in each case.

20.   Do you think it is ethical for children to be involved in research projects? Why or why not? What are your best arguments FOR their involvement? What are your best arguments AGAINST their involvement?

Answer guidelines to these essay questions can be found in the Appendix at the end of the Test Bank.

CHAPTER 2

Theories of Development

MULTIPLE-CHOICE QUESTIONS

What Theories Do

What Theories Do, p. 33
Diff: E, Ans: b
1. A systematic set of principles and generalizations that provides a framework for understanding and examining how and why people change as they get older is referred to as a(n):
   a. hypothesis.
   b. developmental theory.
   c. operational definition.
   d. paradigm.

What Theories Do, pp. 33-34
Diff: H, Ans: a
2. Which of the following is NOT a purpose of a developmental theory?
   a. to provide solutions to most major developmental problems
   b. to offer insight into practical concerns raised by parents, teachers, and therapists
   c. to connect observations with patterns and explanations
   d. to form the basis for hypotheses

What Theories Do, p. 34
Diff: M, Ans: d
3. Which of the following is a true statement about theories in the field of human development?
   a. Theories are unimportant.
   b. One major theory explains everything.
   c. Theories are used only for research purposes.
   d. Theories generate future discoveries.

What Theories Do, p. 34
Diff: M, Ans: c
4. Some theories are called grand theories because they:
   a. are consistently accurate.
   b. offer the only important insights regarding development.
   c. provide a framework for understanding the development of all people.
   d. are considered to be the new theories of the future.

What Theories Do, p. 34
Diff: E, Ans: c

5.   If Greg has a theory that explains only why babies sleep, this would be considered a(n):
      a.   emergent theory.
      b.   psychoanalytic theory.
      c.   minitheory.
      d.   Gregorian theory.

What Theories Do, p. 34
Diff: M, Ans: a

6.   Which of the following is a true statement about emergent theories?
      a.   They include insights from many disciplines.
      b.   They are considered unimportant for understanding the core aspects of human development.
      c.   They are a traditional part of psychology.
      d.   They are fully comprehensive.

What Theories Do, p. 34
Diff: E, Ans: b

7.   Which of the following is NOT considered a grand theory?
      a.   behaviorism
      b.   sociocultural theory
      c.   psychoanalytic theory
      d.   cognitive theory

Grand Theories

Grand Theories, p. 34
Diff: E, Ans: a

8.   Which of the following is NOT a characteristic of grand theories?
      a.   complete accuracy
      b.   wide application
      c.   comprehensiveness
      d.   enduring nature

Psychoanalytic Theory, p. 34
Diff: E, Ans: c

9.   According to psychoanalytic theories, human development is mainly determined by:
      a.   the choices we make for ourselves.
      b.   the environment in which we are raised.
      c.   our unconscious motives and drives.
      d.   the way we think about and understand the world.

Psychoanalytic Theory, pp. 34-35
Diff: M, Ans: d

10.   Psychoanalytic theory views intrinsic drives and motives as the foundation for:
      a.   sexual expression.
      b.   developmental tasks.
      c.   human attachments.
      d.   all of the above.

Psychoanalytic Theory, p. 35
Diff: M, Ans: b

11. Freud believed that all people experience _____ related to various parts of their bodies.
  a. aggressive tendencies
  b. sensual satisfactions
  c. needs for self-control
  d. hidden fears

Psychoanalytic Theory, p. 35
Diff: E, Ans: c

12. In order, Freud's first three stages of development are:
  a. mouth, body, eyes.
  b. trust, autonomy, identity.
  c. oral, anal, phallic.
  d. anal, genital, latent.

Psychoanalytic Theory, p. 35
Diff: M, Ans: b

13. Danielle sucks her thumb because she finds it very pleasurable. She is also becoming emotionally attached to her daddy, Andy, who feeds her. According to Freud, Danielle is most likely in:
  a. the anal stage.
  b. the oral stage.
  c. latency.
  d. the phallic stage.

Psychoanalytic Theory, p. 35
Diff: M, Ans: a

14. Katie's 9-month-old son Jason sucks and chews on just about everything he finds—toys, books, fingers, and so forth. According to psychoanalytic theory, Jason is in which of the following stages?
  a. oral
  b. sensorimotor
  c. attachment
  d. anal

Psychoanalytic Theory, p. 35
Diff: E, Ans: d

15. Freud believed that during the anal stage the most important activity is:
  a. trying to stop thumb-sucking.
  b. developing interest in the opposite sex.
  c. developing friendships.
  d. toilet training.

Psychoanalytic Theory, p. 35
Diff: M, Ans: a

16. According to Freud which of the following occurs in each stage of development?
  a. potential conflicts
  b. inappropriate sexual urges
  c. developmental crises
  d. all of the above

Psychoanalytic Theory, p. 35
Diff: M, Ans: c

17.   According to Freud, which of the following determine individuals' lifelong patterns of behavior?
       a.   the manners in which they were punished and reinforced for particular behaviors
       b.   their attitudes, beliefs, and assumptions
       c.   the ways in which they experience and resolve psychosexual conflicts
       d.   the behaviors modeled by their parents

Psychoanalytic Theory, p. 35
Diff: H, Ans: b

18.   With which of the following statements would Freud be most likely to agree?
       a.   Parents should wean infants from the breast or bottle as soon as possible.
       b.   How conflicts over weaning, toilet training, and sexual curiosity are resolved determine an
            individual's personality.
       c.   Individuals who smoke cigarettes probably had trouble learning how to toilet train.
       d.   People's relationships to their family and culture are more important in determining development
            than are their sexual urges.

Psychoanalytic Theory, p. 35
Diff: E, Ans: c

19.   Sigmund Freud and Erik Erikson are best known for their contributions to _____ theory.
       a.   cognitive
       b.   sociocultural
       c.   psychoanalytic
       d.   behavioral

Psychoanalytic Theory, p. 35
Diff: H, Ans: b

20.   Erikson's theories were influenced by the fact that Erikson:
       a.   lived in Denmark, a country where children are respected.
       b.   studied and worked with a wide diversity of people.
       c.   was a medical doctor with a degree in psychiatry.
       d.   worked exclusively with emotionally disturbed patients.

Psychoanalytic Theory, p. 36
Diff: M, Ans: d

21.   Unlike Freud, Erikson's psychosocial theory emphasizes:
       a.   the logic that underlies thought processes.
       b.   the inherent rewards and punishments of living.
       c.   active mental processes.
       d.   the social and cultural environment.

Psychoanalytic Theory, p. 36
Diff: M, Ans: b

22.   In Erikson's psychosocial theory, resolutions to developmental crises depend on the interaction
       between the individual and:
       a.   his or her genetic predisposition.
       b.   the social environment.
       c.   his or her ability to learn from experience.
       d.   the area of the body where sexual urges are centered.

Psychoanalytic Theory, pp. 35-36
Diff: H, Ans: a

23.   With which of the following statements would *both* Freud and Erikson agree?
      a.   Problems of adult life stem from unresolved conflicts of childhood.
      b.   There are five stages of development.
      c.   People's relationships to their family and culture are of the utmost importance.
      d.   Freud and Erikson would agree with *none* of the above statements.

Psychoanalytic Theory, p. 37 (Table 2.1)
Diff: M, Ans: b

24.   According to Freud, sexual needs are relatively quiet during:
      a.   toddlerhood.
      b.   latency.
      c.   adulthood.
      d.   infancy.

Psychoanalytic Theory, p. 37 (Table 2.1)
Diff: M, Ans: d

25.   According to Freud, who is most likely to be in the genital stage?
      a.   a 6-month-old girl
      b.   a 1-year-old boy
      c.   a 7-year-old girl
      d.   a 16-year-old boy

Psychoanalytic Theory, p. 37 (Table 2.1)
Diff: H, Ans: b

26.   According to Freud's theory, development in the first six years occurs in three:
      a.   two-year stages.
      b.   psychosexual stages.
      c.   unconscious progressions.
      d.   psychosocial stages.

Psychoanalytic Theory, p. 37 (Table 2.1)
Diff: H, Ans: a

27.   Freud believed that the goal of a healthy life is:
      a.   "to love and to work."
      b.   "to bring your unconscious to the surface."
      c.   "to find your one true life partner."
      d.   "to resolve all of your unconscious issues."

Psychoanalytic Theory, p. 37 (Table 2.1)
Diff: M, Ans: b

28.   Which of the following statements regarding Erik Erikson's theory is true?
      a.   There are six stages.
      b.   Developmental challenges continue throughout adulthood.
      c.   The first stage is called the oral stage.
      d.   Autonomy occurs when young adults leave home.

Psychoanalytic Theory, p. 37 (Table 2.1)
Diff: H, Ans: c

29.   The psychosocial stage that occurs at the same time as Freud's anal stage is:
      a.   industry vs. inferiority.
      b.   initiative vs. guilt.
      c.   autonomy vs. shame and doubt.
      d.   trust vs. mistrust.

Psychoanalytic Theory, p. 37 (Table 2.1)
Diff: M, Ans: b
30.   According to Erikson, an infant experiences:
    a.   industry vs. inferiority.
    b.   trust vs. mistrust.
    c.   autonomy vs. shame and doubt.
    d.   independence vs. dependence.

Psychoanalytic Theory, p. 37 (Table 2.1)
Diff: H, Ans: c
31.   In the industry vs. inferiority stage, children try to:
    a.   become accepted by important others.
    b.   figure out who they are.
    c.   master new skills.
    d.   become toilet trained.

Psychoanalytic Theory, p. 37 (Table 2.1)
Diff: H, Ans: d
32.   Erikson believed that the main crisis during adolescence involved:
    a.   trying to find an intimate relationship.
    b.   establishing a sense of self-control.
    c.   learning to trust others in the world.
    d.   trying to determine who one is.

Psychoanalytic Theory, p. 37 (Table 2.1)
Diff: H, Ans: a
33.   A 9-year-old girl learning to be competent at school would be in Erikson's psychosocial stage of:
    a.   industry vs. inferiority.
    b.   identity vs. role confusion.
    c.   autonomy vs. shame and doubt.
    d.   integrity vs. despair.

Psychoanalytic Theory, p. 37 (Table 2.1)
Diff: H, Ans: c
34.   The psychosocial stage in which people try to see their lives as a worthy and justifiable whole is:
    a.   identity vs. role confusion.
    b.   the formal operational stage.
    c.   integrity vs. despair.
    d.   the genital stage.

Behaviorism, p. 37
Diff: E, Ans: b
35.   Which of the following theories arose in direct opposition to psychoanalytic theory?
    a.   cognitive theory
    b.   behaviorism
    c.   sociocultural theory
    d.   ecological theory

Behaviorism, p. 37
Diff: E, Ans: a
36.   Behaviorism focuses on which of the following?
    a.   actions
    b.   unconscious urges
    c.   thoughts
    d.   emotions

Behaviorism, p. 37
Diff: M, Ans: d
37.   Who helped initiate behaviorism by saying, "Why don't we make what we can observe the real field of psychology? Let us limit ourselves to the things that can be observed . . ."?
   a.   Lev Vygotsky
   b.   Erik Erikson
   c.   B. F. Skinner
   d.   John B. Watson

Behaviorism, p. 38
Diff: E, Ans: c
38.   Behaviorism is also called:
   a.   motivational theory.
   b.   emotional theory.
   c.   learning theory.
   d.   analysis theory.

Behaviorism, p. 38
Diff: H, Ans: d
39.   Diana, a toddler, is throwing a temper tantrum. Behaviorists would say Diana is doing this because she:
   a.   is a toddler, and toddlers are learning how to control their environment.
   b.   believes this will get her parents to give her what she wants.
   c.   is egocentric and cannot think about how other people will be upset by her behavior.
   d.   has gradually learned that this type of behavior gets rewarded.

Behaviorism, p. 38
Diff: E, Ans: a
40.   The scientist who first demonstrated classical conditioning was:
   a.   Ivan Pavlov.
   b.   B. F. Skinner.
   c.   John B. Watson.
   d.   Lev Vygotsky.

Behaviorism, p. 38
Diff: M, Ans: c
41.   In classical conditioning, an organism learns:
   a.   a reflex.
   b.   that reinforcement follows responses.
   c.   to associate a neutral stimulus with a meaningful one.
   d.   how to become self-sufficient.

Behaviorism, p. 38
Diff: M, Ans: b
42.   Pavlov's dogs salivated at the sound of the bell because they:
   a.   were rewarded with a pat on the back each time they salivated on command.
   b.   learned to associate the bell with food.
   c.   learned to enjoy the music of the bell.
   d.   believed the bell was food.

Behaviorism, p. 38
Diff: H, Ans: c

43.   Which of the following could be an example of classical conditioning?
        a. laughing at a funny movie
        b. crying with the pain of a stubbed toe
        c. feeling happy at the smell of baking cookies
        d. wearing layers in the winter

Behaviorism, p. 38
Diff: H, Ans: d

44.   Rachel is a young child who has been given a vaccination each time she has been to the doctor's office.
        She now starts to scream and cry each time she sees the doctor's office building. According to the
        principles of classical conditioning, she is screaming and crying because she:
        a. is trying to discourage her parents from taking her to the doctor.
        b. would prefer to go to the park and play.
        c. is angry at the doctor and her mother for giving her shots.
        d. has learned to associate the building with the pain she feels when she gets a shot.

Behaviorism, p. 38
Diff: E, Ans: b

45.   The researcher most associated with operant conditioning is:
        a. Ivan Pavlov.
        b. B. F. Skinner.
        c. John B. Watson.
        d. Lev Vygotsky.

Behaviorism, p. 38
Diff: M, Ans: d

46.   In operant conditioning, an organism learns that:
        a. a neutral stimulus is associated with a meaningful stimulus.
        b. punishment always follows a reinforcer.
        c. classically conditioned responses are learned for life.
        d. a particular behavior usually produces a particular consequence.

Behaviorism, pp. 38-39
Diff: H, Ans: b

47.   According to behaviorists, a child who frequently hits other children is doing this because:
        a. of the child's innate tendencies.
        b. the child has been reinforced for this behavior.
        c. the child is expressing unconscious aggression.
        d. the child has been classically conditioned to do this.

Behaviorism, p. 38
Diff: M, Ans: c

48.   Operant conditioning is also known as:
        a. classical conditioning.
        b. respondent conditioning.
        c. instrumental conditioning.
        d. reciprocal determinism.

Behaviorism, pp. 38-39
Diff: M, Ans: b

49. A dog learns to "shake paws" on command because it has been given dog biscuits for doing so. This is an example of:
    a. classical conditioning.
    b. operant conditioning.
    c. cognitive conditioning.
    d. stimulus conditioning.

Behaviorism, p. 39
Diff: H, Ans: a

50. Which of the following is the best example of operant conditioning?
    a. playing a slot machine
    b. crying when hurt
    c. feeling tired after a long day
    d. puckering up after tasting a dill pickle

Behaviorism, p. 39
Diff: H, Ans: a

51. Bob, a psychologist, has been testing the effectiveness of operant conditioning in regard to study habits. Which of the following is most likely to be the title of Bob's latest study?
    a. "How to reinforce good study habits"
    b. "Why some children develop good study habits by themselves"
    c. "Ways a parent can be a role model for good study habits"
    d. "The unconscious reasons for good study habits"

Behaviorism, p. 39
Diff: M, Ans: c

52. A reinforcer is:
    a. always pleasant, such as a smile or a piece of candy.
    b. the same thing as a punishment.
    c. something that increases the likelihood that a behavior will be repeated.
    d. all of the above.

Behaviorism, p. 39
Diff: E, Ans: a

53. In operational conditioning, reinforcements have what effect on an individual's behavior?
    a. make the behavior more likely
    b. make the behavior less likely
    c. ensure that the behavior will remain constant
    d. cause an individual to think harder about his or her behavior

Behaviorism, p. 39
Diff: E, Ans: b

54. In operational conditioning, punishment has what effect on an individual's behavior?
    a. makes the behavior more likely
    b. makes the behavior less likely
    c. ensures that the behavior will completely disappear
    d. causes an individual to think harder about his or her behavior

Behaviorism, p. 39
Diff: H, Ans: c
55. Lori always yells at her 5-year-old son Jake when he won't get dressed for school. Although she has been yelling at him to get dressed nearly every day for months, he still does not comply when she asks him to get dressed. Operant conditioning would explain this by pointing out that:
    a. 5-year-olds are trying to exert their independence.
    b. Jake has come to associate mornings with yelling.
    c. Lori's yelling is serving as a reinforcer.
    d. Jake is fearful that he will appear incompetent at school.

Behaviorism: Thinking Like a Scientist, p. 40
Diff: H, Ans: b
56. Which of the following hypotheses did psychoanalytic theory and behaviorism agree on before Harlow's research?
    a. Infants are genetically programmed to bond with their mothers.
    b. Infants' attachments to their mothers result from the fact that their mothers feed them.
    c. Infants need to learn to love their mothers over the first several years of life because their mothers are kind toward them.
    d. Infants have no true love for their mothers, as infants are not cognitively advanced enough to understand love.

Behaviorism: Thinking Like a Scientist, p. 40
Diff: E, Ans: a
57. Harlow conducted his research on children's attachments to their mothers on:
    a. monkeys.
    b. turtles.
    c. humans.
    d. dogs.

Behaviorism: Thinking Like a Scientist, p. 40
Diff: M, Ans: b
58. What did Harlow notice in his monkeys that led him to question psychoanalytic and learning theories?
    a. Some of them showed no love for their mothers.
    b. They showed a stronger attachment to their cloth diapers than to their bottles.
    c. Some of them refused to eat from a bottle.
    d. They seemed to be comforted by their bottles in times of fear.

Behaviorism: Thinking Like a Scientist, p. 41
Diff: M, Ans: c
59. What did Harlow's research demonstrate about infants' attachments to their mothers?
    a. They are based on food supply.
    b. They rarely occur naturally.
    c. They are based on comfort and touch.
    d. They are genetically programmed.

Behaviorism: Thinking Like a Scientist, p. 41
Diff: E, Ans: d
60. What does Harlow's research demonstrate about theories?
    a. They rarely lead to any new insights.
    b. They are always accurate.
    c. They are useful only in sciences focusing on animals, not on humans.
    d. They lead to intriguing observations and hypotheses.

Behaviorism, p. 42
Diff: E, Ans: a
61.   Social learning involves:
    a.   copying a model.
    b.   learning how to be polite.
    c.   following the rules.
    d.   understanding one's own family.

Behaviorism, p. 42
Diff: E, Ans: b
62.   Social learning theory emphasizes learning through:
    a.   cooperation with others.
    b.   observation and imitation.
    c.   reinforcers.
    d.   understanding how one's behavior affects other people.

Behaviorism, p. 42
Diff: M, Ans: d
63.   After watching a new Jackie Chan movie, Rob tries some of the karate moves he saw in the film. Social
    learning theorists would say that _____ has occurred.
    a.   operant conditioning
    b.   classical conditioning
    c.   reinforcement
    d.   modeling

Behaviorism, p. 42
Diff: M, Ans: c
64.   A father wants his son to help his mother wash the dishes every night. According to social learning
    theory, the father should:
    a.   explain that a mother's love is greater than any other love.
    b.   promise the boy a new basketball if he helps wash the dishes.
    c.   help out with the dishes himself.
    d.   tell his son that he can't have dessert unless he helps with the dishes.

Cognitive Theory, p. 43
Diff: M, Ans: a
65.   Cognitive theories emphasize the:
    a.   development of thought processes and their effect on behavior.
    b.   role of unconscious urges and impulses.
    c.   control that external forces have over the direction of human development.
    d.   crisis that each individual must resolve at each stage of life.

Cognitive Theory, p. 43
Diff: E, Ans: c
66.   Cognitive theory focuses on which of the following?
    a.   actions
    b.   unconscious urges
    c.   thoughts
    d.   all of the above

Cognitive Theory, p. 43
Diff: E, Ans: b

67.   Which of the following is the predominant perspective in contemporary psychology?
    a.   psychoanalytic theory
    b.   cognitive theory
    c.   behaviorism
    d.   social learning theory

Cognitive Theory, p. 43
Diff: H, Ans: b

68.   Martina is a cognitive psychologist studying children's violence. Which of the following is most likely to be the title of her latest study?
    a.   "Unconscious motivations of violent children"
    b.   "Children's understanding of the world that leads them to violence"
    c.   "Societies that produce violent children"
    d.   "How parenting causes children to act violently"

Cognitive Theory, p. 43
Diff: E, Ans: d

69.   A major pioneer in cognitive theory was:
    a.   Freud.
    b.   Vygotsky.
    c.   Pavlov.
    d.   Piaget.

Cognitive Theory, p. 43
Diff: M, Ans: a

70.   Piaget's theory of development focused primarily on:
    a.   how our thinking changes as we grow older.
    b.   biological and physical changes.
    c.   our unconscious issues.
    d.   the ways in which our environment influences us.

Cognitive Theory, p. 43
Diff: H, Ans: c

71.   While testing questions for an intelligence test, Piaget became interested in the:
    a.   ability of young children to remember what they had been taught.
    b.   fact that children of well-educated parents had greater intelligence.
    c.   mistakes that children made that demonstrated how they thought.
    d.   importance of testing for specific knowledge.

Cognitive Theory, p. 43
Diff: E, Ans: a

72.   Piaget was most interested in:
    a.   studying how children think.
    b.   how parents discipline their children.
    c.   measuring what children know.
    d.   how peers influence each other.

Cognitive Theory, p. 43
Diff: M, Ans: b

73.   Piaget's view of cognitive development includes the idea that:
    a.   children learn best when they are rewarded for learning.
    b.   cognitive development follows age-related changes in understanding.
    c.   young children learn everything they know from their parents.
    d.   culture determines cognitive growth.

Cognitive Theory, p. 43
Diff: E, Ans: d
74.   Piaget's concept of cognitive equilibrium is:
   a.   learning to remain steady while walking or standing.
   b.   seeing the world from both your own and others' perspective.
   c.   behaving in ethical ways.
   d.   a state of mental balance.

Cognitive Theory, p. 43
Diff: E, Ans: d
75.   According to Piaget, cognitive growth is promoted by a need for:
   a.   assimilation.
   b.   models.
   c.   reinforcement.
   d.   equilibrium.

Cognitive Theory, p. 43
Diff: M, Ans: c
76.   When we adjust our old ways of thinking in order to fit in new information, Piaget calls this:
   a.   operating.
   b.   assimilating.
   c.   accommodating.
   d.   equilibrating.

Cognitive Theory, p. 43
Diff: M, Ans: d
77.   According to Piaget, the two elements of adaptation are:
   a.   object permanence and decentering.
   b.   concrete and formal operations.
   c.   equilibrium and disequilibrium.
   d.   assimilation and accommodation.

Cognitive Theory, p. 44 (Table 2.2)
Diff: E, Ans: c
78.   During the sensorimotor stage, the main task is to:
   a.   learn to use language to express sensations.
   b.   think of past and future events.
   c.   use senses and motor skills to understand the world.
   d.   think logically and critically.

Cognitive Theory, p. 44 (Table 2.2)
Diff: E, Ans: b
79.   Piaget's second stage of cognitive development is called:
   a.   formal operational.
   b.   preoperational.
   c.   concrete operational.
   d.   sensorimotor.

Cognitive Theory, p. 44 (Table 2.2)
Diff: M, Ans: a
80.   A child begins to think symbolically, including using language, in Piaget's _____ stage.
   a.   preoperational
   b.   sensorimotor
   c.   concrete operational
   d.   abstract intelligence

Cognitive Theory, p. 44 (Table 2.2)
Diff: H, Ans: d
81.   Olaf can reason consistently about real and tangible things. However, he cannot yet reason about abstract ideas or situations. Olaf is probably in Piaget's _____ stage.
a.   rational logic
b.   preoperational
c.   formal operational
d.   concrete operational

Cognitive Theory, p. 44 (Table 2.2)
Diff: E, Ans: c
82.   Piaget calls the most advanced stage of cognitive development:
a.   concrete operational.
b.   abstract operational.
c.   formal operational.
d.   symbolic operational.

Cognitive Theory, p. 45
Diff: E, Ans: b
83.   According to Piaget, when a new experience or idea does not fit a person's existing understanding, the person experiences cognitive:
a.   disbelief.
b.   disequilibrium.
c.   disarray.
d.   disorganization.

Cognitive Theory, p. 45
Diff: M, Ans: b
84.   If you were to see a man from the nation of Fiji, but had never seen someone from there before, you would still recognize him as a human being. This cognitive process is called:
a.   accommodation.
b.   assimilation.
c.   object permanence.
d.   disequilibrium.

Cognitive Theory, p. 45
Diff: H, Ans: d
85.   A 1-year-old likes to pull his cat's tail because the cat meows and moves away. One day he pulls another cat's tail and gets scratched. From that day on, he is cautious around cats. What cognitive process has probably occurred?
a.   decentering
b.   modeling
c.   assimilation
d.   accommodation

Cognitive Theory, p. 45
Diff: H, Ans: a
86.   A baby places all new objects into her mouth. However, after she places a shiny object into her mouth and it hurts her tongue, she no longer places shiny objects into her mouth. Piaget would say that the child has:
a.   experienced accommodation.
b.   demonstrated object permanence.
c.   experienced assimilation.
d.   demonstrated egocentrism.

Cognitive Theory, p. 45
Diff: H, Ans: d

87.   Imagine you and your friend are having a discussion about politics. Your friend makes an argument that puts your views into disequilibrium. If you respond by believing that your friend is simply uninformed or dumb, Piaget would say that you have _____ your friend's argument.
      a.   accommodated
      b.   disequilibrated
      c.   reinterpreted
      d.   assimilated

Emergent Theories

Sociocultural Theory, pp. 45-46
Diff: E, Ans: b

88.   The central thesis of sociocultural theory is that human development is the result of a dynamic interaction between developing persons and their:
      a.   genetic heritage.
      b.   surrounding society and culture.
      c.   physical well-being.
      d.   parents.

Sociocultural Theory, p. 46
Diff: E, Ans: b

89.   Lev Vygotsky is best known for his contributions to _____ theory.
      a.   cognitive
      b.   sociocultural
      c.   psychoanalytic
      d.   behavioral

Sociocultural Theory, p. 46
Diff: E, Ans: d

90.   According to the sociocultural theory, how do society and culture relate to development?
      a.   They are irrelevant.
      b.   They frame development but do not influence it.
      c.   They are external variables that impinge on the developing person.
      d.   They are integral to development.

Sociocultural Theory, p. 46
Diff: M, Ans: a

91.   According to the sociocultural theory, the primary means of learning is:
      a.   from more knowledgeable members of our society.
      b.   by observing others.
      c.   by learning at the same time as others.
      d.   through one's own discoveries.

Sociocultural Theory, p. 46
Diff: E, Ans: c

92.   According to Vygotsky, novices learn from mentors through a process termed an apprenticeship in:
      a.   career selection.
      b.   learning.
      c.   thinking.
      d.   development.

Sociocultural Theory, p. 46
Diff: M, Ans: a

93.   Vygotsky was particularly interested in the development of:
      a.   cognitive competencies.
      b.   family relationships.
      c.   genetic adaptations.
      d.   self-efficacy.

Sociocultural Theory, pp. 46-48
Diff: H, Ans: b

94.   Mr. McGinty works with his child, Edward, to put together a new puzzle. Each time Edward tries the puzzle, his father helps him less and less, and he requires less help from his father. This example best supports the view of development put forth by:
      a.   Piaget.
      b.   Vygotsky.
      c.   Skinner.
      d.   Freud.

Sociocultural Theory, p. 46
Diff: E, Ans: a

95.   The process by which a skilled person helps a novice learn by engaging the learner in joint activities is referred to as:
      a.   guided participation.
      b.   instruction.
      c.   selective adaptation.
      d.   assisted growth.

Sociocultural Theory, p. 46
Diff: H, Ans: d

96.   Which of the following is an example of guided participation?
      a.   A teacher lectures about rain, snow, and sleet in front of a class.
      b.   A child learns how to tie a knot through trial and error.
      c.   A parent demonstrates repeatedly how to zip a zipper.
      d.   An older child works together with a younger child to build a sand castle.

Sociocultural Theory, p. 46
Diff: M, Ans: d

97.   According to sociocultural theory, which of the following is a true statement about adult and child learning?
      a.   Adults learn from children.
      b.   Children learn from adults.
      c.   Children learn from peers.
      d.   All of the above are true statements.

Sociocultural Theory, p. 47
Diff: E, Ans: a

98.   According to sociocultural theory, the zone of proximal development refers to the skills that:
      a.   the learner can master with assistance.
      b.   overwhelm the learner.
      c.   the learner wants to learn.
      d.   the learner can perform independently.

Sociocultural Theory, p. 47
Diff: E, Ans: b

99.   According to sociocultural theory, learning occurs when the skills are:
   a.   more simple than those in the zone of proximal development.
   b.   in the zone of proximal development.
   c.   more complex than those in the zone of proximal development.
   d.   any of the above.

Sociocultural Theory, p. 47
Diff: E, Ans: c

100.   In Vygotsky's idea of social apprenticeship, a mentor draws the child into a zone of:
   a.   possibilities.
   b.   distal development.
   c.   proximal development.
   d.   potentiality.

Sociocultural Theory, pp. 47-48
Diff: M, Ans: c

101.   The concept of the zone of proximal development suggests that the parent or teacher do all of the following EXCEPT:
   a.   become attuned to the child's abilities.
   b.   urge the child to new levels of competence.
   c.   hold the child back until he or she can perform the skills independently.
   d.   provide support as the child takes on new challenges.

Sociocultural Theory, pp. 47-48
Diff: H, Ans: d

102.   With which of the following statements would a sociocultural theorist NOT agree?
   a.   It is important for the mentor to ensure that the novice is neither bored nor overwhelmed.
   b.   The teaching process must be under continuous modification.
   c.   Learning must be active.
   d.   The same manner of teaching can work for any individual.

Sociocultural Theory, p. 48
Diff: M, Ans: c

103.   Vygotsky's theory has been criticized for:
   a.   overlooking how people learn from one another.
   b.   failing to recognize how much children can learn when encouraged.
   c.   neglecting neurological maturation.
   d.   ignoring the dynamic interaction that occurs between people.

Epigenetic Theory, p. 48
Diff: E, Ans: a

104.   The newest developmental theory, the epigenetic theory, emphasizes:
   a.   how genetics and environment interact.
   b.   the various cultures in which we grow up.
   c.   how learning occurs within social interactions.
   d.   the "free will" individuals have to make decisions.

Epigenetic Theory, p. 49
Diff: M, Ans: d

105.   Epigenetic theory holds that:
   a.   environmental influences are much more important than genetics.
   b.   individuals can change their genes by behaving in particular ways.
   c.   every aspect of development is set in advance by genes.
   d.   all traits are influenced by genes.

Epigenetic Theory, p. 49
Diff: H, Ans: b

106.   Which of the following is an example of the influence of an epigenetic factor?
    a.   School-age children who were well-nourished in infancy are more intelligent.
    b.   Only individuals with a gene for schizophrenia and a traumatic early life event are likely to develop schizophrenia.
    c.   Teenagers who spend time with delinquent peers demonstrate more delinquency.
    d.   People who live in smog-filled cities and smoke are more likely to develop lung cancer.

Epigenetic Theory, p. 50
Diff: M, Ans: a

107.   If we find that over the past few centuries, humans have come to run faster than previous generations did and that this ability is important for survival, we might say that _____ has occurred.
    a.   selective adaptation
    b.   reciprocal determinism
    c.   genetic reduction
    d.   systematic elimination

In Person: My Beautiful, Hairless Babies, p. 51
Diff: E, Ans: c

108.   The study of patterns of animal behavior, particularly as the behavior relates to evolution, is referred to as:
    a.   epigenetics.
    b.   behaviorism.
    c.   ethology.
    d.   zoology.

In Person: My Beautiful, Hairless Babies, p. 51
Diff: H, Ans: d

109.   Jan is a psychologist with a strong interest in attachment and ethology. What is likely to be the title of her newest study?
    a.   "The unconscious reasons why children form attachments"
    b.   "How mothers can encourage attachment"
    c.   "The long-term impact of secure attachment in childhood"
    d.   "Why attachment is necessary for survival"

What Theories Can Contribute

What Theories Can Contribute, p. 53 (Table 2.3)
Diff: E, Ans: c

110.   All of the following are stage theories EXCEPT:
    a.   Piaget's cognitive theory.
    b.   Freud's psychosexual theory.
    c.   Skinner's behaviorism.
    d.   Erikson's psychosocial theory.

What Theories Can Contribute, p. 53 (Table 2.3)
Diff: H, Ans: d

111.   The theory that most strongly emphasizes nurture as important in development is:
    a.   Piaget's cognitive theory.
    b.   Erikson's psychosocial theory.
    c.   epigenetic theory.
    d.   behaviorism.

What Theories Can Contribute, p. 53
Diff: E, Ans: b

112.   Most developmental psychologists are:
   a.   Freudian, because early experiences are so important.
   b.   eclectic, because each theory of human development has its limitations.
   c.   sociocultural theorists, because many factors influence development.
   d.   learning theorists, because behaviorism is the most scientific.

What Theories Can Contribute, p. 53
Diff: M, Ans: c

113.   A researcher in human development who takes an eclectic approach:
   a.   emphasizes the role of ecosystems.
   b.   believes that social learning is the best descriptor of human behavior.
   c.   uses parts of several theories rather than sticking to one particular theory.
   d.   does not use any theories.

The Nature-Nurture Controversy, p. 53
Diff: E, Ans: d

114.   Developmentalists' argument over the relative importance of hereditary and environmental influences
        is called the:
   a.   social-context controversy.
   b.   genetic-engineering controversy.
   c.   social-engineering controversy.
   d.   nature-nurture controversy.

The Nature-Nurture Controversy, p. 53
Diff: E, Ans: c

115.   When psychologists say that a given trait is due more to nature than nurture, they mean that the trait:
   a.   is universal; that is, it is found in everyone.
   b.   is a result of experiences.
   c.   is mostly influenced by the traits inherited at the moment of conception.
   d.   cannot be influenced by the environment.

The Nature-Nurture Controversy, p. 53
Diff: M, Ans: a

116.   Parents who spend great deal of time and money trying to find the best school for their children are
        emphasizing the importance of:
   a.   nurture.
   b.   the zone of proximal development.
   c.   nature.
   d.   operant conditioning.

The Nature-Nurture Controversy, p. 54
Diff: M, Ans: b

117.   Which of the following statements best reflects developmentalists' current thinking on the nature-
        nurture controversy?
   a.   Nurture is the predominant influence in determining human traits.
   b.   The interaction between nature and nurture is crucial to the production of every trait.
   c.   Few significant discoveries will be made until this controversy is settled.
   d.   Some traits are due entirely to nurture, and some are entirely due to nature.

Theoretical Perspectives on Hyperactivity and Homosexuality, p. 54
Diff: H, Ans: c
118. Which of the following is evidence for the influence of nature on attention-deficit/hyperactivity disorder (AD/HD)?
    a. AD/HD is diagnosed at a higher rate now than it was 50 years ago.
    b. Rates of AD/HD are much higher in some classrooms than in others.
    c. AD/HD children are usually boys.
    d. All of the above are evidence for the influence of nature on AD/HD.

Theoretical Perspectives on Hyperactivity and Homosexuality, p. 55
Diff: H, Ans: d
119. Which of the following is evidence for the influence of nature on homosexuality?
    a. Children raised by homosexual couples have the same rate of homosexuality as children raised by heterosexuals.
    b. Many people have homosexual impulses that they do not act on.
    c. There is no evidence for the role of parental relationship or personality characteristics.
    d. All of the above are evidence for the influence of nature on homosexuality.

TRUE-FALSE QUESTIONS

What Theories Do

Ans: F, p. 33
1. A developmental theory is information that has been proven to be true by extensive research.

Ans: F, p. 34
2. Emergent theories have traditionally inspired thinking in the developmental psychology field.

Ans: T, pp. 33-34
3. The three grand theoretical approaches described in the chapter (psychoanalytic, behaviorism, and cognitive) are NOT the only theories that contribute to the study of human development.

Grand Theories

Ans: T, p. 34
4. Psychoanalytic theory views irrational and unconscious inner drives and motives as influencing even the smallest details of daily life.

Ans: F, p. 35
5. The theory of childhood sexuality was first proposed by Erikson.

Ans: F, p. 35
6. Psychoanalytic theories are most concerned with how often (and under what circumstances) we have been punished and reinforced.

Ans: T, p. 35
7. According to Freud, the development of even young infants involves sensual pleasures.

Ans: F, p. 36
8. Erikson's theory of development is a sociocultural theory because it stresses the importance of both society and the culture in which we live.

Ans: T, p. 36
9. Erikson's theory involves developmental crises that involve two opposite outcomes, but most people end up somewhere in the middle.

Ans: F, p. 37 (Table 2.1)

10.   According to Freud, during the latency stage, sexual interests are vigorous.

Ans: T, p. 37 (Table 2.1)

11.   Erikson's first five stages of psychosocial development are closely related to Freud's psychosexual stages.

Ans: T, p. 37 (Table 2.1)

12.   According to Erikson, during the industry vs. inferiority stage, the child is learning to feel competent and to master new skills.

Ans: F, p. 37 (Table 2.1)

13.   According to Erikson, if a young adult is able to find love and companionship in a relationship with another person, he or she will resolve the sixth crisis by achieving intimacy. If he or she is not able to do this, he or she will resolve the sixth crisis by achieving a sense inferiority.

Ans: F, pp. 37-38

14.   Watson would agree with the statement, "Genetics are very important in determining what path an individual will take in life."

Ans: T, p. 38

15.   The basic laws of behavior, as formulated by behaviorists, apply to any individual, from newborn to octogenarian.

Ans: T, p. 38

16.   Conditioning refers to any process in which a behavior is learned.

Ans: F, p. 38

17.   When a dog begins to bark at the sound of his owner's keys jingling outside the door, operant conditioning has occurred.

Ans: F, p. 39

18.   Only a few human behaviors can be understood as a result of operant conditioning.

Ans: T, p. 39

19.   Earning a paycheck is the result of operant conditioning.

Ans: F, p. 39

20.   In classical conditioning, individuals become more or less likely to do a behavior based on the consequences of the behavior.

Ans: T, p. 39

21.   Within operant conditioning, what might appear to be a punishment could actually serve as a reinforcer.

Ans: F, p. 39

22.   For operant conditioning to work, reinforcers must be given each and every time the individual performs the behavior.

Ans: F, p. 42

23.   According to social learning theory, individuals model any behavior they see repeatedly.

Ans: T, p. 42

24.   According to social learning theory, modeling is more likely to occur if the model is respected and admired by the observer.

Ans: T, p. 43

25.   According to Piaget, disequilibrium represents a cognitive imbalance that initially produces confusion and ultimately results in growth.

Ans: T, pp. 43-44

26.   According to Piaget, there are four age-related periods of cognitive development, each with a different type of knowing and understanding.

Emergent Theories

Ans: T, p. 46

27.   A major pioneer of the sociocultural perspective was Lev Vygotsky.

Ans: F, p. 46

28.   Vygotsky believed the most universally important learning tool was television.

Ans: T, p. 46

29.   According to sociocultural theory, the process of learning continues throughout life, with adults learning from individuals of all ages.

Ans: F, p. 46

30.   According to sociocultural theory, individuals very often learn skills on their own, through a process of trial and error.

Ans: F, p. 48

31.   According to sociocultural theory, learning can be either active or passive.

Ans: T, p. 48

32.   Preformism refers to the belief that every aspect of development is set in advance by genes.

Ans: F, p. 49

33.   Epigenetic theory posits that most human traits are genetic; only a few can be influenced by the environment.

Ans: T, p. 49

34.   According to epigenetic theory, food, loving care, and freedom to play can affect the expression of genetic instructions.

Ans: F, p. 50

35.   Selective adaptation is a process important to behaviorism.

Ans: T, p. 50

36.   According to epigenetic theory, a particular trait will become more common in the population if the trait contributes to the survival of the species.

Ans: T, p. 51 (In Person: My Beautiful, Hairless Babies)

37.   Ethology is particularly interested in the instinctive behaviors of infants and their caregivers.

What Theories Can Contribute

Ans: F, p. 53

38.   Most developmentalists today are strongly committed to one of the theories described in this chapter.

Ans: F, p. 53

39.   To be eclectic means to be practical and to use no theory.

Ans: F, p. 53

40. Nature refers to those traits that are evident at birth, whereas nurture refers to all traits that emerge after birth.

Ans: T, p. 54

41. Prenatal medical care is considered to be part of nurture.

Ans: F, p. 54

42. The important question in the nature-nurture debate is whether nature or nurture influences a trait rather than how much nature and nurture each influence a trait.

Ans: F, p. 55

43. When researchers began to test hypotheses about the roots of homosexuality, nurture was revealed to be crucial in determining sexual orientation.

FILL-IN-THE-BLANK QUESTIONS

What Theories Do

Ans: Emergent, p. 34

1. _____ theories bring together information from various disciplines but have not yet cohered into fully comprehensive theories.

Grand Theories

Ans: Psychoanalytic, p. 35

2. _____ theory interprets human behavior in terms of unconscious drives and motives.

Ans: oral; anal; phallic, p. 36

3. The first psychosexual stage identified by Freud is the _____ stage, the second is the _____ stage, and the third is the _____ stage.

Ans: crisis (or challenge), p. 36

4. According to Erikson, each psychosocial stage is characterized by a particular _____ that must be resolved.

Ans: psychosocial, p. 37 (Table 2.1)

5. Whereas Freud described psychosexual stages of development, Erikson described _____ stages.

Ans: adolescence, p. 37 (Table 2.1)

6. According to Freud, the last psychosexual stage, the genital stage, is reached at _____.

Ans: mistrust, p. 37 (Table 2.1)

7. According to Erikson, if infants learn that others will provide for their basic needs, they will resolve the first crisis with trust. If infants do not learn this, they will resolve the first crisis with _____.

Ans: despair, p. 37 (Table 2.1)

8. According to Erikson, if older adults look back on their life and believe it has meaning, they will resolve the final crisis with integrity. If they are not able to do this, they will resolve the final crisis with _____.

Ans: observed, pp. 37-38

9. Behaviorists believe that psychologists should limit their study to behaviors that can be _____ and measured.

Ans: neutral, p. 38

10.   In classical conditioning, an animal or person comes to associate a(n) _____ stimulus with a meaningful one.

Ans: classical, p. 38

11.   Your palms sweat when you see exam booklets even on days that you do not have an exam; this is an example of _____ conditioning.

Ans: operant, p. 38

12.   B. F. Skinner was an American behaviorist who believed that _____ conditioning explained much of human behavior.

Ans: reinforcement, p. 39

13.   A consequence that increases the likelihood that a behavior will be repeated is called a(n) _____.

Ans: modeling, p. 42

14.   Your son has just repeated the swear word you used when you stubbed your toe. A social learning theorist would say that your son has just demonstrated _____.

Ans: self-efficacy, p. 42

15.   In social learning theory, the belief that one is effective is referred to as _____.

Ans: senses; motor, p. 44 (Table 2.2)

16.   According to Piaget, in the first stage of cognitive development, the infant uses his or her _____ and _____ abilities to understand the world.

Ans: accommodate, p. 45

17.   According to Piaget, when individuals cannot reinterpret new experiences to fit into old ideas, they must _____ the experiences by altering their ideas.

Emergent Theories

Ans: Sociocultural, pp. 45-46

18.   _____ theory seeks to explain growth of individual knowledge and competencies in terms of guidance, support, and structure provided by the broader cultural context.

Ans: guided participation, p. 46

19.   Vygotsky believed that parents and teachers mentor children in various skills by using _____, in which the mentor and child engage in joint activities.

Ans: proximal development, p. 47

20.   Vygotsky said the mentor draws the child into the zone of _____.

Ans: biological (or genetic), p. 48

21.   Sociocultural theory has been criticized for neglecting _____ processes that guide development.

Ans: genetic; environmental, p. 49

22.   Epigenetic theory stresses the interaction between _____ and _____ factors in development.

Ans: selective adaptation, p. 50

23.   The process by which some genes are more likely to pass from one generation to the next because they contribute to the survival of the species is referred to as _____.

What Theories Can Contribute

Ans: eclectic, p. 53

24. A developmentalist who draws from many theories, using what is most helpful from each, is said to have a(n) _____ perspective.

Ans: Nurture, p. 53

25. _____ refers to all of the environmental influences that affect development after an individual is conceived.

ESSAY QUESTIONS

1. Describe three functions of a developmental theory.

2. Describe two ways in which Erikson's psychoanalytic theory differs from Freud's psychoanalytic theory.

3. Name, describe, and give the approximate ages for the five stages of Freud's psychosexual theory of development.

4. Imagine that you are a developmental psychologist who wants to understand a 15-year-old boy from a little-known area of the world. What would you expect to learn by applying Freud's psychosexual theory of development? By applying Erikson's psychosocial theory of development? Which theory do you think will prove most useful in this case, and why?

5. Describe how classical conditioning can explain why a cat comes running at the sound of an electric can opener.

6. Briefly describe what is learned in classical conditioning and what is learned in operant conditioning, and give an example of each type of conditioning. What do you think is the biggest difference between the two types of conditioning?

7. Give a detailed description of how you could use operant conditioning to get your roommate to make her bed more often.

8. How does social learning theory differ from traditional behaviorism?

9. Name, describe, and give the approximate ages for the four stages of cognitive development as outlined by Piaget.

10. Define the terms assimilation and accommodation. Describe one way in which these processes are similar and one way in which they are different.

11. Give an example of a time when you assimilated a new experience and an example of a time when you accommodated to it.

12. A person is confronted with an event that is out of the ordinary; for example, the betrayal by a friend, or the devastating effects of an earthquake, or an encounter with an extraterrestrial being. Describe the person's possible reaction to one of these experiences, using the terms from cognitive theory (for example, *equilibrium*, *disequilibrium*, *adaptation*, and *assimilation*).

13. A fourth-grade class includes several children who are disruptively aggressive. In detail, explain how a behaviorist would define the problem and help the disruptive children, the teacher, and the other students.

14.   Dina, a child in her first year of nursery school, refuses to share her toys with other children. She always grabs what she wants and screams and hits when something is taken away. She does not respond to the teacher's lessons about sharing. In three separate statements, describe what a psychoanalytic theorist, a behaviorist, and a cognitive theorist would say about Dina's behavior and how to remedy it.

15.   Imagine you want to teach a child how to do a jigsaw puzzle. Following sociocultural theory, describe the steps you should take to try to help the child learn how to do the jigsaw puzzle independently. How will you know if the child is learning?

16.   Give an example of an epigenetic factor that you think might influence an individual's intelligence.

17.   You are a psychologist who wants to explain each of the following problems or behaviors. Identify which of the three major theoretical perspectives examined in this chapter will be most useful to you in each case, and briefly explain why.
        a.   Randy finds it difficult to stop smoking, especially when he is studying.
        b.   Alec has an irrational fear of thunderstorms.
        c.   Anne always misbehaves in the supermarket, but is perfectly well-behaved in the car.
        d.   Debra thinks that girls can change into men when they grow up.
        e.   Coco, a cocker spaniel, has learned to sniff out narcotics at the airport.

18.   Briefly describe one of your personal characteristics or abilities that you believe is primarily the result of nature and one that you believe is primarily the result of nurture. Then, demonstrate how nurture has had an influence on the "natural" characteristic and how nature has had an influence on the "nurtured" characteristic.

Answer guidelines to these essay questions can be found in the Appendix at the end of the Test Bank.

CHAPTER 3 — Heredity and Environment

MULTIPLE-CHOICE QUESTIONS

The Genetic Code

What Genes Are, p. 59
Diff: E, Ans: c
1. The molecular basis of heredity, constructed of a double helix, is:
    a. the gene.
    b. thymine.
    c. DNA.
    d. the cell.

What Genes Are, p. 59
Diff: E, Ans: d
2. Molecules of DNA are referred to as:
    a. cells.
    b. adenine.
    c. genes.
    d. chromosomes.

What Genes Are, p. 60
Diff: E, Ans: a
3. A genome is:
    a. the full set of genes for a particular organism.
    b. a molecule of DNA.
    c. the basic unit of heredity.
    d. the manufacturer of protein.

What Genes Are, p. 59
Diff: E, Ans: c
4. The genes in our cells are segments of:
    a. adenine.
    b. thymine.
    c. DNA.
    d. cytosine.

The Beginnings of Human Life, p. 60
Diff: H, Ans: a
5. The instructions on each gene are written in a chemical code made up of:
    a. four bases.
    b. a dozen or so base pairs.
    c. 23 chromosome pairs.
    d. 10 trillion cells.

The Beginnings of Human Life, p. 60
Diff: M, Ans: a
6.   The genetic code directs the synthesis of hundreds of different kinds of:
      a.   proteins.
      b.   genes.
      c.   chromosomes.
      d.   cytosines.

What Genes Are, p. 60
Diff: H, Ans: b
7.   Which of the following is a true statement?
      a.   There are four types of protein, symbolized as A, T, C, and G.
      b.   A gene is a section of DNA that contains instructions for a particular protein.
      c.   Every cell contains 46 pairs of genomes.
      d.   Each triplet is the genetic code for a human being.

What Genes Are, p. 60
Diff: E, Ans: a
8.   Every normal human body cell contains how many chromosomes?
      a.   23 pairs
      b.   23
      c.   46 pairs
      d.   about 1,000

What Genes Are, p. 61
Diff: M, Ans: c
9.   Approximately how many genes are contained in the human genome?
      a.   3
      b.   300
      c.   30,000
      d.   3 million

The Beginnings of Human Life, p. 61
Diff: E, Ans: b
10.   The sperm and the ovum are:
      a.   chromosomes.
      b.   gametes.
      c.   eggs.
      d.   zygotes.

The Beginnings of Human Life, p. 61
Diff: M, Ans: a
11.   A sperm has _____ as many genes as a normal body cell.
      a.   half
      b.   four times
      c.   twice
      d.   just

The Beginnings of Human Life, p. 61
Diff: H, Ans: c
12.   About how many chromosomally different ova or sperm can be produced by a single individual?
      a.   100
      b.   10,000
      c.   8 million
      d.   60 billion

The Beginnings of Human Life, p. 61
Diff: E, Ans: a

13. Human development begins when a sperm penetrates the membrane of:
    a. an ovum.
    b. the ovary.
    c. the placenta.
    d. an amino acid.

The Beginnings of Human Life, p. 61
Diff: E, Ans: c

14. When two human reproductive cells combine at the moment of conception, the result is a:
    a. fetus.
    b. pair of twins.
    c. zygote.
    d. gamete.

The Beginnings of Human Life, p. 61
Diff: E, Ans: d

15. An organism's entire genetic inheritance is referred to as its:
    a. gamete.
    b. genome.
    c. zygote.
    d. genotype.

The Beginnings of Human Life, p. 61
Diff: H, Ans: c

16. A karyotype is a:
    a. person's demonstrated traits.
    b. chart of the generations in a family.
    c. chromosomal portrait.
    d. single cell containing all of a person's genes.

The Beginnings of Human Life, p. 62
Diff: E, Ans: b

17. A person's sex is determined by:
    a. nurture during prenatal development.
    b. the 23rd pair of chromosomes.
    c. the first pair of chromosomes.
    d. hormones released during prenatal development.

The Beginnings of Human Life, p. 62
Diff: E, Ans: b

18. An XX pattern in the 23rd pair of chromosomes indicates the a fetus will:
    a. have Down syndrome.
    b. be female.
    c. be male.
    d. be homosexual.

The Beginnings of Human Life, p. 62
Diff: E, Ans: a

19. In the twenty-third pair, a normal girl has:
    a. two X chromosomes.
    b. two Y chromosomes.
    c. one X and Y chromosome.
    d. one X chromosome.

The Beginnings of Human Life, p. 62
Diff: M, Ans: c

20.   An individual with at least one X chromosome in the twenty-third pair:
        a.   must be a boy.
        b.   must be a girl.
        c.   might be a boy.
        d.   cannot be a boy.

The Beginnings of Human Life, p. 62
Diff: M, Ans: a

21.   One difference between sperm cells and ova is that:
        a.   ova carry an X chromosome, whereas sperm carry either an X or a Y chromosome.
        b.   ova carry two X chromosomes, whereas sperm carry two Y chromosomes.
        c.   sperm carry more genetic material than ova do.
        d.   ova always carry an X chromosome, whereas sperm always carry a Y chromosome.

The Beginnings of Human Life, p. 62
Diff: M, Ans: c

22.   The chromosomal make-up of a normal male is _____; the chromosomal make-up of a normal female
        is _____.
        a.   YY; XY
        b.   XX; XY
        c.   XY; XX
        d.   YY; XX

The Beginnings of Human Life, p. 62
Diff: E, Ans: b

23.   The determining factor in a zygote's sex is:
        a.   which ovum becomes fertilized.
        b.   which sperm reaches the ovum first.
        c.   the time it takes the sperm and ovum to meet.
        d.   the number of sperm the father has.

The Beginnings of Human Life, p. 62
Diff: E, Ans: a

24.   An allele is:
        a.   a normal variation of a particular gene.
        b.   either an X or a Y.
        c.   the gene that causes twins to develop.
        d.   an individual's actual appearance and behavior.

The Beginnings of Human Life, p. 62
Diff: H, Ans: d

25.   Some families have only male offspring generation after generation. Given what you know about
        genetics, which of the following could be the explanation?
        a.   The women produce ova with healthy X, but unhealthy Y chromosomes.
        b.   The men produce sperm with healthy X, but unhealthy Y chromosomes.
        c.   The women produce ova with healthy Y, but unhealthy X chromosomes.
        d.   The men produce sperm with healthy Y, but unhealthy X chromosomes.

The Beginnings of Human Life, pp. 64-65
Diff: M, Ans: c

26.   Monozygotic twins are produced when:
        a.   two ova are fertilized by a single sperm.
        b.   two ova are fertilized by different sperm.
        c.   one ovum is fertilized by one sperm, but then splits to form two halves.
        d.   one ovum is fertilized by two sperm, which causes a split.

The Beginnings of Human Life, pp. 64-65
Diff: E, Ans: b

27. Monozygotic twins:
    a. can be both male, both female, or one male and one female.
    b. originate from one zygote.
    c. are also known as fraternal twins.
    d. are all of the above.

The Beginnings of Human Life, p. 64
Diff: M, Ans: a

28. Fraternal twins usually result from:
    a. two ova that were fertilized at about the same time.
    b. sperm from two different fathers.
    c. a zygote splitting during the first two weeks after conception.
    d. none of the above.

The Beginnings of Human Life, p. 64
Diff: E, Ans: b

29. Monozygotic twins are also known as:
    a. fraternal twins.
    b. identical twins.
    c. half-siblings.
    d. Down syndrome children.

The Beginnings of Human Life, p. 64
Diff: M, Ans: a

30. Dizygotic twins result when:
    a. two ova are fertilized by two different sperm.
    b. one ovum splits and is then fertilized by two different sperm.
    c. one ovum is fertilized by a single sperm and the fertilized egg splits.
    d. monozygotic twins are of different sexes.

The Beginnings of Human Life, p. 64
Diff: M, Ans: c

31. The most important reason that dizygotic twins are less alike than monozygotic twins is that dizygotic twins share fewer common:
    a. experiences.
    b. parents.
    c. genes.
    d. environments.

The Beginnings of Human Life, p. 64
Diff: H, Ans: a

32. A woman has just had twins, a boy and a girl. That means they came from:
    a. two ova fertilized by two sperm.
    b. one ovum fertilized by two sperm.
    c. a zygote that split into two.
    d. two ova fertilized by one sperm.

The Beginnings of Human Life, p. 64
Diff: H, Ans: b
33.   Given a set of quadruplets consisting of two girls and two boys, AT LEAST how many ova had to be
       fertilized?
       a.   one
       b.   two
       c.   three
       d.   four

Duplication, Division, and Differentiation, pp. 64-65
Diff: M, Ans: a
34.   The first hours and days of human development involve the processes of:
       a.   duplication, division, and differentiation.
       b.   duplication, specialization, and progression.
       c.   division, multiplication, and specialization.
       d.   differentiation, division, and centralization.

Duplication, Division, and Differentiation, pp. 64-65
Diff: H, Ans: c
35.   Which of the following is a true statement about the zygote in the first few hours after conception?
       a.   It is in the process of becoming either a male zygote or a female zygote.
       b.   The single cell splits suddenly into 46 similar cells.
       c.   Its chromosomes duplicate and then split, forming two identical cells, then four, and so on.
       d.   Its gamete is forming.

Duplication, Division, and Differentiation, p. 65
Diff: H, Ans: a
36.   Differentiation refers to the process by which:
       a.   zygotic cells specialize depending on where they are located.
       b.   the single zygotic cell splits into two cells, then four cells, and so on.
       c.   identical twins attempt to make a distinction between themselves.
       d.   sperm and ova are formed.

Duplication, Division, and Differentiation, p. 65
Diff: E, Ans: d
37.   The sum total of all the genes a person inherits is called the:
       a.   dominant pattern.
       b.   additive pattern.
       c.   phenotype.
       d.   genotype.

Duplication, Division, and Differentiation, p. 65
Diff: E, Ans: c
38.   Phenotype refers to:
       a.   a person's total genetic inheritance.
       b.   the recessive genes a person carries.
       c.   the actual expression of traits.
       d.   the dominant genes a person carries.

Duplication, Division, and Differentiation, p. 65
Diff: H, Ans: d
39.   Genotype is to phenotype as:
       a.   feminine is to masculine.
       b.   feminine is to human.
       c.   frequent is to rare.
       d.   hidden is to observable.

Duplication, Division, and Differentiation, p. 65
Diff: M, Ans: c
40.   Phenotype is a result of:
a.   genetics only.
b.   environment only.
c.   both genetics and environment.
d.   neither genetics nor environment.

Gene-Gene Interactions, p. 65
Diff: M, Ans: c
41.   Because most traits are polygenic, they are:
a.   the result of dominant genes.
b.   constantly changing.
c.   produced by many genes.
d.   unaffected by the environment.

Gene-Gene Interactions, p. 65
Diff: E, Ans: d
42.   Traits affected by many genes are said to be:
a.   genotypic.
b.   multifactorial.
c.   phenotypic.
d.   polygenic.

Gene-Gene Interactions, p. 65
Diff: M, Ans: a
43.   If a human characteristic is the result of the interaction of genes and the environment, the characteristic
is considered to be:
a.   multifactorial.
b.   mosaical.
c.   dominant.
d.   additive.

Gene-Gene Interactions, pp. 65-66
Diff: M, Ans: c
44.   If your mom's family members all have very dark skin and your dad's family members all have very
light skin, your skin color may be somewhere in between. Each parent's genes contributed in a(n)
_____ fashion.
a.   dominant-recessive
b.   dizygotic
c.   additive
d.   nonadditive

Gene-Gene Interactions, p. 66
Diff: H, Ans: a
45.   Raquel's mother is very tall and comes from a family in which almost everyone is above average in
height. Raquel's father is quite short and comes from a family where almost everyone is below average
in height. We would expect that Raquel will be of _____ height because the genes that affect height
relate in a(n) _____ pattern.
a.   average; additive
b.   average; dominant-recessive
c.   above average; additive
d.   above average; dominant-recessive

Gene-Gene Interactions, p. 66
Diff: H, Ans: c

46.   The difference between additive and nonadditive genetic patterns is whether:
      a.   they are present in twins.
      b.   the trait is observable.
      c.   all alleles contribute.
      d.   whether environment has an effect.

Gene-Gene Interactions, p. 66
Diff: M, Ans: d

47.   The dominant-recessive pattern is:
      a.   monozygotic.
      b.   dizygotic.
      c.   additive.
      d.   nonadditive.

Gene-Gene Interactions, p. 66
Diff: E, Ans: a

48.   When a particular inherited characteristic is controlled more by one gene of a pair than by the other, the stronger gene is called:
      a.   dominant.
      b.   phenotypic.
      c.   recessive.
      d.   genotypic.

Gene-Gene Interactions, p. 66
Diff: M, Ans: b

49.   A gene is recessive when:
      a.   it skips a generation.
      b.   its influence can be hidden by a more powerful gene.
      c.   it is smaller than the other genes.
      d.   it does not appear in the genotype.

Gene-Gene Interactions, p. 66
Diff: H, Ans: b

50.   When a dominant gene influences a phenotype, but the recessive gene also has some influence, this is referred to as:
      a.   a recessive interaction.
      b.   incomplete dominance.
      c.   an additive factor.
      d.   incomplete recessiveness.

Gene-Gene Interactions, p. 66
Diff: H, Ans: c

51.   Imagine that eye color is determined by only one pair of genes and that brown eyes are dominant over blue eyes. If you are blue-eyed and both your parents are brown-eyed, you know that:
      a.   you have at least one gene for brown eyes.
      b.   all your siblings will be brown-eyed.
      c.   both your parents are carriers for blue eyes.
      d.   you were adopted.

Gene-Gene Interactions, p. 66
Diff: H, Ans: d
52. A blue-eyed man marries a brown-eyed woman. They have four children. If eye color is determined by only one pair of genes and brown eyes are dominant over blue eyes, how many will have blue eyes?
    a. none
    b. one
    c. two
    d. impossible to predict

Gene-Gene Interaction, p. 66
Diff: M, Ans: a
53. You can be a carrier of a recessive gene as part of your:
    a. genotype.
    b. phenotype.
    c. nurture.
    d. genotype and phenotype.

Gene-Gene Interactions, pp. 66-67
Diff: H, Ans: a
54. Color blindness is more common among males because:
    a. most color blindness is inherited by a recessive gene on the X chromosome.
    b. males have only one Y chromosome.
    c. most color blindness is inherited by a recessive gene on the Y chromosome.
    d. the gene for color blindness is a dominant gene.

Gene-Gene Interactions, pp. 66-67
Diff: M, Ans: a
55. Recessive X-linked genes are:
    a. more likely to be expressed in a man's phenotype.
    b. more likely to be expressed in a woman's phenotype.
    c. carried on all chromosomes.
    d. never expressed in a phenotype.

Gene-Gene Interactions, pp. 66-67
Diff: M, Ans: a
56. Boys can inherit an X-linked trait from their:
    a. mother only.
    b. father only.
    c. mother or father.
    d. father's mother only.

Gene-Gene Interactions, pp. 66-67
Diff: H, Ans: b
57. The recessive gene for a certain learning disability is X-linked. This means that:
    a. females are twice as likely as males to have this disability.
    b. females will have this disability only if they inherit the gene from both parents.
    c. males will have this disability only if they inherit the gene from both parents.
    d. males can carry for the gene but will not have the disability.

Gene-Gene Interactions, p. 68
Diff: H, Ans: d
58. Which statement about genetic interaction is accurate?
    a. Patterns of gene interaction are usually straightforward.
    b. The presence of a dominant gene will always suppress any recessive genes.
    c. The final product of additive genes is always the average of all the contributions.
    d. Some genes behave differently depending on whether they come from the mother or the father.

Gene-Gene Interactions, p. 68
Diff: H, Ans: c

59.   Genetic "imprinting" refers to genes whose expressions are affected by whether they are:
      a.   phenotypes or genotypes.
      b.   dominant or recessive.
      c.   from mother or father.
      d.   additive or nonadditive.

Genetic Diversity, p. 68
Diff: M, Ans: d

60.   When you were conceived, the particular chromosomes that you received represented 1 out of about
      how many possible combinations of chromosomes your parents could produce?
      a.   4
      b.   about 100
      c.   1 million
      d.   64 trillion

Genetic Diversity, p. 68
Diff: H, Ans: b

61.   All of the following factors contribute to genetic diversity EXCEPT the:
      a.   variety of chromosomal combinations possible from each parent.
      b.   varying number of chromosomes possible in each cell.
      c.   mutations of genetic information caused by environmental factors.
      d.   crossing-over of genes before chromosome division.

Genetic Diversity, p. 68
Diff: M, Ans: a

62.   Which of the following statements is true of genetic diversity?
      a.   It maintains the species.
      b.   It cannot be influenced by environmental factors.
      c.   It is more important for females than for males.
      d.   It exists for behavioral traits but not for physiological traits.

Thinking Like a Scientist: The Human Genome Project, p. 69
Diff: M, Ans: b

63.   Which of the following was learned from the Human Genome Project?
      a.   Humans have about 1 million genes.
      b.   All living creatures share genes.
      c.   Humans and chimpanzees share about 25 percent of their genes.
      d.   All of the above were learned.

From Genotype to Phenotype

From Genotype to Phenotype, pp. 70–71
Diff: E, Ans: c

64.   Physical traits such as height are:
      a.   totally determined by genetics.
      b.   totally determined by environment.
      c.   determined by environmental influences and genetic potential.
      d.   not attributable to either genetics or environment.

Behavior Genetics, p. 71
Diff: E, Ans: d

65. Behavior genetics is the study of:
    a. how an individual's genes can change with behavior.
    b. what genes cause individuals to mate with poor genetic counterparts.
    c. why zygotes copy their genetic material and then split.
    d. the genetic origins of psychological characteristics.

Behavior Genetics, p. 71
Diff: H, Ans: d

66. Which of the following is a true statement about insights that have been made from research in behavior genetics?
    a. Many behavior patterns can be caused by more than one genotype.
    b. Many genotypes can result in more than one phenotype.
    c. Genetic origins of behavior patterns do not imply that it is fixed or unalterable.
    d. All of the above are true.

Senility Caused by Alzheimer's Disease, p. 72
Diff: E, Ans: d

67. Which of these statements regarding Alzheimer's disease is true?
    a. It is entirely a genetic disorder.
    b. It is genetic for men, but not for women.
    c. It is entirely determined by your upbringing.
    d. It is determined by both genetics and environment.

Senility Caused by Alzheimer's Disease, p. 72
Diff: M, Ans: d

68. Which of the following affect an individual's likelihood of developing senility caused by Alzheimer's disease?
    a. the ApoE genes
    b. diet, exercise, and not smoking
    c. level of emotional expression in childhood
    d. all of the above

Schizophrenia, p. 73
Diff: M, Ans: c

69. Which of the following individuals has the highest risk of developing schizophrenia?
    a. an individual who has a sibling with schizophrenia
    b. an individual who has a mother with schizophrenia
    c. an individual who has a monozygotic twin with schizophrenia
    d. none of the above, since schizophrenia is determined only by environmental factors.

Schizophrenia, p. 73
Diff: H, Ans: a

70. If you learned that schizophrenia is more highly correlated among monozygotic twins than among dizygotic twins, you could conclude that:
    a. schizophrenia is at least partly genetic.
    b. schizophrenia is affected by having a twin.
    c. monozygotic twins are usually schizophrenic.
    d. schizophrenia is polygenic.

Alcoholism, pp. 73-74
Diff: M, Ans: c
71.   All of the following affect the development of alcoholism EXCEPT:
      a.   biochemical make-up.
      b.   cultural beliefs about appropriate alcohol use.
      c.   moral make-up.
      d.   temperamental traits.

Alcoholism, pp. 73-74
Diff: E, Ans: d
72.   Which of these statements regarding alcoholism is true?
      a.   Alcoholism is entirely a genetic disorder.
      b.   Alcoholism is genetic for men, but not for women.
      c.   Alcoholism is entirely determined by your upbringing.
      d.   Alcoholism is determined by both genetics and environment.

Chromosomal and Genetic Abnormalities

Chromosomal and Genetic Abnormalities, p. 75
Diff: E, Ans: d
73.   Developmentalists study genetic abnormalities in order to:
      a.   better understand the complexities of genetic interaction generally.
      b.   be better equipped to limit their harmful effects.
      c.   remove the misunderstandings and prejudices surrounding such abnormalities.
      d.   do all of the above.

Chromosomal Abnormalities, p. 75
Diff: H, Ans: b
74.   Which of the following is most associated with chromosomal abnormalities?
      a.   paternal age
      b.   maternal age
      c.   environmental agents
      d.   none of the above

Chromosomal Abnormalities, p. 75
Diff: M, Ans: d
75.   Among the most common correlates of chromosomal abnormalities such as Down syndrome and
      Klinefelter syndrome is:
      a.   father's age.
      b.   child's age.
      c.   ethnic background.
      d.   mother's age.

Chromosomal Abnormalities, p. 75
Diff: M, Ans: d
76.   Between ages 20 and 50, a woman's chances of conceiving a fetus with Down syndrome:
      a.   remain about the same.
      b.   increase slightly.
      c.   decrease slightly.
      d.   increase greatly.

Chromosomal Abnormalities, p. 75
Diff: E, Ans: b
77.   A condition in which an individual has a mixture of cells, some normal and some with an incorrect
       number of chromosomes, is referred to as being:
       a.   a carrier.
       b.   mosaic.
       c.   eclectic.
       d.   trisomic.

Chromosomal Abnormalities, p. 76
Diff: H, Ans: c
78.   The proportion of all zygotes that have an abnormal number of chromosomes is about:
       a.   one-fourth.
       b.   one-third.
       c.   one-half.
       d.   three-fourths.

Chromosomal Abnormalities, p. 76
Diff: E, Ans: b
79.   Most zygotes with serious chromosomal problems are:
       a.   born prematurely.
       b.   do not even begin to develop or are aborted spontaneously.
       c.   stillborn.
       d.   born after a full-term pregnancy.

Chromosomal Abnormalities, p. 76
Diff: H, Ans: c
80.   About how many newborns have 45, 47, or more chromosomes?
       a.   1 in 2
       b.   1 in 20
       c.   1 in 200
       d.   1 in 500

Chromosomal Abnormalities, p. 76
Diff: M, Ans: b
81.   Trisomy-21 is called:
       a.   fragile-X syndrome.
       b.   Down syndrome.
       c.   muscular dystrophy.
       d.   Klinefelter syndrome.

Chromosomal Abnormalities, p. 76
Diff: M, Ans: b
82.   People with Down syndrome:
       a.   have a third chromosome in the 19th pair.
       b.   have a third chromosome in the 21st pair.
       c.   are missing a chromosome.
       d.   are missing two chromosomes.

Chromosomal Abnormalities, p. 76
Diff: E, Ans: d
83.   Children with Down syndrome are generally:
       a.   antisocial.
       b.   so mentally retarded that they need to live in an institution.
       c.   deaf.
       d.   slower to develop mentally than other children.

Chromosomal Abnormalities, p. 77
Diff: M, Ans: a

84.   If individuals with Down syndrome survive to middle age, they often develop:
       a.   Alzheimer's disease.
       b.   eccentric speech patterns.
       c.   a variation of Klinefelter syndrome.
       d.   spinal defects and coordination problems.

Chromosomal Abnormalities, p. 77
Diff: M, Ans: c

85.   Which of the following is NOT a possible 23rd chromosome pair for a surviving human?
       a.   XX
       b.   XXY
       c.   Y
       d.   X

Chromosomal Abnormalities, p. 77
Diff: H, Ans: b

86.   Children born with Klinefelter syndrome characteristically:
       a.   have ambiguous sex organs—that is, a blending of male and female genitals.
       b.   do not develop normally once they hit puberty.
       c.   are physically normal males, but are cognitively impaired.
       d.   are physically normal females, but are antisocial.

Genetic Abnormalities, p. 77
Diff: M, Ans: d

87.   A person with Huntington's disease:
       a.   is unable to conceive children.
       b.   is likely to shout curses and obscenities.
       c.   gets better as he or she grows older.
       d.   has a central nervous system disorder.

Genetic Abnormalities, p. 77
Diff: H, Ans: a

88.   Which of the following statements helps to explain why many more people carry abnormal genes than
       are affected by them?
       a.   Many genetic problems are recessive.
       b.   Good medical care prevents their expression.
       c.   Most genetic disorders are phenotypic.
       d.   Many genetic diseases are dominant.

Genetic Abnormalities, p. 80
Diff: M, Ans: a

89.   The chief chromosomal feature of fragile-X syndrome is that:
       a.   the gene has more than 200 CGG repetitions.
       b.   the X chromosome carries dangerous recessive genes.
       c.   the X chromosome carries dangerous dominant genes.
       d.   the X chromosome is missing.

Genetic Abnormalities, p. 80
Diff: H, Ans: b

90.   Greta carries the fragile-X chromosome. This means that she:
       a.   will be perfectly normal.
       b.   might be normal or mentally retarded.
       c.   will be severely retarded mentally.
       d.   will be moderately retarded mentally.

Genetic Abnormalities, p. 80
Diff: M, Ans: d

91. Mental retardation caused by a fragile-X chromosome appears:
    a. in males only.
    b. in females only.
    c. in both sexes equally.
    d. more frequently in males than in females.

Genetic Abnormalities, p. 80
Diff: H, Ans: c

92. Which of the following is a true statement about individuals with fragile-X syndrome?
    a. The intensity of the mutation remains the same from generation to generation.
    b. Females with fragile-X syndrome are always normal because they also have a normal X chromosome.
    c. Males with fragile-X syndrome tend to show mental deficiency and inadequate social skills.
    d. All of the above are true.

Genetic Abnormalities, p. 80
Diff: H, Ans: d

93. Which of the following is a true statement about recessive disorders?
    a. They can pass unnoticed from generation to generation.
    b. They are less likely to be recognized than dominant disorders.
    c. The genes causing some of them are protective.
    d. All of the above are true statements.

Genetic Testing and Genetic Counseling, p. 82
Diff: M, Ans: a

94. Which of the following couples is LEAST likely to need genetic counseling before pregnancy?
    a. The man is 39, the woman 30; they have no children.
    b. The man and woman are both 27; they have had two spontaneous abortions.
    c. The man and woman are both 37; the man has one normal child from his first marriage.
    d. The man and woman are both 20; they are cousins.

Genetic Testing and Genetic Counseling, p. 82
Diff: H, Ans: d

95. Genetic counseling is recommended for people:
    a. with a history of infertility.
    b. who have had several spontaneous abortions.
    c. whose relatives have genetic problems.
    d. who have one or all of the above characteristics.

Genetic Testing and Genetic Counseling, pp. 82, 84
Diff: E, Ans: d

96. Genetic counseling involves which of the following?
    a. explaining conditions for which a couple is at-risk
    b. constructing a couple's family histories
    c. discussing the options if testing reveals a high risk of serious disorders
    d. all of the above

Genetic Testing and Genetic Counseling, p. 83 (Table 3.3)
Diff: H, Ans: c

97. Alpha-fetoprotein assay is useful in detecting all of the following conditions EXCEPT:
    a. neural-tube defects.
    b. Down syndrome.
    c. diabetes.
    d. multiple embryos.

Genetic Testing and Genetic Counseling, p. 83 (Table 3.3)
Diff: H, Ans: a

98.   Talia is having her alpha-fetoprotein level tested. If the results show an unexpected AFP level, she probably:
    a.   will undergo further testing.
    b.   has a damaged fetus.
    c.   is pregnant with twins.
    d.   has a fetus with neural-tube defects of some type.

Genetic Testing and Genetic Counseling, p. 83 (Table 3.3)
Diff: M, Ans: c

99.   A prenatal diagnostic procedure that entails a risk of spontaneous abortion is:
    a.   AFP testing.
    b.   fetal heart monitoring.
    c.   amniocentesis.
    d.   ultrasound.

Genetic Testing and Genetic Counseling, p. 83 (Table 3.3)
Diff: E, Ans: c

100.   In an amniocentesis:
    a.   blood samples are taken from the fetus.
    b.   a type of x-ray is used to check fetal development.
    c.   fluid from the amniotic sac is examined.
    d.   a sample of placental tissue is taken.

Genetic Testing and Genetic Counseling, pp. 84-85
Diff: M, Ans: d

101.   If a couple learns that they are carriers of a genetic disorder, which of the following is NOT an alternative for them?
    a.   avoid pregnancy
    b.   artificial insemination with donor sperm
    c.   have a child naturally
    d.   none of the above

Genetic Testing and Genetic Counseling, p. 85
Diff: E, Ans: a

102.   Suppose a particular couple has a 50/50 chance of having a child with a lifelong, painful disease that will require expensive medical care. Who makes the decision about whether the couple tries to conceive?
    a.   the couple
    b.   their genetic counselor
    c.   their doctor
    d.   a judge and the law of the land

TRUE-FALSE QUESTIONS

The Genetic Code

Ans: F, pp. 59-60
1.   Genes contain instructions for making DNA.

Ans: T, p. 60
2.   Each human has 23 pairs of chromosomes in each cell.

Ans: F, p. 60

3.   A, T, G, and C are referred to as gametes.

Ans: F, p. 61

4.   All of the gametes belonging to a particular individual are exactly the same.

Ans: T, p. 61

5.   A zygote is formed when a sperm enters an ovum.

Ans: T, p. 61

6.   An individual's genotype is set at conception and remains the same throughout its entire life.

Ans: F, p. 62

7.   If the 23rd chromosomal pair is XY, the zygote is female; if it is YY, the zygote is male.

Ans: F, p. 64

8.   Dizygotic twins are also known as identical twins.

Ans: T, p. 64

9.   Fraternal twins are more common than identical twins.

Ans: F, p. 64

10.   Dizygotic twins are always very similar in appearance.

Ans: F, p. 64

11.   The term "trizygotic" refers to the birth of three individuals who have an identical genetic endowment.

Ans: F, p. 65

12.   Zygotic cells differentiate and then split.

Ans: T, p. 65

13.   Some genes code for proteins that act as on-off switching mechanisms.

Ans: F, p. 65

14.   An individual's genotype is the result of both genetics and environment.

Ans: F, p. 66

15.   Dominant-recessive traits depend on all of the genes for that trait an individual inherits.

Ans: F, p. 66

16.   X-linked diseases are more common for females than for males, because females have two X chromosomes.

Ans: T, p. 67

17.   That an individual's genotype contains a particular gene does not mean it will be expressed in the phenotype.

Ans: F, p. 67

18.   Mothers cannot pass down X-linked diseases to their sons.

Ans: T, p. 68

19.   "Crossing over" refers to the reshuffling of chromosome segments, thus contributing to genetic diversity.

Ans: T, p. 68
20.   A few people have a difference in the code of one gene that causes them not to become infected with HIV even when repeatedly exposed to the virus.

Ans: F, p. 69
21.   Geneticists have yet to make significant progress on the map of the human genome.

Ans: T, p. 69
22.   The same gene produces legs in butterflies, centipedes, and humans.

From Genotype to Phenotype

Ans: T, pp. 70-71
23.   Psychological traits, such as shyness, are the result of genetic influences as well as environmental influences.

Ans: F, p. 70
24.   A carrier is a person whose phenotype contains a particular gene.

Ans: T, p. 71
25.   Environment affects every human characteristic.

Ans: T, p. 71
26.   Every human behavioral tendency is affected by many genes, some interacting in dominant-recessive patterns and some in additive fashion.

Ans: F, p. 72
27.   The senility caused by Alzheimer's disease is entirely genetic.

Ans: F, p. 73
28.   If one monozygotic twin suffers from a disease known to have a genetic component, such as schizophrenia, the other twin will develop the disease, too.

Ans: T, p. 73
29.   Schizophrenia may be partially caused by a virus that is more common in late winter.

Ans: F, p. 73
30.   Many mental illnesses are caused purely by genetics.

Ans: T, p. 74
31.   Personality traits, such as having a quick temper and being anxious, are associated with increased risk of alcoholism.

Ans: T, p. 74
32.   Selective adaptation is part of the explanation for the fact that individuals from the British Isles are particularly likely to become alcoholics and individuals from East Asia are particularly unlikely to become alcoholics.

Chromosomal and Genetic Abnormalities

Ans: T, p. 75
33.   The age of the mother is the variable that most often correlates with the likelihood of chromosomal abnormalities in the fetus.

Ans: F, p. 75

34.   Chromosomal abnormalities occur when one of an individual's genes code for a protein that can cause serious problems or when it fails to code for a protein needed to prevent problems.

Ans: F, p. 76

35.   Individuals with Down syndrome tend to be severely mentally retarded, regardless of whether they live at home or are institutionalized.

Ans: T, p. 76

36.   When a zygote has an abnormal number of chromosomes, it usually does not even begin to develop.

Ans: T, p. 77

37.   An embryo cannot develop without at least one X chromosome.

Ans: T, p. 77

38.   More people are born with genetic abnormalities than with chromosomal abnormalities.

Ans: F, p. 77

39.   Most of the known genetic disorders are recessive.

Ans: F, p. 77

40.   Severely disabling dominant disorders often get passed on from one generation to the next.

Ans: F, p. 80

41.   Girls are more likely to have fragile-X syndrome than are boys.

Ans: T, p. 80

42.   Recessive and multifactorial disorders claim more victims than do dominant disorders because they can pass unnoticed for generations.

Ans: F, p. 80

43.   Many conditions affecting human health are purely genetic.

Ans: F, p. 82

44.   All couples should seek out genetic counseling before attempting a pregnancy.

Ans: F, p. 82

45.   Genetic counseling is strongly recommended for prospective parents who are of different races.

Ans: T, p. 82

46.   Prospective parents should receive genetic counseling if the woman is 35 years of age or older or if the man is 40 years of age or older.

Ans: T, pp. 82-83

47.   High-risk individuals often do not want information about their own genetic potential; they want genetic information only as it applies to their pregnancy or prospective pregnancy.

Ans: T, p. 83 (Table 3.3)

48.   Alpha-fetoprotein and ultrasound are two tests that may be recommended by genetic counselors.

Ans: F, p. 85

49.   One option that many couples who are at-risk for having children with a genetic disorder turn to is gene therapy.

Ans: T, p. 87

50.	About 50 percent of couples who learn that their fetus has Klinefelter syndrome abort, and about 50 percent carry the fetus to term.

FILL-IN-THE-BLANK QUESTIONS

The Genetic Code

Ans: genome, p. 60

1.	The full set of instructions for making a human being is called the human _____.

Ans: DNA, p. 60

2.	Genes are segments of _____ molecules.

Ans: one, p. 61

3.	When cells divide to produce gametes, they do so in such a way that each sperm or ovum receives _____ member(s) of each chromosome pair.

Ans: sperm; ova, p. 61

4.	Male gametes are called _____; female gametes are called _____.

Ans: zygote, p. 61

5.	When a sperm and an ovum fuse, they form a cell called a(n) _____.

Ans: 46, p. 61

6.	The number of chromosomes in a zygote is _____.

Ans: identical; fraternal, p. 64

7.	Monozygotic twins are also known as _____ twins; dizygotic twins are also known as _____ twins.

Ans: monozygotic (or identical), p. 64

8.	Every person is genetically unique, with the exception of _____ twins, triplets, quadruplets, and so on.

Ans: differentiation, p. 65

9.	The process of _____ follows the duplication and division of the zygote.

Ans: genotype; phenotype, p. 65

10.	The sum total of all the genes a person inherits is called the person's _____; the person's actual appearance and behavior is called the person's _____.

Ans: polygenic; multifactorial, p. 65

11.	A characteristic that is determined by many genes is called _____; one that is the result of the interaction of many genetic and environmental factors is called _____.

Ans: Additive, p. 65

12.	_____ traits depend on *all* of the genes for that trait that an individual inherits.

Ans: dominant, p. 66

13.	A gene that has more influence in the phenotype than its interacting allele is considered _____.

Ans: X-linked, p. 66

14.	Genes that are located in the X chromosome are referred to as _____.

Ans: mutation, p. 68
15.   A change in a gene caused by environmental factors is referred to as a(n) _____.

Ans: Human Genome Project, p. 69
16.   The scientists who worked to map the entire human genetic code are part of the _____.

From Genotype to Phenotype

Ans: potential, p. 70
17.   We must differentiate between a person's genetic inheritance, or _____, and the actual expression of that inheritance.

Ans: carrier, p. 70
18.   A girl who has normal color vision but who also has the recessive gene for color blindness in her genotype is said to be a(n) _____ of the recessive gene.

Ans: behavior genetics, p. 71
19.   The study of the genetic origins of psychological characteristics is _____.

Chromosomal and Genetic Abnormalities

Ans: chromosomal, p. 75
20.   A(n) _____ abnormality occurs when a zygote's cells have more or fewer chromosomes than the usual number.

Ans: mosaic, p. 75
21.   If duplication does not occur correctly during the development of a zygote such that some of the cells have the normal number of chromosomes and some have the incorrect number, the result is a person who is _____.

Ans: Down syndrome (or trisomy-21), p. 76
22.   The most common of the extra-chromosome conditions, caused by an extra chromosome at the 21st pair, is _____.

Ans: males, p. 80
23.   Although both males and females suffer from fragile-X syndrome, the retardation that is characteristic of this syndrome is more common among _____.

Ans: Alpha-fetoprotein assay, p. 83
24.   _____ is a prenatal test that is actually a test of the mother's blood.

Ans: genetic engineering (or gene therapy), p. 85
25.   The altering of an organism's genetic instructions through the insertion of additional genetic instruction is referred to as _____.

ESSAY QUESTIONS

1.   Name the four bases on each gene. What are the four possible pairings?

2.   What is the difference between monozygotic and dizygotic twins?

3.   Imagine that you are an adopted child who has received no information about your biological parents. From your observable characteristics, or phenotype, what, if anything, could you determine about your biological parents? Explain your reasoning.

4.   Describe how additive genes work and how dominant-recessive genes work. Give an example of each, and describe how the characteristic is inherited from an individual's parents.

5.   Describe two things scientists have learned from the results of the Human Genome Project.

6.   Describe three factors influencing an individual's likelihood of developing alcoholism. Be specific.

7.   Are there more recessive or more dominant abnormal genes? Explain why this is the case.

8.   Do you think that our new capabilities in prenatal testing and genetic counseling will result in a decrease in the number of individuals born with serious genetic defects, or could it result in an increase? Explain your reasoning.

9.   A couple at high risk for a genetic abnormality wants to undergo prenatal tests to determine if their unborn child is abnormal. Discuss the benefits of genetic counseling for this couple.

10.   Why is it important to study genetics in a course on child development? List three specific reasons.

11.   Using the information provided in Chapter 3, develop a profile of two different couples who would be at risk for transmitting genetic disorders to their children.

12.   Briefly outline a set of guidelines that you would like to see developed to govern the use and handling of genetic information in the world community.

13.   Who should receive genetic counseling?

14.   What factors determine whether an at-risk couple should have children?

Answer guidelines to these essay questions can be found in the Appendix at the end of the Test Bank.

CHAPTER 4

Prenatal Development and Birth

MULTIPLE-CHOICE QUESTIONS

From Zygote to Newborn

From Zygote to Newborn, p. 91
Diff: E, Ans: c
1. The germinal period ends approximately:
    a. two days after conception.
    b. two months after conception.
    c. two weeks after conception.
    d. twelve weeks after conception.

From Zygote to Newborn, p. 91
Diff: E, Ans: d
2. The period of the fetus lasts:
    a. during the last three months before the child's birth.
    b. from the midway point of prenatal development until birth.
    c. from the second until the eighth week after conception.
    d. from nine weeks after conception until birth.

From Zygote to Newborn, pp. 91, 92
Diff: M, Ans: b
3. The longest period of prenatal development is the:
    a. period of the embryo.
    b. period of the fetus.
    c. first trimester.
    d. germinal period.

Germinal: The First 14 Days, p. 92
Diff: M, Ans: c
4. Within hours after conception, the zygote travels toward the uterus down the:
    a. umbilical cord.
    b. vaginal wall.
    c. fallopian tube.
    d. ovarian wall.

Table 4.1: Timing and Terminology, p. 92
Diff: M, Ans: c
5. Full-term pregnancies last:
    a. 34 weeks.
    b. 36 weeks.
    c. 38 weeks.
    d. 40 weeks.

Germinal: The First 14 Days, p. 92
Diff: H, Ans: b
6.   The germinal stem cells first take on distinct characteristics and move toward particular locations
      during:
      a.   implantation.
      b.   differentiation.
      c.   assimilation.
      d.   fertilization.

Germinal: The First 14 Days, p. 92
Diff: M, Ans: a
7.   About a week after conception, the outer layer of the multiplying cells forms a protective circle or shell
      that will become the:
      a.   placenta.
      b.   umbilical cord.
      c.   vernix.
      d.   infant.

Germinal: The First 14 Days, p. 92
Diff: M, Ans: a
8.   By one week after conception, the multiplying cells have divided into outer cells enclosing a mass of
      inner cells. The inner cells will become the:
      a.   embryo.
      b.   amnion.
      c.   placenta.
      d.   digestive system.

Germinal: The First 14 Days, p. 92
Diff: E, Ans: c
9.   The placenta:
      a.   screens the embryo from all harmful substances.
      b.   provides the fetus with its first taste of breast milk.
      c.   surrounds and protects the developing organism.
      d.   mixes the blood supply of mother and fetus.

Germinal: The First 14 Days, p. 92
Diff: E, Ans: c
10.   During the germinal period, the first task of the outer cells is to:
      a.   divide as rapidly as possible.
      b.   differentiate into different types of tissue.
      c.   implant in the uterus.
      d.   find a permanent location in the ovaries.

Germinal: The First 14 Days, p. 92
Diff: M, Ans: b
11.   Which occurs about 7 days after conception?
      a.   deposit of the male's sperm into the body of the female
      b.   nestling of the developing organism into the lining of the uterus
      c.   fertilization of the ovum by sperm
      d.   the placenta begins to function

Germinal: The First 14 Days, p. 92
Diff: E, Ans: c
12.   Which of the following is a true statement?
   a.   All infants of HIV-positive women contract the HIV virus as well.
   b.   A teratogen is a substance or disease that, when present, always results in a birth defect.
   c.   Months 4, 5, and 6 are referred to as the second or middle trimester of pregnancy.
   d.   There is no real evidence that the fetus can hear anything.

Table 4.1: Timing and Terminology, p. 92
Diff: H, Ans: c
13.   What percentage of babies are actually born on their exact due date?
   a.   1
   b.   3
   c.   5
   d.   7

Germinal: The First 14 Days, pp. 92-93
Diff: H, Ans: b
14.   About what percentage of zygotes successfully become implanted?
   a.   15-20 percent
   b.   30-40 percent
   c.   60-70 percent
   d.   90-95 percent

Embryo: From the Third Through the Eighth Week, p. 93
Diff: E, Ans: d
15.   The first organ system that shows any sign of activity is the:
   a.   respiratory system.
   b.   digestive system.
   c.   nervous system.
   d.   cardiovascular system.

Germinal: The First 14 Days, p. 93
Diff: H, Ans: a
16.   Pregnancy is most likely to end:
   a.   before the germinal period.
   b.   in spontaneous abortion in the period of the embryo.
   c.   in spontaneous abortion in the period of the fetus.
   d.   in induced abortion in the second trimester.

Embryo: From the Third Through the Eighth Week, p. 93
Diff: E, Ans: c
17.   What begins about 14 days after conception?
   a.   cell differentiation
   b.   implantation
   c.   the period of the embryo
   d.   the period of the fetus

Embryo: From the Third Through the Eighth Week, p. 93
Diff: M, Ans: c
18.   The neural tube will become the:
   a.   reproductive organs.
   b.   intestinal tract.
   c.   brain and spinal cord or column.
   d.   backbone, legs, and arms.

Embryo: From the Third Through the Eighth Week, p. 93
Diff: M, Ans: a

19.   The head begins to take shape in the _____ week after conception.
       a.   fourth
       b.   fifth
       c.   sixth
       d.   seventh

Embryo: From the Third Through the Eighth Week, p. 93
Diff: M, Ans: c

20.   Buds that will become arms and legs appear by the _____ week.
       a.   third
       b.   fourth
       c.   fifth
       d.   sixth

Embryo: From Third Through the Eighth Week, p. 93
Diff: E, Ans: d

21.   Which of the following begins to develop last during prenatal development?
       a.   legs
       b.   hands
       c.   head
       d.   toes

Table 4.2: Vulnerability During Prenatal Development, p. 94
Diff: H, Ans: a

22.   Which statistic accurately reflects the vulnerability of prenatal development?
       a.   Only 31 percent of all conceptions become living newborn babies.
       b.   Only 75 percent of fetuses reach the age of viability.
       c.   50 percent of fetuses are spontaneously aborted or stillborn.
       d.   10 percent of all fetuses die during birth.

Table 4.2: Vulnerability During Prenatal Development, p. 94
Diff: E, Ans: d

23.   The third period of prenatal development is the period of the:
       a.   embryo.
       b.   ovum.
       c.   trimester.
       d.   fetus.

Table 4.2: Vulnerability During Prenatal Development, p. 94
Diff: H, Ans: b

24.   What percentage of embryos are aborted spontaneously?
       a.   5
       b.   20
       c.   31
       d.   40

Embryo: From the Third Through the Eighth Week, p. 94
Diff: E, Ans: c

25.   At eight weeks after conception, the embryo has not yet formed:
       a.   intestines.
       b.   lungs.
       c.   sex organs.
       d.   kidneys.

Embryo: From the Third Through the Eighth Week, p. 94
Diff: H, Ans: b
26. About eight weeks after conception, the embryo:
     a.   weighs about 5 ounces (142 g).
     b.   has distinct fingers and toes.
     c.   has a visible tail.
     d.   is about 1/4 inch long (.64 cm).

Fetus: The Third Month, p. 94
Diff: H, Ans: a
27. The fetus begins to develop male sex organs if:
     a.   the Y chromosome sends a biochemical signal.
     b.   the master signal from the Y chromosome overrides the X signal.
     c.   the X chromosome sends a biochemical signal.
     d.   no biochemical signal is received.

Fetus: The Third Month, p. 94
Diff: H, Ans: c
28. External sex organs are fully formed by the:
     a.   fourth week after conception.
     b.   sixth week after conception.
     c.   twelfth week after conception.
     d.   fifth month after conception.

The Middle Three Months, p. 95
Diff: E, Ans: a
29. The "age of viability" refers to the point when the preterm newborn:
     a.   might survive if born.
     b.   begins to move.
     c.   will survive if born.
     d.   has developed all its major organs.

The Middle Three Months, p. 95
Diff: H, Ans: b
30. What was the weight of the smallest newborn on record?
     a.   8 oz.
     b.   10 oz.
     c.   20 oz.
     d.   26 oz.

The Middle Three Months, p. 95
Diff: H, Ans: b
31. The critical factor in attaining the age of viability is:
     a.   weighing at least 5 pounds (2.3 kg).
     b.   having adequate brain development.
     c.   having functioning digestive and respiratory systems.
     d.   surviving at least 28 weeks past conception.

The Middle Three Months, p. 95
Diff: H, Ans: b
32. With excellent medical care, a fetus can survive if it is born as early as what week?
     a.   16
     b.   22
     c.   27
     d.   30

The Middle Three Months, p. 96
Diff: H, Ans: c
33.   Lung expansion and contraction, maturation of the heart, and weight gain of about 4 1/2 pounds occur in the:
      a.   first trimester.
      b.   critical period.
      c.   third trimester.
      d.   second trimester.

Table 4.3: Average Prenatal Weights, p. 96
Diff: H, Ans: b
34.   A birth weight of between 2 and 3 1/2 lbs. would be classified as:
      a.   low birth weight.
      b.   very low birth weight.
      c.   extremely low birth weight.
      d.   normal, though low.

The Final Three Months, p. 96
Diff: E, Ans: b
35.   Which of these statements is a *true* one?
      a.   The development of the central nervous system is completed during the period of the embryo.
      b.   In the last months of prenatal life, the lungs begin to expand and contract and the valves of the heart undergo final maturation.
      c.   A baby cannot be both preterm and small-for-date.
      d.   The cry of the newborn can earn a 3, the highest score for respiratory effort on the Apgar scale.

The Final Three Months: From Viability to Full Term, p. 96
Diff: E, Ans: c
36.   Viability is most closely associated with which of the following?
      a.   probability
      b.   predictability
      c.   possibility
      d.   likelihood

Risk Reduction

Risk Reduction, p. 97
Diff: M, Ans: c
37.   What percentage of fetuses are born with major structural anomalies?
      a.   1
      b.   2
      c.   3
      d.   4

Risk Reduction, p. 97
Diff: M, Ans: c
38.   About what percent of newborns will develop behavioral difficulties that could be related to behavioral teratogens?
      a.   3-5
      b.   5-10
      c.   10-20
      d.   20-25

Risk Reduction, p. 97
Diff: E, Ans: b

39.   Teratology refers to:
       a.   abnormalities in the birth process.
       b.   the study of the factors involved in birth defects.
       c.   research in new forms of birth control.
       d.   the study of chromosomal abnormalities.

Risk Reduction, p. 97
Diff: E, Ans: c

40.   Teratogens that harm the prenatal brain are called _____ teratogens, because they can make the child
       hyperactive, antisocial, or retarded.
       a.   cognitive
       b.   cephalic
       c.   behavioral
       d.   remedial

Determining Risk, p. 97
Diff: H, Ans: d

41.   The science of teratology can best be compared to:
       a.   mathematics, because it is just as precise.
       b.   psychology, because it is devoted to human behavior.
       c.   chemistry, because all teratogens are chemicals.
       d.   insurance, because it deals with risk analysis.

Risk Reduction, p. 97
Diff: E, Ans: b

42.   A teratogen is:
       a.   damage sustained to the placenta.
       b.   a substance or a condition that can increase the risk of prenatal abnormalities.
       c.   a cell with extra chromosomes.
       d.   waste products from the embryo.

Determining Risk, pp. 97-98
Diff: H, Ans: a

43.   Research in teratology has found that:
       a.   the effects of teratogens vary greatly.
       b.   most hazards cannot be avoided.
       c.   prenatal exposure to teratogens is always damaging.
       d.   very few agents can harm the embryo.

Determining Risk, p. 98
Diff: E, Ans: a

44.   Maria used a prescription medicine for two weeks while she was pregnant. The potential damage:
       a.   depends partly on when during her pregnancy she took the medicine.
       b.   is the same throughout the pregnancy.
       c.   is greater for structures that are fully developed.
       d.   is highest during the last trimester.

Amount of Exposure, p. 98
Diff: E, Ans: d
45.   The condition whereby the risk of a teratogen causing harm increases when it occurs at the same time
      as another teratogen or risk defines the:
      a.   critical period effect.
      b.   threshold effect.
      c.   fetal teratogen effect.
      d.   interaction effect.

Amount of Exposure, p. 98
Diff: H, Ans: d
46.   More than 50,000 units of this vitamin can cause fetal abnormalities:
      a.   E
      b.   B12
      c.   B6
      d.   A

Timing of Exposure, p. 98
Diff: M, Ans: a
47.   During prenatal development, a particular organ or body part is most vulnerable during the:
      a.   critical period.
      b.   vulnerability period.
      c.   period of viability.
      d.   period of the fetus.

Amount of Exposure, pp. 98-99
Diff: H, Ans: d
48.   Jan used several prescription drugs in early pregnancy, before she missed her first period. Her doctor
      will probably say:
      a.   have an abortion because the embryo is damaged.
      b.   the placenta ensured that no harm was done.
      c.   prescription drugs never hurt a developing embryo.
      d.   most drugs are harmless in low doses, but the doctor needs more specifics.

Amount of Exposure, pp. 98-99
Diff: H, Ans: d
49.   Because Suzanne is pregnant, she drinks only one glass of wine a day and smokes fewer cigarettes than
      previously. She should be told that:
      a.   this will definitely cause serious damage.
      b.   she is taking careful precautions.
      c.   only her smoking may represent a risk.
      d.   each drug might intensify the effects of the other.

Genetic Vulnerability, p. 99
Diff: H, Ans: b
50.   The enzyme crucial to the breakdown of alcohol in the human body is called alcohol:
      a.   amylase.
      b.   dehydrogenase.
      c.   carbohydrase.
      d.   lipase.

Fig. 4.3: Birth Defects From Teratogens, p. 99
Diff: H, Ans: b

51.   The heart is the most susceptible to developing birth defects:
        a. during the first two weeks after conception.
        b. between the third and sixth weeks after conception.
        c. between the eighth and twelfth weeks after conception.
        d. during the two months immediately before birth.

Table 4.4: Teratogens: Effects of Exposure, p. 100
Diff: H, Ans: b

52.   Rubella is the:
        a. researcher who was the first to scientifically study teratogens.
        b. other name for German measles.
        c. tissue mass connecting the embryo to the umbilical cord.
        d. most common birth defect in the United States.

Table 4.4: Teratogens: Effects of Exposure, p. 100
Diff: H, Ans: b

53.   Sandra has a very small head in contrast with the proportions of the rest of her body. As otherwise she
        is a normal baby, her pediatrician would be astute in asking her mother:
        a. Have you been using pesticides on your lawn, lately?
        b. Have you recently had a large number of X-Rays to diagnose a health problem?
        c. Do you have a urinary tract infection that you haven't told me about?
        d. Have you been exhausting yourself in the gym lately?

Table 4.4: Teratogens: Effects of Exposure, p. 100
Diff: H, Ans: b

54.   Which of the following is likely to cause a spontaneous abortion?
        a. syphilis
        b. a high level of stress
        c. toxoplasmosis
        d. malnutrition

Table 4.4: Teratogens: Effects of Exposure, p. 100
Diff: H, Ans: d

55.   Brain damage, loss of vision, and mental retardation which may be caused by eating undercooked meat
        and handling cat feces or garden dirt is attributable to:
        a. lead or mercury pollution.
        b. German measles.
        c. syphilis.
        d. Toxoplasmosis.

Table 4.4: Teratogens: Effects of Exposure, p. 101
Diff: M, Ans: d

56.   Which of the following is a psychoactive drug?
        a. lithium
        b. streptomycin
        c. retinoic acid
        d. tobacco

Table 4.1: Teratogens: Timing and Terminology, p. 101
Diff: E, Ans: c
57.   The best policy regarding prescription drugs during pregnancy is:
       a.   avoid taking any medicines, because all do serious damage.
       b.   prescription drugs are safe because they have to pass strict FDA testing.
       c.   take drugs only if medically necessary, prescribed by a knowledgeable doctor.
       d.   drugs are safe when taken in low doses for short periods of time.

Table 4.4: Teratogens: Effects of Exposure, p. 101
Diff: M, Ans: c
58.   Which of the following is classified as a psychoactive drug?
       a.   lithium
       b.   Phenobarbital
       c.   caffeine
       d.   thalidomide

Table 4.4: Teratogens: Effects of Exposure, p. 101
Diff: E, Ans: b
59.   Which of the following is a psychoactive drug?
       a.   thalidomide
       b.   cocaine
       c.   Valium
       d.   estrogen

Genetic Vulnerability, p. 101
Diff: E, Ans: b
60.   The condition which causes part of the brain *not* to form is known as:
       a.   microcephaly.
       b.   anencephaly.
       c.   macrocephaly.
       d.   encephalitis.

Genetic Vulnerability, p. 101
Diff: H, Ans: c
61.   Martha Ann was still-born. The doctors told her mother that the part of the brain above her eyebrow-level had failed to form, prenatally. This sad problem was probably caused by:
       a.   a sexually transmitted disease.
       b.   toxoplasmosis.
       c.   a lack of folic acid in her mother's diet.
       d.   household cleaning compounds.

Genetic Vulnerability, p. 102
Diff: H, Ans: d
62.   Research in genetic vulnerability to teratogens has found that:
       a.   fraternal twins are equally vulnerable.
       b.   female embryos are more vulnerable than males.
       c.   genetic vulnerability guarantees a birth defect of some sort.
       d.   the XY chromosome pattern is more susceptible to damage.

Specific Teratogens, p. 102
Diff: M, Ans: d
63.   Precise prediction of interaction between genes and teratogens is possible for:
       a.   male embryos but not female embryos.
       b.   all embryos.
       c.   monozygotic twins.
       d.   none of the above.

Changing Policy, p. 102
Diff: M, Ans: c
64. HIV-infected babies usually die by age:
   a. 3.
   b. 4.
   c. 5.
   d. 6.

Changing Policy, p. 102
Diff: E, Ans: a
65. One of the first teratogens to be recognized was:
   a. rubella.
   b. alcohol.
   c. heroin.
   d. the common cold.

Changing Policy, p. 102
Diff: E, Ans: a
66. The agent responsible for deformed limbs in the newborns in the late 1950s was:
   a. thalidomide.
   b. tetracycline.
   c. toxoplasmosis.
   d. tobacco.

Changing Policy, p. 102
Diff: H, Ans: a
67. Monique contracted rubella early in her pregnancy. Damage is most likely to affect the embryo's:
   a. eyes.
   b. arms or legs.
   c. breathing.
   d. bloodstream.

Changing Policy, p. 102
Diff: M, Ans: b
68. If a pregnant woman is HIV-positive, the HIV virus:
   a. will not be passed on to her newborn.
   b. has about a 25 percent chance of being passed to the baby.
   c. will always infect the fetus.
   d. can be avoided through Cesarean section.

Changing Policy, p. 102
Diff: H, Ans: c
69. Human immunodeficiency virus (HIV):
   a. is one of the least dangerous teratogens.
   b. affects most babies born to HIV-positive mothers.
   c. affects less than 30 percent of all babies born to HIV-positive mothers.
   d. can be acquired prenatally but not during birth.

Changing Policy, p. 102
Diff: E, Ans: b
70. Pregnant women who are HIV-positive:
   a. always have abortions.
   b. can reduce the risk of infecting their fetus by taking AZT.
   c. can reduce the risk of infecting their fetus by having monthly HIV tests.
   d. can reduce the risk of infecting their fetus by avoiding a Cesarean delivery.

Changing Policy, p. 103
Diff: M, Ans: b
71.   Approximately how many HIV-positive children are born each year?
       a.   1/2 million
       b.   1 million
       c.   1 1/2 million
       d.   2 million

Changing Policy, p. 103
Diff: M, Ans: a
72.   A cluster of birth defects, including abnormal facial characteristics, slow physical growth, and retarded
       mental development is associated most closely with which of the following?
       a.   fetal alcohol syndrome
       b.   fetal alcohol effects
       c.   polychlorinated biphenyls (PCBs)
       d.   toxoplasmosis

Low Birth Weight, p. 104
Diff: E, Ans: a
73.   The international definition for *low birth weight* is weighing less than:
       a.   2,500 grams/5 1/2 lbs.
       b.   3,400 grams/7 1/2 lbs.
       c.   1,400 grams/3 lbs.
       d.   2,700 grams/6 lbs.

Low Birth Weight, p. 104
Diff: E, Ans: d
74.   The international definition for *extremely low birth weight* is weighing below:
       a.   5 1/2 lbs.
       b.   4 1/2 lbs.
       c.   3 lbs.
       d.   2 lbs.

Low Birth Weight, p. 104
Diff: E, Ans: b
75.   Low birth weight:
       a.   means weighing less than three pounds (1,400 g) at birth.
       b.   affects more than 7 percent of all U.S. newborns.
       c.   affects at least 8 percent of the babies in every nation of the world.
       d.   means a newborn is more likely to die than to live.

Low Birth Weight, p. 104
Diff: M, Ans: c
76.   The international definition for *very low birth weight* is weighing below:
       a.   5 1/2 lbs.
       b.   4 1/2 lbs.
       c.   3 lbs.
       d.   2 lbs.

Low Birth Weight, p. 106
Diff: M, Ans: b
77.   Births that occur at _____ or fewer weeks after conception are referred to as preterm.
       a.   34
       b.   35
       c.   36
       d.   37

Low Birth Weight, p. 106
Diff: M, Ans: c
78.   Which psychoactive drug slows fetal growth the most?
      a.   marijuana
      b.   cocaine
      c.   tobacco
      d.   alcohol

Low Birth Weight, p. 106
Diff: M, Ans: b
79.   Which psychoactive drug is the most prevalent?
      a.   alcohol
      b.   tobacco
      c.   marijuana
      d.   crack

Low Birth Weight, p. 106
Diff: M, Ans: d
80.   Cigarette smoking is implicated in _____ percent of all low birth weight births worldwide.
      a.   10
      b.   15
      c.   20
      d.   25

Low Birth Weight, p. 106
Diff: M, Ans: b
81.   Smoking among women of childbearing age is _____ in the United States, and it is _____ in many
      other nations.
      a.   rising; rising
      b.   declining; rising
      c.   rising; declining
      d.   declining; declining

Fig. 4.7: Why Babies Die, p. 106
Diff: M, Ans: d
82.   In causes of infant mortality, which of these has seen a marked downturn over the past 15 years due to
      medical technological advances and intense research?
      a.   low birth weight
      b.   maternal complications of pregnancy
      c.   accidents
      d.   SIDS

Fig. 4.7: Why Babies Die, p. 106
Diff: M, Ans: b
83.   Which of these in the past 15 years has markedly decreased due to modern technological advances and
      a heavy research focus?
      a.   maternal complications of pregnancy
      b.   respiratory distress
      c.   low birth weight
      d.   accidents

Low Birth Weight, p. 106
Diff: H, Ans: d
84.   Infants born more than three weeks early are called:
      a.   low birth weight.
      b.   premature.
      c.   miracles
      d.   preterm.

Fig. 4.7: Why Babies Die, p. 106
Diff: M, Ans: c
85.   Which of the following causes of infant mortality has taken a marked downturn over the past 15 years
      due to intense research and medical technological advances?
      a.   low birth weight
      b.   maternal complications of pregnancy
      c.   congenital abnormalities
      d.   accidents

Low Birth Weight, p. 106
Diff: E, Ans: a
86.   Babies considered small for their gestational age (SGA):
      a.   weigh less than expected, given the length of pregnancy.
      b.   have major structural deformities.
      c.   are born buttocks or legs first.
      d.   are addicted to drugs.

The Birth Process

The Birth Process, p. 107
Diff: H, Ans: c
87.   A breech baby is:
      a.   lodged against the mother's back when labor begins.
      b.   head first going into the cervix when labor begins.
      c.   buttocks first going into the cervix when labor begins.
      d.   larger than the mother's pelvic opening.

The Birth Process, p. 107
Diff: E, Ans: a
88.   In a normal uncomplicated birth, the position of presentation is:
      a.   head first.
      b.   knees first.
      c.   buttocks first.
      d.   feet first.

The Birth Process, p. 107
Diff: E, Ans: c
89.   In a first birth, the first stage of labor usually lasts:
      a.   several days.
      b.   10 to 12 hours.
      c.   about 8 hours.
      d.   only a few minutes.

The Newborn's First Minutes, p. 107
Diff: M, Ans: a
90. Bonita is in medical school and plans to become an obstetrician. She will be taught to do all of the following as soon as the baby is born *except*:
     a. routinely spank the neonate so that it begins to breathe.
     b. remove any mucus from its throat.
     c. cut the umbilical cord.
     d. wrap the baby to preserve body heat.

Fig. 4.8: A Normal, Uncomplicated Birth, p. 108
Diff: H, Ans: c
91. The time during labor when the fetal head descends from the uterus and is visible to the birth attendant is called:
     a. descent.
     b. transition.
     c. the second stage.
     d. the third stage.

Fig. 4.8: A Normal, Uncomplicated Birth, p. 108
Diff: M, Ans: c
92. The second stage of labor begins when the:
     a. mother starts experiencing contractions.
     b. cervix begins dilating.
     c. baby's head appears at the opening of the vagina.
     d. placenta is expelled.

Fig. 4.8: A Normal, Uncomplicated Birth, p. 108
Diff: M, Ans: c
93. The baby is born at the end of:
     a. the first stage of labor.
     b. transition.
     c. the second stage of labor.
     d. the third stage of labor.

Fig. 4.8: A Normal, Uncomplicated Birth, p. 108
Diff: E, Ans: d
94. Normally, during birth:
     a. the placenta is expelled first.
     b. the labor process takes two hours.
     c. the labor process takes two days.
     d. the head emerges first.

The Newborn's First Minutes, p. 108
Diff: H, Ans: b
95. The five characteristics that are evaluated in the Apgar are:
     a. the Babinski, Moro, stepping, swimming, and grasping reflexes.
     b. heart rate, breathing, muscle tone, color, and reflexes.
     c. cuddling, startling, irritability, vocal response, and visual response.
     d. sucking reflex, breathing reflex, size, weight, and disease symptoms.

The Newborn's First Minutes, p. 108
Diff: E, Ans: d
96.   A total Apgar score of 3 indicates that a newborn is:
        a.   of very low birth weight.
        b.   irritable and may be coughing and crying.
        c.   in excellent condition.
        d.   in critical condition.

The Newborn's First Minutes, p. 108
Diff: E, Ans: d
97.   The Apgar is used one minute and five minutes after birth to:
        a.   measure sensory abilities.
        b.   measure the health of the new mother.
        c.   help the mother recover from childbirth.
        d.   determine whether the newborn needs immediate medical care.

Variations, p. 109
Diff: M, Ans: d
98.   Which of the following countries has the highest percent of cesarean deliveries?
        a.   Ghana
        b.   England
        c.   the United States
        d.   Brazil

Table 4.5: Criteria and Scoring of the Apgar Scale, p. 109
Diff: H, Ans: c
99.   On the Apgar scale, a newborn heartbeat that is rapid (over 100) indicates that the:
        a.   baby needs immediate help to slow the heart rate.
        b.   baby is suffering from anoxia.
        c.   heart is beating normally.
        d.   baby has a heart defect.

Table 4.5: Criteria and Scoring of the Apgar Scale, p. 109
Diff: H, Ans: a
100.   Matthew is an obstetrical nurse who is administering the Apgar. Which of the following reactions
        should be rated as a 2?
        a.   coughing or sneezing
        b.   pulse of 90
        c.   slow respiration
        d.   inactive or weak muscle tone

Birth Complications, pp. 111-112
Diff: E, Ans: c
101.   Anoxia refers to:
        a.   cerebral hemorrhaging.
        b.   signs of cerebral palsy.
        c.   lack of oxygen.
        d.   toxic substances in the bloodstream.

Birth Complications, pp. 111-112
Diff: H, Ans: c
102.   High-risk infants, such as preterm, low-birth weight babies tend to:
        a.   be more active than full-term babies.
        b.   be girls more often than boys.
        c.   be slower to talk than other babies.
        d.   smile more at the parents than do full-term infants.

Mothers, Fathers, and a Good Start, p. 115
Diff: M, Ans: a
103.   Kyoto's daughter is five days old. Kyoto is feeling sad and inadequate. She may be experiencing:
        a.   postpartum depression.
        b.   isolette.
        c.   vernix.
        d.   postnatal anoxia.

Mothers, Fathers, and a Good Start, p. 115
Diff: M, Ans: d
104.   Postnatal depression is partly influenced by:
        a.   the amount of time spent in labor.
        b.   having a Cesarean section.
        c.   giving birth to a preterm infant.
        d.   the mother's beliefs about her ability to care for her infant.

TRUE-FALSE QUESTIONS

From Zygote to Newborn

Ans: T, p. 91
1.   The first two weeks of prenatal development are called the germinal period.

Ans: T, p. 93
2.   The cardiovascular system is the first organ system to show any sign of activity.

Ans: F, p. 94
3.   The development of the central nervous system is completed during the period of the embryo.

Ans: T, p. 96
4.   In the last months of prenatal life, the lungs begin to expand and contract and the valves of the heart undergo final maturation.

Ans: F, p. 97
5.   There is no evidence that the fetus can hear anything.

Risk Reduction

Ans: F, p. 97
6.   A teratogen is a substance or disease that, when present, always results in a birth defect.

Ans: T, pp. 98-99
7.   The effect of one teratogen is increased when taken in combination with other drugs.

Ans: F, p. 102
8.   All infants of HIV-positive women contract the virus as well.

Ans: T, p. 103
9.   Alcohol is a teratogen whose damage is dose-related.

Ans: T, p. 106
10.   A baby cannot be both preterm and small-for-date.

Ans: T, p. 107

11.   One of the first teratogens to be recognized was German measles.

Ans: T, p. 109

12.   The cry of the newborn can earn a 2, the highest score for respiratory effort on the Apgar scale.

The Birth Process

Ans: T, p. 110

13.   Today, about 1 percent of all American births occur at home.

Ans: T, p. 112

14.   Unless special arrangements are made, preterm infants in the intensive care nursery are less likely than other infants to receive stimulation from parents.

Ans: T, p. 115

15.   Between 10 to 20 percent of all women experience postpartum depression in the days and weeks after giving birth.

Ans: F, p. 115

16.   Studies show that early skin contact between parents and newborns is necessary for the development of a strong parent-infant bond.

FILL-IN-THE-BLANK QUESTIONS

From Zygote to Newborn

Ans: implantation, p. 92

1.   The process by which the developing organism embeds itself into the lining of the uterus is _____.

Ans: second (or middle), p. 92

2.   Months 4, 5, and 6 are referred to as the _____ trimester of pregnancy.

Ans: placenta, umbilical cord, p. 92

3.   The fetus depends on the _____ and _____ for survival.

Ans: cardiovascular, p. 93

4.   The first organ system to show any sign of activity is the _____ system.

Ans: fetus, p. 94

5.   The period of the _____ lasts from the ninth week until birth.

Ans: Y, p. 94

6.   The indifferent organism develops into a male if and when a biochemical signal is received from the _____ chromosome.

Ans: fetus, p. 94

7.   The sex organs develop during the period of the _____.

Ans: brain, spinal column, p. 98

8.   The neural tube in the embryo will eventually form the _____ and _____ _____.

Risk Reduction

Ans: teratology, p. 97
9.   The science of _____ is a science of risk analysis.

Ans: critical, p. 98
10.   A developing organ is most susceptible to damage from a teratogen during the _____ period of its formation.

Ans: spina bifida, anencephaly, pp. 100-101
11.   Severe folic acid deficiency can cause neural-tube defects such as _____, in which the lower spine does not close, and _____, in which part of the brain does not form.

Ans: rubella, p. 102
12.   One of the first teratogens to be identified was German measles, or _____.

Ans: HIV, p. 102
13.   The most devastating viral teratogenic disease is _____.

Ans: psychoactive, p. 103
14.   Alcohol, tobacco, and heroin are called _____ drugs.

Ans: Fetal Alcohol Syndrome, p. 103
15.   FAS is an abbreviation for _____.

Ans: preterm; small-for-dates (or small for gestational age), p. 106
16.   Infants born three or more weeks early are called _____; those infants weighing less than they should, given the amount of time that has passed since conception, are called _____.

The Birth Process

Ans: Apgar; 10, p. 108
17.   A measure called the _____ is used to assess the newborn's physical condition; the highest score a newborn can get is _____.

Ans: Cesarean section, p. 109
18.   In about 22 percent of all births in the United States, a surgical procedure called a(n) _____ is used to remove the fetus from the uterus through the abdomen.

Ans: anoxia, pp. 111-112
19.   A cause for brain damage in the newborn is repeated and prolonged lack of oxygen, which is called _____.

Ans: parent-newborn bond, p. 115
20.   A psychologist studies the amount of time mothers spend with newborns in the first few hours of life; the psychologist is probably interested in the concept of the _____ between mother and infant.

ESSAY QUESTIONS

1.   In Chapter 4 you learned that the age of viability of the fetus was about 22 weeks, and you learned about the preterm infant. Medical advances are helping to push back the age of viability, enabling younger and smaller infants to survive preterm birth. What effect do you think an earlier age of viability will have on our experience with preterm infants?

2.   Despite the complexity of prenatal development, the large majority of all babies are born without serious congenital abnormalities. Explain the reasons for this high incidence of normality, and tell what, if anything, we can do to increase it.

3.   With the recent appearance on the market of early home pregnancy tests, the pregnant woman can tell almost immediately—before her first missed period—if she is pregnant. Discuss the possible advantages and disadvantages of these tests to pregnant women.

4.   Imagine that you and your spouse are planning to adopt a child. A lawyer specializing in adoption, and her associate, a social worker, tell you about a woman due to deliver in a few months who has agreed to release the infant for adoption. Like any expectant parent you are concerned about the health of the fetus. What questions do you ask the lawyer and social worker? What, if anything, will the answers tell you?

5.   In Chapter 4, you learned about some of the factors that contribute to low birth weight and prematurity. Among these are low socioeconomic status, poor nutrition, and teratogens that increase the risk of a mother's having a low-birth weight or preterm infant. From the material in this chapter, develop a profile of a mother who is at risk for having a low-birth weight infant, and tell what she might do to reduce the risk.

6.   What is known about infants' prenatal senses? How do we know?

7.   Pregnant women in Michigan who ate larger amounts of PCB-polluted fish from Lake Michigan had newborns with more problems than pregnant women who ate lesser amounts of the fish. Give examples of other teratogens and what their effects tend to be.

8.   Taking into account the long incubation period of HIV, what do you think should be done to help prevent the spread of HIV to unborn children? Should there be mandatory testing of all women of childbearing age, or just those women who are at high risk of contracting the virus?

9.   What do you think about laws that would prevent pregnant women from taking recreational drugs, such as alcohol, cocaine, or marijuana?

10.   What do you think doctors should do if medical intervention is needed to save the life of the fetus, but the intervention places the mother's life at risk?

11.   What control do you think society should have over a pregnant woman in order to protect the fetus? What rights does the mother have? When should the fetus get "protective custody"? Be specific in your answer.

12.   What are some of the causes of low-birth weight babies?

13.   The majority of births occur safely without medical intervention. Knowing this, many couples explore the possibility of giving birth at home. What medical interventions are usually not available in a home birth, and under what circumstances would they be necessary or desirable?

14.   At the first interview between a new mother, her baby, and the pediatrician, information about the birth will be elicited. The pediatrician will ask the mother how long she was in labor, whether labor was easy or difficult, and whether or not pain medication was given. Similarly, when the child enters nursery school, the admissions interview may include questions about the birth history, specifically, questions about the child's birth weight, and whether the child was preterm or full term. On the basis of what you have learned in Chapter 4, tell what the pediatrician and the nursery school hope to learn from the birth history.

15.   What occurs during the first stage of labor?

16.   What occurs during the second stage of labor?

17.   What is the Apgar scale? What does it measure? How are scores determined? What do the scores mean?

18.   What are some of the benefits of medical attention for childbirth?

19.   What are some of the costs and risks involved with medically aided childbirth?

20.   What are some of the pros and cons of encouraging immediate bonding between parent and child?

21.   You have a close friend who wishes to adopt a baby. However, the adoption agency has told her that it is unlikely that she will be able to adopt a newborn. She and her husband are apprehensive about continuing with their plans for adoption because they fear that if they do not know their infant from birth, they will not be able to establish a good parent-infant bond. What have you learned about parent-infant bonding, specifically, that might be reassuring to your friend?

Answer guidelines to these essay questions can be found in the Appendix at the end of the Test Bank.

CHAPTER 5   The First Two Years: Biosocial Development

MULTIPLE-CHOICE QUESTIONS

Body Changes

Body Size, p. 121
Diff: E, Ans: c
1. The average North American newborn measures:
   a. 14 inches (36 cm).
   b. 16 inches (41 cm).
   c. 20 inches (51 cm).
   d. 24 inches (60 cm).

Body Size, p. 122
Diff: H, Ans: b
2. The average newborn doubles her birth weight in:
   a. two months.
   b. four months.
   c. six months.
   d. the first year.

Body Size, p. 122
Diff: M, Ans: b
3. A well-nourished newborn gains weight:
   a. continuously from birth onward.
   b. to triple its birth weight by age 1 year.
   c. mostly of bone and water.
   d. to double its birth weight by age 1 year.

Body Size, p. 122
Diff: M, Ans: d
4. Early weight gain is mainly:
   a. bone growth.
   b. muscle growth.
   c. internal organ growth.
   d. increase in fat.

Body Size, p. 122
Diff: H, Ans: b
5. A typical child at 24 months weighs about:
   a. 19 pounds.
   b. 30 pounds.
   c. 41 pounds.
   d. 52 pounds.

Body Size, p. 122
Diff: M, Ans: b

6.   An average, or standard, measurement, calculated from many individuals within a specific group or population is know as a:
      a.   normal score.
      b.   standard deviation.
      c.   percentile.
      d.   norm.

Body Size, p. 122
Diff: E, Ans: a

7.   Half of the subjects rank higher and half of them rank lower than the 50th:
      a.   percentile.
      b.   stanine.
      c.   standard deviation.
      d.   T-score.

Body Size, p. 122
Diff: E, Ans: c

8.   The biological protection of the brain when malnutrition temporarily affects body growth is known as:
      a.   the blood-brain barrier.
      b.   brain-override.
      c.   head-sparing.
      d.   cephalo-sequential primary default.

Body Size, p. 122
Diff: M, Ans: a

9.   Children reach half their adult height by age:
      a.   2 years.
      b.   3 years.
      c.   4 years.
      d.   6 years.

Body Size, p. 122
Diff: H, Ans: a

10.   By age 2, the typical child weighs about _____ and is about _____ inches tall.
      a.   30; 35
      b.   35; 40
      c.   35; 45
      d.   40; 40

Sleep, p. 123
Diff: E, Ans: d

11.   The text indicates that one of the possible reasons that growing infants sleep as much as they do is that:
      a.   they are generating new leukocytes to fight infection during that time.
      b.   their parasympathetic nervous system develops with the help of sleep neurotransmitters.
      c.   sleep is the only time when memories can be consolidated into permanency.
      d.   more growth hormones are released during sleep than during wakefulness.

Sleep, p. 123
Diff: M, Ans: a

12.   Slow-wave or so-called "quiet" sleep:
      a.   increases significantly at about 3 or 4 months.
      b.   is known as "REM" sleep.
      c.   is known as "paradoxical" sleep.
      d.   does not truly establish itself until after 2 years of age.

Sleep, p. 123
Diff: H, Ans: b
13. REM sleep:
    a. is also known as "transitional sleep."
    b. declines after the first months of life.
    c. is somewhat less essential than "transitional sleep."
    d. can be equated to slow-wave sleep.

Sleep, p. 124
Diff: H, Ans: d
14. What percent of 1-year-olds in North America currently "sleep through the night"?
    a. 55
    b. 60
    c. 70
    d. 80

Sleep, p. 124
Diff: M, Ans: c
15. By the time one reaches 60 years of age, they are dreaming approximately _____ minutes each night while asleep.
    a. 30
    b. 45
    c. 60
    d. 75

Early Brain Development

Early Brain Development, p. 125
Diff: H, Ans: d
16. A newborn's brain weight is _____ that of an adult's.
    a. greater than
    b. the same as
    c. about one-half
    d. about one-quarter

Basic Brain Structures, p. 125
Diff: H, Ans: c
17. The frontal areas of the cortex:
    a. are responsible for visual functions.
    b. help us understand spoken words.
    c. assist with self-control.
    d. are well-developed in newborns.

Basic Brain Structures, p. 125
Diff: H, Ans: d
18. The cortex:
    a. is the brain's outer layer.
    b. is also called the gray matter.
    c. is the location of most feeling and sensing.
    d. all of the above.

Fig. 5.3: Early Brain Development, p. 125
Diff: M, Ans: a
19.   The slowest-to-mature brain lobe is the:
        a.   Frontal cortex.
        b.   Parietal cortex.
        c.   Temporal cortex.
        d.   Striate cortex.

Basic Brain Structures, p. 125
Diff: E, Ans: b
20.   The nerve cells of the brain are called:
        a.   axons.
        b.   neurons.
        c.   dendrites.
        d.   the cortex.

Basic Brain Structures, p. 126
Diff: H, Ans: a
21.   Axons are to dendrites as:
        a.   sending is to receiving.
        b.   small is to large.
        c.   baby is to adult.
        d.   controllable is to automatic.

Basic Brain Structures, p. 126
Diff: M, Ans: a
22.   The part of a neuron which acts as a tiny antennae and conducts signals toward the axon of that cell is
        called the:
        a.   dendrite.
        b.   myelin sheath.
        c.   axon terminal.
        d.   synapse, or synaptic cleft.

Exuberance, p. 127
Diff: M, Ans: c
23.   In the process of *transient exuberance*, great brain growth is seen, especially in the area of the:
        a.   axons.
        b.   nucleus.
        c.   dendrites.
        d.   axon terminals.

Exuberance, p. 127
Diff: H, Ans: c
24.   From birth until age 2 years, the density of dendrites in the cortex increases:
        a.   twofold.
        b.   threefold.
        c.   fivefold.
        d.   tenfold.

Experience Enhances the Brain

Experience Enhances the Brain, p. 127
Diff: E, Ans: c

25.   The process by which underused neurons are inactivated is known as:
   a.   transient exuberance.
   b.   plasticity.
   c.   pruning.
   d.   neuron deactivation.

Experience Enhances the Brain, p. 127
Diff: E, Ans: a

26.   A synonym for "pruning" is:
   a.   "sculpting."
   b.   "shaping."
   c.   "honing."
   d.   "deactivation."

Experience Enhances the Brain, p. 127
Diff: H, Ans: d

27.   The fine-tuning process of the human brain implies that:
   a.   infants should be constantly stimulated during infancy.
   b.   compared to other infant animals, the human brain is more mature.
   c.   language and emotion mature very slowly in the first two years of life.
   d.   stimulation helps neural connections develop.

Fig. 5.5: Experience Enhances the Brain, p. 127
Diff: H, Ans: a

28.   When is the peak growth period of synapses for the senses?
   a.   3 months
   b.   4 months
   c.   5 months
   d.   6 months

Fig. 5.5: Experience Enhances the Brain, p. 127
Diff: H, Ans: d

29.   When is the peak growth rate of synapses for higher brain functions, such as analysis?
   a.   6 months
   b.   8 months
   c.   10 months
   d.   12 months

Fig. 5.5: Experience Enhances the Brain, p. 127
Diff: H, Ans: c

30.   When is the peak growth period of synapses for language?
   a.   4 months
   b.   6 months
   c.   8 months
   d.   10 months

Experience Enhances the Brain, p. 128
Diff: M, Ans: d
31.   After proliferation and neural pruning occurs, the type of brain experiences which occur are typically:
    a.   trifling, or insignificant.
    b.   those dealing with abstract, general, or universal statements or laws of behavior.
    c.   experience-expectant.
    d.   experience-dependent.

The Senses and Motor Skills

Sensation and Perception, p. 130
Diff: H, Ans: b
32.   Sensation is demonstrated when a person:
    a.   understands what someone is telling him.
    b.   is able to hear someone whispering.
    c.   solves a math problem correctly.
    d.   believes that two pizzas are the same size, regardless of the number of slices.

Sensation and Perception, p. 130
Diff: H, Ans: b
33.   When a body system first detects an external stimulus, what is the process involved?
    a.   perception
    b.   sensation
    c.   interpretation
    d.   cognition

Sensation and Perception, p. 130
Diff: H, Ans: c
34.   Which indicates that cognition has occurred?
    a.   paying no attention to a plane flying overhead
    b.   your eyes' response when the light turns on
    c.   coming to the kitchen when you smell dinner cooking
    d.   dropping a dish that is too hot

Sensation and Perception, p. 130
Diff: M, Ans: b
35.   A newborn:
    a.   is virtually deaf and blind.
    b.   has all the senses but is immature.
    c.   perceives the world as alarming and confusing.
    d.   has all the senses functioning as well as those of an adult.

Sensation and Perception, pp. 130-131
Diff: H, Ans: a
36.   The newborn's perceived world is:
    a.   immature.
    b.   overwhelming, which is why he or she cries so much.
    c.   very similar to the perceived world of an adult.
    d.   blooming, buzzing confusion.

Looking, p. 131
Diff: E, Ans: c
37. Binocular vision refers to the ability to:
     a. focus on objects at a distance.
     b. bring an object in and out of focus.
     c. focus on an object with both eyes.
     d. visually distinguish colors.

Looking, p. 131
Diff: H, Ans: c
38. The average infant's visual systems:
     a. cannot tolerate much stimulation.
     b. benefits from stimulation after 1 year of age.
     c. benefits from stimulation in the early months of life.
     d. cannot process events that are out of the ordinary.

Looking, p. 131
Diff: E, Ans: b
39. The sense that is the *least* developed at birth is:
     a. hearing.
     b. vision.
     c. taste.
     d. smell.

Looking, p. 131
Diff: E, Ans: a
40. The neonate's vision:
     a. is clearest when objects are 4 to 30 inches away.
     b. is clearest when objects are about 10 feet away.
     c. does not improve until age 1.
     d. is the most developed of the senses.

Looking, p. 131
Diff: M, Ans: d
41. Newborns can focus best on:
     a. clouds moving in the sky.
     b. a bookcase across the room.
     c. a mobile hung three feet above its crib.
     d. their mothers' face while she is feeding them.

Looking, p. 131
Diff: H, Ans: c
42. A 1-month-old infant has all of the following *except*:
     a. imperfect ability to scan objects.
     b. a tendency to look at peripheral features.
     c. binocular vision.
     d. a wandering gaze.

Listening, Looking, p. 131
Diff: E, Ans: a
43. Tom will find that his newborn son's hearing is:
     a. more sensitive than his vision.
     b. sensitive only to sudden noises.
     c. too immature to distinguish human voices.
     d. more acute than that of adults.

Reflexes, p. 132
Diff: E, Ans: b
44.   All reflexes:
a.   are essential for life.
b.   are involuntary.
c.   disappear by 4 months.
d.   all of the above are true.

Reflexes, p. 132
Diff: E, Ans: c
45.   Which reflex ensures an adequate supply of oxygen?
a.   Babinski
b.   anoxia
c.   breathing
d.   respiratory

Reflexes, p. 132
Diff: E, Ans: a
46.   An involuntary response to a stimulus is known as a:
a.   reflex.
b.   perception.
c.   habit.
d.   marasmus.

Reflexes, p. 132
Diff: M, Ans: c
47.   The sucking reflex explains why babies:
a.   spend so much time sucking their thumbs.
b.   are able to learn how to suck on the mother's breast.
c.   suck anything that touches their lips.
d.   learn to coordinate sucking with oxygen intake.

Reflexes, p. 132
Diff: H, Ans: a
48.   When infants are cold, they:
a.   cry, shiver, and tuck their legs close to their bodies.
b.   cry, shiver, and kick their legs vigorously.
c.   shiver and kick their legs vigorously.
d.   cry and pull their legs up close to their bodies.

Reflexes, p. 132
Diff: H, Ans: c
49.   A 3-day-old infant has sneezed. It is most likely that he:
a.   has a cold.
b.   smelled something he did not like.
c.   did so as a reflex.
d.   has asthma.

Reflexes, pp. 132-133
Diff: M, Ans: b
50.   When infants turn their heads and suck in response to a touch on the cheek, that is the:
a.   Moro reflex.
b.   rooting reflex.
c.   sucking reflex.
d.   Babinski reflex.

Reflexes, p. 133
Diff: H, Ans: d
51. Which reflex allows newborns to grip so tightly that they can carry their weight?
    a. Moro reflex
    b. rooting reflex
    c. wrestlers reflex
    d. grasping reflex

Reflexes, p. 133
Diff: H, Ans: a
52. When one-month-old Lily is held upright with her feet touching a flat surface, she should:
    a. move her legs as if to walk.
    b. curl up her toes.
    c. kick out her legs.
    d. move her legs upward toward her body.

Gross Motor Skills, p. 133
Diff: E, Ans: d
53. Children first walk with their legs spread apart, unsteady and unbalanced. Because of this they are called:
    a. waddlers.
    b. infants.
    c. tipplers.
    d. toddlers.

Gross Motor Skills, p. 133
Diff: E, Ans: b
54. The average child can walk well unassisted at about:
    a. 6 months.
    b. 1 year.
    c. 18 months.
    d. 2 years.

Gross Motor Skills, p. 133
Diff: E, Ans: b
55. When newborns are held horizontally on their stomachs, their arms and legs stretch out. This response is known as the:
    a. flying motor skill.
    b. swimming motor skill.
    c. Moro reflex.
    d. Babinski reflex.

Gross Motor Skills, p. 133
Diff: M, Ans: a
56. Most infants are able to crawl on their bellies by age:
    a. 4 to 6 months.
    b. 6 to 8 months.
    c. 8 to 10 months.
    d. 10 to 12 months.

The Senses and Motor Skills, pp. 133-134
Diff: M, Ans: a

57.   The difference between gross and fine motor skills is whether they:
       a.   involve bigger or smaller muscles.
       b.   involve mental or physical skills.
       c.   are controllable.
       d.   are due more to nature or nurture.

Fine Motor Skills, p. 134
Diff: H, Ans: b

58.   Sam is able to grab objects but he sometimes closes his hand too early or too late. Sam is probably
       about:
       a.   2 months old.
       b.   4 months old.
       c.   6 months old.
       d.   8 months old.

Fine Motor Skills, p. 134
Diff: M, Ans: c

59.   Babies learn to grab and hold onto objects by about:
       a.   2 months.
       b.   4 months.
       c.   6 months.
       d.   8 months.

Fine Motor Skills, p. 134
Diff: E, Ans: c

60.   Fine motor skills are those that:
       a.   are due to brain damage or trauma.
       b.   require practice.
       c.   require small body movements.
       d.   use three or more muscles.

Table 5.1: The Senses and Motor Skills, p. 134
Diff: H, Ans: d

61.   Ann-Marie started walking when she was 10 months old; Cynthia is just beginning to take steps by
       herself at 13 months. Which of the following is most likely?
       a.   Ann-Marie is very intelligent.
       b.   Cynthia is malnourished.
       c.   Cynthia is retarded.
       d.   Both girls are developing normally.

Table 5.1: The Senses and Motor Skills, p. 134
Diff: H, Ans: b

62.   At 6 months, Andrew is finally able to sit up unsupported. Probably Andrew is:
       a.   being breastfed.
       b.   a healthy infant.
       c.   brain damaged.
       d.   malnourished.

Variations and Ethnic Differences, p. 134
Diff: H, Ans: a

63.   Healthy infants usually develop:
      a.   the same motor skills in the same sequence.
      b.   the same motor skills at the same age.
      c.   motor skills only if they are taught.
      d.   motor skills in unpredictable sequences.

Variations and Ethnic Differences, p. 134
Diff: H, Ans: b

64.   According to recent norms, which skill develops last in the sequence?
      a.   walking while holding on
      b.   standing momentarily without holding on
      c.   sitting without support
      d.   standing while holding on

Variations and Ethnic Differences, p. 134
Diff: E, Ans: c

65.   Among the following, the skill that is generally the first to develop is:
      a.   kicking a ball forward.
      b.   walking backward.
      c.   walking well alone.
      d.   walking up steps.

Variations and Ethnic Differences, p. 135
Diff: E, Ans: d

66.   If all of these children are healthy, the first child to walk is probably:
      a.   Renee, from Canada.
      b.   Michelle, from France.
      c.   Kim, from Korea.
      d.   Kynashi, from Uganda.

Variations and Ethnic Differences, p. 135
Diff: E, Ans: a

67.   That genes affect motor skill is shown by the fact that:
      a.   identical twins are likely to master skills at the same time.
      b.   fraternal twins are more alike than other brothers or sisters.
      c.   undernourished children walk later than other children.
      d.   boys are likely to reach milestones before girls.

Variations and Ethnic Differences, p. 135
Diff: E, Ans: c

68.   Louise wants to know when her baby boy will develop various skills. The answer depends on:
      a.   his genetic programming.
      b.   the home environment.
      c.   the interaction between genes and environment.
      d.   his father's involvement.

Public Health Measures

Public Health Measures, p. 136
Diff: M, Ans: c
69.   Approximately _____ children were born between 1950 and the year 2000, according to textbook supposition.
       a.   4 billion
       b.   5 billion
       c.   6 billion
       d.   7 billion

Immunization, p. 137
Diff: E, Ans: b
70.   A process stimulating the body's immune system to defend the body against a contagious disease is called:
       a.   exuberance.
       b.   immunization.
       c.   pertussis.
       d.   head-sparing.

Immunization, p. 137
Diff: M, Ans: b
71.   Which of the following stimulates the production of antibodies?
       a.   pruning
       b.   immunization
       c.   head-sparing
       d.   allergies

Immunization, p. 137
Diff: M, Ans: b
72.   The most lethal disease for all children in past centuries has been:
       a.   polio.
       b.   smallpox.
       c.   rubeola.
       d.   anencephaly.

Immunization, p. 138
Diff: E, Ans: c
73.   One of the natural consequences of "chicken pox" is:
       a.   death.
       b.   deafness.
       c.   encephalitis.
       d.   blindness.

Table 5.2: Public Health Measures, p. 138
Diff: M, Ans: a
74.   The oldest childhood vaccine is that of:
       a.   diphtheria.
       b.   tetanus.
       c.   measles.
       d.   polio.

Immunization, p. 139
Diff: M, Ans: d
75.   A _____ percent immunization rate is sufficient to halt common childhood diseases.
       a.   60
       b.   70
       c.   80
       d.   90

Table 5.2: Public Health Measures, p. 139
Diff: M, Ans: c
76.   A fetus whose mother contracts _____ may be born blind, deaf, and brain-damaged.
       a.   mumps
       b.   measles
       c.   rubella
       d.   the chicken pox

SIDS, p. 139
Diff: M, Ans: b
77.   In order to be included in the statistics for SIDS, a seemingly healthy infant dying in its sleep must be at least _____ of age.
       a.   2 weeks
       b.   2 months
       c.   3 months
       d.   8 days

SIDS, p. 139
Diff: M, Ans: a
78.   Of the following, which country has had the highest infant mortality rate in the past 30 years?
       a.   India
       b.   Chile
       c.   Mexico
       d.   Poland

Ethnicity and SIDS, p. 140
Diff: M, Ans: c
79.   Most Chinese infants are _____, which makes them sleep _____ soundly.
       a.   bottle-fed; less
       b.   bottle-fed; more
       c.   breast-fed; less
       d.   breast-fed; more

Ethnicity and SIDS, p. 140
Diff: M, Ans: c
80.   Benjamin Spock's book on child-rearing recommended which position for sleeping babies?
       a.   on the back
       b.   on the side
       c.   on the stomach
       d.   the prenatal position

Ethnicity and SIDS, p. 140
Diff: H, Ans: a
81.   Research on SIDS has shown that babies should be:
       a.   put to sleep on their backs.
       b.   swaddled tightly before being put to bed.
       c.   kept in a warm bedroom.
       d.   fed right before being put to bed.

Ethnicity and SIDS, p. 141
Diff: E, Ans: a
82.   SIDS rates in the United States are:
   a.   declining rapidly.
   b.   staying steady.
   c.   increasing slightly.
   d.   increasing rapidly.

Breast Is Best, p. 140
Diff: H, Ans: d
83.   Cow's milk is _____ to digest than breast milk, so it causes _____ tiredness and a _____ sleep.
   a.   easier; more; deeper
   b.   easier; less; shallower
   c.   harder; less; shallower
   d.   harder; more; deeper

Breast Is Best, p. 141
Diff: E, Ans: c
84.   Breast milk:
   a.   is deficient in iron and vitamin C.
   b.   is more likely than formula to produce allergies.
   c.   provides more iron and vitamins C and A than cow's milk.
   d.   upsets the baby's digestive system more often than formulas.

Breast Is Best, p. 141
Diff: E, Ans: c
85.   In deciding how to feed a baby, a mother should consider that:
   a.   alcohol or nicotine are never present in breast milk.
   b.   employers encourage working mothers who want to breast-feed.
   c.   breast milk contains antibodies that provide some protection against disease.
   d.   breast-feeding will make the baby always love her.

Breast Is Best, p. 141
Diff: M, Ans: a
86.   Studies comparing breast-feeding with bottle-feeding show that:
   a.   breast-fed babies have fewer allergies and stomach aches.
   b.   breast-feeding is recommended for all mothers and babies.
   c.   scientific improvements make bottle-feeding a better choice.
   d.   breast-feeding should stop when the baby gets the first tooth.

Breast Is Best, p. 141
Diff: M, Ans: b
87.   Which substance is secreted into the mother's milk in the first day or two after childbirth?
   a.   ocytocin
   b.   colostrum
   c.   pertussin
   d.   DTaP

Breast Is Best, p. 141
Diff: M, Ans: c
88.   The World Health Organization (WHO) suggested than infants should be fed only breast milk for the first:
   a.   2 months.
   b.   2 to 4 months.
   c.   4 to 6 months.
   d.   6 to 8 months.

Breast Is Best, p. 141
Diff: E, Ans: d
89.   The first solid foods that should be given to an infant are:
        a.   meats.
        b.   eggs.
        c.   vegetables.
        d.   cereals.

Malnutrition, p. 142
Diff: M, Ans: b
90.   Birth weight should _____ by age 1 year.
        a.   double
        b.   triple
        c.   quadruple
        d.   quintuple

Malnutrition, p. 142
Diff: E, Ans: d
91.   Marasmus results from:
        a.   lack of specific vitamin.
        b.   protein-calorie malnutrition in middle childhood.
        c.   iodine malnutrition during pregnancy.
        d.   protein-calorie malnutrition in early infancy.

Malnutrition, p. 142
Diff: E, Ans: d
92.   Untreated protein-calorie malnutrition in infancy will eventually result in:
        a.   dwarfism and underweight.
        b.   SIDS.
        c.   hyperactivity.
        d.   sickness and perhaps death.

Malnutrition, p. 142
Diff: E, Ans: c
93.   In this terrible disease, one's essential organs use the available nutrients shared with the body so that
        the rest of the body becomes degraded. This is a condition called:
        a.   SIDS.
        b.   marasmus.
        c.   kwashiorkor.
        d.   pertussis.

Malnutrition, p. 143
Diff: E, Ans: a
94.   Unusual swelling of a toddler's face and abdomen and thin, colorless hair are symptoms of:
        a.   kwashiorkor.
        b.   marasmus.
        c.   rickets.
        d.   hypoglycemia.

TRUE-FALSE QUESTIONS

Body Changes

Ans: F, p. 121
1.   The average American newborn weighs about 7 pounds and is about 27 inches in length.

Ans: T, p. 122
2.   Two-year-olds are about 20 percent of their adult weight.

Ans: T, p. 122
3.   Infants usually triple their birth weight by the end of their first year.

Ans: T, p. 122
4.   Between 12 and 24 months, infant growth is generally slower than it was in the first year.

Ans: T, p. 122
5.   Norms are closely tied to percentiles.

Ans: T, p. 122
6.   Most two-year-olds weigh 30 pounds.

Ans: F, p. 122
7.   The speed of physical growth in the first year is continued during the second year.

Ans: T, p. 123
8.   "Transitional sleep" and the period of dozing are synonymous.

Ans: F, p. 123
9.   More human growth hormones are released during the waking state than during sleep.

Ans: T, p. 123
10.   The infant's brain is too immature for some infants to be able to sleep through the night.

Ans: T, Fig. 5.1, p. 124
11.   At age 60, we only dream a total of 60 minutes during a typical night's sleep.

Early Brain Development

Ans: F, p. 125
12.   The skull and brain of the newborn are the same size as those of an adult and are therefore disproportionately large.

Ans: T, p. 125
13.   The neonate's body weight is only 5 percent of that of the adult.

Ans: T, p. 126
14.   Axons and dendrites meet at the synapse.

Ans: T, p. 127
15.   Proliferation and pruning of neural connections improve neural communication and increase thinking ability.

Experience Enhances the Brain

Ans: T, p. 127
16.   Neural connections which are not used shrink and disappear.

The Senses and Motor Skills

Ans: F, p. 130
17.   Sensation occurs when the brain tries to make sense out of a stimulus.

Ans: T, p. 130

18.   Sensation begins when an outer sense organ detects an incoming stimulus.

Ans: F, p. 130

19.   Cognition cannot occur in the absence of perception or sensation.

Ans: T, p. 131

20.   Vision is not as well-developed as hearing at birth.

Ans: T, p. 131

21.   Newborns are responsive to a variety of sounds; for example, rhythmic sounds or lullabies are often soothing to them.

Ans: F, p. 131

22.   Perception takes place in the corpus callosum.

Ans: T, p. 131

23.   Perception requires experience, in addition to normal brain functioning.

Ans: T, pp. 132-133

24.   The rooting reflex is a reflex that helps the newborn infant find a nipple.

Ans: T, p. 133

25.   A child who begins walking well unassisted at 12 months is close to the average age for mastering this skill.

Ans: T, p. 134

26.   By one year of age, most infants can coordinate both hands to hold an object that is too big for just one hand.

Ans: T, p. 134

27.   An example of a fine motor skill is transferring objects from one hand to the other.

Ans: F, p. 135

28.   Identical twins are more likely than fraternal twins to take their first step on the same day. This indicates that parental encouragement is more important than genetic endowment in the timing of motor development.

Ans: F, p. 141

29.   The thick, high-calorie fluid secreted by the mother's breasts at childbirth is known as callosum.

Ans: T, p. 142

30.   The problem with infant formula (bottle-feeding) in many poor or developing countries is that the formula is prepared improperly, often under unsanitary conditions.

Ans: T, p. 143

31.   The child's abdomen typically swells with water with the disorder kwashiorkor.

FILL-IN-THE-BLANK QUESTIONS

Body Changes

Ans: fat, p. 122

1.   In the first months after birth, much of the infant's weight gain is _____, which provides both insulation and a source of nourishment.

Ans: Eighty, p. 124

2.   _____ percent of North American one-year-olds sleep through the night.

Early Brain Development

Ans: neurons, p. 125

3.   The nervous system is made up of nerve cells called _____.

Ans: synapse, p. 126

4.   The _____ is the point where the axon of one neuron meets the dendrites of another neuron.

Ans: binocular, p. 131

5.   The ability to use both eyes together to focus on an object is called _____ vision.

The Senses and Motor Skills

Ans: perception, p. 130

6.   Sensation occurs when a sensory system detects a stimulus; _____ occurs when the brain processes the sensory information.

Ans: human face, p. 131

7.   Human infants are "pre-programmed" to be especially attentive to the _____.

Ans: Sugar, p. 132

8.   _____ is an effective pain reliever for newborns.

Ans: breast milk, p. 132

9.   Early _____ acts as a mild anesthetic for the newborn.

Motor Skills

Ans: reflexes, p. 132

10.   When newborns are cold, they shiver, cry, and tuck their legs close to the body. These are examples of _____ that help maintain constant body temperature.

Ans: toddler, p. 133

11.   A baby who walks in the characteristically unsteady manner of an 18-month-old is called a(n) _____.

Ans: norms, p. 134

12.   A table that shows the age at which infants usually master certain motor skills, gives averages, or _____, for these skills.

Ans: sequence, p. 134

13.   Although the exact age at which motor skills are mastered varies from one individual to another, the _____ is the same for all individuals.

Public Health Measures

Ans: immunization, p. 137

14.   The single most important cause of improvement in child survival in the twentieth century is _____.

Ans: smallpox, p. 137

15.   Widespread immunization eradicated _____, the most lethal disease of all for children.

Ans: breast, p. 141
16.   When breast milk and cow's milk are compared, _____ milk is found to contain more vitamin A and vitamin C and more antibodies against disease.

Ans: cereal, p. 141
17.   The first solid foods that should be added to the infant's diet are _____ and fruits.

Ans: protein-calorie, p. 142
18.   When a child does not consume food of any kind, _____ malnutrition occurs.

Ans: kwashiorkor; marasmus, pp. 142-143
19.   A toddler in a country affected by famine suffers from a protein-calorie deficiency that causes the disease _____; in his sister, who is 6 months old, the same deficiency results in a disease called _____.

ESSAY QUESTIONS

1.   Draft a profile of an infant at high risk for SIDS. Suggest ways to prevent SIDS.

2.   What kinds of changes are occurring within the brain during the first years of life?

3.   In the United States, newborns are not allowed to appear on television. This means that if a baby is "born" on a soap opera, for example, the part of the newborn must be played by a much older baby. Why do you think that newborns are not allowed on the set, and why might they not be welcome even if regulations permitted?

4.   Based on what is known about infants' visual abilities and visual preferences, what can parents do to set up the child's environment? What should parents expect?

5.   Imagine that you are a psychologist who wants to determine the earliest point in human development at which an infant can demonstrate specific skills, such as the ability to judge distances or to differentiate between lines at different angles. Suggest research approaches and techniques that might be helpful in studying these questions. Note the difficulties that might be expected.

6.   What are some of the short-term and long-term results of nutritional problems?

7.   Discuss the advantages and disadvantages of breast-feeding over bottle-feeding and suggest ways in which more women can be encouraged to breast-feed.

8.   What can parents do to prevent undernutrition?

9.   Design a program to help prevent infant undernutrition domestically and globally. Discuss who would run the program, where it would get its funding, and who it is intended to help.

Answer guidelines to these essay questions can be found in the Appendix at the end of the Test Bank.

CHAPTER 6

**The First Two Years:
Cognitive Development**

MULTIPLE-CHOICE QUESTIONS

Sensorimotor Intelligence

Sensorimotor Intelligence, p. 147
Diff: E, Ans: d

1. What Swiss scientist emphasized that infants are active learners and that early learning is based on sensory and motor skills?
    a. Noam Chomsky
    b. Eleanor Gibson
    c. Sigmund Freud
    d. Jean Piaget

Sensorimotor Intelligence, p. 147
Diff: E, Ans: a

2. Piaget called the active intellectual functioning of infants:
    a. sensorimotor intelligence.
    b. adaptation.
    c. object awareness.
    d. imitative learning.

Sensorimotor Intelligence, p. 147
Diff: H, Ans: b

3. Assimilation is to accommodation as:
    a. small is to large.
    b. incorporating is to readjusting.
    c. difficult is to easy.
    d. alone is to united.

Sensorimotor Intelligence, p. 147
Diff: M, Ans: a

4. Piaget believed that infants:
    a. actively seek to comprehend their world.
    b. learn mostly through reinforcement.
    c. possess concepts and ideas.
    d. are passive receptors of stimulation.

Sensorimotor Intelligence, p. 147
Diff: H, Ans: b

5.   If you were to see a man from the nation of Fiji, but had never seen one before, you would be able to recognize him as a human being. This cognitive process is:
a.   accommodation.
b.   assimilation.
c.   object permanence.
d.   egocentric thinking.

Sensorimotor Intelligence, p. 147
Diff: H, Ans: d

6.   A 1-year-old likes to pull his cat's tail because the cat meows and moves away. One day he pulls another cat's tail and is scratched. From that day on he is cautious around cats. What cognitive process has occurred?
a.   habituation
b.   trial and error
c.   assimilation
d.   accommodation

Sensorimotor Intelligence, p. 147
Diff: M, Ans: c

7.   When we revamp our old ways of thinking because of new information, Piaget calls this:
a.   historical context.
b.   assimilation.
c.   accommodation.
d.   imitation.

Sensorimotor Intelligence, p. 147
Diff: H, Ans: c

8.   According to Jean Piaget, the two elements of adaptation are:
a.   mental combinations and trial and error.
b.   goal-directed behavior and habituation.
c.   assimilation and accommodation.
d.   object permanence and circular reactions.

Sensorimotor Intelligence, p. 147
Diff: M, Ans: c

9.   During the sensorimotor stage, the main task is to:
a.   learn to use language to express sensations.
b.   think of past and future events.
c.   use senses and motor skills to understand the world.
d.   think logically and critically.

Sensorimotor Intelligence, p. 147
Diff: E, Ans: b

10.   Which person, according to Piaget, is rigid, "stuck, unable or unwilling to adapt his or her cognitive processes"?
a.   a rigid one
b.   an unintelligent one
c.   a convergent one
d.   a divergent one

Sensorimotor Intelligence, p. 147
Diff: M, Ans: a

11.   Sensorimotor intelligence is characterized as:
       a.   perceiving and doing.
       b.   manipulating and evaluating.
       c.   symbol manipulating.
       d.   building schemes.

Sensorimotor Intelligence, pp. 147-153
Diff: E, Ans: a

12.   Piaget's theory of development focused primarily on:
       a.   how our thinking changes as we grow older.
       b.   biological and physical changes.
       c.   our unconscious issues.
       d.   the ways in which our environment influences us.

Sensorimotor Intelligence, pp. 147-153
Diff: E, Ans: a

13.   Jean Piaget was most interested in:
       a.   studying how children think.
       b.   measuring what children know.
       c.   how parents discipline their children.
       d.   how peers influence each other.

Sensorimotor Intelligence, p. 148
Diff: E, Ans: d

14.   Piaget believed children begin to develop cognitively at:
       a.   18 months.
       b.   1 year.
       c.   6 months.
       d.   birth.

Sensorimotor Intelligence, p. 148
Diff: E, Ans: a

15.   Piaget called the active intellectual functioning of infants:
       a.   sensorimotor intelligence.
       b.   adaptation.
       c.   object awareness.
       d.   imitative learning.

Table 6.1: The Six Stages of Sensorimotor Intelligence, p. 148
Diff: M, Ans: b

16.   In which Piagetian sensorimotor stage would one find the *first acquired adaptation*, such as grabbing a bottle to suck on it?
       a.   stage one
       b.   stage two
       c.   stage three
       d.   stage four

Table 6.1: The Six Stages of Sensorimotor Intelligence, p. 148
Diff: M, Ans: c
17.   In which Piagetian sensorimotor stage would one find *an awareness of things – responding to people and objects*?
   a.   stage one
   b.   stage two
   c.   stage three
   d.   stage four

Table 6.1: The Six Stages of Sensorimotor Intelligence, p. 148
Diff: M, Ans: d
18.   In which Piagetian sensorimotor stage would one find *new adaptation and anticipation – becoming more deliberate and purposeful in responding to people and objects*?
   a.   stage one
   b.   stage two
   c.   stage three
   d.   stage four

Table 6.1: The Six Stages of Sensorimotor Intelligence, p. 148
Diff: H, Ans: b
19.   In which Piagetian sensorimotor stage involves the infant's responses to its own body?
   a.   stage one
   b.   stage three
   c.   stage four
   d.   stage five

Table 6.1: The Six Stages of Sensorimotor Intelligence, p. 148
Diff: H, Ans: c
20.   Which Piagetian sensorimotor stage involves the infant's responses to objects and people?
   a.   stage one
   b.   stage two
   c.   stage three
   d.   stage five

Table 6.1: The Six Stages of Sensorimotor Intelligence, p. 148
Diff: H, Ans: b
21.   Just before a child develops "new means through experimentation," which of these has most recently occurred?
   a.   stage one
   b.   new awareness of things
   c.   new adaptation and anticipation
   d.   new means through mental combinations

Table 6.1: The Six Stages of Sensorimotor Intelligence, p. 148
Diff: M, Ans: d
22.   In which of the following Piagetian sensorimotor stages is the child the most creative?
   a.   stage one
   b.   stage two
   c.   stage three
   d.   stage five

Table 6.1: The Six Stages of Sensorimotor Intelligence, p. 148
Diff: M, Ans: c

23.   In which Piagetian sensorimotor stage would one find *new means through active experimentation*?
   a.   stage three
   b.   stage four
   c.   stage five
   d.   stage six

Table 6.1: The Six Stages of Sensorimotor Intelligence, p. 148
Diff: M, Ans: d

24.   In which Piagetian sensorimotor stage would one find *new means through mental combinations*?
   a.   stage three
   b.   stage four
   c.   stage five
   d.   stage six

Stages One and Two: Primary Circular Reactions, p. 148
Diff: M, Ans: d

25.   The first two stages of sensorimotor thought involve:
   a.   creative actions.
   b.   creative thoughts.
   c.   objects and people.
   d.   the infant's own body.

Stages One and Two: Primary Circular Reactions, p. 148
Diff: H, Ans: b

26.   A baby kicks its legs, smiles, and deliberately kicks its legs again. These actions are repeated for several minutes. According to Piaget, this is an example of:
   a.   repetitious behavior.
   b.   a primary circular reaction.
   c.   a secondary circular reaction.
   d.   accommodation.

Stages One and Two: Primary Circular Reactions, p. 148
Diff: M, Ans: c

27.   In Piaget's terminology, sensorimotor stage two is known as:
   a.   the stage of reflexes.
   b.   procedures for making interesting sights last.
   c.   the first acquired adaptations.
   d.   new adaptation and anticipation.

Stages One and Two: Primary Circular Reactions, p. 148
Diff: E, Ans: a

28.   The infant's first sensorimotor activities are:
   a.   reflexes.
   b.   first acquired adaptations.
   c.   anticipation.
   d.   active experimentation.

Stages One and Two: Primary Circular Reactions, p. 148
Diff: M, Ans: c

29.   Piaget would say that the use of a reflex such as grasping provides:
   a.   an infant with a way to survive until thought can begin.
   b.   physical exercise as well as social contact.
   c.   information about the world that is used for learning.
   d.   little benefit to the infant.

Stages One and Two: Primary Circular Reactions, p. 149
Diff: E, Ans: d

30.   During sensorimotor stage two, an infant:
   a.   begins to understand object permanence.
   b.   learns to talk.
   c.   experiments with toys and animals.
   d.   begins to adapt reflexes to the environment.

Stages Three and Four: Secondary Circular Reactions, p. 149
Diff: H, Ans: c

31.   A baby sticks out its tongue and another person laughs. The baby joins in the laughter and deliberately sticks out its tongue again. Piaget would call this:
   a.   social circular reactions.
   b.   primary circular reactions.
   c.   secondary circular reactions.
   d.   rudimentary circular reactions.

Stages Three and Four: Secondary Circular Reactions, p. 149
Diff: H, Ans: c

32.   Jean Piaget focused heavily on the child's ability and use of feedback loops of activity. To which of these does this most specifically refer?
   a.   assimilation
   b.   tertiary reactions
   c.   circular reactions
   d.   deferred reactions

Stages Three and Four: Secondary Circular Reactions, p. 149
Diff: H, Ans: d

33.   An example of stage-three behavior is:
   a.   thumb-sucking and self-soothing.
   b.   searching for a teddy bear hidden under a blanket.
   c.   trying to dress like Mommy or Daddy.
   d.   making a noise, looking for a smile, and smiling back.

Stages Three and Four: Secondary Circular Reactions, p. 149
Diff: H, Ans: b

34.   Hugh enjoys playing with your keys. When you take them away and place them in your pocket, Hugh does not search for them. Piaget would say that Hugh does not understand:
   a.   conservation.
   b.   object permanence.
   c.   egocentrism.
   d.   affordances.

Stages Three and Four: Secondary Circular Reactions, p. 149
Diff: M, Ans: d

35.   Sensorimotor stage four is the stage of:
   a.   procedures for making interesting sights last.
   b.   new means through active experimentation.
   c.   new means through mental combinations.
   d.   new adaptation and anticipation.

Stages Three and Four: Secondary Circular Reactions, p. 149
Diff: H, Ans: b

36.   A baby sees a white bakery bag for the first time and screams with joy. The baby is most likely in the sensorimotor stage:
a.   five.
b.   four.
c.   three.
d.   two.

Stages Three and Four: Secondary Circular Reactions, p. 150
Diff: E, Ans: a

37.   That objects continue to exist when they cannot be seen is:
a.   object permanence.
b.   an acquired adaptation.
c.   mental representation.
d.   object continuity.

Stages Three and Four: Secondary Circular Reactions, p. 150
Diff: H, Ans: c

38.   Makesha is 8 months old. Research on object permanence would suggest that she:
a.   will not yet search for hidden objects.
b.   can find an object that has been transferred to a second hiding place.
c.   has limited search abilities.
d.   will acquire complete object permanence by 10 months.

Stages Three and Four: Secondary Circular Reactions, p. 150
Diff: M, Ans: b

39.   Identify the *accurate* statement:
a.   A single-word utterance that expresses a complete thought is called an idiom.
b.   With goal-directed behavior, children will initiate motor activities to fulfill their own needs.
c.   The hybrid theory of language development during infancy combines valid aspects of other theories and is called the behaviorist theory.
d.   According to Skinner, a grandfather who smiles whenever the baby says "pa-pa" is providing a model for talking.

Stages Three and Four: Secondary Circular Reactions, p. 150
Diff: E, Ans: d

40.   The principle of object permanence is demonstrated by an infant's:
a.   laughing when a sibling makes faces.
b.   grasping a rattle and banging it on the floor.
c.   being willing to let go of an object.
d.   searching for a toy that has fallen from sight.

Stages Three and Four: Secondary Circular Reactions, p. 150
Diff: M, Ans: b

41.   A particular stage-four baby does not like to get wet. If his mother turned on the faucet and got out his bath towel, the baby might:
a.   be curious about the water.
b.   howl and move away from her and the bathroom.
c.   take the towel and throw it in the bathtub.
d.   bring a rubber duck and want to give it a bath.

Stages Three and Four: Secondary Circular Reactions, p. 150
Diff: M, Ans: c
42.   The behavior of an infant in sensorimotor stage four might best be described as:
        a. creative.
        b. anxious.
        c. deliberate or purposeful.
        d. experimental.

Stages Three and Four: Secondary Circular Reactions, p. 150
Diff: E, Ans: c
43.   You roll a ball across the floor to a baby. The ball rolls out of sight behind a chair. For the first time, the baby crawls to search for it. The baby is probably about:
        a. 6 months old.
        b. 12 months old.
        c. 8 months old.
        d. 15 months old.

Thinking Like a Scientist, p. 150
Diff: E, Ans: d
44.   A baby trying to pry his/her Dad's fingers apart to get to a toy demonstrates accomplishment of:
        a. synchrony.
        b. accommodation.
        c. mutuality.
        d. object permanence.

Thinking Like a Scientist, p. 150
Diff: M, Ans: b
45.   Piaget's basic test for object permanence involves:
        a. seeing how babies play with their mothers.
        b. showing a baby an interesting toy and then covering it with a cloth.
        c. placing a toe in a baby's hand and seeing how the baby responds to it.
        d. seeing if a baby can imitate a facial expression it has been shown.

Stages Five and Six: Tertiary Circular Reactions, p. 151
Diff: E, Ans: b
46.   The last stage of circular reactions occurs in:
        a. secondary circular reactions.
        b. tertiary circular reactions.
        c. deferred circular reactions.
        d. stage five.

Stages Five and Six: Tertiary Circular Reactions, p. 151
Diff: H, Ans: d
47.   A toddler experimentally varies the way she handles a ball—first squeezing it, then throwing it—in order to learn what effect each variation has. This child is demonstrating:
        a. secondary circular reactions.
        b. primary circular reactions.
        c. quaternary circular reactions.
        d. tertiary circular reactions.

Stages Five and Six: Tertiary Circular Reactions, p. 152
Diff: M, Ans: a
48.   Stage five of the sensorimotor period is known as the stage of:
        a. experimentation.
        b. first adaptations.
        c. new adaptation and anticipation.
        d. mental combinations.

Stages Five and Six: Tertiary Circular Reactions, p. 152
Diff: H, Ans: c

49. Which of these statements is a *true* one?
  a. According to Piaget, the first period of cognitive development is the sensorimotor period, which lasts from birth until about age 4.
  b. The theory of infant language development that holds that communication with others is the crucial element is referred to as the behaviorism theory.
  c. In the final stage of sensorimotor intelligence, toddlers begin to anticipate and solve simple problems by using mental combinations.
  d. The child's first word combinations, for example, "More cookie," or "My ball," are called *holophrases*.

Stages Five and Six: Tertiary Circular Reactions, p. 152
Diff: E, Ans: d

50. According to Piaget, the stage-five infant is like a:
  a. child in the "terrible twos."
  b. neurotic who cannot take no for an answer.
  c. mime who imitates behavior of all kinds.
  d. scientist who experiments in order to see.

Stages Five and Six: Tertiary Circular Reactions, p. 152
Diff: H, Ans: c

51. Attempting to eat spaghetti by trying to put a piece in the ears as well as in the mouth is typical of sensorimotor stage:
  a. three.
  b. four.
  c. five.
  d. six.

Stages Five and Six: Tertiary Circular Reactions, p. 152
Diff: M, Ans: a

52. The scientific method of the stage-five infant is:
  a. trial and error.
  b. considered anticipation of results.
  c. theoretical.
  d. behavioral conditioning.

Stages Five and Six: Tertiary Circular Reactions, p. 152
Diff: E, Ans: a

53. Piaget's stage six of sensorimotor intelligence is known as:
  a. mental combinations.
  b. interesting observations.
  c. primary reactions.
  d. new adaptation and anticipation.

Stages Five and Six: Tertiary Circular Reactions, p. 152
Diff: H, Ans: a

54. Becka is trying to figure out a place to hide her doll. She considers putting it under the kitchen table, but then realizes it would still be in sight. She decides to hide the doll in the closet instead. Becka is using:
  a. mental combinations.
  b. trial and error.
  c. object permanence.
  d. invisible displacements.

Stages Five and Six: Tertiary Circular Reactions, p. 152
Diff: H, Ans: a
55.   Fourteen-month-old Tony would most likely be in a sensorimotor stage that involves:
       a.   experimentation.
       b.   discovering his own body parts.
       c.   generating creative ideas.
       d.   learning to use words to explain his ideas.

Piaget and Modern Research, p. 152
Diff: E, Ans: c
56.   "Becoming used to an experience after repeated exposure to it, as when infants hear the same sound or see the same picture again and again until they seem to lose interest," defines:
       a.   assimilation.
       b.   accommodation.
       c.   habituation.
       d.   equilibration.

Piaget and Modern Research, p. 152
Diff: E, Ans: a
57.   The process of getting used to an object or event through repeated exposure to it is referred to as:
       a.   habituation.
       b.   assimilation.
       c.   accommodation.
       d.   equilibration.

Table 6.2: Some Techniques Used by Neuroscientists, p. 153
Diff: E, Ans: b
58.   The amplitude and frequency of electrical activity in specific cortical sections of the brain can best be detected by use of the:
       a.   *EEG.*
       b.   *ERP.*
       c.   *fMRI.*
       d.   *PET* scan.

Information Processing

Information Processing, p. 154
Diff: H, Ans: a
59.   Which of the following is a *false* statement?
       a.   The perspective of cognition modeled on computer functioning is called cognitive theory.
       b.   The Gibsons used the term "affordances" to indicate the diverse opportunities offered for interaction by all objects.
       c.   The "language acquisition device" is a term Chomsky used to refer to the infant's inborn ability to learn language.
       d.   The social reason for language is communication.

Affordances, p. 154
Diff: M, Ans: b
60.   Eleanor and James Gibson would describe perception as:
       a.   an automatic phenomenon.
       b.   a cognitive process.
       c.   a reflex.
       d.   a sensation.

Affordances, p. 154
Diff: M, Ans: b

61.   Which of these statements is a *true* one?
       a.   The sequence in which language development occurs depends on the language spoken.
       b.   All objects have many affordances, which means that what a person perceives depends partly on the individual's motivation and experiences.
       c.   The *fMRI* measures electrical activity in the cortex of the brain.
       d.   Pretending tends to diminish when children reach the stage of metal combinations and are able to plan their actions.

Affordances, p. 154
Diff: H, Ans: c

62.   If we give a 6-month-old infant a furry toy dog and a rubber rattle, probably the baby will:
       a.   try to suck on both objects.
       b.   squeeze both the rattle and the dog.
       c.   shake the rattle and pat the dog.
       d.   shake both the dog and the rattle.

Affordances, p. 154
Diff: H, Ans: d

63.   Eleanor and James Gibson believed that perception:
       a.   is an automatic human phenomenon.
       b.   is something everyone experiences in the same basic way.
       c.   cannot be controlled by the individual.
       d.   is something each individual experiences in his or her own way.

Affordances, p. 154
Diff: H, Ans: a

64.   Objects offer various opportunities, termed by the Gibsons:
       a.   affordances.
       b.   circular reactions.
       c.   deep structures.
       d.   offerings.

Affordances, p. 154
Diff: E, Ans: b

65.   The affordances that are actually perceived depend on the individual's:
       a.   present needs, education, and financial opportunities.
       b.   sensory awareness, past experiences, and immediate motivation.
       c.   age, familiarity, and family.
       d.   sensitivity to the needs of others.

Affordances, p. 154
Diff: H, Ans: a

66.   Which of the following sentences is a *false* statement?
       a.   Affordances reside solely in the objective qualities of the object itself.
       b.   The EEG measures electrical activity in the top layers of the brain.
       c.   Among the first acquired adaptations is accommodation of reflexes – for example, the reflexes involved in sucking a pacifier.
       d.   A baby who delights in squeezing his rubber duck to produce a noise has probably reached Piaget's stage three sensorimotor period.

Affordances, p. 154
Diff: M, Ans: d

67.   I like to make popcorn because I like the noise, I enjoy the taste, and it makes me think of seeing a movie. For me, popcorn has many:
       a.   potentiations.
       b.   sensibilities.
       c.   myelinations.
       d.   affordances.

Sudden Drops, p. 155
Diff: H, Ans: c

68.   Three-month-old Rob might demonstrate that he has perceived the "graspability" of an object by:
       a.   crying when he sees the object.
       b.   following the object with his eyes.
       c.   reaching for the object.
       d.   looking at the object.

Sudden Drops, p. 155
Diff: E, Ans: d

69.   An apparent (but not actual) drop between one surface and another is called a(n):
       a.   illusion drop.
       b.   actual cliff.
       c.   zone of danger.
       d.   visual cliff.

Sudden Drops, p. 155
Diff: M, Ans: d

70.   An infant's reaction to the visual cliff is supposed to measure her:
       a.   locomotion.
       b.   perceptual constancy.
       c.   culture.
       d.   depth perception.

Sudden Drops, p. 155
Diff: H, Ans: c

71.   Salma is a 10-month-old who is being tested on the visual cliff. We would expect her to:
       a.   cry throughout the testing.
       b.   cross over the "visual cliff."
       c.   refuse to cross over the "visual cliff."
       d.   slide down the slope.

Sudden Drops, p. 155
Diff: H, Ans: a

72.   An infant's growing awareness of vertical depths and their dangers is mostly due to:
       a.   the experience of walking.
       b.   reaching the age of 12 months.
       c.   having previous experience with the visual cliff.
       d.   the mother's reaction to those things.

Movement and People, p. 156
Diff: E, Ans: a

73.   Which of the following would an infant least prefer to look at?
       a.   the family dog sleeping on the floor
       b.   a mobile rotating above the crib
       c.   her mother's face as she talks to her
       d.   her flexing toes

Movement and People, p. 156
Diff: M, Ans: c

74.   According to dynamic perception, 1-year-old Diane would most prefer to look at which of the following:
      a.   a brightly colored beach ball.
      b.   a cassette tape with the music of Barney.
      c.   a mobile spinning over her head.
      d.   the puzzle being held by her Aunt Cynthia.

Movement and People, p. 156
Diff: E, Ans: d

75.   Perception primed to focus on movement and change is called:
      a.   motion perception.
      b.   active perception.
      c.   perceptual constancy.
      d.   dynamic perception.

Memory, p. 157
Diff: E, Ans: d

76.   If you teach a 3-month-old how to move a mobile over the crib, you would expect the baby to forget if retested after:
      a.   one hour.
      b.   one day.
      c.   one week.
      d.   two weeks.

Reminders and Repetition, p. 157
Diff: H, Ans: d

77.   New research on infant long-term memory has shown that infants can remember, if the researchers:
      a.   use situations that are different from real life.
      b.   do not let the baby move during the memory event.
      c.   use highly emotional events.
      d.   use special measures to aid memory retrieval.

A Little Older, a Little More Memory, p. 157
Diff: H, Ans: d

78.   Because of _____, a 10-month-old may later pick up and try to use the scissors that his brother used to cut paper.
      a.   cross-modal perception
      b.   overextensions
      c.   LAD
      d.   deferred imitation

A Little Older, a Little More Memory, p. 157
Diff: M, Ans: c

79.   Billy is 10 months old and has been watching his brother play with a toy piano. The next day Billy crawls over to the piano, which his brother left on the floor, and:
      a.   does not recognize it.
      b.   recognizes it but does not know how to "play" it.
      c.   pushes the keys the way his brother did.
      d.   pushes it like a truck.

Language: What Develops in Two Years?

The Universal Sequence of Language Development, p. 159
Diff: M, Ans: d
80.   Children all over the world usually:
    a.   follow the same timing in the development of language.
    b.   understand sounds only from their native language.
    c.   fail to discriminate the sound of the human voice from other sounds.
    d.   follow the same sequence of language development.

The Universal Sequence of Language Development, p. 159
Diff: H, Ans: d
81.   What percent of all 2-year-olds have a vocabulary of at least 100 words?
    a.   10
    b.   25
    c.   50
    d.   90

First Noises and Gestures, p. 159
Diff: E, Ans: d
82.   Choose the *false* statement in the following list:
    a.   Stage one of sensorimotor intelligence is characterized by sucking, grasping, and other reflexes.
    b.   After repeated exposures to an event or an object, the child tends to experience habituation.
    c.   The distinct form of language used by adults to communicate with babies is called baby talk, or child-directed speech.
    d.   A 3-month-old infant who sucks her thumb, discovers that it is pleasurable, and sucks it again is demonstrating Piaget's concept of tertiary circular reactions.

First Noises and Gestures, p. 159
Diff: H, Ans: d
83.   Which of the following sentences is a *false* statement?
    a.   The realization that it is possible to "fall" off the edge in the visual cliff experiment does not come until after an infant has started crawling.
    b.   Two general principles of perception are shared by all infants: one is dynamic perception and the other is a fascination with people.
    c.   Reminder sessions can prolong young infants' memories of earlier events.
    d.   "Baby talk" refers to the sounds made by babies and imitated by parents in the first few weeks after birth.

First Noises and Gestures, p. 159
Diff: E, Ans: a
84.   Newborns prefer:
    a.   speech over most other sounds.
    b.   animal sounds over speech.
    c.   normal speech over baby talk.
    d.   traffic noises more than music.

First Noises and Gestures, p. 159
Diff: E, Ans: c
85.   The distinct language form known as "baby talk" is a(n):
    a.   verbal collection of facts and myths about having and caring for babies.
    b.   enrichment teaching technique used to accelerate language acquisition.
    c.   simplified language that adults use when talking to babies.
    d.   preverbal sound (like "ga ga" and "goo goo" that mothers often make).

First Noises and Gestures, p. 159
Diff: M, Ans: b
86.   Research has found that "baby talk" is:
       a.   confined to females; males do not use it.
       b.   characterized by a high pitch, simple vocabulary, and short sentences.
       c.   unique to English-speaking parents.
       d.   characterized by a lower pitch and use of nonsense words.

First Noises and Gestures, p. 159
Diff: E, Ans: d
87.   Which statement in this list is an *incorrect* one?
       a.   A psychologist who hides a toy under a blanket to see if an infant will try to uncover it is testing for object permanence.
       b.   The initials LAD, as proposed by Chomsky, stand for "language acquisition device."
       c.   Noting that infants between 12 and 18 months engage in actual experimentation and exploration, Piaget described the toddler of this age as "the little scientist."
       d.   Compared to ordinary speech, baby talk has a lower pitch and a shorter sentence length.

Table 6.3: The Development of Spoken Language, p. 159
Diff: H Ans: b
88.   The usual order of the development of spoken language is:
       a.   cooing, babbling, reflexes, spoken words.
       b.   reflexes, cooing, babbling, spoken words.
       c.   babbling, cooing, spoken words, reflexes.
       d.   cooing, reflexes, babbling, spoken words.

Babbling, p. 160
Diff: E, Ans: d
89.   Infants' repetition of certain syllables at the age of about 6 or 7 months is called:
       a.   cooing.
       b.   holophrasing.
       c.   gurgling.
       d.   babbling.

Babbling, p. 160
Diff: M, Ans: d
90.   Babbling:
       a.   is found only in infants from the Western Hemisphere.
       b.   occurs only if the infant can hear.
       c.   precedes cooing.
       d.   is universal.

Babbling, p. 160
Diff: E, Ans: a
91.   Vanna is 14 months old and does not yet respond to any specific words. When she began to babble, she did not respond to her parents' voices and soon she stopped. Her parents should:
       a.   have her hearing tested.
       b.   relax, she is just a slow talker.
       c.   assume she has nothing to say.
       d.   assume she is retarded.

Babbling, p. 160
Diff: H, Ans: c
92.   Greti's little girl is deaf and, therefore, we would expect that she would:
a.   not communicate until she has speech therapy.
b.   babble several months earlier than hearing children.
c.   babble manually at about the same time normal children babble.
d.   learn sign language about 6 months later than hearing children begin to speak.

First Words, p. 160
Diff: E, Ans: c
93.   On average, children begin saying recognizable words at about:
a.   3 months old.
b.   6 months old.
c.   12 months old.
d.   24 months old.

First Words, p. 160
Diff: H, Ans: b
94.   After the child's vocabulary has reached about 50 words, the vocabulary increases approximately _____ words per month.
a.   25-50
b.   50-100
c.   100-125
d.   125-150

The Language Explosion and Early Grammar, p. 161
Diff: E, Ans: b
95.   The term "holophrase" is used to denote:
a.   a word that is empty of meaning.
b.   the infant's use of one word to express a whole thought.
c.   the relationship of object permanence to language development.
d.   the use of two words to take the place of one.

The Language Explosion and Early Grammar, p. 161
Diff: H, Ans: b
96.   Using the word "more" to mean "I want another cookie" is a(n):
a.   preverbal communication.
b.   holophrase.
c.   overextension.
d.   reflexive communication.

The Language Explosion and Early Grammar, p. 162
Diff: M, Ans: c
97.   The first two-word sentences appear, on the average, at:
a.   12 months.
b.   16 months.
c.   21 months.
d.   27 months.

Theory One: Infants Are Taught, p. 162
Diff: M, Ans: b
98.   The theorist who believed that children learn language when they are reinforced by parental attention was:
a.   Jean Piaget.
b.   B. F. Skinner.
c.   Noam Chomsky.
d.   Leo Vygotsky.

Theory One: Infants Are Taught, p. 162
Diff: M, Ans: c

99.   By 10 months of age, Alan has a vocabulary of a dozen words. B.F. Skinner would have attributed
        Alan's rapid speech development mainly to his:
        a.   unusually high I.Q.
        b.   unusual language-acquisition talent.
        c.   parents' talking to him frequently.
        d.   rapid physical development.

Theory Two: Infants Teach Themselves, p. 164
Diff: M, Ans: b

100.   According to Chomsky's theory of language acquisition:
        a.   children learn language through a complex process of imitation and reinforcement.
        b.   children have an inborn ability to learn language.
        c.   the inability to learn language is due to specific brain dysfunctions.
        d.   language learning depends on specific structure in the brain.

Theory Two: Infants Teach Themselves, p. 164
Diff: E, Ans: c

101.   The language acquisition device (LAD) was proposed by Chomsky to explain:
        a.   vocabulary spurts.
        b.   the difference between surface structure and deep structure.
        c.   the universal inborn ability to learn language.
        d.   the systematic differences among languages.

Social Impulses, p. 165
Diff: M, Ans: c

102.   The language-learning theory which focuses on communication as an explanation is the:
        a.   behaviorism model.
        b.   epigeneticists' theory.
        c.   social-pragmatic theory.
        d.   emergentist coalition theory.

Social Impulses, p. 165
Diff: E, Ans: d

103.   Bill constantly talks to his 3-month-old infant. His friend Ted tells him that it is useless to do so,
        because an infant cannot understand language. Social-pragmatists would:
        a.   agree with Ted, since cooing and babbling are reflexive.
        b.   suggest that Bill's behavior indicates he needs therapy.
        c.   agree with Ted, since too much listening slows talking.
        d.   disagree with Ted, because Bill's behavior teaches communication.

Social Impulses, p. 165
Diff: M, Ans: d

104.   Identify the *true* statement:
        a.   An infant who misses her teddy bear at bedtime and will not go to sleep without it is demonstrating
              that she does not yet understand the concept of object permanence.
        b.   There are five (only) stages of sensorimotor intelligence.
        c.   Deaf babies begin making babbling sounds at the same age as hearing infants.
        d.   The first two-word sentence appears at about 21 months of age.

A Note for Caregivers, p. 167
Diff: E, Ans: b

105.   To support infants in their acquisition of language, the text suggest that parents:
        a.   avoid baby talk.
        b.   provide infants with object, words, and social play.
        c.   let the baby watch television.
        d.   wait for the child to make a sound before talking to the child.

TRUE-FALSE QUESTIONS

Sensorimotor Intelligence

Ans: F, p. 148

1.   There are five (only) stages of sensorimotor intelligence.

Ans: F, p. 148

2.   The period of sensorimotor intelligence, according to Piaget, comes to an end shortly after the first birthday.

Ans: T, p. 148

3.   Among the first acquired adaptations is accommodation of reflexes – for example, the reflexes involved in sucking a pacifier.

Ans: T, p. 149

4.   A baby who delights in squeezing her rubber duck to produce a noise has probably reached Piaget's stage three.

Ans: F, p. 150

5.   An infant who misses her teddy bear at bedtime and will not go to sleep without it is demonstrating that she does not yet understand the concept of object permanence.

Ans: F, p. 150

6.   By 8 months of age, infants have a firm grasp of object permanence.

Ans: F, p. 152

7.   The "little scientist" was a term affectionately applied to Piaget by some of the children he studied.

Ans: F, p. 152

8.   Pretending tends to diminish when children reach the stage of mental combinations and are able to plan their actions.

Ans: T, p. 152

9.   The term for getting used to an object by becoming disinterested in that object is "habituation."

Table 6.2: Some Techniques Used by Neuroscientists to Understand Brain Function

Ans: F, p. 153

10.   The *fMRI* measures electrical activity in the cortex of the brain.

Ans: T, p. 153

11.   The *EEG* measures electrical activity in the top layers of the brain.

Ans: T, p. 153

12.   *PET* scans require injection of radioactive dye to get a reading.

Information Processing

Ans: F, p. 154
13.   According to the Gibsons, all people perceive the same affordances in an object.

Ans: T, p. 154
14.   All objects have many affordances, which means that what a person perceives depends partly on the individual's motivation and experiences.

Ans: F, p. 154
15.   Affordances reside solely in the objective qualities of the object itself.

Ans: T, p. 155
16.   The realization that it is possible to "fall" off the edge in the visual cliff experiment does not come until after an infant has started crawling.

Ans: T, p. 156
17.   Two general principles of perception are shared by all infants: one is *dynamic perception* and the other is *fascination with people*.

Ans: T, p. 157
18.   Reminder sessions can prolong young infants' memory of earlier events.

Language: What Develops in Two Years?

Ans: F, p. 159
19.   The sequence in which language development occurs depends on the language spoken.

Ans: F, p. 159
20.   "Baby talk" refers to the sounds made by babies and imitated by parents in the first few weeks after birth.

Ans: T, p. 159
21.   Preverbal infants show a preference for "baby talk" over ordinary adult speech.

Ans: F, p. 160
22.   Deaf babies begin making babbling sounds at the same age as hearing infants.

Ans: T, p. 160
23.   After the child's vocabulary has reached about 50 words, the vocabulary increases dramatically, building 50 to 100 words per month.

Ans: F, p. 161
24.   A child's first word combinations, for example, "More cookie," or "My toy," are called *holophrases*.

Ans: T, p. 162
25.   The first two-word sentence appears at about 21 months of age.

Ans: T, p. 162
26.   According to Skinner, a grandfather who smiles whenever the baby says "pa-pa" is providing reinforcement for talking.

Ans: T, p. 164
27.   The "language acquisition device" is a term Chomsky used to refer to the infant's inborn ability to learn language.

Ans: T, p. 165

28.   The social reason for language is *communication*.

FILL-IN-THE-BLANK QUESTIONS

Sensorimotor Intelligence

Ans: Sensorimotor: 2 years/age 2, p. 148

1.   According to Piaget, the first period of cognitive development is the _____ period, which lasts from birth until about _____.

Ans: object permanence, p. 150

2.   A psychologist who hides a toy under a blanket to see if an infant will try to uncover it is testing for _____.

Ans: primary, p. 148

3.   A 3-month-old infant who sucks her thumb, discovers that it is pleasurable, and sucks it again is demonstrating Piaget's concept of _____ circular reactions.

Ans: reflexes, p. 148

4.   Stage one of sensorimotor intelligence is characterized by sucking, grasping, and other _____.

Ans: goal-directed, p. 150

5.   With _____ behavior, children will initiate motor activities to fulfill their own needs.

Ans: "the little scientist," p. 152

6.   Noting that infants between 12 and 18 months engage in actual experimentation and exploration, Piaget described the toddler of this age as _____.

Ans: mental, p. 152

7.   In the final stage of sensorimotor intelligence, toddlers begin to anticipate and solve simple problems by using _____ combinations.

Ans: habituation, p. 152

8.   After repeated exposures to an event or an object, the child tends to experience _____ as he/she becomes used to it.

Information Processing

Ans: information processing, p. 154

9.   The perspective of cognition modeled on computer functioning is called _____ theory.

Ans: affordances, p. 154

10.   The Gibsons used the term _____ to indicate the diverse opportunities offered for interaction by all objects.

Language: What Develops in Two Years?

Ans: child-directed speech, p. 159

11.   The distinct form of language used by adults to communicate with babies is called baby talk, or _____.

Ans: higher; shorter, p. 159

12.   Compared to ordinary speech, baby talk has a _____ pitch and _____ sentence length.

Ans: babbling, p. 160

13.   The infant's repetition of syllables such as "ba-ba" is called _____.

Ans: holophrase, p. 161

14.   A single-word utterance that expresses a complete thought is called a(n) _____.

Ans: language acquisition device, p. 164

15.   The initials LAD, as proposed by Chomsky, stand for _____.

Ans: social-pragmatic, p. 165

16.   The theory of infant language development that holds that communication with others is the crucial element is referred to as the _____ theory.

Ans: emergentist coalition, p. 165

17.   The hybrid theory of language development during infancy, which combines valid aspects of other theories, is called the _____.

ESSAY QUESTIONS

1.   Describe the research on infant perceptual abilities. Discuss the areas that you think are valid and those you feel are questionable.

2.   What are affordances and how do they help infants adjust to the world?

3.   What is the visual cliff? What does it tell us about infants' vision? Be sure to describe the task and how it is performed.

4.   Describe a standard test that a developmentalist might use to determine whether an infant has attained object permanence. Why might the test not work? Use your answer to explain why some of Piaget's findings have been challenged by other researchers.

5.   What is known about infants' memory ability?

6.   Piaget's last two stages of sensorimotor intelligence are the most creative. Imagine two 18-month-olds playing in a sandbox; describe activities that would be typical of their stage of sensorimotor intelligence.

7.   Describe the development of spoken communication during the first two years of life.

8.   You have been asked to baby-sit for a 10-month-old infant in your home. What kinds of activities would you plan for an infant of this age?

9.   What reasons can you think of to explain the fact that baby talk seems to have the same characteristics all over the world?

10.   Your friend writes to tell you that her 18-month-old baby, whom you have never seen, has not yet uttered a recognizable word. What are the possible explanations for this?

11.   How do the views of Skinner and Chomsky differ in their explanation of infant language acquisition? Explain each view, and then determine which one seems most convincing to you.

12.   Briefly describe the perceptual, cognitive, and language skills an infant will acquire in the first two years of life.

13.   How concerned should parents be if their 15-month-old still has not emitted her first word?

14.   What is "baby talk"?

15.   Briefly describe each of the six stages of sensorimotor intelligence and give an example of what an infant learns in each stage.

Answer guidelines to these essay questions can be found in the Appendix at the end of the Test Bank.

CHAPTER **7**   **The First Two Years:**
Psychosocial Development

MULTIPLE-CHOICE QUESTIONS

A Case to Study: Parents on Autopilot, p. 172
Diff: M, Ans: b
1.   The child Jacob, who was unable to relate to his parents for his first two years, was diagnosed as
      having:
      a.   a conduct disorder.
      b.   pervasive developmental disorder.
      c.   attention-deficit disorder.
      d.   autism.

Theories About Early Psychosocial Development

Psychoanalytic Theory, p. 173
Diff: E, Ans: c
2.   Sigmund Freud was a(n):
      a.   ethological theorist.
      b.   behaviorist.
      c.   psychoanalytic theorist.
      d.   humanistic theorist.

Freud: The Oral and Anal Stages, p. 173
Diff: E, Ans: a
3.   Which of the following describes an activity typical of the oral stage?
      a.   breast-feeding
      b.   toilet training
      c.   feeling a blanket using the fingers
      d.   playing peek-a-boo

Freud: The Oral and Anal Stages, p. 173
Diff: E, Ans: a
4.   According to psychoanalytic theory, what is the prime focus of pleasure in early infancy?
      a.   the mouth
      b.   the anus
      c.   the stomach
      d.   the hands and feet

Freud: The Oral and Anal Stages, p. 173
Diff: E, Ans: b
5.   Freud's second stage is called:
      a.   a new adaptation.
      b.   the anal stage.
      c.   trust versus mistrust.
      d.   the oral stage.

Freud: The Oral and Anal Stages, p. 173
Diff: M, Ans: c
6.   Freud claimed that during the anal stage:
      a.   infants often find urinating and defecating to be quite painful.
      b.   toilet training leads to positive mother-child interactions.
      c.   there is pleasure in stimulating and controlling the bowels.
      d.   the infant is striving to develop a sense of trust in the parents.

Freud: The Oral and Anal Stages, p. 173
Diff: H, Ans: b
7.   How do people become fixated in a Freudian stage?
      a.   They are excessively emotional.
      b.   Their normal developmental urges are frustrated.
      c.   Their mother is not the primary caregiver.
      d.   They fail to undergo a normal "cognitive metamorphosis."

Freud: The Oral and Anal Stages, p. 173
Diff: E, Ans: a
8.   A child fixated in the oral stage may become an adult who:
      a.   eats excessively.
      b.   is excessively neat.
      c.   is a homosexual.
      d.   has intense fears.

Freud: The Oral and Anal Stages, p. 173
Diff: M, Ans: b
9.   Freud would attribute an adult's fingernail biting and overeating to problems during the:
      a.   sensorimotor period.
      b.   oral stage.
      c.   anal stage.
      d.   Oedipus complex.

Erikson: Trust and Autonomy, p. 173
Diff: H, Ans: a
10.   A toddler in Freud's anal stage would also be at Erikson's:
      a.   autonomy versus shame and doubt stage.
      b.   oral stage.
      c.   trust versus mistrust stage.
      d.   object permanence stage.

Erikson: Trust and Autonomy, p. 173
Diff: E, Ans: d
11.   In Erikson's theory, the infant's earliest task is described as that of:
      a.   obtaining oral gratification.
      b.   controlling bodily functions.
      c.   learning pain and pleasure.
      d.   learning trust or mistrust.

Erikson: Trust and Autonomy, p. 173
Diff: H, Ans: d

12.   If a child successfully resolves Erikson's first stage, she or he can be expected to:
   a.   be increasingly self-confident.
   b.   greet strangers with a smile.
   c.   be an easy baby.
   d.   explore his or her world.

Erikson: Trust and Autonomy, p. 173
Diff: E, Ans: d

13.   Which of these is a stage of development invented by Erik Erikson?
   a.   attachment vs. self-awareness
   b.   pride vs. shame
   c.   synchrony vs. attachment
   d.   autonomy vs. shame and doubt

Erikson: Trust and Autonomy, p. 173
Diff: E, Ans: c

14.   The first "crisis of life," according to Erikson, is:
   a.   industry vs. inferiority.
   b.   autonomy vs. shame and doubt.
   c.   trust vs. mistrust.
   d.   the oral stage.

Erikson: Trust and Autonomy, p. 173
Diff: E, Ans: b

15.   The second "crisis of life," according to Erikson, is:
   a.   industry vs. inferiority.
   b.   autonomy vs. shame and doubt.
   c.   trust vs. mistrust.
   d.   the oral stage.

Erikson: Trust and Autonomy, p. 173
Diff: M, Ans: a

16.   According to Erikson, toddlers usually:
   a.   want to control their own bodies.
   b.   want to keep sucking on a pacifier.
   c.   stay very close to their mothers.
   d.   learn how to express their ideas through language.

Erikson: Trust and Autonomy, p. 173
Diff: M, Ans: c

17.   Another name for "self-rule" is:
   a.   governed.
   b.   synchrony.
   c.   autonomy.
   d.   controlled.

Erikson: Trust and Autonomy, p. 173
Diff: M, Ans: d

18.   Failure to develop self-rule over one's own actions is most closely identified with:
   a.   mistrust.
   b.   autonomy.
   c.   the oral stage.
   d.   shame and doubt.

Erikson: Trust and Autonomy, p. 173
Diff: M, Ans: b

19.   The autonomy versus shame and doubt crisis involves the child:
       a.   exhibiting self-control.
       b.   trying to rule his or her own actions.
       c.   developing a sense of self.
       d.   getting along with other children.

Erikson: Trust and Autonomy, p. 174
Diff: E, Ans: c

20.   Freud and Erikson agree on the:
       a.   importance of early weaning.
       b.   need for the mother to be permissive and noncritical.
       c.   importance of early experience.
       d.   need for parents to stimulate their children.

Behaviorism, p. 174
Diff: H, Ans: a

21.   According to traditional behaviorism, personality is:
       a.   molded by parents.
       b.   due to nature.
       c.   in the unconscious mind.
       d.   unchangeable.

Behaviorism, p. 174
Diff: H, Ans: d

22.   Who stated that parents determine whether a child "is to grow into a happy person, an anger-driven,
       vindictive, over-bearing slave driver, or one whose every move in life is definitely controlled by fear"?
       a.   Erikson
       b.   Freud
       c.   Skinner
       d.   Watson

Behaviorism, p. 174
Diff: M, Ans: d

23.   The early behaviorist who strongly believed that a child's personality is "created" or largely determined
       by his or her parents was:
       a.   Erikson.
       b.   Freud.
       c.   Skinner.
       d.   Watson.

Behaviorism, p. 174
Diff: M, Ans: c

24.   Dr. Hoemann believes that a child's behavior problems are caused entirely by the parents' use of
       reinforcements and punishments. Dr. Hoemann is most likely a(n):
       a.   psychoanalyst.
       b.   information-process theorist.
       c.   behaviorist.
       d.   sociologist.

Epigenetic Theory, p. 174
Diff: H, Ans: b

25. Epigenetic theory suggests that:
    a. emotions of the infant are universal in their emergence.
    b. change is possible because genes permit selective adaptation to the environment.
    c. some human behavior is imbedded in a social and biological context.
    d. all of the above are accurate statements.

Epigenetic Theory, p. 174
Diff: E, Ans: d

26. "Constitutionally based individual differences in emotions, activity, and self-control" would be a useful and appropriate definition of:
    a. the unconscious.
    b. personality.
    c. self-awareness.
    d. temperament.

Epigenetic Theory, p. 175
Diff: H, Ans: c

27. Concerning temperament and personality, research has found that:
    a. personality dimensions are quite different from one country to the next.
    b. temperament and personality are determined almost entirely by parenting.
    c. temperament is linked to biological patterns that appear in infancy.
    d. all of the above are accurate statements.

Research on Temperament, p. 175
Diff: E, Ans: a

28. The most famous and comprehensive ongoing study of innate temperament is the:
    a. New York Longitudinal Study.
    b. California Study of Temperament.
    c. Australian Infant Survey.
    d. British Research Schedule.

Research on Temperament, p. 175
Diff: H, Ans: b

29. Research in temperament reveals that:
    a. temperament remains consistent throughout life.
    b. temperament evolves and changes over time.
    c. rhythmicity and quality of mood are its most stable characteristics.
    d. as the child goes through new stages, temperamental qualities become more stable.

Research on Temperament, p. 175
Diff: M, Ans: c

30. Threshold of responsiveness, approach-withdrawal, and intensity of reaction, all of which shape an individual's personality are part of what psychologists call:
    a. personality.
    b. mood.
    c. temperament.
    d. frame of mind.

Research on Temperament, p. 175
Diff: M, Ans: c

31. Six-month-old Juan's mother has not been able to get him on a regular sleeping and eating schedule. NYLS researchers would say that Juan is low in:
    a. adaptability.
    b. distractibility.
    c. rhythmicity.
    d. intensity of reaction.

Research on Temperament, p. 175
Diff: M, Ans: c

32. Delilah loves new food and people, whereas Laura tends to get tense when new items are presented. The New York Longitudinal Study considers these to be differences in:
    a. rhythmicity.
    b. distractibility.
    c. approach-withdrawal.
    d. attention span.

Research on Temperament, p. 175
Diff: H, Ans: b

33. "Threshold of responsiveness" refers, for example, to:
    a. how active the child is.
    b. noticing noises.
    c. whether we can shift a child's attention easily.
    d. how predictable a child is.

Research on Temperament, p. 175
Diff: H, Ans: a

34. Smiling and whimpering belong to which of Thomas and Chess's temperament characteristics?
    a. intensity of reaction
    b. threshold of responsiveness
    c. quality of mood
    d. rhythmicity

Research on Temperament, p. 175
Diff: H, Ans: d

35. A baby who delights in everything new thrust at her is evidencing which of Thomas and Chess's temperament characteristics?
    a. intensity of reaction
    b. threshold of responsiveness
    c. quality of mood
    d. approach-withdrawal

Research on Temperament, p. 175
Diff: E, Ans: b

36. Ginny goes to the "potty" at about the same time every afternoon and also goes to bed at 8:30 each night. Her Mom says, "You can set your watch by Ginny, she has such a regular pattern." Ginny's habits would fit nicely into Thomas and Chess's category of:
    a. level of activity.
    b. rhythmicity.
    c. attention span.
    d. threshold of responsiveness.

Research on Temperament, p. 175
Diff: H, Ans: c

37.   Lupe has always been easy to care for. While waiting for food she can be amused with a toy, and her parents have always been able to divert her attention from dangerous to safe objects. The NYLS would categorized Lupe as high in:
   a.   attention span.
   b.   adaptability.
   c.   distractibility.
   d.   quality of mood.

Research on Temperament, p. 175
Diff: M, Ans: d

38.   Which is *not* one of the temperament characteristics defined by the NYLS to categorize babies in the first few months of life?
   a.   activity level
   b.   adaptability
   c.   distractibility
   d.   irritability

Research on Temperament, p. 175
Diff: M, Ans: d

39.   The identical twins of Mrs. Willey have different temperaments, she has discovered: Jill is very sensitive to every noise in the house, while June appears to ignore or not care about the small noises like her sister. Which temperament dimension would this easily fit into?
   a.   attention span
   b.   adaptability
   c.   distractibility
   d.   threshold of responsiveness

Research on Temperament, p. 175
Diff: M, Ans: c

40.   Kevin is a "grouch," while his older brother seems more of a happy child, on the whole. Which temperament dimension would this easily fit into?
   a.   distractibility
   b.   rhythmicity
   c.   quality of mood
   d.   threshold of responsiveness

Research on Temperament, p. 175
Diff: E, Ans: a

41.   Once little Arthur gets a dangerously sharp object in his hand, it is quite difficult to distract him with something else so his attention can be diverted long enough to extricate the item from his grasp. Which temperament dimension would this easily fit into?
   a.   distractibility
   b.   rhythmicity
   c.   attention span
   d.   threshold of responsiveness

Research on Temperament, pp. 175-176
Diff: E, Ans: a

42.   Thomas and Chess believe that temperamental individuality is well established as early as:
   a.   2 or 3 months of age.
   b.   8 months of age.
   c.   2 years of age.
   d.   5 years of age.

Temperament and Caregiving, p. 176
Diff: H, Ans: c
43. Re-examinations of Thomas & Chess's infants showed either consistently negative, inhibited, or positive temperamental response types. Which group showed the *greatest* tendency to change in their temperament in a day-care setting where they could learn to control their fear?
   a.   the positive-temperament children
   b.   the negative-temperament children
   c.   the inhibited-temperament children
   d.   the exuberant children

Temperament and Caregiving, p. 176
Diff: H, Ans: d
44. Re-examinations of Thomas & Chess's infants showed either consistently negative, inhibited, or positive temperamental response types. Which group showed the *least* tendency to change in their temperament?
   a.   the slightly positive temperament children
   b.   the negative-temperament children
   c.   the inhibited-temperament children
   d.   the exuberant children

Temperament and Caregiving, p. 176
Diff: E, Ans: a
45. Regina is irregular, disturbed easily, unhappy, hard to distract, and emotionally tense. Thomas and Chess would say that Regina is:
   a.   difficult.
   b.   challenging.
   c.   experiencing asynchrony.
   d.   typical.

Temperament and Caregiving, p. 176
Diff: H, Ans: b
46. Research in temperament reveals that:
   a.   temperament remains consistent throughout life.
   b.   temperament evolves and changes over time.
   c.   rhythmicity and quality of mood are the most stable characteristics.
   d.   as the child goes through new stages, temperamental qualities become more stable.

Temperament and Caregiving, p. 177
Diff: E, Ans: a
47. A match between a child's temperament and the demands of the environment is called:
   a.   goodness of fit.
   b.   synchrony.
   c.   organismic specificity.
   d.   temperamental enhancement.

Sociocultural Theory, p. 177
Diff: H, Ans: b
48. Which of the following is *false*, as it relates to temperament?
   a.   A child's temperamental style affects the parenting style of his parents.
   b.   The parents' level of poverty directly affects the infant.
   c.   When parents modify their child-rearing expectations in response to their offspring's temperamental style, the result is a more harmonious "goodness of fit" between them.
   d.   Rhythmicity, attention span, and threshold of responsiveness are three of the nine characteristics of temperament considered by Thomas and Chess.

Emotional Development

The First Year, p. 178
Diff: M, Ans: a

49. The first recognizable emotion in an infant is:
     a. distress.
     b. anger.
     c. happiness, indicated by a social smile.
     d. wariness in the presence of strangers.

The First Year, p. 178
Diff: H, Ans: d

50. Which of the following is a true statement?
     a. The social smile, in response to another person, begins to appear about 12 weeks after birth.
     b. Very young infants seem incapable of expressing distress and contentment.
     c. A 5-month-old baby is likely to display both fear of strangers and separation anxiety.
     d. An 11-month-old baby may show anxiety when its mother goes into another room.

The First Year, p. 178
Diff: M, Ans: c

51. At 6 weeks, Jessica's most recent emotional reaction is likely to be:
     a. fear of strangers.
     b. a wide-eyed look of surprise.
     c. a social smile.
     d. a squeal of delight at her favorite toy.

The First Year, p. 178
Diff: M, Ans: c

52. Typically, stranger wariness is first noticeable at:
     a. 3 months and it fades by 9 months of age.
     b. 4 months and it remains steady during the next year.
     c. 9 months.
     d. 9 months and it increases in intensity throughout the next two years.

The First Year, p. 178
Diff: E, Ans: b

53. When a baby is upset because a caregiver is leaving, the baby is exhibiting:
     a. general anxiety.
     b. separation anxiety.
     c. solitary fear.
     d. fear of isolation.

The First Year, p. 178
Diff: E, Ans: a

54. An infant's distress at an unfamiliar person is called:
     a. stranger wariness.
     b. extrafamilial fear.
     c. fear of the unknown.
     d. separation anxiety.

The First Year, p. 178
Diff: M, Ans: b
55.   Separation anxiety:
      a.   is not affected by caregiver behaviors.
      b.   emerges at about the 9th month.
      c.   occurs after a favorite toy is taken away.
      d.   peaks at about 24 months of age.

The First Year, p. 178
Diff: M, Ans: b
56.   Separation anxiety is strongest at about:
      a.   8 months.
      b.   14 months.
      c.   20 months.
      d.   26 months.

The First Year, p. 178
Diff: M, Ans: b
57.   The new emotions that appear toward the end of the second year are:
      a.   joy, distress, fear, and anger.
      b.   pride, shame, embarrassment, and guilt.
      c.   joy, fear, shame, and guilt.
      d.   pride, shame, joy, and anger.

The First Year, p. 178
Diff: M, Ans: b
58.   Tammi, age 4 months, and Dawn, age 13 months, are left with a baby-sitter. How will they react?
      a.   Tammi will be more upset than Dawn.
      b.   Dawn will probably show more distress than Tammi.
      c.   Both Tammi and Dawn will be similar in experiencing separation anxiety.
      d.   Neither is likely to show distress.

Self-Awareness, p. 179
Diff: E, Ans: c
59.   The emotions of shame, pride, and embarrassment require that a person first:
      a.   develop long-term memory skills.
      b.   become aware that there are people nearby.
      c.   gain self-awareness.
      d.   have experienced punishment.

Self-Awareness, p. 179
Diff: E, Ans: d
60.   Which emotion depends on self-awareness?
      a.   fear
      b.   anxiety
      c.   anger
      d.   shame

Table 7.1: Ages When Emotions Emerge, p. 178
Diff: H, Ans: c
61.   Which emotion requires the greatest sophistication in an infant?
      a.   fear of strangers
      b.   anger
      c.   pride
      d.   curiosity

Self-Awareness, p. 179
Diff: H, Ans: b

62.   Children have a limited sense of self in their early months, as is shown by their:
      a.   failure to respond to their own names.
      b.   lack of awareness of their own bodies as being theirs.
      c.   love of the game "peek-a-boo."
      d.   inability to talk.

Self-Awareness, p. 179
Diff: E, Ans: d

63.   If we place a dot of rouge on an 18-month-old's nose and stand the child in front of a mirror, she may then touch her nose. This shows that the child has some:
      a.   dynamic perception.
      b.   perceptual constancy.
      c.   social referencing.
      d.   self-awareness.

Self-Awareness, p. 179
Diff: E, Ans: d

64.   Researchers placed a dot of rouge on babies' noses and then had them look into a mirror. At what age did most babies touch their nose when they saw their reflection?
      a.   3 months
      b.   6 months
      c.   9 months
      d.   15 months

Pride and Shame, p. 179
Diff: H, Ans: a

65.   A study by Belsky and others found that self-evaluation is key to developing pride and shame. What interesting fact did they also discover?
      a.   Toddler boys who received less praise from their parents became more proud of themselves.
      b.   Toddler girls who received less praise from their parents became more proud of themselves.
      c.   Toddler boys who received more praise from their parents became more proud of themselves.
      d.   Toddler girls who received more praise from their parents became more proud of themselves.

The Development of Social Bonds

Synchrony, p. 180
Diff: E, Ans: b

66.   Coordinated interaction between caregiver and infant is called:
      a.   psychosocialization.
      b.   synchrony.
      c.   symbiosis.
      d.   interplay.

Synchrony, p. 180
Diff: H, Ans: b

67.   Jimmy's Dad comes home from grocery shopping and sees Jimmy sitting on the sofa, eating chips and says "Where's that boy of mine?" Immediately, Jimmy gives his Dad the biggest smile, which spreads across his entire face. Now, Dad responds with an exaggerated surprised look. What is this an example of?
      a.   psychosocialization
      b.   synchrony
      c.   symbiosis
      d.   polarization

Synchrony, p. 180
Diff: E, Ans: a
68. Synchrony can be best described as a:
    a. duet.
    b. lecture.
    c. command.
    d. tornado.

Synchrony, pp. 180-181
Diff: M, Ans: c
69. Victor and Rosa want to enhance their synchrony with their 6-month-old daughter. They can best do this by:
    a. watching her imitate their mouth movements and smiles.
    b. listening to her vocalizations.
    c. imitating her vocal and facial expressions.
    d. none of the above.

Synchrony, p. 181
Diff: E, Ans: b
70. A baby searches the faces of her parents to see how to respond in unfamiliar situations. This is called:
    a. separation anxiety.
    b. social referencing.
    c. stranger anxiety.
    d. uncertainty checking.

Synchrony, p. 181
Diff: H, Ans: c
71. The most critical element in determining synchrony is:
    a. attention span.
    b. mood.
    c. timing.
    d. love.

Synchrony, p. 181
Diff: M, Ans: b
72. When caregivers play with 3-month-olds, they:
    a. try to calm those babies down.
    b. exaggerate expressions of mock delight or surprise.
    c. speak in a steady, low voice.
    d. try to avoid eye contact.

Attachment, p. 181
Diff: M, Ans: d
73. An enduring emotional connection between people is known as:
    a. synchrony.
    b. love.
    c. unionization.
    d. attachment.

Attachment, p. 181
Diff: M, Ans: d
74. Who defined attachment as a "tie that binds one person with another in space and endures over time"?
    a. Skinner
    b. Erikson
    c. Freud
    d. Ainsworth

Attachment, p. 181
Diff: M, Ans: c
75. Proximity-seeking behavior in a secure infant occurs when a baby:
    a. clings to the mother.
    b. refuses to be put down.
    c. crawls behind the mother.
    d. watches the mother respond to a stranger.

Attachment, p. 181
Diff: E, Ans: a
76. Bob quietly watches his infant son, Hamilton, while he sleeps. Bob is engaging in:
    a. contact-maintaining behavior.
    b. social referencing.
    c. synchrony.
    d. goodness of fit.

Attachment, p. 181
Diff: E, Ans: c
77. "Proximity-seeking" and "contact-maintaining" behaviors are displays of:
    a. love.
    b. insecurity.
    c. attachment.
    d. friendliness.

Attachment, p. 182
Diff: M, Ans: d
78. Which of these is a sign of secure attachment?
    a. refusing to let go of the caregiver's arm
    b. playing aimlessly with no contact with the caregiver
    c. fear and anger
    d. attempts to be close to the caregiver

Attachment, p. 182
Diff: E, Ans: a
79. Secure attachment makes a toddler:
    a. willing to explore.
    b. self-centered.
    c. cling to the mother.
    d. try to talk.

Measuring Attachment, p. 182
Diff: E, Ans: c
80. All of the following are expressions of insecure attachment *except*:
    a. fear.
    b. anger.
    c. exploring a new toy.
    d. ignoring the caretaker.

Measuring Attachment, pp. 182-183
Diff: M, Ans: d
81. Basically, the Strange Situation measures how a child:
    a. responds to a stranger.
    b. plays with a parent.
    c. plays with toys he or she has never seen before.
    d. responds to separations and reunions with a caregiver.

Measuring Attachment, p. 183
Diff: E, Ans: d
82. Attachment studies find that most infants are:
a. avoidant.
b. disoriented.
c. resistant.
d. securely attached.

Measuring Attachment, p. 183
Diff: E, Ans: c
83. What proportion of all normal infants tested in the Strange Situation demonstrate secure attachment?
a. a quarter
b. half
c. two-thirds
d. three-fourths

Measuring Attachment, p. 183
Diff: M, Ans: a
84. In the Strange Situation, a sign of secure attachment is:
a. smiling at Mother when she returns to the room.
b. crying and not being comforted when Mother comes back.
c. ignoring Mother when she returns to the room.
d. reluctance to leave Mother to play with new toys.

Measuring Attachment, p. 183
Diff: E, Ans: a
85. Secure attachment (type B) makes a toddler:
a. willing to explore.
b. self-centered.
c. cling to the mother.
d. want to talk.

Measuring Attachment, p. 183
Diff: E, Ans: c
86. Dr. Berkowitz is doing research using the Strange Situation. He is attempting to measure:
a. fear.
b. love.
c. attachment.
d. depth perception.

Measuring Attachment, p. 183
Diff: M, Ans: b
87. Harry's mother left him for a few minutes. When she returned, Harry climbed into her lap and then resumed playing. Harry is probably a(n):
a. insecure child.
b. secure child.
c. abused child.
d. neglected child.

Measuring Attachment, p. 184
Diff: M, Ans: b
88. In the Strange Situation, a sign of insecure attachment might be:
a. smiling at Mother when she returns to the room.
b. crying and not being comforted when Mother comes back.
c. seeking contact with Mother when reunited.
d. plays happily as long as Mother is present.

Table 7.1: Ages When Emotions Emerge, p. 178
Diff: H, Ans: d
89.   Which of these is the infant at birth capable of?
    a.   laughter and social smiling
    b.   responsive smiling and anger
    c.   contentment and fear of strangers
    d.   crying and contentment

Table 7.1: Ages When Emotions Emerge, p. 178
Diff: H, Ans: c
90.   Which of these is the infant of 6 weeks capable of?
    a.   laughter and curiosity
    b.   anger
    c.   a social smile
    d.   stranger wariness

Table 7.1: Ages When Emotions Emerge, p. 178
Diff: H, Ans: c
91.   The emotion of *anger* usually appears at what age?
    a.   1-2 months
    b.   2-4 months
    c.   4-8 months
    d.   8 months to 1 year

Table 7.1: Ages When Emotions Emerge, p. 178
Diff: H, Ans: d
92.   The emotion of *pride* usually appears at what age?
    a.   2-4 months
    b.   6-8 months
    c.   8 months to 1 year
    d.   1 1/2 years

Table 7.2: Patterns of Attachment in Infancy, p. 183
Diff: E, Ans: a
93.   A 9-month-old explores new environments when her mother is present but shows distress when her
        mother leaves the room. The child's behavior illustrates:
    a.   secure attachment.
    b.   insecure-resistant attachment.
    c.   insecure-avoidant attachment.
    d.   disoriented and ambivalent attachment.

Table 7.2: Patterns of Attachment in Infancy, p. 183
Diff: M, Ans: d
94.   Which of these is a sign of secure attachment?
    a.   refusing to let go of the caregiver's arm
    b.   playing aimlessly with no contact with the caregiver
    c.   fear and anger
    d.   attempts to be close to the caregiver

Table 7.2: Patterns of Attachment in Infancy, p. 183
Diff: H, Ans: a

95.   Ruby does not notice when her mother leaves the day-care center and ignores her mother when she returns. Ruby's behavior is:
        a.   insecure-avoidant attachment.
        b.   insecure-resistant attachment.
        c.   secure attachment.
        d.   disoriented attachment.

Table 7.2: Patterns of Attachment in Infancy, p. 183
Diff: H, Ans: b

96.   Select the *false* statement in the following choices:
        a.   The securely attached infant is likely to explore an unfamiliar environment when the mother is present.
        b.   An inconsistent mixture of behavior toward the mother is found in resistant infants.
        c.   A toddler's refusal to obey his mother's request is sometimes an indicator of emotional maturity.
        d.   Following the mother's orders even after she was out of sight, accepting her judgment, is called *committed compliance*.

Table 7.2: Patterns of Attachment in Infancy, p. 183
Diff: H, Ans: b

97.   Jerome clings to his mother and can't be soothed when she returns. Jerome is exhibiting:
        a.   insecure-avoidant attachment.
        b.   insecure-resistant attachment.
        c.   secure attachment.
        d.   disoriented attachment.

Insecure Attachment as a Warning Sign, p. 184
Diff: H, Ans: b

98.   What percentage of all mothers of young infants are clinically depressed?
        a.   5
        b.   10
        c.   15
        d.   20

Insecure Attachment as a Warning Sign, p. 184
Diff: H, Ans: d

99.   What percentage of low-income mothers of young infants are clinically depressed?
        a.   5
        b.   10
        c.   15
        d.   20

Insecure Attachment as a Warning Sign, p. 184
Diff: H, Ans: c

100.   Attachment status appears to be determined by:
        a.   the mother's poverty level.
        b.   the mother's depth of depression.
        c.   the mother's responses to her child.
        d.   the mother's state of mind.

Insecure Attachment as a Warning Sign, p. 184
Diff: M, Ans: a
101.   Which type of attachment leads to the most difficulty in adjustment during later childhood?
a.   Type D
b.   Type C
c.   Type B
d.   Type A

How Disturbed Mothers Develop Type D Attachment in Their Infants

Table 7.3: How Disturbed Mothers…, p. 185
Diff: H, Ans: c
102.   An indication of type D (disorganized infants) is their mothers':
a.   depressed mental state.
b.   attitudes toward her infant.
c.   sudden changes in mood.
d.   none of the above

Table 7.3: How Disturbed Mothers…, p. 185
Diff: H, Ans: d
103.   Four-month-old Janie begins to cry in her mother's arms in the mall. Her mother tells her to hush, as people are beginning to stare at them. Which type of attachment is Janie likely to have as a result of this and other similar responses from her mother?
a.   A
b.   B
c.   C
d.   D

Table 7.3: How Disturbed Mothers…, p. 185
Diff: H, Ans: b
104.   One of the things a disturbed mother does *not* do to develop Type D attachment in their infant is:
a.   display a frightened expression.
b.   consistently hug the infant.
c.   tease the infant.
d.   withhold a toy.

Social Referencing, pp. 185-186
Diff: E, Ans: b
105.   A baby searches the faces of her parents to see how she should respond in unfamiliar situations. This is called:
a.   separation anxiety.
b.   social referencing.
c.   stranger anxiety.
d.   uncertainty checking.

Social Referencing, p. 186
Diff: E, Ans: a
106.   A parent and a toddler meet someone the baby does not know, but who makes the parent nervous. The baby will probably:
a.   act anxious.
b.   smile and reach for the person.
c.   start crying and hit the person.
d.   not show any reaction.

Social Referencing, p. 186
Diff: M, Ans: a
107.   Geoffrey enjoys spending time with his 1-year-old son. Compared to his wife, Geoffrey's interaction to their son is likely to be:
    a.   more playful.
    b.   less noisy and boisterous.
    c.   more involved with basic care.
    d.   less active and energetic.

Referencing Mom, p. 186
Diff: M, Ans: b
108.   Infants accepting their mother's judgment and following her rules even after she is out of sight is called:
    a.   moral referencing.
    b.   committed compliance.
    c.   restricted obedience.
    d.   synchrony.

Referencing Dad, p. 187
Diff: M, Ans: d
109.   When playing with their children, mothers are more likely than fathers to:
    a.   engage in physical play.
    b.   provide less basic care.
    c.   engage in noisy play.
    d.   use standard sequences that involve only one part of the body.

Referencing Dad, p. 187
Diff: M, Ans: b
110.   When playing with their children, fathers are more likely than mothers to:
    a.   read stories.
    b.   engage in physical play.
    c.   help them play with their toys.
    d.   give them food.

Referencing Dad, p. 187
Diff: E, Ans: b
111.   Compared to mothers, fathers are more likely to make their infants:
    a.   cry less.
    b.   laugh more.
    c.   go to sleep.
    d.   say "please."

Referencing Dad, p. 187
Diff: H, Ans: a
112.   Arnie, who is 18 months old, is in a room when a stranger enters. Arnie is most likely to smile if:
    a.   dad is with him.
    b.   mom is with him.
    c.   he is alone in the room.
    d.   the stranger begins talking.

Referencing Dad, p. 187
Diff: H, Ans: c
113.   One clear difference between father-infant and mother-infant interactions is that:
   a.   fathers foster insecure attachment.
   b.   babies find their mothers more fun.
   c.   babies seem to show more excitement for their fathers.
   d.   fathers do not affect their babies' cognitive development.

Cultural Differences

Cultural Differences, p. 187
Diff: H, Ans: c
114.   The father's involvement in infant care specifically benefits:
   a.   the child's vocabulary.
   b.   the father's self-confidence.
   c.   the mother's self-confidence.
   d.   the cognitive aspects of the father's synchronous behaviors.

Cultural Differences, p. 187
Diff: H, Ans: c
115.   Identify the *true* statement from the following list:
   a.   Studies show that there are no significant differences between mother-child play and father-child play with infants under 12 months of age.
   b.   *Family day care* usually has 15 children or more in a place set aside for early child care.
   c.   The father's involvement in infant care boosts the mother's self-confidence and his own emotional strength.
   d.   In-home day care is always preferable to out-of-home day care.

Infant Day Care, p. 188
Diff: E, Ans: a
116.   Most of today's researchers agree that:
   a.   high-quality day care from ages 3 to 5 produces positive long-term outcomes.
   b.   all day care puts children at risk for insecure attachments.
   c.   mothers are the best caregivers for children under 5 years of age.
   d.   day care has no impact on the child.

Table 7.4: High-Quality Day Care, p. 188
Diff: M, Ans: d
117.   Infant day care is of high quality if caregivers emphasize, among other things:
   a.   a regular nap and quiet time for all infants.
   b.   a variety of caregivers every day.
   c.   each infant having his or her own playpen.
   d.   sensorimotor exploration.

TRUE-FALSE QUESTIONS

Theories About Early Psychosocial Development

Ans: T, p. 173
1.   According to Freud, preventing sucking or early weaning during infancy may have lasting effects on personality development later.

Ans: T, p. 174
2.   Like Freud, Erikson felt that problems and conflicts that arise in early childhood could adversely affect later adult personality.

Ans: T, p. 174

3.   Behaviorists after Watson emphasized the role of social learning in infancy.

Ans: T, p. 174

4.   Values and thoughts determine one's perspective on the world, according to cognitive theorists.

Ans: F, p. 175

5.   Rhythmicity, adaptability, and assertiveness are among the nine temperament characteristics of infants.

Ans: T, p. 177

6.   When parents modify their child-rearing expectations to their offspring's temperamental style, the result is a more harmonious "fit" between them.

Ans: T, p. 177

7.   A child's temperamental style affects the parenting style of his or her parents.

Ans: T, p. 177

8.   Poverty does not directly affect infants.

Emotional Development

Ans: T, p. 178

9.   The social smile, in response to another person, begins to appear about 6 weeks after birth.

Ans: T, p. 178

10.   Very young infants seem capable of expressing distress and contentment.

Ans: T, p. 178; Table 7.1

11.   An 11-month-old baby is likely to display both fear of strangers and separation anxiety.

The Development of Social Bonds

Ans: T, pp. 180-181

12.   An example of synchrony is the interaction that occurs when a father makes a silly face and his infant widens her eyes in surprise.

Ans: T, p. 182

13.   The securely attached infant is likely to explore an unfamiliar environment when mother is present.

Ans: F, p. 183

14.   An inconsistent mixture of behavior toward the mother is found in resistant infants.

Ans: T, p. 186

15.   A toddler's refusal to obey his mother's request is sometimes an indicator of emotional maturity.

Ans: T, p. 186

16.   Following Mother's orders even after she was out of sight, accepting her judgment, is called *committed compliance*.

Ans: F, p. 187

17.   Studies show that there are no significant differences between mother-child play and father-child play with infants under 12 months of age.

Ans: T, p. 187

18.   Play with the father may contribute to the growth of social skills and emotional expressions.

Ans: T, p. 187

19.   The father's involvement in infant care boosts the mother's self-confidence and his own emotional strength.

Ans: F, p. 188

20.   *Family day care* usually has 15 children or more in a place set aside for early child care.

Ans: F, p. 189

21.   In-home day care is always preferable to out-of-home day care.

FILL-IN-THE-BLANK QUESTIONS

Theories About Early Psychological Development

Ans: trust; mistrust, p. 173

1.   When a baby discovers that her world is a fairly predictable place in which her needs are met by a responsive caregiver, Erikson would say she has resolved the crisis of _____ vs. _____.

Ans: autonomy: shame and doubt, p. 173

2.   According to Erikson, the central crisis of toddlerhood is _____ versus _____.

Behaviorism

Ans: John Watson, p. 174

3.   The early behaviorist who strongly believed that a child's personality is "created" or largely determined by his or her parents was _____.

Ans: social, p. 174

4.   Later theorists in the behaviorist tradition incorporated the role of _____ learning to explain how personality traits are formed.

Ans: temperament, p. 175

5.   Activity level, attention span, and other basis dispositions that shape an individual's personality are part of what psychologists call _____.

Ans: 2 or 3 months, pp. 175-176

6.   Thomas and Chess, members of the research team that carried out the most extensive study of temperament, believe that temperament is well established by the time the infant is _____ old.

Ans: "slow to warm up", p. 176

7.   In their study of "temperamental individuality," Thomas and Chess found that most infants can be characterized as "easy," "difficult," or _____.

Ans: "goodness of fit", p. 177

8.   When the child's temperamental pattern matches the demands of the home and social environment, there is _____.

Emotional Development

Ans: social, p. 178
9.   The infant's smile that appears whenever mother peeks over the side of the crib and makes a funny face is called a(n) _____ smile.

Ans: fear of strangers or stranger wariness, p. 178
10.   An infant who cries when an unknown person approaches is displaying _____.

Ans: separation anxiety, p. 178
11.   An infant's fear of being left alone by a parent or other caregiver is called _____.

Ans: self-awareness, p. 179
12.   One's realization that they are a separate person with a mind, body, and behavior separate from those around them is _____.

The Development of Social Bonds

Ans: synchrony, pp. 180-181
13.   A term for the patterned "waltz" of exquisite precision between parent and infant is _____.

Ans: attachment, p. 181
14.   The "proximity-seeking" and "contact-maintaining" behaviors of the 12-month-old infant are evidence of the affectional tie that Ainsworth called _____.

Ans: John Bowlby, p. 182
15.   The research responsible for the invention of the concept of attachment was _____.

Ans: insecure-avoidant, Table 7.2: Patterns of Attachment in Infancy, p. 183
16.   A 12-month-old who shows no distress at her mother's departure and is also indifferent to her return is probably displaying _____ attachment.

Table 7.2: Patterns of Attachment in Infancy

Ans: insecure-resistant, Table 7.2: Patterns of Attachment in Infancy, p. 183
17.   A 12-onth-old who clings anxiously to her mother and cries loudly every time the mother moves toward the door is probably demonstrating _____ attachment.

Ans: disorganized, p. 184
18.   The child who first hits her mother, then kisses her with a blank expression, would be classified as _____.

Ans: depressed, p. 184
19.   Twenty percent of low-income mothers of young infants are clinically _____.

Ans: social referencing, pp. 185-186
20.   When infants watch other people for emotional cures in uncertain situations, they are engaging in _____.

Ans: earning more money, p. 187
21.   For fathers, there may be a trade-off between spending more time on child care and _____.

Ans: family day, p. 188
22.   The two choices of infant day are *center care* and _____ care.

ESSAY QUESTIONS

1.   Diana is meeting her friend's 1-year-old for the first time. How should she approach the child? What factors will determine the child's response?

2.   The room is quiet when music suddenly starts playing. If a 1-year-old and a parent are in the room, how will the child respond?

3.   Compare and contrast the traditional roles of mothers and fathers in child care. What do you think are the advantages and disadvantages of these roles? How would you change the parenting roles to improve the child's chances for healthy development?

4.   Hugh and Rebecca are having a baby. They are considering having Hugh be a stay-at-home father, while Rebecca works full-time. How would you advise them?

5.   What is the behaviorist theory regarding the development of our personalities? What do you think of this theory?

6.   Compare and contrast the behavioral and psychoanalytic perspectives on early childhood development.

7.   Compare and contrast Freud's and Erikson's concepts regarding the importance of feeding.

8.   Some families and cultures are much more restrictive than others of their toddler's autonomy. What are the possible consequences of raising a child with a strong sense of autonomy? With a strong sense of shame and doubt?

9.   Your best friend is considering leaving his son in day care. How would you advise him? Is this a good idea? What kinds of things should he look for that indicate a high-quality setting?

10.   Distinguish between cognitive and epigenetic theories.

11.   Explain the role poverty might play in development of the infant-caregiver relationship.

12.   Discuss the role that self-awareness has in the development of pride and shame.

Answer guidelines to these essay questions can be found in the Appendix at the end of the Test Bank.

CHAPTER 8   The Play Years: Biosocial Development

MULTIPLE-CHOICE QUESTIONS

Body and Brain

Body Shape and Growth Rates, p. 197
Diff: H, Ans: b
1. The average 6-year-old from a developed nation weighs about:
   a. 35 pounds.
   b. 46 pounds.
   c. 55 pounds.
   d. 66 pounds.

Body Shape and Growth Rates, p. 197
Diff: H, Ans: b
2. How much *total* growth is seen between ages 2 and 6?
   a. 26 pounds; 18 inches
   b. 18 pounds; 12 inches
   c. 13 pounds; 9 inches
   d. 10 pounds; 6 inches

Ethnic and Cultural Differences, p. 198
Diff: H, Ans: c
3. In general, for all children around the world, the factors that affect growth are:
   a. appetite and the family's income.
   b. genetic disorders, social deprivation, and illness.
   c. genetic background, nutrition, and health care.
   d. gender, hormone levels, and nutrition.

Ethnic and Cultural Differences, p. 197
Diff: M, Ans: a
4. In which ethnic group do children tend to be tallest?
   a. Africans
   b. Europeans
   c. Asians
   d. Latinos

Ethnic and Cultural Differences, pp. 197-198
Diff: H, Ans: a
5. Choose the ethnic group in which height among children is particularly variable:
   a. Africans
   b. Europeans
   c. Asians
   d. Latinos

Ethnic and Cultural Differences, pp. 197-198
Diff: H, Ans: c
6.	Which factor is largely responsible for the great differences in height between children in developed and underdeveloped nations?
	a.	genes
	b.	health
	c.	nutrition
	d.	exercise

Ethnic and Cultural Differences, p. 198
Diff: H, Ans: b
7.	Which of the following preschoolers is *most likely* to be taller than average?
	a.	Benji, who is Asian
	b.	Chuck, who is the oldest child in his family
	c.	Hunter, who lives high above sea level
	d.	Ross, who lives in a rural area

Eating Habits, p. 198
Diff: M, Ans: b
8.	Parents of a 5-year-old girl are likely to say:
	a.	"She eats too much."
	b.	"She isn't eating enough."
	c.	"She has no control over her appetite."
	d.	"She is suffering from malnutrition."

Eating Habits, p. 198
Diff: E, Ans: c
9.	As a measure of weight gain or loss, percentiles:
	a.	show the percent of daily requirements for vitamins.
	b.	let parents know the percent of body fat in their child.
	c.	compare a child's weight to that of their peers.
	d.	all of the above are correct answers.

Eating Habits, p. 198
Diff: M, Ans: d
10.	Most importantly, young children get an insufficient intake of:
	a.	fruits.
	b.	vitamins.
	c.	vegetables.
	d.	iron, zinc, and calcium.

Eating Habits, p. 199
Diff: H, Ans: d
11.	The most common disease of young children in developed nations is:
	a.	anemia.
	b.	AIDS.
	c.	insomnia.
	d.	early tooth decay.

Eating Habits, p. 199
Diff: E, Ans: b
12.	The best advice for parents to improve their child's diet and promote healthy eating habits is to:
	a.	eliminate all "snacks."
	b.	offer many healthy foods as alternatives when they become hungry.
	c.	not set the child up to expect "treats."
	d.	cut down on the availability of desserts at the end of lunch and evening meals.

Eating Habits, p. 199
Diff: M, Ans: a
13.   To prevent tooth decay, the most important thing parents can do is ensure that their children:
       a.   don't eat too much sugar.
       b.   brush regularly.
       c.   visit the dentist regularly.
       d.   floss every day.

Brain Development, p. 199
Diff: H, Ans: d
14.   Which part of the body develops most quickly?
       a.   the heart
       b.   the eyes
       c.   the lungs
       d.   the brain

Brain Development, p. 199
Diff: M, Ans: c
15.   The 2-year-old human brain weighs _____ percent of the adult brain.
       a.   55
       b.   65
       c.   75
       d.   80

Brain Development, p. 199
Diff: H, Ans: d
16.   By age 5, the brain has reached about _____ of its adult weight.
       a.   30 percent
       b.   60 percent
       c.   75 percent
       d.   90 percent

Brain Development, p. 199
Diff: M, Ans: b
17.   The process of myelination involves:
       a.   bone growth.
       b.   nerve insulation.
       c.   muscle growth.
       d.   parents' teaching their children.

Speed of Thought, p. 199
Diff: E, Ans: d
18.   Myelination:
       a.   connects the two halves of the brain.
       b.   compensates for loss of brain function due to injury.
       c.   promotes regular childhood sleep patterns.
       d.   speeds up the transmission of neural impulses.

Speed of Thought, p. 199
Diff: M, Ans: d
19.   The process of myelination continues through:
       a.   infancy.
       b.   late childhood.
       c.   mid-adolescence.
       d.   early adulthood.

Speed of Thought, p. 199
Diff: E, Ans: b
20.   The ability to generate several thoughts in rapid succession is most specifically related to:
    a.   eating healthy foods.
    b.   myelination.
    c.   frontal cortex maturation.
    d.   development of new axons.

Speed of Thought, p. 199
Diff: H, Ans: b
21.   Which of the following most directly facilitates the rate of myelination?
    a.   eating healthy foods
    b.   experience
    c.   frontal cortex maturation
    d.   genetics

Speed of Thought, p. 199
Diff: E, Ans: b
22.   The ability to generate several thoughts in rapid succession is most specifically related to:
    a.   eating healthy foods.
    b.   myelination.
    c.   frontal cortex maturation.
    d.   development of new axons.

Connecting the Brain's Hemispheres, p. 199
Diff: H, Ans: d
23.   Which sections of the brain are among the earliest to become myelinated?
    a.   the temporal lobes
    b.   the parietal cortexes
    c.   the thalamic pathways
    d.   the visual and auditory cortexes

Connecting the Brain's Hemispheres, p. 200
Diff: E, Ans: b
24.   The differentiation and specialization of the functioning of the two halves of the brain is called:
    a.   linearization.
    b.   lateralization.
    c.   equalization.
    d.   disequilibrium.

Connecting the Brain's Hemispheres, p. 200
Diff: M, Ans: b
25.   When their 3-month-old daughter Amber lies down to take a nap, she usually turns her head and bends her limbs to the right. Her parents think this may predict later:
    a.   academic excellence.
    b.   right-handedness.
    c.   poor coordination.
    d.   creativity.

Connecting the Brain's Hemispheres, p. 200
Diff: E, Ans: b
26.   In which culture is it an insult to give someone something and then try to pass it to his or her left hand?
    a.   Latino
    b.   African
    c.   European
    d.   Asian

Planning and Analyzing, p. 201
Diff: H, Ans: b
27.   After a head injury, 15-year-old Jack started having temper tantrums. Most likely his _____ was injured.
a.   temporal cortex
b.   prefrontal cortex
c.   corpus callosum
d.   parietal lobe

Planning and Analyzing, p. 201
Diff: E, Ans: a
28.   Impulsiveness and perseveration are the same in that they both represent:
a.   an underdeveloped prefrontal cortex.
b.   too much emotional control.
c.   strict discipline.
d.   bad parenting.

Planning and Analyzing, p. 201
Diff: M, Ans: d
29.   The part of the brain responsible for the coordination of thoughts matures during:
a.   infancy.
b.   the toddler years.
c.   late childhood.
d.   late adolescence.

Planning and Analyzing, p. 201
Diff: M, Ans: b
30.   The ability to control one's impulsiveness appears to be directly related to the development of the:
a.   parietal cortex.
b.   prefrontal cortex.
c.   striate cortex.
d.   frontal cortex.

Planning and Analyzing, p. 201
Diff: M, Ans: b
31.   Janie just cannot seem to keep from becoming extremely angry when she does not get her way. Her ability to reign in this tendency toward tantrums will get better when her _____ has further matured.
a.   parietal cortex
b.   prefrontal cortex
c.   striate cortex
d.   frontal cortex

Planning and Analyzing, p. 201
Diff: M, Ans: b
32.   Hamilton asks his Dad to put on a "Thomas the Train" DVD and his Dad complies. No more than 3 minutes into the movie, Hamilton wants to play with his toy cars on the floor. This inability to stay focused on one thing at a time is due to the immaturity of his:
a.   parietal cortex.
b.   prefrontal cortex.
c.   striate cortex.
d.   frontal cortex.

Planning and Analyzing, p. 201
Diff: E, Ans: a

33.   Once a young child starts to cry, it tends to continue to do so long after, whatever the initial cause, sometimes frustrating the parent. This behavior is an example of:
   a.   perseveration.
   b.   myelination.
   c.   lateralization.
   d.   transubstantiation.

Educational Implications of Brain Development, 202
Diff: M, Ans: d

34.   The reason 6-year-olds are ready to start school is that:
   a.   they can sit for an hour.
   b.   their brains have matured sufficiently.
   c.   they think before talking.
   d.   all of the above are good reasons.

Educational Implications of Brain Development, 202
Diff: M, Ans: d

35.   The reason 6-year-olds are ready to start school is that:
   a.   they can scan a page of print.
   b.   they can balance the sides of the body.
   c.   they can draw and write with one hand.
   d.   all of the above are good reasons.

Educational Implications of Brain Development, 202
Diff: M, Ans: d

36.   The reason 6-year-olds are ready to start school is that:
   a.   they can scan a page of print.
   b.   they can remember important facts and instructions for more than a few seconds.
   c.   they can control their emotions.
   d.   all of the above are good reasons.

Motor Skills and Avoidable Injuries

Gross Motor Skills, p. 203
Diff: E, Ans: d

37.   An example of a gross motor skills is:
   a.   painting a picture.
   b.   dialing a phone.
   c.   picking up a bug.
   d.   swimming across a pool.

Gross Motor Skills, p. 203
Diff: M, Ans: c

38.   Gross motor skills such a riding a tricycle are acquired:
   a.   solely through many opportunities for practice.
   b.   automatically when brain maturation occurs.
   c.   through a combination of brain maturation and practice.
   d.   only if the parents are well coordinated.

Gross Motor Skills, p. 203
Diff: H, Ans: a

39. The members of the city council want to provide play areas especially designed to improve the gross motor skills of preschoolers. Which factor is *least* important?
a. modern, state-of-the-art play equipment
b. adequate space
c. the opportunity to play with other children
d. safety precautions to prevent accidents

Fine Motor Skills, p. 203
Diff: E, Ans: d

40. Writing your name is a _____, whereas kicking a ball is a(n) _____.
a. sensorimotor skill; preoperational skill
b. physical skill; cognitive skill
c. coordination skill; inter-coordination skill
d. fine motor skill; gross motor skill

Fine Motor Skills, p. 203
Diff: E, Ans: a

41. The best example of a fine motor skill in this list is:
a. using scissors to cut paper.
b. swimming across a pool.
c. roller-skating around the block.
d. playing catch with a football.

Fine Motor Skills, p. 203
Diff: H, Ans: d

42. Children have difficulty with fine motor skills because:
a. they lack the necessary muscular control.
b. they lack the necessary patience.
c. they lack the necessary judgment.
d. all of the above are reasons.

Fine Motor Skills, pp. 203-204
Diff: E, Ans: a

43. Which of the following requires fine motor skills?
a. buttoning a coat
b. kicking a ball
c. climbing a tree
d. playing tag

Fine Motor Skills, pp. 203, 204
Diff: M, Ans: b

44. Preschoolers often have trouble tying their shoelaces because they have inadequate:
a. forearm strength.
b. fine motor skill development.
c. coordination and balance.
d. gross motor skill development.

Fine Motor Skills, p. 204
Diff: H, Ans: a
45. Many preschoolers have trouble dressing themselves, writing, or stringing small beads. This can be explained by a lack of:
    a. brain maturation and having short, fat fingers.
    b. practice and motivation.
    c. encouragement and having short, fat fingers.
    d. motivation and brain maturation.

Serious Injuries, p. 205
Diff: H, Ans: a
46. A male child under age 15 in the United States has about a 1 in _____ chance of dying accidentally.
    a. 500
    b. 1,000
    c. 5,000
    d. 10,000

Serious Injuries, p. 205
Diff: M, Ans: d
47. Public health experts think the phrase "accident prevention" is inaccurate because:
    a. no one can prevent people from making mistakes.
    b. accidents are a result of chance, not of poor judgment.
    c. "accident" implies that no one was at fault.
    d. all of the above are true.

Three Levels of Prevention, p. 206
Diff: H, Ans: c
48. Which is an example of tertiary prevention?
    a. establishing parenting courses for expectant parents
    b. when high-risk families receive home visits from trained visitors
    c. taking a child away from parents who have repeatedly abused her
    d. removing the second child if the first has been abused

Three Levels of Prevention, p. 206
Diff: E, Ans: d
49. Which of these describes primary prevention?
    a. actions that avert harm in the immediate situation, such as stopping a car before it hits a pedestrian
    b. actions that are taken after an adverse event occurs, aimed at reducing the harm or preventing disability
    c. immediate and effective medical treatment of illness or injury
    d. actions that change overall background conditions to prevent some unwanted event or circumstance, such as injury, disease, or abuse

Three Levels of Prevention, p. 206
Diff: H, Ans: a
50. Which of these describes tertiary prevention?
    a. making laws against hit-and-run drivers
    b. insisting that children walk with adults
    c. emergency room procedures that reduce brain swelling
    d. requiring flashing lights on stopped school buses

Child Maltreatment

Changing Definitions of Maltreatment, p. 208
Diff: E, Ans: d
51. The term "child maltreatment" includes:
    a. intentional harm.
    b. avoidable endangerment.
    c. abuse and neglect.
    d. all of the above categories.

Changing Definitions of Maltreatment, p. 209
Diff: E, Ans: c
52. A mistreated child who is startled at any noise and is continually looking around to see who is coming up to them is showing symptoms of:
    a. ADD/HD.
    b. OCD.
    c. PTSD.
    d. ADD.

Changing Definitions of Maltreatment, p. 209
Diff: E, Ans: b
53. Symptoms of post-traumatic stress disorder include:
    a. an "out-of-body" feeling.
    b. hyper vigilance.
    c. hypo-manic reactions.
    d. depersonalization.

Changing Definitions of Maltreatment, pp. 209-210
Diff: H, Ans: b
54. According to statistics regarding substantiated cases of child maltreatment, about 1 out of every _____ children is maltreated each year.
    a. 45
    b. 70
    c. 125
    d. 360

Changing Definitions of Maltreatment, p. 210
Diff: M, Ans: d
55. There are more reported than substantiated cases of child maltreatment because:
    a. cases may be reported numerous times.
    b. even when a report is accurate, it may be difficult to find proof.
    c. since reports are based only on suspicion, some reports are subsequently disproven.
    d. all of these reasons.

Fig. 8.5: Rates of Substantiated Child Maltreatment, United States, 1990-2001
Diff: H, Ans: b
56. The peak year for substantiated cases of child maltreatment in the United States was:
    a. 1989.
    b. 1993.
    c. 1995.
    d. 1999.

Changing Definitions of Maltreatment, p. 210
Diff: E, Ans: b
57.   Children who are hyperactive, hypervigilant, and confused between reality and fantasy are expressing symptoms of:
a.   child abuse.
b.   post-traumatic stress disorder.
c.   neglect.
d.   battered child syndrome.

Brain Damage and Consequences for Learning, p. 212
Diff: M, Ans: c
58.   Victims of serious prolonged child abuse are most likely to:
a.   become abusive parents themselves.
b.   show no permanent damage.
c.   suffer from depression.
d.   be unemployed.

Brain Damage and Consequences for Learning, p. 212
Diff: E, Ans: d
59.   Children who are neglected because their mothers are clinically depressed:
a.   are hyperactive.
b.   become hypervigilant.
c.   are confused about reality.
d.   have the right side of their prefrontal cortexes develop more than the left.

Brain Damage and Consequences for Learning, p. 212
Diff: E, Ans: d
60.   Children of mothers who are depressed:
a.   are more likely to experience fear, sadness, and anxiety.
b.   have difficulty learning.
c.   develop asymmetrical prefrontal cortexes.
d.   all of the above.

Impaired Social Skills, p. 213
Diff: H, Ans: d
61.   Tracy is a 21-year-old woman who was abused by her stepfather during the six years that her mother was married to him. Today, Tracy is most likely to do which of the following?
a.   avoid drinking alcohol
b.   be happily married
c.   engage in theft
d.   eat too much or too little

Impaired Social Skills, p. 213
Diff: M, Ans: c
62.   Over time, victims of serious maltreatment are most likely as adults to do which of the following?
a.   choose a supportive relationship
b.   set unrealistic goals
c.   become victims
d.   grow out of it

Three Levels of Prevention, Again, p. 213
Diff: E, Ans: c
63.   In contemporary society, foster care generally means:
a.   that the children are preparing for adoption.
b.   neighborhood support for the family.
c.   children's removal from the original parents.
d.   children's placement in an institution.

Three Levels of Prevention, Again, p. 213
Diff: E, Ans: d
64.   The goal in dealing with child maltreatment is to:
       a.   decide if legal action is needed.
       b.   provide family counseling.
       c.   restore children's health.
       d.   prevent future problems.

Three Levels of Prevention, Again, p. 213
Diff: H, Ans: c
65.   The three requirements of not stigmatizing the family as inadequate, not undermining atypical family or
       cultural patterns which nurture a child, and not creating a sense of helplessness in the family are
       associated with:
       a.   initial prevention.
       b.   primary prevention.
       c.   secondary prevention.
       d.   tertiary prevention.

Three Levels of Prevention, Again, p. 213
Diff: H, Ans: c
66.   Spotting warning signs of abuse, such as slow weight gain and insecure disorganized attachment, is
       associated with:
       a.   initial prevention.
       b.   primary prevention.
       c.   secondary prevention.
       d.   tertiary prevention.

Three Levels of Prevention, Again, p. 213
Diff: M, Ans: b
67.   Secondary prevention always involves:
       a.   stopping a problem before it begins.
       b.   responding to the first symptoms of a problem.
       c.   getting children out of abusive situations.
       d.   removing the second child if the first has been abused.

Three Levels of Prevention, Again, pp. 213-214
Diff: H, Ans: a
68.   In the United States, foster care families:
       a.   have been rising in numbers over the last ten years.
       b.   keep children longer than in past generations.
       c.   are more willing to care for unrelated children.
       d.   are usually trained and willing to take in troubled children.

Three Levels of Prevention, Again, p. 214
Diff: E, Ans: c
69.   An example of kinship care is:
       a.   Michelle baby-sits her brother Tommy.
       b.   Patti and Rob adopt two brothers.
       c.   Eric and Sherral provide foster care for their neglected nephew.
       d.   Mari is placed in a group home with other abused children.

Three Levels of Prevention, Again, p. 214
Diff: M, Ans: a

70.   The final choice available to child-care specialists in cases of child abuse is:
       a.   adoption.
       b.   foster care.
       c.   kinship care.
       d.   return to the family after rigorous counseling and parental re-education.

TRUE-FALSE QUESTIONS

Body and Brain

Ans: T, p. 197

1.   By age 6, most children have nearly adult-like proportions; that is, they no longer have the large heads, short limbs, and protruding stomachs characteristic of toddlers.

Ans: T, p. 197

2.   The range of weight in normal preschoolers is quite broad.

Ans: F, p. 197

3.   The total body weight of a 6-year-old is about 20 percent of that of the average adult.

Ans: T, p. 198

4.   The major nutritional problem in early childhood is insufficient intake of iron, zinc, and calcium.

Ans: F, p. 198

5.   The essential nutrients for a growing child have been recently identified.

Ans: F, p. 198

6.   Failure to brush the teeth is the primary cause of early tooth decay.

Ans: F, p. 199

7.   By age 5, the brain has attained about half of its adult weight.

Ans: T, p. 199

8.   The 2-year-old brain weighs about 75 percent of its adult weight.

Ans: F, p. 199

9.   Myelination is essential for basic communication between neurons.

Ans: T, p. 199

10.   During the play years, myelination proceeds most rapidly in the area of the brain dedicated to memory and reflection.

Ans: T, p. 200

11.   The left hemisphere of the brain is where language abilities are located in most people.

Ans: T, p. 200

12.   The corpus callosum is comprised of 250 to 800 million fibers that do nothing.

Ans: F, p. 201

13.   Impulsiveness and perseveration are opposites.

Ans: T, p. 201

14.   Maturation of the prefrontal cortexes is directly related to cessation of temper tantrums.

Ans: F, p. 201

15.   The part of the brain that specializes in planning, selecting, and coordinating thoughts is the cerebellum.

Ans: T, p. 201

16.   Perseveration is the tendency to continue an activity even when it has become inappropriate to do so.

Ans: F, p. 202

17.   Brain development is smooth and linear.

Ans: T, p. 202

18.   Most 6-year-olds are ready to draw and write with one hand, accurately copying shapes or letters.

Motor Skills and Avoidable Injuries

Ans: T, p. 203

19.   For the most part, preschool children teach themselves motor skills or learn them from other children.

Ans: F, p. 203

20.   For most preschoolers, gross motor skills are more difficult to master than fine motor skills.

Ans: T, p. 204

21.   Mastery of drawing skills is related to overall intellectual growth.

Ans: F, p. 205

22.   In the United States, the odds are about 1 in 5,000 of a child dying due to an accident.

Ans: T, p. 205

23.   During childhood, the odds of dying in an accident are about three times greater than the odds of dying due to cancer.

Ans: F, p. 205

24.   Two-thirds of all accidental deaths among children involve vehicles.

Ans: T, p. 205

25.   Boys tend to have more injuries than girls do.

Ans: T, p. 205

26.   The word "accident" implies that an injury is an unpredictable act of God.

Ans: T, p. 205

27.   Injuries and accidental deaths are more likely to befall boys than girls.

Ans: T, p. 206

28.   Secondary prevention reduces the danger of high-risk situations and people.

Ans: T, p. 206

29.   Tertiary prevention reduces damage after the impact of abuse.

Ans: F, p. 206

30.   Primary prevention reduces the danger of high-risk situations and people.

Ans: T, p. 207

31.   Deaths resulting from accidents to children between ages 1 and 5 in the United States have decreased by 50 percent during the past 20 years.

Child Maltreatment

Ans: F, p. 208

32.   Failure to provide adequate food to a child is considered a type of abuse.

Ans: F, p. 208

33.   Child neglect is a type of child abuse.

Ans: F, p. 209

34.   Most child maltreatment involves serious physical abuse.

Ans: T, p. 209

35.   About one-third of all reported cases of maltreatment are substantiated annually.

Ans: F, p. 209

36.   About 2 million new cases of child maltreatment are substantiated annually.

Ans: F, p. 210

37.   The peak of substantiated cases of child maltreatment in the United States was in 1999.

Ans: T, p. 210

38.   The peak of substantiated cases of child maltreatment in the United States was in 1993.

Ans: F, p. 212

39.   Maltreated children are friendlier than other children are.

Ans: T, p. 212

40.   Maltreated children are more aggressive than other children are.

Ans: F, p. 213

41.   Primary, secondary, and tertiary prevention are all targeted at preventing child maltreatment before it ever occurs.

Ans: F, p. 214

42.   It is estimated that about 70 percent of all foster children are staying with relatives.

Ans: T, p. 214

43.   Long-term adoption is usually the best solution for young children in inadequate families.

Ans: T, p. 214

44.   Adoption is generally better than foster care for maltreated children.

FILL-IN-THE-BLANK QUESTIONS

Body and Brain

Ans: myelination, p. 199

1.   The increase in brain size in early childhood is due to the proliferation of communication pathways and the ongoing process of _____.

Ans: transmission, p. 199

2.   Myelination results in more rapid _____ of neural impulses.

Ans: corpus callosum, p. 200

3.   The band of nerve fibers connecting the two halves of the brain is known as the _____.

Ans: corpus callosum, p. 200

4.   The brain part that allows children to coordinate functions that involve both halves of the body is the _____.

Ans: left, p. 200

5.   In most adults, the brain is organized in such a way that the areas of language development are located in the _____ hemisphere of the brain.

Ans: Lateralization, p. 200

6.   _____ is the term used to describe the specialization of the brain so that one side of the body or brain is dominant for certain functions.

Ans: prefrontal cortex (or frontal brain lobe), p. 201

7.   The "executive function" area of the brain where planning, selecting, and coordinating thoughts are carried out is the _____.

Ans: perseveration, p. 201

8.   A child crying herself to sleep would be an example of _____.

Motor Skills and Avoidable Injuries

Ans: gross; fine, p. 203

9.   Pumping a swing is an example of a(n) _____ motor skill; buttoning a sweater is an example of a(n) _____ motor skill.

Ans: accidents, p. 205

10.   In all but the most disease-ridden or war-torn countries of the world, the leading cause of childhood death is _____.

Ans: injury control, p. 205

11.   In dealing with childhood accidents, it would be more useful to focus on _____ rather than on accident prevention.

Child Maltreatment

Ans: child maltreatment, p. 208

12.   The text defines _____ as all intentional harm to, or avoidable endangerment of, someone under the age of 18.

Ans: abuse; neglect, p. 208

13.   The definition of child maltreatment includes both _____ and _____.

Ans: neglect, p. 208

14.   Failure to meet a child's basic needs is called _____.

Ans: shaken baby syndrome, p. 212

15.   Infants who are held by the shoulders and shaken back and forth may experience _____.

Ans: foster care, p. 213

16.   With _____, children are taken from their original parents and placed temporarily in the custody of another caregiver.

Ans: primary, p. 213

17.   With _____ prevention, we try to prevent maltreatment from ever occurring.

Ans: tertiary, p. 213

18.   With _____ prevention, we try to halt ongoing maltreatment and treat the child.

Ans: secondary, p. 213

19.   With _____ prevention, we try to intervene during ongoing maltreatment to keep it from getting any worse.

Ans: foster care, p. 213

20.   The transfer of care of a mistreated child from parents to someone else is known as _____.

Ans: kinship care, p. 214

21.   When relatives care for the mistreated child, it is referred to as _____.

ESSAY QUESTIONS

1.   Discuss how growth rate affects the eating habits of preschool children, and discuss the most common nutritional problem of preschoolers.

2.   A friend is worried that her 4-year-old daughter is not developing on schedule. What can you tell her about the physical development of preschoolers that would help your friend?

3.   Design a program to help decrease the number of serious accidents to children.

4.   Based on what you have learned from this chapter, design a preschool program that will foster optimal development of children.

5.   What are some of the reasons why children of low socioeconomic status are more likely to die in accidents than children of other income groups?

6.   What are some of the gross motor skills that most 5-year-olds have mastered?

7.   What is the difference between abuse and neglect?

8.   What are some of the factors that contribute to maltreatment?

9.   What are some of the consequences of having been maltreated?

10.   Briefly describe the Healthy Start program utilized in Hawaii. Do you think it would be successful in other states? Why?

11.   What can be done to reduce the risk of child maltreatment?

12.   If you had limited funds and could only afford to support a primary, secondary, or tertiary prevention program regarding maltreatment, where would you target your money? Why?

13.   Discuss the effect of the coinage of the terms "snack" and "treat" on the health of American children.

14.   Distinguish between the terms "child abuse" and "child neglect."

15.   Explain the usefulness of myelination.

16.   Give one method parents can use to determine the handedness of their infant.

17.   Although the issue is more complicated than a simple or reductionistic description, identify some of the functions loosely identified with the left and right hemispheres of the brain.

Answer guidelines to these essay questions can be found in the Appendix at the end of the Test Bank.

CHAPTER 9   The Play Years: Cognitive Development

MULTIPLE-CHOICE QUESTIONS

How Children Think: Piaget and Vygotsky

How Children Think: Piaget and Vygotsky, p. 217
Diff: E, Ans: b
1. The Piagetian term for centration in which the child thinks about the world exclusively from his or her personal perspective is called:
    a. theory-theory.
    b. egocentrism.
    c. static perspective.
    d. world view.

Piaget: Preoperational Thought, p. 218
Diff: H, Ans: c
2. To Piaget, the difference between cognition during infancy and the preschool years is:
    a. understanding object permanence.
    b. the reduction in egocentrism.
    c. symbolic thought.
    d. abstract and scientific thinking.

Piaget: Preoperational Thought, p. 218
Diff: E, Ans: c
3. Piaget called cognitive development between the ages of two and six _____ thought.
    a. operational
    b. egocentric
    c. preoperational
    d. symbiotic

Piaget: Preoperational Thought, p. 218
Diff: H, Ans: c
4. Piaget believed that between the ages of two and six, it is difficult for children to think:
    a. subjectively.
    b. egocentrically.
    c. operationally.
    d. all of the above.

Piaget: Preoperational Thought, p. 218
Diff: M, Ans: d

5.   Using logical principles to think is referred to as:
     a.   symbolic thought.
     b.   centration.
     c.   pragmatic reasoning.
     d.   operational thought.

Obstacles to Logical Operations, p. 218
Diff: E, Ans: a

6.   Thinking about one idea at a time, ignoring other ideas, is known as:
     a.   centration.
     b.   animism.
     c.   conservation.
     d.   egocentrism.

Obstacles to Logical Operations, p. 218
Diff: E, Ans: d

7.   Which of these is a preoperational characteristic?
     a.   decentration
     b.   reversibility
     c.   deductive reasoning
     d.   focus on appearance

Obstacles to Logical Operations, p. 218
Diff: H, Ans: a

8.   Arnie wants "more juice" when the straw pulls out of his apple juice and he sucks only air. Mom
     pretends to fill his sippy cup by unscrewing the lid and acting as if she is adding more juice. In reality,
     all Mom does is push the straw back down to the bottom of Arnie's cup. He acts pleased as he sucks on
     the straw, pulling the juice into his mouth. Mom is wise not to tell Arnie that he has plenty of juice,
     because he is preoperationally:
     a.   centering on his original experience.
     b.   unable to reverse the operation.
     c.   fixed in his static reasoning.
     d.   engaging in magical thinking.

Obstacles to Logical Operations, p. 218
Diff: E, Ans: c

9.   To focus on one aspect of a situation and simultaneously exclude all others is called:
     a.   magical thinking.
     b.   static reasoning.
     c.   centration.
     d.   focusing on appearances only.

Obstacles to Logical Operations, p. 218
Diff: M, Ans: a

10.   When Jennie sees her third-grade teacher in the grocery store, she does not recognize her. This is likely
      due to Jennie's:
      a.   static reasoning.
      b.   abstract reasoning.
      c.   concrete thinking.
      d.   irreversibility.

Obstacles to Logical Operations, p. 218
Diff: H, Ans: c
11.   The characteristic *irreversibility* refers to the preoperational child's tendency to:
      a.   focus on something other than appearances.
      b.   use deductive reasoning to solve a problem.
      c.   be unable to think backwards from a conclusion to the beginning.
      d.   engage in centration when another solution is needed.

Obstacles to Logical Operations, p. 218
Diff: H, Ans: c
12.   A magician's stock and trade is getting the audience to focus on one aspect of his demonstration while
      he is manipulating another. This is most easy with preoperational children, as they are easily fooled
      with their tendency to:
      a.   be static thinkers.
      b.   reverse things in their perception.
      c.   centrate.
      d.   equilibrate.

Obstacles to Logical Operations, p. 218
Diff: E, Ans: b
13.   To assume that the world is unchanging is to engage in:
      a.   magical thinking.
      b.   static reasoning.
      c.   centration.
      d.   a focus on appearances only.

Obstacles to Logical Operations, p. 218
Diff: E, Ans: d
14.   When children demonstrate centration, they:
      a.   are in the formal operational stage.
      b.   cannot make a decision.
      c.   cannot solve math problems in their heads.
      d.   only look at one aspect of a problem.

Obstacles to Logical Operations, p. 218
Diff: H, Ans: d
15.   Nine-year-old Bobby has no problem understanding that the 20-year-old who sometimes stays with him
      is both a student and a baby-sitter. According to Piaget, Bobby's thinking is no longer characterized by:
      a.   conservation.
      b.   object permanence.
      c.   overregularization.
      d.   centration.

Obstacles to Logical Operations, p. 218
Diff: E, Ans: c
16.   If a preschool child thinks a tall 20-year-old is older than a 40-year-old dwarf, this is an example of:
      a.   egocentrism.
      b.   static thinking.
      c.   focus on appearance.
      d.   symbolic thinking.

Obstacles to Logical Operations, p. 218
Diff: E, Ans: c

17.   Not understanding that undoing a sequence of events will bring about the original conditions or situation is called:
  a.   concrete operations.
  b.   conservation.
  c.   irreversibility.
  d.   symbolic thought.

Obstacles to Logical Operations, p. 218
Diff: H, Ans: a

18.   Romy understands that if she has four pieces of pizza and we give her two more, she will have six. However, she does not know what happens if she has six and we take away two. Piaget would say that Romy:
  a.   has demonstrated irreversible thinking.
  b.   has exhibited centration.
  c.   is thinking in a static way.
  d.   has demonstrated a scaffold.

Obstacles to Logical Operations, p. 218
Diff: M, Ans: a

19.   Krista understands that $4 + 6 = 10$ but does not understand that $10 - 6 = 4$. She is displaying:
  a.   irreversibility.
  b.   centration.
  c.   egocentrism.
  d.   animism.

Obstacles to Logical Operations, p. 218
Diff: M, Ans: d

20.   Which of these aspects of preoperational thought focuses on transformations?
  a.   centration
  b.   focus on appearances
  c.   static reasoning
  d.   irreversibility

Obstacles to Logical Operations, p. 218
Diff: E, Ans: b

21.   The idea that children tend to focus on only one aspect of a problem is called:
  a.   focus on appearance.
  b.   centration.
  c.   static reasoning.
  d.   irreversibility.

Obstacles to Logical Operations, p. 218
Diff: H, Ans: c

22.   Evelyn asks to leave school so she can change her skirt which she got a tiny amount of catsup on during lunchtime. Evelyn is acting like a preoperational child suffering from:
  a.   irreversibility.
  b.   static reasoning.
  c.   focus on appearance.
  d.   overregularization.

Fig. 9.1: Conservation, Please, p. 219
Diff: E, Ans: b
23.   A child is shown two identical tall containers, half-filled with water. The contents of one container are
      then poured into a short, wide container. If the child states that both containers still have the same
      amount, that phenomenon would be called:
      a.   classification.
      b.   conservation.
      c.   centration.
      d.   transformation.

Fig. 9.1: Conservation, Please, p. 219
Diff: M, Ans: c
24.   The young child's inability to grasp conservation explains his or her:
      a.   inability to see more than one person's point of view at a time.
      b.   tendency to draw a picture of a dime three times its normal size.
      c.   belief that an 8-oz. soup bowl holds less liquid than an 8-oz. glass.
      d.   inability to understand that both a collie and a beagle are dogs.

Fig. 9.1: Conservation, Please, p. 219
Diff: H, Ans: c
25.   An experimenter lines up pairs of checkers into two identical rows. Then the experimenter elongates
      one of the rows by spacing the checkers farther apart. This is a classic test of:
      a.   conservation of volume.
      b.   conservation of area.
      c.   conservation of numbers.
      d.   conservation of matter.

Fig. 9.1: Conservation, Please, p. 219
Diff: E, Ans: c
26.   The example of having two equal lines of checkers and then increasing the spacing of checkers in one
      line and asking which line has more checkers is meant to test for:
      a.   theory of mind.
      b.   scaffolding.
      c.   conservation.
      d.   egocentrism.

Fig. 9.1: Conservation, Please, p. 219
Diff: M, Ans: b
27.   Daryl has a ball of Silly Putty. His 6-year-old son, John, watches as Daryl flattens the Silly Putty into a
      thin "pancake." When Daryl asks John if there is now more Silly Putty, John replies, "Yes." Piaget
      would say that John has:
      a.   demonstrated scaffolding.
      b.   not mastered the concept of conservation.
      c.   an understanding of object permanence.
      d.   demonstrated fast mapping.

Vygotsky: Children as Apprentices, p. 220
Diff: H, Ans: d
28.   Whereas Piaget saw cognitive development as a result of individual discovery, Vygotsky attributed
      it to:
      a.   biological changes in the brain.
      b.   unconscious factors.
      c.   watching others complete activities.
      d.   social activities guided by others.

Vygotsky: Children as Apprentices, p. 220
Diff: M, Ans: c

29. Preschoolers have a tendency to try to make up a reason why things occur as they do around them. This tendency is known as:
    a. reversibility.
    b. focus on appearances.
    c. theory-theory.
    d. logical reasoning.

Vygotsky: Children as Apprentices, p. 220
Diff: M, Ans: d

30. Humans seek reasons, causes, and underlying principles to explain the world around them. The research term for this is:
    a. deductive reasoning.
    b. conservation.
    c. scaffolding.
    d. theory-theory.

Vygotsky: Children as Apprentices, p. 221
Diff: E, Ans: d

31. Vygotsky's theory includes the ideas of:
    a. young children as "apprentices in thinking."
    b. guided participation.
    c. scaffolding.
    d. all of the above.

Vygotsky: Children as Apprentices, p. 221
Diff: M, Ans: c

32. The stimulation of intellectual growth in children as guided by older and more skilled society members is:
    a. guided participation.
    b. equilibration.
    c. an apprenticeship in thinking.
    d. child-centeredness.

Vygotsky: Children as Apprentices, p. 221
Diff: M, Ans: d

33. The process that depends heavily on exploration and social experiences is:
    a. proximal development.
    b. scaffolding.
    c. active learning.
    d. guided participation.

Vygotsky: Children as Apprentices, p. 221
Diff: H, Ans: b

34. Each time Juan puts a puzzle together, his father gives him a little less help. Which theorist would be happy with Juan's father?
    a. Piaget
    b. Vygotsky
    c. Skinner
    d. Freud

Vygotsky: Children as Apprentices, p. 221
Diff: M, Ans: a

35.   In the least-developed nations, the most common teachers are:
    a.   older siblings.
    b.   parents.
    c.   extended family members.
    d.   special government-funded program instructors.

Vygotsky: Children as Apprentices, p. 221
Diff: M, Ans: a

36.   According to Vygotsky, guided participation requires that a child:
    a.   interact with an adult to accomplish the task.
    b.   is told instructions for a task only once.
    c.   is allowed to discover the solution to a task on his or her own.
    d.   be assisted by an adult until the child can perform the task well alone.

How to Solve a Puzzle, p. 221
Diff: E, Ans: b

37.   The crucial element involved in the guided participation with a mentor is:
    a.   that both child and adult cognitively operate on the same level.
    b.   mutuality.
    c.   egocentrism.
    d.   reversibility.

Scaffolding, p. 221
Diff: E, Ans: c

38.   Vygotsky suggested that each individual is surrounded by a zone of:
    a.   possibilities.
    b.   distal development.
    c.   proximal development.
    d.   potentiality.

Scaffolding, p. 221
Diff: H, Ans: a

39.   Mrs. Suttman helps her 2-year-old daughter count blocks and measure teaspoons of cocoa. Mrs. Suttman is providing:
    a.   scaffolding and structure.
    b.   overstimulation.
    c.   conservation skills.
    d.   peer tutoring.

Scaffolding, p. 221
Diff: H, Ans: d

40.   Skills that the person can accomplish with assistance but is not yet ready to perform independently are part of:
    a.   private speech.
    b.   the gap between heredity and learning.
    c.   distal development.
    d.   the zone of proximal development.

Scaffolding, p. 221
Diff: H, Ans: d

41.   The child not being able to read on her own, gets assistance from an adult to accomplish the skill. This is only possible if the child is in:
a.   a static reasoning period.
b.   a scaffold.
c.   the period of preoperations.
d.   the zone of proximal development.

Scaffolding, p. 221
Diff: M, Ans: c

42.   One of Vygotsky's most famous concepts was the *zone of proximal development*, which asserts that:
a.   there is a certain place in a school where most learning occurs.
b.   children can only reach a certain level of intelligence.
c.   child can master some tasks with the help of others.
d.   certain parts of the brain need to be activated.

Scaffolding, p. 221
Diff: H, Ans: b

43.   A teacher who carefully plans each child's participation in the learning process is:
a.   reinforcing good behavior.
b.   scaffolding.
c.   teaching new skills.
d.   constructing.

Scaffolding, p. 221
Diff: E, Ans: a

44.   Which of the following examples *best* demonstrates scaffolding?
a.   Elizabeth helps her son prepare meatloaf for dinner. She gives him specific instructions and simplifies whenever possible.
b.   Roberto buys his daughter ice cream when she rides her two-wheel bike successfully.
c.   Carla decides not to ask her daughter for help, because she knows her daughter does not have much patience.
d.   Jason makes his son, Peter, go to bed early, because Peter swore at school.

Scaffolding, p. 222
Diff: E, Ans: a

45.   The function of speech by which a person's cognitive skills are refined and extended is:
a.   social mediation.
b.   guided participation.
c.   overregularization.
d.   theory of mind.

Scaffolding, p. 222
Diff: E, Ans: d

46.   When a person talks to herself or himself, it is referred to as:
a.   theory of mind.
b.   a river of consciousness.
c.   mentally disturbed.
d.   private speech.

Scaffolding, p. 222
Diff: M, Ans: c
47. According to Vygotsky, the difference between private speech in preschoolers and private speech in adults is whether it is:
    a. coherent.
    b. useful.
    c. out loud.
    d. embarrassing.

Scaffolding, p. 222
Diff: M, Ans: a
48. Marie talks out loud to herself in school as she puts a puzzle together. She is probably:
    a. 4 years old.
    b. 7 years old.
    c. 10 years old.
    d. 12 years old.

Scaffolding, p. 222
Diff: E, Ans: c
49. Preschoolers do *not* use private speech to:
    a. review what they know.
    b. decide what to do.
    c. communicate with those around them.
    d. explain events to themselves.

Scaffolding, p. 222
Diff: H, Ans: d
50. According to Vygotsky, language:
    a. serves as a mediator of social interaction.
    b. refines and extends a person's skills.
    c. is essential in traversing the zone of proximal development.
    d. serves all of the above functions.

Table 9.1: Comparing Piaget and Vygotsky, p. 223
Diff: M, Ans: c
51. Piaget's view of development included:
    a. guided participation.
    b. scaffolding.
    c. active learning.
    d. apprenticeship.

Table 9.1: Comparing Piaget and Vygotsky, p. 223
Diff: E, Ans: a
52. Researcher Vygotsky suggested that the preschooler:
    a. work hand-in-hand with an adult who coordinates the learning episodes.
    b. work from an internal "voice" of curiosity when attempting new learning.
    c. be single-minded in approaching difficult lessons.
    d. build and rebuild mental structures when working through problems.

Theory of Mind

Theory of Mind, p. 223
Diff: E, Ans: c
53. A person's understanding of the emotions, intentions, thoughts, and perceptions of other people is called:
    a. intuitive psychology.
    b. psychological schemata.
    c. theory of mind.
    d. self schemes.

Theory of Mind, p. 223
Diff: H, Ans: c
54. Britney understands that her father is crying because his best friend died. This shows that Britney:
    a. is egocentric.
    b. has a script for crying.
    c. has a theory of mind.
    d. has learned conservation.

Emergence at Age 4, p. 223
Diff: M, Ans: b
55. Shana is 4 years old, so her parents can probably expect her to:
    a. not be egocentric.
    b. have a theory of mind.
    c. understand metaphors.
    d. all of the above.

Emergence at Age 4, p. 223
Diff: H, Ans: d
56. When 3-year-old Eric is shown a candy box and asked what is inside, he will probably answer, "Candy." When he is shown that there are actually pencils inside, Eric will probably:
    a. not be surprised that there are pencils inside.
    b. predict that other children would expect to find candy inside.
    c. say that he thought there would be candy inside.
    d. say that he thought there would be pencils inside.

Emergence at Age 4, p. 223
Diff: H, Ans: a
57. After being shown a candy box that turns out to be holding pencils, a 3-year-old is *not* likely to say:
    a. "But I thought it was candy!"
    b. "I knew it was pencils all along."
    c. "My friend will know it is pencils."
    d. "I knew it wasn't candy all the time."

Table 9.2: Age at Which Theory of Mind Emerges, p. 223
Diff: M, Ans: a
58. The youngest children to demonstrate theory of mind in experiments are age:
    a. 3 1/2.
    b. 5.
    c. 7.
    d. 9.

Table 9.2: Age at Which Theory of Mind Emerges, p. 223
Diff: H, Ans: c
59.   When children in Peru were tested on theory of mind, they:
        a.   were ahead of U.S. children.
        b.   were at the same level as U.S. children.
        c.   were behind U.S. children.
        d.   refused to answer the questions.

Contextual Influences on Theory of Mind, p. 224
Diff: M, Ans: b
60.   The underlying factor allowing the development of theory of mind is:
        a.   the simultaneous development of magical thinking.
        b.   maturation of the prefrontal cortexes.
        c.   static reasoning.
        d.   centration.

Contextual Influences on Theory of Mind, p. 224
Diff: H, Ans: a
61.   In one study, 4- to 8-year-olds in Peru were tested on a version of the candy-box situation. What did the researcher(s) discover?
        a.   Many Peruvian children answered the theory-of-mind questions incorrectly.
        b.   Only the 8-year-olds were proficient at answering correctly.
        c.   Most of both groups answered the theory-of-mind questions correctly.
        d.   Overall, the Peruvian children in this study were superior to their Western counterparts.

Contextual Influences on Theory of Mind, pp. 224-225
Diff: H, Ans: b
62.   Which is *not* one of the key factors that strengthens theory of mind at about age 4?
        a.   having a sibling
        b.   whether or not the child is adopted
        c.   language ability
        d.   culture

Language

Language, p. 225
Diff: H, Ans: b
63.   A "critical period" view of language learning refers to:
        a.   the sensitive time for prefrontal cortex development.
        b.   the only time language can be learned.
        c.   the best time to learn a language.
        d.   second-language acquisition.

Language, p. 225
Diff: E, Ans: b
64.   The skills needed to learn to read are called:
        a.   grammar.
        b.   emergent literacy.
        c.   syntax.
        d.   fast-mapping skills.

Vocabulary, p. 226
Diff: H, Ans: c
65.   By age 6, how many words does the average child know?
a.   about 2,000
b.   about 5,000
c.   more than 10,000
d.   a little less than 75,000

Vocabulary, p. 226
Diff: E, Ans: a
66.   A child's ability to add new vocabulary words very quickly is called:
a.   fast mapping.
b.   word mapping.
c.   mental language.
d.   word charting.

Vocabulary, p. 226
Diff: E, Ans: d
67.   When children hear a new word in a familiar context, they can simply add the word to the general category without fully understanding the word. This is called:
a.   lexical addition.
b.   categorical embellishment.
c.   vocabulary expansion.
d.   fast mapping.

Vocabulary, p. 226
Diff: H, Ans: a
68.   Fast mapping explains how children are able to:
a.   understand new words.
b.   add words into their vocabulary.
c.   learn how to pronounce new words.
d.   follow simple instructions.

Vocabulary, p. 226
Diff: M, Ans: d
69.   Because of "fast mapping," a preschooler:
a.   needs several experiences with a word in order to learn it.
b.   grasps the meaning of words describing emotions.
c.   has a clear understanding of all the words he uses.
d.   learns some words after a single exposure to them.

Vocabulary, p. 226
Diff: M, Ans: a
70.   Logical extension involves:
a.   applying a newly learned word to other objects in the same category.
b.   mentally charting new words.
c.   applying a new concept to a preexistent category.
d.   equilibration.

Vocabulary, p. 226
Diff: E, Ans: a
71.   Words are learned after being heard only once through the process of:
a.   fast mapping.
b.   centration.
c.   theory of mind.
d.   theory-theory.

Vocabulary, p. 226
Diff: M, Ans: c
72.   The term most closely associated with fast mapping is:
a.   overregularization.
b.   the language shift.
c.   logical extension.
d.   theory-theory.

Vocabulary, p. 227
Diff: M, Ans: c
73.   At age 5 children:
a.   cannot correctly use difficult words.
b.   usually have very small vocabularies.
c.   can learn almost any word if carefully taught.
d.   usually learn verbs before nouns.

Vocabulary, p. 227
Diff: H, Ans: c
74.   A problem with fast mapping is that:
a.   the child forgets most words learned this way.
b.   when words are learned this way, good grammar is lost.
c.   the child may misuse the word.
d.   it interferes with other aspects of cognitive development.

Vocabulary, p. 227
Diff: H, Ans: d
75.   Among the most difficult words for preschoolers to learn are:
a.   egocentric words.
b.   action verbs.
c.   concrete nouns.
d.   abstract nouns.

Vocabulary, p. 227
Diff: H, Ans: b
76.   Most young children:
a.   understand every word they hear.
b.   have trouble understanding metaphors.
c.   learn the literal and metaphorical meanings at the same time.
d.   say a lot more words than they can understand.

Grammar, p. 228
Diff: M, Ans: a
77.   When do children first use some rules of grammar?
a.   before age 3
b.   by the time the child has a vocabulary of about 300 words
c.   by the time the child has a vocabulary of about 600 words
d.   by about age 5

Grammar, p. 228
Diff: H, Ans: d
78.   By age 3, most children can:
a.   form the plural of words.
b.   use past, present, and future tenses of verbs.
c.   use possessive forms of pronouns.
d.   do all of the above.

Grammar, p. 228
Diff: E, Ans: c

79. The structures, rules, and techniques used to communicate meaning are referred to as:
    a. inflections.
    b. logical extensions.
    c. grammar.
    d. theory-theory.

Grammar, p. 228
Diff: M, Ans: b

80. The formation of overregularization in a child's speech patterns indicates:
    a. that he or she is entering a sensitive period of language development.
    b. he or she is able to apply grammatical rules to her vocalizations.
    c. logical extension is now possible.
    d. that fast mapping has occurred.

Grammar, p. 228
Diff: E, Ans: b

81. "I catched two mices in a trap" is an example of:
    a. egocentric speech.
    b. overregularization.
    c. literal translation.
    d. the past imperfect.

Grammar, p. 228
Diff: M, Ans: c

82. Which of the following is an example of overregularization?
    a. "It's snowing so I can build a snowman."
    b. "The moon looks happy tonight."
    c. "He hitted me with the stick."
    d. "Yesterday, I want to go to the park."

Grammar, p. 228
Diff: H, Ans: d

83. Overregularization occurs because children:
    a. tend to regress briefly before progressing to new forms of language.
    b. have no understanding of past, present, and future.
    c. assume that the language is less regular than it actually is.
    d. assume their language always follows the rules.

Grammar, p. 228
Diff: M, Ans: a

84. "I falled down and I hurted myself" is typical of a child when they first are learning grammar. Of what is this an example?
    a. overregularization
    b. egocentrism
    c. conservation
    d. scaffolding

Early-Childhood Education

Topic, pp. 230-232
Diff: M, Ans: d
85.   Of the many types of early-childhood programs from which to choose, which of the following was a common element?
   a.   readiness
   b.   academics
   c.   direct instruction by a teacher
   d.   a special focus on children in a prime period for intellectual growth

Child-Centered and Readiness Programs, p. 231
Diff: M, Ans: b
86.   "Readiness" programs for preschoolers focus on:
   a.   child-centeredness.
   b.   structure in the learning episodes.
   c.   Montessori projects.
   d.   artistic expression within the zone of proximal development.

Reggio-Emilia and Kindergarten, p. 231
Diff: M, Ans: c
87.   The Reggio-Emilia early-childhood program focuses on:
   a.   reinforcements for academic accomplishments.
   b.   assimilation and accommodation skills.
   c.   master of skills not typically accomplished until age 7.
   d.   self-esteem and self-concept.

Head Start, p. 232
Diff: E, Ans: d
88.   Low-income children are given preschool education classes under which program?
   a.   the War on Poverty
   b.   Three, Two, One Contact
   c.   Sesame Street
   d.   Project Head Start

Quality Learning, p. 234
Diff: E, Ans: b
89.   To find a good preschool, a parent should look for:
   a.   a curriculum geared toward behavioral control; experienced teachers.
   b.   teachers with degrees in early childhood education; low teacher-child ratios.
   c.   a desk and a chair for each child; a curriculum geared toward cognitive development.
   d.   experienced teachers; curriculum that teaches children as a whole group.

Quality Learning, p. 234
Diff: E, Ans: d
90.   An excellent early childhood program would *not* have:
   a.   a low teacher-child ratio.
   b.   space that facilitates creative play.
   c.   a staff trained in early childhood education.
   d.   a curriculum geared toward behavioral control.

TRUE-FALSE QUESTIONS

How Children Think: Piaget and Vygotsky

Ans: T, p. 217
1. Egocentrism is Piaget's term for centration in which the child thinks about the world from his or her own personal perspective.

Ans: T, p. 218
2. A preschooler's approach to the world is often dictated more by their own subjective views of the world than by the world's reality.

Ans: T, p. 218
3. Preoperational thought involves magical, self-centered imagination disallowing logic.

Ans: T, p. 218
4. Centration is an obstacle to developing logical operations.

Ans: T, p. 218
5. The preoperational child is incapable of engaging in reversibility.

Ans: F, p. 219
6. Conservation refers to a person's tendency to act cautiously in uncertain situations.

Ans: T, p. 219
7. Piaget believed that it was impossible for preoperational children to grasp the concept of conservation, even with training.

Ans: F, p. 220
8. For quite a while, developmentalists overestimated children's thinking skills.

Ans: T, p. 221
9. The process of learning to think by having social experiences and by exploration is called guided participation.

Ans: F, p. 221
10. The sensitive structuring provided by others to the developing child in learning encounters is known as the zone of proximal development.

Ans: T, p. 221
11. Older and more skilled society members help the child to learn new things through an apprenticeship in thinking.

Ans: F, p. 222
12. In children, private speech is usually silent.

Ans: F, p. 223
13. Vygotsky believed cognitive growth was a process of individual discovery, propelled by experience and biological maturation.

Ans: T, p. 223
14. Mental assumptions and scenarios the child creates to help organize an understanding of the world are known as structures.

Ans: F, p. 223
15.   Vygotsky believed that the nature of the child was primarily egocentric.

Ans: F, p. 223
16.   The learning process support by Piagetians involves mentors who guide the child using scaffolding.

Theory of Mind

Ans: T, p. 223
17.   A "theory of mind" is one's own personal understanding of mental processes, of the complex interaction among emotions, perceptions, thoughts, and intentions in others and ourselves.

Emergence at Age 4
Ans: T, p. 223
18.   All developmental researchers agree that preschoolers develop a theory of mind.

Ans: F, p. 224
19.   The underlying factor allowing the development of theory of mind is static reasoning.

Language

Ans: F, p. 225
20.   The language "explosion" typically occurs at about 1 year.

Ans: F, p. 226
21.   The child by age six has a vocabulary of about 20,000 words.

Ans: T, p. 226
22.   The charting of new vocabulary words by associating them with words children already know the definitions of is called fast mapping.

Ans: T, p. 227
23.   Abstract nouns and metaphors are some of the hardest concepts for young children to grasp.

Ans: T, p. 228
24.   Overregularization is actually a sign of verbal sophistication.

Ans: F, p. 228
25.   The text recommends using and explaining no more than one new word per day to your child.

Ans: T, p. 229
26.   The best time to learn a second language is in early childhood.

Ans: F, p. 229
27.   The *language shift* occurs when the child becomes equally fluent in their new language as they are in their home language.

Early-Childhood Education

Ans: T, p. 231
28.   The Montessori schools focus on using materials and projects in such a way so that children would get a strong sense of accomplishment.

Ans: T, p. 232
29.   Studies suggest that preschool education, such as that provided by Head Start, advances the behavioral and academic development of disadvantaged children.

FILL-IN-THE-BLANK QUESTIONS

How Children Think: Piaget and Vygotsky

Ans: egocentrism, p. 217

1.   The preschooler's prevailing tendency to view the world and others exclusively from their own personal perspective is _____.

Ans: egocentrism, p. 218

2.   Another name or term for *ego-centration* is _____.

Ans: static reasoning, p. 218

3.   The four aspects of preoperational thought include centration, focus on appearance, irreversibility, and _____.

Ans: centration, p. 218

4.   Jana always chooses the taller glass of grape juice when her older brother pours them both a glass of juice. In this process, Jana is applying the concept of _____.

Ans: number, p. 219

5.   The conservation experiment in which the child is shown two equal lines of checkers and, after one line has been spread out, is asked which line has more checkers, is a test for conservation of _____.

Ans: conservation, p. 219

6.   Perceiving that there is the same amount of modeling clay as before when it is rolled out into a Tootsie roll shape is known as _____.

Ans: appearances, p. 219

7.   In conservation problems, preschoolers make mistakes because they ignore the transformations that have taken place and focus on _____.

Ans: Vygotsky, pp. 220-221

8.   The view of the child as an "apprentice in thinking" was inspired by the work of _____.

Ans: private, p. 222

9.   The internal dialogue in which a person talks to herself or himself is called _____ speech.

Theory of Mind

Ans: theory of mind, p. 223

10.   The change in thinking 4-year-old children go through which allows them to understand that just because one believes something does not necessarily mean that it is also true is called _____.

Language

Ans: fast mapping, p. 226

11.   Learning vocabulary by connecting a word to words and categories that are already understood is called _____.

Ans: fast mapping, p. 226

12.   When 9-year-old Sam tells 5-year-old Flo, "Don't have a cow," Flo might say, "I won't because Daddy says we can't have any animals." This response is because of _____.

Ans: metaphors, p. 227
13.   The text mentions two types of concepts that young children have a lot of trouble comprehending. One is *abstract nouns* and the other is _____.

Ans: overregularization, p. 228
14.   The child who says, "I cutted myself," or "I unremembered it," is demonstrating a tendency called _____.

Ans: Maria Montessori, p. 231
15.   The special program developed to focus on structured, individualized projects designed to give children a sense of accomplishment was developed by _____.

Early-Childhood Education

Ans: college; jail, pp. 232-233
16.   As they enter adulthood, Head Start graduates are more likely to be in _____ and are less likely to be in _____ than non-Head-Start peers.

ESSAY QUESTIONS

1.   What is conservation? Describe two examples of how conservation tasks are done.

2.   If a parent or teacher wished to try scaffolding with a child, what steps should he or she take in order to provide the most effective scaffolding?

3.   Francesca is frustrated trying to learn to tie her shoelaces. According to Vygotsky, should the parents get involved or should they let her try to master this task on her own? If they decide to get involved, what should her parents do?

4.   According to Vygotsky, what role does the culture play in determining what things a child will learn? Provide an example.

5.   Compare and contrast the theories of Piaget and Vygotsky. Include examples of children's behavior from research and from your own personal experience to support the views of each.

6.   Based on what you learned in this chapter, describe an ideal preschool in some detail.

7.   You have been hired as an educational consultant to the president of the United States. What policy would you recommend to the federal government concerning preschool education? What children should be targeted? How much government involvement should there be? Who will bear the cost of these programs? Be sure to take into consideration the research presented in this chapter.

8.   Explain the difference between Piaget's concept of *egocentric* and the word *selfish*.

9.   Explain the "theory of mind" the text discusses at length.

10.   Distinguish between a *critical period* and a *sensitive period* for the development of language.

11.   Explain and discuss the process of *fast mapping* and the related idea of *logical extension*.

12.   Contrast the two views on learning a second language in childhood.

13.   Briefly identify the unique differences of the Reggio-Emilia early-childhood education program that separates it from other programs already in place.

Answer guidelines to these essay questions can be found in the Appendix at the end of the Test Bank.

CHAPTER 10   The Play Years: Psychosocial Development

MULTIPLE-CHOICE QUESTIONS

The Play Years: Psychosocial Development, p. 237
Diff: M, Ans: b
1. When do 2-year-olds typically need direct supervision?
   a. in familiar settings, they can play safely unsupervised
   b. they need supervision almost every waking moment
   c. they can play unsupervised with familiar peers
   d. they should be able to feed and dress themselves without supervision

Emotional Development

Initiative Versus Guilt, p. 237
Diff: E, Ans: a
2. Erikson's stage that occurs between 3 and 6 years is called:
   a. initiative versus guilt.
   b. phallic pride versus penis envy.
   c. the preoperational stage.
   d. autonomy versus inferiority.

Initiative Versus Guilt, p. 237
Diff: H, Ans: c
3. If a 6-year-old girl has a high self-esteem, one could say she has successfully resolved Erikson's stage of:
   a. trust vs. mistrust.
   b. autonomy versus shame and doubt.
   c. initiative vs. guilt.
   d. industry vs. inferiority.

Initiative Versus Guilt, p. 238
Diff: H, Ans: b
4. One difference between shame and guilt is that:
   a. toddlers feel guilt but not shame.
   b. guilt comes from within the child.
   c. during childhood, we acquire more shame and less guilt.
   d. guilt is based on how others judge our performance.

Initiative Versus Guilt, p. 238
Diff: H, Ans: a

5.   In Erikson's third psychosocial stage, a child:
      a.   eagerly takes on new tasks.
      b.   has not yet developed a sense of failure.
      c.   does not react to criticism.
      d.   does things from the pure joy of being alive.

Initiative Versus Guilt, p. 238
Diff: M, Ans: c

6.   Toby, a 4-year-old, accidentally dropped a glass vase while trying to bring it to his mother. According
      to Erikson, Toby will:
      a.   experience no change in emotion.
      b.   be proud of himself for having tried to do something nice.
      c.   feel a sense of guilt.
      d.   be sad that his mother did not get the flowers.

Initiative Versus Guilt, p. 238
Diff: H, Ans: c

7.   When a preschooler judges his or her own skills, he or she:
      a.   tends to underestimate his or her own abilities.
      b.   has a realistic idea about his or her own abilities.
      c.   tends to overestimate his or her own abilities.
      d.   asks other people their opinions about his or her abilities.

Emotional Regulation, p. 239
Diff: E, Ans: d

8.   An angry 5-year-old might stop herself from hitting another child, because she has developed:
      a.   social referencing.
      b.   self-esteem.
      c.   identification.
      d.   emotional regulation.

Emotional Regulation, p. 239
Diff: E, Ans: b

9.   When 4-year-old Karen is angry, she lashes out by hitting. This is an example of:
      a.   an internalizing problem.
      b.   an externalizing problem.
      c.   modulated emotional expression.
      d.   frustration management.

Neurons and Nurture, p. 239
Diff: M, Ans: c

10.   Emotional regulation develops due to:
      a.   changes within the brain.
      b.   learning.
      c.   both brain changes and learning.
      d.   peer interaction.

Neurons and Nurture, p. 239
Diff: E, Ans: c

11.   Emotional regulation develops due to:
      a.   changes within the brain.
      b.   learning.
      c.   both brain changes and learning.
      d.   peer interaction.

Neurons and Nurture, pp. 239-240
Diff: H, Ans: c

12.   Emotional regulation in preschool children is affected by:
   a.   genes and early care.
   b.   stress and current care.
   c.   both a. and b.
   d.   neither a. nor b.

Cognition and Emotions, p. 241
Diff: H, Ans: a

13.   Five-year-old Fred brought a dead bird to his mother. Crying he said, "I'm so sad this little bird died." His mother might conclude that Fred is:
   a.   developing emotional intelligence.
   b.   overly sensitive.
   c.   aware of his self-concept.
   d.   precocious.

Empathy and Antipathy, p. 241
Diff: H, Ans: d

14.   Of the following, which behavior is considered pro-social?
   a.   Savannah takes out the garbage for a quarter.
   b.   Selena helps her mother so that her mother will take her to the park.
   c.   Jana says "please" when asking her mother for the car keys.
   d.   Beth feeds her baby brother because her mother is sick.

Empathy and Antipathy, p. 241
Diff: H, Ans: c

15.   Sara, 3, seeing a little boy fall and hurt himself, gets a look of concern on her face. She is probably experiencing:
   a.   fear.
   b.   sadness.
   c.   empathy.
   d.   frustration.

Empathy and Antipathy, p. 242
Diff: E, Ans: b

16.   Which is an example of antisocial behavior?
   a.   Jamie tries to share his toys with Jill.
   b.   Mark intentionally knocks over Simon's blocks.
   c.   Holly watches while other children are playing jump rope.
   d.   Courtney helps her mom rake the leaves.

Table 10.1: The Four Forms of Aggression, p. 243
Diff: E, Ans: b

17.   Aggression used to obtain or retain a toy or other object is called:
   a.   bullying.
   b.   instrumental aggression.
   c.   reactive aggression.
   d.   personal aggression.

Table 10.1: The Four Forms of Aggression, p. 243
Diff: M, Ans: b

18.   Which is the best example of reactive aggression?
       a.   Ralph spanks his daughter when he gets mad.
       b.   Joanie hits Beth because Beth grabbed her coloring book.
       c.   Arthur wrestles Richie for fun.
       d.   Marion punches Arnold for no apparent reason.

Table 10.1: The Four Forms of Aggression, p. 243
Diff: H, Ans: d

19.   Three girls start a rumor that 7-year-old Heather is a bed-wetter who still uses a pacifier. What kind of aggression is this?
       a.   instrumental
       b.   reactive
       c.   bullying
       d.   relational

Table 10.1: The Four Forms of Aggression, p. 243
Diff: H, Ans: d

20.   One thing bullies and their victims have in common is:
       a.   low tolerance for frustration.
       b.   future involvement in aggression.
       c.   a false image of maleness.
       d.   inadequate emotional regulation.

Aggression, p. 243
Diff: M, Ans: c

21.   The difference between relational and reactive aggression is that relational aggression is _____, whereas reactive aggression is _____.
       a.   retaliatory; bullying
       b.   physical behavior; social
       c.   social; physical behavior
       d.   verbal; social

Active Play, p. 244
Diff: M, Ans: c

22.   Enzio and Ramon are "wrestling" in the preschool playground. This is probably:
       a.   a fight.
       b.   mastery play.
       c.   rough-and-tumble play.
       d.   sociodramatic play.

Active Play, p. 244
Diff: E, Ans: b

23.   When deciding if kids are really fighting, one should look for:
       a.   their mothers.
       b.   a play face.
       c.   their hands wagging.
       d.   a difference in size.

Active Play, p. 244
Diff: M, Ans: c

24.   Rough-and-tumble play is *least* likely to take place:
       a.   when there is plenty of room for each child to play in.
       b.   when there are no adults nearby.
       c.   when children have little social experience.
       d.   among groups of boys.

Active Play, p. 244
Diff: M, Ans: a
25. The type of child's play that resembles that of baby monkeys is called:
   a. rough-and-tumble play.
   b. imaginative play.
   c. parallel play.
   d. solitary play.

Imaginative Play, p. 244
Diff: E, Ans: b
26. In sociodramatic play, children:
   a. play physically with other children.
   b. act out roles and create stories.
   c. coordinate senses and motions.
   d. cooperate with other children to help build something.

Imaginative Play, p. 244
Diff: E, Ans: b
27. One child pretends to be the mother while the other pretends to be a baby who will not eat his dinner. Such play is called:
   a. representative.
   b. sociodramatic.
   c. family.
   d. psychosocial.

Imaginative Play, p. 245
Diff: M, Ans: c
28. Sociodramatic play becomes more interactive and greatly increases in frequency and complexity between the ages of:
   a. 1 and 2.
   b. 2 and 4.
   c. 2 and 6.
   d. 6 and 8.

Parenting Patterns

Baumrind's Three Styles of Parenting, p. 246
Diff: E, Ans: c
29. Diana Baumrind is famous for her work on:
   a. the Electra complex.
   b. types of play.
   c. styles of parenting.
   d. cognitive stages.

Baumrind's Three Styles of Parenting, p. 246
Diff: M, Ans: b
30. The four dimensions of parenting style are warmth, discipline, communication, and:
   a. physical contact.
   b. expectations for maturity.
   c. trust.
   d. supportiveness.

Baumrind's Three Styles of Parenting, p. 246
Diff: M, Ans: d

31.   When parents expect unquestioning obedience from their children, this is what style of parenting?
       a.   tyrannical
       b.   authoritative
       c.   dictatorial
       d.   authoritarian

Baumrind's Three Styles of Parenting, pp. 246-247
Diff: H, Ans: a

32.   As a father, Mr. Wallace was rated low on nurturance and communication and high on maturity demands. He would most closely fit the parenting style that is identified as:
       a.   authoritarian.
       b.   democratic.
       c.   authoritative.
       d.   rejecting.

Baumrind's Three Styles of Parenting, p. 247
Diff: M, Ans: c

33.   Authoritarian parents:
       a.   are affectionate with their children and often praise them.
       b.   allow children to question their decisions but punish misconduct.
       c.   seem aloof from their children.
       d.   make few maturity demands on their children.

Baumrind's Three Styles of Parenting, p. 247
Diff: H, Ans: b

34.   Mrs. Kaminsky is a very nurturing parent and has good communication with her children whom she never disciplines. Her parenting style is:
       a.   authoritative.
       b.   permissive.
       c.   neglectful.
       d.   authoritarian.

Baumrind's Three Styles of Parenting, p. 247
Diff: M, Ans: c

35.   Parents who set limits, enforce rules, and listen receptively to their children are exhibiting what parenting style?
       a.   autocratic
       b.   authoritarian
       c.   authoritative
       d.   democratic

Baumrind's Three Styles of Parenting, p. 247
Diff: M, Ans: a

36.   A young girl's parents have made a rule but then they make an exception when their daughter gives a good reason. Their parenting style is:
       a.   authoritative.
       b.   permissive.
       c.   authoritarian.
       d.   inconsistent.

Baumrind's Three Styles of Parenting, p. 247
Diff: H, Ans: c
37.   Strict and aloof parents tend to have children who are:
a.   abusive.
b.   overcontrolling.
c.   authoritarian.
d.   permissive.

Baumrind's Three Styles of Parenting, p. 247
Diff: H, Ans: d
38.   Children who lack self-control are most likely to have parents who are:
a.   abusive.
b.   over-controlling.
c.   authoritarian.
d.   permissive.

Baumrind's Three Styles of Parenting, p. 247
Diff: H, Ans: c
39.   Which child is most likely to have permissive parents?
a.   Richard, who is obedient but not very happy.
b.   George, who is happy and successful.
c.   Paul, who is unhappy and lacks self-control.
d.   Peter, who is generous, but a drug user.

Baumrind's Three Styles of Parenting, p. 247
Diff: H, Ans: c
40.   At least among the majority of families, adolescents who are successful, generous individuals are from what kind of homes?
a.   authoritarian
b.   permissive
c.   authoritative
d.   traditional

Baumrind's Three Styles of Parenting, p. 247
Diff: E, Ans: d
41.   Child-rearing patterns are affected by:
a.   the child's temperament.
b.   the parents' ethnicity.
c.   the culture.
d.   all of the above.

Baumrind's Three Styles of Parenting, p. 248
Diff: E, Ans: d
42.   Comparing children in different nations and various ethnic groups suggests that the "best" parenting style:
a.   is authoritarian.
b.   is authoritative.
c.   is traditional.
d.   varies according to the culture and community.

Table 10.2: Characteristics of Parenting Styles Identified by Baumrind, p. 248
Diff: E, Ans: b
43.   Which of these parenting styles is high on warmth?
       a.   authoritarian
       b.   authoritative and permissive
       c.   indulgent
       d.   uninvolved

Techniques of Discipline, p. 249
Diff: M, Ans: a
44.   Compared to Japanese families, North American families of preschool children:
       a.   encourage more expression that is emotional.
       b.   encourage less emotional expression.
       c.   have less aggressive children.
       d.   have children that are more intelligent.

Techniques of Discipline, p. 249
Diff: H, Ans: d
45.   The "Time-out" discipline technique is harsh for the child who is:
       a.   an only child.
       b.   fearful of public shame.
       c.   seeking approval of others.
       d.   both b. and c. answers are correct.

What About Spanking?, p. 250
Diff: H, Ans: c
46.   Research on spanking suggests that it is quick and efficient at age 2 or 3, and that:
       a.   the child will become more self-controlled.
       b.   the spanking is less harmful if the parent expressed honest anger at the child's negative emotions.
       c.   it may have negative repercussions later.
       d.   the child will be less likely to shove or hit as retaliation.

What About Spanking?, p. 250
Diff: M, Ans: c
47.   Which of these is a true statement?
       a.   Only authoritarian parents physically punish their children.
       b.   Harsh physical punishment and frequent speaking is likely to produce an over-controlled child.
       c.   Physical punishment of child is unlawful for teachers as well as parents.
       d.   Ninety-eight percent of North American children were spanked as children.

The Challenge of Video, p. 251
Diff: M, Ans: c
48.   Four-year-old Bill watches television violence at least two hours a day. Most likely, as he grows older:
       a.   this experience will have no effect on him.
       b.   he will sympathize with the victims of violence.
       c.   he will become aggressive himself.
       d.   he will get tired of such programs.

The Challenge of Video, p. 251
Diff: E, Ans: b
49.   The television program most likely to have the approval of psychologists among the following is:
       a.   *Sponge Bob Square Pants.*
       b.   *Sesame Street.*
       c.   *Zoids.*
       d.   *Transformers.*

The Evidence on Content, p. 252
Diff: E, Ans: b

50.   Video violence:
   a.   has not been actually proven to increase aggression in children.
   b.   makes children more violent.
   c.   has the most effect on children over 6.
   d.   has less of a deleterious effect on children over 6.

Boy or Girl: So What?

The Development of Gender Awareness, p. 253
Diff: E, Ans: c

51.   Choose the correct statement:
   a.   Sex differences and gender differences are synonymous.
   b.   Epigeneticists focus only on genetics as a cause of behavior.
   c.   Children between 2 and 6 confuse gender and sex.
   d.   Boys appear to be more advanced in emotional regulation than girls.

The Development of Gender Awareness, p. 253
Diff: M, Ans: a

52.   Most American children develop traditional gender-role beliefs, such as that girls "become nurses," by what age?
   a.   4
   b.   6
   c.   10
   d.   12

The Development of Gender Awareness, p. 253
Diff: M, Ans: c

53.   When Sam wanted to play with dolls, his friend teased him. Sam was probably:
   a.   2 years old.
   b.   3 years old.
   c.   4 years old.
   d.   any of the above ages.

The Development of Gender Awareness, p. 253
Diff: E, Ans: a

54.   Boys prefer to play with older boys beginning at age:
   a.   2.
   b.   4.
   c.   6.
   d.   8.

The Development of Gender Awareness, p. 253
Diff: M, Ans: a

55.   The tendency for girls to prefer to play with other girls is first evident at age:
   a.   2.
   b.   4.
   c.   6.
   d.   8.

Psychoanalytic Theory, p. 254
Diff: E, Ans: b

56.   At what stage would Freud put a typical 5-year-old?
   a.   latency
   b.   phallic
   c.   genital
   d.   superego

Psychoanalytic Theory, p. 254
Diff: E, Ans: c

57.   In Freudian theory, when a little boy develops sexual feelings toward his mother and becomes jealous of his father, this is called:
   a.   the Electra complex.
   b.   penis envy.
   c.   the Oedipus complex.
   d.   identification.

Psychoanalytic Theory, p. 254
Diff: H, Ans: b

58.   Freud believed that preschool boys:
   a.   are openly angry with their fathers.
   b.   secretly want to replace their fathers.
   c.   disrespect their mothers.
   d.   believe their fathers are perfect.

Psychoanalytic Theory, p. 254
Diff: H, Ans: a

59.   Which of the following scenarios is most likely to occur during the phallic stage?
   a.   John stands between his mother and father, but he only looks at his mother.
   b.   Paul is constantly fighting with his mother.
   c.   George copies everything his mother does.
   d.   Richard is struggling with toilet training.

Psychoanalytic Theory, p. 254
Diff: M, Ans: a

60.   In order to successfully resolve the Oedipus complex, the child must:
   a.   strive to be like the father.
   b.   strive to be like the mother.
   c.   be jealous of the father.
   d.   love both parents equally.

Psychoanalytic Theory, p. 254
Diff: M, Ans: b

61.   According to Freud, how do little boys cope with the guilt of wanting to kill their fathers?
   a.   They want to kill themselves.
   b.   They identify with their father.
   c.   They become angry with their father.
   d.   They are envious of their father's penis.

Psychoanalytic Theory, p. 254
Diff: H, Ans: b

62.   The phrase that best describes the resolution of the Oedipus complex is:
   a.   "People who live in glass houses shouldn't throw stones."
   b.   "If you can't beat them, join them."
   c.   "Don't cry over spilt milk."
   d.   "Out of sight, out of mind."

Psychoanalytic Theory, p. 254
Diff: M, Ans: b

63. Freud's term for our self-critical conscience that internalizes social and parental morals is:
    a. identification.
    b. superego.
    c. ego.
    d. schema.

Psychoanalytic Theory, p. 254
Diff: E, Ans: b

64. The Electra complex is characterized by:
    a. frustration in peer relations.
    b. sexual feelings towards the father.
    c. feelings of low self-esteem and inadequacy.
    d. boys wishing they were girls.

Psychoanalytic Theory, p. 254
Diff: M, Ans: b

65. The Electra complex causes girls to:
    a. resent their father because he has a penis.
    b. adore their father and resent their mother.
    c. prefer their mother to their father.
    d. try to make peace when parents fight.

Psychoanalytic Theory, p. 254
Diff: H, Ans: d

66. According to Freud, little girls are jealous that boys have:
    a. attention from the father.
    b. attention from the mother.
    c. power in the home and in society.
    d. penises.

Psychoanalytic Theory, p. 255
Diff: M, Ans: b

67. When Professor Berger's daughters said, "When I grow up, I'm going to marry Daddy," that was an example of:
    a. modeling.
    b. the Electra complex.
    c. gender stereotyping.
    d. the Oedipus complex.

Behaviorism, p. 256
Diff: E, Ans: b

68. To understand gender attitudes and roles, learning theorists stress:
    a. biological mechanisms.
    b. reinforcement.
    c. reasoning ability.
    d. unconscious motivations.

Behaviorism, p. 256
Diff: H, Ans: d

69. Which scenario is most in line with learning theories?
    a. Lindsey has some hostility toward his father.
    b. Stevie is a 6-year-old girl who is trying to act like her father.
    c. Mick realizes that he is male and that he will always be male.
    d. Christine wears a dress, and both her parents tell her how pretty she looks.

Behaviorism, p. 256
Diff: H, Ans: c
70.   Research on parents' punishment and reinforcement of their children's nontraditional behaviors has found that:
a.   girls today are encouraged to act aggressively.
b.   mothers expect gender-appropriate behavior more than fathers do.
c.   boys are more criticized than girls are for playing with toys associated with the other sex.
d.   most parents treat their sons and daughters in the same way.

Behaviorism, p. 256
Diff: H, Ans: b
71.   A theorist who believes gender roles are learned through role models is a:
a.   cognitive theorist.
b.   behaviorist theorist.
c.   psychoanalytic theorist.
d.   neo-Freudian theorist.

Behaviorism, p. 256
Diff: E, Ans: c
72.   Behaviorist theorists believe that children learn their gender behavior by:
a.   gaining a better understanding of the world.
b.   resolving the Oedipus and the Electra complexes.
c.   observing others.
d.   doing what their parents tell them to do.

Behaviorism, p. 256
Diff: H, Ans: a
73.   According to behaviorist theorists, parents are:
a.   models for behavior.
b.   reinforcers and punishers.
c.   socializing agents.
d.   sources of identification.

Cognitive Theory, p. 256
Diff: E, Ans: d
74.   Which group of theorists supports a focus on children's understanding as opposed to observable behavior?
a.   sociocultural
b.   psychoanalytic
c.   behavioristic
d.   cognitive

Cognitive Theory, p. 257
Diff: E, Ans: c
75.   Which specialty group of researchers would best explain the concept of mental set?
a.   behaviorists
b.   epigenetic theorists
c.   cognitive theorists
d.   sociocultural theorists

Cognitive Theory, p. 257
Diff: E, Ans: b
76.   Perception of one's experiences in childhood is the focus of which theory?
a.   cognitive
b.   behavioral
c.   epigenetic
d.   sociocultural

Sociocultural Theory, p. 257
Diff: M, Ans: b

77. Which theory of childhood development would be most likely to discuss the concept of androgyny in a conversation concerning their beliefs?
   a. cognitive
   b. sociocultural
   c. psychoanalytic
   d. epigenetic

Epigenetic Theory, p. 258
Diff: E, Ans: c

78. "Every aspect of human behavior is the result of interaction between genes and early experience" is the textbook quote for the _____ theory of childhood development.
   a. cognitive
   b. sociocultural
   c. epigenetic
   d. behavioral

Epigenetic Theory, p. 258
Diff: H, Ans: d

79. Which view of childhood development asserts that girls tend to be more responsive to language than boys not because of experience?
   a. sociocultural
   b. psychoanalytic
   c. behavioral
   d. epigenetic

TRUE-FALSE QUESTIONS

Emotional Development

Ans: T, p. 237

1. Self-concept turns from factual to evaluative in becoming self-esteem.

Ans: T, p. 238

2. The typical 3-year-old might believe that she can run as fast as her 6-year-old sister can.

Ans: T, p. 238

3. Preschoolers are likely to overestimate their abilities.

Ans: T, p. 239

4. Both genes and early care experiences contribute to the regulation of emotions.

Ans: T, p. 240

5. Early extreme stress, such as chronic malnourishment, can change electrical activity, dendrite growth, and production of various hormones in the brain.

Ans: F, p. 241

6. Much of a child's passion is governed by the prefrontal cortex.

Ans: F, p. 241

7. For a child's behavior to be called *prosocial*, it must be a self-benefiting social behavior.

Ans: T, p. 242

8. It is the child's *intent* that defines hurtful behavior as antisocial.

Ans: T, p. 242

9.   Children tend to be more aggressive at age 2.

Ans: F, p. 242

10.   Japanese mothers emphasize individuality in training their children to share.

Ans: F, p. 242

11. . *Active aggression* involves forceful behavior that is an angry retaliation for someone else's actions.

Ans: T, p. 243

12.   Of the types of aggression described, instrumental aggression is common and the most likely to increase from 2 to 6 years of age.

Ans: F, p. 244

13.   Although common in North America, rough-and-tumble play is seldom seen in many other countries of the world.

Ans: T, p. 245

14.   Boys engage in more rough-and-tumble play than girls do.

Ans: T, p. 245

15.   Girls engage in more sociodramatic play than boys do.

Parenting Patterns

Ans: F, p. 246

16.   Baumrind suggested that the four features of parenting are warmth, discipline, communication, and sharing.

Ans: F, pp. 246-247

17.   Parents who make few maturity demands on their children would be considered authoritarian.

Ans: T, p. 247

18.   Parents who are nurturing, communicative, and demanding of maturity would be called authoritative.

Ans: T, p. 247

19.   Authoritarian parenting tends to produce conscientious, obedient children.

Ans: T, p. 248

20.   More authoritarian parenting is required when families live in stressful and violent neighborhoods.

Ans: F, p. 249

21.   Japanese parents allow and even encourage emotional expression of all sorts, including anger.

Ans: F, p. 250

22.   Only two out of every three American adults were spanked when they were young.

Ans: T, p. 250

23.   Most parents in North America, Asia, Africa, and South American believe that spanking is acceptable and occasionally necessary.

Ans: T, p. 250

24.   Children who are spanked are more likely to use aggression to retaliate against a peer.

Ans: F, p. 250

25. Children who experience physical punishment tend to be less aggressive than other children are.

Ans: T, p. 251

26. Children who watch many violent television shows tend to behave more aggressively than other children do.

Ans: F, p. 251

27. In television cartoons, the "bad guys" are about three times as violent as the "good guys."

Ans: T, p. 252

28. Current research on the effect of violent video programs and games indicate that these programs push children to be more violent than they would be without them.

Boy or Girl: So What?

Ans: F, p. 253

29. Children usually cannot apply gender labels with any consistency until they are 5 or 6 years old.

Ans: T, p. 253

30. By school age, children with a friend of the opposite sex will rarely play with that child while other children are around.

Ans: T, p. 253

31. In a group of 4-year-olds, a child who chooses a toy traditionally associated with the other sex is likely to be criticized by peers.

Ans: T, p. 254

32. Freud believed that homosexuality is evidence of a poorly resolved phallic stage.

Ans: T, p. 255

33. According to psychoanalytic theory, a girl in the throws of penis envy identifies with women her father finds attractive.

Ans: T, p. 256

34. Fathers are more likely than mothers to expect their sons to be tough and their daughters to be feminine.

Ans: F, p. 257

35. The sex differences remaining after the feminist revolution are biological in nature.

Ans: T, p. 258

36. According to epigenetic theory, many gender differences are genetically based.

Ans: F, p. 258

37. Boys tend to be more responsive to language than girls are, while mothers are typically more verbal than fathers are.

Ans: T, p. 258

38. Epigenetic theory stresses that the environment shapes genetic impulses.

FILL-IN-THE-BLANK QUESTIONS

Emotional Development

Ans: initiative, p. 237

1.   According to Erik Erikson, the crisis experienced by children during the play years is _____ versus guilt.

Ans: impulses; inhibitions, p. 239

2.   Externalizing problems are to _____ as internalizing problems are to _____.

Ans: antisocial, p. 242

3.   Behavior that is _____ is intended to harm someone else.

Ans: bullying, instrumental p. 243

4.   An unprovoked attack on a peer is called _____ aggression, whereas aggression used to obtain an object is called _____ aggression.

Ans: facial expressions, p. 244

5.   Adults can distinguish between a fight and rough-and-tumble play by looking at the children's _____.

Parenting Patterns

Ans: warmth, discipline, communication, maturity p. 246

6.   The four features of parenting considered by Baumrind are _____, _____, _____, and _____ expectations.

Ans: love and concern, p. 247

7.   Although Baumrind's three styles of parenting are different, they all reflect _____.

Ans: Time-out, p. 249

8.   _____ is a method of discipline that requires the child to stop all activity and sit quietly for a few minutes.

Boy Or Girl: So What?

Ans: sex, p. 253

9.   If we find that boys tend to be taller than girls are, we are discussing _____ differences.

Ans: phallic, p. 254

10.   Freud called the period from age 3 to 6 the _____ stage.

Ans: Oedipus, p. 254

11.   While experiencing Freud's _____ complex, a boy begins to masturbate, fear castration, and develops sexual feelings toward his mother.

Ans: identification, pp. 254, 255

12.   According to Freudian theory, children resolve the Oedipus and Electra complex by means of _____, a defense mechanism through which people ally themselves with a person more powerful than themselves.

Ans: reinforced/rewarded, p. 256

13.   According to learning theorists, a preschool boy learns to behave like a boy because he is _____ for gender-appropriate behaviors.

Ans: cognitive, p. 257

14.	Children develop a mental set, a _____ perception, which biases their viewpoint of the world around them.

Ans: early experience, p. 258

15.	Epigenetic theory espouses the idea that every aspect of human behavior is the result of the interaction between genes and _____.

ESSAY QUESTIONS

1.	Your preschooler has been having frequent nightmares in which he is being beaten up by another child. What should you do?

2.	Briefly describe what happens during Erikson's initiative versus guilt stage.

3.	Suggest three ways a parent might provide opportunities for social play for a 3-year-old child who has no siblings. Note at least two social skills that the child might acquire through play with peers.

4.	What is the difference between sociodramatic and rough-and-tumble play?

5.	Provide an example of sociodramatic play. Why do children engage in this type of play?

6.	You have been asked by the president of the United States to chair a special task force that is to write a national policy statement on children's exposure to television. What recommendations would you make concerning viewing hours and type of shows to be aired?

7.	From your own childhood or adolescence, provide an example of one type of aggression. This example can be something that happened to you or something you witnessed. What type of aggression was it?

8.	By what methods did Diana Baumrind measure parenting styles?

9.	Compare and contrast the three parenting styles originally described by Baumrind. Cite examples of families that you know are representative of each style and discuss how their children are developing.

10.	Which parenting style(s) did your parents use most frequently? In what ways would you say that they were typical examples of that style? Be sure to provide enough evidence of the parenting style chosen.

11.	What factors influence parenting style?

12.	Your best friend is considering having only one child. What advice would you give her?

13.	What is the difference between sex differences and gender differences? Provide some examples of each.

14.	A nursery-school teacher in New York State reports a changing attitude on the part of preschool boys. "Boys play in the kitchen more than they used to. Some of them even take on feminine personas. They'll say, 'I'll be the grandma.' On the other hand, right in the middle of this play, they will often revert to boyish behavior. They'll pick up the mops and start using them as guns." Discuss and explain the developments noted by this nursery-school teacher.

15.	According to Freud, what occurs during the phallic stage?

16.	What is penis envy? What is your opinion of it?

17.   Explain why gender-role stereotypes of men and women persist. What, if any, do you believe these
        roles should be? Be certain to support your ideas with appropriate examples.

18.   What is the core belief of the epigeneticist?

Answer guidelines to these essay questions can be found in the Appendix at the end of the Test Bank.

CHAPTER 11 The School Years: Biosocial Development

MULTIPLE-CHOICE QUESTIONS

A Healthy Time

A Healthy Time, p. 267
Diff: M, Ans: c
1. As far as physical ailments are concerned, the age range in which humans are the healthiest is:
    a. 2 to 5 years.
    b. 5 to 7 years.
    c. 7 to 11 years.
    d. 12 to 15 years.

Typical Size and Shape, p. 267
Diff: M, Ans: a
2. When you look at the rate of growth for children from ages 7 to 11, you see that:
    a. children grow more slowly than they did in early childhood.
    b. children grow faster than they did in early childhood.
    c. the rate is about the same from ages 2 to 12.
    d. children have a tremendous growth spurt during the school years.

Typical Size and Shape, p. 268
Diff: H, Ans: c
3. Gabriella, an average 10-year-old, can probably throw a ball _____ she could when she was six.
    a. the same distance as
    b. a little bit farther than
    c. twice as far as
    d. four times as far as

Childhood Obesity, p. 268
Diff: E, Ans: a
4. Being overweight means that one is _____ above the ideal weight for age and height, whereas obese means one is _____ or more above this benchmark.
    a. 20 percent; 30 percent
    b. 15 percent; 25 percent
    c. 20 pounds; 30 pounds
    d. 15 pounds; 25 pounds

Childhood Obesity, p. 268
Diff: M, Ans: b

5.   The rate of obesity in the United States has increased _____ since 1980.
     a.   50 percent
     b.   100 percent
     c.   150 percent
     d.   200 percent

Childhood Obesity, p. 268
Diff: E, Ans: b

6.   The way in which parents can best help their obese child is by:
     a.   purchasing healthier foods to bring home.
     b.   exercising with them.
     c.   not keeping microwavable food in the pantry.
     d.   not rewarding their victories with foods.

Childhood Obesity, p. 268
Diff: M, Ans: a

7.   Childhood obesity is made more complicated by:
     a.   the interaction of genes and the environment.
     b.   the number of government agencies involved.
     c.   the number of hours children watch TV.
     d.   improper health habits.

Childhood Obesity, p. 269
Diff: H, Ans: d

8.   In the United States, certain cultural groups are more likely to have obese children than are other groups because:
     a.   their children are rewarded for cleaning their plates.
     b.   American food is too high in calories.
     c.   the abundance of food is new to them.
     d.   they continue customs that previously protected against death.

Childhood Obesity, p. 269
Diff: H, Ans: d

9.   The ethnic group with the highest rate of obesity in the United States are the most recent immigrants from:
     a.   Japan.
     b.   England.
     c.   Africa.
     d.   Mexico.

Chronic Illness: The Case of Asthma, p. 269
Diff: E, Ans: c

10. The once-common childhood operation, until after 1980, was:
     a.   Beer's operation.
     b.   thyroidotomy.
     c.   tonsillectomy.
     d.   intubation of the eardrum.

Chronic Illness: The Case of Asthma, p. 269
Diff: E, Ans: b

11. The disorder that causes uncontrollable movements or noises is:
     a.   Asperger syndrome.
     b.   Tourette syndrome.
     c.   autism.
     d.   Alzheimer's.

Causes of Asthma, p. 270
Diff: M, Ans: b
12.   Asthma is a disorder caused by _____ of the airways.
  a.   enlargement
  b.   inflammation
  c.   destruction
  d.   missing portions

Causes of Asthma, p. 270
Diff: E, Ans: c
13.   Chronic inflammation of the airways is diagnosed as:
  a.   pulmonary edema.
  b.   bronchitis.
  c.   asthma.
  d.   COPD.

Causes of Asthma, p. 270
Diff: H, Ans: c
14.   The disorder having genetic contributors on chromosomes 2, 11, 12, 13, and 21 is:
  a.   Alzheimer's.
  b.   autism.
  c.   asthma.
  d.   automatization.

Prevention of Asthma, p. 270
Diff: E, Ans: a
15.   The changes made in traffic patterns in Atlanta, Georgia, for the Summer Olympics represented an unexpected _____ level of prevention for asthma.
  a.   primary
  b.   secondary
  c.   tertiary
  d.   none of the above.

Prevention of Asthma, p. 271
Diff: E, Ans: c
16.   Mary, age 10, has asthma. Her parents bought a HEPA filter for her bedroom. This represents which level of prevention?
  a.   primary
  b.   secondary
  c.   tertiary
  d.   none of the above.

Prevention of Asthma, p. 271
Diff: E, Ans: c
17.   An asthmatic child who gets shots in the doctor's office is operating at the _____ level of prevention.
  a.   primary
  b.   secondary
  c.   tertiary
  d.   none of the above.

Brain Development

Attention and Automatization, p. 272
Diff: E, Ans: c

18. One of the major differences in brain development that distinguishes middle childhood is the development of:
   a. lateralization.
   b. myelination.
   c. automatization.
   d. left-right coordination.

Attention and Automatization, p. 272
Diff: M, Ans: d

19. Extensive neural myelination allows:
   a. sensory neurons to carry messages faster than motor neurons.
   b. the normal brain to correct errors made in the genetic code for autism.
   c. academic intelligence to develop.
   d. selective attention to improve.

Attention and Automatization, p. 272
Diff: E, Ans: c

20. The process by which thoughts and actions are repeated in sequence enough times to no longer require much conscious thought is called:
   a. habituation.
   b. practice.
   c. automatization.
   d. coordination.

Attention and Automatization, p. 272
Diff: M, Ans: d

21. Growth in brain sophistication during middle childhood allows the child to direct his or her focus on certain self-chosen environmental elements to the exclusion of others. This ability is known as:
   a. automatization.
   b. decentration.
   c. transduction.
   d. selective attention.

Motor Skills, p. 273
Diff: E, Ans: a

22. The time it takes for someone to respond to a particular stimulus is:
   a. reaction time.
   b. response time.
   c. reflex time.
   d. about 2 seconds.

Motor Skills, p. 273
Diff: H, Ans: c

23. In a game of dodge ball played by a large group of second-graders, the same children regularly get hit with the ball. This probably is due to:
   a. sex differences in motor skills.
   b. poor gross-motor skills.
   c. slow reaction time.
   d. lack of practice.

Motor Skills, p. 273
Diff: E, Ans: d
24. Which group of children would have the quickest reaction time?
  a. 2-year-olds
  b. 6-year-olds
  c. 9-year-olds
  d. 12-year olds

Motor Skills, p. 273
Diff: E, Ans: a
25. The time it takes for someone to respond to a particular stimulus is:
  a. reaction time.
  b. response time.
  c. reflex time.
  d. about 2 seconds.

Motor Skills, p. 273
Diff: M, Ans: d
26. One researcher believes that allowing boys to play in an active, rough-and-tumble fashion may:
  a. make them fidgety in school.
  b. increase aggressiveness in school.
  c. teach them to be bullies.
  d. help them overcome learning disabilities.

Tests of Ability, p. 274
Diff: E, Ans: b
27. The terms "MA" and "CA" were used to compute:
  a. achievement on the WAIS.
  b. the intelligence quotient in children.
  c. the intelligence quotient in adults.
  d. intelligence on the WPPSI.

Tests of Ability, p. 274
Diff: M, Ans: a
28. April is tested on her mastery of college chemistry. What kind of test is this?
  a. achievement
  b. IQ
  c. field
  d. aptitude

Tests of Ability, p. 274
Diff: H, Ans: a
29. Although the test you are now taking measures many things, it is supposed to be a test of:
  a. achievement.
  b. aptitude.
  c. intelligence.
  d. general knowledge.

Tests of Ability, p. 274
Diff: E, Ans: b
30. Aptitude tests are designed to measure:
  a. how much has been learned.
  b. potential for accomplishment.
  c. capacity for divergent thinking.
  d. verbal abilities.

Tests of Ability, p. 274
Diff: E, Ans: a

31. Achievement tests are designed to measure:
    a. how much has been learned.
    b. potential for accomplishment.
    c. capacity for divergent thinking.
    d. verbal abilities.

Tests of Ability, p. 274
Diff: H, Ans: c

32. Achievement tests are to aptitude tests as:
    a. long is to short.
    b. intelligence is to creativity.
    c. knowledge is to potential.
    d. fruit is to apple.

Tests of Ability, p. 274
Diff: M, Ans: a

33. Both the Stanford-Binet and Wechsler are:
    a. intelligence scales.
    b. performed entirely with pencil and paper.
    c. achievement tests.
    d. used only for children born in the United States.

Tests of Ability, p. 274
Diff: E, Ans: c

34. How much a child has actually learned is measured by a(n):
    a. aptitude test.
    b. Piagetian test.
    c. achievement test.
    d. intelligence test.

Tests of Ability, p. 274
Diff: H, Ans: a

35. Which group are there no Wechsler tests in?
    a. adolescents
    b. adults
    c. school-age children
    d. preschoolers

Tests of Ability, p. 274
Diff: H, Ans: a

36. The IQ test specifically designed for school-aged children is the:
    a. WISC.
    b. WAIS.
    c. Stanford-Binet.
    d. Lorge-Thorndike.

Tests of Ability, p. 274
Diff: H, Ans: d

37. The item which was defined originally as the mental age divided by one's chronological age and multiplied by 100 is the:
    a. PIQ.
    b. VIQ.
    c. concept of aptitude.
    d. IQ.

Tests of Ability, p. 274
Diff: M, Ans: d
38. Which of these IQ tests is specific for preschoolers?
 a. the WISC
 b. the WAIS
 c. the Stanford-Binet
 d. the WPPSI

Fig. 11.2: In Theory, Most People Are Average, p. 274
Diff: H, Ans: b
39. About two-thirds of all those who take IQ tests score in the "average" range, that is, between 85 and:
 a. 100.
 b. 115.
 c. 125.
 d. 135.

Fig. 11.2: In Theory, Most People Are Average, p. 274
Diff: H, Ans: b
40. Sara has an IQ of 90, and Chuck's IQ is 114. Sara would be classified as _____ and Chuck as _____.
 a. a slow learner; gifted
 b. average; average
 c. mentally retarded; gifted
 d. average; gifted

Fig. 11.2: In Theory, Most People Are Average, p. 274
Diff: H, Ans: b
41. About 70 percent of all those who take IQ test score in the "average" range, that is, between 85 and:
 a. 100.
 b. 115.
 c. 125.
 d. 135.

Fig. 11.2: In Theory, Most People Are Average, p. 274
Diff: H, Ans: b
42. With an IQ of 118, Alan would be classified as _____. Ginny, whose IQ is 113, would be classified as _____.
 a. gifted; average
 b. superior; average
 c. superior; superior
 d. average; a slow learner

Criticisms of IQ Testing, p. 275
Diff: H, Ans: b
43. Which of the following is *not* one of the three distinct types of intelligence described by Robert Sternberg?
 a. academic
 b. self-knowledge
 c. creative
 d. practical

Criticisms of IQ Testing, p. 275
Diff: M, Ans: d

44.   Howard Gardner believes that:
        a.   there are twelve distinct intelligences.
        b.   everyone is equal in all types of intelligence.
        c.   IQ tests are the best way to measure intelligence.
        d.   musical ability is a type of intelligence.

Criticisms of IQ Testing, p. 275
Diff: M, Ans: b

45.   The description of an aptitude test as giving a score for *spatial intelligence* belongs to the suggestions
        and theory of:
        a.   Robert Sternberg.
        b.   Howard Gardner.
        c.   David Wechsler.
        d.   Alfred Binet.

Criticisms of IQ Testing, p. 275
Diff: M, Ans: b

46.   Robert Sternberg suggested three types of intelligence, *creative*, *practical*, and:
        a.   *divergent*.
        b.   *academic*.
        c.   *linguistic*.
        d.   *kinesthetic*.

Children with Special Needs

Children with Special Needs, p. 277
Diff: H, Ans: c

47.   In 1999, approximately what percentage of all 7- to 11-year-olds in the United States were special-
        needs children (including those who were not formally identified)?
        a.   15
        b.   22
        c.   26
        d.   34

Children with Special Needs, p. 277
Diff: M, Ans: d

48.   Aggression, anxiety, Asperger syndrome, depression, attention-deficit disorder, and attachment
        disorder are all diagnoses which describe a(n):
        a.   biological anomaly.
        b.   child with special needs.
        c.   inherited tendency.
        d.   all of the above.

Children with Special Needs, p. 277
Diff: H, Ans: a

49.   Down syndrome, Asperger syndrome, and depression all begin with:
        a.   a biological anomaly.
        b.   slowed reaction time in answering questions.
        c.   attention-deficit.
        d.   a broken chromosome.

Developmental Psychopathology, p. 277
Diff: E, Ans: c
50.   Insights from normal development are applied to the study of childhood disorders in:
      a.   abnormal psychology of childhood.
      b.   pediatric pathology.
      c.   developmental psychopathology.
      d.   special education.

Developmental Psychopathology, p. 278
Diff: E, Ans: b
51.   Developmental psychopathology has given us the following lesson applicable to all children:
      a.   Pathology as it relates to children is a static issue.
      b.   Abnormality is normal.
      c.   Most childhood disorders have been misdiagnosed.
      d.   Adulthood is an exaggeration of childhood disorders.

Developmental Psychopathology, p. 278
Diff: M Ans: c
52.   Having a developmental perspective on any special problem that a child might have makes it clear that the symptoms of the problem:
      a.   intensify as the child grows older.
      b.   remain stable across the life span.
      c.   change as the child grows older.
      d.   are apparent in the first year of life.

Developmental Psychopathology, p. 278
Diff: M, Ans: d
53.   When children with special needs become adults, their disability usually:
      a.   disappears.
      b.   gets worse.
      c.   gets better.
      d.   changes—for better or worse.

Developmental Psychopathology, p. 279
Diff: E, Ans: b
54.   The DSM-IV-R is a manual for:
      a.   comparing schools on compliance with laws regarding special education in the United States.
      b.   diagnosing mental disorders.
      c.   educating children with special needs.
      d.   none of the above.

Developmental Psychopathology, p. 279
Diff: E, Ans: c
55.   The current manual for diagnosing childhood and other psychiatric disorders is the:
      a.   DSM IIIR.
      b.   DSM-IV.
      c.   DSM-IV-R.
      d.   DSM V.

Table 11.1: Prevalence of Some Categories of Childhood Psychopathology, p. 278
Diff: H, Ans: b
56.   The DSM-IV-R category containing both autism and Asperger syndrome is:
      a.   Conduct Disorder.
      b.   Pervasive Developmental Disorder.
      c.   Communicative Disorders.
      d.   Serious Emotional Disturbance.

Table 11.1: Prevalence of Some Categories of Childhood Psychopathology, p. 278
Diff: H, Ans: c

57.   Bullying, cruelty to animals, and lying belongs to the pathological category of:
      a.   communicative disorder.
      b.   pervasive developmental disorder.
      c.   conduct disorder.
      d.   serious emotional disturbance.

Table 11.1:Prevalence of Some Categories of Childhood Psychopathology, p. 278
Diff: E, Ans: d

58.   Hostility toward authorities is one of the basic indicators of _____, according to the DSM-IV-R.
      a.   attention-deficit disorder
      b.   conduct disorder
      c.   mental retardation
      d.   oppositional defiant disorder

Table 11.1: Prevalence of Some Categories of Childhood Psychopathology, p. 278
Diff: E, Ans: a

59.   Stuttering is an example of a(n):
      a.   communicative disorder.
      b.   attention-deficit disorder.
      c.   culture-bound disorder.
      d.   serious emotional disturbance.

Pervasive Developmental Disorders, p. 279
Diff: E, Ans: b

60.   Severe problems affecting many aspects of a young child's psychological growth are called:0
      a.   school phobias.
      b.   pervasive developmental disorders.
      c.   attention-deficit disorders.
      d.   culture-bound syndromes.

Incidence, p. 280
Diff: H, Ans: b

61.   Which of the following is a true statement concerning autism?
      a.   Autism rates are twice as high among girls as among boys.
      b.   Autism rates are four times as high among boys as among girls.
      c.   Autism is no longer a "rare" disorder in children.
      d.   About 1 out of every 500 children shows autistic traits.

Incidence, p. 280
Diff: H, Ans: b

62.   Kanner's definition describes autistic children as:
      a.   easily bored by predictable routines.
      b.   unable to relate to people in an ordinary way.
      c.   suffering from severe depression.
      d.   excessively talkative and active.

Incidence, p. 280
Diff: H, Ans: a

63.   The disorder mentioned in the text that affects only girls is:
      a.   Rett syndrome.
      b.   Tourette syndrome.
      c.   Asperger syndrome.
      d.   echolalia.

Possible Causes, p. 280
Diff: H, Ans: c
64.   Most likely, autism is caused by:
   a.   genetic factors alone.
   b.   parents' early child-care methods.
   c.   genetic vulnerability coupled with other factors.
   d.   uncaring, cold parents, especially the mother.

Possible Causes, p. 280
Diff: M, Ans: b
65.   The belief that childhood immunization sometimes causes a pervasive developmental disorder:
   a.   has finally been established with the case of "Billy" (A Case to Study).
   b.   has been disproved.
   c.   shows how delicate and susceptible some children are to this disorder.
   d.   goes far in explaining how many of these childhood disorders are caused.

Changes over Time, p. 280
Diff: M, Ans: b
66.   Children with Asperger syndrome:
   a.   are severely malnourished.
   b.   might be viewed as "high-functioning autistics."
   c.   have the most severe form of autism.
   d.   constantly repeat certain words and phrases.

Changes over Time, p. 280
Diff: E, Ans: c
67.   Individuals with Asperger syndrome:
   a.   have classic autism.
   b.   are mute for life.
   c.   function better than most autistics.
   d.   need to be institutionalized.

Changes over Time, p. 280
Diff: H, Ans: b
68.   Research on autism has revealed that:
   a.   Kanner's original definition was too broad.
   b.   some autistic children are quite intelligent.
   c.   autism is more common in girls than in boys.
   d.   symptoms usually first appear at about age 9.

Changes over Time, p. 280
Diff: M, Ans: d
69.   Many autistic infants are:
   a.   bored by routine.
   b.   disturbed by pain.
   c.   affectionate to other children.
   d.   disturbed by noise.

Changes over Time, pp. 280-281
Diff: H, Ans: b
70.   In early childhood, autistic children have difficulty:
   a.   with fine motor skills.
   b.   in communication ability.
   c.   having to play by themselves.
   d.   all of the above.

Changes over Time, p. 281
Diff: M, Ans: a
71.   Children engaging in echolalia tend to repeat:
      a.   whatever they have just heard.
      b.   the same words and phrases over and over.
      c.   certain motions.
      d.   whatever they just saw someone else doing.

Changes over Time, p. 281
Diff: H, Ans: a
72.   The most devastating problem for autistic individuals as they grow up is their lack of:
      a.   social understanding.
      b.   motor skills.
      c.   intelligence.
      d.   imagination.

Changes over Time, p. 281
Diff: E, Ans: c
73.   The best way to help autistic children is to provide:
      a.   psychoanalysis of their parents.
      b.   the same set of expectations for them as for normal children.
      c.   early, preventative intervention for their language difficulties.
      d.   an active social environment.

Changes over Time, p. 281
Diff: M, Ans: c
74.   On intelligence tests, young autistic individuals tend to score:
      a.   so poorly that they cannot be scored.
      b.   on the low end of the average range.
      c.   mentally retarded, with good scores in certain areas.
      d.   mentally retarded, with all scores equally low.

Changes over Time, p. 281
Diff: H, Ans: c
75.   During adolescence, most autistic children:
      a.   do not talk.
      b.   do not go to school.
      c.   are deficient in social skills.
      d.   exhibit echolalia.

Changes over Time, p. 281
Diff: M, Ans: b
76.   A child with Asperger syndrome, as an adult:
      a.   will function well socially.
      b.   may function well in a business environment.
      c.   will likely do poorly in work demanding attention to small details.
      d.   will most likely be unable to function in any environment.

Changes over Time, p. 281
Diff: H Ans: c
77.   Four-year-old Carla is autistic. An early sign was probably that she:
      a.   was a very difficult baby.
      b.   stuttered when she first started talking.
      c.   did not like playing with others.
      d.   expressed terrifying fantasies.

Changes over Time, p. 281
Diff: M, Ans: b
78. In dealing with children with autism, most experts in behavioral genetics would most prefer:
     a. that the disorder turn out to have a genetic basis.
     b. early prevention intervention.
     c. quick intervention when language problems affect other developmental areas.
     d. none of the above.

Attention-Deficit Disorders, p. 281
Diff: M, Ans: d
79. Children with attention-deficit disorders:
     a. are always impulsive.
     b. are always objective.
     c. are able to concentrate momentarily.
     d. experience difficulty in concentrating.

Attention-Deficit Disorders, p. 281
Diff: E, Ans: b
80. The main symptom of ADHD is:
     a. hyperactivity.
     b. poor concentration.
     c. poor reading skills.
     d. inability to play normally.

Attention-Deficit Disorders, p. 281
Diff: E, Ans: c
81. Todd runs around the classroom, can't seem to sit still or concentrate, and is easily excited. He is most likely to be diagnosed as having:
     a. mental retardation.
     b. a sensory deficit.
     c. attention-deficit hyperactivity disorder.
     d. childhood schizophrenia.

Attention-Deficit Disorders, p. 281
Diff: E, Ans: c
82. David is excitable, impulsive, and very active in addition to having difficulty concentrating. He probably has:
     a. ADD.
     b. ADDA.
     c. ADHD.
     d. an anxiety disorder.

Attention-Deficit Disorders, p. 281
Diff: M, Ans: d
83. Who is the most likely to be diagnosed as ADHD?
     a. Hayley, a British girl who is highly excitable and always seems to be in motion.
     b. Howard, an aggressive British boy who seems bored in class.
     c. Mimi, a North American girl who is depressed because of her concentration difficulties.
     d. Scott, a North American boy who has concentration difficulties and is very impulsive.

Attention-Deficit Disorders, p. 282
Diff: H, Ans: c
84.   The underlying problem in ADHD is most likely:
    a.   lack of motivation.
    b.   poor schooling.
    c.   a neurological difficulty involving neurotransmitters.
    d.   poor parental discipline.

Attention-Deficit Disorders, p. 282
Diff: H, Ans: a
85.   The brain neurotransmitters believed, in some way, to be responsible for attention-deficit disorder are:
    a.   norepinephrine and dopamine.
    b.   GABA and acetylcholine.
    c.   histamine and epinephrine.
    d.   substance P and endorphins.

Attention-Deficit Disorders, p. 282
Diff: H, Ans: b
86.   The sex ratio of children with ADHD is _____ boy(s) to one girl.
    a.   ten
    b.   four
    c.   two
    d.   one

Learning Disabilities, p. 282
Diff: M, Ans: d
87.   According to the usual definition, a child with a learning disability often:
    a.   has notable vision or hearing problems.
    b.   is of low intelligence.
    c.   lives in stressful environments.
    d.   has no real physical handicap.

Learning Disabilities, p. 282
Diff: E, Ans: c
88.   If an intelligent 8-year-old could not read, this might be attributed to:
    a.   dysgraphia.
    b.   dysphonemia.
    c.   dyslexia.
    d.   dyscalcula.

Learning Disabilities, p. 282
Diff: E, Ans: a
89.   Expressing a significant delay in a specific area of learning not associated with a physical handicap, mental retardation, or stressful environment is known as having a(n):
    a.   learning disability.
    b.   dyslexia.
    c.   disapproprio externalis.
    d.   ADD disorder.

Learning Disabilities, p. 282
Diff: M, Ans: a
90.   The most common learning disorder is:
    a.   dyslexia.
    b.   discalcula.
    c.   autism.
    d.   Asperger syndrome.

Treatment of Attention-Deficit Disorders, p. 283
Diff: M, Ans: a
91.   When hyperactive children are given stimulants such as amphetamines, many of them respond by:
      a.   calming down.
      b.   having hallucinations.
      c.   becoming depressed and angry.
      d.   becoming even more active.

Treatment of Attention-Deficit Disorders, p. 283
Diff: E, Ans: a
92.   Psychoactive drugs that are given to hyperactive children:
      a.   enable some children to sit still and concentrate.
      b.   typically cause addiction later on, including addiction to heroin.
      c.   make psychological therapy unnecessary.
      d.   are used as reinforcement.

Treatment of Attention-Deficit Disorders, p. 283
Diff: H, Ans: b
93.   In 1999, approximately how many new prescriptions for Ritalin were prescribed in the United States?
      a.   4 million
      b.   11 million
      c.   15 million
      d.   19.6 million

Treatment of Attention-Deficit Disorders, p. 283
Diff: M, Ans: c
94.   The drug Ritalin is actually a(n):
      a.   chemical depressant.
      b.   anti-anxiety medication.
      c.   brand name for methylphenidate.
      d.   cleansing chemical used in processing meat.

Educating Children with Special Needs, p. 284
Diff: H, Ans: a
95.   A friend's child has just been diagnosed with ADHD. Based on what you have learned from the text, you might emphasize to your friend the importance of:
      a.   finding the proper classroom environment.
      b.   avoiding prescription drugs.
      c.   accepting that the child will always be a slow learner.
      d.   keeping sugar and caffeine out of the child's diet.

Educating Children with Special Needs, p. 284
Diff: M, Ans: c
96.   Maria has dyslexia. Maria is taught in the regular classroom, where she has her own reading tutor for part of the day. This is an example of:
      a.   mainstreaming.
      b.   resource room.
      c.   inclusion.
      d.   indoctrination.

TRUE-FALSE QUESTIONS

A Healthy Time

Ans: T, p. 267
1.   Ages 7 to 11 are the healthiest time of life in the United States, as far as physical ailments are concerned.

Ans: T, fig. 11.1, p. 267
2.   In developed nations, children aged 7 to 11 are generally the healthiest humans of all. They are least likely to die or become seriously ill or injured.

Ans: T, p. 268
3.   Lung capacity increases each year during the school years.

Ans: T, p. 268
4.   A typical 8-year-old weighs 55 pounds.

Ans: F, p. 268
5.   The weight at which a child is considered obese is the same for all children of the same age.

Ans: T, p. 268
6.   The rate of obesity among American children has doubled since 1980.

Ans: F, p. 268
7.   Overweight adults who were obese as children have fewer psychophysiological problems than those who became overweight in adulthood.

Ans: T, p. 268
8.   Children are overweight if their weight is 20 percent above their ideal weight for their age and height.

Ans: F, p. 268
9.   Parents should do nothing about the weight of an obese child because the child will usually outgrow the obesity by adolescence.

Ans: F, pp. 268-269
10.   The increased rate of obesity in the United States is primary due to heredity.

Ans: F, p. 270
11.   Asthma rates have stayed relatively constant since 1980.

Ans: F, p. 269
12.   Tonsillectomies are no longer performed on young children.

Ans: T, p. 269
13.   Tourette syndrome creates uncontrollable noises and/or movements.

Ans: F, p. 270
14.   As of 2003, 28 percent of all school-age children had physical problems that limited their performance.

Ans: F, p. 270
15.   Pet hair, dust mites, and pollution are causes of asthma.

Ans: T, p. 270
16.   Asthma is associated with crowded urban living conditions.

Brain Development

Ans: T, p. 271
17.   Less than one-half of U.S. children with asthma are receiving adequate tertiary prevention of the disorder.

Ans: F, p. 273
18.   A child's reaction time is determined by his or her level of muscular development.

Ans: F, p. 273
19.   In determining competence for physical activities in middle childhood, sex is as much of a factor as are age and experience.

Ans: F, p. 273
20.   During the elementary school years, boys tend to be more flexible than girls.

Ans: T, p. 273
21.   Continuing development of the corpus callosum allows for improved development of motor coordination in the school years.

Ans: T, p. 273
22.   About 6 percent of children have motor coordination problems that cause them to have difficulty in school achievement.

Ans: F, p. 274
23.   An intelligence test is an example of an achievement test.

Ans: T, p. 274
24.   An intelligence test is an example of an aptitude test.

Ans: T, fig. 11.2, p. 274
25.   About 70 percent of all people score between 85 and 115 on IQ tests.

Ans: F, fig. 11.2, p. 274
26.   All those scoring below 90 on IQ tests are classified as being mentally retarded.

Ans: T, p. 275
27.   Sternberg's 3 types of intelligence were *academic*, *creative*, and *practical*.

Children with Special Needs

Ans: T, p. 276
28.   Clumsiness in motor skill areas is one of the first problems noticed in children with special needs.

Ans: F, p. 277
29.   Sensitive parents should be able to detect almost all of their children's problems while they are at home.

Ans: F, p. 277
30.   Special needs children are created as a direct consequence of an obvious physical handicap in 22 percent of cases in the United States.

Ans: T, Table 11.1, p. 278
31.   The greatest percentage of special needs children lie within the category of communicative disorders.

Ans: T, p. 280

32.   Autism rates are four times as high among boys as among girls.

Ans: F, p. 280

33.   About 1 out of every 500 children shows autistic traits.

Ans: F, p. 280

34.   Autism rates are twice as high among girls as among boys.

Ans: T, p. 280

35.   It is clear from twin studies that genetic factors probably play a role in autism.

Ans: T, p. 280

36.   The autistic-like category which is sometimes called high-functioning autism is known as Asperger syndrome.

Ans: F, p. 281

37.   Autistic children are invariably less skilled than normal children in all areas of development.

Ans: F, p. 281

38.   Children repeating verbatim television jingles or phrases said to them is an example of *echopraxia*.

Ans: F, p. 282

39.   According to the DSM-IV, about 10 percent of all children have dyslexia.

Ans: T, p. 282

40.   In a sample of 100 children with attention-deficit hyperactivity disorder, chances are that 80 of them will be boys.

Ans: T, p. 282

41.   Children with *dyslexia* have trouble reading.

Ans: F, p. 284

42.   Mainstreaming involves placing children with special needs in the regular classroom while also having the child receive special individualized instruction.

Ans: F, p. 285

43.   Learning disabilities are frequently caused by a lack of effort on the child's part.

FILL-IN-THE-BLANK QUESTIONS

A Healthy Time

Ans: exercise, p. 268

1.   One of the best things parents can do for their overweight or obese child is to _____ with them.

Ans: overweight, p. 268

2.   To be 20 percent over one's ideal weight for age and height is called being _____.

Ans: obese, p. 268

3.   To be 30 percent over one's ideal weight for age and height is called being _____.

Ans: television watching, p. 269

4.   One leisure activity that is directly correlated with obesity in children is _____.

Ans: tonsillectomy, p. 269
5.   The type of surgery quite common before 1980 that "practically every child" experienced is _____.

Ans: primary prevention, p. 270
6.   The best approach level for prevention of asthma is _____.

Brain Development

Ans: reaction time, p. 273
7.   The length of time it takes a person to respond to a particular stimulus is called _____.

Ans: brain, p. 273
8.   The key factor in determining reaction time is the level of maturation of the _____.

Ans: age, p. 273
9.   When it comes to sports in which reaction time is crucial, a child's _____ has a more important effect on performance than does sex or body size.

Ans: achievement, p. 274
10.   A test designed to see how well a child is reading in the third grade is called a(n) _____ test.

Ans: achievement, p. 274
11.   We should use a(n) _____ test to measure how much a person knows about a particular subject.

Ans: aptitude, p. 274
12.   The ability to master a certain skill is referred to as a(n) _____.

Ans: Wechsler, p. 274
13.   One of the two highly regarded IQ tests mentioned in the text is the Stanford-Binet. The other is the _____.

Children with Special Needs

Ans: special needs, p. 277
14.   Children with _____ have difficulties learning new skills and developing friendships because of a psychological or physical disorder.

Ans: psychopathology, p. 277
15.   The new field that studies the development of childhood psychological disorders is developmental _____.

Ans: Diagnostic and Statistical Manual of Mental Disorders (or DSM-IV), p. 279
16.   To diagnose emotional and behavioral disorders psychologists rely on the diagnostic guide called _____, which is published by the American Psychiatric Association.

Ans: stimulation or noise, p. 280
17.   Many autistic children are unusually sensitive to _____.

Ans: attention-deficit hyperactivity disorder, p. 281
18.   ADHD stands for _____.

Ans: learning disability, p. 282
19.   A failing in a specific cognitive skill that is not attributable to an overall intellectual slowness, a physical condition, or an environmental problem is a(n) _____.

Ans: performance, p. 282

20.   The key criterion for diagnosing a learning disability is a significant disparity between expected and actual _____ in a particular area.

Ans: learning disability, p. 282

21.   A failing in a specific cognitive skill that is not attributable to an overall intellectual slowness, a physical condition, or an environmental problem is a(n) _____.

Ans: Ritalin, p. 283

22.   Certain psychoactive drugs that stimulate adults have a reverse effect on hyperactive children; among these is the drug _____.

Ans: resource, p. 284

23.   With a ____ room, a special needs child spends part of the day with a specially trained teacher in a designated room.

ESSAY QUESTIONS

1.   What are the major causes of obesity?

2.   You have been hired as a consultant by your local Department of Health to develop a program of education, counseling, and activities to promote healthy eating and weight loss in your community. What would you suggest?

3.   You are trying to design a new athletic program for your daughter's elementary school. You want to make the program fun for all children. Besides cost, what kinds of things should you keep in mind while designing the program?

4.   Five-year-old Karla is interested in dancing and wants to be a ballerina. Her dance teacher, however, offers her only "creative movement." "No classical ballet training at this age," says the teacher. What is the likely reason behind the teacher's decision? What general principle does it reflect? Do you agree?

5.   Discuss what intelligence tests evaluate, what the scores tend to predict, and what factors can affect the score obtained.

6.   What kinds of things are measured with the Stanford-Binet and Wechsler tests? Be specific.

7.   How concerned should a parent be if his child scores 82 on an I.Q. test?

8.   What are some of the symptoms of autism?

9.   You are asked to write an article, aimed at nonprofessionals, to appeal for help for learning-disabled children. What would you say to help them understand these disabilities?

10.   Seven-year-old Brian has been diagnosed as having attention-deficit hyperactivity disorder. What can his parents and teachers do to help him cope with this disability?

11.   You have a child with special needs. Where would you like to see your child placed in the school? What would you say if you were the teacher?

Answer guidelines to these essay questions can be found in the Appendix at the end of the Test Bank.

CHAPTER 12

The School Years: Cognitive Development

MULTIPLE-CHOICE QUESTIONS

Building on Piaget and Vygotksy

Building on Piaget and Vygotksy, p. 289
Diff: E, Ans: c
1. According to Piaget, the distinguishing characteristic of school-age children is that they are:
   a. imaginative.
   b. friendly.
   c. logical.
   d. fearless.

Building on Piaget and Vygotksy, p. 289
Diff: E, Ans: c
2. According to Piaget, a child between the ages of 7 and 11 can apply logical principles to:
   a. abstractions, such as truth and justice.
   b. chemistry and physics.
   c. concrete and visible examples.
   d. questions of social justice, such as in capitalism and in socialism.

Building on Piaget and Vygotksy, p. 289
Diff: E, Ans: d
3. Between the ages of 7 and 11, Piaget believed that children are in the period of:
   a. latency.
   b. preoperational thought.
   c. metacognitive thought.
   d. concrete operational thought.

Building on Piaget and Vygotksy, p. 289
Diff: M, Ans: b
4. When capable of concrete operational thought, children:
   a. are limited to intuitive, perceptual focusing.
   b. can apply their reasoning to real situations.
   c. can reason about abstractions.
   d. are likely to be misled by appearances.

Building on Piaget and Vygotksy, p. 289
Diff: M, Ans: a
5. With concrete operational thought, children can:
   a. think logically about tangible things.
   b. think logically about tangible things and abstract ideas.
   c. consistently make good decisions.
   d. solve most problems on their own.

Logical Principles, pp. 290-291
Diff: M, Ans: a

6.   The cognitive concept called "identity" is best illustrated by which statement?
        a.   "Even though they are an omelet now, they are still two eggs."
        b.   "If you'll let me have one of your cookies, I'll let you use my new crayons."
        c.   "If you give back my doll, we can be friends again."
        d.   "Mommy can make my scraped knee well again."

Logical Principles, p. 290
Diff: H, Ans: a

7.   The Piagetian concept that certain characteristics of an object remain the same despite changes in the object's appearance is:
        a.   identity.
        b.   reversibility.
        c.   reciprocity.
        d.   object permanence.

Logical Principles, p. 290
Diff: H, Ans: d

8.   Because she understands that categories are _____, Jeanette understands that basketball is a sport, a game, a participatory activity, and a spectator activity.
        a.   hierarchical
        b.   separate
        c.   propagated
        d.   overlapping

Logical Principles, p. 291
Diff: E, Ans: a

9.   Which of the following demonstrates the principle of reversibility?
        a.   Addition can be used to undo subtraction.
        b.   There is still only one pizza regardless of how many slices we make.
        c.   The teenager in the photograph is Grandpa.
        d.   A frog was once a tadpole.

Logical Principles, pp. 290-291
Diff: M, Ans: d

10.   Greta has recently grasped the idea that the sum of 25 can be achieved in a variety of ways (24+1, 10+15, etc.). Greta has grasped the principle of:
        a.   conservation.
        b.   reversibility.
        c.   reciprocity.
        d.   identity.

Logical Principles, p. 291
Diff: E, Ans: a

11.   Because she understands reversibility, Darcie believes that:
        a.   if she doesn't like her snowman, she can always tear it apart and redistribute the snow.
        b.   her brother will get in trouble if he breaks his mother's favorite vase.
        c.   adults never grow younger.
        d.   she can wear her sweater inside out or backwards.

Logic and Culture, p. 290
Diff: M, Ans: d
12. Piaget has provided us with the _____ of children's concepts, whereas Vygotsky has provided us with the _____.
    a. how; why
    b. developmental steps; cultural influence
    c. individual context; social context
    d. all of the above

Logic and Culture, p. 292
Diff: M, Ans: c
13. When Brazilian children in middle childhood were tested on mathematical ability:
    a. their skills were far superior to those of North American schoolchildren.
    b. their skills were far inferior to those of North American schoolchildren.
    c. they did poorly when given a pencil-and-paper test, but did well orally.
    d. they did well when given a pencil-and-paper test, but were shy about answering spoken questions.

Logic and Culture, p. 292
Diff: E, Ans: d
14. Piaget underestimated the influence of _____ in understanding cognitive development in children:
    a. context
    b. instruction
    c. culture
    d. all of the above

Logic and Culture, p. 292
Diff: E, Ans: c
15. Because Piaget underestimated the influence of context, he _____ the differences between children.
    a. didn't consider
    b. overestimated
    c. underestimated
    d. none of the above

Logic and Culture, p. 292
Diff: E, Ans: b
16. Lawrence Kohlberg built on the theories of _____ in his description of the stages of moral development.
    a. Sigmund Freud
    b. Jean Piaget
    c. Erik Erikson
    d. Carol Gilligan

Kohlberg's Stages, p. 293
Diff: E, Ans: b
17. Identify the stage *not* belonging with the others:
    a. postconventional
    b. unconventional
    c. preconventional
    d. conventional

Kohlberg's Stages, p. 293
Diff: E, Ans: b

18.   Which Piagetian stage of development matches Kohlberg's stage of preconventional morality?
        a.   the sensorimotor period
        b.   the preoperational stage
        c.   concrete operations
        d.   formal operations

Kohlberg's Stages, p. 293
Diff: E, Ans: d

19.   Which Piagetian stage of development matches Kohlberg's stage of postconventional morality?
        a.   the sensorimotor period
        b.   the preoperational stage
        c.   concrete operations
        d.   formal operations

Kohlberg's Stages, p. 294
Diff: E, Ans: d

20.   The most famous study of the ethical dilemmas of moral development was conducted by:
        a.   Lev Vygotsky.
        b.   Erik Erikson.
        c.   Jean Piaget.
        d.   Lawrence Kohlberg.

Kohlberg's Stages, p. 293
Diff: E, Ans: c

21.   Kohlberg developed a famous story in a study of the development of:
        a.   moral actions.
        b.   cultural differences in ethics.
        c.   moral reasoning.
        d.   how a person acts toward others.

Kohlberg's Stages, p. 294
Diff: H, Ans: a

22.   To measure a person's stage of moral development, Kohlberg examined:
        a.   how the person thinks about moral questions.
        b.   what a person concludes about moral questions.
        c.   overall intelligence.
        d.   how a person acts with others.

Kohlberg's Stages, p. 294
Diff: H, Ans: b

23.   Kohlberg measured morality by:
        a.   determining what people felt was right or wrong.
        b.   analyzing how people reason about what is right and wrong.
        c.   watching how people behave in morally ambivalent situations.
        d.   analyzing the words people choose when explaining their answers.

Kohlberg's Three Levels and Six Stages of Moral Reasoning (Table 12.1), p. 293
Diff: M, Ans: c

24.   Preconventional morality involves:
        a.   the careful consideration of all options.
        b.   an emphasis on laws and social order.
        c.   an emphasis on reward and punishment.
        d.   trying to gain the approval of others.

Kohlberg's Three Levels and Six Stages of Moral Reasoning (Table 12.1), p. 293
Diff: E, Ans: b

25.   Carla is usually good because she is afraid that she will be punished if she isn't. Carla is in which level of Kohlberg's view of moral development?
      a.   conventional
      b.   preconventional
      c.   premoral
      d.   postconventional

Kohlberg's Three Levels and Six Stages of Moral Reasoning (Table 12.1), p. 293
Diff: H, Ans: b

26.   Karl wants to know what his father will give him if he gets a good report card. According to Kohlberg, this is stage _____ of moral development.
      a.   1
      b.   2
      c.   3
      d.   4

Kohlberg's Three Levels and Six Stages of Moral Reasoning (Table 12.1), p. 293
Diff: H, Ans: a

27.   Concerning speeding on the highway, who is expressing a stage 5 response?
      a.   Janet does not speed because, "If I did, everyone else could speed too."
      b.   Chrissy speeds because she is in a big hurry.
      c.   Jack does not speed because he knows that he could get a ticket.
      d.   Stanley speeds because his passenger loves going fast and is impressed by him.

Kohlberg's Three Levels and Six Stages of Moral Reasoning (Table 12.1), p. 293
Diff: H, Ans: c

28.   Susan decides not to tell the teacher that her classmate Ian is cheating on the math exam because she's afraid the other kids will call her a snitch. This is an example of stage _____ of moral development.
      a.   1
      b.   2
      c.   3
      d.   4

Kohlberg's Three Levels and Six Stages of Moral Reasoning (Table 12.1), p. 293
Diff: H, Ans: c

29.   If Max responds that "Heinz shouldn't steal because stealing is against the law," what Kohlberg stage is exemplified?
      a.   2
      b.   3
      c.   4
      d.   5

Kohlberg's Three Levels and Six Stages of Moral Reasoning (Table 12.1), p. 293
Diff: H, Ans: d

30.   Which statement best reflects moral reasoning at the preconventional level?
      a.   "I obey a higher power."
      b.   "Every citizen should obey the rules."
      c.   "I want everyone to like me."
      d.   "I am careful not to get caught."

Kohlberg's Three Levels and Six Stages of Moral Reasoning (Table 12.1), p. 293
Diff: H, Ans: d
31.   A Florida man killed a doctor who performed abortions. The man knew this was a crime, and he knew
        he could be convicted of murder. He said stopping abortion was worth dying for. This is an example of:
        a.   insanity.
        b.   preconventional morality.
        c.   conventional morality.
        d.   postconventional morality.

Kohlberg's Critics, p. 294
Diff: M, Ans: c
32.   Kohlberg's theory has been criticized because:
        a.   his "universal" stages do not reflect liberal, Western values.
        b.   his theory doesn't emphasize stages strongly enough.
        c.   the theory is seen as not taking into account cultural differences.
        d.   the theory emphasize differences between men and women.

Kohlberg's Critics, pp. 294-295
Diff: M, Ans: c
33.   Who argued that Kohlberg's work ignored the female perspective?
        a.   Erikson
        b.   Freud
        c.   Gilligan
        d.   Piaget

Kohlberg's Critics, p. 294
Diff: M, Ans: d
34.   Gilligan believed that women are more likely to follow the morality of care because they are socialized
        to be:
        a.   nurturant.
        b.   compassionate.
        c.   nonjudgmental.
        d.   all of the above.

Kohlberg's Critics, p. 295
Diff: H, Ans: d
35.   When 11-year-old Amy responded to the question of whether a man should steal to obtain a drug that
        could save his wife's life, Gilligan found that Amy:
        a.   took a strong, firm stand against stealing.
        b.   took a firm stand that any act is justified if it saves a life.
        c.   was unable to think of a response.
        d.   saw good and bad in stealing and hesitated about making a judgment.

Information Processing

Information Processing, p. 296
Diff: E, Ans: b
36.   Compared to 7-year-olds, children age 11 are much:
        a.   more egocentric.
        b.   better thinkers.
        c.   more intuitive.
        d.   less teachable.

Information Processing, p. 296
Diff: H, Ans: d

37.   The speed and capacity of thought increases for school-aged children primarily because of the:
   a.   myelination of neural axons.
   b.   development of the frontal cortex.
   c.   brain's increased size.
   d.   child's ability to use the brain more efficiently.

Information Processing, p. 296
Diff: E, Ans: c

38.   The information-processing theory likens many aspects of human thinking to that of:
   a.   animals.
   b.   high-level business companies.
   c.   computers.
   d.   athletic teams.

Information Processing, p. 296
Diff: H, Ans: b

39.   Which information is most likely to be in your current working memory?
   a.   everything you see right now
   b.   the answer to this question
   c.   where you saw the term "working memory" in the text
   d.   the musical theme of your favorite television show

Information Processing, p. 296
Diff: H, Ans: c

40.   What is the main reason 11-year-olds are better thinkers than 7-year-olds?
   a.   They can search, analyze, and express themselves better.
   b.   They have better attention.
   c.   They have better access strategies.
   d.   Their brains process faster.

Information Processing, p. 296
Diff: M, Ans: c

41.   The memory system in which signals are held for less than a second, yet long enough for one to process them further, if so desired is:
   a.   the short-term memory system.
   b.   the working memory.
   c.   the sensory register.
   d.   none of the above.

Speed of Processing, p. 297
Diff: M, Ans: a

42.   When learning to drive, Jim concentrated so much on his driving that he didn't want anyone to talk to him. A year later, he can carry on a conversation with a passenger while driving safely. What has probably occurred?
   a.   His driving has become automated.
   b.   His working memory has increased.
   c.   His driving has become unconscious.
   d.   He understands the value of friendship.

Speed of Processing, p. 297
Diff: M, Ans: c
43.   Which is the best example of automatization?
       a.   Nicholas concentrates intensely while tying his shoelaces.
       b.   Zachary's mother allows him to pick out his own clothes for the day.
       c.   Madeline immediately knows that $8 \times 9 = 72$.
       d.   Kristen chooses a different route home from school each day.

Speed of Processing, p. 297
Diff: M, Ans: c
44.   For a person to successfully accomplish the automatization of mental skills, the task must be:
       a.   explicit.
       b.   memorized.
       c.   overlearned.
       d.   implicit.

Control Processes, p. 298
Diff: M, Ans: d
45.   The brain part(s) allowing one to regulate the analysis and flow of information is:
       a.   the anterior cingulate (cortex).
       b.   the prefrontal cortex.
       c.   the hypothalamus.
       d.   all of the above.

Control Processes, p. 298
Diff: H, Ans: b
46.   If one wishes to use a rule of thumb strategy from long-term memory, which of these would be most
       directly involved?
       a.   the knowledge base
       b.   the control processes
       c.   the auditory cortexes of the brain
       d.   the automatization processes

Control Processes, p. 298
Diff: H, Ans: a
47.   The hypothalamus, the anterior cingulate (cortex), the orbital prefrontal cortex, and the medial
       prefrontal cortex are collectively referred to as the:
       a.   executive function.
       b.   knowledge base of the brain.
       c.   unconscious mind.
       d.   metacognitive area of the brain.

Selective Attention, p. 298
Diff: M, Ans: d
48.   Kindergartners are not usually able to complete a page of work because they:
       a.   concentrate too hard.
       b.   do not take the task seriously.
       c.   are uncooperative.
       d.   are easily distracted.

Selective Attention, p. 298
Diff: E, Ans: c
49. Sonja is studying for an exam while her roommate is talking to her boyfriend on the phone. Sonja cannot concentrate on her books because she is unable to use:
  a. metacognition.
  b. divided attention.
  c. selective attention.
  d. common sense.

Selective Attention, p. 298
Diff: E, Ans: b
50. Ignoring distractions and focusing on essential information is called:
  a. incidental learning.
  b. selective attention.
  c. intentional learning.
  d. concentrative attention.

Selective Attention, p. 298
Diff: M, Ans: a
51. Which is the best example of selective attention?
  a. Ryan reads while other children in the room are singing.
  b. Shelley decides to do her math homework before going outside to play.
  c. Bill is drawing a picture, but he is distracted by his brother's radio.
  d. Karen is fixing a snack, trying to work on puzzles, and listening to the radio.

Selective Attention, pp. 298-299
Diff: M, Ans: d
52. Children in the fifth grade with AD/HD are likely to:
  a. study independently at their desk without being distracted.
  b. quietly follow a chalkboard demonstration.
  c. seek assistance without distracting.
  d. shout out the answer instead of raising a hand and waiting to be called on.

Metacognition, p. 299
Diff: E, Ans: c
53. Evaluating a cognitive task to determine how best to accomplish and monitor one's performance is called:
  a. automatization.
  b. decentration.
  c. metacognition.
  d. social standards.

Metacognition, p. 299
Diff: E, Ans: c
54. Metacognition refers to:
  a. better problem-solving strategies.
  b. better problem-solving abilities.
  c. thinking about one's thinking processes.
  d. considering multiple alternatives.

Metacognition, p. 299
Diff: H, Ans: d

55. Given the importance of metacognition, educators should probably:
    a. teach children in small groups.
    b. stress phonics in learning to read.
    c. focus on helping children learn facts.
    d. teach cognitive strategies.

Metacognition, p. 299
Diff: H, Ans: d

56. In their learning and problem-solving abilities, school-age children differ from preschoolers in that they:
    a. devote equal time to all tasks, easy or difficult.
    b. use fewer external aids such as making lists.
    c. rely mainly on memory skills in problem solving.
    d. can evaluate their own progress.

The Pragmatics of Language, p. 299
Diff: H, Ans: b

57. John has the ability to talk informally with his friends and more formally to his teachers when called on in class. This is because John understands the:
    a. metacognitive aspects of intellect.
    b. pragmatics of his language.
    c. automatized view of social interaction.
    d. control processes of regulation.

The Pragmatics of Language, p. 299
Diff: H, Ans: d

58. When Kitana wants her teacher to repeat the question asked her, she asks: "Would you please repeat the question?", but when she responds to a classmate's question, she says: "Huh?" This example shows that Kitana understands:
    a. at the formal operational stage of Piaget.
    b. metacognitive processes.
    c. the control processes in speech.
    d. the pragmatics of language.

The Pragmatics of Language, p. 300
Diff: E, Ans: d

59. In middle childhood, evidence of children's joy with language includes their:
    a. poetry.
    b. jokes.
    c. secret languages.
    d. all of the above

The Pragmatics of Language, p. 300
Diff: H, Ans: c

60. The sudden understanding that one's tone of voice, word selection, and the context in which the language is used may override the literal content of one's speech requires a complex knowledge of:
    a. metacognition.
    b. automatization.
    c. the pragmatics of language.
    d. working memory.

Teaching and Learning

Teaching and Learning, p. 301
Diff: H, Ans: a

61. What percentage of the world's children spends at least some time in school?
   a. 95 percent
   b. 85 percent
   c. 78 percent
   d. 67 percent

Which Curriculum?, p. 302
Diff: E, Ans: b

62. Jefferson High School has rules and regulations that guarantee student representation in school affairs. John, a senior, has learned that the administration of his high school wants obedience. Obedience at John's school is a/an:
   a. hidden agenda.
   b. hidden curriculum.
   c. hidden value.
   d. hidden assumption.

Which Curriculum?, p. 302
Diff: M, Ans: d

63. The unspoken and often unrecognized lessons that children learn in school which are the unofficial, unstated, or implicit rules and priorities that influence the academic curriculum and every other aspect of learning in school is called the:
   a. territorial imperative.
   b. whole language theory.
   c. socioeconomic divide.
   d. hidden curriculum.

Thinking Like a Scientist, p. 303
Diff: E, Ans: c

64. The problem with smaller school classes is that:
   a. politicians won't support them.
   b. they are too costly.
   c. there is weak research supporting their advantages.
   d. evidence supporting them is correlational.

The Reading Wars, p. 303
Diff: E, Ans: d

65. Clashes between the phonics and whole language approach to reading have been waged without concern for:
   a. children's needs.
   b. scientific evidence.
   c. developmental changes.
   d. all of the above.

The Reading Wars, p. 303
Diff: H, Ans: b

66. The so-called *reading wars* most specifically are related to:
   a. memorization vs. comprehension.
   b. whole language vs. phonics.
   c. abstract conceptualization vs. concrete comprehension.
   d. metacognition vs. the hidden curriculum.

Phonics vs. Whole-Language, p. 304
Diff: E, Ans: d

67. Despite the battles, both approaches to the teaching of reading share in common the knowledge that:
     a. motivation is important.
     b. reading is experience-dependent.
     c. many strategies need to be used.
     d. all of the above.

The Socioeconomic Divide, p. 305
Diff: H, Ans: c

68. The best predictor of school achievement and overall intelligence is:
     a. the level of understanding of the pragmatics of language.
     b. a bright spirit.
     c. vocabulary size.
     d. none of the above.

Ranks on Math Achievement Scores, Selected Countries (Table 12.3), p. 306
Diff: M, Ans: d

69. In the rankings on math achievement (TIMSS), which of the countries scored *lowest*?
     a. Korea
     b. The United States
     c. Canada
     d. New Zealand

Ranks on Math Achievement Scores, Selected Countries (Table 12.3), p. 306
Diff: M, Ans: a

70. In the rankings on math achievement (TIMSS), which of these scored *highest*?
     a. Korea
     b. The United States
     c. Canada
     d. New Zealand

The Math Wars, p. 306
Diff: M, Ans: c

71. The fact that children progress in math faster when they are taught strategies, not mere facts, and when they learn through teacher guidance and peer collaborations support which theory of cognitive development?
     a. Piaget
     b. information processing
     c. Vygotsky
     d. none of the above

The Math Wars, pp. 306-307
Diff: M, Ans: a

72. Which controversial approach has shown promise in helping U.S. children raise their skill levels in mathematics?
     a. the program developed by the National Council of Teachers of Mathematics
     b. the historical program of rote learning in math
     c. the digital math program developed at UCLA
     d. none of the above

Bilingual Education, p. 308
Diff: M, Ans: b
73.   To teach a child a second language, the most effective approach is to start during:
a.   infancy.
b.   middle childhood, about age 7.
c.   early adolescence, about age 12.
d.   adolescence, about age 15.

Various Approaches, p. 309
Diff: E, Ans: a
74.   Total immersion is an approach to learning a second language in which:
a.   the child is taught entirely in his or her second language.
b.   the child is taught entirely in his or her original language.
c.   the second language is taught as a foreign language in middle adulthood.
d.   all children receive bilingual and bicultural education.

Various Approaches, p. 309
Diff: M, Ans: c
75.   The approach in teaching a second language in which children are taught in their first language for several years and then learn the second language as a "foreign" language is the:
a.   additive bilingual approach.
b.   total immersion approach.
c.   reverse immersion approach.
d.   partial immersion approach.

Various Approaches, p. 309
Diff: H, Ans: d
76.   The label given to the language-learning approach in which children have been made to feel shy, stupid or socially isolated because of their language difference has been referred to as the:
a.   partial immersion approach.
b.   total immersion approach.
c.   reverse immersion approach.
d.   submersion approach.

Various Approaches, p. 309
Diff: M, Ans: d
77.   Immersion is unlikely to succeed when the child:
a.   is shy.
b.   is socially isolated.
c.   made to feel stupid.
d.   is all of the above.

Two Strategies for Teaching English (Table 12.4), p. 309
Diff: H, Ans: d
78.   In the English as a second language (ESL) approach:
a.   the teacher speaks in the child's native language.
b.   the goal is to master English in about two years.
c.   children typically work one-on-one with a tutor.
d.   the teacher may not speak the child's native language.

TRUE-FALSE QUESTIONS

Building on Piaget and Vygotsky

Ans: F, p. 289
1.   Piaget's concept of the logical principle of classification is valid in only North America and England.

Ans: F, p. 290
2.   The logical principle by which things are organized into groupings or categories is known as *identity*.

Ans: F, p. 291
3.   A child's statement that "Mommy was a good girl when she was my age" shows that the child has some grasp of reciprocity.

Ans: F, p. 292
4.   Kohlberg based his theory of moral development on the work of Erikson.

Ans: F, p. 293
5.   The stage called "good girl" and "nice boy" is in the preconventional level of Kohlberg's theory of moral development.

Ans: T, p. 293
6.   The "law and order" stage is listed under the conventional moral reasoning level in Kohlberg's moral reasoning system.

Ans: T, p. 294
7.   A person's *reasoning* level, rather than *behavior*, is the critical element in placing him or her within Kohlberg's moral reasoning stages.

Ans: F, p. 294
8.   During middle childhood, children's moral reasoning is usually at the third level of Kohlberg's theory.

Ans: F, p. 295
9.   Studies in which males and females are compared on moral reasoning find consistent gender differences.

Information Processing

Ans: T, p. 296
10.   Long-term memory is virtually limitless by the end of middle childhood.

Ans: F, p. 297
11.   Processing speed affects performance time but not capacity (mental).

Ans: T, p. 298
12.   Control processes help you determine what you will pay attention to and what problem-solving strategies you will use.

Ans: F, p. 299
13.   Preschoolers and school-age children have equal difficulties in judging how challenging a task is.

Ans: F, p. 299
14.   Preschoolers intuitively realize that they must devote more effort to challenging tasks than to easy ones.

Ans: T, p. 300
15.   Understanding and using secret languages, jokes, and metaphors depends on a level of cognitive development that is typically attained during middle childhood.

Teaching and Learning

Ans: T, p. 301
16.   95 percent of the world's children now spend at least some time in school.

Ans: T, p. 302
17.   The evidence supporting the view that class size affects learning is mainly correlational.

Ans: F, p. 303
18.   The whole-language approach focuses on drilling children on letter sounds before learning words.

Ans: T, p. 304
19.   Children from lower-income families have smaller vocabularies and use simpler grammar.

Ans: T, p. 305
20.   Vocabulary size is the best predictor of school achievement and overall intelligence.

Ans: T, p. 306
21.   Children from the United States score among the lowest in rankings on math achievement.

Ans: T, p. 307
22.   Math process must be explicitly taught rather than "discovered" by children.

Ans: T, p. 308
23.   The best time to learn a second language through exposure is during early childhood.

Various Approaches

Ans: T, p. 309
24.   In the reverse immersion approach to bilingual education, social communication in both languages is encouraged.

Ans: F, p. 309
25.   In the total immersion approach to bilingual education, social communication in both languages is encouraged.

FILL-IN-THE-BLANK QUESTIONS

Building on Piaget and Vygotsky

Ans: logic, p. 289
1.   The root of Piaget's concrete operational thought lies in the concept of _____.

Ans: logical, pp. 290-291
2.   Beginning at about 7 or 8 years, the child becomes capable of concrete operational thought and is able to grasp identity, reversibility, and other _____ principles.

Ans: hierarchies, p. 290
3.   An understanding that categories involve _____ means that we know that a banana is a fruit and that fruits are foods.

Ans: cultural, p. 291

4.   Vygotsky's view of how children learn focused on adult guidance as well as the child's _____ context.

Ans: (Jean) Piaget, p. 292

5.   The well-known researcher who was criticized as underestimating the influence of culture in the learning of logical principles was _____.

Ans: Kohlberg, p. 293

6.   The basic framework for moral development has been most clearly described by _____.

Ans: obedience, p. 293

7.   In Kohlberg's moral development stage 1, the most important value is _____ to authority.

Ans: care, justice, p. 294

8.   According to Gilligan, women develop a morality of _____, whereas men develop a morality of _____.

Information Processing

Ans: long-term, p. 296

9.   Our _____ memory has a virtually limitless capacity.

Ans: retrieving; conscious, pp. 296-297

10.   When I recall plans I have made for this weekend, I am _____ them from long-term memory and bringing them to my _____ mind.

Ans: processing, p. 297

11.   Children in the school years have a larger _____ capacity than preschoolers do.

Ans: automatic, p. 297

12.   As children get older, processing capacity is freed for other things, as more mental activities become routine or _____.

Ans: automatization, p. 297

13.   Behaviors or thoughts that are repeated frequently require less and less processing capacity because of _____.

Ans: control, p. 298

14.   The analysis and flow of information within the information-processing system is regulated by _____ processes.

Ans: selective, p. 298

15.   Many preschoolers fail at simple problem solving because their _____ attention is inconsistent.

Ans: metacognition, p. 299

16.   The ability to evaluate a cognitive task to determine what to do and to monitor one's progress while working on the task is called _____.

Teaching and Learning

Ans: knowledge, p. 301

17.   Children become better learners in middle childhood because they have an established and expanded _____ base.

Ans: phonics, p. 303

18. When children learn to read by first learning the sounds of each letter before deciphering words, they are learning to read by the _____ method.

Ans: whole-language, p. 303

19. When children are encouraged to write, inventing the spelling, to communicate their ideas and emotions, the _____ approach to learning to read is being used.

Ans: total immersion, p. 309

20. An approach to learning a new language in which instruction occurs exclusively in the new language is called _____ .

Ans: bilingual, p. 309

21. Teachers instruct children in their native language as well as in English with _____ education.

ESSAY QUESTIONS

1. What are (a) the parts of memory in the information-processing system and (b) What is the function of each?

2. According to the information-processing perspective, what cognitive advances do schoolchildren make in terms of selective attention, memory skills, processing capacity, knowledge, and metacognition? Given these changes, how should a sixth-grade classroom differ from a first-grade classroom?

3. What are some of the differences between preschoolers' and elementary school children's memory abilities and strategies?

4. Briefly describe the Heinz story used to measure moral reasoning. How do you think Heinz should respond? Why?

5. What are some criticisms of Kohlberg's theory of moral development? What do you think of these criticisms?

6. How did Gilligan explain differences in moral reasoning that exist between men and women? Do you agree with her?

7. Explain what is involved in the Piagetian concrete operation of reciprocity.

8. Distinguish between the "immersion," "English as a second language," and "bilingual education" approaches to teaching another language. Briefly describe each.

9. What are some of the advantages and disadvantages to using immersion?

10. Nancy is a fully bilingual adult and the first member of her family to seek a college education. Nancy remembers as a child, being told by her teacher not to speak Spanish to her best friend. "We don't talk that way in school," the teacher said. Nancy became very proficient in English, but the memory remains painful. Comment on Nancy's story.

11. What should be done to help a child learn a second language but still achieve school and personal success while limiting family disruption and cultural alienation?

12. Describe how you would handle a second-language program in your local school system. Be sure to include how you would teach English to non-English-speaking students and how you would go about introducing a second language to English-speaking students.

13. Discuss the relationship of the ability to establish hierarchies to the Piagetian concept of classification.

Answer guidelines to these essay questions can be found in the Appendix at the end of the Test Bank.

CHAPTER 13   The School Years: Psychosocial Development

MULTIPLE-CHOICE QUESTIONS

The Child's Emotions and Concerns

Theories of Development During Middle Childhood, p. 313
Diff: M, Ans: d
1.   During the latency stage, children:
   a.   develop sexual feelings toward the opposite-sex parent.
   b.   seek to establish their identity.
   c.   try to learn self-control.
   d.   assimilate cultural values.

Theories of Development During Middle Childhood, p. 313
Diff: M, Ans: a
2.   According to Freud, 8-year-old Sven will experience:
   a.   repression of psychosexual needs.
   b.   emergence of many unconscious conflicts.
   c.   increased emotional drives.
   d.   new interest in girls.

Theories of Development During Middle Childhood, p. 313
Diff: E, Ans: b
3.   According to Erikson, if 9-year-old Anita is successful in solving her psychosocial conflict, she should be developing a view of herself as:
   a.   emotional.
   b.   industrious.
   c.   incompetent.
   d.   inferior.

Theories of Development During Middle Childhood, p. 313
Diff: H, Ans: a
4.   Who is typical of the industry versus inferiority stage?
   a.   Rudy is having difficulty in learning math.
   b.   Vanessa says, "My parents never let me do anything!"
   c.   Cliff says that his girlfriend, Clair, doesn't understand him.
   d.   Theo decides to take piano lessons.

Theories of Development During Middle Childhood, p. 314
Diff: E, Ans: d
5.   Social cognition refers to:
   a.   the ability to act as a leader.
   b.   mastery of the basic concepts of classification and causality.
   c.   the ability to learn about various societies.
   d.   the abilities in learning, dealing with culture, and thinking.

Theories of Development During Middle Childhood, p. 314
Diff: E, Ans: d

6. Which theory would suggest that because 10-year-olds can explain their emotions, make decisions to study or not, and think logically, they are more active than passive in the social context and thus display social efficacy?
    a. Freudian
    b. Piagetian
    c. Eriksonian
    d. social cognitive

Theories of Development During Middle Childhood, pp. 314-315
Diff: M, Ans: a

7. Most developmentalists agree that middle childhood is important for:
    a. meeting challenges and taking responsibilities.
    b. figuring out who you are.
    c. trying to understand your family.
    d. coping with your aggressive urges.

Understanding Self and Others, p. 315
Diff: E, Ans: c

8. When asked to describe another child, a 5-year-old child would probably *not*:
    a. mention whether the child was male or female.
    b. focus on the child's outward appearance.
    c. think of the child's personality.
    d. focus on the child's observable behavior.

Understanding Self and Others, p. 315
Diff: M, Ans: a

9. Chris, who is 12 years old, is likely to predict a person's future based on:
    a. personality traits.
    b. age.
    c. observable behavior.
    d. appearance.

Understanding Self and Others, p. 316
Diff: H, Ans: b

10. Compared with a 7-year-old, a 10-year-old would be more likely to:
    a. tell you frankly that you smell bad.
    b. describe a friend as very smart and very funny.
    c. insist that a photograph of a young woman couldn't be that of Grandma.
    d. believe that a teenager would like the same things that he or she does.

Understanding Self and Others, p. 316
Diff: M, Ans: b

11. Which decreases during the school years?
    a. self-understanding
    b. self-esteem
    c. self-regulation
    d. self-criticism

Understanding Self and Others, p. 316
Diff: H, Ans: b

12. Because schoolchildren judge their own talents and limitations more realistically than preschoolers:
    a. they should decide which reading and math groups they wish to join.
    b. their self-confidence may suffer as they compare themselves with others.
    c. following a failure, they are less pessimistic about future failure.
    d. they are less likely to concede that they're not good at something.

Understanding Self and Others, p. 316
Diff: M, Ans: b
13.   In social comparison, children do *not* compare themselves with standards set by:
       a.   parents.
       b.   their own past behavior.
       c.   teachers.
       d.   peers.

The Peer Group

The Peer Group, p. 317
Diff: E, Ans: c
14.   A group of individuals roughly the same age who play or learn together are known as the:
       a.   society of children.
       b.   social context.
       c.   peer group.
       d.   sociocultural unit.

The Peer Group, p. 317
Diff: M, Ans: d
15.   The peer group does *not* usually provide:
       a.   companionship.
       b.   self-validation.
       c.   advice.
       d.   a zone of proximal development.

The Peer Group, p. 317
Diff: E, Ans: b
16.   School-age children would most admire:
       a.   Timmy, whose mother kisses him good-bye at school.
       b.   Marla, who was punished for not telling who threw a paper airplane.
       c.   Mary, who is the third-grade teacher's favorite.
       d.   Billy, who spends a lot of time with adults.

Friendship, p. 317
Diff: H, Ans: b
17.   Which of these is a *false* statement?
       a.   Older children tend to choose friends who are of the same sex, race, and economic background as themselves.
       b.   Being accepted by the entire group is more important than having a close friend.
       c.   Aggressive-rejected children tend to misinterpret the words and behavior of others.
       d.   Aggressive-rejected children tend to interpret ambiguous situations as hostile.

Friendship, p. 318
Diff: E, Ans: d
18.   Compared with younger children, older children:
       a.   change friends frequently.
       b.   make new friends easily.
       c.   choose friends from both sexes.
       d.   demand more from their friends.

Friendship, p. 318
Diff: M, Ans: c
19. Unlike younger children, older children:
    a. believe that friends are people who do things together.
    b. believe that friends should be helpful to each other.
    c. find it harder to make new friends.
    d. have friendships that are less intense.

Friendship, p. 318
Diff: H, Ans: c
20. Compared to younger children, older children:
    a. change friends more often.
    b. find it easier to make new friends.
    c. more often choose friends of the same sex and background as themselves.
    d. have larger friendship groups.

Friendship, p. 318
Diff: E, Ans: c
21. The child who is most likely to have one "best" friend is a:
    a. 7-year-old girl.
    b. 7-year-old boy.
    c. 10-year-old girl.
    d. 10-year-old boy.

Friendship, p. 319
Diff: E, Ans: d
22. Liv is an extremely shy and anxious 8-year-old. Other children seem to dislike her. She appears to be a(n):
    a. aggressive-rejected child.
    b. controversial child.
    c. neglected child.
    d. withdrawn-rejected child.

Friendship, p. 318
Diff: M, Ans: b
23. Ten-year-old Mary caught Anne, her best friend, lying to her own mom. Mary will probably:
    a. tell Anne's mother about the lie.
    b. keep quiet about it.
    c. no longer have Anne as a friend.
    d. none of the above.

Friendship, p. 318
Diff: E, Ans: c
24. If Fred is neither picked as a friend nor avoided, the effect on his self-esteem may be buffered if:
    a. Fred can talk to his parents about it.
    b. Fred can play the violin well.
    c. both a and b.
    d. none of the above.

Friendship, p. 319
Diff: E, Ans: a
25. Who is the best example of an aggressive-rejected child?
    a. Veru is disliked by most children because she is so uncooperative.
    b. Theresa is popular, but hated by many children.
    c. Greg is ignored by most children.
    d. Maher changes friends often.

Types of Bullying, p. 320
Diff: E, Ans: a
26.   Research shows that a child is most likely to be a victim of bullying if the child is:
        a.   withdrawn-rejected.
        b.   a girl.
        c.   homely.
        d.   obese.

Types of Bullying, p. 320
Diff: M, Ans: b
27.   Males bullies are often:
        a.   smaller than average in size.
        b.   above average in size.
        c.   below average in verbal assertiveness.
        d.   above average in verbal assertiveness.

Types of Bullying, p. 320
Diff: M, Ans: b
28.   Girls who bully typically:
        a.   use threat of force.
        b.   mock and ridicule their victim.
        c.   are larger than average in size.
        d.   have older sisters who are aggressive.

Types of Bullying, p. 320
Diff: M, Ans: b
29.   The key word in the definition of bullying is:
        a.   attacks.
        b.   repeated.
        c.   abused.
        d.   intolerant.

Types of Bullying, p. 320
Diff: E, Ans: c
30.   The bully who has been a victim of bullying himself is called a:
        a.   "modeled" bully.
        b.   "rejected" bully.
        c.   "bully-victim."
        d.   "familial" bully.

Bullying in Many Nations, pp. 320-321
Diff: M, Ans: c
31.   A prominent researcher in the area of bullying is:
        a.   Lawrence Kohlberg.
        b.   William Plollack.
        c.   Dan Olweus.
        d.   Jonathan Kozol.

Bullying in Many Nations, p. 321
Diff: H, Ans: d
32.   It is typical of bullying that there is a sudden increase in that behavior at about age:
        a.   8.
        b.   9.
        c.   10.
        d.   11.

Bullying in Many Nations, p. 321
Diff: H, Ans: a
33.   In Japan, the primary bullying tactic of both sexes is:
    a.   social shunning.
    b.   deliberately embarrassing the bullied child.
    c.   physical bullying.
    d.   direct bullying.

Thinking Like A Scientist, p. 322
Diff: M, Ans: d
34.   Both bullies and their victims assume that:
    a.   the current situation is fine.
    b.   classmates will intervene.
    c.   it is not serious.
    d.   adults will not intervene.

Thinking Like A Scientist, pp. 322-323
Diff: H, Ans: d
35.   A government-funded campaign to reduce bullying in Norway reduced bullying overall by _____ percent.
    a.   20
    b.   30
    c.   40
    d.   50

Thinking Like A Scientist, p. 322
Diff: E, Ans: c
36.   The only country to have a nationwide effort to reduce bullying is:
    a.   the United States.
    b.   Spain.
    c.   Norway.
    d.   England.

Thinking Like A Scientist, p. 323
Diff: E, Ans: c
37.   The most dramatic nationwide effort to reduce bullying is:
    a.   the United States.
    b.   Spain.
    c.   Norway.
    d.   England.

Families and Children

Children Need Families, pp. 324-325
Diff: H, Ans: c
38.   Parents' belief that they mold their children's personalities may be diminished by the finding that:
    a.   half of personality traits may be genetic.
    b.   half of personality traits may be environmental.
    c.   most of the environmental effects may be from the "nonshared" environment.
    d.   none of the above is true.

Family Function, p. 325
Diff: H, Ans: c
39.   Developing self-esteem, nurturing friendships with peers, and encouraging learning are three of the:
   a.   family structures.
   b.   measurements of family harmony.
   c.   functions of a family.
   d.   suggestions for stress resilience.

Family Function, p. 325
Diff: M, Ans: d
40.   Which family is considered to be the one that functions perfectly?
   a.   the nuclear family
   b.   the extended family
   c.   the blended family
   d.   none of these

Family Structure, Connecting Structure & Function, Family Income, & Harmony At Home, pp. 325-329
Diff: M, Ans: a
41.   The crucial question regarding family structure is:
   a.   Whatever the structure, does it fulfill the five essential functions for school-age children?
   b.   What structure will our culture prefer?
   c.   Which structure best meets the needs of its members?
   d.   Which of the five essential functions are fulfilled in which structure?

Family Structure, p. 326
Diff: E, Ans: b
42.   Family structure refers to:
   a.   how well a family raises its children.
   b.   legal and genetic relationships of family members.
   c.   how the family's house is constructed.
   d.   how the various generations interact.

Family Structure, p. 326
Diff: M, Ans: d
43.   A family's structure is likely to change over time due to:
   a.   divorce.
   b.   marriage.
   c.   the adoption of a child.
   d.   all of the above.

Common Family Structures (Table 13.2), p. 327
Diff: E, Ans: c
44.   Which is the most common type of family for children in the United States?
   a.   extended
   b.   single-parent
   c.   nuclear
   d.   blended

Common Family Structures (Table 13.2), p. 326
Diff: M, Ans: b
45.   Compared to nuclear families, extended families typically:
   a.   are more chaotic.
   b.   involve more people.
   c.   feature less structure.
   d.   are better for children.

Common Family Structures (Table 13.2), p. 326
Diff: H, Ans: c
46. What percentage of school-age children live in households headed by a single father?
  a. 1 percent
  b. 2 1/2 percent
  c. 5 percent
  d. 6 percent

Common Family Structures (Table 13.2), p. 326
Diff: H, Ans: a
47. Foster families account for ____ percent of school-age children's family structure.
  a. 1
  b. 2
  c. 2.5
  d. 2.7

Common Family Structures (Table 13.2), p. 326
Diff: H, Ans: b
48. In 2000, _____ percent of school-age children were living in adoptive families.
  a. 1
  b. 2
  c. 3
  d. 4

Common Family Structures (Table 13.2), p. 326
Diff: H, Ans: c
49. At any one time, _____ percent of school-age children live with one biological parent and a stepparent.
  a. 8
  b. 9
  c. 10
  d. 12

Common Family Structures (Table 13.2), p. 326
Diff: H, Ans: c
50. Approximately what percentage of school-age children live in a two-parent (husband and wife) family?
  a. 26 percent
  b. 48 percent
  c. 58 percent
  d. 63.5 percent

Common Family Structures (Table 13.2), p. 326
Diff: H, Ans: c
51. Which family structure is the most rare in the United States?
  a. nuclear
  b. homosexual
  c. polygamous
  d. single father, divorced or never married

Connecting Structure and Function, p. 327
Diff: M, Ans: b
52. Compared with single-parent homes, nuclear families usually have:
  a. higher moral values.
  b. psychologically healthier parents.
  c. fewer children.
  d. better discipline.

Connecting Structure and Function, p. 327
Diff: M, Ans: b
53.   Compared with single-parent homes, two-parent homes usually have:
        a.   higher moral values.
        b.   higher income.
        c.   fewer children.
        d.   better discipline.

Connecting Structure and Function, p. 327
Diff: E, Ans: b
54.   A positive correlation has been found between being raised by both biological parents and becoming
        a(n):
        a.   drug addict.
        b.   success.
        c.   rebellious teenager.
        d.   anxious adult.

Harmony at Home, p. 328
Diff: H, Ans: d
55.   Approximately _____ of all divorces that involve children end marriages in which the parents were
        openly hostile to each other and actually benefit the children as a result.
        a.   one-eighth
        b.   two-fifths
        c.   one-quarter
        d.   one-third

Harmony at Home, p. 329
Diff: E, Ans: c
56.   Which parenting style has consistently shown to be the most effective?
        a.   democratic
        b.   permissive
        c.   authoritative
        d.   authoritarian

Harmony at Home, p. 329
Diff: E, Ans: a
57.   Parenting which involves harsh discipline is usually _____ in design.
        a.   authoritarian
        b.   authoritative
        c.   permissive-indulgent
        d.   democratic

Coping with Problems

Coping with Problems, p. 330
Diff: E, Ans: b
58.   The child who weathers severe family problems, even abuse, and somehow have remained unscathed in
        the process is termed in your text as:
        a.   buoyant.
        b.   resilient.
        c.   parasympathetic.
        d.   unflappable.

Dominant Ideas About Challenges and Coping in Children, 1965–Present (Table 13.3), p. 331
Diff: H, Ans: d
59.   The statement: "All children are *not* the same. Some children are resilient, coping easily with stressors that cause harm in other children," describes the prevailing view in America in what year?
      a.   1960
      b.   1965
      c.   1970
      d.   1975

Dominant Ideas About Challenges and Coping in Children, 1965 – Present (Table 13.3), p. 331
Diff: H, Ans: c
60.   In what time-period in the United States was the idea of "risk-benefit analysis" of children's living conditions popular?
      a.   1975
      b.   1985
      c.   1990
      d.   2000

The Impact of Stress, p. 331
Diff: H, Ans: b
61.   In childhood, how children react to a serious stressor depends primarily on:
      a.   what the stressor is.
      b.   how many other stressors are present.
      c.   whether the stress is economic.
      d.   whether the stressor affects other siblings too.

The Impact of Stress, p. 332
Diff: M, Ans: a
62.   Research suggests that an important aspect of a stressor is how the child appraises it. Therefore, it would make sense to:
      a.   help the child reinterpret the stressor.
      b.   reduce the number of stressors.
      c.   involve the community.
      d.   determine how the stressor affects the child's daily life.

The Impact of Stress, p. 332
Diff: H, Ans: d
63.   Which issue is the most critical in dealing with the impact of stressors?
      a.   the child's genetic inheritance
      b.   the parents' personalities
      c.   the objective nature of the stress triggers
      d.   the child's attitude in response to the stressors

When Parents Fight and Children Blame Themselves (Figure 13.4), p. 332
Diff: H, Ans: d
64.   When parents fight and the children somehow blame themselves for the situation, what sort of problems are to be expected?
      a.   nightmares
      b.   stomach aches
      c.   panic attacks
      d.   all of the above

Social Support and Coping, p. 333
Diff: M, Ans: a
65.   The most dominant coping measure used by East Asian immigrants to combat difficulties related to immigration was:
a.   social support.
b.   a stress-resilient nature.
c.   having a naturalized mentor.
d.   psychological denial.

Religious Faith and Coping, p. 334
Diff: E, Ans: d
66.   Who is most likely to overcome serious problems in the family?
a.   Kurt, who lacks confidence
b.   Rolf, who stays home because he hates school
c.   Liesl, who has three brothers
d.   Maria, who is very religious

TRUE-FALSE QUESTIONS

The Child's Emotions and Concerns

Ans: F, p. 313
1.   According to Freud, children between the ages of 6 and 11 experience the crisis of industry versus inferiority.

Ans: T, p. 314
2.   The social-cognitive theory of development focuses heavily on maturation and experience in its explanation of advances in culture, cognition, and learning.

Ans: T, p. 315
3.   School-age children have a more elaborate understanding of abilities and traits than those under age 7.

Ans: T, p. 316
4.   As schoolchildren begin to use social comparison rather than simply comparing their own past and present performance abilities, their self-esteem tends to suffer.

The Peer Group

Ans: F, p. 317
5.   The "peer group" is a term that refers to a specific club or group.

Ans: F, p. 317
6.   Being accepted by the entire group is more important than having a close friend.

Ans: T, p. 318
7.   Older children tend to choose friends who are of the same sex, race, and economic background as themselves.

Ans: T, p. 318
8.   By age 10, most children have one "best" friend to whom they are quite loyal.

Ans: T, p. 319
9.   Aggressive-rejected children tend to misinterpret the words and behavior of others.

Ans: T, p. 319

10.   Aggressive-rejected children tend to interpret ambiguous situations as hostile.

Ans: F, p. 320

11.   Relational aggression includes hitting and shoving other children.

Ans: T, p. 320

12.   Girls more often use relational aggression than do boys.

Ans: T, p. 320

13.   Spreading a rumor about someone is a type of indirect bullying.

Ans: T, p. 320

14.   Two types of bully are: *direct* and *indirect*.

Ans: T, p. 321

15.   Bullying may lie in brain abnormalities present at birth and strengthened by insecure attachments and other defects.

Ans: F, p. 321

16.   Worldwide, girls bully other girls more than boys bully other boys, except in Japan.

Ans: T, p. 322

17.   Children are more likely to stop incidents of bullying than are teachers.

Ans: F, p. 323

18.   Cooperative learning groups increase bullying because children in them are in close contact with one another.

Families and Children

Ans: T, p. 324

19.   Environmental influences from different teachers and peer groups reflect one's nonshared influences.

Ans: F, p. 325

20.   Families do not need to provide opportunities for the development of peer relationships.

Ans: T, p. 326

21.   How family members are genetically connected is a concern of the family structure.

Ans: F, p. 326

22.   Blended families represent the background of nearly 10 percent of school-age children.

Ans: T, p. 326

23.   Fewer adoptable children are available in the United States today.

Ans: F, p. 326

24.   About 5 percent of children in the United States live in a "homosexual family."

Ans: T, p. 326

25.   About 9 percent of school-age children live in their grandparent's homes.

Ans: T, p. 327

26.   Children who live in a nuclear family tend to do better than children in other family structures.

Ans: T, p. 327
27.   Children who live with both biological parents tend to do better than children in other family structures.

Ans: T, p. 328
28.   There is no one type of family structure that is always the best.

Ans: F, p. 328
29.   Not all family functions are enhanced by adequate family income.

Ans: T, p. 329
30.   Most unmarried mothers are involved in a series of romances, which may include several episodes of cohabitation, marriage, and divorce.

Coping with Problems

Ans: F, p. 330
31.   Resilience to stress is a stable or static trait describing a child's responses under adverse situations.

Ans: T, pp. 331-332
32.   Having an emotionally dysfunctional parent may not affect a child if the other parent protects and nurtures the child.

Ans: T, p. 333
33.   Immigrant Asian children are more likely to keep to themselves and endure their stressors than to actually confront them.

Ans: F, p. 334
34.   School-age children develop a theology identical to that of their parents.

FILL-IN-THE-BLANK QUESTIONS

The Child's Emotions and Concerns

Ans: latency, p. 313
1.   Freud placed school-age children in the stage of _____.

Ans: social cognitive theory, p. 314
2.   The perspective that highlights how the school-age child advances in learning, cognition, and culture, building on maturation and experience to become more articulate, insightful, and competent is called _____.

Ans: social comparison, p. 316
3.   The ability to compare oneself with others is called _____.

The Peer Group

Ans: peer group, p. 317
4.   Perhaps the most influential system in which the school-age child receives his or her self-validation is the _____.

Ans: aggressive, withdrawn, p. 319
5.   Children who are disliked because of their antagonistic, confrontational behavior are _____ -rejected and those who are disliked because of their timid, anxious demeanor are _____ -rejected.

Ans: prosocial skills, p. 319

6.   Insight into human relationships, the tendency to help rather than attack others, and having benign social perceptions are collectively referred to as _____.

Ans: direct, p. 320

7.   Physical and verbal attacks are types of _____ bullying.

Ans: indirect bullying, p. 320

8.   Social shunning by a ringleader and spreading a rumor about someone describes _____.

Families and Children

Ans: nonshared, p. 324

9.   Aspects of the environment such as school and friendship are called _____ because children in the same family do not share them.

Ans: function, p. 325

10.   Family _____ refers to how well the family nurtures its members and satisfies their needs.

Ans: stress, p. 330

11.   Children who overcome severe problems in childhood are sometimes referred to as "invincible," or _____ resilient.

ESSAY QUESTIONS

1.   Compare and contrast the Freudian, behaviorist, sociocultural, and social-cognitive on middle childhood.

2.   A psychologist you know is working on an exciting research project: She is attempting to expand the scope of the standard IQ test by including a new section on "social IQ." Evaluate the idea of including such a section, and list at least two specific skills that it would measure.

3.   In what ways does a child's understanding of others' emotions develop during childhood?

4.   Define the "peer group" and give an example of a fad, style of dress, or hero that is currently popular in this subculture and one that was popular when you were a child.

5.   Imagine that you have been asked to write a self-help article for children ages 9 to 12. Your working title is "How to Be the Most Popular Kid in Your Class!" Begin your article by describing, in a few sentences, the kind of child who tends to be popular. Then suggest the ways that the less popular, or rejected, child can improve his or her social skills.

6.   Your son has been constantly bullied. How concerned should you be? Should you get involved or let your child resolve his own conflicts?

7.   What are the five main ways in which a functional family nurtures school-age children? In which area did your family do the best? The worst?

8.   Psychologists observe that the effect of divorce on one child in a family may be very different from the effect on another. What factors might account for the differing reactions of siblings?

9.   You are a judge trying to decide a custody case. What factors should you consider when deciding where to place the child?

10.   What factors will determine how well a child does in a single-parent home?

11.   The existence of a network of social support is crucial to the adjustment of the parent and child(ren) in a single-parent home. Give at least four specific examples of people, agencies, or institutions that might function as social supports for a single-parent family, and tell what each might provide.

12.   Researchers have suggested that some children are stress-resilient or invulnerable. Describe the traits and behaviors that such a child would display and suggest at least three ways that a child could be helped to be more stress-resilient.

13.   What can adults do to ensure that children can deal with stress?

14.   How would you address the problem of homeless children? Imagine that you were able to change laws and summon whatever financial support you night need to do this.

Answer guidelines to these essay questions can be found in the Appendix at the end of the Test Bank.

CHAPTER 14   Adolescence: Biosocial Development

MULTIPLE-CHOICE QUESTIONS

Puberty Begins

Puberty Begins, p. 341
Diff: E, Ans: c
1.   The period when children's bodies become adultlike is called:
   a.   the growth spurt.
   b.   secondary sex development.
   c.   puberty.
   d.   youth.

Puberty Begins, p. 341
Diff: E, Ans: b
2.   Bill noticed that he has some pubic hair. His next growth event will probably be:
   a.   beard development.
   b.   growth of penis.
   c.   spermarche.
   d.   voice change.

Puberty Begins, p. 341
Diff: H, Ans: c
3.   The process of puberty spans approximately _____ years after the initial signs of puberty.
   a.   1 to 2.
   b.   2 to 3.
   c.   3 to 4.
   d.   5 to 6.

The Sequence of Puberty (Table 14.1), p. 342
Diff: M, Ans: d
4.   Adolescence:
   a.   lasts for about ten years.
   b.   begins at about age 9.
   c.   usually ends at about age 19.
   d.   all of the above.

The Sequence of Puberty (Table 14.1), p. 342
Diff: M, Ans: b

5.   According to the text, in healthy children, puberty typically begins at age _____ for girls and at age _____ for boys.
a.   8; 12
b.   9; 9 1/2
c.   12; 12
d.   11; 9

The Sequence of Puberty (Table 14.1), p. 342
Diff: M, Ans: a

6.   In girls, the average age for the breast bud stage is:
a.   10.
b.   12.
c.   13.
d.   15.

The Sequence of Puberty (Table 14.1), p. 342
Diff: E, Ans: c

7.   For boys, the first ejaculation generally occurs:
a.   when facial hair first appears.
b.   after the weight and height spurt.
c.   following growth of the testes and penis.
d.   when the final pubic hair pattern is established.

The Sequence of Puberty (Table 14.1), p. 342
Diff: M, Ans: b

8.   The first sign of puberty in a typical girl is:
a.   a spurt in height.
b.   the onset of breast growth.
c.   an increase in weight.
d.   the development of muscular strength.

The Sequence of Puberty (Table 14.1), p. 342
Diff: H, Ans: b

9.   For girls, the usual sequence of physical changes in puberty is:
a.   menarche, the growth spurt, and the beginning of breast development.
b.   the beginning of breast development, the growth spurt, and menarche.
c.   the growth spurt, menarche, and the beginning of breast development.
d.   the growth spurt, the beginning of breast development, and menarche.

The Sequence of Puberty (Table 14.1), p. 342
Diff: M, Ans: c

10.   Nancy has just experienced a sudden growth spurt. Soon she will notice:
a.   the appearance of pubic hair.
b.   breast development.
c.   her first menstrual period.
d.   an increase in her shoe size.

The Sequence of Puberty (Table 14.1), p. 342
Diff: H, Ans: c

11.   In girls, the onset of puberty brings the lowering of the voice at approximately age:
a.   11.
b.   13.
c.   14.
d.   15.

The Sequence of Puberty (Table 14.1), p. 342
Diff: E, Ans: b
12.   John noticed that his testes have grown larger. His next growth event will probably be:
        a.   his beard develops.
        b.   his pubic hair begins to appear.
        c.   he has his first ejaculation.
        d.   his voice changes.

Hormones, p. 342
Diff: H, Ans: d
13.   The sequence of the release of hormones in puberty is:
        a.   gonads, pituitary, hypothalamus.
        b.   hypothalamus, gonads, pituitary.
        c.   pituitary, gonads, hypothalamus.
        d.   hypothalamus, pituitary, gonads.

Hormones, p. 342
Diff: H, Ans: b
14.   The biological events that begin puberty involve a hormonal signal from the:
        a.   cerebellum.
        b.   hypothalamus.
        c.   hippocampus.
        d.   ovaries or testes.

Hormones, p. 342
Diff: E, Ans: b
15.   The first hormones to begin the process of puberty are triggered in the child's:
        a.   adrenal glands.
        b.   brain.
        c.   gonads.
        d.   penis or uterus.

Hormones, p. 342
Diff: M, Ans: c
16.   The sex glands are also known as:
        a.   the reproductive system.
        b.   estrogen and testosterone.
        c.   the ovaries and testes.
        d.   the penis and the vagina.

Hormones, p. 342
Diff: H, Ans: c
17.   The hormone that causes the ovaries and testes to greatly increase their production of estrogen and
        testosterone is:
        a.   the growth hormone.
        b.   the follicle-stimulating hormone.
        c.   the gonadotropin-releasing hormone.
        d.   none of the above.

Hormones, p. 342
Diff: H, Ans: a
18.   The hormone that causes gonads to increase dramatically the production of estrogen and testosterone is:
      a.   GnRH.
      b.   GH.
      c.   RNA.
      d.   RTE.

Hormones, p. 342
Diff: E, Ans: c
19.   During puberty, testosterone increases:
      a.   in males.
      b.   only in females.
      c.   in both males and females.
      d.   in neither males nor females.

Hormones, p. 342
Diff: H, Ans: a
20.   The gland(s) producing hormones that regulate growth and also directly activate the adrenal glands
      is (are) the:
      a.   pituitary.
      b.   gonads.
      c.   hypothalamus.
      d.   thyroid.

Hormones, p. 342
Diff: E, Ans: d
21.   In females, the glands that are sometimes perceived as the "sex" glands are the:
      a.   hypothalamus and the pituitary.
      b.   pituitary and adrenals.
      c.   HPA axis.
      d.   ovaries.

Hormones, p. 342
Diff: H, Ans: a
22.   The gland(s) located just above the kidneys which secrete(s) norepinephrine in a stress response
      is (are) the:
      a.   adrenals.
      b.   pituitary.
      c.   hypothalamus.
      d.   gonads.

Hormones, pp. 342-343
Diff: H, Ans: d
23.   Which of the following is a *false* statement?
      a.   Both boys and girls produce testosterone and estrogen.
      b.   During puberty, girls' estrogen production increases up to eight times as much as during
           childhood.
      c.   The changes of puberty are initiated by a part of the brain called the hypothalamus.
      d.   During puberty, boys' testosterone production increases up to five times as much as during
           childhood.

Hormones, pp. 342, 343
Diff: M, Ans: a
24.   For males, the hormone that produces most sexual changes is:
   a.   testosterone.
   b.   progesterone.
   c.   estrogen.
   d.   adrenaline.

Hormones, p. 343
Diff: E, Ans: b
25.   The sex hormone secreted in greater amounts by males than females is:
   a.   progesterone.
   b.   testosterone.
   c.   estrogen.
   d.   noradrenaline.

Hormones, p. 343
Diff: M, Ans: a
26.   In males, the onset of puberty brings:
   a.   dramatic increases in testosterone and slight increases in estrogen.
   b.   dramatic increases in estrogen and slight increases in testosterone.
   c.   dramatic increases in both testosterone and estrogen.
   d.   an increase in testosterone only.

Hormones, p. 343
Diff: M, Ans: c
27.   Chris is just starting to experience an eightfold increase in the amount of estrogen. Chris is most
      likely a:
   a.   very feminine boy.
   b.   normal 10-year-old boy.
   c.   normal 9-year-old girl.
   d.   typical 12-year-old girl.

Indirect Effects on Emotions, p. 343
Diff: H, Ans: c
28.   The most powerful effect on adolescent joy or anger usually comes from:
   a.   fluctuating hormones.
   b.   parents.
   c.   the indirect psychological effects of puberty.
   d.   the influence of television.

Indirect Effects on Emotions, pp. 343-344
Diff: H, Ans: c
29.   Hormones have their greatest impact on moods:
   a.   directly, by changing moods more quickly.
   b.   directly, by making pubescent children more unpredictable.
   c.   indirectly, by the responses of adults and others to these biological signs.
   d.   all of the above

The Timing of Puberty, p. 344
Diff: H, Ans: d
30.   Besides gender, the three main factors that affect the timing of puberty are:
   a.   parental involvement, genes, and nutrition.
   b.   genes, drug usage, and stress.
   c.   nutrition, drug usage, and parental involvement.
   d.   genes, body fat or nutrition, and stress.

Sex, Genes and Weight, p. 345
Diff: E, Ans: c

31.   The term "menarche" refers to:
      a.   the beginning of growth of the uterus.
      b.   the first ovulation of a mature egg.
      c.   a girl's first menstrual period.
      d.   the first year of menstruation, which is usually anovulatory.

Sex, Genes and Weight, p. 345
Diff: E, Ans: b

32.   Which of the following 10-year-old girls will probably experience menarche first?
      a.   Brooke, who weighs 85 pounds (6 kg)
      b.   Amanda, who watches a lot of television
      c.   Allison, who is seriously malnourished
      d.   Sydney, who is a runner

Sex, Genes and Weight, p. 345
Diff: M, Ans: d

33.   Genetics probably do *not* account for which variation in age of puberty?
      a.   African Americans begin puberty earlier.
      b.   Some girls develop breast buds at 8 years old.
      c.   Puberty occurs later in Belgium than in other European countries.
      d.   Female athletes experience later onset of puberty than inactive girls.

Sex, Genes and Weight, p. 345
Diff: M, Ans: b

34.   For boys, the event that most closely parallels menarche is the:
      a.   growth of the penis.
      b.   first ejaculation of live sperm.
      c.   first intercourse.
      d.   discharge of enough sperm to fertilize an ovum.

Stress in Families, p. 345
Diff: H, Ans: c

35.   A man, unrelated to a young girl but living in her home, was a factor in:
      a.   more chores being done in the home.
      b.   a lower level of conflict in the home.
      c.   a tendency to earlier onset of the girl's puberty, related to the longer the length of his stay.
      d.   all of the above.

Stress in Families, pp. 345-346
Diff: M, Ans: a

36.   Family conflict and stress:
      a.   may cause the early onset of puberty.
      b.   may cause the late onset of puberty.
      c.   typically increase after puberty.
      d.   typically decrease after puberty.

Too Early or Too Late, p. 346
Diff: E, Ans: c

37.   Ellie is 10 years old and well into puberty. She will probably experience:
      a.   welcome attention from boys.
      b.   pride that she is ahead of her friends.
      c.   teasing and name-calling from her classmates.
      d.   a better body image than her peers.

Too Early or Too Late, p. 346
Diff: M, Ans: d
38.   Who will probably find puberty most difficult?
        a.   Eric, an on-time maturer
        b.   Trisha, a late maturer
        c.   Hans, an early maturer
        d.   Katya, an early maturer

The Growth Spurt, p. 347
Diff: E, Ans: d
39.   One of the first signs of the growth spurt is:
        a.   lengthening of the torso.
        b.   increased muscle mass.
        c.   growth of arms and legs.
        d.   growth of fingers and toes.

The Growth Spurt, p. 347
Diff: E, Ans: b
40.   During the growth spurt, the last part(s) of the body to grow:
        a.   are the limbs.
        b.   is the torso.
        c.   are the nose, lips, and ears.
        d.   are the hands and feet.

The Growth Spurt, p. 347
Diff: E, Ans: d
41.   A 14-year-old boy has disproportionately large feet and hands and a big nose. He most likely:
        a.   is at the end of his growth spurt.
        b.   has not started his growth spurt.
        c.   has reached his full adult body size.
        d.   is near the beginning of his growth spurt.

Wider, Taller, Then Stronger, p. 347
Diff: M, Ans: a
42.   The growth spurt begins with a(n):
        a.   increase in bone length.
        b.   rapid growth of muscle tissue.
        c.   increase in skull size.
        d.   increase in torso length.

Wider, Taller, Then Stronger, p. 347
Diff: E, Ans: b
43.   Janet and Carlos are both in their growth spurt. If they are typical of their sex, compared with Carlos, Janet will:
        a.   retain less fat.
        b.   have a higher proportion of body fat.
        c.   have an increase in upper body muscle.
        d.   burn off all her baby fat.

Wider, Taller, Then Stronger, p. 347
Diff: H, Ans: c

44. Georgette is in her adolescent growth spurt. If she is typical, she will probably accumulate the most fat on her:
    a. face and arms.
    b. arms and hips.
    c. legs and hips.
    d. torso and face.

Wider, Taller, Then Stronger, p. 347
Diff: M, Ans: a

45. In what order does the growth spurt typically occur during puberty?
    a. weight, height, muscle
    b. weight, muscle, height
    c. height, weight, muscle
    d. muscle, height, weight

Wider, Taller, Then Stronger, p. 347
Diff: H, Ans: c

46. During puberty, boys:
    a. increase muscle strength by about 20 percent.
    b. increase muscle strength most noticeably in the legs.
    c. more than double their arm strength.
    d. experience all of the above.

Other Body Changes, p. 347
Diff: M, Ans: a

47. In adolescence, changes in heart and lung capacity include:
    a. greater lung capacity.
    b. increased heart rate.
    c. the heart tripling in size.
    d. the lungs doubling in weight.

Other Body Changes, p. 347
Diff: H, Ans: b

48. Which of the following changes typically occurs during adolescence?
    a. The lungs increase to about five times their earlier weight.
    b. The heart doubles in size.
    c. The tonsils increase in size.
    d. Acne occurs in about 98 percent of all adolescents.

Other Body Changes, p. 347
Diff: M, Ans: d

49. Some teenagers seem able to skate, play basketball, or dance for hours without rest. This increased endurance is best explained by:
    a. increased hormone output.
    b. increases in muscle tissue.
    c. better digestive processes.
    d. the growth of the heart and lungs.

Other Body Changes, p. 347
Diff: M, Ans: c

50. Barry is taking a weight-lifting class in high school. The weights he lifts should:
    a. match his projected size for next year.
    b. force him to maximum exertion.
    c. match his size of one year ago.
    d. reflect that his muscles were the first part of his body to develop.

Other Body Changes, p. 348
Diff: H, Ans: d
51.   Ever since he began puberty, Barry has been staying awake late at night and craving sleep in the mornings. His parents should:
   a.   get Barry professional help.
   b.   realize that this is due to his avoiding them.
   c.   realize that this is due to changes in the brain.
   d.   realize that this is due to hormonal shifts.

Other Body Changes, p. 348
Diff: E, Ans: d
52.   Adolescent acne is usually brought on by:
   a.   changes in diet.
   b.   changes in the lymphoid system.
   c.   sexual frustration.
   d.   increased activity of oil and sweat glands.

Other Body Changes, p. 348
Diff: M, Ans: b
53.   One undesirable change during the adolescent growth spurt is a(n):
   a.   enlargement in heart size.
   b.   change in eye shape, causing nearsightedness.
   c.   increased likelihood of asthma.
   d.   decrease in lung capacity.

Other Body Changes, p. 348
Diff: M, Ans: a
54.   If our culture were responsive to the physical changes occurring in adolescence:
   a.   schools would begin at 10:00 A.M.
   b.   English and History classes would be at 9:00 A.M.
   c.   we would have adolescents rise early.
   d.   we would be more supportive of rigorous sports training.

Primary Sex Characteristics, p. 348
Diff: M, Ans: c
55.   Changes in primary sex characteristics during puberty include:
   a.   pubic hair and underarm hair start to grow.
   b.   height increases rapidly.
   c.   the uterus and the testes begin to grow.
   d.   all of the above.

Secondary Sex Characteristics, p. 349
Diff: M, Ans: d
56.   Secondary sex characteristics are those characteristics that:
   a.   occur later in development.
   b.   are harder to detect.
   c.   are inside the body.
   d.   are not directly related to reproduction.

Secondary Sex Characteristics, p. 349
Diff: E, Ans: d
57.   Breast development in girls:
   a.   begins toward the end of puberty.
   b.   is complete in about six months.
   c.   precedes puberty.
   d.   continues throughout puberty.

Secondary Sex Characteristics, p. 349
Diff: M, Ans: a
58.   If a boy's breast increases during puberty, he probably:
      a.   is quite normal.
      b.   has an extra chromosome.
      c.   eats too much beef and pork.
      d.   needs to exercise more.

Secondary Sex Characteristics, p. 349
Diff: M, Ans: a
59.   What has the greatest effect on an adolescent's beard growth?
      a.   heredity
      b.   sexual activity
      c.   nutrition
      d.   overall growth rate

Hazards to Health

Poor Nutrition, p. 350
Diff: E, Ans: c
60.   Because Cassie is 15 years old, she most likely needs more:
      a.   magnesium.
      b.   potassium.
      c.   iron.
      d.   vitamin C.

Poor Nutrition, p. 350
Diff: E, Ans: c
61.   Janice is worried that her son will indulge in behaviors that will cause him to be shorter and fatter as an
      adult than he would be normally. The only behavior that she does *not* need to worry about is his:
      a.   drug use.
      b.   cigarette smoking.
      c.   overexercising.
      d.   overeating.

Poor Nutrition, p. 351
Diff: H, Ans: d
62.   Sharon is concerned about deficiencies in her daughter Alana's diet. If Alana is a typical teen, Sharon
      should prepare:
      a.   potatoes to increase her starch.
      b.   carrots to increase her calcium.
      c.   orange juice to increase her vitamin C.
      d.   a steak to increase her iron.

Poor Nutrition, p. 351
Diff: M, Ans: d
63.   Amy feels apathetic and lazy. Those are symptoms of insufficient:
      a.   calcium.
      b.   zinc.
      c.   vitamin D.
      d.   iron.

Sexually Transmitted Infections, p. 352
Diff: E, Ans: d
64.   The younger people are when they contract a STI:
        a.   the less likely they are to seek treatment.
        b.   the less likely they are to alert their sexual partners.
        c.   the higher the rate of reinfection.
        d.   all of the above

Teenage Pregnancy, pp. 352-353
Diff: H, Ans: a
65.   The problems of teenage pregnancy before age 15 are _____, whereas, the problems of teenage
        pregnancy after age 15 are _____.
        a.   physical; cultural
        b.   cultural; physical
        c.   psychological; sociological
        d.   sociological; psychological

Sexual Abuse, p. 354
Diff: E, Ans: a
66.   A mother is sexually abusive when she:
        a.   teases and fondles her sons.
        b.   reports her husband's abuse of their daughters.
        c.   talks to her son about birth control.
        d.   tells her daughter not to have sex.

Sexual Abuse, p. 354
Diff: H, Ans: a
67.   Most sexual abuse is done:
        a.   by men.
        b.   by strangers to the child.
        c.   to boys.
        d.   all of the above.

Sexual Abuse, p. 355
Diff: E, Ans: d
68.   Because 14-year-old Nannette has been sexually abused, she is at risk of:
        a.   use of drugs and alcohol.
        b.   having an eating disorder.
        c.   developing delinquent behaviors.
        d.   all of the above.

The Gateway Drugs, p. 355
Diff: M, Ans: b
69.   Which of the following is considered a "gateway" drug?
        a.   LSD
        b.   alcohol
        c.   heroin
        d.   cocaine

The Gateway Drugs, p. 356
Diff: E, Ans: a
70.   Girls use tobacco _____ boys.
        a.   as much as
        b.   less than
        c.   more than
        d.   much more than

The Gateway Drugs, p. 356
Diff: E, Ans: d
71.   Drinking is more harmful in adolescence than adulthood because it:
        a.   damages the prefrontal cortex.
        b.   impairs judgment.
        c.   loosens inhibitions.
        d.   all of the above.

Patterns of Adolescent Drug Use, p. 357
Diff: H, Ans: b
72.   Annual nationwide surveys of high school seniors show that about _____ percent have tried alcohol and about _____ percent have smoked at least one cigarette.
        a.   90; 57
        b.   80; 67
        c.   70; 37
        d.   60; 97

Drug Use By U.S. High School Seniors in the Past 30 Days (Fig. 14.4), p. 357
Diff: M, Ans: c
73.   Trends in drug use by adolescents in the United States show:
        a.   steady increases from the mid-1970s on.
        b.   steady decreases from the mid-1970s on.
        c.   after decreases in the 1980s, a recent increase.
        d.   less use of alcohol, more use of marijuana.

Changing Policy: Postponing Teenage Drug Experimentation, p. 358
Diff: H, Ans: c
74.   Three factors that protect against drug use are: a problem-solving style of coping, a sense of competence and well-being, and _____.
        a.   a drug-awareness program at school put on by police officers.
        b.   an independent personality.
        c.   cognitive maturity.
        d.   a high level of alcohol dehydrogenase in the body.

Changing Policy: Postponing Teenage Drug Experimentation, p. 358
Diff: E, Ans: a
75.   The experimental antidrug program that has police officers go into classrooms and teach children and adolescents about the harmfulness of drug usage is called:
        a.   D.A.R.E.
        b.   H.O.P.E.
        c.   S.T.O.P.
        d.   S.A.Y.N.O.

Cultural Differences in Drug Use, p. 359
Diff: E, Ans: c
76.   Although it is true that smoking decreases one's appetite, it also:
        a.   decreases stress responses.
        b.   increases body injury rates.
        c.   stunts growth.
        d.   lowers self-esteem.

Cultural Differences in Drug Use, p. 359
Diff: H, Ans: b
77.   Most teenage girls who smoke are:
   a.   of Asian extraction.
   b.   of European extraction.
   c.   of African extraction.
   d.   none of the above.

Cultural Differences in Drug Use, p. 359
Diff: E, Ans: c
78.   The all-time high for lifetime drug usage in the United States was in:
   a.   1969.
   b.   1971.
   c.   1978.
   d.   1992.

Cultural Differences in Drug Use, p. 359
Diff: E, Ans: d
79.   The all-time low for drug usage in the United States was in:
   a.   1969.
   b.   1971.
   c.   1978.
   d.   1992.

Cultural Differences in Drug Use, p. 359
Diff: H, Ans: b
80.   Drug use appears to be:
   a.   an expected part of the transitional experience of puberty.
   b.   part of the peer culture from time to time.
   c.   a genetically triggered event involving a rush of hormones.
   d.   all of the above.

TRUE-FALSE QUESTIONS

Puberty Begins

Ans: F, p. 341
1.   The major events of growth and sexual maturation associated with puberty typically are completed a year or two after puberty begins.

Ans: T, p. 341
2.   Beard development is among the last visual signs of pubertal changes in males.

Ans: F, p. 342
3.   In boys, final pubic-hair pattern is established at age 14.

Ans: T, p. 342
4.   The changes of puberty are initiated by a part of the brain called the hypothalamus.

Ans: F, p. 343
5.   During puberty, boys' testosterone production increases up to five times the level in childhood.

Ans: T, p. 343
6.   During puberty, girls' estrogen production increases up to eight times as much as it was during childhood.

Ans: T, p. 343

7.   Both boys and girls produce testosterone and estrogen.

Ans: T, p. 343

8.   For boys during puberty, hormonal increases directly lead to more thoughts about sex and more masturbation.

Ans: T, p. 344

9.   Differing reactions to sexual urges are primarily cultural in nature.

Ans: T, p. 344

10.   It is usual and typical for children to begin seeing pubertal changes in their bodies between ages 8 and 14.

Ans: T, p. 345

11.   Studies suggest that genes influence the timing of menarche.

Ans: T, p. 345

12.   It appears that the timing of menarche is related to the accumulation of a certain amount of body fat, which is why tall thin, athletic girls generally menstruate later than other girls do.

Ans: T, p. 345

13.   Menarche does not usually occur until a girl weighs 100 pounds (45–48 kg).

Ans: T, p. 345

14.   In 2000, boys in the United States were beginning puberty about a year earlier than boys did in the 1960s.

Ans: F, p. 346

15.   Girls who reach menarche later experience more stress than girls who develop earlier.

Ans: F, p. 346

16.   Late-maturing girls tend to have a worse body image than their early-maturing peers do.

Ans: T, p. 347

17.   During the growth spurt, females gain more fat than males do.

Ans: F, p. 347 (picture caption)

18.   Most teens are fairly satisfied with their physical appearance.

Ans: F, p. 347

19.   During adolescence, the total volume of blood decreases.

Ans: T, p. 348

20.   For some adolescents, growth and elongation of the eyeball result in nearsightedness.

Ans: T, p. 348

21.   Primary sex characteristics are those parts of the body involving reproductive organs, such as the uterus and testes.

Ans: F, p. 349

22.   About 10 percent of all boys experience some breast enlargement during puberty.

Ans: T, p. 349

23.   Some breast development takes place in males as well as females during puberty.

Hazards to Health

Ans: T, p. 350

24.   During adolescence, the major diseases of adulthood are rare, due to the strength of the immune system.

Ans: F, p. 350

25.   Because of rapid weight gain during the growth spurt, most adolescents should reduce their caloric intake.

Ans: F, p. 351

26.   Most American high school seniors eat the daily recommended amount of fruits and vegetables.

Ans: F, p. 352

27.   STI stands for syphilis-type infection.

Ans: F, p. 352

28.   Most STIs are fatal if not treated properly.

Ans: T, p. 352

29.   By their senior year of high school, about 20 percent of U.S. teens have had four or more sexual partners.

Ans: T, p. 352

30.   About half of all U.S. teens used a condom the last time they had intercourse.

Ans: T, p. 353

31.   Young adolescent pregnancy slows down or stops growth in height and increases in bone density for the mother-to-be.

Ans: F, p. 353

32.   About 95 percent of all teenage mothers are unmarried.

Ans: T, p. 353

33.   Teen motherhood reduces the teenager's likelihood of marriage.

Ans: T, p. 353

34.   Babies of teenagers have a higher risk of birth complications.

Ans: T, p. 353

35.   Babies of teenagers are more likely than other babies to eventually become delinquents or, if female, teen mothers themselves.

Ans: T, p. 354

36.   Men who are known to the victim are the perpetrators in the majority of cases of sexual abuse of children and adolescents.

Ans: F, p. 355

37.   "Addiction" is another word for "drug abuse."

Ans: T, p. 356

38.   Marijuana slows down the thinking process.

Ans: F, p. 356

39.   Repeated marijuana usage typically leads to an increase in motivation and energy level.

Ans: F, p. 357

40.   Nearly 75 percent of adolescents have tried at least one illegal drug.

Ans: F, p. 358

41.   Project D.A.R.E., which puts on programs in the schools to emphasize the harmfulness of drugs, has
       led to a rejection of drug use in U.S. schools.

Ans: T, p. 359

42.   In many adolescent peer groups, drug use and abuse are admired as signs of maturity.

FILL-IN-THE-BLANK QUESTIONS

Puberty Begins

Ans: puberty, p. 341

1.   The transitional process that ends childhood is called _____.

Ans: HPA axis, p. 342

2.   Crucial to triggering puberty is a confluence of hormonal activity known as _____.

Ans: testes; ovaries, p. 342

3.   The term "gonads" refers to the sex glands, that is, to the _____ in the male and the _____ in the
       female.

Ans: testosterone; estrogen, p. 343

4.   In the male, the first invisible signs of puberty are a dramatic increase in the hormone _____ and a
       slight increase in the hormone _____.

Ans: menarche, p. 345

5.   The first menstrual period is called _____ and usually occurs between the ages of 9 and 15.

Ans: earlier, p. 346

6.   Those girls who develop _____ than their friends tend to be the most upset.

Ans: spermarche; masturbation, p. 349

7.   An event usually taken to signify the beginning of reproductive potential in boys is _____. It can
       occur during sleep, through sexual intercourse, or through _____.

Ans: secondary, p. 349

8.   Breast development and voice change during adolescence are examples of changes involving the
       _____ sex characteristics.

Ans: lower; lower, p. 349

9.   During adolescence, a boy's voice becomes _____ due to growth of the larynx; during the same years,
       a girl's voice becomes _____.

Hazards to Health

Ans: 50, p. 350

10.   The typical adolescent needs about _____ percent more zinc, iron, and calcium during the growth
       spurt than he or she did two years earlier.

Ans: sexually transmitted infection, p. 352

11.   "STI" stands for _____.

ESSAY QUESTIONS

1.   What are the similarities and differences in the male and female experience of puberty? Include specific biological and psychological information in your answer.

2.   What kinds of changes occur in boys concerning estrogen and/or testosterone production? What about girls?

3.   You are a family counselor. Describe the advice you would give to parents of each of the following: an early-maturing adolescent boy, a late-maturing adolescent boy, an early-maturing adolescent girl, and a late-maturing adolescent girl. Explain the positive and negative impact each condition can have on the adolescent.

4.   Joshua has a slightly deformed ear that can be corrected by plastic surgery. Although at age 11, Joshua is quite conscious of the defect, he has been told that it would be best to postpone surgery until he is at least 15. Discuss the possible advantages and disadvantages of this recommendation.

5.   Explain why an 18-year-old is likely to outperform the most athletic 13-year-olds in sports such as swimming, tennis, and skiing.

6.   You have been asked to speak to a group of boys and girls who are nearing puberty about their new sexuality, the changes they are experiencing, and the chances of pregnancy occurring. Briefly describe what you would say.

7.   What sorts of changes occur in primary sex characteristics during puberty?

8.   What sorts of changes occur in secondary sex characteristics during puberty?

9.   Discuss the physical, social, and cultural factors that make the typical adolescent boy or girl feel dissatisfied with his or her appearance.

10.   What are some of the consequences of having been sexually abused?

11.   You have been asked to create a comprehensive plan to reduce teen usage of drugs. What will you do?

Answer guidelines to these essay questions can be found in the Appendix at the end of the Test Bank.

CHAPTER 15

Adolescence: Cognitive Development

MULTIPLE-CHOICE QUESTIONS

Intellectual Advances

More and Better Cognition, p. 363
Diff: E, Ans: d
1. Which of the following cognitive skills develops (or continues to develop) during adolescence?
    a. metacognition
    b. memory
    c. selective attention
    d. all of the above

More and Better Cognition, pp. 363-364
Diff: E, Ans: b
2. Which of the following may be the underlying reason for the improved cognitive skills of adolescence?
    a. drug experimentation
    b. brain maturation
    c. better nutrition
    d. all of the above

More and Better Cognition, pp. 363-364
Diff: H, Ans: c
3. Cognitive advances in adolescence generally include all of the following EXCEPT:
    a. using selective attention more skillfully.
    b. developing a personal writing style.
    c. focusing on others more than on oneself.
    d. analyzing one's own mental processes.

More and Better Cognition, p. 364
Diff: M, Ans: a
4. The executive functions of the brain, which originate primarily in the prefrontal cortex:
    a. improve markedly in adolescence.
    b. improve slightly in adolescence.
    c. slow down in adolescence.
    d. remain stable in adolescence.

New Logical Abilities, p. 364
Diff: E, Ans: a

5.   Piaget called the reasoning that characterizes adolescence:
        a. formal operational thought.
        b. the game of thinking.
        c. metacognition.
        d. concrete operational thinking.

New Logical Abilities, p. 364
Diff: M, Ans: b

6.   Juanita is able to think hypothetically about abstract ideas. Piaget would say she has developed:
        a. concrete operational thought.
        b. formal operational thought.
        c. concrete conjectural thought.
        d. postoperational thought.

Thinking Like a Scientist, p. 365
Diff: H, Ans: c

7.   When Piaget and Inhelder asked children of different ages to balance a scale using several different weights, they found that:
        a. very young children tended to use logical deduction.
        b. 7-year-old children tended to use spatial relationships.
        c. by age 10, children tended to use trial-and-error strategies.
        d. adolescents failed to see the complexities of the problem.

Thinking Like a Scientist, p. 365
Diff: H, Ans: b

8.   Jeremy is 7-years-old and has been asked to balance a scale with weights that can be hooked to the arms of the scale. Jeremy will probably:
        a. solve the problem through a trial-and-error strategy.
        b. put weights on both sides without considering distance from the center of the scale.
        c. understand the inverse relationship between distance and weight.
        d. put all the weights on one side of the scale.

Thinking Like a Scientist, p. 365
Diff: E, Ans: b

9.   In Inhelder and Piaget's balance experiment, trial-and-error problem solving was most characteristic of:
        a. unrealistic thought.
        b. concrete operational thought.
        c. logical thought.
        d. formal operational thought.

Thinking Like a Scientist, p. 365
Diff: E, Ans: d

10.   In Inhelder and Piaget's balance experiment, a child who systematically tests the idea that weight and distance are inversely related is probably:
        a. 4 years old.
        b. 7 years old.
        c. 10 years old.
        d. 14 years old.

Thinking Like a Scientist, p. 365
Diff: M, Ans: b

11. Compared to that of preadolescents, adolescents' thinking about science is more likely to:
     a. be logically inconsistent.
     b. recognize alternative possibilities.
     c. be concretely tied to the situation.
     d. maintain traditional ideas.

Thinking Like a Scientist, p. 365
Diff: E, Ans: d

12. Adolescents apply formal logic:
     a. in all situations.
     b. in very few situations.
     c. only when encouraged to do so.
     d. in some situations but not in others.

Thinking Like a Scientist, p. 365
Diff: H, Ans: a

13. More recent research examining the development of formal logic has demonstrated that:
     a. development may be far less stagelike than Piaget believed.
     b. those who have developed this capability use it consistently in every situation.
     c. development occurs much more quickly than Piaget believed.
     d. adolescents across cultures develop this capability at the same age.
     e. all of the above

Thinking Like a Scientist, p. 365
Diff: M, Ans: e

14. According to recent research, which of the following influences individuals' ability to reason formally?
     a. age
     b. intelligence
     c. talents
     d. emotional factors
     e. all of the above

Hypothetical-Deductive Thought, p. 366
Diff: E, Ans: d

15. Which of the following is typical of formal operational thought?
     a. thinking about what is possible
     b. thinking about what is hypothetical
     c. thinking about what is abstract
     d. all of the above

Hypothetical-Deductive Thought, p. 366
Diff: H, Ans: c

16. Gary is an adolescent living in the United States. After learning about social injustice in some underdeveloped countries, which of the following is Gary LEAST likely to say?
     a. "That is not the way things should be."
     b. "Humans shouldn't be treated that way."
     c. "I guess that's just how things are."
     d. Gary would be unlikely to say any of the above.

Hypothetical-Deductive Thought, p. 366
Diff: H, Ans: b
17.   One of the most prominent aspects of adolescent thought is the ability to:
       a.   reject adult thoughts and values.
       b.   think in terms of possibilities.
       c.   take another person's point of view.
       d.   use practical problem-solving skills.

Hypothetical-Deductive Thought, p. 366
Diff: M, Ans: c
18.   Compared to younger children, when thinking about historical or political problems, adolescents tend
       to:
       a.   be less consistent in their reasoning.
       b.   bring in more unrelated arguments.
       c.   consider more possibilities.
       d.   make judgments based only on the facts.

Hypothetical-Deductive Thought, p. 366
Diff: H, Ans: a
19.   Which of the following is NOT true of hypothetical thought?
       a.   It is tied to the everyday world as the individual knows it.
       b.   It entails reasoning about propositions that may or may not reflect reality.
       c.   It involves imagined possibilities.
       d.   It is an aspect of formal operational thinking.

Hypothetical-Deductive Thought, p. 366
Diff: M, Ans: d
20.   A teenager who can use hypothetical thinking will tend to:
       a.   accept the values of his or her culture.
       b.   accept the world as it is.
       c.   be confident about the future.
       d.   reflect about serious issues.

Hypothetical-Deductive Thought, p. 366
Diff: E, Ans: c
21.   Does the ability to use deductive reasoning tend to develop at the same time as the ability to use
       inductive reasoning?
       a.   Yes, deductive reasoning and inductive reasoning tend to develop at the *same time*.
       b.   No, deductive reasoning tends to develop *before* inductive reasoning.
       c.   No, deductive reasoning tends to develop *later* than inductive reasoning.
       d.   No, these two types of reasoning tend to develop *randomly*, with deductive reasoning sometimes
            developing first and inductive reasoning sometimes developing first.

Hypothetical-Deductive Thought, p. 366
Diff: M, Ans: c
22.   Which of the following refers to the ability to begin with a logical idea and then use logic to draw
       specific conclusions?
       a.   hypothetical reasoning
       b.   inductive reasoning
       c.   deductive reasoning
       d.   adolescent egocentrism

Hypothetical-Deductive Thought, p. 366
Diff: M, Ans: b
23.   Which of the following refers to the ability to begin with specifics, such as accumulated facts, and then make general conclusions?
a.   hypothetical reasoning
b.   inductive reasoning
c.   deductive reasoning
d.   adolescent egocentrism

Hypothetical-Deductive Thought, p. 366
Diff: E, Ans: d
24.   Using inductive thinking, a person might think, "If it barks like a dog, and wags its tail like a dog, it must be a _____."
a.   mammal
b.   animal
c.   dogfish
d.   dog

Hypothetical-Deductive Thought, p. 366
Diff: H, Ans: b
25.   Brian has met three girls who tell him that *Titanic* is their all-time favorite movie. He concludes that all girls love *Titanic*. Brian has just used:
a.   hypothetical reasoning.
b.   inductive reasoning.
c.   deductive reasoning.
d.   adolescent egocentrism.

Hypothetical-Deductive Thought, p. 366
Diff: H, Ans: d
26.   Elle, an adolescent, believes that government should pay for citizens' health care. From this premise, she reasons about the particulars of how and why government-funded health care would work. This is an example of:
a.   adolescent egocentrism.
b.   intuitive thinking.
c.   inductive reasoning.
d.   deductive reasoning.

Hypothetical-Deductive Thought, p. 367
Diff: H, Ans: a
27.   Imagine a group of students who support the death penalty being asked the following question: "Would you still support the death penalty even if you learned that low-income individuals have a harder time defending against it than do higher income individuals?" Which of the following is the most likely result?
a.   Preadolescents would be more likely than adolescents to change their minds.
b.   Adolescents would be more likely than preadolescents to change their minds.
c.   Both preadolescents and adolescents would tend to continue supporting the death penalty.
d.   Neither preadolescents nor adolescents would tend to continue supporting the death penalty.

Hypothetical-Deductive Thought, p. 367
Diff: M, Ans: a
28.   Unlike individuals who possess formal operational thought, those who possess only concrete operational thought tend to have a great deal of difficulty arguing:
a.   a point of view with a false premise.
b.   with their parents or other authority figures.
c.   when they have tangible evidence.
d.   none of the above.

Hypothetical-Deductive Thought, p. 367
Diff: H, Ans: c
29.   A professor asks a group of 8-year-olds and a group of 16-year-olds to argue that they should receive a
       reduction in their allowance, an argument with which they all surely disagree. Which of the following is
       a likely result of this study?
       a.   Almost *none* of the students will be able to do this.
       b.   8-year-olds will be able to do this, but 16-year-olds will be unable to do this.
       c.   16-year-olds will be able to do this, but 8-year-olds will be unable to do this.
       d.   Almost *all* of the students will be able to do this easily.

Hypothetical-Deductive Thought, p. 367
Diff: H, Ans: d
30.   When faced with a dilemma between religious freedom and economic justice, mid-adolescents
       tended to:
       a.   engage in egocentric thought.
       b.   abandon the principle of religious freedom.
       c.   have a difficult time following the logical argument.
       d.   believe that religious freedom should prevail.

More Intuitive, Emotional Thought, p. 367
Diff: E, Ans: a
31.   Which of the following is NOT an example of analytic thought?
       a.   intuitive thought
       b.   deductive thought
       c.   logical thought
       d.   formal thought

More Intuitive, Emotional Thought, pp. 367-368
Diff: E, Ans: b
32.   Which of the following is a way of referring to intuitive thought?
       a.   conscious
       b.   emotional
       c.   intellectual
       d.   factual

More Intuitive, Emotional Thought, pp. 367-368
Diff: E, Ans: a
33.   The type of thought supported by a "feeling" that a belief is right is referred to as:
       a.   intuitive thought.
       b.   factual thought.
       c.   experimental thought.
       d.   logical thought.

More Intuitive, Emotional Thought, pp. 367-368
Diff: M, Ans: c
34.   Which of the following is a true statement about adolescents' intuitive thought?
       a.   It almost always ends up at the same conclusion as analytic thought.
       b.   It is slower than analytic thought.
       c.   It is considered a separate pathway from analytic thought.
       d.   It begins with a logical premise.

More Intuitive, Emotional Thought, p. 368
Diff: H, Ans: e
35. Which of the following is a true statement about adolescents' analytic and intuitive thought "tracks"?
a. They generally agree.
b. Analytic thought is better than intuitive thought.
c. Intuitive thought is better than analytic thought.
d. The two tracks are so dependent on one another that it is impossible to say whether they agree or disagree.
e. None of the above is a true statement.

Adolescent Egocentrism, p. 368
Diff: E, Ans: d
36. In general, adolescent egocentrism refers to which of the following?
a. the belief that one is destined to have a legendary life
b. the notion that one cannot be harmed by unprotected sex
c. the viewpoint that everyone else is smarter than oneself
d. the view that one is noticed by everyone

Adolescent Egocentrism, p. 368
Diff: E, Ans: b
37. Adolescent egocentrism is evident when teenagers believe:
a. their own ethnic group is superior to others.
b. they personally are much more socially significant than they actually are.
c. they receive adequate attention from their family and friends.
d. their generation is similar to previous generations.

Adolescent Egocentrism, p. 368
Diff: M, Ans: c
38. A characteristic of adolescent egocentrism is:
a. the belief that all people think the same thoughts.
b. the controlling of the id and the superego by the ego.
c. the belief that one's emotional experience is unique.
d. an attempt to live up to the standards of society.

Adolescent Egocentrism, p. 368
Diff: H, Ans: b
39. Which of the following is true of adolescent egocentrism?
a. It stems from an inability to think abstractly.
b. It involves distorted inductions and deductions.
c. It develops in late adolescence.
d. all of the above

Adolescent Egocentrism, p. 368
Diff: M, Ans: b
40. A 15-year-old girl realizes that the dress she has worn to school has a small stain on it. Her belief that everyone will notice it is an example of:
a. the personal fable.
b. adolescent egocentrism.
c. clothes consciousness.
d. school phobia.

Adolescent Egocentrism, p. 368
Diff: M, Ans: d
41.   An adolescent's statement that, "But, Mother, you just don't understand; nobody understands!" is indicative of:
    a. formal operational thought.
    b. poor person-environment fit.
    c. belief in the imaginary audience.
    d. adolescent egocentrism.

Adolescent Egocentrism, p. 368
Diff: E, Ans: a
42.   The belief that one cannot be harmed by things that would hurt a normal person is referred to as:
    a. the invincibility fable.
    b. a personal fable.
    c. an imaginary audience.
    d. deductive reasoning.

Adolescent Egocentrism, p. 368
Diff: M, Ans: d
43.   Sixteen-year-old Paul drinks heavily and drives dangerously fast, believing that he cannot be hurt. Paul is demonstrating:
    a. the personal fable.
    b. deductive reasoning.
    c. self-awareness.
    d. the invincibility fable.

Adolescent Egocentrism, p. 368
Diff: H, Ans: b
44.   The personal fable refers to an adolescent's imagining that he or she is:
    a. playing a role rather than living a real life.
    b. destined to live a heroic life.
    c. the center of attention wherever he or she goes.
    d. much smarter and wiser than his or her parents.

Adolescent Egocentrism, p. 368
Diff: M, Ans: c
45.   Terence began playing guitar three months ago. He now plans to be a big-time rock star. Terence:
    a. is demonstrating the invincibility fable.
    b. is utilizing an imaginary audience.
    c. has a personal fable.
    d. is in the concrete operational stage.

Adolescent Egocentrism, p. 368
Diff: M, Ans: a
46.   An example of a personal fable would be an adolescent girl who:
    a. believes she will become a famous actress.
    b. writes a story with a moral message.
    c. lies about her past.
    d. believes that Cinderella really lived.

Adolescent Egocentrism, p. 368
Diff: E, Ans: d
47.   Which of the following is NOT an aspect of adolescent egocentrism?
    a. the invincibility fable
    b. the personal fable
    c. the imaginary audience
    d. intuitive thinking

Adolescent Egocentrism, p. 368
Diff: E, Ans: b

48. The term "imaginary audience" refers to adolescents':
    a. ability to understand how others perceive them.
    b. false belief that everyone is constantly attending to their behavior and appearance.
    c. constant posing and posturing before mirrors.
    d. belief that others spy on them.

Adolescent Egocentrism, p. 368
Diff: M, Ans: c

49. Marsha says, "There is no way I am going to school today with this bruise on my cheek. Everybody is going to laugh at me." Marsha is demonstrating:
    a. a volatile mismatch.
    b. implicit judgment.
    c. her belief in an imaginary audience.
    d. an invincibility fable.

Adolescent Egocentrism, p. 369
Diff: M, Ans: d

50. When adolescents fantasize about how others will react to their new hairstyle, they are creating a(n):
    a. personal fable.
    b. abstract audience.
    c. personal identity.
    d. imaginary audience.

Adolescent Egocentrism, p. 369
Diff: M, Ans: d

51. At what age do humans have a "self-serving bias"?
    a. childhood
    b. adolescence
    c. adulthood
    d. all of the above

Adolescent Egocentrism, p. 369
Diff: H, Ans: b

52. Which of the following is a true statement about adolescent egocentrism?
    a. It is destructive, by definition.
    b. It may signal growth toward cognitive maturity.
    c. It has little in common with adult thinking.
    d. All of the above are true of adolescent egocentrism.

Intuitive Conclusions

Intuitive Conclusions, pp. 369-370
Diff: H, Ans: b

53. In adolescence, analytical thinking is sometimes overshadowed by intuitive thinking because:
    a. intuitive thinking is quick and emotional.
    b. analytical thinking is more complex.
    c. analytical thinking is egocentric.
    d. intuitive thinking is generally wrong.

Intuitive Conclusions, pp. 369-370
Diff: E, Ans: a

54. In Klaczynski's studies of adolescents' analytical thinking, those who jumped ahead to what experience had taught them, rather than sticking to the logical task at hand, used:
   a. intuitive thinking.
   b. analytical thinking.
   c. egocentric thinking.
   d. logical thinking.

Intuitive Conclusions, pp. 369-370
Diff: H, Ans: c

55. Klaczynski's studies of adolescents' analytical thinking used the story of Timothy, a good-looking, strong high school senior. Which of the following statements is most likely to be true about Timothy?
   a. Timothy has a girlfriend and is a teacher's pet.
   b. Timothy is popular and an athlete.
   c. Timothy is a teacher's pet.
   d. All of the above are equally likely to be true.

Intuitive Conclusions, pp. 369-370
Diff: H, Ans: c

56. Klaczynski's studies of younger and older adolescents' analytical thinking indicated that:
   a. younger adolescents were rarely logical, whereas older adolescents were nearly always logical.
   b. individuals who were analytical on some problems were analytical on all problems.
   c. most adolescents do not think as analytically as their capabilities would allow.
   d. younger adolescents were more biased toward dismissing research that was contrary to their own beliefs.

Intuitive Conclusions, p. 370
Diff: M, Ans: b

57. Using mental resources in the most efficient and effective manner is referred to as:
   a. analytic thinking.
   b. cognitive economy.
   c. fast processing.
   d. intuitive thinking.

Intuitive Conclusions, pp. 370-371
Diff: H, Ans: c

58. Which of the following is a true statement about intuitive thinking?
   a. It is rarely correct.
   b. It is inefficient when used for personal issues.
   c. It can become analytic and logical with guidance.
   d. All of the above are true.

Adolescent Decision Making

Adolescent Decision Making, p. 372
Diff: M, Ans: b

59. Adolescents rarely make important decisions by rationally exploring all of the options and then deciding on the best one because they:
   a. are likely to be concrete operational thinkers.
   b. think about possibilities more than practicalities.
   c. are often impaired by drug or alcohol use.
   d. do all of the above.

Adolescent Decision Making, p. 372
Diff: E, Ans: a

60.   Which of the following is a *practical* reason to understand that adolescent thinking is both analytical and intuitive?
    a.   to help them make wise decisions
    b.   to understand the growth of cognitive processes into adulthood
    c.   neither a nor b
    d.   both a and b

Weighing Risks and Benefits, p. 372
Diff: H, Ans: c

61.   Which of the following is a true statement about the decision-making skills of adolescents and adults?
    a.   Adults nearly always make wise decisions for themselves.
    b.   The worst outcomes, including drug addiction and accidental death, are more common among adolescents than among adults.
    c.   Adolescents are particularly likely to overrate the joys of the moment and disregard potential risks.
    d.   All of the above are true statements.

Weighing Risks and Benefits, p. 372
Diff: M, Ans: d

62.   Which of the following is a true statement about the decision-making skills of adolescents?
    a.   Adolescents need special protection from poor judgment.
    b.   Adolescents are particularly likely to overrate the joys of the moment and disregard potential risks.
    c.   The younger an individual, the more serious are the consequences of risk taking.
    d.   All of the above are true statements.

Weighing Risks and Benefits, p. 373
Diff: H, Ans: a

63.   Good decision making involves:
    a.   avoiding both overly risky and overly cautious choices.
    b.   basing decisions on the opinions of adults.
    c.   never doing anything that may be too risky.
    d.   waiting until adulthood to make all important decisions.

Weighing Risks and Benefits, p. 373
Diff: M, Ans: e

64.   Which of the following is NOT related to an individual's likelihood of engaging in risky behavior?
    a.   age
    b.   situation
    c.   culture
    d.   gender
    e.   none of the above

Making Decisions About School, Jobs, and Sex, p. 373
Diff: E, Ans: d

65.   Compared to individuals who do not graduate from high school, high school graduates:
    a.   earn less money.
    b.   are less likely to marry.
    c.   die younger.
    d.   are more likely to buy homes.

Making Decisions About School, Jobs, and Sex, p. 373
Diff: E, Ans: b

66. A lack of fit between an individual and his or her environment that causes the individual to become angry, hostile, or depressed is referred to as a(n):
      a. ineffectual environment.
      b. volatile mismatch.
      c. unfortunate arrangement.
      d. misaligned interaction.

Making Decisions About School, Jobs, and Sex, p. 373
Diff: E, Ans: c

67. A volatile mismatch occurs between:
      a. many adolescent boy-girl couples.
      b. stepparents and stepchildren.
      c. teenagers and traditional high schools.
      d. athletes and nonathletes.

Making Decisions About School, Jobs, and Sex, pp. 373-374
Diff: M, Ans: d

68. In the United States, which of the following ethnic groups has the highest high school drop-out rate?
      a. African American
      b. European American
      c. Asian American
      d. Hispanic American

Making Decisions About School, Jobs, and Sex, pp. 374-375
Diff: M, Ans: a

69. Which of the following contributes to the poor fit between current adolescent needs and the traditional structure of high schools?
      a. large school size
      b. low levels of competition
      c. flexible behavioral demands
      d. high levels of student-adult interaction

Making Decisions About School, Jobs, and Sex, p. 375
Diff: E, Ans: c

70. From a psychological perspective, which of the following is a good reason for starting high school instruction later than the before-8:00 A.M. first bell that is common in the United States?
      a. to allow for before-school employment
      b. to encourage students to spend more unsupervised time with their peers
      c. to permit adolescent minds to wake up
      d. all of the above

Making Decisions About School, Jobs, and Sex, p. 375
Diff: H, Ans: a

71. The common high school schedule that involves deeply divided disciplines being taught in separate 40-minute blocks has the effect of:
      a. inhibiting formal operational thought.
      b. increasing teacher-student interaction.
      c. improving student grades.
      d. influencing all of the above.

Making Decisions About School, Jobs, and Sex, p. 375
Diff: M, Ans: d

72. Karen is entering high school. Compared to her 10-year-old sister, she will probably have:
     a. increased academic self-confidence.
     b. better relationships with her teachers.
     c. higher motivation.
     d. lower grades.

Making Decisions About School, Jobs, and Sex, p. 375
Diff: H, Ans: b

73. Which of the following is necessary for adolescent cognitive development?
     a. independent learning
     b. personal involvement
     c. high grades on report cards
     d. all of the above

Making Decisions About School, Jobs, and Sex, p. 375
Diff: H, Ans: c

74. Which of the following recommendations would you make to a school district that is trying to structure its high schools to enhance adolescent cognitive development?
     a. cut the length of subject periods from 40 minutes to 25 minutes so that students do not have to pay attention for such a long time
     b. enlarge schools so that students have more opportunities to find a group of friends
     c. create more opportunities for students to be involved in school clubs and sports
     d. discourage teachers and students from talking about personal matters by keeping teachers' lunch rooms, parking lots, and bathrooms separate from those of students
     e. Do all of the above.

Making Decisions About School, Jobs, and Sex, p. 375
Diff: M, Ans: b

75. Which of the following is a true statement about the association between high school size and student involvement?
     a. The larger the school, the *more* involved individual students are.
     b. The larger the school, the *less* involved individual students are.
     c. The association between school size and student involvement depends entirely on the ethnicity of the students.
     d. There is no association between school size and student involvement.

Working Outside of School, p. 376
Diff: M, Ans: b

76. LeAnn is a 16-year-old who has just started working 25 hours a week at a local ice cream store. If she is like the average employed adolescent, she is more likely than students who are not employed to:
     a. refrain from sex.
     b. get poor grades.
     c. avoid drug use.
     d. feel appreciative of her family.

Working Outside of School, p. 376
Diff: H, Ans: a

77. Which of the following is a true statement about adolescent employment in the United States?
     a. No matter how few hours adolescents are employed, their grades are negatively influenced.
     b. It generally prepares students for adult employment.
     c. Teenage girls who are employed are less likely to be sexually active than teenage girls who are not employed.
     d. All of the above are true.

Working Outside of School, p. 376
Diff: E, Ans: d
78.   Compared to high school seniors who are not employed, those who are employed are more likely to:
   a.   smoke cigarettes.
   b.   have poor relationships with parents.
   c.   have low grades.
   d.   do all of the above.

Working Outside of School, p. 376
Diff: E, Ans: c
79.   In which of the following countries are adolescents expected to fulfill their obligation to study and thus are rarely employed?
   a.   United States
   b.   Germany
   c.   Japan
   d.   all of the above

Working Outside of School, p. 377
Diff: M, Ans: d
80.   In the United States today, adolescent employment:
   a.   helps families meet their expenses.
   b.   teaches money-management skills.
   c.   keeps adolescents out of trouble.
   d.   does none of the above.
   e.   does all of the above.

Working Outside of School, p. 377
Diff: M, Ans: c
81.   When adolescents are employed more than 20 hours per week, they:
   a.   are gaining valuable real-world experience.
   b.   tend to save a great deal of money for college.
   c.   are more likely to engage in risk-taking behaviors.
   d.   learn how to balance their academic goals with their employment responsibilities.

What Teenagers Decide About Sex, p. 377
Diff: H, Ans: a
82.   Which of the following facts suggests that adolescent decisions about sex are NOT biologically inevitable?
   a.   The age of onset of puberty varies across racial groups.
   b.   Teen birth rates vary widely across cultures.
   c.   The use of contraceptives has increased.
   d.   Cultural differences in the onset of sexual intercourse are vast.

What Teenagers Decide About Sex, p. 377
Diff: M, Ans: d
83.   Which of the following is a true statement about adolescent sexual behavior?
   a.   The teen birth rate worldwide is increasing.
   b.   The use of contraceptives is decreasing.
   c.   Teen birth rates are comparable across a variety of cultures.
   d.   The age of onset of sexual intercourse varies widely across cultures.

What Teenagers Decide About Sex, p. 377
Diff: E, Ans: b

84. The country with the highest teen birth rate is:
    a. Sweden.
    b. the United States.
    c. England.
    d. Japan.

What Teenagers Decide About Sex, p. 377
Diff: M, Ans: c

85. Which of the following contributes to the high teen birth rate in the United States, in comparison with that of other developed countries?
    a. earlier puberty
    b. poorer health care
    c. less contraceptive use
    d. higher rates of teen marriage

What Teenagers Decide About Sex, p. 377
Diff: E, Ans: e

86. Compared to teenagers in other developed countries, teens in the United States:
    a. use less contraception.
    b. are more sexually active.
    c. have fewer abortions.
    d. have more babies.
    e. do all of the above.

What Teenagers Decide About Sex, p. 377
Diff: E, Ans: a

87. Since 1990, the rate of condom use among adolescent boys has:
    a. increased.
    b. decreased.
    c. remained stable.
    d. varied randomly.

What Teenagers Decide About Sex, p. 378
Diff: H, Ans: d

88. Which of the following is a true statement about scientific research on adolescents' thoughts about sexual decisions and their differences from those of the previous generation?
    a. A great deal of research has been conducted, and it is clear why patterns of behavior have changed.
    b. A great deal of research has been conducted, but it still is *not* clear why patterns of behavior have changed.
    c. Researchers have conducted some research in this area, but the research has been of poor quality, and thus little is known.
    d. Solid research in this area has been difficult, because it has been hindered by political disagreements and federal law.

What Teenagers Decide About Sex, p. 378
Diff: E, Ans: e

89. Adolescents who are engaging in which of the following do NOT need to be concerned about STIs and contraception?
    a. sexual intercourse
    b. mutual masturbation
    c. shared bathing
    d. oral sex
    e. none of the above

Sex Education in School, pp. 378-379
Diff: H, Ans: b
90.   From a developmental perspective, school sex education programs are to be commended because
       teenagers need:
       a.   to understand what it means to be sexually active.
       b.   practice with the emotional expression that reflects their intuitive thinking.
       c.   experience with concrete operational thinking.
       d.   help finding appropriate sexual partners.

Sex Education in School, p. 379
Diff: H, Ans: d
91.   In the United States during the past decade, there has been an increase in the number of schools
       teaching:
       a.   the correct use of condoms.
       b.   various methods of contraception.
       c.   about sexual orientation.
       d.   how to avoid AIDS and pregnancy.
       e.   all of the above.

Sex Education in School, p. 379
Diff: E, Ans: c
92.   In the United States, what percent of schools teach students about sex and health?
       a.   11
       b.   55
       c.   93
       d.   100

Sex Education in School, p. 379
Diff: E, Ans: b
93.   In the United States, the number of schools teaching the correct use of condoms has:
       a.   increased.
       b.   decreased.
       c.   remained stable.
       d.   varied randomly.

Sex Education in School, p. 379
Diff: M, Ans: c
94.   In the United States in the year 2000, what percent of school districts required that schools teach sexual
       abstinence as the only acceptable alternative to marriage and forbade mention of contraception?
       a.   0
       b.   9
       c.   35
       d.   95

Sex Education in School, p. 379
Diff: M, Ans: a
95.   Teaching adolescents about contraception increases which of the following?
       a.   condom use
       b.   frequency of sexual intercourse
       c.   number of sexual partners
       d.   sexual activity
       e.   none of the above
       f.   all of the above

Sex Education in School, p. 379
Diff: H, Ans: a

96.   Which of the following is a true statement about adolescent thinking?
   a.   It is hypothetical.
   b.   It causes adolescents to try out whatever they learn.
   c.   It is not capable of comprehending how to say "no" to sexual activity.
   d.   All of the above are true.

Risk Taking, Decision Making, and Cultures, p. 380
Diff: E, Ans: d

97.   Demonstrating condom use at soccer games in Cameroon worked _____, as the approach was _____ suited to that culture.
   a.   poorly; poorly
   b.   poorly; well
   c.   well; poorly
   d.   well; well

Risk Taking, Decision Making, and Cultures, p. 380
Diff: H, Ans: d

98.   Which of the following is *required* for people to make responsible, healthy decisions about sex?
   a.   being an adult
   b.   knowing the facts
   c.   having access to confidential services
   d.   b and c
   e.   all of the above

Risk Taking, Decision Making, and Cultures, pp. 380-381
Diff: M, Ans: b

99.   Which of the following is the most important factor in predicting whether an individual adolescent will engage in risk-taking behavior?
   a.   ethnicity
   b.   family and peers
   c.   income
   d.   family structure

Risk Taking, Decision Making, and Cultures, pp. 380-381
Diff: H, Ans: c

100.   Knowing a person's ethnicity, income, and family structure:
   a.   makes it possible to predict how likely it is for an individual to take any particular risk.
   b.   makes family and peers irrelevant in predicting risky behavior.
   c.   is less relevant than an individual's thought processes and immediate social context in predicting risky behavior.
   d.   does none of the above.

TRUE-FALSE QUESTIONS

Intellectual Advances

Ans: F, pp. 363-364

1.   Psychologists agree that brain maturation has little to do with the cognitive advances of adolescence.

Ans: T, p. 365

2.   In an experiment by Inhelder and Piaget that involved balancing a scale with weights, the age at which children were first able to use the trial-and-error method to achieve some understanding of balancing was approximately 10 years.

Ans: F, p. 365

3.   The cognitive gains needed for such tasks as balancing a scale with weights are gradually acquired by all people, usually during adolescence.

Ans: F, p. 365

4.   Once adolescents develop their capacity for formal logic, they tend to use it consistently across situations.

Ans: F, p. 366

5.   Hypothetical thought involves reasoning only about propositions that reflect reality.

Ans: T, p. 366

6.   As adolescents develop their capacity for hypothetical thinking, they become more capable of deductive reasoning.

Ans: F, p. 367

7.   In a debate, adolescents are less able than 8-year-olds to argue against their personal interests, largely because of egocentrism.

Ans: T, p. 367

8.   Analytic thinking generally takes more time than intuitive thinking.

Ans: F, p. 368

9.   Analytic thinking and intuitive thinking nearly always come up with the same conclusion.

Ans: F, p. 368

10.   Adolescents tend to think logically about themselves.

Ans: T, p. 368

11.   Both the invincibility fable and the personal fable reflect adolescent egocentrism.

Ans: F, pp. 368-369

12.   Adolescents' belief that others are as intensely interested in them as they are in themselves is referred to as the personal fable.

Ans: T, p. 369

13.   Being self-conscious because of a belief in an imaginary audience is indicative of adolescents' lack of comfort in the broader social world.

Ans: T, p. 369

14.   Adolescent egocentrism is not necessarily destructive.

Ans: T, p. 370

15.   As adolescents' knowledge base increases and their thinking processes accelerate, their thinking becomes more efficient.

Ans: F, pp. 370-371

16.   Adolescents geared toward cognitive economy will always use intuitive thinking.

Ans: T, pp. 371-372

17.   Although formal operational thought may be universally possible after age 11, it is not universally used.

Adolescent Decision Making

Ans: F, p. 372
18. Once adolescents reach adulthood, they always make wise, logical decisions.

Ans: T, p. 373
19. Adolescent boys are more likely to engage in thrill-seeking behavior than are adolescent girls.

Ans: F, p. 373
20. Many critics blame high school drop-out rates on widespread poor-quality teaching.

Ans: F, p. 375
21. Report card grades tend to rise as students move from elementary school to high school.

Ans: T, p. 375
22. Student commitment to schools enhances academic performance.

Ans: F, p. 376
23. When teachers and students believe that learning is the result of inborn intelligence, students seem to perform better in school.

Ans: F, p. 376
24. Realistic career expectations are typical during high school.

Ans: T, p. 376
25. In the United States, part-time jobs do little to prepare students for adult employment.

Ans: T, p. 376
26. Cigarettes are considered a gateway drug.

Ans: F, p. 376
27. In Japan, it is common to find that almost all teens are employed.

Ans: F, p. 377
28. In the United States, the money earned by adolescents often goes toward saving for college.

Ans: T, p. 377
29. Adolescence should be a time for academic learning, not vocational experience.

Ans: F, p. 377
30. It is clear from research in the United States and other countries that adolescent decisions regarding sex are biologically inevitable.

Ans: F, p. 377
31. STI stands for syphilis-type infection.

Ans: T, p. 377
32. In some cultures, girls are more sexually experienced than boys.

Ans: T, p. 377
33. In the United States, the teen birth rate is decreasing for every age group and every ethnic group.

Ans: F, p. 377
34. Condom use among adolescent boys has decreased dramatically in the last decade.

Ans: T, p. 378
35.   Federal law has hindered scientific research on adolescent decision making about sex.

Ans: F, p. 378
36.   Traditionally, the term "sexually active" has referred to individuals who have engaged in either oral sex or sexual intercourse.

Ans: T, p. 378
37.   Many adolescents who have oral sex do not consider themselves to be having sex.

Ans: T, p. 379
38.   Fewer than half of all schools in the United States teach the correct use of condoms.

Ans: F, p. 379
39.   Teaching students about contraception increases adolescent sexual activity.

Ans: F, p. 380
40.   The success of the condom education program in Cameroon has led U.S. high school coaches to imitate the program.

Ans: T, p. 380
41.   The pattern of risk-taking behavior is different for Whites, Blacks, and Hispanics.

Ans: F, pp. 380-381
42.   Knowing an individual's age and ethnicity makes it possible to predict how likely the individual is to engage in any particular risk.

FILL-IN-THE-BLANK QUESTIONS

Intellectual Advances

Ans: formal operational thought, p. 364
1.   Piaget referred to the stage of cognitive development that involves the ability to think logically about abstract ideas as _____.

Ans: hypothetical, p. 366
2.   When thinking about possibilities that may or may not reflect reality, for the first time an adolescent is now using _____ thought.

Ans: Inductive, p. 366
3.   _____ reasoning involves using specific cases to form a general conclusion.

Ans: deductive, p. 366
4.   In _____ reasoning, one begins with a general premise and draws logical conclusions from it.

Ans: inductive reasoning, p. 366
5.   The statement, "If it walks like a duck and quacks like a duck, it must be a duck," is an example of _____.

Ans: Intuitive (or Heuristic or Experiential), p. 367
6.   _____ thought arises not from a logical premise, but from memories and feelings.

Ans: invincibility, p. 368

7.   A survivor of a Nazi concentration camp writes that as a teenager in the camp he took large risks, never considering the consequences of being caught, and ignoring the advice of others. His behavior can, in part, be explained by the _____ fable of adolescence.

Ans: personal, p. 368

8.   An adolescent who fantasizes about his success as a world-famous song composer has created a(n) _____ fable about his heroic future.

Ans: imaginary audience, pp. 368-369

9.   An adolescent girl suffers great discomfort at having to go to math class with wet hair after her swimming class, because she feels that all eyes are on her. This girl, like many adolescents, is responding to a(n) _____, which she supposes will judge her appearance harshly.

Ans: self-consciousness, p. 369

10. Adolescent egocentrism enables adolescents to reflect more thoughtfully about their lives, but often at the cost of greater _____.

Ans: Cognitive economy, p. 370

11. _____ refers to the most efficient and effective use of mental resources.

Adolescent Decision Making

Ans: brave (cool/sexy), p. 373

12. In adolescent culture, caution is considered "goody-goody," whereas risk-taking behavior is considered _____.

Ans: education (high school graduation), p. 373

13. Even once variables such as family background and IQ are equalized, _____ is a significant predictor of success, including employment, income, and life span.

Ans: volatile mismatch, pp. 373-374

14. The rigid behavioral demands and intense competition of secondary schools often result in a(n) _____ between adolescents and their schools.

Ans: effort, p. 376

15. Believing that learning is a result of _____ enhances student motivation.

Ans: heuristic (intuitive/experiential), p. 376

16. Adolescents generally use _____ thinking when making the decision to work outside school.

Ans: less, p. 377

17. The more hours of after-school employment adolescents work, the _____ learning they do in school.

Ans: sexually transmitted infection, p. 377

18. STI stands for _____.

Ans: culture (cohort/environment), p. 377

19. The fact that teen birth rates and the age of onset of sexual intercourse vary widely across countries indicates that adolescent decision making about sex is largely due to _____.

Ans: sexually active, p. 378

20. The term _____ has traditionally referred to individuals who have had sexual intercourse.

Ans: factual information, p. 379

21. High school students want schools to provide more _____ about sex.

Ans: confidential services, p. 380

22.   A review of family planning across the globe indicates that people of all ages make responsible decisions about sex if the facts and _____ are available.

Ans: Family (Individual), p. 380

23.   _____ factors outweighed ethnic differences predicting teenager risk-taking behaviors.

ESSAY QUESTIONS

1.   Language development is covered extensively in the chapters devoted to cognitive development in the first two years, the play years, and the school years. Because the growth of language is not as striking in adolescence, a section on language development was not included. From what you have learned about cognitive development in general, hypothesize (or make some guesses about) language development in adolescence.

2.   If given some weights and asked to balance a scale by hooking the weights onto the scale's arms, how will the most cognitively advanced adolescents determine where to place the weights in order to balance the scale? How about preadolescents?

3.   Define analytic thinking and intuitive thinking, and give an example of each. Why do you think adolescents tend to use intuitive thinking to such a great extent?

4.   Provide an example of a time when you exhibited adolescent egocentrism in your own life. What type of adolescent egocentrism was it?

5.   Several years ago, a movie (*The Program*) was released in which some of the teenage characters would lie down on top of the white lines on a road. Using what you have learned about adolescent cognitive processes, explain why teenagers might engage in risky behavior like this.

6.   Give an example of an important decision that an adolescent must make, and describe the types of thought processes he or she may undergo in making this decision. Would these thought processes be more likely to be rational or intuitive?

7.   Imagine you are a consultant working for a school board. The school board is concerned about the drop-out rate in the district's high schools. Describe *three* recommendations you would make to the school board about changes it can make to try to improve the drop-out rate.

8.   Imagine your teenager wants to get an after-school job. Do you think this is a good idea or a bad idea? Why?

9.   Describe one way in which sex education in school provides adolescents with experience in formal operational thinking and one way in which it provides experience in intuitive thinking.

10.   Even though teens know many facts about sex, they do not always engage in responsible sexual behavior. Provide *two* reasons why this may be the case.

11.   Develop an outline for a sex-education course to be implemented in your local school district. Be sure to include what ages it should reach and the topics it should cover.

12.   Describe how knowledge of an individual's culture and ethnicity helps to predict in what risk-taking behaviors he or she will engage. How accurate is this prediction? Describe *two* other pieces of information you could use to improve your prediction.

Answer guidelines to these essay questions can be found in the Appendix at the end of the Test Bank.

MULTIPLE-CHOICE QUESTIONS

The Self and Identity

The Self and Identity, p. 385
Diff: E, Ans: c
1. Psychosocial development during adolescence is often seen as a quest to answer the question:
    a. "What am I going to do with my life?"
    b. "Will I ever find someone to love?"
    c. "Who am I?"
    d. "Why don't my parents understand me?"

The Self and Identity, p. 385
Diff: M, Ans: d
2. Identity refers to:
    a. all of the possible selves that an individual tries out.
    b. the group of peers with whom an individual spends time.
    c. a set of behaviors adopted in order to please others.
    d. a consistent definition of the self as a unique individual.

The Self and Identity, p. 385
Diff: M, Ans: c
3. The first step in the process of self-definition involves:
    a. separating from parents emotionally and physically.
    b. finding a sexual partner.
    c. establishing consistency of emotions, thoughts, and actions.
    d. setting a career goal.

Multiple Selves, p. 386
Diff: E, Ans: a
4. Which of the following is NOT one of the common types of false selves noted by Harter and her colleagues?
    a. religious false self
    b. experimental false self
    c. acceptable false self
    d. pleasing false self

Multiple Selves, p. 386
Diff: M, Ans: b
5. The pleasing false self typically arises from:
    a. the perception that the real self is rejected by parents and peers.
    b. a desire to impress others.
    c. the belief that one is fake.
    d. an attempt to see how it feels to behave differently.

Multiple Selves, p. 386
Diff: M, Ans: a
6.   The acceptable false self typically arises from:
        a.   the perception that the real self is rejected by parents and peers.
        b.   a desire to impress others.
        c.   the belief that one is fake.
        d.   an attempt to see how it feels to behave differently.

Multiple Selves, p. 386
Diff: H, Ans: b
7.   Eddie feels that others do not like him, and he does not like himself much either. He has little understanding of who he really is, and he behaves in ways that hide his true nature. Eddie is:
        a.   behaving in a deviant manner.
        b.   demonstrating an acceptable false self.
        c.   experiencing identity moratorium.
        d.   a victim of low parental monitoring.

Multiple Selves, p. 386
Diff: H, Ans: c
8.   Which is most typical of a 15-year-old boy?
        a.   He has not even begun to think about who he is.
        b.   He has already found his "true self."
        c.   He is exploring several "possible selves."
        d.   He is rarely, if ever, disappointed in himself.

Identity Status, p. 386
Diff: E, Ans: a
9.   Which of the following is NOT one of the four aspects of identity highlighted by Erikson?
        a.   hairstyle
        b.   politics
        c.   vocation
        d.   sex

Identity Status, p. 387
Diff: E, Ans: a
10.   According to Erikson, adolescents are in the stage of:
        a.   identity versus role confusion.
        b.   intimacy versus isolation.
        c.   independence versus neediness.
        d.   integration versus separation.

Identity Status, p. 387
Diff: M, Ans: b
11.   According to Erikson, the goal of adolescence is to:
        a.   abandon parental goals.
        b.   form a coherent identity.
        c.   attain independence from the peer group.
        d.   form an intimate relationship with a member of the other sex.

Identity Status, p. 387
Diff: H, Ans: c
12.   Mary is an adolescent. According to Erikson, her new identity will be established by choosing:
        a.   an appropriate adult "hero figure."
        b.   values and goals opposite to the destructive identities of music stars.
        c.   some parental and societal values and abandoning others.
        d.   one sexual, political, and vocational role and sticking with it, regardless of the consequences.

Identity Status, p. 387
Diff: M, Ans: c

13. Following Erikson's lead, _____ distinguished four identity statuses.
     a. Baumrind
     b. Freud
     c. Marcia
     d. Skinner

Identity Status, pp. 387-388
Diff: E, Ans: b

14. Adoption of parents' or society's roles and values, rather than questioning and exploring a personal identity, is referred to as identity:
     a. moratorium.
     b. foreclosure.
     c. diffusion.
     d. achievement.

Identity Status, pp. 387-388
Diff: H, Ans: d

15. Which of the following is most likely to be a form of identity foreclosure?
     a. dropping out of school
     b. taking a career path very different from that urged by parents and counselors
     c. refusing to vote
     d. joining a religious cult

Identity Status, pp. 387-388
Diff: H, Ans: a

16. Angel's parents always wanted him to be part of the family business—and Angel never questioned this. At 21, Angel decided to leave the business to become a teacher. Angel is resisting:
     a. identity foreclosure.
     b. forced conversion.
     c. role repudiation.
     d. negative identity.

Identity Status, p. 388 (Table 16.1)
Diff: H, Ans: b

17. The identity status that is characterized by not questioning and high commitment is:
     a. achievement.
     b. foreclosure.
     c. diffusion.
     d. moratorium.

Identity Status, p. 388 (Table 16.1)
Diff: H, Ans: c

18. According to Erikson, the least satisfactory identity status, characterized by not questioning and no commitment, is:
     a. achievement.
     b. foreclosure.
     c. diffusion.
     d. moratorium.

Identity Status, p. 388
Diff: E, Ans: a

19.   An identity that is opposite to the one that is expected, adopted as a way of rebelling against
        expectations, is considered a(n):
        a.   negative identity.
        b.   autocratic identity.
        c.   transpositional identity.
        d.   reverse identity.

Identity Status, p. 388
Diff: M, Ans: d

20.   In the movie called *Footloose*, the son of a religious leader grows up to be rebellious and defiant. He:
        a.   has attained identity achievement.
        b.   is experiencing foreclosure.
        c.   is in a state of identity diffusion.
        d.   has established a negative identity.

Identity Status, p. 388
Diff: H, Ans: d

21.   Imagine an adolescent who is part of an ethnic or social group with the reputation of being overweight.
        If this adolescent rejects the dominant culture and adopts and exaggerates this stereotype by becoming
        obese, he or she has adopted a(n):
        a.   stereotyped identity.
        b.   diffused identity.
        c.   reversed identity.
        d.   oppositional identity.

Identity Status, p. 388
Diff: E, Ans: c

22.   Identity diffusion refers to the identity status in which adolescents:
        a.   take a pause in identity formation that allows for exploration of alternatives.
        b.   form their identity prematurely.
        c.   have few commitments to goals or values and fail to take on any role.
        d.   understand who they are, connected to everything they have learned.

Identity Status, p. 388
Diff: E, Ans: a

23.   Identity diffusion is typically characterized by:
        a.   apathy.
        b.   foreclosure.
        c.   following one's heart.
        d.   all of the above.

Identity Status, p. 388
Diff: H, Ans: c

24.   Which of the following adolescents appears to be experiencing identity diffusion?
        a.   Jeannine, who runs away from a pressured home environment and joins a commune
        b.   Fred, who is pressured by his parents to go into medicine
        c.   Zachary, who spends most of his time hanging out and seems apathetic about life
        d.   Barbara, a college student who frequently changes majors

Identity Status, p. 388
Diff: E, Ans: d
25. The term for a pause in identity formation, when alternatives are explored before final choices are made, is known as:
    a. identity diffusion.
    b. role confusion.
    c. negative identity.
    d. moratorium.

Identity Status, p. 388
Diff: H, Ans: b
26. During an identity moratorium, adolescents typically:
    a. ignore their future roles and responsibilities.
    b. attempt to fill the role they are in, but consider it temporary.
    c. think in very simple, uncomplicated ways.
    d. experience a type of adolescent schizophrenia.

Identity Status, p. 388
Diff: M, Ans: a
27. In the United States, one way for some to legitimatize an identity moratorium is to:
    a. join the army.
    b. get married.
    c. have a baby.
    d. smoke marijuana.

Identity Status, p. 388
Diff: H, Ans: a
28. Which of the following is probably the most typical sequence of identity status?
    a. diffusion, moratorium, achievement
    b. moratorium, achievement, foreclosure
    c. foreclosure, diffusion, moratorium
    d. achievement, moratorium, foreclosure

Status Versus Process, pp. 388-389
Diff: H, Ans: b
29. Individuals with which of the following identity status or statuses are considered to have an identity?
    a. achievement only
    b. achievement and foreclosure
    c. achievement and moratorium
    d. achievement, foreclosure, and moratorium

Status Versus Process, p. 389
Diff: M, Ans: b
30. In the United States in the twenty-first century, it is not uncommon for adolescents to be in moratorium in which of the following domains?
    a. religious identity
    b. vocational identity
    c. sexual identity
    d. moral identity

Status Versus Process, p. 389
Diff: E, Ans: c
31.   Is identity formed from within, when an individual recognizes his or her true nature, or from without, after social forces push an adolescent toward a particular identity?
      a.   from within only
      b.   from without only
      c.   from a combination of the two
      d.   from none of the above

Gender and Ethnic Identity, p. 389
Diff: E, Ans: a
32.   An individual's acceptance of the roles and behaviors that society associates with the biological category of male or female is referred to as:
      a.   gender identity.
      b.   ethnic identity.
      c.   heterosexual identity.
      d.   foreclosed identity.

Gender and Ethnic Identity, p. 389
Diff: M, Ans: d
33.   Which of the following is involved in an individual's gender identity?
      a.   with whom the individual is sexually active
      b.   what clothing the individual wears
      c.   how the individual talks and moves
      d.   all of the above

Gender and Ethnic Identity, p. 389
Diff: E, Ans: b
34.   Ethnic identity and gender identity are often connected because:
      a.   some cultures have only one sex.
      b.   male and female roles are defined differently by different cultures.
      c.   they are essentially the same thing.
      d.   males have an easier time forming an ethnic identity than females have.

Gender and Ethnic Identity, p. 390
Diff: H, Ans: a
35.   Laura is a minority adolescent who lives in the United States. She grew up in a neighborhood with others of a similar ethnic background. As Laura grows older, she will probably tend to:
      a.   take pride in the heritage of her broad ethnic category.
      b.   define herself only as part of the majority European-American culture.
      c.   strictly adhere to the ethnic patterns she learned in her family and neighborhood.
      d.   have difficulty defining her ethnic identity at all.

Sadness and Anger

Sadness and Anger, p. 391
Diff: E, Ans: b
36.   Emotional difficulties that are manifested inward, inflicting harm on the troubled individual, are referred to as:
      a.   externalizing problems.
      b.   internalizing problems.
      c.   suicidal ideations.
      d.   parasuicidal attempts.

Sadness and Anger, p. 391
Diff: E, Ans: d
37.   The term "externalizing problems" refers to:
    a.   individuals' feelings of incompetence.
    b.   deliberate acts of self-destruction that do not end in death.
    c.   thinking about killing oneself.
    d.   emotional difficulties that are manifested in acting out behaviors.

Sadness and Anger, p. 391
Diff: M, Ans: a
38.   Which of the following is considered an internalizing problem?
    a.   clinical depression
    b.   destroying property
    c.   injuring others
    d.   defying authority

Sadness and Anger, p. 391
Diff: M, Ans: b
39.   Which of the following is considered an externalizing problem?
    a.   clinical depression
    b.   property destruction
    c.   overuse of sedative drugs
    d.   bulimia

Sadness and Anger, p. 391
Diff: H, Ans: c
40.   Which of the following is a true statement about suicide as an internalizing problem or an externalizing problem?
    a.   It is always considered an *externalizing* problem.
    b.   It is always considered an *internalizing* problem.
    c.   It is generally considered an *internalizing* problem, except when it is used as a strategy to get back at someone.
    d.   It is generally considered an *externalizing* problem, except when it is used as a strategy to get back at someone.

Sadness and Anger, p. 391
Diff: E, Ans: a
41.   Do internalizing problems and externalizing problems increase, decrease, or stay the same from childhood to adolescence?
    a.   Both internalizing problems and externalizing problems increase.
    b.   Both internalizing problems and externalizing problems decrease.
    c.   Both internalizing problems and externalizing problems stay the same.
    d.   Internalizing problems increase, whereas externalizing problems decrease.
    e.   Internalizing problems decrease, whereas externalizing problems increase.

Sadness and Anger, p. 391
Diff: M, Ans: b
42.   Which of the following is a true statement about the prevalence of internalizing problems and externalizing problems among adolescent males and females?
    a.   Internalizing problems are more common among males, and externalizing problems are more common among females.
    b.   Internalizing problems are more common among females, and externalizing problems are more common among males.
    c.   Both internalizing problems and externalizing problems are more common among males than among females.
    d.   Both internalizing problems and externalizing problems are more common among females than among males.

The Usual Dip, pp. 391-392
Diff: E, Ans: b

43.   In general, as children become adolescents, their feelings of competence:
       a.   rise.
       b.   decline.
       c.   rise then decline.
       a.   remain stable.

The Usual Dip, p. 392 (Figure 16.2)
Diff: M, Ans: d

44.   In which of the following areas do feelings of competence decrease from grade one to grade nine?
       a.   sports
       b.   math
       c.   language arts
       d.   all of the above

The Usual Dip, p. 392
Diff: M, Ans: c

45.   Individuals with which of the following perspectives on their competence are most likely to effectively
       handle the declines in feelings of competence that come with adolescence?
       a.   those who have extreme self-doubt
       b.   those who have extreme self-confidence
       c.   those who are realistic
       d.   all of the above

The Usual Dip, p. 392
Diff: H, Ans: a

46.   Your adolescent cousin is asking for your advice about her low feelings of competence in athletics and
       academics. Which of the following would be the best advice you could give her?
       a.   "Be realistic."
       b.   "You are the best in everything you do. Don't listen to anyone who tells you otherwise."
       c.   "It is good to doubt your abilities. You are probably not that good at everything."
       d.   "I had so much trouble with my own adolescence; I can't help you at all."

Depression, p. 392
Diff: E, Ans: b

47.   Approximately 1 in _____ adolescent girls is affected by clinical depression.
       a.   2
       b.   5
       c.   10
       d.   100

Depression, p. 392
Diff: H, Ans: e

48.   Which of the following does NOT influence an individual's risk of experiencing clinical depression in
       adolescence?
       a.   having been cared for as an infant by a depressed mother
       b.   hormonal changes of puberty
       c.   genes
       d.   stresses of school
       e.   none of the above

Adolescent Suicide, p. 393
Diff: E, Ans: b

49.   Suicidal ideation refers to:
    a.   a deliberate act of self-destruction that does not end in death.
    b.   thinking about suicide.
    c.   the belief that suicide is an effective way of getting back at one's parents or peers.
    d.   feelings of sadness or hopelessness.

Adolescent Suicide, p. 393
Diff: M, Ans: c

50.   Which of the following is NOT an accurate explanation for why many people believe that adolescent suicides are common?
    a.   Suicide attempts are more common in adolescence than in adulthood.
    b.   Statistics often group adolescents together with young adults.
    c.   Adolescents commit suicide more frequently than do adults.
    d.   The rate of adolescent suicide has increased over the past 40 years.

Adolescent Suicide, p. 393 (Figure 16.3)
Diff: H, Ans: d

51.   Which of the following statements regarding suicide in the United States is true?
    a.   The rate of suicides in young adolescents aged 10 to 14 is higher than is the rate for older adolescents aged 15 to 19.
    b.   The suicide rate for adolescents has stayed essentially constant since 1962.
    c.   More than 2 percent of adolescents aged 15 to 19 committed suicide in 2000.
    d.   In 2000, the suicide rate for the elderly was about twice the rate for teenagers.

Adolescent Suicide, p. 393 (Figure 16.3)
Diff: M, Ans: c

52.   Which of the following groups had the highest suicide rate in the United States in 2000?
    a.   young adolescents aged 10 to 14
    b.   older adolescents aged 15 to 19
    c.   young adults aged 20 to 24
    d.   older adults aged 65 to 69

Adolescent Suicide, p. 393
Diff: M, Ans: c

53.   Parasuicide refers to:
    a.   any self-destructive behavior.
    b.   the serious consideration of suicide as an option.
    c.   a deliberate act of self-destruction that does not end in death.
    d.   all of the above.

Adolescent Suicide, p. 393
Diff: H, Ans: d

54.   Which of the following is a true statement about parasuicide?
    a.   Experts prefer the term *failed attempt* over the term *parasuicide*.
    b.   Parasuicide only includes acts that are intended to take one's own life.
    c.   Parasuicide only includes acts that are well thought-out.
    d.   None of the above are true statements.

Adolescent Suicide, p. 393
Diff: M, Ans: a
55.   The term "parasuicide" is used rather than the term "failed suicide" because "failed suicide":
a.   assumes that the individual intended to kill himself or herself.
b.   is too explicit.
c.   makes the individual feel like he or she failed at one more thing.
d.   inhibits coverage by medical insurance companies.

Adolescent Suicide (Figure 16.3), pp. 393-394
Diff: M, Ans: b
56.   Which of the following is a true statement about adolescent suicide?
a.   The adolescent suicide rate is about twice that of adults.
b.   The adolescent rate in 2000 is double what it was in 1962.
c.   Almost all teens who seriously consider suicide attempt suicide.
d.   The present adolescent suicide rate is about 1 in 500 each year.

Adolescent Suicide, pp. 393-394
Diff: H, Ans: d
57.   Adolescents who perform acts of parasuicide:
a.   have clear intentions of killing themselves.
b.   are almost always disappointed that they did not kill themselves.
c.   will tend to try again if authority figures assume the attempt was serious.
d.   perform the act in the role of the possible self.

Adolescent Suicide, p. 394
Diff: M, Ans: b
58.   An adolescent you know has experienced suicidal ideation. All of the following will increase this adolescent's likelihood of parasuicide or death EXCEPT:
a.   availability of guns.
b.   being female.
c.   lack of parental supervision.
d.   alcohol and drug use.

Adolescent Suicide (Table 16.2), p. 394
Diff: E, Ans: c
59.   Suicidal ideation is more common in:
a.   boys than in girls.
b.   older adolescents than in younger adolescents.
c.   girls than in boys.
d.   adults than in adolescents.

Adolescent Suicide (Table 16.2), p. 394
Diff: H, Ans: c
60.   Which of the following is more common in adolescent boys than it is in adolescent girls?
a.   seriously considering attempting suicide
b.   parasuicide
c.   actual suicide
d.   all of the above

Adolescent Suicide, p. 394
Diff: H, Ans: c
61.   Which of the following is NOT a true statement about sex differences in adolescent suicide?
a.   Male suicides are more likely to be externalizing.
b.   Male suicides are more likely to involve the use of guns.
c.   Depressed boys are more likely to engage in parasuicide, signaling distress.
d.   China is the only country in which females complete suicide more often than males.

Adolescent Suicide, p. 394
Diff: M, Ans: a
62.   A teenager in which of the following nations is MOST likely to commit suicide?
   a.   Hungary
   b.   Canada
   c.   United States
   d.   Japan

Adolescent Suicide (Table 16.3), p. 394
Diff: M, Ans: d
63.   In the United States, which of the following ethnic groups has the highest adolescent suicide rate?
   a.   Hispanic American
   b.   African American
   c.   European American
   d.   Native American
   e.   Asian American

Adolescent Suicide (Table 16.3), p. 394
Diff: H, Ans: e
64.   In the United States, which of the following ethnic groups has the highest proportion of *female*
      suicides?
   a.   Hispanic American
   b.   African American
   c.   European American
   d.   Native American
   e.   Asian American

Adolescent Suicide, p. 395
Diff: E, Ans: d
65.   Several suicides committed within the same group of people in a brief period are referred to as:
   a.   cult suicides.
   b.   pact suicides.
   c.   planned suicides.
   d.   cluster suicides.

Adolescent Suicide, p. 395
Diff: H, Ans: c
66.   Because of cluster suicides, experts recommend:
   a.   large public memorials following a suicide.
   b.   public statements blaming the suicide on others.
   c.   reporting the suicide without emotional overtones.
   d.   glorification of the life of the individual who committed suicide.

Adolescent Rebellion, p. 395
Diff: M, Ans: b
67.   How would Anna Freud describe adolescent rebellion and defiance?
   a.   They signify developmental delay.
   b.   They are normal.
   c.   They are problematic.
   d.   They are evidence of being stuck in the latency period.

Adolescent Rebellion, p. 395
Diff: H, Ans: c
68.   In the United States, about _____ percent of all arrests for serious crimes involve people between the ages of 10 and 20.
       a.   5
       b.   15
       c.   45
       d.   75

Adolescent Rebellion, p. 395
Diff: M, Ans: a
69.   A person is most likely to be arrested at what age?
       a.   16
       b.   18
       c.   20
       d.   22

Adolescent Rebellion, p. 395
Diff: E, Ans: b
70.   How often a particular behavior or circumstance occurs is referred to as:
       a.   likelihood.
       b.   incidence.
       c.   odds.
       d.   prevalence.

Adolescent Rebellion, p. 395
Diff: E, Ans: d
71.   How widespread a particular behavior or circumstance is within a population is referred to as:
       a.   likelihood.
       b.   incidence.
       c.   odds.
       d.   prevalence.

Adolescent Rebellion, p. 395
Diff: H, Ans: d
72.   The number of people within a population who have cancer is referred to as the _____ of cancer.
       a.   likelihood
       b.   incidence
       c.   odds
       d.   prevalence

Adolescent Rebellion, p. 395
Diff: E, Ans: a
73.   In a certain city, there are only a small number of criminals. In that city, crime has:
       a.   a low prevalence rate.
       b.   a high prevalence rate.
       c.   a low commitment rate.
       d.   a high commitment rate.

Adolescent Rebellion, p. 395
Diff: H, Ans: c
74.   Many big cities' "crack-down" policies for young criminals have been fueled by the incorrect supposition that adolescent crime has a:
       a.   low incidence rate.
       b.   high incidence rate.
       c.   low prevalence rate.
       d.   high prevalence rate.

Adolescent Rebellion, pp. 395-396
Diff: M, Ans: d

75. Developmentalists have proven that adolescent crime has:
    a. a high incidence rate and a low prevalence rate.
    b. a low incidence rate and a high prevalence rate.
    c. low incidence and prevalence rates.
    d. high incidence and prevalence rates.

Adolescent Rebellion, pp. 395-396
Diff: H, Ans: b

76. Which of the following is a true statement about adolescent crime?
    a. It is quite low, involving less than 20 percent of arrests for serious crimes.
    b. There are many one-time offenders.
    c. Chronic offenders tend to be convicted of many repeated violent offenses.
    d. The average girl has committed more crimes than the average boy, but she has not been arrested.

Adolescent Rebellion, p. 396
Diff: M, Ans: b

77. Arrest statistics do not accurately reflect the prevalence of adolescent delinquency because:
    a. older criminals lie about their age.
    b. many offenses never come to police attention.
    c. more juvenile offenses lead to arrest than do adult crimes.
    d. police exaggerate juvenile crimes.

Adolescent Rebellion, p. 396
Diff: E, Ans: c

78. Arrests are more likely to occur among adolescents who are:
    a. ages 12 to 14 rather than 15 to 17.
    b. females rather than males.
    c. European Americans rather than Asian Americans.
    d. all of the above.

Adolescent Rebellion, p. 396
Diff: M, Ans: a

79. Which of the following is a true statement about victimization rates?
    a. Most victims of adolescent crime are adolescents.
    b. Children are more likely to be victims than adolescents.
    c. Few adolescents are offenders or victims of crime.
    d. Adults are more likely than adolescents to be victims of violent crimes.

Adolescent Rebellion, p. 396
Diff: E, Ans: b

80. An adolescent-limited offender is someone who:
    a. attacks only adolescents.
    b. stops committing crimes by age 21.
    c. is never arrested.
    d. is a juvenile delinquent.

Adolescent Rebellion, p. 396
Diff: E, Ans: d

81. An individual who commits crimes during adolescence but stops by the age of 21 is considered a(n):
    a. repeat offender.
    b. career criminal.
    c. life-course-persistent offender.
    d. adolescence-limited offender.

Adolescent Rebellion, p. 396
Diff: M, Ans: a
82.   Which of the following is true of life-course-persistent offenders?
        a.   They show signs of brain damage.
        b.   They are late to have sex.
        c.   They tend to be involved in school activities.
        d.   They are unlikely to end up in prison.

Adolescent Rebellion, p. 397
Diff: M, Ans: a
83.   In order to reduce the number of life-course-persistent offenders, the text suggests:
        a.   implementing more programs for violence prevention before adolescence.
        b.   hiring more police officers and building more prisons.
        c.   increasing the sentences for juvenile offenders.
        d.   enforcing greater punishment of adult criminals.

Adolescent Rebellion, p. 397
Diff: M, Ans: c
84.   Which of the following is true about reform school and residential incarceration for juvenile offenders?
        a.   They reduce the likelihood that individuals will become career criminals.
        b.   They provide better hope than do foster homes.
        c.   They can encourage temporary externalizing behavior to become permanent.
        d.   They effectively remove at-risk teens from environments that teach aggression.

Family and Friends

Parents, p. 397
Diff: E, Ans: c
85.   The distance between parents and children in values, behaviors, and knowledge is referred to as:
        a.   generational stake.
        b.   the family stake.
        c.   a generation gap.
        d.   intergenerational strife.

Parents, p. 398
Diff: M, Ans: d
86.   Generational stake refers to the:
        a.   distance between parents and children in values, behaviors, and knowledge.
        b.   petty, peevish arguing between adolescents and their parents.
        c.   fact that parents have a time and emotional investment in their children.
        d.   need of parents and children to view family interactions from their own perspective.

Parents, p. 398
Diff: M, Ans: a
87.   That parents want adolescents to be loyal to the family and that adolescents want to become independent reflects:
        a.   generational stake.
        b.   the family stake.
        c.   a generation gap.
        d.   intergenerational strife.

Parents, p. 398
Diff: M, Ans: c
88.   Which of the following is true of generational stake?
      a.   Adolescents want to carry on family traditions.
      b.   Adolescents readily accept their parents' restrictions.
      c.   Parents want to believe that all is well despite superficial shows of rebellion.
      d.   Parents exaggerate differences between themselves and their adolescents.

Parents, p. 398
Diff: H, Ans: b
89.   Which of the following is a true statement about adolescents' generational stake?
      a.   It is completely inaccurate.
      b.   It is in line with human evolution.
      c.   It is generally in agreement with that of adults'.
      d.   It leads adolescents to eventually take on their parents' values and beliefs.

Parents, p. 398
Diff: H, Ans: a
90.   Who among the following adolescents is *most* likely to be in conflict with her parent(s)?
      a.   Shirley, a European-American girl in early adolescence
      b.   Julie, who is having a discussion with her father
      c.   Shelley, who is a late-maturing teen
      d.   Helen, a Chinese girl in late adolescence

Parents, p. 398
Diff: M, Ans: a
91.   Bickering between parents and teenagers is most common for which pair?
      a.   mother-daughter
      b.   mother-son
      c.   father-daughter
      d.   father-son

Parents, p. 398
Diff: M, Ans: b
92.   In the United States, parent-child conflict peaks in:
      a.   late childhood.
      b.   early- to mid-adolescence.
      c.   late adolescence.
      d.   none of the above; it remains stable.

Parents, p. 398
Diff: E, Ans: c
93.   Bickering between parents and teenagers:
      a.   usually concerns politics and religion.
      b.   is a signal of pathology.
      c.   usually concerns clothes and personal habits.
      d.   increases steadily between the ages of 12 and 19.

Parents, p. 398
Diff: E, Ans: d
94.   Parent-child arguments during the teen years indicate:
      a.   a disturbed parent-child relationship.
      b.   poor parenting skills.
      c.   teenage depression.
      d.   children's desire to make their own decisions.

Parents, pp. 398-399
Diff: H, Ans: d

95.   Which of the following delays the peak of parent-child conflict?
      a.   school achievement
      b.   parental lack of concern
      c.   single parenthood
      d.   cultural encouragement of child dependency

Parents, p. 399
Diff: E, Ans: c

96.   Your cousin is the parent of a teenager. Now that you have taken this course, your cousin asks you for advice on how strict she should be with her adolescent. What advice would you give her?
      a.   "Avoid conflict at all costs."
      b.   "Keep your child in line at all times."
      c.   "Be sure to avoid being extremely lax or extremely strict."
      d.   "Children tend to raise themselves. Don't worry about it."

Parents, p. 399
Diff: H, Ans: c

97.   Which of the following is true concerning parental connectedness and control in parent-adolescent interactions?
      a.   These aspects are always constructive.
      b.   These aspects are always destructive.
      c.   Whether these aspects are constructive or destructive depends on the context.
      d.   Whether these aspects are constructive or destructive depends on the sex of the child.

Parents, p. 399
Diff: H, Ans: a

98.   Bob's parents insist that he study for three hours each night, keep his room clean, and be home by 10 P.M. on weekends. Judging from this description, you can conclude that Bob's parents are high in:
      a.   control.
      b.   connectedness.
      c.   communication.
      d.   all of the above.

Parents, p. 399
Diff: E, Ans: a

99.   Parents' awareness of where their children are, what they are doing, and with whom they are doing it is referred to as:
      a.   parental monitoring.
      b.   generational stake.
      c.   control.
      d.   connectedness.

Parents, p. 399
Diff: M, Ans: c

100. Abbie is aware of where her son is whenever he goes out, and she requires him to call if there is any change in plans. Abbie is demonstrating:
      a.   a strong generational stake.
      b.   foreclosure for her son.
      c.   parental monitoring.
      d.   negative control.

Parents, p. 399
Diff: E, Ans: b
101.   A great deal of parental interference and control is a strong predictor of:
   a.   a well-behaved adolescent.
   b.   adolescent depression.
   c.   adolescent achievement.
   d.   closeness with parents.

Parents, p. 399
Diff: H, Ans: d
102.   Nate's parents engage in very high parental monitoring and control. Compared to Nate's peers whose parents engage in less parental monitoring, Nate is more likely to:
   a.   avoid using drugs and alcohol.
   b.   not be involved with weapons.
   c.   be depressed.
   d.   show all of the above.

Peers, p. 401
Diff: M, Ans: a
103.   Which of the following statements about adolescent friendships is NOT true?
   a.   They tend to be fleeting, even once trust and intimacy have been established.
   b.   They are even more crucial than they were during middle childhood.
   c.   They are vital for the transition from childhood to adulthood.
   d.   All of the above are true statements about adolescent friendships.

Peers, p. 401
Diff: E, Ans: d
104.   Pressure to conform to one's friends or contemporaries in behavior, dress, and attitude is referred to as:
   a.   conformance.
   b.   adolescent burden.
   c.   generation gap.
   d.   peer pressure.

Peers, p. 401
Diff: M, Ans: c
105.   Which of the following statements is true of peer pressure?
   a.   It always involves activities that are negative.
   b.   It increases throughout adolescence.
   c.   It involves the desire to conform to one's friends or contemporaries.
   d.   All of the above are true.

Peers, p. 401
Diff: M, Ans: b
106.   At what age is the pressure to conform to peers greatest?
   a.   12
   b.   14
   c.   18
   d.   21

Peers, p. 401
Diff: E, Ans: d

107.   Most adolescents need a bridge in their transition from childhood to young adulthood, easing the shift from childish behaviors to more independent ones. This bridge is generally provided by:
a.   a romantic partner.
b.   permissive parents.
c.   favorite teachers.
d.   peers at their level.

Peers, p. 401
Diff: H, Ans: c

108.   Mr. and Mrs. Cortina have discovered that their son has been skipping classes and cutting school with a group of boys. Probably:
a.   the group has led their innocent son astray.
b.   the behavior is nothing to worry about.
c.   their son chose this group because he shares their interests.
d.   when they are all together, they are less rebellious than when they are alone.

Peers, p. 402
Diff: E, Ans: a

109.   Adolescents often use the behaviors of their peer group as a way of experimenting with:
a.   possible selves.
b.   impossible selves.
c.   actual selves.
d.   deviant selves.

Peers, p. 402
Diff: E, Ans: b

110.   The peer group can be particularly helpful for adolescents whose parents are:
a.   poor.
b.   recent immigrants.
c.   overly permissive.
d.   older.

Peers, pp. 402-403
Diff: H, Ans: b

111.   Which of the following is a true statement about ethnic gangs?
a.   They are common in homogenous (single ethnicity) areas of the country.
b.   They satisfy a need for self-identity for adolescents who experience conflict between the majority culture and their strict family traditions.
c.   They are a big draw for ethnic youth, even those whose parents have provided a great deal of supervision and affection.
d.   All of the above are true statements about ethnic gangs.

Peers, pp. 402-403
Diff: H, Ans: c

112.   Which of the following adolescents from immigrant families is most likely to be pushed toward either becoming extremely rebellious or extremely obedient?
a.   Jimmy, whose parents provide a great deal of affection and supervision
b.   Gina, whose parents do not strongly enforce the traditions of their culture
c.   Joanne, whose parents are from a region that promotes early marriage and childbearing
d.   All of the above adolescents are equally likely to becoming extremely rebellious or extremely obedient.

Peers, p. 403
Diff: M, Ans: c
113.   Which of the following is the general pattern of heterosexual attraction, as described by Dunphy?
   a.   small mixed-sex group, pairing off of couples, loose association of boys' and girls' same-sex groups
   b.   small mixed-sex group, loose association of boys' and girls' same-sex groups, pairing off of couples
   c.   loose association of boys' and girls' same-sex groups, small mixed-sex group, pairing off of couples
   d.   loose association of boys' and girls' same-sex groups, pairing off of couples, small mixed-sex group

Peers, p. 403
Diff: M, Ans: b
114.   Who is likely to spend the greatest percentage of waking time with members of the other sex?
   a.   Rebecca, a female ninth-grade student
   b.   Carla, a female eleventh-grade student
   c.   Norm, a male ninth-grade student
   d.   Sam, a male eleventh-grade student

Peers (Figure 16.4), p. 403
Diff: M, Ans: d
115.   As other-sex companionship develops, time spent with same-sex peers:
   a.   increases slightly.
   b.   increases sharply.
   c.   decreases.
   d.   remains essentially stable.

Peers, p. 404
Diff: E, Ans: b
116.   Heterosexual attraction usually begins with:
   a.   a sudden passion.
   b.   a seeming dislike.
   c.   intense sexual drive.
   d.   the pairing up of couples.

Peers, p. 404
Diff: M, Ans: a
117.   Which of the following influences adolescents to reach out to other-sex peers earlier?
   a.   maturing early
   b.   having happily married parents
   c.   being physically unattractive
   d.   all of the above

Peers, p. 404
Diff: E, Ans: c
118.   In comparison with heterosexual attachments, romantic homosexual attachments tend to happen:
   a.   at a slightly earlier age.
   b.   at a much earlier age.
   c.   at a later age.
   d.   at the same age.

Peers, p. 404
Diff: M, Ans: d

119.   A retrospective study of homosexual adults demonstrated that, on average, they first became aware of their sexual interests at age _____ and told people at age _____.
   a.   8; 12
   b.   9; 25
   c.   11; 11
   d.   11; 17

Peers, p. 405
Diff: E, Ans: c

120.   In comparison with heterosexual youth, homosexual youth have a _____ rate of depression and a _____ rate of suicide.
   a.   lower; lower
   b.   lower; similar
   c.   higher; higher
   d.   higher; similar

TRUE-FALSE QUESTIONS

The Self and Identity

Ans: T, pp. 385-386

1.   Adolescents often take on behavioral styles that are not consistent with their sense of who they are.

Ans: F, p. 386

2.   Adolescents who display a false self will be unlikely to develop a true identity in late adolescence or adulthood.

Ans: F, p. 387

3.   Identity achievement involves a complete repudiation of past experiences and childhood identifications.

Ans: T, p. 388

4.   One negative outcome in the crisis of identity is identity diffusion.

Ans: T, p. 388

5.   An identity status that is sometimes associated with finding a mature identity is moratorium.

Ans: F, p. 389

6.   Developmentalists are typically more interested in identity status than in the ongoing process of identity formation.

Ans: F, p. 389

7.   Gender identity includes *only* whether one identifies oneself as male or female.

Ans: T, p. 389

8.   Gender identity and ethnic identity are often intertwined.

Ans: T, p. 390

9.   In a multicultural society, minority youth tend to take on generational attitudes toward drugs and sex as soon as they are able.

Sadness and Anger

Ans: F, p. 391

10.   Externalizing problems include self-mutilation and eating disorders.

Ans: T, p. 391

11.   Many angry attempts by adolescents to harm others are an outgrowth of depression.

Ans: T, p. 392

12.   The overall trend that children's feelings of competence decrease with age is consistent across culture, cohort, or the particular domain of life examined.

Ans: F, p. 392

13.   Adolescents with extreme levels of self-confidence tend to stand up well to the changes in peers', coaches', and teachers' feedback that generally come with adolescence.

Ans: F, p. 392

14.   The rate of clinical depression is higher for teenage boys than it is for teenage girls.

Ans: T, p. 392

15.   Social and cultural factors can either increase or decrease an individual's likelihood of experiencing clinical depression.

Ans: T, p. 393

16.   Young adults are more likely to commit suicide than are adolescents.

Ans: T, p. 393

17.   Suicide attempts are more common in adolescence than in young adulthood.

Ans: T, p. 393

18.   Over the past few decades, adolescence has become a more vulnerable period for suicide.

Ans: F, p. 393

19.   Experts prefer the term "failed attempt" over "parasuicide."

Ans: F, pp. 393-394

20.   A failed attempt at suicide is only a plea for help and should not be seen as an indication that a young person actually wants to take his or her own life.

Ans: F, p. 394

21.   For U.S. 15- to 19-year-olds, Hispanic-American and African-American males are more likely than are other teens to commit suicide.

Ans: T, p. 394

22.   At every age and in all ethnic groups in the United States, the suicide rate is higher for males than for females.

Ans: T, p. 394

23.   The recent increase in adolescent suicide parallels the increase in availability of guns.

Ans: T, pp. 394-395

24.   Cultural attitudes toward suicide can influence suicide rates.

Ans: F, p. 394

25.   Parasuicide among girls is more likely to be externalizing, whereas parasuicide among boys is more likely to be internalizing.

Ans: T, p. 394

26.   Among males in the United States, Asian Americans have the lowest suicide rate.

Ans: T, p. 395

27.   Illegal activity peaks when a person is about 16 years of age.

Ans: T, p. 395

28.   Most adolescent criminals have no more than one serious brush with the law.

Ans: F, p. 396

29.   The high rate of adolescent crime is caused by a few very active delinquents.

Ans: T, p. 396

30.   The overall victimization rate of adolescents is two to three times that of adults.

Ans: T, p. 396

31.   Nearly all adolescents engage in some law-breaking behaviors.

Ans: F, p. 396

32.   Most adolescence-limited offenders become career criminals.

Ans: T, p. 396

33.   Nearly all life-course-persistent offenders are antisocial as early as preschool.

Ans: F, p. 397

34.   For most adolescent delinquents, prison seems to be the best solution.

Family and Friends

Ans: F, pp. 397-398

35.   Most research indicates a wide generation gap between parents and their children.

Ans: F, p. 398

36.   Part of the parental generational stake is working to ensure that one's children strive for and discover their own niche in the world.

Ans: T, p. 398

37.   Parents and adolescents often view the same interaction completely differently, because of generational stake.

Ans: F, p. 398

38.   Mother-son pairs tend to bicker more than mother-daughter pairs.

Ans: T, pp. 398-399

39.   For Chinese teens, stormy relations with parents may not surface until late adolescence.

Ans: F, p. 399

40.   Adolescents tend to benefit from homes where the parents have few house rules.

Ans: F, p. 399

41.   The worse a neighborhood is, the less it matters if parents are lax with their adolescents.

Ans: F, pp. 399-400

42.   There is really no such thing as too much parental monitoring, even when it becomes intrusive, as parents cannot ensure their adolescents are safe without it.

Ans: T, p. 400

43.   Parents should make sure they discuss their values regarding sex when they discuss the biological aspects of sex with their adolescents.

Ans: F, p. 401

44.   The pressure to conform to the peer group rises dramatically throughout adolescence, declining only in the twenties.

Ans: T, p. 401

45.   Positive examples of peer-group pressure that have been noted in research include pressure to study and to avoid cigarette smoking.

Ans: T, p. 401

46.   Peer pressure is likely to be particularly negative when an adolescent is experiencing a period of uncertainty.

Ans: T, p. 403

47.   Early other-sex interactions are done mostly in groups; intimacy with a member of the other sex usually does not occur until late adolescence.

Ans: T, p. 403

48.   By the junior or senior year of high school, most adolescents are happier when they are with members of the other sex than when they are with members of the same sex.

Ans: F, p. 404

49.   Homosexual pairings tend to develop earlier than heterosexual pairings.

Ans: T, pp. 404-405

50.   Lesbian females are likely to spend their adolescence oblivious to, or in denial of, their sexual interests.

FILL-IN-THE-BLANK QUESTIONS

The Self and Identity

Ans: identity, p. 385

1.   An individual's _____ is his or her unique and consistent self-definition.

Ans: possible selves, p. 385

2.   In the process of trying to find their true selves, many adolescents try out _____.

Ans: false self, p. 386

3.   A _____ is a set of behaviors adopted by a person to cope with rejection, to please others, or to try out as a possible self.

Ans: statuses, p. 387

4.   Achievement, foreclosure, diffusion, and moratorium are the four major identity _____ defined in detail by James Marcia.

Ans: foreclosure, p. 387

5.   A premature identity formation that involves wholesale acceptance of parental values is called _____.

Ans: negative identity, p. 388

6.   A minister's daughter who becomes a prostitute has adopted a _____.

Ans: achievement (Table 16.1), p. 388
7.   The identity status characterized by high commitment and questioning is identity _____.

Ans: Gender identity, p. 389
8.   _____ includes the roles and behaviors that society associates with the biological category of male or female.

Sadness and Anger

Ans: internalizing, p. 391
9.   Clinical depression and self-mutilation are examples of _____ problems.

Ans: Clinical depression, p. 391
10.   _____ is defined as marked feelings of sadness and worthlessness leading to lack of interest in, and isolation from, normal activities for two weeks or more.

Ans: realistic, p. 392
11.   Adolescents who are _____ about their competence are most likely to fare well during the commonly experienced decline in self-esteem during adolescence.

Ans: ideation, p. 393
12.   Suicidal _____ refers to thinking about suicide.

Ans: attempts, p. 393
13.   Suicide _____ are more common in adolescence than in adulthood.

Ans: Parasuicide, p. 393
14.   _____ includes any self-destructive act that does not end in death, regardless of whether the individual's intent was clear.

Ans: cluster, p. 394
15.   When an adolescent suicide is well publicized and seems to make a strong impression on other adolescents in the community, adults in order to prevent _____ suicides must be particularly sensitive to not sentimentalize the death.

Ans: incidence; prevalence, p. 395
16.   The amount of crime committed by adolescents in a community is referred to as the _____ of adolescent crime. The number of offenders committing these crimes is referred to as the _____ of adolescent crime.

Ans: high; high, p. 395
17.   Adolescent crime has a _____ incidence and a _____ prevalence.

Ans: limited, p. 396
18.   The term adolescence-_____ offender refers to individuals whose criminal activity stops by age 21.

Family and Friends

Ans: generational, p. 398
19.   Each generation has a tendency to view the family and its interests in a special way; in other words, each group has a(n) _____ stake in the family.

Ans: monitoring, p. 399
20.   Parental _____ refers to parents being watchful and aware of where their children are and what they are doing.

Ans: mixed, p. 400
21.   If parents only talk about ways to avoid pregnancy and disease and fail to talk about the social, emotional, and moral consequences of intercourse, teens may hear a "_____ message" and infer that their parents approve of sexual activity.

Ans: peer pressure, p. 401
22.   In adolescence, _____ can be negative, such as when it promotes conformance to deviant standards, or positive, such as when it promotes refraining from smoking.

Ans: peers, p. 402
23.   For an adolescent whose parents are recent immigrants, _____ can help him or her negotiate conflicting cultural demands.

Ans: early, p. 404
24.   Adolescents who mature _____ are more likely to be among the first to reach out to other-sex peers.

Ans: homophobic, p. 404
25.   Especially in a(n) _____ culture, males with homosexual feelings are likely to deny their feelings or try to conceal them with heterosexual relationships.

ESSAY QUESTIONS

1.   Consider the following biographical facts about Erik Erikson, and discuss how they might have influenced his theories of adolescent development: He grew up as Erik Homberger, named for the kindly pediatrician-stepfather who married his mother when Erik was an infant. He changed his name to Erikson, retaining Homberger as his middle name. As a young man, he spent a few years hiking through Europe, sketching and reading philosophy, before he joined the circle of psychologists around Anna Freud.

2.   In which of the four identity statuses would you say that you currently are? Provide evidence to demonstrate your conclusion.

3.   Define the four identity statuses and identify for each whether it is characterized by *no commitment* or *commitment* and by *not questioning* or *questioning*.

4.   Think about the changes in roles for women and men from the 1950s to today. How do you think identity formation has changed for adolescents over this period? How do you think the changes have been different for women and men?

5.   How might alcohol or drug use among adolescents contribute to their forging a negative identity or to their experiencing identity diffusion?

6.   Describe how feelings of competence and self-esteem change from childhood through adolescence. Do the same patterns of change exist for all areas of competence? Do the same patterns of change exist for males and females and for members of different cultures?

7.   What are some of the conditions or warning signs of adolescents who may take their own lives?

8.   How do the rates of suicidal ideation, parasuicide, and actual suicide compare for adolescent males and females in the United States? Why do these rates differ?

9.   Define the terms "incidence" and "prevalence" as they apply to adolescent crime rates. Does adolescent crime have a high or low incidence? Does it have a high or low prevalence? Do the answers to these two questions suggest that "crack downs" on adolescent repeat offenders will bring the adolescent crime rate down significantly? Explain your answer.

10.   What factors influence individuals to become life-course-persistent offenders? If the federal government offered you a large grant of money to help prevent children from becoming life-course-persistent offenders, on which children would you focus? Describe one thing you would do with the money.

11.   What do you think are the major causes of delinquency? What do you think ought to be done to prevent it?

12.   Consider the following statement: "Teenagers probably need as much support at age 13 or 14 as do toddlers." Compare the differences and similarities in the amount and kind of parental support needed by the developing person at these two stages.

13.   In some cultures, children are sent away to school at puberty. How would this influence the level of parent-adolescent conflict?

14.   Imagine you are writing an article for a parenting magazine on parental monitoring of adolescents. What advice would you give to readers about which level of monitoring is ideal, as well as what the effects are of effective parental monitoring and of interfering parental monitoring?

15.   Imagine that an acquaintance of yours claims that he or she "fell in with the wrong crowd" in adolescence, and as a result engaged in many delinquent activities he or she shouldn't have done and wouldn't have done otherwise. (1) Do you agree or disagree with the statement about falling in with the wrong crowd? Explain why. (2) Do you agree or disagree with the statement about doing things he or she wouldn't have done otherwise? Explain why.

16.   Describe what you believe to be two of the main functions of the peer group for adolescents. Did your peer group provide this for you? Give examples.

17.   Describe the four steps identified by Dunphy as making up the sequence of heterosexual attraction.

Answer guidelines to these essay questions can be found in the Appendix at the end of the Test Bank.

CHAPTER 17

Early Adulthood:
Biosocial Development

MULTIPLE-CHOICE QUESTIONS

Early Adulthood: Biosocial Development

Early Adulthood: Biosocial Development, p. 413
Diff: E, Ans: b

1. In terms of biosocial development, early adulthood, from age _____, can be considered the prime of life.
   a. 15 to 30
   b. 20 to 35
   c. 35 to 45
   d. 30 to 50

Early Adulthood: Biosocial Development, p. 413
Diff: M, Ans: c

2. Most serious declines in health and strength during young adulthood are caused by:
   a. normal aging processes.
   b. genetic inheritance.
   c. poor lifestyle choices.
   d. physiological changes.

Growth, Strength, and Health

Norms and Peaks, p. 413
Diff: E, Ans: c

3. Most girls reach their maximum height by age _____, and most boys reach their maximum height by age _____.
   a. 14; 16
   b. 16; 14
   c. 16; 18
   d. 18; 16

Norms and Peaks, p. 413
Diff: M, Ans: d

4. Tim is in his early twenties. He can expect:
   a. an increase in height.
   b. infertility and reproductive problems.
   c. an increase in infections and colds.
   d. weight gain and muscle growth.

Norms and Peaks, p. 413
Diff: M, Ans: a
5.   Jessica is 24 years old, and her cousin Rachel is 16 years old. If Jessica and Rachel race up a flight of
     stairs, what is the likely outcome?
     a.   Jessica will win.
     b.   Rachel will win by a slight margin.
     c.   Rachel will win by a large margin.
     d.   They will tie.

Norms and Peaks, p. 413
Diff: M, Ans: a
6.   For which of the following is a woman in her mid-20s most likely to consult a doctor?
     a.   pregnancy
     b.   cancer
     c.   senescence
     d.   colds and flu

Norms and Peaks, p. 414
Diff: H, Ans: c
7.   Of the fatal diseases, the leading killer of adults under age 75 is:
     a.   heart disease.
     b.   pneumonia.
     c.   cancer.
     d.   tuberculosis.

Norms and Peaks, p. 414
Diff: M, Ans: d
8.   Homicide, suicide, and motor-vehicle deaths account for what percent of deaths in young adulthood?
     a.   4
     b.   13
     c.   22
     d.   43

Signs of Senescence, p. 414
Diff: E, Ans: b
9.   The gradual age-related physical decline that begins in early adulthood is called:
     a.   aging.
     b.   senescence.
     c.   senility.
     d.   maturational decline.

Signs of Senescence, p. 414
Diff: E, Ans: d
10. The rate of senescence is due to:
     a.   genetics.
     b.   environmental influences.
     c.   personal choices.
     d.   all of the above.

Signs of Senescence, p. 414
Diff: E, Ans: a
11. The efficiency of most body functions:
     a.   begins to decline before age 30.
     b.   begins to decline after age 30.
     c.   declines by six percent each year in the 20s.
     d.   declines more rapidly in women than in men.

Signs of Senescence, p. 414
Diff: M, Ans: b
12.   Marge is in her late 20s. The first sign of aging she is likely to notice is:
   a.   increased vulnerability to disease.
   b.   wrinkles around the eyes.
   c.   declining muscular strength.
   d.   a decrease in sexual desire.

Signs of Senescence, p. 414
Diff: E, Ans: d
13.   At age 27, Ruth is most likely to notice age-related changes in:
   a.   organ reserve.
   b.   muscular strength.
   c.   maximum heart rate.
   d.   physical appearance.

Signs of Senescence, p. 414
Diff: E, Ans: c
14.   Graying of hair is due to:
   a.   the bleaching out of color by the sun.
   b.   thinning of individual hair strands making them more translucent.
   c.   a decrease in the number of pigment-producing cells.
   d.   excessive worry about aging and family problems.

Signs of Senescence, p. 416
Diff: H, Ans: a
15.   Presbyopia results when the eyes are less able to focus on objects near the face because:
   a.   the lens becomes less elastic.
   b.   the cornea does not open fully.
   c.   the fovea slowly becomes misshapen.
   d.   skin around the eyes wrinkles causing vision-obstructive folds.

Signs of Senescence, p. 416
Diff: E, Ans: c
16.   By age 60, most adults have the vision problem known as:
   a.   nearsightedness.
   b.   myopia.
   c.   presbyopia.
   d.   astigmatism.

Gender Differences in Health and Senescence, p. 416
Diff: M, Ans: a
17.   Which of the following is associated with faster aging?
   a.   being from an ethnic minority
   b.   being female
   c.   being from a high socioeconomic status
   d.   all of the above

Gender Differences in Health and Senescence, p. 416
Diff: H, Ans: b
18.   Which of the following individuals is likely to age most quickly?
   a.   Grace, a poor woman from an ethnic majority
   b.   Don, a poor man from an ethnic minority
   c.   Sally, a wealthy woman from an ethnic minority
   d.   Harold, a wealthy man from the ethnic majority

Gender Differences in Health and Senescence, p. 416
Diff: H, Ans: c

19. Which of the following is a true statement about gender differences in senescence?
    a. In terms of health, women age more quickly than do men.
    b. Men spend more money combating wrinkled skin and covering gray hair than do women.
    c. Women feel middle-aged sooner than do men.
    d. Men are more likely to seek out preventative care than are women.

Gender Differences in Health and Senescence, pp. 416-417
Diff: E, Ans: d

20. Compared to men, women:
    a. eat more vegetables.
    b. live longer.
    c. have more reproductive system problems.
    d. do all of the above.

Gender Differences in Health and Senescence, p. 417
Diff: H, Ans: a

21. Which of the following is NOT a possible explanation for sex differences in death rates?
    a. Women are more likely to die from cancer.
    b. Women are more likely to be married.
    c. Men are taught to be independent and tough.
    d. Men have lower levels or estrogen.

Homeostasis, p. 417
Diff: E, Ans: b

22. Which of the following is the goal of homeostasis?
    a. organ depletion
    b. equilibrium
    c. pregnancy
    d. weight loss

Homeostasis, p. 417
Diff: M, Ans: c

23. An example of homeostasis is the:
    a. increase in maximum heart rate with age.
    b. reserve that allows a person to do without a night of sleep.
    c. increase in heart rate and breathing that occurs during physical exertion.
    d. loss of muscle tone that occurs in the absence of exercise.

Homeostasis, p. 418
Diff: H, Ans: b

24. Larry is 30 years old and will play tennis with 18-year-old Chris. They are equally matched in ability. Larry will probably:
    a. spend less time in warm-up because he is more mature.
    b. need more rest afterward to allow bodily functions to return to normal.
    c. need less rest afterward because he is stronger.
    d. lose; he cannot keep up with an 18-year-old.

Homeostasis, p. 418
Diff: M, Ans: b

25. Compared to 20-year-olds, 35-year-olds are less likely to:
    a. engage in energy-demanding sports.
    b. bounce back quickly after a physiologically stressful activity.
    c. perform any job requiring manual labor.
    d. require a warm-up period before exercise.

Reserve Capacity, p. 418
Diff: M, Ans: c
26.   If they maintain their bodies adequately, most adults can function quite well until their:
       a.   50s.
       b.   60s.
       c.   70s
       d.   80s.

Reserve Capacity, p. 418
Diff: E, Ans: d
27.   The term "organ reserve" refers to:
       a.   a decline in functioning of major organs, such as the heart.
       b.   the practice of conserving and transplanting solid organs.
       c.   the mechanism that automatically maintains physiological balance.
       d.   the extra capacity available to an organ when subjected to stress.

Reserve Capacity, p. 418
Diff: M, Ans: a
28.   A 50-year-old will most likely be slower than a 20-year-old in:
       a.   running up several flights of stairs.
       b.   mowing the yard.
       c.   cleaning the house.
       d.   routine activities at work.

Reserve Capacity, p. 418
Diff: H, Ans: d
29.   Fifty-year-olds can expect to retain _____ percent of the muscle strength they had at age 20.
       a.   30
       b.   50
       c.   70
       d.   90

Reserve Capacity, pp. 418-419
Diff: H, Ans: c
30.   At age 50, a man can expect to:
       a.   feel exhausted after doing routine chores.
       b.   notice that his resting heart rate is slower.
       c.   feel almost as strong as he did at age 20.
       d.   experience severe loss of cartilage in his knees.

Reserve Capacity, p. 419
Diff: M, Ans: c
31.   As we age, the resting heart rate:
       a.   slows precipitously.
       b.   fluctuates a great deal.
       c.   remains stable.
       d.   increases greatly.

Reserve Capacity, p. 419
Diff: H, Ans: c
32.   The age-related biological changes that occur during the first decades of adulthood:
       a.   affect all areas of functioning equally.
       b.   increase the risk of death.
       c.   are of little consequence under normal circumstances.
       d.   affect athletic performance but not sexual performance.

Sports Stars and the Rest of Us, p. 419
Diff: E, Ans: b

33. Athletic performance generally peaks sometimes between the ages of:
    a. 10 and 25.
    b. 15 and 35.
    c. 20 and 40.
    d. 25 and 40.

Sports Stars and the Rest of Us, p. 419
Diff: H, Ans: d

34. Which of the following is true of age differences in athletic ability?
    a. It takes two to three years of preparation to reach peak performance.
    b. Gross motor skills peak earlier than fine motor skills.
    c. Superior performance correlates with small differences in specific skills.
    d. Peak performance is attained years after peak physical maturity.

Sexual Responsiveness, p. 420
Diff: M, Ans: c

35. Until late adulthood, the capacity for sexual pleasure is:
    a. about the same for all adults.
    b. likely to increase each decade of adulthood.
    c. determined by gender and aging.
    d. unaffected by choice of partner.

Sexual Responsiveness, p. 420
Diff: E, Ans: a

36. Compared to his sexual responses when he was younger, a 40-year-old man usually needs:
    a. more time to attain a full erection.
    b. less direct stimulation to initiate sexual arousal.
    c. a shorter refractory period.
    d. to be more careful with birth control.

Sexual Responsiveness, p. 420
Diff: H, Ans: b

37. Decline in sexual activity over the adult years is:
    a. especially rapid during the 20s and 30s.
    b. at least partially age-related.
    c. more apparent for women than for men.
    d. caused exclusively by social factors.

Sexual Responsiveness, p. 420
Diff: H, Ans: c

38. Age-related trends in sexual responsiveness are:
    a. the same for men and women.
    b. a major problem for most young adults.
    c. not as clear-cut for women as for men.
    d. affected by culture, not by biology.

Sexual Responsiveness, p. 420
Diff: E, Ans: a

39. In sexual responses, a woman approaching middle age often becomes:
    a. more sexually responsive than at age 25.
    b. less sexually responsive than at age 25.
    c. as sexually responsive as she was in adolescence.
    d. less interested in the sex act.

Sexual Responsiveness, p. 420
Diff: H, Ans: d
40. Which of the following is NOT a possible explanation for sex differences in age-related changes in sexual responsiveness?
   a. With experience, couples learn how to intensify the woman's sexual responses.
   b. Young women are conditioned to believe that sex is victimizing.
   c. Evolution has caused women to restrain their sexual urges during their prime reproductive years.
   d. Women's maximum heart rate increases to a greater degree than does men's.

Fertility, p. 421
Diff: E, Ans: b
41. The most common time for males and females to have a baby is during:
   a. adolescence.
   b. young adulthood.
   c. middle adulthood.
   d. late adulthood.

Fertility, p. 421
Diff: M, Ans: c
42. In the United States, about _____ percent of all couples experience infertility.
   a. 5
   b. 10
   c. 15
   d. 20

Fertility, p. 421
Diff: M, Ans: b
43. Infertility is defined as not conceiving after regular intercourse without contraception for:
   a. six months.
   b. one year.
   c. two years.
   d. six years.

Fertility, p. 421
Diff: H, Ans: c
44. Which of the following is a true statement about a couple's source of infertility?
   a. The prospective mother is most likely to be the source.
   b. The prospective father is most likely to be the source.
   c. Both the prospective mother and the prospective father are equally likely to be the source.
   d. Environmental influences, not the prospective parents, are most likely to be the source.

Fertility, p. 421
Diff: M, Ans: d
45. The most common reason for male infertility is:
   a. too little sexual activity.
   b. blockage of the tubes in which sperm are produced.
   c. incompatibility with a sexual partner.
   d. too few sperm that are normal and active.

Fertility, p. 421
Diff: H, Ans: c

46. Exposure to drugs, radiation, and other toxins can influence the number, shape, and motility of sperm for several _____.
    a. hours
    b. days
    c. months
    d. years

Fertility, p. 421
Diff: M, Ans: a

47. Forty-year-old women who are trying to become pregnant will:
    a. have more twins if they do conceive.
    b. conceive more quickly than do younger women.
    c. require long periods of bed rest in order to ovulate.
    d. often experience pelvic inflammatory disease.

Fertility, p. 421
Diff: M, Ans: c

48. Pelvic inflammatory disease is a primary cause of:
    a. irregular ovulation.
    b. high fevers that impair sperm production.
    c. blocked Fallopian tubes.
    d. sterility as a side effect of drugs used for treatment.

Fertility, p. 421
Diff: M, Ans: b

49. Pelvic inflammatory disease occurs when:
    a. women are underweight.
    b. infections of female reproductive organs are not treated properly.
    c. women are overweight.
    d. a woman has irregular menstrual cycles.

Fertility, p. 421
Diff: M, Ans: b

50. Most physicians recommend that would-be mothers begin their efforts at conception before age _____ and would-be fathers, before age _____.
    a. 20; 30
    b. 30; 40
    c. 40; 50
    d. 40; 60

Fertility, p. 421
Diff: E, Ans: d

51. The incidence of which of the following increases with maternal and paternal age?
    a. stillbirth
    b. miscarriage
    c. chromosomal abnormalities
    d. all of the above

Fertility, p. 422
Diff: H, Ans: a

52. Varicoceles are:
    a. varicose veins in the testes.
    b. fibrous tumors in the uterus.
    c. blocked genital ducts.
    d. closings in the fallopian tubes.

Fertility, p. 422
Diff: H, Ans: b
53. Which of the following is NOT a common way of treating infertility caused by problems with ovulation?
    a. surgery on the Fallopian tubes
    b. artificial insemination
    c. in vitro fertilization
    d. drug therapy

Fertility, p. 422
Diff: M, Ans: c
54. A woman with blocked Fallopian tubes has gone to a doctor for help in conceiving a child. The doctor removes some ova, fertilizes them with sperm from her husband, and inserts them into her uterus. Which treatment has been used?
    a. surgery on the Fallopian tubes
    b. artificial insemination
    c. in vitro fertilization
    d. drug therapy

Fertility, p. 422
Diff: M, Ans: b
55. In vitro fertilization is successful approximately _____ percent of the time.
    a. 10
    b. 30
    c. 60
    d. 90

Fertility, p. 422
Diff: E, Ans: d
56. The typical cost of assisted reproductive technology for a woman under the age of 35 is approximately:
    a. $5,000
    b. $10,000
    c. $20,000
    d. $30,000

Emotional Problems in Early Adulthood Dieting as a Disease, p. 423
Diff: M, Ans: a
57. Which of the following is a true statement about eating habits in young adulthood?
    a. Almost half of all North American women who diet to lose weight are not overweight.
    b. The majority of females begin adulthood overweight.
    c. It is easy for young women to maintain their "girlish figure" of adolescence.
    d. All of the above are true.

Dieting as a Disease, p. 423
Diff: M, Ans: b
58. Distorted ideas about food and food consumption are especially common among women of _____ descent.
    a. African
    b. European
    c. Hispanic
    d. Asian
    e. Native American

Dieting as a Disease, p. 424 (Table 17.2)
Diff: M, Ans: d
59. The ratio of a person's weight in kilograms divided by his or her height in meters squared is that person's:
   a. DSM.
   b. IVF.
   c. AID.
   d. BMI.

Dieting as a Disease, p. 424 (Table 17.2)
Diff: M, Ans: b
60. A body mass index between _____ and _____ is considered normal.
   a. 5; 15
   b. 19; 25
   c. 25; 29
   d. 30; 35

Dieting as a Disease, p. 424
Diff: E, Ans: c
61. An eating disorder involving self-starvation, sometimes to the point of death, is:
   a. fasting.
   b. dieting.
   c. anorexia nervosa.
   d. bulimia nervosa.

Dieting as a Disease, pp. 424-425
Diff: H, Ans: b
62. The person most likely to suffer from anorexia nervosa is:
   a. Mark, who is in the top 10 percent of his high school junior class.
   b. Sara, who is 13 years old and a high achiever.
   c. Warren, who is on a diet recommended by his doctor.
   d. Noreen, who is doing poorly in school.

Dieting as a Disease, p. 424
Diff: E, Ans: b
63. Members of which of the following groups are most likely to suffer from anorexia?
   a. high-school-age males who drop out of school
   b. female young adults and athletes
   c. male athletes
   d. middle-aged women

Dieting as a Disease, p. 426
Diff: E, Ans: d
64. MaryBeth frequently goes on compulsive eating binges and then follows them with vomiting. She is suffering from:
   a. anorexia nervosa.
   b. diet pill addiction.
   c. cocaine withdrawal.
   d. bulimia nervosa.

Dieting as a Disease, p. 426
Diff: H, Ans: c
65. Which of the following is a true statement about bulimia nervosa?
   a. Individuals suffering from it often starve to death.
   b. It is less common than anorexia nervosa.
   c. It can cause cardiac arrest and severe damage to the gastrointestinal system.
   d. Unlike anorexia nervosa, it does not generally involve a distorted body perception.

Dieting as a Disease, p. 426
Diff: E, Ans: a
66.   Which of the following is good advice for parents who want to encourage healthy eating habits in their infants and young children and discourage development of eating disorders?
   a.   Allow children to develop self-control of eating patterns.
   b.   Make sure that children eat exactly what parents tell them to eat.
   c.   Prohibit all unhealthy foods.
   d.   Require children to finish all of the food that is on their plates.

Dieting as a Disease, p. 427
Diff: H, Ans: d
67.   According to the epigenetic perspective, eating disorders can be explained by:
   a.   a woman's desire to compete with men in the workforce by projecting a strong, masculine image.
   b.   cultural pressures that influence a female to present a slim, model-like appearance.
   c.   the inability of the daughter to psychically separate from the mother.
   d.   a girl's avoidance of the stresses of puberty that include developing a womanly body.

Dieting as a Disease, p. 427
Diff: M, Ans: c
68.   According to the psychoanalytic theory, eating disorders can be explained by:
   a.   a woman's desire to compete with men in the workforce by projecting a strong, masculine image.
   b.   cultural pressures that influence a female to present a slim, model-like appearance.
   c.   the inability of the daughter to psychically separate from the mother.
   d.   a girl's avoidance of the stresses of puberty that include developing a womanly body.

Drug Abuse and Addiction, p. 427
Diff: E, Ans: c
69.   Ingestion of a drug, regardless of how much or how often, is called:
   a.   drug abuse.
   b.   drug addiction.
   c.   drug use.
   d.   intoxication.

Drug Abuse and Addiction, p. 427
Diff: E, Ans: a
70.   Using a drug in a quantity or a manner that harms physical, cognitive, or psychosocial well-being is called drug:
   a.   abuse.
   b.   use.
   c.   addiction.
   d.   dependence.

Drug Abuse and Addiction, p. 427
Diff: E, Ans: c
71.   When the absence of a drug creates a craving to satisfy a physiological or psychological need, that is a sign of drug:
   a.   use.
   b.   abuse.
   c.   addiction.
   d.   overdose.

Drug Abuse and Addiction, p. 427
Diff: M, Ans: b

72. Most marijuana smokers and cocaine users quit by the age of:
     a. 20.
     b. 30.
     c. 40.
     d. none of the above; once use is started, quitting is rare.

Drug Abuse and Addiction, pp. 427-428
Diff: H, Ans: a

73. Which of the following is a true statement about drug use and abuse in the United States?
     a. Drug abuse is more prevalent in early adulthood than in adolescence.
     b. Women use drugs more than men do.
     c. Young adult African Americans use drugs more than do European Americans.
     d. Abuse of most drugs, including cigarettes, eases before age 30.

Drug Abuse and Addiction, p. 428
Diff: M, Ans: d

74. Who is most likely to misuse drugs? A person:
     a. with a high tolerance for frustration.
     b. who is not vulnerable to depression.
     c. with a relaxed attitude toward life.
     d. who is constantly seeking new sensations.

Drug Abuse and Addiction, p. 428
Diff: H, Ans: c

75. Which of the following is a potential explanation for the decrease in rates of drug use during young adulthood?
     a. decreasing genetic vulnerability
     b. increasing legal consequences
     c. changing social norms
     d. none of the above

Drug Abuse and Addiction, p. 428
Diff: M, Ans: b

76. Which of the following is NOT a potential source of the increased rate of drug use in early adulthood?
     a. increased vulnerability to depression
     b. increased genetic vulnerability
     c. settings in which young adults commonly congregate
     d. lack of supervision by parents

Drug Abuse and Addiction, p. 429
Diff: E, Ans: d

77. Compared with their peers, young adults who use and abuse drugs are more likely to:
     a. drop out of college.
     b. be involved in transitory sexual relationships.
     c. die violently.
     d. do all of the above.

Psychopathology, p. 429
Diff: M, Ans: c

78. Psychopathology in young adulthood is generally caused by all of the following EXCEPT:
     a. environmental stress.
     b. biological problems.
     c. being female.
     d. childhood trauma.

Psychopathology, p. 430
Diff: M, Ans: b
79.   During young adulthood, are males or females more likely to suffer from depression?
      a.   Males are more likely than females.
      b.   Females are more likely than males.
      c.   Males and females are equally likely.
      d.   Research on this is controversial, and thus it is impossible to determine which sex is more likely to suffer from depression.

Psychopathology, p. 430
Diff: M, Ans: a
80.   Many medications for depression:
      a.   regulate the brain's neurotransmitters.
      b.   change the genetic predisposition for depression.
      c.   are stimulants.
      d.   are generally ineffective.

Psychopathology, p. 430
Diff: M, Ans: d
81.   The best treatment for depression is:
      a.   medication.
      b.   cognitive therapy.
      c.   gene therapy.
      d.   medication and cognitive therapy.

Psychopathology, p. 430
Diff: M, Ans: c
82.   Symptoms of schizophrenia typically begin in _____ and come to full force in _____.
      a.   childhood; adolescence
      b.   childhood; early adulthood
      c.   adolescence; early adulthood
      d.   adolescence; late adulthood

Violence, p. 431
Diff: E, Ans: c
83.   Which of the following groups has the highest rate of violent death?
      a.   middle-aged females
      b.   young adult females
      c.   young adult males
      d.   middle-aged males

Violence, p. 431
Diff: E, Ans: a
84.   The rate of violent deaths among young men is highest in:
      a.   the United States.
      b.   Australia.
      c.   Canada.
      d.   all of the above.

Violence, p. 431
Diff: M, Ans: c
85.   An important explanation for the high rate of violent death among young men lies in:
      a.   chromosomal factors.
      b.   the "If you can't join them, beat them" theory.
      c.   stereotypes about "manly" behavior.
      d.   insufficient protein in the diet.

Violence, p. 431
Diff: M, Ans: a

86.   Young men are more likely to die violently than young women because:
        a.   testosterone is associated with impulsive and angry reactions.
        b.   they drive more frequently.
        c.   they are more likely to blame themselves for their problems.
        d.   they do all of the above.

Violence, p. 431
Diff: M, Ans: d

87.   Eric is a 25-year-old American male. If he dies in the next year, which of the following is the most likely cause?
        a.   leukemia.
        b.   a drug overdose.
        c.   an accident on the job.
        d.   homicide.

TRUE-FALSE QUESTIONS

Early Adulthood: Biosocial Development

Ans: T, p. 413

1.   In terms of biosocial development, early adulthood is considered to be the prime of life.

Growth, Strength, and Health

Ans: T, p. 413

2.   Weight typically increases in both men and women during their early 20s.

Ans: F, p. 413

3.   Physical strength for both sexes decreases during early adulthood from its adolescent peak.

Ans: F, p. 413

4.   Young adults require more medical attention for disease than any other age group except the elderly.

Ans: T, p. 414

5.   In the United States, young adults are the age group least likely to have health insurance.

Ans: F, p. 414

6.   In adulthood, chronological age and the aging process are highly correlated.

Ans: F, pp. 414-415

7.   The rate of senescence is fairly constant from person to person and organ to organ.

Ans: T, pp. 414-415

8.   The efficiency of the lungs declines earlier than that of the kidneys.

Ans: T, p. 416

9.   Women tend to take better care of themselves than do men.

Ans: F, p. 417

10.   At age 80, there are nearly as many men as there are women; it is not until age 90 that a sex difference in death rate appears.

Ans: F, p. 417

11.   It is clear that sex differences in death rates are due entirely to lifestyle choices.

Ans: T, p. 417

12.   The body weight that an individual's homeostatic processes are striving to maintain is referred to as the individual's set point.

Ans: T, p. 418

13.   An older adult has less stamina and recovers less quickly from physical exertion than a young adult because of decreased homeostatic functioning.

Ans: F, p. 418

14.   As muscle strength declines, arms and hands are affected more than leg muscles.

Ans: F, pp. 418-419

15.   Most adults feel the aging process powerfully from age 30 on.

Ans: T, p. 419

16.   Conditioned older adults perform better on physical tasks than most unconditioned younger persons.

Ans: T, p. 420

17.   Women's sexual responsiveness tends to intensify throughout early adulthood.

Ans: F, p. 421

18.   A couple is considered infertile if they are unable to conceive after six months of unprotected sexual intercourse.

Ans: T, p. 421

19.   Half of all women in their 40s who try to become pregnant do not succeed.

Ans: T, p. 421

20.   If they do succeed in conceiving, women in their 40s are more likely than younger women to conceive twins.

Ans: F, p. 421

21.   Infertility in young couples is most often caused by age-related physical problems of the woman.

Ans: T, p. 421

22.   Untreated sexually transmitted infections are a leading cause of female infertility.

Ans: T, p. 422

23.   In vitro fertilization is one option for couples whose fertility problems are due to blocked Fallopian tubes in the woman.

Emotional Problems in Early Adulthood

Ans: F, pp. 424-426

24.   Anorexia nervosa is characterized by binge eating followed by purging.

Ans: T, p. 425

25.   Rates of anorexia nervosa are much higher among runners, gymnasts, and dancers than among other groups of women.

Ans: T, p. 426

26.   Some research has indicated that half of all college women have binged and purged at least once.

Ans: T, p. 426
27.   People who suffer from bulimia are usually close to normal in weight.

Ans: T, p. 427
28.   An explanation for women's increased risk of eating disorders based on the cognitive theory is that fasting, bingeing, and purging are powerful reinforcers.

Ans: T, p. 427
29.   Older adolescents and young adults are the chief initiators and heaviest users of drugs.

Ans: F, p. 427
30.   The only difference between use and abuse of drugs is the quantity of drugs taken.

Ans: T, p. 427
31.   Drug addiction can be either physiological or psychological in nature.

Ans: F, p. 427
32.   Drug abuse usually eases by the early 20s.

Ans: F, p. 428
33.   Drug abuse is not at all genetic.

Ans: T, p. 428
34.   Informing college students that most adults do not use illegal drugs or drink to excess can help deter college students from drug use.

Ans: T, p. 429
35.   A deterrent to serious drug and alcohol abuse is religious faith and practice.

Ans: T, p. 430
36.   Not all monozygotic twins share psychopathologies.

Ans: F, p. 430
37.   Medication is usually all that is necessary to cure depression.

Ans: F, p. 430
38.   If people experience no schizophrenic symptoms by age 20, they almost never become schizophrenic later on.

Ans: T, p. 431
39.   Trauma at birth is a cause of schizophrenia.

Ans: F, p. 431
40.   The high rate of violent death among young adult males is found only in the United States.

Ans: T, p. 431
41.   Testosterone may be a cause of males' higher rates of violent death in comparison with females.

Ans: F, p. 431
42.   Aggression may be the result of an "explosive combination" of low self-esteem and dashed expectations.

FILL-IN-THE-BLANK QUESTIONS

Growth, Strength, and Health

Ans: injuries (or accidents), p. 413

1.   Medical attention during early adulthood is less often needed for disease than for pregnancy and
     _____.

Ans: Cancer, p. 414

2.   _____ is the leading killer of adults under the age of 75.

Ans: 20, p. 414

3.   Most adults notice the first signs of aging when they are in their _____s.

Ans: presbyopia, p. 416

4.   The farsightedness of middle and late adulthood is called _____.

Ans: appearance, p. 416

5.   Women tend to feel middle-aged before men, probably because of the increased importance they place
     on their _____.

Ans: homeostasis, p. 417

6.   When we exert ourselves, our breathing and heart rate speed up, an example of the body's
     physiological balance called _____.

Ans: homeostasis, p. 417

7.   The processes of _____ work to maintain body weight and normal body temperature.

Ans: set point, p. 417

8.   Each person has a certain _____ for his or her weight that his/her body strives to maintain.

Ans: organ reserve, p. 418

9.   The extra capacity of the heart or kidneys to respond to higher than normal or stressful physiological
     demands is called _____.

Ans: reserve, p. 418

10. The declines of aging primarily affect organ _____.

Ans: maximum, p. 419

11. In adulthood, _____ heart rate, the number of times the heart can beat under extreme stress, declines
     steadily.

Ans: refractory, p. 419

12. For both men and women, orgasm is followed by a period of time during which sexual arousal is not
     possible; this is called the _____ period.

Ans: increases; decreases, p. 420

13. With age, women's sexual responsiveness _____, and men's sexual responsiveness _____.

Ans: one year, p. 421

14. Infertility is defined as being unable to conceive a child after _____ or more of regular intercourse
     without contraception.

Ans: ovulation, p. 421

15. Older women usually take longer to conceive because _____ becomes less regular as middle age
     approaches.

Ans: pelvic inflammatory disease, p. 421
16.   A common cause of infertility in women is blocked Fallopian tubes caused by _____.

Ans: 30, p. 421
17.   Most physicians recommend that would-be mothers begin their efforts at conception before age _____.

Ans: in vitro fertilization, p. 422
18.   The medical procedure in which ova are surgically removed from the ovaries and fertilized by sperm in the laboratory and then placed into the uterus is called _____.

Emotional Problems in Early Adulthood

Ans: body-mass index, p. 424 (Table 17.2)
19.   A person's weight in kilograms divided by his/her height in meters squared is referred to as that person's BMI or _____.

Ans: bulimia nervosa, p. 426
20.   An eating disorder characterized by compulsive binge eating, followed by compulsive vomiting or use of laxatives, is called _____.

Ans: psychoanalytic, p. 427
21.   A _____ hypothesis to explain women's increased risk of eating disorders is that women develop eating disorders because of a conflict with their mothers.

Ans: sociocultural, p. 427
22.   A _____ explanation for eating disorders is that contemporary culture pressures women to be "slim and trim" and model-like.

Ans: Drug addiction, p. 427
23.   _____ refers to the condition in which absence of a drug leads to a drive for more of the drug.

Ans: multifactorial, p. 430
24.   Psychopathologies are _____; that is, they have many causes.

Ans: young men, p. 431
25.   Most murdered young men are murdered by _____.

ESSAY QUESTIONS

1.   In earlier chapters, we learned that the male is more vulnerable, biologically, than the female over the life span. Describe two special vulnerabilities of the male in early adulthood and explain the causes of each.

2.   Your friend has just celebrated her 21st birthday, and she is concerned that "it is all downhill from here." You want to be honest with her about what you have learned. Give your friend two pieces of good news and two pieces of bad news about the physical effects of young adulthood.

3.   How does the prevalence of drug abuse in early adulthood compare to that in other periods? Discuss three factors that contribute to the likelihood of drug use in early adulthood.

4.   You are a physician who specializes in treating fertility disorders. A couple is worried about having no children in their first two years of marriage. What could you tell them about the possible causes and available treatments?

5.   Discuss two factors that lead women to be more likely than men to try to lose an unhealthy amount of weight. What do you think can be done to change this situation?

6.   Compare and contrast the physiological and psychological experiences of senescence, from the ages of 20 to 50, for two adults, one of whom is progressing more rapidly than the other.

7.   You tell your uncle who is 50, wears reading glasses, is slightly overweight, and has recently stopped playing on his company's softball team that you are a mind reader. Even though you are only 20, you can describe the physical changes that he has experienced over the past 30 years and even give him the time frames for when these changes occurred. He does not believe you. Keeping in mind that he will probably not appreciate you talking about his sex life, what else can you tell him?

8.   Define the process of homeostasis, and then describe two homeostatic functions that our bodies perform.

Answer guidelines to these essay questions can be found in the Appendix at the end of the Test Bank.

CHAPTER 18

Early Adulthood: Cognitive Development

MULTIPLE-CHOICE QUESTIONS

Early Adulthood: Cognitive Development

Early Adulthood: Cognitive Development, p. 435
Diff: E, Ans: d
1. The cognitive growth of adults is:
   a. straightforward and direct.
   b. characterized by questioning about everything.
   c. unrelated to childhood cognition.
   d. fostered by life situations in many contexts.

Early Adulthood: Cognitive Development, p. 435
Diff: M, Ans: c
2. Understanding adult cognitive development involves which of the following?
   a. focusing on how adults learn in the classroom
   b. tying cognitive development directly to chronological age
   c. examining how abilities improve, decline, and remain stable
   d. none of the above

Early Adulthood: Cognitive Development, p. 435
Diff: M, Ans: a
3. Which approach to adult cognitive development is an outgrowth of Piaget's theory?
   a. postformal
   b. information processing
   c. psychometric
   d. behavioral

Early Adulthood: Cognitive Development, p. 435
Diff: M, Ans: b
4. The psychometric approach to cognition emphasizes:
   a. developmental stages of cognitive growth.
   b. components of intelligence as measured by IQ tests.
   c. encoding, memory, and output.
   d. the effects of life events on cognition.

Early Adulthood: Cognitive Development, p. 435
Diff: E, Ans: d
5.   Dr. Marquette is a researcher who studies the encoding, storage, and retrieval of information throughout life. What approach to cognitive development does she take?
     a.   psychometric
     b.   multidirectional
     c.   postformal
     d.   information-processing

Postformal Thought

Postformal Thought, p. 436
Diff: M, Ans: c
6.   Compared to formal operational thinking, postformal thought is all of the following EXCEPT more:
     a.   flexible.
     b.   practical.
     c.   rational.
     d.   dialectical.

A Fifth Stage of Cognitive Development?, p. 436
Diff: H, Ans: d
7.   Mark has finished graduate school, and at age 30 he is established in his career and is married with two children. His approach to problems has changed since he was an adolescent. Now, he is more likely to:
     a.   act without exploring the consequences.
     b.   engage in the "game of thinking."
     c.   stay up all night to debate.
     d.   see life's answers as conditional rather than permanent.

The Practical and the Personal, p. 437
Diff: E, Ans: a
8.   In solving a real-life problem, Ben takes into account his subjective feelings and personal experience. Developmentalists refer to this as:
     a.   postformal thought.
     b.   formal thought.
     c.   an absolutist approach.
     d.   hypothetical deductive reasoning.

The Practical and the Personal, p. 437
Diff: M, Ans: b
9.   Traditional models of advanced thought overvalued:
     a.   subjective thought.
     b.   objective thought.
     c.   personal faith.
     d.   emotional experiences.

The Practical and the Personal, p. 437
Diff: H, Ans: d
10. Which of the following is a true statement about objective, logical thinking as part of the scientific method?
     a.   It is necessary to counteract subjective thinking.
     b.   It is can be verified through replication.
     c.   It is useful in overcoming culture-bound perspectives.
     d.   All of the above are true.

The Practical and the Personal, p. 437
Diff: M, Ans: a

11. Which of the following abilities is a hallmark of adult adaptive thought?
    a. applying both objective and subjective thinking to real-life problems
    b. recognizing the logic of an argument
    c. ignoring subjective feelings and personal experience
    d. reasoning abstractly

The Practical and the Personal, p. 437
Diff: H, Ans: b

12. Who would most likely require postformal thinking in order to solve his or her problem?
    a. an accountant who must keep track of the many governmental changes from the IRS
    b. a full-time student who needs to study while caring for her two small children
    c. a man who must memorize information to pass the bar examination
    d. a computer hacker who is developing a program that will transmit a virus

The Practical and the Personal, pp. 437-438
Diff: E, Ans: d

13. Does adult thinking utilize both objective and subjective thought?
    a. No, it only utilizes objective thought.
    b. No, it only utilizes subjective thought.
    c. Yes, it uses both objective thought and subjective thought, but only one type at a time.
    d. Yes, it combines objective and subjective thought.

The Practical and the Personal, p. 438
Diff: H, Ans: b

14. In the study by Blanchard-Fields on the progression in reasoning ability, the least mature level was an approach that:
    a. recognized discrepancies in people's interpretations of events.
    b. was absolute and recognized only one perspective as correct.
    c. weakly insisted on external truth.
    d. looked at the multiple perspectives and weighed discrepant sources of information.

The Practical and the Personal, p. 438
Diff: M, Ans: b

15. In Blanchard-Fields' study of the progression of reasoning, _____ percent of adolescents and _____ percent of young adults scored above level three.
    a. 5; 81
    b. 16; 36
    c. 57; 57
    d. 84; 12

The Practical and the Personal, p. 438
Diff: M, Ans: c

16. Which of the following is a true statement about adolescents' and young adults' reasoning on the emotional questions in Blanchard-Fields' study of the progression of reasoning?
    a. Adults found it particularly difficult to reason on emotional questions.
    b. Adults found it particularly difficult to reason on practical questions.
    c. Adolescents found it particularly difficult to reason on emotional questions.
    d. Adolescents found it particularly difficult to reason on practical questions.

The Practical and the Personal, p. 438
Diff: E, Ans: b
17.   Adult thought can be characterized as which of the following?
       a.   extreme
       b.   balanced
       c.   absolute
       d.   either/or

The Practical and the Personal, p. 438
Diff: E, Ans: a
18.   Young adults will usually exhibit more mature reasoning ability than adolescents when a topic is:
       a.   emotionally charged.
       b.   age-related.
       c.   political in nature.
       d.   objectively stated.

The Practical and the Personal, p. 438
Diff: H, Ans: c
19.   An adolescent doing which of the following is most likely to reason less maturely than a young adult?
       a.   learning about the workings of refrigerators
       b.   researching the history of the U.S. presidency
       c.   debating whether teens should be allowed to drink
       d.   studying for a calculus exam

Cognitive Flexibility, p. 438
Diff: H, Ans: d
20.   Which of the following is characteristic of postformal thought?
       a.   the ability to characterize experience in a stable way
       b.   understanding that information is absolute
       c.   objective, logical thinking that devalues personal experience
       d.   understanding that one's own perspective is one of many potentially valid views

Cognitive Flexibility, p. 439
Diff: E, Ans: a
21.   In comparison with adolescent thinking, adult thinking requires more:
       a.   flexibility.
       b.   stability.
       c.   persistence.
       d.   rationality.

Cognitive Flexibility, p. 439
Diff: M, Ans: b
22.   The study in which adults were asked to suggest solutions to 15 real-life problems demonstrated that:
       a.   it was very difficult for adults to generate more than one solution.
       b.   familiarity with situations enabled adults to be more flexible.
       c.   problems that were particularly emotional immobilized many adults.
       d.   all of the above were true.

Cognitive Flexibility, p. 439
Diff: E, Ans: c
23.   The possibility that one's appearance or behavior will be misused to confirm another person's oversimplified, prejudiced attitude is referred to as:
       a.   overcompensation.
       b.   dialectical thought.
       c.   stereotype threat.
       d.   disidentification.

Cognitive Flexibility, pp. 440-441
Diff: H, Ans: d
24.   Which of the following responses to stereotype threat requires cognitive flexibility?
    a.   counteridentification
    b.   identification
    c.   disidentification
    d.   none of the above

Cognitive Flexibility, p. 441
Diff: M, Ans: d
25.   In the study of young adults who were asked to solve difficult math problems, which of the following groups did the most poorly?
    a.   men who were not told that sex differences would be assessed
    b.   women who were not told that sex differences would be assessed
    c.   men who were told that sex differences would be assessed and who identified strongly as men
    d.   women who were told that sex differences would be assessed and who identified strongly as women

Cognitive Flexibility, p. 441
Diff: H, Ans: a
26.   Which of the following is a possible reaction to stereotype threat?
    a.   the comparatively high drop-out rate for African American males
    b.   many young girls' preferences for playing with dolls over trucks
    c.   married couples' arguments about money
    d.   college students' practice of referring to professors by their last names

Thinking Like a Scientist: Reducing Stereotype Threat, p. 442
Diff: H, Ans: c
27.   Which of the following is probably the best way for colleges to improve the academic achievement of groups whose potential may be hindered by stereotype threat?
    a.   requiring all students to take upper-level mathematics courses
    b.   reducing the academic requirements for high grades
    c.   restricting admission to either females or minorities
    d.   all of the above

Thinking Like a Scientist: Reducing Stereotype Threat, pp. 442-443
Diff: H, Ans: b
28.   In the stereotype-threat study in which college students were taught about intelligence research, which group showed the most improvement in attitudes about academic achievement and grades?
    a.   white students who were taught that intelligence is malleable
    b.   black students who were taught that intelligence is malleable
    c.   white students who were taught that there are multiple intelligences
    d.   black students who were taught that there are multiple intelligences

Dialectical Thought, p. 443
Diff: E, Ans: c
29.   The adult thinking process in which every idea implies an opposite idea, and both the idea and its opposite can be integrated into a synthesis is referred to as:
    a.   formal operational thought.
    b.   adaptive logic.
    c.   dialectical thought.
    d.   moral reasoning.

Dialectical Thought, p. 443
Diff: M, Ans: d
30.   Dialectical thinking involves:
    a.   the view that everything is relative.
    b.   a rejection of logical principles.
    c.   a closed system with an inevitable outcome.
    d.   the integration of an idea with its opposite.

Dialectical Thought, p. 443
Diff: E, Ans: a
31.   A new idea that integrates an original idea and its opposite is referred to as a(n):
    a.   synthesis.
    b.   thesis.
    c.   antithesis.
    d.   counterthesis.

Dialectical Thought, p. 443
Diff: H, Ans: c
32.   In an essay, Michelle begins by writing that knowing the truth sets people free. In her next paragraph, she opposes this with the idea that knowing the truth often involves learning about limitations and constraints on freedom. In her third paragraph, Michelle integrates these two perspectives. Michelle's essay best demonstrates:
    a.   inconsistent thinking.
    b.   moral reasoning.
    c.   dialectical thinking.
    d.   subjective thinking.

Dialectical Thought, p. 443
Diff: M, Ans: b
33.   Geraldine is a medical intern who believes that all people deserve the highest quality of medical care. However, she realizes that someday she may need to make decisions about which patients will receive a scarce, life-saving medication. Reconciling these two thoughts requires:
    a.   intuitive-projective faith.
    b.   dialectical thinking.
    c.   relativism.
    d.   ideological reasoning.

Dialectical Thought, p. 444
Diff: M, Ans: b
34,   A dialectical thinker is likely to recognize the:
    a.   true nature of most relationships.
    b.   changing nature of human relationships.
    c.   need to explain human actions logically.
    d.   insincerity of most human relationships.

Dialectical Thought, p. 494
Diff: M, Ans: a
35.   Marge's marriage is troubled. She and her husband find very little joy in being with each other. If Marge and her husband are capable of dialectical thinking, they will:
    a.   adjust their relationship to accommodate the changes in themselves.
    b.   realize that divorce is the only solution.
    c.   try to find out which one of them is to blame.
    d.   try to reinstate their relationship as it was when they were first married.

Dialectical Thought, pp. 444-445
Diff: H, Ans: d

36.   Cross-cultural research on thinking has demonstrated that compared to Americans, Asians are more likely to:
   a.   perceive a picture in its entirety, rather than simply the object in the middle.
   b.   seek compromises between two extremes.
   c.   try to find a holistic, balanced synthesis.
   d.   do all of the above.

Adult Moral Reasoning

Adult Moral Reasoning, p. 446
Diff: M, Ans: b

37.   According to James Rest's research, the most useful type of college experience:
   a.   prepares one for an occupation that provides a decent living.
   b.   involves problem-solving strategies used to deal with ethical issues.
   c.   includes study abroad in order to foster learning a second language.
   d.   allows a person to work first in order to learn to serve others.

Adult Moral Reasoning, p. 446
Diff: M, Ans: c

38.   To be capable of "truly ethical" reasoning, according to Kohlberg, a person must have:
   a.   the experience of failure and disillusionment.
   b.   faith and religious insight.
   c.   sustained responsibility for the welfare of others.
   d.   a low tolerance for hypocrisy in others.

Addressing Specific Dilemmas, p. 446
Diff: E, Ans: d

39.   In which of the following circumstances do adults confront moral issues?
   a.   parenthood
   b.   intimate relationships
   c.   career
   d.   all of the above
   e.   none of the above

Addressing Specific Dilemmas, p. 447
Diff: M, Ans: a

40.   According to Gilligan's view of moral development:
   a.   adult decisions particularly advance moral thinking.
   b.   most moral development occurs prior to adulthood.
   c.   women's ethics are more concerned about justice than relationships.
   d.   men tend to put human needs above legal principles.

Addressing Specific Dilemmas, p. 447
Diff: H, Ans: b

41.   Carol Gilligan would probably say that choices about which of the following are most likely to advance moral thinking?
   a.   politics
   b.   child rearing
   c.   financial matters
   d.   religion

Measuring Moral Growth, p. 447
Diff: E, Ans: d
42.   The Defining Issues Test (DIT) was developed by:
      a. Gilligan.
      b. Kohlberg.
      c. Fowler.
      d. Rest.

Measuring Moral Growth, p. 447
Diff: M, Ans: c
43.   Research using the Defining Issues Test (DIT) has demonstrated that which of the following is associated with moral growth?
      a. ethnicity
      b. gender
      c. education
      d. none of the above

Measuring Moral Growth, p. 448
Diff: E, Ans: b
44.   A detailed six-stage description of the development of faith has been proposed by:
      a. Kohlberg.
      b. Fowler.
      c. Gilligan.
      d. Piaget.

Measuring Moral Growth, p. 448
Diff: H, Ans: a
45.   Four-year-old Davis believes that God gave his little brother to his mother because she stayed overnight at the hospital. Davis is at the _____ stage of religious faith.
      a. intuitive-projective
      b. universalizing
      c. synthetic-conventional
      d. individual-reflective

Measuring Moral Growth, p. 448
Diff: M, Ans: d
46.   The stage of faith that is based on God rewarding those who follow His laws and punishing others is referred to as:
      a. universalizing faith.
      b. synthetic-conventional faith.
      c. conjunctive faith.
      d. mythic-literal faith.

Measuring Moral Growth, p. 448
Diff: H, Ans: d
47.   Favoring what feels right over what makes intellectual sense is typical of _____ faith.
      a. conjunctive
      b. universalizing
      c. mythic-literal
      d. synthetic-conventional

Measuring Moral Growth, p. 448
Diff: M, Ans: a

48.   The stage in which faith becomes an active commitment, detached from the expectations of culture and parents, is referred to as the stage of:
   a.   individual-reflective faith.
   b.   intuitive-projective faith.
   c.   universalizing faith.
   d.   mythic-literal faith.

Measuring Moral Growth, p. 448
Diff: H, Ans: b

49.   The type of faith in which people can accept contradictions and incorporate both powerful unconscious ideas and rational, conscious values is:
   a.   mythic-literal faith.
   b.   conjunctive faith.
   c.   synthetic-conventional faith.
   d.   individual-reflective faith.

Measuring Moral Growth, p. 448
Diff: M, Ans: d

50.   Which statement is true of Fowler's sixth stage of Universalizing Faith?
   a.   It develops during adolescence.
   b.   People act in accordance with their own personal welfare.
   c.   All people eventually achieve it.
   d.   People have a vision of universal compassion, justice, and love.

Measuring Moral Growth, p. 448
Diff: E, Ans: b

51.   According to Fowler, Mother Teresa, Martin Luther King Jr., and Mohandas Gandhi exhibited which stage of faith?
   a.   mythic-literal
   b.   universalizing
   c.   synthetic-conventional
   d.   individual-reflective

Measuring Moral Growth, p. 448
Diff: M, Ans: c

52.   Which of the following is a true statement about developmentalists' view of faith and religion?
   a.   It is rarely helpful when people are confronted with stressful situations.
   b.   It remains static throughout adulthood.
   c.   It progresses from a self-centered perspective to a multisided, altruistic view.
   d.   It involves taking the myths and symbols of religion literally.

Cognitive Growth and Higher Education

Cognitive Growth and Higher Education, p. 449
Diff: E, Ans: a

53.   Which of the following correlates with depth and flexibility of thought in adulthood?
   a.   college education
   b.   age
   c.   ethnicity
   d.   sex

The Effects of College on Cognition, p. 449
Diff: E, Ans: d
54. Compared to individuals without a college education, those with a college education tend to be more:
    a. healthy.
    b. wealthy.
    c. flexible.
    d. all of the above.
    e. none of the above.

The Effects of College on Cognition, p. 450
Diff: M, Ans: b
55. The first phase of college students' thinking is:
    a. questioning personal and social values.
    b. believing in the existence of clear and perfect truths.
    c. carefully considering many opposing ideas.
    d. becoming committed to a set of personal values.

The Effects of College on Cognition, p. 451
Diff: E, Ans: d
56. According to Perry, students in which year of college are the most likely to be open-minded?
    a. first
    b. second
    c. third
    d. fourth

The Effects of College on Cognition, p. 451
Diff: H, Ans: d
57. Perry found that over the four years of their college careers, students:
    a. move from a relativistic to a dualistic approach.
    b. change very little.
    c. stick to their own views when faced with conflicts.
    d. progress through nine levels of complexity in their thinking.

The Effects of College on Cognition, p. 451 (Table 18.3)
Diff: H, Ans: a
58. Joe is at the low end of Perry's scheme of cognitive development. He believes that:
    a. authorities know what is right.
    b. everyone has the right to his or her own opinion.
    c. authorities don't know everything.
    d. we all must make our own decisions.

The Effects of College on Cognition, p. 451 (Table 18.3)
Diff: H, Ans: b
59. Which statement illustrated Perry's concept of Relativism Discovered?
    a. It is difficult to make sense out of life's dilemmas.
    b. Everyone has the right to their opinion when authorities don't know the right answer.
    c. Legitimate opinions are permanent.
    d. Authorities know, and if we work hard, we can learn all of the right answers.

Possible Factors in Cognitive Growth During College, p. 452
Diff: M, Ans: a
60. Describing college students in North America today, it is true that:
    a. there are more females than males.
    b. the number of older students is decreasing.
    c. liberal arts education is becoming more common than career-based programs.
    d. fewer students are attending college part-time.

Possible Factors in Cognitive Growth During College, pp. 452-453
Diff: E, Ans: b
61. Compared to 50 years ago, today's U.S. college population:
     a. has a larger proportion of males.
     b. is more diverse and heterogeneous.
     c. includes more liberal arts majors.
     d. has fewer minority students.

Possible Factors in Cognitive Growth During College, p. 453 (Figure 18.4)
Diff: E, Ans: e
62. Which of the following ethnic groups did NOT have a larger number of individuals earning bachelor's degrees in 2000 than in 1981?
     a. African American
     b. Asian American
     c. Hispanic American
     d. European American
     e. none of the above

Possible Factors in Cognitive Growth During College, p. 453 (Figure 18.5)
Diff: E, Ans: a
63. In a 1999 study, which of the following objectives was rated as essential or very important by the largest number of college freshman?
     a. being better off financially
     b. becoming an authority in their field
     c. developing a philosophy of life
     d. becoming a community leader

Possible Factors in Cognitive Growth During College, p. 453 (Figure 18.5)
Diff: M, Ans: c
64. In surveys of college freshman, _____ percent of students in 1966 rated keeping up to date on politics as important, and _____ percent of students in 1999 rated this as important.
     a. 15; 54
     b. 32; 36
     c. 58; 27
     d. 84; 53

Possible Factors in Cognitive Growth During College, p. 454
Diff: M, Ans: a
65. Which of the following is a true statement about the structure of higher education in the United States currently as compared to several decades ago?
     a. Enrollment in community colleges has increased.
     b. Fewer career programs are being offered.
     c. More instructors are European American men.
     d. There are fewer institutions of higher learning.

In Person: A Dialectical View of Cheating, p. 454
Diff: M, Ans: b
66. According to a survey, about 1 U.S. college student in _____ believes cheating is sometimes necessary to get better grades.
     a. 3
     b. 12
     c. 25
     d. 50

In Person: A Dialectical View of Cheating, p. 454
Diff: E, Ans: c

67.   Students who agree that some cheating is necessary to get the grades they want are more likely to attend:
      a.   two-year colleges.
      b.   four-year colleges.
      c.   universities.
      d.   school part-time.

In Person: A Dialectical View of Cheating, p. 454
Diff: M, Ans: a

68.   Which college students are most likely to accept cheating?
      a.   full-time students who live on campus
      b.   full-time students who commute
      c.   part-time students who commute
      d.   part-time or full-time students who are employed

In Person: A Dialectical View of Cheating, p. 454
Diff: M, Ans: c

69.   _____ percent of college students admit to having cheated at least three times.
      a.   5
      b.   10
      c.   20
      d.   40

In Person: A Dialectical View of Cheating, p. 455
Diff: E, Ans: b

70.   The author of your textbook reported that she used postformal thought in order to determine the best:
      a.   sequence for presenting the information in the textbook.
      b.   way to deal with cheating in her classroom.
      c.   way to convince her students to study more and party less.
      d.   definitions for the key terms at the end of each chapter.

Evaluating the Research, p. 455
Diff: H, Ans: a

71.   Which of the following is a true statement about cohort effects regarding the effect of college on cognitive development?
      a.   The increased diversity of the college atmosphere probably helps to enhance cognitive development.
      b.   A college education may have had positive effects on cognitive development in the past, but it is unlikely that this is the case today.
      c.   Since less-able students are more likely to drop out of school, estimating the effect of college education on cognitive development is complicated.
      d.   Cohort effects are irrelevant, since college students are all approximately the same age.

Evaluating the Research, p. 455
Diff: M, Ans: c

72.   Which of the following could be evidence that a selection effect is responsible for the difference between the cognitive development of college-educated and non-college-educated individuals?
      a.   Intellectually inclined individuals are more likely than others to attend college.
      b.   College students are more diverse than they were several decades ago.
      c.   Some students drop out of college, impairing their ability to mature.
      d.   All of the above could be evidence.

Evaluating the Research, p. 456
Diff: E, Ans: c
73.   Research has revealed that college education leads students to become:
    a.   less committed to values of any kind.
    b.   less tolerant of differing religious and social views.
    c.   more tolerant of differing religious and political views.
    d.   overwhelmingly liberal in political philosophy.

TRUE-FALSE QUESTIONS

Early Adulthood: Cognitive Development

Ans: T, p. 435
1.   The information-processing approach studies advances in the encoding, storage, and retrieval of information.

Ans: F, p. 435
2.   The psychometric approach is the only accurate explanation of cognitive development.

Postformal Thought

Ans: F, p. 436
3.   Adulthood has several distinct stages of cognitive development.

Ans: F, p. 436
4.   Adult cognition is closely tied to chronological age.

Ans: T, p. 436
5.   Adults realize that most of life's answers are not necessarily permanent.

Ans: F, p. 437
6.   Postformal thought involves only objective reasoning, rejecting subjective feelings.

Ans: F, p. 437
7.   The scientific method relies solely on subjective thinking.

Ans: T, p. 437
8.   Purely logical, objective thought can be rigid and impractical when thinking about personal experiences.

Ans: T, p. 438
9.   The difference between the reasoning of adolescents and that of young adults is particularly apparent when the problem is emotionally charged.

Ans: F, p. 438
10.   Adolescent thinking is flexible in comparison with the thinking of young adults.

Ans: T, p. 439
11.   For adults, familiarity with a problem enables them to generate greater numbers of potential solutions.

Ans: F, p. 439
12.   Stereotype threat is often considered as an explanation for the increasing pressure colleges are putting on students to choose a major early in their college career.

Ans: T, p. 442

13.   Adults need to be cognitively flexible to overcome stereotypes and stereotype threat.

Ans: F, p. 443

14.   Dialectical thinkers consider an idea and similar, closely related ideas and integrate them into a new idea.

Ans: F, p. 443

15.   According to dialectical thinkers, everything is always relative.

Ans: T, pp. 443-444

16.   Faced with a troubled romance, nondialectical thinkers usually conclude that one of the partners is at fault.

Ans: F, pp. 444-445

17.   All adults appear to eventually become dialectical thinkers; culture has little influence.

Adult Moral Reasoning

Ans: T, p. 446

18.   Becoming a parent and being a victim of a crime are examples of events that might trigger new patterns of thinking in adulthood.

Ans: T, p. 446

19.   Much of the evidence for the effect of life events on cognition comes from personal experience, biographies, and autobiographies.

Ans: T, pp. 446-447

20.   Adulthood naturally brings moral issues to the forefront of everyone's thinking, but only some adults are able to master their ethical principles.

Ans: F, p. 447

21.   Gilligan believes that issues such as sexuality, reproduction, marriage, and child rearing are particularly likely to hinder individuals' moral growth.

Ans: T, p. 447

22.   Gilligan believes that women have been raised to develop a morality of care, and men have been raised to develop a morality of justice.

Ans: T, p. 448

23.   James Fowler believes that the development of faith follows a path similar to that of moral and cognitive development.

Ans: F, p. 448

24.   According to Fowler, universalizing faith involves nonintellectual acceptance of cultural and religious values.

Ans: T, p. 448

25.   According to Fowler, college may be a facilitator of individual-reflective faith, as individuals learn to question authority and rely on their own understanding of the world.

Ans: T, p. 448

26.   Fowler believes that the level of conjunctive faith is rarely reached before middle adulthood and that most people never reach the level of universalizing faith.

Cognitive Growth and Higher Education

Ans: F, pp. 449-450

27. Most young adults enroll in college because they want to master dialectical thinking and adaptive logic.

Ans: T, p. 450

28. Compared to students two decades ago, college students today are less concerned with developing a philosophy of life and more concerned with being financially well-off.

Ans: T, p. 450

29. Every year of college appears to improve cognitive abilities, including cognitive flexibility.

Ans: F, p. 450

30. The college experience serves as a catalyst for thought primarily for the older or returning college student rather than for the traditional student.

Ans: F, pp. 450-451

31. In the end more than at the beginning of college, students are likely to believe that there are clear and absolute truths to discover.

Ans: T, p. 451

32. Longitudinal research on college students suggests that a college education makes people more tolerant of differing views, as well as more flexible and realistic in their attitudes.

Ans: F, p. 451

33. As students progress through college, they become more open-minded and more able to see multiple perspectives.

Ans: F, p. 451 (Table 18.3)

34. The final position in Perry's scheme of cognitive and ethical development is: "Things are getting contradictory. I can't make sense out of life's dilemmas."

Ans: T, p. 452

35. More of today's college students enroll in career-based studies and fewer in the liberal arts than did students of 20 years ago.

Ans: T, p. 452

36. The cognitive changes that occur during college are probably due to both the intellectual challenge and the social interaction.

Ans: T, p. 453 (Figure 18.4)

37. Across ethnic groups, more individuals are earning bachelor's degrees in U.S. colleges today than they were in the early 1980s.

Ans: F, p. 453 (Figure 18.5)

38. The vast majority of college freshman rate "developing a philosophy of life" as essential or very important to them.

Ans: F, p. 454

39. Fewer students are attending community colleges in the United States today than three decades ago.

Ans: T, p. 454 (In Person)

40. Most college students know classmates who have cheated.

Ans: F, p. 454 (In Person)

41.   College students who are most closely connected to their academic institutions are the least likely to cheat.

Ans: T, p. 455 (In Person)

42.   Students who cheat in college appear to believe that the purpose of school is to get good grades, not to learn.

Ans: F, p. 456

43.   It is likely that a large part of the apparent effect of college education on cognitive development is really a selection effect, in that smarter students are more likely to go to college than are other students.

Ans: T, p. 456

44.   Although 80 percent of community college students plan to earn a bachelor's degree, only fewer than 20 percent actually do so.

Ans: T, p. 456

45.   Students' abilities to adapt to the complexities of a college education are generally developed during the course of a college career, but some students may drop out before they have developed sufficiently to deal with the complexities.

FILL-IN-THE-BLANK QUESTIONS

Early Adulthood: Cognitive Development

Ans: multidirectional, p. 435

1.   The cognitive achievements of childhood and adolescence are rather linear; the cognitive achievements of adulthood are _____.

Ans: postformal, p. 435

2.   The _____ approach to cognitive development begins where Piaget left off, exploring new thinking that builds on earlier cognitive skills.

Postformal Thought

Ans: Subjective; objective, p. 437

3.   _____ thought arises from personal experiences and perceptions; whereas _____ thought follows abstract, impersonal knowledge.

Ans: emotions, p. 438

4.   Blanchard-Fields found that _____ can cloud adolescents' thinking in a problem-solving task.

Ans: stereotype threat, p. 439

5.   The possibility that one's appearance or behavior will be misused to confirm another person's oversimplified, prejudiced attitude is referred to as _____.

Ans: dialectical, p. 443

6.   Thinking that recognizes and synthesizes contradictions is called _____ thinking.

Ans: antithesis (opposite), p. 443

7.   Dialectical thinking involves integrating a thesis and its _____.

Ans: evolving, p. 494

8.   The picture of adaptive, dialectical thinking presented views people and relationships as constantly
        _____.

Adult Moral Reasoning

Ans: college (or education), p. 446

9.   According to Rest, _____ is a catalyst for shifts in moral reasoning.

Ans: cognitive, p. 446

10.   Becoming a new parent, receiving a job promotion or dismissal, or being the victim of a violent attack
        can all further _____ development.

Ans: disequilibrium, p. 446

11.   Experiencing the illness or death of a loved one can create cognitive _____ and reflection.

Ans: women; men, p. 447

12.   Gilligan believes that in young adulthood, men and women differ in their approach to moral reasoning,
        with _____ being more interested in relationships and the personal implications of a moral decision,
        and _____ being more interested in the principles of justice and rights.

Ans: moral dilemmas, pp. 447-448

13.   The Defining Issues Test consists of a series of questions about _____.

Ans: James Fowler, p. 448

14.   A detailed description of the development of faith has been suggested by _____.

Ans: mythic-literal, p. 448

15.   Myths and stories of religion are taken literally in the _____ stage of faith.

Ans: detachment, p. 448

16.   According to Fowler, individual-reflective faith is characterized by _____ from the values of the
        culture and the approval of significant other people.

Cognitive Growth and Higher Education

Ans: years of education, p. 449

17.   Comparing age, ethnicity, and years of education, the variable that would be expected to correlate most
        strongly with adults' scores on measures of cognition is _____.

Ans: William Perry, p. 451 (Table 18.3)

18.   _____ suggests that over the course of their college careers, students' thinking progresses through
        nine levels of complexity.

Ans: dualism modified, p. 451 (Table 18.3)

19.   College students at Perry's level of _____ are trying to learn the right answers that authorities know.

Ans: relativism discovered, p. 451 (Table 18.3)

20.   At the level of _____, Perry states that college students realize that authorities may not know the right
        answers.

Ans: dialectical (or flexible), p. 451

21.   Research shows that the more years of higher education a person has, the deeper and more _____ the
        person's reasoning is likely to become.

Ans: career, p. 452

22.   Over the past several decades, a larger proportion of students are choosing _____-based programs rather than liberal arts programs.

Ans: diverse, pp. 452-454

23.   The college population and the colleges themselves have become more _____ in recent years.

Ans: selection, p. 455

24.   If the difference between the cognitive development of college-educated and non-college-educated individuals is really due to the fact that smarter and wealthier individuals are more likely to attend college, this would be referred to as a _____ effect.

ESSAY QUESTIONS

1.   Consider the many kinds of problem-solving skills that arise in the life of a college student. Give three examples of problems that would benefit most from postformal thinking. Explain your choices.

2.   Describe two findings from Blanchard-Fields' research on reasoning.

3.   Define stereotype threat and provide an example of it that is different from the examples provided in the text. How might it explain women's comparatively low participation in technological fields?

4.   What is dialectical thinking? Give an example (not the ones in the text) of the use of dialectical thinking in daily life. Explain how dialectical thinking contributes to an evolving view of oneself or of the world.

5.   Describe how the decisions with which adults are faced influence their moral development. Provide two examples to support your description.

6.   Do you agree or disagree with Fowler's theory of faith development? Describe the level of faith development of two people you know (one may be yourself), and explain why understanding these people's faith causes you to believe that Fowler is correct or incorrect.

7.   Describe the current trends in college education: type of student, major, type of instruction, etc. Discuss whether or not you believe today's college students are getting the same opportunities for cognitive growth as were college students of 40 years ago.

8.   Compare and contrast the three approaches to cognitive development: postformal, psychometric, and information-processing.

Answer guidelines to these essay questions can be found in the Appendix at the end of the Test Bank.

CHAPTER 19

Early Adulthood:
Psychosocial Development

MULTIPLE-CHOICE QUESTIONS

Early Adulthood: Psychosocial Development

Early Adulthood: Psychosocial Development, p. 459
Diff: E, Ans: b
1. Between the ages of 20 and 35, the average adult in the United States:
    a. spends 10 to 15 years unmarried.
    b. changes jobs nine times.
    c. has two to three children.
    d. has a 20 percent chance of divorce.

Theories of Adulthood

Love and Work, p. 459
Diff: E, Ans: a
2. Freud defined the healthy adult as a person who is able to:
    a. love and work.
    b. achieve success and esteem.
    c. find love and belonging.
    d. achieve affiliation and wealth.

Love and Work, p. 460
Diff: E, Ans: d
3. Maslow conceptualized human need as a(n):
    a. spreadsheet.
    b. plateau.
    c. circle.
    d. hierarchy.

Love and Work, p. 460
Diff: M, Ans: a
4. According to Maslow, which needs must be met before an adult can focus on the need for love and belonging?
    a. physiological needs and safety needs.
    b. safety needs and self-actualization needs.
    c. physiological needs and success and esteem needs.
    d. self-actualization needs and success and esteem needs.

Love and Work, p. 460
Diff: H, Ans: b

5.   Larry is striving for success in his career field. According to Maslow, Larry would already have satisfied his need for all of the following EXCEPT:
     a.   love and belonging.
     b.   self-actualization.
     c.   safety needs.
     d.   physiological needs.

Love and Work, p. 460
Diff: M, Ans: d

6.   According to Erikson, young adults first face which of the following crises?
     a.   generativity vs. stagnation
     b.   love vs. work
     c.   identity vs. role confusion
     d.   intimacy vs. isolation

Love and Work, p. 460
Diff: M, Ans: c

7.   According to Erikson, the stage of intimacy vs. isolation:
     a.   is followed by the search for identity.
     b.   is characterized by a need for generativity.
     c.   involves the need to share one's personal life with someone else.
     d.   occurs only if one avoids stagnation.

Love and Work, p. 460
Diff: H, Ans: b

8.   According to Erikson, failure to achieve generativity results in:
     a.   intermittent feelings of loneliness.
     b.   stagnation and personal impoverishment.
     c.   childlessness and a career orientation.
     d.   difficulties in mate selection or friendship.

Ages and Stages, p. 461
Diff: E, Ans: a

9.   Grand theorists in the mid-twentieth century based their stages of adulthood on:
     a.   financially secure men from Western Europe or North America.
     b.   financially secure homemakers.
     c.   poor men from Africa and Asia.
     d.   all of the above.

Ages and Stages, p. 462 (Table 19.1)
Diff: H, Ans: d

10. According to research by Levinson, the period of adult life in which neglected talents, desires, and aspirations seek expression is referred to as the:
     a.   entering the adult world stage.
     b.   age 30 transition stage.
     c.   settling down stage.
     d.   midlife transition stage.

Ages and Stages, p. 462
Diff: M, Ans: a

11. Most developmental theorists today believe that:
     a.   stages of adult development are not entirely orderly and predictable.
     b.   adulthood is divided into a specific sequence of stages.
     c.   intimacy always precedes generativity.
     d.   generativity cannot appear before the age of 40.

The Social Clock, p. 462
Diff: M, Ans: c

12. The "social clock" tells us the:
    a. age at which marriages become biologically feasible.
    b. average age for first marriages.
    c. appropriate or "best" age for a first marriage in our society.
    d. marriage age that correlates with mental health in later adulthood.

The Social Clock, p. 462
Diff: M, Ans: a

13. Cross-culturally, social clock norms:
    a. vary in scope and rigidity.
    b. are much stronger for children than for adults.
    c. generally apply only to legal ages.
    d. are consistent across cohort and gender.

The Social Clock, pp. 462-463
Diff: E, Ans: d

14. In the United States today, the social clock:
    a. affects only people of low socioeconomic status.
    b. is fairly specific about the best times for marriage and parenthood.
    c. no longer operates.
    d. allows for greater diversity than in the past.

The Social Clock, p. 463
Diff: E, Ans: c

15. Researchers have found that the social clock is:
    a. the same for all cultures and subcultures.
    b. particularly important in determining retirement age worldwide.
    c. greatly influenced by socioeconomic status.
    d. biologically determined.

The Social Clock, p. 463
Diff: E, Ans: a

16. The woman most likely to be married a year after high school graduation is:
    a. of low socioeconomic status.
    b. planning on getting an advanced degree.
    c. a German citizen.
    d. one who refuses to be influenced by the social clock.

The Social Clock, p. 463
Diff: M, Ans: b

17. On the average, North American adults start a career and family between the ages of:
    a. 15 to 30.
    b. 20 to 35.
    c. 25 to 30.
    d. 25 to 40.

Intimacy

Intimacy, p. 464
Diff: E, Ans: a
18. Intimacy is best defined as:
     a. affiliation.
     b. generativity.
     c. sexuality.
     d. self-esteem.

Intimacy, p. 464
Diff: M, Ans: b
19. During adulthood, intimacy:
     a. stems from a need for self-protection.
     b. is found primarily in friendship and sexual partnership.
     c. is limited to lovers and spouses.
     d. requires little personal sacrifice.

Friendship, p. 465
Diff: E, Ans: c
20. How do friends differ from family members?
     a. Friends are less of a buffer against stress.
     b. Families attest more to one's personal worthiness.
     c. Friends are chosen for qualities that make them good companions.
     d. Friendships are generally lifelong.

Friendship, p. 465
Diff: E, Ans: d
21. Which is one of the four "gateways to attraction" in friendship?
     a. infrequent exposure
     b. presence of exclusion criteria
     c. average yearly income
     d. apparent availability

Friendship, p. 465
Diff: H, Ans: b
22. Which of the following is *least* true of friendship selection?
     a. Birds of a feather flock together.
     b. Absence makes the heart grow fonder.
     c. You *can* judge a book by its cover.
     d. Love the one you're with.

Friendship, p. 465
Diff: M, Ans: c
23. Which of the following is NOT a "gateway to attraction" in terms of friendship choice?
     a. frequent exposure
     b. absence of unacceptable characteristics
     c. being trustworthy
     d. apparent availability

Friendship, p. 465
Diff: M, Ans: b
24.   Mario is 22 years old and lives alone. If he is typical of his age group, he:
       a.   needs to provide care for older relatives.
       b.   has an extensive social network.
       c.   is less satisfied with friendship than other parts of his life.
       d.   spends more leisure time alone than with friends.

Friendship, pp. 465-466
Diff: H, Ans: c
25.   Which is the best example of self-disclosure?
       a.   discussing a game-deciding call in a national championship
       b.   telling your co-workers how bad weather ruined your vacation
       c.   telling someone about a recurring health problem that limits your activity
       d.   explaining the kind of music you enjoy the most

Friendship, pp. 465-466
Diff: E, Ans: b
26.   Compared to those of women, friendships between men are:
       a.   virtually nonexistent.
       b.   less emotional.
       c.   a significant threat to marriage.
       d.   less likely to be aggressive and competitive.

Friendship, pp. 465-466
Diff: E, Ans: a
27.   When two men converse, they are most likely to discuss:
       a.   politics.
       b.   their families.
       c.   their past.
       d.   health problems.

Friendship, p. 466
Diff: E, Ans: b
28.   When a woman talks about her problems with a friend, she usually wants:
       a.   a solution to her problems.
       b.   sympathy or understanding.
       c.   practical advice.
       d.   someone to tease her about how much she worries.

Friendship, p. 466
Diff: E, Ans: b
29.   If a man talks about his problems to a male friend, he is most likely to expect:
       a.   sympathy.
       b.   practical solutions.
       c.   comfort.
       d.   emotional support.

Friendship, p. 466
Diff: M, Ans: d
30.   Cross-sex friendships result in problems when:
       a.   the male and female meet each others' needs.
       b.   females offer advice to males.
       c.   males offer sympathy to females.
       d.   each gender has different expectations.

Friendship, p. 466
Diff: M, Ans: a
31.   Friendships between men are less intimate than those between women because:
    a.   men are more hesitant to express their vulnerabilities.
    b.   from childhood on, boys are more verbal and less active.
    c.   women have strong fears of homophobia.
    d.   men never show affection for each other.

Friendship, p. 466
Diff: M, Ans: c
32.   Which of the following is a particular advantage of cross-sex friendships?
    a.   the development of similar expectations for the friendship process
    b.   an opportunity to express sexual feelings
    c.   an opportunity to learn practical skills traditionally reserved for the other sex
    d.   a chance to defend each partner's perspective on key social and ethical issues

Friendship, p. 466
Diff: H, Ans: d
33.   Men may have an advantage in their interpersonal relationships at work because they:
    a.   deal with the personal problems of their employees.
    b.   offer advice to females when they need it.
    c.   are often the confidants of other workers.
    d.   keep emotional distance while sharing information.

The Development of Love, p. 467 (Table 19.3)
Diff: M, Ans: a
34.   Which of the following is a true statement about the qualities young adults seek from a romantic partner?
    a.   Culture greatly affects the qualities sought by individuals.
    b.   European American men and women differ greatly in the qualities they seek.
    c.   The qualities sought by men are the same across cultures.
    d.   Wealth ranks highly for women across cultures.

The Development of Love, p. 467
Diff: E, Ans: d
35.   Which of the following is NOT one of the dimensions of love described by Robert Sternberg?
    a.   commitment
    b.   passion
    c.   intimacy
    d.   dependence

The Development of Love, p. 467
Diff: E, Ans: b
36.   According to Sternberg, the three components of love are passion, intimacy, and:
    a.   congeniality.
    b.   commitment.
    c.   compatibility.
    d.   cooperation.

The Development of Love, p. 467
Diff: M, Ans: b
37.   George and Emily are newly engaged to be married. The component of love that is probably most intense at this time is:
    a.   commitment.
    b.   passion.
    c.   intimacy.
    d.   dependence.

The Development of Love, p. 467
Diff: M, Ans: c
38.   Which is associated with passionate love?
   a.   a stable personality
   b.   honesty about oneself
   c.   a new relationship
   d.   trust over the years

The Development of Love, p. 467 (Table 19.4)
Diff: E, Ans: b
39.   Sternberg refers to love in which couples share passion but lack intimacy or commitment as:
   a.   empty love.
   b.   infatuation.
   c.   romantic love.
   d.   companionate love.

The Development of Love, p. 467 (Table 19.4)
Diff: H, Ans: d
40.   Jim and Margaret have been married for 35 years. They feel no passion and share few feelings. Sternberg would say that they have which type of love?
   a.   romantic
   b.   liking
   c.   consummate
   d.   empty

The Development of Love, p. 467 (Table 19.4)
Diff: E, Ans: a
41.   When a couple shares passion and intimacy, but there is no commitment, Sternberg would say they have:
   a.   romantic love.
   b.   fatuous love.
   c.   empty love.
   d.   consummate love.

The Development of Love, p. 467 (Table 19.4)
Diff: M, Ans: d
42.   According to Sternberg, passion and commitment without intimacy result in:
   a.   infatuation.
   b.   empty love.
   c.   romantic love.
   d.   fatuous love.

The Development of Love, p. 467 (Table 19.4)
Diff: M, Ans: c
43.   Clara and Gus have been married for 55 years. They share deep intimacy and commitment but are no longer passionate. According to Sternberg, their love is now:
   a.   fatuous.
   b.   empty.
   c.   companionate.
   d.   consummate.

The Development of Love, pp. 467-468
Diff: E, Ans: d

44. According to Sternberg, when commitment, passion, and intimacy are all present, the form of love is:
     a. romantic.
     b. fatuous.
     c. compassionate.
     d. consummate.

The Development of Love, pp. 467-468
Diff: M, Ans: d

45. Which of the following lists Sternberg's three dimensions of love in the order in which they generally develop in a relationship?
     a. commitment, intimacy, passion
     b. passion, commitment, intimacy
     c. intimacy, passion, commitment
     d. passion, intimacy, commitment

The Development of Love, p. 468
Diff: E, Ans: b

46. The dominant traits of commitment are:
     a. excitement and risk.
     b. devotion and mutual dependence.
     c. passion and freedom.
     d. independence and accomplishment.

The Development of Love, p. 468
Diff: H, Ans: a

47. When we compare Ryan and Barbara, a married heterosexual couple, with Stan and Brett, a homosexual couple, we find that as the years pass:
     a. both couples will probably experience less passion and more commitment.
     b. only Ryan and Barbara will experience growth of commitment.
     c. Ryan and Barbara will have more passion; Stan and Brett will have more intimacy.
     d. both couples will experience more intimacy but the same level of passion.

The Development of Love, p. 468
Diff: E, Ans: d

48. Passion is fueled in part by:
     a. security and familiarity.
     b. the expected and known.
     c. boundaries and safety.
     d. uncertainty and risk.

The Development of Love, p. 468
Diff: H, Ans: e

49. For which of the following types of couples does the developmental pattern of intimacy, commitment, and passion differ from that of others?
     a. married heterosexual couples
     b. unmarried homosexual couples
     c. older remarried couples
     d. cohabitating young couples
     e. none of the above

The Development of Love, p. 468
Diff: E, Ans: c

50.   For which of the following types of couples does commitment nearly always come before intimacy and
      passion?
      a.   older remarried couples
      b.   cohabiting young heterosexual couples
      c.   couples in arranged marriages
      d.   cohabitating young homosexual couples

The Development of Love, p. 469
Diff: M, Ans: b

51.   The typical pattern of courtship in Western cultures is designed to move a couple from:
      a.   commitment to passion.
      b.   passion to intimacy.
      c.   intimacy to passion.
      d.   commitment to intimacy.

The Development of Love, p. 469
Diff: M, Ans: d

52.   Generally, cohabitating young adults:
      a.   do not intend to marry.
      b.   are happier and healthier than married couples.
      c.   have stronger marriages if they marry than do noncohabitating couples if they marry.
      d.   are more likely to have physical abuse in the relationship than are married couples.

The Development of Love, p. 469
Diff: M, Ans: b

53.   How many of all women between the ages of 25 and 40 in the United States have cohabited?
      a.   almost all
      b.   more than half
      c.   nearly one-third
      d.   about 17 percent

The Development of Love, p. 469
Diff: M, Ans: d

54.   A study of adults in 17 nations found that compared to married couples, cohabitants were:
      a.   happier.
      b.   more satisfied with all aspects of their relationship.
      c.   more healthy.
      d.   less satisfied with their financial status.

Marriage, p. 470
Diff: H, Ans: b

55.   Which statistics are currently true in the United States?
      a.   The divorce rate is 60 percent of the marriage rate.
      b.   Nearly one-half of all first births are to single mothers.
      c.   The rate of first marriages is the highest in fifty years.
      d.   Approximately 30 percent of brides are virgins.

Marriage, p. 470
Diff: M, Ans: d

56.   Which of the following is a change that has occurred over the past several decades in virtually every industrialized nation?
       a.   People are marrying younger and younger.
       b.   Divorce rates are lower because cohabiting strengthens marriages.
       c.   Adults are coming to view marriage as the sole avenue for sexual expression.
       d.   Adults now spend half of the years between 20 and 40 single.

Marriage, p. 470
Diff: H, Ans: b

57.   Erikson believes that a healthy intimacy in marriage is more likely to emerge when:
       a.   neither partner has yet established a sense of identity and they can build an identity together.
       b.   both partners have already established a sense of identity.
       c.   one partner has established a sense of identity and the other fits in.
       d.   the couple has already built an identity together.

Marriage, p. 470
Diff: M, Ans: a

58.   In a series of studies of college students, those less advanced on Erikson's identity and intimacy stages were more likely to define love in terms of:
       a.   passion.
       b.   intimacy.
       c.   commitment.
       d.   dependence.

Marriage, p. 470
Diff: E, Ans: b

59.   Marriage between people of different backgrounds is called:
       a.   heterosexuality.
       b.   heterogamy.
       c.   homogamy.
       d.   role incompatibility.

Marriage, p. 470
Diff: E, Ans: c

60.   Heterogamy refers to marriage between two people of:
       a.   different sexes.
       b.   the same sex.
       c.   dissimilar ethnicities, interests, attitudes, and religion.
       d.   similar ethnicities, interests, attitudes, and religion.

Marriage, p. 471
Diff: M, Ans: a

61.   According to research, the chance of any particular partner with the same interest in three favorite leisure activities and with similar opinions about three important role preferences is:
       a.   1 percent.
       b.   10 percent.
       c.   20 percent.
       d.   40 percent.

Marriage, p. 471
Diff: E, Ans: d
62.   The view that marriage is an arrangement in which each partner contributes something useful to the other, is part of the:
a.   equity theory.
b.   equality theory.
c.   complementary theory.
d.   social exchange theory.

Marriage, p. 471
Diff: M, Ans: c
63.   In many modern marriages, individuals seek:
a.   an exchange of gender-specific commodities.
b.   heterogamy.
c.   shared contributions of similar commodities.
d.   all of the above.

Marriage, p. 471
Diff: M, Ans: d
64.   Over the past several decades, wives' incomes and husbands' contribution to housework have _____ and marital satisfaction has _____.
a.   decreased; decreased
b.   decreased; increased
c.   increased; decreased
d.   increased; increased

Marriage, p. 472 (Table 19.5)
Diff: M, Ans: b
65.   Which of the following makes divorce more likely?
a.   low divorce rate for others in cohort
b.   family opposition
c.   financial security
d.   both partners being over 21

Marriage, p. 472
Diff: M, Ans: b
66.   According to the estimate in the text, what percentage of American adults spends some part of their lives in long-term gay or lesbian partnerships?
a.   1 to 2
b.   2 to 5
c.   5 to 10
d.   10 to 20

Marriage, p. 472
Diff: H, Ans: b
67.   Which of the following is a true statement about long-term homosexual couples?
a.   In most countries, their unions can be legally recognized.
b.   Children in these families are likely to experience no negative effects.
c.   Their relationship issues are entirely different from those of heterosexual couples.
d.   None of the above is a true statement.

Divorce, p. 472
Diff: M, Ans: b
68.   What developed country has the highest divorce rate?
      a.   Japan
      b.   United States
      c.   Israel
      d.   Sweden

Divorce, p. 473 (Figure 19.2)
Diff: M, Ans: d
69.   From 1980 to 2000 in the United States, the number of divorces per 1000 people has:
      a.   increased dramatically.
      b.   increased slightly.
      c.   decreased dramatically.
      d.   decreased slightly.

Divorce, p. 473
Diff: M, Ans: b
70.   Compared with couples today, couples in earlier decades:
      a.   expected to really understand each other to a greater extent.
      b.   based marital equity on firmer gender roles.
      c.   expected each other to be both a friend and a lover to a greater extent.
      d.   perceived a smaller difference between masculinity and femininity.

Divorce, p. 473
Diff: H, Ans: c
71.   Compared to 100 years ago, contemporary couples expect _____ from a relationship, and devote
      _____ of themselves to it.
      a.   more; more
      b.   less; less
      c.   more; less
      d.   less; more

Divorce, p. 474
Diff: E, Ans: e
72.   Divorce affects which of the following for the family?
      a.   financial stability
      b.   self-esteem
      c.   health
      d.   achievement
      e.   all of the above

Divorce, p. 474
Diff: H, Ans: d
73.   Ex-spouses find adjustment to divorce more difficult than anticipated because while they were married
      they:
      a.   focused on the needs of the children.
      b.   overestimated their emotional dependence on each other.
      c.   expected the legal system to foster contention over property division.
      d.   focused on what was missing in the marriage not on what needs it served.

Divorce, p. 474
Diff: H, Ans: a
74.   Millie is recently divorced. Probably:
    a.   her social circle is smaller than when she was married.
    b.   friends rally to support her.
    c.   social support from friends and family has increased.
    d.   co-workers help while she adjusts.

Divorce, p. 475
Diff: H, Ans: d
75.   The person most likely to be unhappy is a:
    a.   50-year-old widow.
    b.   married parent of three.
    c.   never-married career woman.
    d.   a recently divorced woman.

Domestic Violence, p. 475
Diff: H, Ans: a
76.   Research shows that _____ is more likely in cohabiting couples than in married couples.
    a.   abuse
    b.   financial security
    c.   interdependence
    d.   fidelity

Domestic Violence, p. 475
Diff: E, Ans: b
77.   Which circumstance in childhood is NOT related to spousal abuse later on?
    a.   harsh physical punishment
    b.   authoritative parents
    c.   sexual abuse
    d.   witnessing of spousal assault

Domestic Violence, p. 475
Diff: M, Ans: d
78.   Which of the following is a characteristic of common couple violence?
    a.   isolation of one spouse
    b.   psychological terrorism
    c.   increasing violence
    d.   both partners arguing

Domestic Violence, p. 475
Diff: M, Ans: c
79.   Which of the following is a result of intimate terrorism?
    a.   common couple violence
    b.   violence on the part of both spouses
    c.   battered-wife syndrome
    d.   deceleration of violence with age

Generativity

Generativity, p. 476
Diff: E, Ans: a
80.   Generativity is achieved primarily through:
       a.   employment and parenthood.
       b.   body image and self-image.
       c.   friendship and romantic partnerships.
       d.   community and culture.

The Importance of Work, p. 477
Diff: E, Ans: a
81.   Job satisfaction correlates LEAST highly with:
       a.   high pay.
       b.   challenge.
       c.   productivity.
       d.   creativity.

The Importance of Work, p. 477
Diff: M, Ans: c
82.   Currently, the economy of developed nations is shifting to:
       a.   agriculture economies.
       b.   industry economies.
       c.   service/information economies.
       d.   labor/clerical economies.

The Importance of Work, p. 477
Diff: H, Ans: a
83.   Which of the following is NOT a characteristic of today's workplace?
       a.   more product-based than service-based
       b.   commonly used strategies such as downsizing and outsourcing
       c.   expanding work hours
       d.   more industry-based than agriculture-based

The Importance of Work, p. 478
Diff: M, Ans: c
84.   What percent of the U.S. labor force is female?
       a.   24
       b.   32
       c.   45
       d.   63

The Importance of Work, p. 479
Diff: M, Ans: c
85.   In the United States today, _____ married mothers are in the labor force.
       a.   very few
       b.   about half
       c.   a majority of
       d.   nearly all

The Importance of Work, p. 479
Diff: E, Ans: c

86. The barrier experienced by many women in male-dominated occupations and by many minority workers in majority-dominated occupations that halts their advancement is referred to as a:
   a. trap door.
   b. steel barricade.
   c. glass ceiling.
   d. faulty access panel.

The Importance of Work, p. 479
Diff: H, Ans: d

87. Kate and Bill, who have full-time jobs, have been described by others as a happy couple. If this is true, probably neither Kate nor Bill:
   a. does domestic chores at home.
   b. works more than five miles from their home.
   c. earns more than $50,000 a year.
   d. works very long hours each week.

The Importance of Work, p. 480
Diff: H, Ans: a

88. Hank has just been dismissed from his new job. The LEAST likely reason is:
   a. he could not learn the work.
   b. he had an attitude problem.
   c. he missed too many days.
   d. he couldn't to adapt to the work environment.

Parenthood, p. 480
Diff: H, Ans: d

89. Erik Erikson suggests that in the parent-child relationship:
   a. mature men and women are those who have completed childbearing.
   b. children and the elderly are the two dependent generations.
   c. child rearing is the "ultimate life experience."
   d. adults need to be needed by children.

Parenthood, pp. 480-481
Diff: H, Ans: b

90. Direct conflict between parents is greatest during which of the following periods of their children's lives?
   a. infancy
   b. preschool
   c. school age
   d. adolescence

Parenthood, p. 481
Diff: M, Ans: b

91. Which of the following tends to increase when married couples become parents?
   a. marital satisfaction
   b. commitment
   c. intimacy
   d. all of the above

Parenthood, p. 481
Diff: E, Ans: c
92.   The stress of multiple obligations is referred to as:
       a.   role buffering.
       b.   work overload.
       c.   role overload.
       d.   financially burdened.

Parenthood, p. 481
Diff: M, Ans: c
93.   Role buffering in dual-earner families refers to:
       a.   children observing the father doing housework and other domestic chores.
       b.   the work roles of mothers and fathers being very different.
       c.   each role reducing the impact of disappointment in another.
       d.   males taking responsibility for housework and females for yard work.

Parenthood, p. 481
Diff: M, Ans: d
94.   Research shows that most adults who balance marital, parental, and vocational roles:
       a.   suffer from role overload.
       b.   fail in every area.
       c.   tend to have large families.
       d.   are healthy, happy, and successful.

Parenthood, p. 481
Diff: H, Ans: c
95.   Tom and Sabrina are married and have three children. Both Tom and Sabrina work full time. Tom
       works a night shift and Sabrina works during the day. Which of the following is likely to be true for
       them?
       a.   Tom and Sabrina's family logistics require about as much mutual agreement and planning as those
            of the families in which they grew up.
       b.   Tom does not care for the children while Sabrina works.
       c.   Tom and Sabrina both engage in role buffering.
       d.   Tom and Sabrina have the same risk of divorce as couples who both work during the day.

Parenthood, p. 482 (Figure 19.3)
Diff: H, Ans: a
96.   Of the following couples who have been married for fewer than five years and who have children,
       which of the following is most likely to be divorced in five years?
       a.   Megan, who works during the day, and Robert, who works at night.
       b.   Karlene and Jim, who both work during the day.
       c.   Brianne, who works evenings, and Greg, who is unemployed.
       d.   Dina, who is unemployed, and Frank, who works rotating shifts.

Parenthood, p. 482
Diff: M, Ans: b
97.   Which of the following is true for divorced couples with children, compared to divorcing couples who
       do not have children?
       a.   They are more likely to remarry.
       b.   They are more likely to need to maintain a relationship with their ex-spouse.
       c.   They have less financial pressure.
       d.   All of the above are true.

Parenthood, pp. 482-483
Diff: M, Ans: b
98.   The presence of children after divorce:
  a.   decreases ties with relatives.
  b.   increases the financial burden of the custodial parent.
  c.   enhances the custodial parent's chances for remarriage.
  d.   decreases stress for the custodial parent.

Parenthood, p. 483
Diff: H, Ans: d
99.   Bill and Barbara have just gotten a divorce. Barbara has custody of their two young children. A year
      after the divorce, it is likely that:
  a.   Barbara's standard of living has dropped significantly while Bill's has risen.
  b.   both Bill and Barbara have experienced a rise in their standard of living.
  c.   because of child support payments, Bill's standard of living has dipped significantly, but Barbara's
       has remained stable.
  d.   both Bill's and Barbara's standard of living has dropped—Barbara's more than Bill's.

Parenthood, p. 483
Diff: M, Ans: d
100. Dave is a new noncustodial father of two children. He will probably find:
  a.   it is easy to adjust to his children's changing needs.
  b.   his children will easily accept his discipline and direction.
  c.   he will remain active in his children's lives.
  d.   the physical and psychological distance distressing.

Parenthood, p. 483
Diff: E, Ans: c
101. Which of the following is true for divorced couples with children?
  a.   The custodial parent suffers while the noncustodial parent does not.
  b.   The noncustodial parent suffers while the custodial parent does not.
  c.   Both the custodial parent and the noncustodial parent suffer.
  d.   Neither the custodial parent nor the noncustodial parent suffers.

Parenthood, p. 483
Diff: H, Ans: c
102. Which of the following is a true statement about divorced couples with children?
  a.   Most noncustodial fathers maintain intimate relationships with their children.
  b.   Divorce is easier for noncustodial fathers who were active parents before the divorce than for those
       who were not active parents.
  c.   The majority of children would benefit from regular overnight visits with their noncustodial
       fathers.
  d.   Contact with noncustodial fathers, even when it is just limited to food and fun, is helpful to both
       the children and adults.

Parenthood, p. 483
Diff: E, Ans: d
103. Compared with families with only biological children, the challenges for adults with stepchildren,
      adoptive children, or foster children are _____; the potential for the feeling of generativity is _____.
  a.   lesser; lesser
  b.   lesser; greater
  c.   greater; lesser
  d.   greater; greater

Parenthood, p. 483

Diff: M, Ans: b

104.   About what percent of all North American adults become stepparents, adoptive parents, or foster parents at some point in their lives?

    a.   10

    b.   33

    c.   45

    d.   60

Parenthood, p. 483

Diff: H, Ans: a

105.   In typical stepparent families:

    a.   stepfathers hope to become benevolent disciplinarians.

    b.   stepmothers become excessively strict.

    c.   stepchildren become disloyal to their biological parents.

    d.   stepparents become intimately involved in the personal lives of stepchildren.

Parenthood, p. 538

Diff: M, Ans: c

106.   In the typical stepfamily, children usually:

    a.   help stabilize the new marriage.

    b.   are very obedient so as not to upset the marriage.

    c.   sabotage the stepparents' efforts.

    d.   become pregnant or get arrested.

Parenthood, p. 484

Diff: M, Ans: d

107.   About what percent of all marriages involving stepchildren end in divorce?

    a.   20

    b.   30

    c.   40

    d.   50

Parenthood, p. 484

Diff: M, Ans: a

108.   Which of the following types of parents are *least* likely to invest in the parent-child relationship?

    a.   stepparents

    b.   adoptive parents

    c.   biological parents

    d.   none of the above; they are all likely to invest equally

Parenthood, p. 484

Diff: H, Ans: b

109.   Of the following children, who is the most likely to leave home latest?

    a.   Chris, who was adopted when he was one year old

    b.   Meg, who lives with her biological mother

    c.   Walter, who lives with foster parents

    d.   Annemarie, who lives with a stepfather

TRUE-FALSE QUESTIONS

Early Adulthood: Psychosocial Development

Ans: F, p. 459

1.   The average young adult holds only two jobs between the ages of 20 and 35.

Theories of Adulthood

Ans: T, p. 459

2.   Many theoretical perspectives focus on love and work as the two psychosocial needs of adulthood.

Ans: F, p. 460 (Figure 19.1)

3.   According to Maslow, adult needs form concentric circles.

Ans: T, p. 460

4.   According to Maslow, basic adult needs, such as food and safety, have to be met before adults can focus on love and belonging needs and success and esteem needs.

Ans: T, p. 460

5.   Erikson believes that a young adult who has achieved identity is eager and willing to fuse his or her identity with others, for example, in intimate relationships.

Ans: F, p. 460

6.   Erikson refers to the search for intimacy with a partner as striving for "generativity."

Ans: T, p. 462

7.   Researchers now realize that traditional theorists' stages of adult development were insensitive and perhaps even racist and sexist.

Ans: T, p. 462

8.   Internationally, the social-clock settings for marriage and childbearing vary greatly.

Ans: F, pp. 462-463

9.   Although the social clock is the same for all subcultures within a culture, it may differ from culture to culture.

Ans: T, p. 463

10.   The lower the SES, the sooner individuals are expected to meet major milestones, such as getting married and beginning a career.

Ans: T, p. 463

11.   Although the speed of the social clock may vary across cultures, the needs for intimacy and generativity are universal.

Intimacy

Ans: F, p. 464

12.   The adult need for intimacy can be fulfilled only by a romantic partner.

Ans: F, p. 465

13.   Most young adults have difficulty finding the time to make friends.

Ans: T, p. 465

14.   Physical attractiveness is considered a gateway to attraction for same-sex friends.

Ans: T, p. 465

15.   Most people have two or three filters they use to exclude people from the possibility of becoming their close friends.

Ans: F, p. 466

16.   Men are more likely than women to reveal their weaknesses and fears to close friends.

398   CHAPTER 19 Early Adulthood: Psychosocial Development

Ans: F, p. 466
17. When women discuss their problems, they seek practical solutions.

Ans: T, p. 466
18. Men are most likely to openly express affection for one another when their masculinity is unlikely to be questioned.

Ans: F, p. 466
19. Men are less likely to openly express affection for one another in military combat or athletic competition than they are in their everyday friendships.

Ans: T, p. 466
20. Overall, the typical female friendship pattern may be better than the typical male pattern in reducing loneliness.

Ans: F, p. 467
21. Sternberg refers to intimacy as the intense physical, cognitive, and emotional connection between two members of a couple.

Ans: T, pp. 467-468
22. The Western ideal of a relationship includes all three of Sternberg's dimensions of love.

Ans: F, p. 468
23. Usually the first aspect of love to develop is commitment.

Ans: F, pp. 468-469
24. The four gateways to attraction are only applicable to friendships and not to romantic partnerships.

Ans: F, p. 469
25. Most developmentalists agree that cohabitation before marriage can strengthen a relationship and ensure a happy marriage.

Ans: T, p. 470
26. In the United States today, the proportion of unmarried adults is higher than at any other time in the previous 100 years.

Ans: T, p. 470
27. In the United States today, single mothers are increasingly unlikely to marry the fathers of their babies.

Ans: T, p. 470
28. Across cultures, married people are happier, healthier, and richer than unmarried people.

Ans: F, p. 470
29. In general, the younger marriage partners are, the more likely the marriage is to succeed.

Ans: F, p. 470
30. Homogamy is defined as marriage between two people who look alike.

Ans: F, p. 470
31. It is quite easy to find a potential mate who shares several of the same interests and values.

Ans: F, p. 471
32. In most modern marriages, social exchange is sought.

Ans: T, p. 472
33. In general long-term homosexual couples have the same relationship issues as heterosexual couples.

Ans: T, p. 472

34. The United States has the highest divorce rate of any large nation.

Ans: F, p. 473

35. Because they expect more from their marriages, couples today devote more of themselves to the marriage than couples did a few decades ago.

Ans: T, p. 474

36. Initially, the consequences of divorce tend to be worse than either partner anticipated for all family members in every way.

Ans: F, p. 475

37. Intimate terrorism refers to abuse in which one or both partners engage in outbursts of verbal and physical attack.

Generativity

Ans: F, p. 477

38. Job satisfaction tends to correlate more highly with ease of work than with challenge.

Ans: T, p. 477

39. Globalization and changes in world economies have led to shifts in the types of economies, in the types of jobs, and in the timing and pace of jobs.

Ans: F, p. 479

40. In the United States today, 26 percent of married mothers whose youngest child is in school are in the labor force.

Ans: F, p. 479

41. The glass ceiling is based on individual skills and abilities.

Ans: F, pp. 479-480

42. Work teams function best when they are made up of people from very similar backgrounds.

Ans: T, p. 480

43. Children affect their parents at least as much as their parents affect them.

Ans: F, p. 481

44. A woman who is simultaneously wife, mother, and employee nearly always experiences role overload.

Ans: T, p. 481

45. Role buffering is more prevalent than role overload in dual-earner families.

Ans: T, p. 482

46. The resilience of many couples in the face of changes in number and ages of children, employment demands, and financial burdens is evidence that marriage can be beneficial to the couple and family.

Ans: T, p. 483

47. Over the years, divorced fathers tend to become less involved with their children.

Ans: F, p. 483

48. Approximately 10 percent of North American adults become stepparents, adoptive parents, or foster parents at some point in their lives.

Ans: T, p. 484

49.   Divorces in remarried families with stepchildren occur 50 percent of the time, typically within the first five years of marriage.

Ans: T, p. 484

50.   Most adoptive and foster parents seek a second child within a few years of the arrival of the first.

FILL-IN-THE-BLANK QUESTIONS

Theories of Adulthood

Ans: love; work, p. 459

1.   Although theories differ in the terms they use, they generally agree with Freud's portrayal of _____ and _____ as the two psychosocial needs of adulthood.

Ans: success, p. 460

2.   According to Maslow, adults experience a need for love and belonging, which, if met, allows adults to focus on their need for _____ and esteem.

Ans: isolation; stagnation, p. 460

3.   Two adulthood crises described by Erikson are intimacy versus _____ and generativity versus _____.

Ans: stages, p. 461

4.   Mid-twentieth century theorists viewed adulthood as being divided into distinct _____.

Ans: socioeconomic, p. 463

5.   A prime influence on the cultural-clock setting worldwide is _____ status.

Intimacy

Ans: friendships; romantic, p. 464

6.   The two main sources of intimacy in early adulthood are close _____ and _____ partnerships.

Ans: gateways, p. 465

7.   Physical attractiveness, frequent exposure, and apparent availability are three _____ to attractiveness.

Ans: aggression, p. 466

8.   Most open expressions of affection between men tend to occur in situations where they are banded together in the name of _____ such as team sports or military combat.

Ans: Cross-sex, p. 466

9.   _____ friendships in young adulthood pose a particular complicating factor, that of unclear sexual boundaries.

Ans: commitment, p. 467 (Table 19.4)

10.   "Companionate love" is characterized chiefly by intimacy and _____.

Ans: Passion, p. 468

11.   _____ is fueled by the very aspects of a relationship that are diminished when a couple achieves intimacy and commitment.

Ans: Arranged, p. 468

12.   _____ marriages are high on commitment but may never include passion or intimacy.

Ans: cohabitation, p. 469

13.   A living pattern in which an unmarried couple lives together is referred to as _____.

Ans: 49, p. 470

14.   The U.S. divorce rate is _____ percent of the marriage rate.

Ans: homogamy, p. 471

15.   One study of young couples found that social _____, defined as similarity in leisure interests and role preferences, is particularly important to marital success.

Ans: intimate, p. 475

16.   In _____ terrorism, the man uses violent methods to isolate, degrade, and punish the woman.

Generativity

Ans: half, p. 478

17.   In developed nations, almost _____ the civilian labor force is female.

Ans: glass ceiling, p. 479

18.   The invisible barrier to career advancement experienced by women and minorities is called the _____.

Ans: generativity, p. 480

19.   According to Erikson, caring for children is an important way in which adults achieve _____.

Ans: logistics, p. 481

20.   The coordination of schedules, housework, job changes, child care, and so forth, is referred to as family _____.

Ans: mothers, p. 483

21.   The financial burden of child rearing usually falls heaviest on custodial _____.

Ans: foster, p. 484

22.   Attachments between _____ parents and children can be especially difficult because both realize that their bond can be suddenly broken for reasons outside of their control.

Ans: leave home, p. 484

23.   Stepchildren, foster children, and adoptive children tend to _____ earlier than adolescents who live with one or both biological parents.

ESSAY QUESTIONS

1.   Describe Maslow's theory of adult needs. Explain why you agree or disagree with Maslow's ideas. Provide an example to support your argument.

2.   Describe two differences between female friendships and male friendships. What types of problems do cross-sex friends have?

3.   Imagine you are an employer who is considering hiring a 26-year-old named Frank. Frank's resume shows that he has never held a full-time job. How might our culture's social clock affect your consideration of him? Would it make a difference for what type of job he was applying? What explanations would you find most acceptable for this circumstance?

4.   Describe Sternberg's three dimensions of love. Provide an example of a type of love that is probably common at the beginning of relationships and a type of love that is probably more common as relationships develop. For each of these examples, indicate whether it does or does not have each of the three dimensions of love.

5.   Describe three factors that make divorce more likely. One factor should relate to the time period before the marriage, one should relate to the time during the marriage, and one should relate to the culture as a whole.

6.   Define the two types of domestic violence described in the text. Which type do you think is more likely to lead to a divorce? Why?

7.   In our present economy, more families have become dual-earner families. Describe two positive effects and two negative effects that this arrangement probably has on families.

8.   If you could change the current social and economic systems in the United States in any way you choose, what three things would you change to help American families? Assume you have no financial limits and are empowered to do anything you choose.

9.   Describe three changes in the U.S. job market over the past several decades, and explain how these changes have affected individuals or families.

10.   What is a social clock? Describe three ways in which your culture's social clock has influenced your life (or will in the future).

Answer guidelines to these essay questions can be found in the Appendix at the end of the Test Bank.

CHAPTER 20   Middle Adulthood: Biosocial Development

MULTIPLE-CHOICE QUESTIONS

Primary and Secondary Aging

Primary and Secondary Aging, p. 491
Diff: E, Ans: a
1. Primary aging refers to age-related changes that:
   a. inevitably take place as time goes by.
   b. occur prior to middle adulthood.
   c. take place as a consequence of a person's unhealthy behaviors.
   d. are entirely genetic in origin.

Primary and Secondary Aging, pp. 491-492
Diff: M, Ans: c
2. Which of the following is a true statement about primary and secondary aging?
   a. Most aspects of primary aging can be reversed by the drugs and surgical interventions of modern medicine.
   b. They are both inevitable.
   c. Most manifestations of aging reflect both types.
   d. They both can be prevented by a healthy lifestyle.

Looking Old, p. 492
Diff: M, Ans: b
3. In middle adulthood, a person is most likely to lose:
   a. a few pounds of weight.
   b. nearly an inch in height.
   c. the ability to run more than a mile.
   d. the ability to experience orgasm.

Looking Old, p. 492
Diff: E, Ans: d
4. The changes in appearance that occur in middle adulthood:
   a. can be made worse by poor lifestyle choices.
   b. are inevitable results of primary aging.
   c. include changes in skin, hair, and fat distribution.
   d. are all of the above.

Looking Old, p. 492
Diff: H, Ans: d
5. For the most part, changes in appearance during middle adulthood:
   a. are dangerous to health.
   b. result in reduced vitality and adaptability.
   c. are greater for men than for women.
   d. do not significantly affect health.

The Senses, p. 492
Diff: M, Ans: e

6.   Which of the senses does NOT begin to decline by the end of middle adulthood?
      a.   smell
      b.   hearing
      c.   vision
      d.   taste
      e.   none of the above

The Senses, p. 492
Diff: E, Ans: c

7.   By the end of middle age, nearly everyone needs:
      a.   a hearing aid.
      b.   a cane or walker.
      c.   reading glasses.
      d.   hormone replacement therapy.

The Senses, p. 492
Diff: M, Ans: c

8.   Laboratory hearing tests of adults reveal that:
      a.   women and men begin to lose their hearing at the same age.
      b.   men show hearing deficits later than women.
      c.   men lose their hearing twice as fast as women.
      d.   men begin losing their hearing around age 60.

The Senses, p. 492
Diff: M, Ans: b

9.   Harry is 65 years old and can hear well enough to understand a whisper spoken three feet away. In a
      sample of 65-year-old men, Harry would be:
      a.   an exception to the rule.
      b.   somewhat unusual.
      c.   slightly worse than average.
      d.   about average.

The Senses, p. 493 (Table 20.1)
Diff: H, Ans: d

10.   David is 50 years old and can hear well enough to understand a whisper. In a sample of 50-year-old
      men, David would be:
      a.   an exception to the rule.
      b.   somewhat unusual.
      c.   in a substantial minority.
      d.   in the majority.

The Senses, p. 493
Diff: M, Ans: c

11.   Which of the following is a true statement about hearing loss in middle adulthood?
      a.   It is entirely a function of primary aging.
      b.   It is entirely a function of secondary aging.
      c.   It is a combination of primary and secondary aging.
      d.   It is a function of neither primary nor secondary aging.

The Senses, p. 493
Diff: E, Ans: a
12. Which of the following is an example of a source of hearing loss due to secondary aging?
    a. construction noise
    b. genes
    c. gender
    d. none of the above; hearing loss is due only to primary aging

The Senses, p. 493
Diff: H, Ans: c
13. Often the first sign of hearing loss in middle adulthood is:
    a. the inability to follow a conversation.
    b. a tendency to speak loudly.
    c. the failure to hear a distant telephone or doorbell.
    d. the failure to respond to music.

The Senses, p. 493
Diff: M, Ans: b
14. Which of the following hearing abilities declines first during middle adulthood?
    a. attending to one voice despite background noises
    b. hearing pure tones
    c. following a conversation
    d. hearing music

Vital Body Systems, p. 493
Diff: E, Ans: d
15. Which of the following is a true statement about declines in vital organs during middle adulthood?
    a. Some decline is caused by lifestyle.
    b. Some decline is inevitable.
    c. Most decline can be minimized until late adulthood.
    d. All of the above are true.

Vital Body Systems, p. 493
Diff: H, Ans: b
16. Which of the following is true of the decline in vital organs during middle adulthood?
    a. The decline tends to become critical before late adulthood.
    b. As organ reserve is depleted, people gradually become more vulnerable to chronic disease if a major stress occurs.
    c. Middle-aged individuals are considerably more likely to catch diseases like the flu and the common cold.
    d. With each passing year, individuals get better at recovering from illnesses.

Vital Body Systems, p. 494 (Table 20.2)
Diff: M, Ans: d
17. How long does it usually take chronic diseases, such as hardening of the arteries, diabetes, and emphysema, to proceed from the earliest stage to the most severe stage?
    a. 3 to 5 years
    b. 10 to 20 years
    c. 20 to 30 years
    d. 40 to 50 years

Vital Body Systems, p. 494 (Table 20.2)
Diff: M, Ans: c
18.   Sugar in the urine is an indication that a person has:
        a.   cancer.
        b.   cirrhosis.
        c.   diabetes.
        d.   atherosclerosis.

Vital Body Systems, p. 494
Diff: E, Ans: c
19.   The current death rate during middle age is _____ what it was in 1940.
        a.   twice
        b.   three times
        c.   half
        d.   just about the same

Vital Body Systems, p. 494
Diff: E, Ans: c
20.   The current death rate during middle adulthood is _____ what it was in 1940.
        a.   twice
        b.   three times
        c.   half
        d.   just about the same

Vital Body Systems, p. 494
Diff: E, Ans: d
21.   Approximately what percentage of U.S. adults who are currently 35 years old will be alive when they
        are 60?
        a.   35
        b.   50
        c.   75
        d.   90

The Sexual-Reproductive System, p. 495
Diff: E, Ans: c
22.   Which of the following is true of the sexual-reproductive system for both sexes during middle
        adulthood?
        a.   Sexual responses become quicker.
        b.   The level of sex hormones increases.
        c.   Reproduction becomes less likely.
        d.   All of the above are true.

The Sexual-Reproductive System, p. 495
Diff: E, Ans: c
23.   The average age of menopause is about:
        a.   40 years.
        b.   45 years.
        c.   50 years.
        d.   60 years.

The Sexual-Reproductive System, p. 495
Diff: E, Ans: a
24.   The many changes of menopause are caused by reduced:
        a.   estrogen.
        b.   lipids.
        c.   protein.
        d.   calcium.

The Sexual-Reproductive System, p. 495
Diff: M, Ans: b

25. The first symptom of the climacteric is:
    a. ovulation moving closer to the midpoint of the menstrual cycle.
    b. shorter menstrual cycles.
    c. longer menstrual cycles.
    d. ovulation of only a single ova during each cycle.

The Sexual-Reproductive System, p. 495
Diff: M, Ans: c

26. The reduction in estrogen production during the climacteric causes:
    a. cancer.
    b. increased testosterone production.
    c. coronary heart disease and osteoporosis.
    d. increased ovulation.

The Sexual-Reproductive System, p. 495
Diff: E, Ans: b

27. During menopause, vasomotor instability is most likely to cause:
    a. depression and mood change.
    b. hot flashes and cold sweats.
    c. brittle bones.
    d. heart attacks.

The Sexual-Reproductive System, p. 495
Diff: M, Ans: b

28. Lower levels of estrogen after menopause are associated with all of the following EXCEPT:
    a. osteoporosis and coronary heart disease.
    b. diabetes and lupus.
    c. vasomotor instability and loss of some breast tissue.
    d. drier skin and decreases in vaginal lubrication.

The Sexual-Reproductive System, p. 495
Diff: H, Ans: d

29. Who will most likely have marked symptoms of menopause?
    a. Claire, who began menopause at age 40
    b. Martha, who began menopause at age 56
    c. Wendy, who is not particularly bothered by her frequent hot flashes
    d. Norma, who just had a hysterectomy

The Sexual-Reproductive System, pp. 495-496
Diff: M, Ans: c

30. Who is most likely to experience clinical depression during menopause?
    a. women whose cultures view menopause as positive
    b. women who are well-rested
    c. women who have a history of depression
    d. women who are moody

The Sexual-Reproductive System, p. 496
Diff: E, Ans: b

31. Hormone replacement therapy (HRT) involves taking:
    a. calcium supplements.
    b. estrogen and progesterone.
    c. long baths to alleviate the stress of menopause.
    d. all of the above.

The Sexual-Reproductive System, p. 496
Diff: M, Ans: a

32.   Most at risk for osteoporosis is a:
     a.   small-framed woman of European descent.
     b.   premenopausal woman.
     c.   woman who has never had children.
     d.   large-boned African-American woman.

The Sexual-Reproductive System, p. 496
Diff: H, Ans: b

33.   Which of the following is a true statement about hormone replacement therapy?
     a.   It involves replacing testosterone that naturally declines with age.
     b.   Researchers now believe that the studies demonstrating its effects were invalid.
     c.   Physicians currently recommend it to a large proportion of menopausal women.
     d.   It increases the risk of osteoporosis.

The Sexual-Reproductive System, p. 497
Diff: E, Ans: c

34.   The term "male menopause" is sometimes used to refer to:
     a.   the sudden loss in fertility in a middle-aged man.
     b.   the sudden drop in testosterone that generally occurs at about age 50.
     c.   a dip in testosterone in response to anxiety or sexual inactivity.
     d.   impotence when a man is aware of his wife's menopause.

The Sexual-Reproductive System, p. 497
Diff: M, Ans: b

35.   Which of the following is a true statement about "male menopause"?
     a.   Similar to women, men experience a sudden age-related drop in hormonal levels.
     b.   Men suffer from sudden, stress-related shifts in hormone levels.
     c.   Viagra prevents declines in sexual desire and speed of intercourse as men age.
     d.   Frequency of intercourse increases during middle adulthood.

The Sexual-Reproductive System, p. 497
Diff: H, Ans: d

36.   The man least likely to experience "male menopause" is:
     a.   Hank, who is 50 and recently has been laid off.
     b.   Carl, who is 48 and having marital problems.
     c.   Mark, who is 47 and recovering from a serious heart attack.
     d.   Bob, who is 55 and has decided to retire early.

Measuring Health

Mortality and Morbidity, p. 498
Diff: E, Ans: a

37.   The most valid international statistic regarding health is:
     a.   mortality.
     b.   morbidity.
     c.   disability.
     d.   vitality.

Mortality and Morbidity, p. 498
Diff: M, Ans: c

38.   The mortality rate for U.S. 35- to 65-year-olds is 1 in:
a.   100.
b.   1000.
c.   2000.
d.   5000.

Mortality and Morbidity, p. 498
Diff: E, Ans: b

39.   A researcher is compiling data on the incidence of all types of diseases. This data reflects:
a.   mortality.
b.   morbidity.
c.   disability.
d.   vitality.

Mortality and Morbidity, p. 498
Diff: M, Ans: c

40.   One measure of health is morbidity, which:
a.   is based on death certificates.
b.   is a person's inability to act normally.
c.   includes both acute and chronic illnesses.
d.   measures how healthy an individual feels.

Disability and Vitality, p. 498
Diff: E, Ans: d

41.   The inability to act in "necessary, expected, and personally desired ways" is called:
a.   mortality.
b.   morbidity.
c.   vitality.
d.   disability.

Disability and Vitality, p. 498
Diff: M, Ans: a

42.   Which is most costly to society?
a.   disability
b.   mortality
c.   morbidity
d.   vitality

Disability and Vitality, p. 498
Diff: M, Ans: b

43.   In the United States, approximately one in _____ middle-aged people is disabled.
a.   2
b.   5
c.   10
d.   20

Disability and Vitality, p. 498
Diff: M, Ans: b

44.   The measure of health most important to the quality of life is:
a.   disability.
b.   vitality.
c.   morbidity.
d.   freedom from mental illness.

Disability and Vitality, p. 498
Diff: H, Ans: b
45.   Wendell has bone cancer and must use a wheelchair to accomplish his daily activities. He feels healthy and energetic and spends his days in a clown costume at the local children's hospital. Which of the following is true for Wendell?
       a.   He is disabled and has a high level of vitality.
       b.   He is not disabled and has a high level of vitality.
       c.   He is disabled and has a low level of vitality.
       d.   He is not disabled and has a low level of vitality.

Disability and Vitality, p. 499
Diff: H, Ans: d
46.   Most experts now agree that which of the following should be the goal of medicine?
       a.   preventing morbidity
       b.   remediating disability
       c.   postponing mortality
       d.   improving vitality

The Burden of Poor Health, p. 499
Diff: E, Ans: a
47.   Combining all four measures of health yields a measure of just how healthy people are called:
       a.   quality-adjusted life years.
       b.   life benefit.
       c.   global disease burden.
       d.   disease/life ratio.

The Burden of Poor Health, p. 499
Diff: E, Ans: d
48.   To measure the QALYs lost due to a particular illness, you need to consider:
       a.   only mortality.
       b.   only morbidity.
       c.   only disability.
       d.   every measure of health.

The Burden of Poor Health, p. 500
Diff: E, Ans: b
49.   Which of the following are the reciprocal of QALYs?
       a.   global disease burden.
       b.   disability-adjusted life years.
       c.   disease/life ratio.
       d.   vitality benefit.

The Burden of Poor Health, p. 500
Diff: M, Ans: c
50.   An individual who is completely well and is enjoying perfect vitality is said to have a QALY score for the year of:
       a.   0.
       b.   0.5.
       c.   1.
       d.   100.

The Burden of Poor Health, p. 500
Diff: M, Ans: c

51.   Which of the following questions is considered when calculating an individual's quality-adjusted life years?
   a.   Did the person die prematurely?
   b.   How much of the person's life fullness is reduced by a particular condition?
   c.   Both a and b are considered.
   d.   Neither a nor b is considered.

The Burden of Poor Health, p. 500
Diff: H, Ans: a

52.   Which of the following is a true statement about QALYs?
   a.   As QALYs decrease, DALYs increase.
   b.   If an individual loses half of his quality of life for the last 10 years of his life, he has lost 10 QALYs.
   c.   Subjective experience of vitality is not considered in the calculation of QALYs.
   d.   QALYs are not very useful in evaluating the costs and benefits of medical interventions.

The Burden of Poor Health, p. 500
Diff: M, Ans: a

53.   If a woman who has a life expectancy of 85 suddenly dies of a heart attack at age 55, how many quality-adjusted life years were lost?
   a.   30
   b.   55
   c.   85
   d.   140

The Burden of Poor Health, p. 500
Diff: M, Ans: d

54.   Which of the following interventions is probably considered the least effective in terms of the impact on QALYs for a large population?
   a.   immunizations
   b.   adequate nutrition
   c.   clean water
   d.   self-examination for breast cancer

The Burden of Poor Health, p. 500
Diff: H, Ans: d

55.   Suppose a medical test for a disease has a high number of false positives, leads to a great deal of surgery and anxiety, and saves a small number of people from dying of the disease. If used on a large population, the test would be considered to _____ quality-adjusted life years and _____ morbidity rates.
   a.   increase; increase
   b.   increase; reduce
   c.   reduce; increase
   d.   reduce; reduce

The Burden of Poor Health, p. 501
Diff: H, Ans: b

56.   If the goal of those concerned with public health is to focus their efforts more on increasing vitality and less on decreasing mortality, morbidity, and disability, they should focus on:
   a.   saving the seriously ill from dying.
   b.   prevention.
   c.   spotting early stages of illness.
   d.   all of the above.

The Burden of Poor Health, p. 502
Diff: H, Ans: b

57. Which of the following individuals would likely rate her vitality lowest?
    a. Pauline, who is 70 years old
    b. Brenda, who is 55 years old
    c. Yolanda, who is 35 years old
    d. Kim, who is 20 years old

Health Habits Through the Years

Health Habits Through the Years, p. 502
Diff: E, Ans: e

58. An individual's health habits during which time period influence healthy aging?
    a. prenatal
    b. childhood
    c. middle adulthood
    d. late adulthood
    e. all of the above

Tobacco, p. 503
Diff: M, Ans: d

59. A woman in the United States today is most likely to die from which type of cancer?
    a. breast
    b. uterine
    c. ovarian
    d. lung

Tobacco, p. 503
Diff: E, Ans: c

60. A known risk factor for most serious diseases that beset adults is:
    a. early retirement.
    b. overactive lifestyle.
    c. cigarette smoking.
    d. drinking red wine.

Tobacco, p. 503
Diff: M, Ans: a

61. All smoking diseases are:
    a. dose and duration sensitive.
    b. decreasing worldwide.
    c. destructive only to the lungs and respiratory system.
    d. less likely to affect African Americans.

Tobacco, p. 503
Diff: H, Ans: b

62. Which of the following is a true statement about the impact of smoking on health?
    a. Lung cancer is not directly related to smoking.
    b. Smoking marijuana accelerates cognitive decline throughout adulthood.
    c. The likelihood of smoking diseases increases with the length of time an individual has smoked, but not with the number of cigarettes smoked.
    d. Exposure to secondhand smoke has little relation to respiratory disabilities.

Tobacco, p. 504
Diff: M, Ans: c
63. Which of the following countries has the highest smoking rate among adult men?
     a.   United States
     b.   Germany
     c.   China
     d.   Canada

Alcohol, p. 504
Diff: M, Ans: c
64. Research studies on alcohol use have shown that:
     a.   alcohol use of any kind is dangerous to health.
     b.   alcohol raises levels of "bad" cholesterol.
     c.   moderate use of alcohol may increase longevity.
     d.   alcohol abuse and dependence are most common in adolescence.

Alcohol, p. 504
Diff: E, Ans: b
65. The disease most closely linked with heavy drinking is:
     a.   atherosclerosis.
     b.   cirrhosis of the liver.
     c.   lupus.
     d.   diabetes.

Alcohol, pp. 504-505
Diff: M, Ans: a
66. Which of the following is NOT associated with alcohol use?
     a.   coronary heart disease
     b.   decreased fertility
     c.   increase in "good" cholesterol
     d.   fatal accidents

Obesity and Overweight, p. 505
Diff: M, Ans: c
67. In middle adulthood, an individual is considered obese who:
     a.   snacks several times a day.
     b.   consumes foods that are high in cholesterol.
     c.   has a BMI higher than 25.
     d.   diets often, but always gains back some weight.

Obesity and Overweight, p. 505
Diff: H, Ans: b
68. Which of the following is a true statement about obesity and overweight?
     a.   Only 1 percent of U.S. adults is morbidly obese.
     b.   Overweight 40-year-olds lose, on average, three years of their lives.
     c.   In 2000, 25 percent of adults in the United States were overweight.
     d.   The rates of obesity are the highest among 20 to 40 year olds.

Obesity and Overweight, p. 506
Diff: M, Ans: a
69. Obesity is LEAST likely to be a contributing factor when a middle-aged adult is diagnosed as having:
     a.   emphysema.
     b.   diabetes.
     c.   arthritis.
     d.   heart disease.

Obesity and Overweight, p. 506
Diff: H, Ans: c
70.   Researchers on obesity agree that in middle age:
        a.   every extra pound is a health hazard.
        b.   it is okay to be overweight as long as one is not obese.
        c.   metabolism slows down by about a third.
        d.   adults need to consume more calories than people in young adulthood.

Obesity and Overweight, p. 506
Diff: E, Ans: d
71.   Developmentalists advocate which of the following to combat overweight?
        a.   surgery
        b.   drugs
        c.   psychotherapy
        d.   lifestyle changes

Exercise, p. 507
Diff: E, Ans: b
72.   Exercise is beneficial because it:
        a.   decreases metabolism.
        b.   burns calories.
        c.   increases appetite.
        d.   reduces HDL in the blood.

Exercise, p. 507
Diff: E, Ans: c
73.   Which of the following is NOT a benefit of regular exercise?
        a.   decreased appetite
        b.   burned calories
        c.   increased blood pressure
        d.   increased metabolism

Exercise, pp. 507-508
Diff: M, Ans: a
74.   Which of the following is NOT a benefit of regular exercise?
        a.   decrease in heart and lung capacity
        b.   decline in risk of almost every serious illness
        c.   decrease in depression
        d.   enhancement of cognitive functioning

Ethnic Variations in Health

Ethnic Variations in Health, p. 509
Diff: H, Ans: a
75.   The 50-year-old man most likely to be in good health is the one who is:
        a.   college-educated and living in Chicago.
        b.   poor and living in rural Virginia.
        c.   a Texan farmer with no college education.
        d.   any of the above; it is unclear who would be in the best health.

Explaining Variations, p. 509
Diff: E, Ans: d
76. Which of the following is associated with variations in health?
    a. income
    b. genes
    c. diet
    d. all of the above

The Influence of Ethnicity on Health, p. 510 (Figure 20.4)
Diff: M, Ans: d
77. Which ethnic group has the highest death rate for 45- to 54-year-olds in the United States?
    a. non-Hispanic whites
    b. Native Americans
    c. Asian Americans
    d. African Americans
    e. Hispanic Americans

The Influence of Ethnicity on Health, p. 510 (Figure 20.4)
Diff: H, Ans: a
78. Which man, living in the United States, is LEAST likely to die in middle age?
    a. Robert Ioki, whose grandparents came from Japan.
    b. Eduard Degas, whose grandparents came from France.
    c. Juan Cortez, whose grandparents came from Cuba.
    d. Jawal Nehru, whose grandparents came from India.

The Influence of Ethnicity on Health, p. 511
Diff: H, Ans: a
79. One explanation for the lower illness and death rates among recent immigrants compared to those who are long-time United States residents is:
    a. only more hardy individuals emigrate.
    b. the higher alcoholism rate among those who speak two languages.
    c. increased family support among long-time residents.
    d. poor health habits among new immigrants.

The Influence of Ethnicity on Health, p. 511
Diff: M, Ans: c
80. The incidence of skin cancer is highest among:
    a. Japanese-Americans.
    b. African-Americans.
    c. European-Americans.
    d. Filipino-Americans.

Three Causes of Ethnic Variations in Health, p. 511
Diff: E, Ans: a
81. Which of the following is NOT a social contextual factor influencing ethnic variations in health?
    a. genes
    b. poverty
    c. prejudice
    d. stress

Three Causes of Ethnic Variations in Health, p. 511
Diff: M, Ans: b
82.   Most genes act:
       a.   single-handedly.
       b.   epigenetically.
       c.   inefficiently.
       d.   unpredictably.

Three Causes of Ethnic Variations in Health, p. 512
Diff: E, Ans: d
83.   The study examining doctors' recommendations for treatment of supposed heart patients demonstrated that the best care was recommended for which group?
       a.   younger African-American women
       b.   older European-American women
       c.   older African-American men
       d.   younger European-American men

Three Causes of Ethnic Variations in Health, p. 513
Diff: M, Ans: d
84.   Diseases of affluence are those that occur more among:
       a.   European-Americans than among Americans of minority groups.
       b.   rich people than among poor people.
       c.   educated people than among less educated people.
       d.   all of the above.

Three Causes of Ethnic Variations in Health, p. 514
Diff: H, Ans: c
85.   The link between income and ethnic differences in health is LEAST likely to be due to differences in:
       a.   exposure to pollution.
       b.   stress in daily life.
       c.   the amounts of fruits and vegetables eaten.
       d.   the likelihood of seeking medical care.

TRUE-FALSE QUESTIONS

Primary and Secondary Aging

Ans: F, p. 491
1.   Primary aging involves changes that occur as a result of smoking, drinking, and eating.

Ans: T, p. 492
2.   In middle adulthood, a person typically gains weight and loses nearly an inch in height.

Ans: F, p. 492
3.   Mid-life changes in appearance have significant health consequences.

Ans: F, p. 492
4.   Of the sensory systems, only hearing and vision decline in middle adulthood.

Ans: F, p. 492
5.   Women typically experience hearing loss at younger ages than men.

Ans: T, p. 493
6.   Some hearing losses experienced by middle-aged adults are due to exposure to noise.

Ans: F, p. 493

7.   The first sign of hearing loss is usually trouble understanding conversations of people with high-pitched voices.

Ans: F, p. 493

8.   The depletion in organ reserve during middle adulthood is apparent on a daily basis.

Ans: T, p. 494

9.   Flu shots are generally recommended for middle-aged adults only when they already have other illnesses that deplete organ reserve.

Ans: T, p. 494 (Table 20.2)

10.   Leg pain while exercising is an indication of atherosclerosis.

Ans: T, p. 495

11.   The mood changes of menopause may actually be caused by fatigue.

Ans: F, p. 496

12.   A combination of progesterone and estrogen (HRT) is commonly used to treat immune system disorders.

Ans: T, p. 496

13.   It is now generally believed by the medical profession that the risks of hormone replacement therapy outweigh the benefits for most women.

Ans: F, p. 497

14.   Men experience the same sudden downward shift in reproductive ability as women, but it is called climacteric.

Ans: T, p. 497

15.   A middle-aged man who is anxious or worried about his self-worth or virility may experience a reduction in testosterone.

Measuring Health

Ans: T, p. 498

16.   Mortality is usually measured by the number of deaths per year per 1,000 individuals.

Ans: T, p. 499

17.   For society as a whole, disability is more costly than mortality or morbidity.

Ans: F, p. 498

18.   Disability refers to how healthy and energetic a person actually feels.

Ans: F, pp. 499-500

19.   The quality-adjusted life years measure is determined by the ratio of morbidity to vitality.

Ans: T, p. 500

20.   When DALYs increase, QALYs are reduced.

Ans: T, p. 500

21.   When the impact of a screening procedure on QALYs for a broad population is calculated, the procedure could be more harmful than helpful.

Ans: F, p. 501 (Table 20.3)

22.   Cancer, the leading cause of death in North America, is among the top 10 causes of DALYs worldwide.

Health Habits Through the Years

Ans: T, p. 502

23.   Prevention of disease adds more QALYs than do treatments for illness.

Ans: T, p. 502

24.   The death of a parent may cause one to reassess and then improve his or her health habits.

Ans: T, p. 503

25.   Smoking accelerates cognitive decline in adulthood.

Ans: F, pp. 503-504 (Table 20.4)

26.   Once an individual has smoked more than one pack a day for more than 10 years, quitting will not substantially improve health.

Ans: F, p. 504

27.   Because most people drink in moderation, alcohol abuse is not a major health problem in the United States.

Ans: T, p. 505

28.   A longitudinal study of Scottish men demonstrated that those who drank two to three drinks per day had a lower rate of heart disease, but higher mortality from almost all other causes.

Ans: T, p. 505

29.   The World Health Organization had declared that there is a worldwide epidemic of obesity and overweight.

Ans: F, pp. 505-506

30.   About the same percentage of North Americans are obese now as was forty years ago.

Ans: F, p. 506

31.   As long as middle-aged adults continue to eat the same amounts they ate in young adulthood, they will have no problems with weight gain as they age.

Ans: T, p. 506

32.   Developmentalists advocate cultural and lifestyle changes to combat overweight.

Ans: F, p. 507

33.   Whether exercise benefits middle-aged adults remains controversial.

Ans: T, pp. 507-508

34.   Regular exercise helps cognitive as well as physical functioning.

Ethnic Variations in Health

Ans: F, p. 510

35.   Ethnic patterns in rates of morbidity and disability are quite different from ethnic patterns in mortality.

Ans: T, p. 511

36.   In minority groups, the illness and death rates among immigrants are usually lower than among long-time U.S. residents of the same ethnicity.

Ans: F, p. 511
37.   Self-selection is unlikely to be a source of the difference between the health of long-time U.S. residents and recent immigrants.

Ans: F, pp. 512-513
38.   Overall, individuals in ethnic minority groups are receiving similar health care in the United States as are individuals in the ethnic majority.

Ans: T, p. 513
39.   In the United States, lung cancer used to be a disease of affluence; now it afflicts the poor more than the wealthy.

Ans: T, p. 514
40.   The reason why immigrants tend to be healthier than native-born individuals in the same group is that the immigrants spent their childhoods in a higher socioeconomic status.

FILL-IN-THE-BLANK QUESTIONS

Primary and Secondary Aging

Ans: primary; secondary, p. 491
1.   Some researchers divide aging into _____ aging, which inevitably takes place as time goes by, and _____ aging, which occurs as a consequence of unhealthy behaviors or society's failure to eliminate unhealthy conditions.

Ans: tones; conversation, p. 493
2.   In middle adulthood, the ability to distinguish pure _____ declines faster than the ability to understand _____.

Ans: autoimmune, p. 494
3.   Rheumatoid arthritis and lupus are _____ diseases, in which the body attacks itself.

Ans: smoke cigarettes, p. 494 (Table 20.2)
4.   To prevent, postpone, or minimize the risk of atherosclerosis, certain kinds of cancer, and emphysema, a person should not _____.

Ans: menstrual periods, p. 495
5.   Technically, a woman is considered to have reached menopause when her _____ ceased one year ago.

Ans: climacteric, p. 495
6.   A term for the three years before and the three years after menopause is the _____.

Ans: vasomotor, p. 495
7.   During the climacteric, _____ instability results in hot flashes and other disruptions of the mechanisms that control body temperature.

Ans: hormone replacement therapy, p. 496
8.   HRT refers to _____.

Ans: reduces; increases, p. 496
9.   Hormone replacement therapy _____ the risk of osteoporosis and _____ the incidence of breast cancer, heart disease, and stroke.

Ans: testosterone, p. 497

10.   Male menopause refers to the problems associated with a decrease in _____ .

Ans: Viagra (or Levitra), p. 497

11.   The drug used by middle-aged men to increase the sexual response is _____ .

Measuring Health

Ans: Mortality, p. 498

12.   _____ statistics are based on legally required death certificates.

Ans: disability, p. 499

13.   One in eight residents of the U.S. population aged 50 to 65 has difficulty walking three city blocks. For those who need to walk farther than that distance for work, this is an example of a(n) _____ .

Ans: burden of disease, p. 501

14.   The total reduction in vitality that is caused by disease-induced disability in a given population is referred to as the _____ .

Health Habits Through the Years

Ans: decreased, pp. 502-503

15.   The rate of smoking among U.S. male adults has _____ .

Ans: tobacco, p. 503

16.   Worldwide, the use of _____ is expected to cause more deaths in the year 2020 than any other single condition.

Ans: moderation, p. 504

17.   Individuals who drink alcohol in _____ tend to live longer than those who never drink.

Ans: body mass index, p. 505

18.   BMI refers to _____ .

Ans: overweight; obese; morbidly obese, p. 505

19.   A BMI of below 25 is considered normal; a BMI of above 25 is considered _____ ; a BMI of 30 or more is considered _____ ; and a BMI of 40 or more is considered _____ .

Ans: arthritis, p. 506

20.   Being overweight contributes to _____ , the most common disability among adults.

Ans: Vigorous exercise, p. 507

21.   _____ reduces the ratio of body fat to body weight.

Ethnic Variations in Health

Ans: health care, p. 509

22.   Income and education are two important determinants of community support and quality of _____

Ans: Africa, p. 510 (Figure 20.3)

23.   The American ethnic group with the highest death rate in middle age has ancestors from _____ .

Ans: melanin, p. 511

24.   European Americans have the highest incidence of skin cancer in part because their genetic makeup gives them less protective _____ in their skin.

Ans: affluence, p. 513
25.   Illnesses that are, or once were, more common in wealthier people and nations than in poorer ones are referred to as diseases of _____ .

ESSAY QUESTIONS

1.   Describe five biosocial changes that occur during middle adulthood.

2.   Primary aging refers to the age-related changes that take place in a person as time goes by. Secondary aging refers to the age-related changes that take place as a consequence of a person's unhealthy behaviors or a society's failure to eliminate unhealthy conditions. Examples will vary.

3.   For a public health pamphlet, develop a five-point list of recommendations for preventing chronic illness in adulthood. Conclude your list with a paragraph that summarizes evidence for the benefits of ONE of your recommendations.

4.   Describe three biosocial differences between middle-aged men and women, one referring to normal aging, one to the sexual-reproductive system, and one to fatal or chronic illness.

5.   Describe the four measures of health discussed in the text. On which measure do you think the medical profession should focus? Why?

6.   Consider the QALY that you yourself experience. How many QALYs have you lived so far? How many do you expect to live? Demonstrate in your answer that you know how to calculate QALYs and what affects health over the course of adulthood.

7.   Describe three causes of ethnic variations in health. Be specific, and be sure to explain why each factor causes ethnic variations.

Answer guidelines to these essay questions can be found in the Appendix at the end of the Test Bank.

CHAPTER **21**   **Middle Adulthood:**
Cognitive Development

MULTIPLE-CHOICE QUESTIONS

What Is Intelligence?

What Is Intelligence?, p. 519
Diff: E, Ans: a
1.   Who proposed the existence of *g*?
     a.   Spearman
     b.   Thurstone
     c.   Gardner
     d.   Sternberg

What Is Intelligence?, p. 519
Diff: E, Ans: b
2.   The term *g* refers to:
     a.   grand intelligence.
     b.   general intelligence.
     c.   great intelligence.
     d.   gross intelligence.

What Is Intelligence?, pp. 519-520
Diff: M, Ans: d
3.   The idea that intelligence is a single entity has been:
     a.   suggested only recently.
     b.   contradicted by Spearman's idea of a *g* factor.
     c.   supported by most psychologists.
     d.   implied by tests of intelligence that result in an overall IQ.

Studying Intelligence During the Twentieth Century, p. 520
Diff: M, Ans: c
4.   Early studies of adult intelligence led researchers to the conclusion that intelligence in adulthood:
     a.   is plastic and variable, and may either increase or decrease.
     b.   increases slowly during the 20s and early 30s, and declines thereafter.
     c.   peaks at about age 18, remains stable until the mid-20s, and declines thereafter.
     d.   is most significantly affected by experience, such as war traumas.

Studying Intelligence During the Twentieth Century, p. 520
Diff: E, Ans: b
5.   Tests of all literate American draftees in World War I indicated that intelligence peaks at age:
     a.   14.
     b.   18.
     c.   30.
     d.   42.

Studying Intelligence During the Twentieth Century, p. 520
Diff: H, Ans: c

6. A study of 1,191 subjects between the ages of 10 and 60 from several New England villages indicated that:
   a. intelligence peaks at 30 years of age.
   b. intelligence is unstable and unpredictable.
   c. the average 55-year-old scores the same as a 14-year-old.
   d. most 30-year-olds have not reached their peak intelligence.

Studying Intelligence During the Twentieth Century, p. 520
Diff: M, Ans: a

7. The idea that intelligence always declines throughout adulthood was:
   a. supported by early cross-sectional studies.
   b. supported by early longitudinal studies.
   c. proposed by Schaie and Baltes.
   d. never seriously considered by psychologists.

Studying Intelligence During the Twentieth Century, p. 520
Diff: M, Ans: a

8. The first evidence to contradict the assumption that intelligence declines with age was demonstrated by:
   a. Bayley and Oden.
   b. Schaie.
   c. Terman and Binet.
   d. Wechsler.

Studying Intelligence During the Twentieth Century, p. 520
Diff: H, Ans: b

9. When Bayley tested a group of adults who had been child geniuses, she found:
   a. performance peaked at age 21 and declined thereafter.
   b. scores increased between ages 20 and 50.
   c. scores decreased on analogies but increased on the other components of intelligence.
   d. no difference between 20- and 50-year-olds.

Studying Intelligence During the Twentieth Century, p. 520
Diff: H, Ans: d

10. When Bayley retested adults who had been part of a Berkeley, California study when they were children, she found that the typical 36-year-old was still improving on:
    a. comprehension and picture completion.
    b. arithmetic and vocabulary.
    c. arithmetic and picture completion.
    d. vocabulary and comprehension.

Studying Intelligence During the Twentieth Century, p. 521
Diff: E, Ans: c

11. Research that analyzes the cognitive development of the same individuals as they develop over the years is called:
    a. cross-sectional research.
    b. representative samples.
    c. longitudinal research.
    d. sequential research.

Studying Intelligence During the Twentieth Century, p. 521
Diff: M, Ans: a

12.   A problem with cross-sectional research is that:
    a.   cohort differences can make it difficult to differentiate between developmental change and cohort differences.
    b.   retesting leads older subjects to do better.
    c.   the most intelligent people are most likely to drop out of the study.
    d.   the results tend not to be worth the large investment.

Studying Intelligence During the Twentieth Century, p. 521
Diff: H, Ans: c

13.   Which is a cohort difference that might emerge in research on adult intelligence?
    a.   The typical middle-aged man is better at reasoning ability than he is at math.
    b.   A 75-year-old man shows a marked decrease in all five primary mental abilities.
    c.   Today's middle-aged women have better verbal skills than the middle-aged women of a different generation did because more of them today are employed.
    d.   High school seniors who plan to attend college score higher in verbal comprehension and mathematical ability than do their classmates.

Studying Intelligence During the Twentieth Century, p. 521
Diff: E, Ans: c

14.   The Flynn effect refers to the:
    a.   rise in an individual's IQ over the years.
    b.   decrease in an individual's IQ over the years.
    c.   rise in average IQ over the generations.
    d.   decrease in average IQ over the generations.

Studying Intelligence During the Twentieth Century, p. 521
Diff: H, Ans: b

15.   Which of the following is a true statement about the Flynn effect?
    a.   It validates the comparison of the IQs of older and younger people.
    b.   It necessitates the renorming of IQ tests every 15 years or so.
    c.   It is probably caused by genetic differences in intelligence.
    d.   It indicates that adults lose some intellectual power as they age.

Studying Intelligence During the Twentieth Century, p. 521
Diff: E, Ans: d

16.   The Flynn effect is probably due to changes in:
    a.   nutrition.
    b.   education.
    c.   family size.
    d.   all of the above.

Studying Intelligence During the Twentieth Century, p. 521
Diff: M, Ans: d

17.   A problem with longitudinal research on intelligence is that:
    a.   it is usually distorted by cohort effects, especially in older participants.
    b.   few people participate in such research voluntarily.
    c.   people of lesser intelligence tend to volunteer for retesting.
    d.   practice on the test items may produce learning.

Studying Intelligence During the Twentieth Century, pp. 521-522
Diff: M, Ans: c
18.   A psychologist who is studying the mathematical abilities of adults finds significant differences
      between the scores of adults born 50 years ago, when rote learning was stressed, and those born 25
      years ago, when more "progressive" approaches to education were popular. This is an example of a(n):
      a.   failure of longitudinal research.
      b.   advantage of cross-sectional research.
      c.   cohort difference.
      d.   intellectual decline in middle adulthood.

Studying Intelligence During the Twentieth Century, p. 522
Diff: M, Ans: b
19.   When Schaie conducted cross-sectional research comparing the cognitive abilities of adults of different
      ages, he found:
      a.   a gradual increase in intellectual ability with age.
      b.   a gradual decline in intellectual ability with age.
      c.   a sudden decline in intelligence in middle adulthood.
      d.   no age-related patterns of intellectual development.

Studying Intelligence During the Twentieth Century, p. 522
Diff: E, Ans: c
20.   The research design that involves testing groups of subjects of different ages multiple times and
      comparing their scores with their own scores in previous periods and with the scores of new groups of
      adults of the same ages is called:
      a.   longitudinal or long-term research.
      b.   cross-sectional research.
      c.   cross-sequential research.
      d.   retesting research.

Studying Intelligence During the Twentieth Century, p. 522
Diff: M, Ans: b
21.   Schaie's cross-sequential research on intellectual development demonstrated that:
      a.   there is a decline in most abilities after age 30.
      b.   individuals improve in most mental abilities during adulthood.
      c.   cohort differences make it appear that older people are more intelligent than younger people.
      d.   women are smarter than men.

Studying Intelligence During the Twentieth Century, p. 522 (Figure 21.1)
Diff: M, Ans: d
22.   When 36-year-old Bettina takes an intelligence test, which of her scores is likely to be lower than when
      she was 20?
      a.   word fluency
      b.   verbal meaning
      c.   inductive reasoning
      d.   number ability

Studying Intelligence During the Twentieth Century, p. 522
Diff: M, Ans: d
23.   Schaie demonstrated that the average adult at age _____ falls below the middle range of performance
      for young adults.
      a.   35
      b.   50
      c.   65
      d.   80

Components of Intelligence: Many and Varied, p. 523
Diff: E, Ans: b

24.   The researchers who concluded that fluid and crystallized intelligence are the two crucial aspects of intelligence were:
     a.   Bayley and Oden.
     b.   Cattell and Horn.
     c.   Jones and Conrad.
     d.   Sternberg and Gardner.

Components of Intelligence: Many and Varied, p. 523
Diff: E, Ans: a

25.   The type of basic intelligence that makes learning quick and thorough is referred to as:
     a.   fluid.
     b.   crystallized.
     c.   practical.
     d.   creative.

Components of Intelligence: Many and Varied, pp. 523-524
Diff: M, Ans: d

26.   Which of the following is NOT true of fluid intelligence?
     a.   It allows people to process new facts.
     b.   It is quick and flexible.
     c.   It involves basic mental abilities.
     d.   It includes the size of one's vocabulary.

Components of Intelligence: Many and Varied, p. 524
Diff: E, Ans: b

27.   Fluid intelligence includes:
     a.   a knowledge of geographical facts.
     b.   the speed of processing mathematical information.
     c.   the size of one's science vocabulary.
     d.   the ability to recognize and name famous paintings.

Components of Intelligence: Many and Varied, p. 524
Diff: M, Ans: b

28.   Of the following, the best example of fluid intelligence is:
     a.   knowledge of the names and dates of the monarchs of Great Britain.
     b.   the ability to quickly perceive logical relationships between words.
     c.   knowledge of computer terminology.
     d.   the ability to read and interpret an electrocardiogram.

Components of Intelligence: Many and Varied, p. 524
Diff: M, Ans: a

29.   To test fluid intelligence, a psychologist would be LEAST likely to measure:
     a.   definitions of technical words.
     b.   abstract thinking.
     c.   the timed assembly of a puzzle.
     d.   inductive reasoning.

Components of Intelligence: Many and Varied, p. 524
Diff: M, Ans: b

30.   The ability that involves crystallized intelligence to the greatest extent is:
     a.   solving an intellectual puzzle.
     b.   interpreting a chemical formula.
     c.   using words in an unusually creativity manner.
     d.   analyzing relations between concepts.

Components of Intelligence: Many and Varied, p. 524
Diff: M, Ans: c

31.   During adulthood, fluid intelligence:
       a.   remains about the same.
       b.   increases.
       c.   decreases.
       d.   decreases only if crystallized intelligence also declines.

Components of Intelligence: Many and Varied, p. 524
Diff: M, Ans: d

32.   Which of the following is a true statement about changes in intelligence?
       a.   Overall, intelligence decreases gradually throughout adulthood.
       b.   Schooling has relatively little to do with the development of intelligence.
       c.   Adult intelligence follows a single pattern of development.
       d.   Age-related declines are first noted for skills that require speed of response.

Components of Intelligence: Many and Varied, p. 524
Diff: H, Ans: d

33.   Carlos is 35 years old and is trying to learn English for the first time. He will experience more difficulty
       than if he were 5 years old because:
       a.   the ability to learn language is gone by 5 years of age.
       b.   he has significantly reduced crystallized intelligence.
       c.   crystallized intelligence is needed to learn new materials.
       d.   his fluid intelligence has declined.

Components of Intelligence: Many and Varied, p. 524
Diff: M, Ans: c

34.   The decline in fluid intelligence during middle adulthood:
       a.   does not affect the majority of adults.
       b.   does not affect speed of response.
       c.   is temporarily counteracted by increases in crystallized intelligence.
       d.   leads to a marked decrease in crystallized intelligence.

Components of Intelligence: Many and Varied, p. 525
Diff: E, Ans: b

35.   Analytic intelligence involves:
       a.   the skills used in everyday problem solving.
       b.   abstract planning, focused attention, and verbal and logical skills.
       c.   the accumulation of facts and knowledge as a result of experience and planning.
       d.   the capacity to be intellectually flexible and innovative.

Components of Intelligence: Many and Varied, p. 525
Diff: E, Ans: a

36.   Analytic intelligence is particularly valued in:
       a.   early adulthood.
       b.   early middle age.
       c.   late middle age.
       d.   late adulthood.

Components of Intelligence: Many and Varied, p. 525
Diff: M, Ans: d

37.   When students take multiple-choice exams, they are using the part of intelligence that Sternberg calls:
       a.   academic.
       b.   creative.
       c.   practical.
       d.   analytic.

Components of Intelligence: Many and Varied, p. 525
Diff: M, Ans: a

38.   Creative intelligence requires _____ thinking.
       a.   divergent
       b.   convergent
       c.   adaptive
       d.   practical

Components of Intelligence: Many and Varied, p. 525
Diff: M, Ans: a

39.   Over the long run, _____ intelligence is prized whenever life circumstances change or new challenges
       arise.
       a.   creative
       b.   crystallized
       c.   analytic
       d.   practical

Components of Intelligence: Many and Varied, p. 525
Diff: H, Ans: b

40.   The Mullers have just had a baby. Both parents must now adapt to the new demands of caring for an
       infant. This will require the part of intelligence that Sternberg calls:
       a.   formal.
       b.   creative.
       c.   analytic.
       d.   practical.

Components of Intelligence: Many and Varied, p. 525
Diff: E, Ans: b

41.   Which of Sternberg's three aspects of intelligence could be called "street smarts"?
       a.   creative
       b.   practical
       c.   analytic
       d.   general

Components of Intelligence: Many and Varied, p. 525
Diff: M, Ans: d

42.   Practical intelligence would be most needed to:
       a.   study vocabulary for a foreign language test.
       b.   take a standard intelligence test.
       c.   improve reading speed.
       d.   understand the needs of family members.

Components of Intelligence: Many and Varied, p. 525
Diff: H, Ans: a

43.   Betty is a retired registered nurse who fills in at the local hospital when the staff is in need of nurses.
       She is frequently called in without advance notice and must take over without any time to get oriented.
       Betty must rely on intelligence that Sternberg calls:
       a.   practical.
       b.   creative.
       c.   flexible.
       d.   analytic.

Components of Intelligence: Many and Varied, p. 525
Diff: H, Ans: c

44.   Who is using practical intelligence?
       a.   Rebecca, who is studying for final exams at college
       b.   Tracy, who is figuring out how to stretch a small family budget
       c.   John, who is trying to introduce a new policy to his coworkers
       d.   Kirsten, who is learning to program a computer

Components of Intelligence: Many and Varied, p. 525
Diff: H, Ans: b

45.   Who is using creative intelligence to the greatest extent?
       a.   Rebecca, who is studying for final exams at college
       b.   Tracy, who is figuring out how to stretch a small family budget
       c.   John, who is trying to introduce a new policy to his coworkers
       d.   Kirsten, who is learning to program a computer

Components of Intelligence: Many and Varied, pp. 525-526
Diff: M, Ans: d

46.   Which of the following is a true statement about practical intelligence?
       a.   The demands of daily life during middle adulthood make it particularly useful at this age.
       b.   Abstract IQ tests cannot assess it.
       c.   Its importance relative to analytic intelligence varies across cultures.
       d.   All of the above are true.

Components of Intelligence: Many and Varied, p. 526
Diff: E, Ans: c

47.   K. Warner Schaie traced which of the following over the years of adulthood?
       a.   eight distinct intelligences
       b.   fluid and crystallized intelligence
       c.   five primary abilities
       d.   general intelligence

Components of Intelligence: Many and Varied, p. 526
Diff: E, Ans: d

48.   Which of the following primary abilities begins its decline earliest in adulthood?
       a.   special orientation
       b.   inductive reasoning
       c.   word fluency
       d.   number ability

Components of Intelligence: Many and Varied, p. 526
Diff: H, Ans: a

49.   When Schaie tested adult intelligence using a cross-sequential research design, he found:
       a.   a gain until the late 50s in all but one ability.
       b.   moderately large decrements in all areas from ages 40 to 50.
       c.   stability until the mid-30s and decline thereafter.
       d.   beyond age 60, only some abilities decrease.

Components of Intelligence: Many and Varied, pp. 526-527
Diff: H, Ans: b

50.   Which of the following is a true statement about age-related differences in Schaie's five primary abilities?
a.   Only one of the abilities increases from ages 20 to 50.
b.   Cohort effects may have been the result of younger generations completing more education taught by educators who valued logic over facts.
c.   After age 35, there were moderate decreases in all of the abilities.
d.   Each successive cohort tended to score lower than previous generations in verbal memory and inductive reasoning but higher in number ability.

Components of Intelligence: Many and Varied, p. 527
Diff: H, Ans: d

51.   Schaie's study of Americans born over a 77-year-period found that each successive cohort scored higher in:
a.   creativity and analysis.
b.   fluid and crystallized intelligence.
c.   motor and verbal skills.
d.   verbal meaning and inductive reasoning.

Components of Intelligence: Many and Varied, p. 527
Diff: M, Ans: a

52.   Number skills are best for cohorts that attended elementary school between:
a.   1920-1940.
b.   1940-1960.
c.   1960-1980.
d.   1980-2000.

Components of Intelligence: Many and Varied (Thinking Like a Scientist), pp. 527-528
Diff: H, Ans: d

53.   Who has the best chance of maintaining intellectual abilities into late adulthood?
a.   Harriet, who is experiencing the "empty nest" syndrome
b.   Bert, who has recently retired and is planning "to do nothing but rest"
c.   Carol, who is well educated, recently divorced, and in financial difficulties
d.   Martin, who has a college education, happy marriage, and good retirement plan

Components of Intelligence: Many and Varied (Thinking Like a Scientist), pp. 527-528
Diff: M, Ans: d

54.   Which of the following would Schaie say affects changes in intellectual functioning in adulthood?
a.   health condition
b.   marital status
c.   occupation
d.   all of the above
e.   none of the above

Components of Intelligence: Many and Varied (Thinking Like a Scientist), pp. 527-528
Diff: H, Ans: c

55.   Schaie's case studies of adult intelligence indicated that:
a.   retirement signals a decrease in performance.
b.   intelligence is stable throughout adulthood.
c.   intellectual growth is affected by the unique experiences of adult life.
d.   women uniformly outperform men.

Components of Intelligence: Many and Varied, p. 528
Diff: E, Ans: a

56.   Who described eight distinct intelligences, each with its own neurological network in the brain?
      a.   Howard Gardner
      b.   Raymond Cattel
      c.   Charles Spearman
      d.   K. Warner Schaie

Components of Intelligence: Many and Varied, p. 528
Diff: M, Ans: d

57.   The intelligence most valued in contemporary Western cultures is:
      a.   social understanding.
      b.   bodily-kinesthetic.
      c.   musical.
      d.   logical-mathematical.

Components of Intelligence: Many and Varied, pp. 528-529
Diff: H, Ans: c

58.   With which of the following statements would Gardner DISAGREE?
      a.   Families and communities value some intellectual abilities more than others, leading to their development.
      b.   Brain-damaged people can be skilled in some intellectual abilities despite deficits in others because each has its own neurological network in the brain.
      c.   Standard IQ tests that have been developed and refined in Western Europe and the United States should be applicable to people elsewhere and to other skills.
      d.   Historical context is important in recognizing which intelligences may never get an opportunity to develop.

Components of Intelligence: Many and Varied, p. 529
Diff: M, Ans: d

59.   Which of the following is affected by culture?
      a.   the abilities that are favored
      b.   the assumptions of psychometricians
      c.   the design of education
      d.   all of the above

Selective Gains and Losses

Optimization with Compensation, p. 530
Diff: E, Ans: b

60.   What did Baltes and Baltes call the capacity of adults to use their intellectual strengths to compensate for declining capacities?
      a.   compensatory thinking.
      b.   selective optimization with compensation.
      c.   maturation of compensation.
      d.   optimization of maturation and wisdom.

Optimization with Compensation, pp. 530-531
Diff: E, Ans: a

61.   For a typical middle-aged adult, intelligence increases:
      a.   in the specific areas that reflect his or her interest.
      b.   in all areas throughout adulthood.
      c.   only in areas associated with work and employment.
      d.   in none of the above.

What Is Expert Cognition?, p. 532
Diff: E, Ans: d
62.   When developmentalists use the term "expert," they usually mean a person who:
   a.   is extraordinarily gifted in one area.
   b.   has earned advanced credentials in his or her special area.
   c.   is innately skilled.
   d.   is significantly better than others at performing a certain task.

What Is Expert Cognition?, p. 532
Diff: M, Ans: b
63.   Expert physicians interpret X-rays more accurately than young doctors because:
   a.   they rely on known procedures and rules.
   b.   of their accumulated knowledge.
   c.   they are less flexible and experimental.
   d.   they work slowly and deliberately.

What Is Expert Cognition?, p. 532
Diff: M, Ans: a
64.   In his or her special area, the expert is more likely than the novice to:
   a.   experiment or deviate from the usual way of doing things.
   b.   give conscious attention to all aspects of performance.
   c.   rely on formal procedures to solve a problem.
   d.   verbalize exactly how he or she achieves results.

What Is Expert Cognition?, p. 532
Diff: E, Ans: c
65.   Compared to novices, experts:
   a.   work more slowly.
   b.   are less flexible.
   c.   are more intuitive.
   d.   are all of the above.

Expertise and Age, p. 535
Diff: E, Ans: e
66.   Which of the following affects the development of expertise?
   a.   age
   b.   practice
   c.   talent
   d.   training
   e.   all of the above

Expertise and Age, p. 535
Diff: H, Ans: a
67.   Which of the following is a true statement about age and expertise?
   a.   Expertise can overcome some effects of age but not others.
   b.   Expertise can nearly always compensate for the deterioration that comes with age.
   c.   Female experts are better than male experts at keeping their level of expertise stable.
   d.   The effects of age apply equally to experts and novices.

Expertise on the Job, pp. 535-536
Diff: M, Ans: a

68.   Data from the Seattle Longitudinal Study demonstrated that as adults grow older, their intellectual functioning increases if they:
   a.   do paid work that is intellectually challenging.
   b.   do any type of work as long as they are paid for it.
   c.   do work that represents an increase in their previous pay level.
   d.   perform the tasks of everyday life.

Expertise on the Job, p. 536
Diff: H, Ans: a

69.   Perlmutter's research on older and younger restaurant employees revealed that:
   a.   older employees served more customers during "rush" and "nonrush" periods.
   b.   age was not a factor in performance.
   c.   prior work experience was a major determinant of job performance.
   d.   younger employees were better during "rush" periods.

Expertise on the Job, p. 536
Diff: H, Ans: c

70.   Katherine, age 50, and her daughter Lisa, age 20, have recently taken jobs as waitresses. Compared to Lisa, Katherine will probably:
   a.   rely more on her ability to memorize orders.
   b.   perform less well.
   c.   employ more time-management strategies.
   d.   wait on fewer tables.

Expertise on the Job, p. 536
Diff: M, Ans: d

71.   Perlmutter's interviews with restaurant managers revealed that older employees did better on the job because they:
   a.   could ignore the criticisms of restaurant patrons.
   b.   were better at remembering customers' orders.
   c.   did not waste time socializing on the job.
   d.   combined several tasks when possible.

Expertise on the Job, p. 537
Diff: H, Ans: c

72.   Research on office workers has demonstrated that:
   a.   the physical and mental capacities required are often too demanding for older workers.
   b.   the most successful workers are the ones who score highest on standard measures of performance.
   c.   skilled older workers use different strategies than younger workers to obtain the same result.
   d.   all of the above are true.

Expertise in Daily Life, p. 538
Diff: E, Ans: b

73.   Attempting to solve problems by attacking them in some way is referred to as:
   a.   ineffective coping.
   b.   problem-focused coping.
   c.   strategy-based coping.
   d.   emotion-focused coping.

Expertise in Daily Life, pp. 538-539
Diff: M, Ans: c
74.   Compared to younger adults, older adults:
        a.   are more likely to attack a problem head-on.
        b.   respond better to stressors because of increased organ reserve.
        c.   are more likely to change their feelings about problems.
        d.   do all of the above.

TRUE-FALSE QUESTIONS

What Is Intelligence?

Ans: T, p. 519
1.   Spearman proposed that intelligence is a single entity, which he called *g*.

Ans: T, p. 519
2.   Spearman believed that general intelligence cannot be measured directly; it must be inferred from various abilities.

Ans: F, p. 520
3.   For most of the twentieth century, psychologists were convinced that intelligence peaked in middle adulthood.

Ans: T, p. 520
4.   When Bayley retested a group of representative adults who had been tested as children, she found that intelligence was still improving at age 36.

Ans: F, p. 520
5.   Bayley's retesting of the intelligence of a group of gifted adults who had been tested as children is an example of cross-sequential design.

Ans: T, p. 521
6.   The rise in average IQ over the generations that has been demonstrated in cross-sectional research is probably most clearly due to evolution.

Ans: F, p. 521
7.   An individual's increasing intelligence with age is termed the Flynn effect.

Ans: F, p. 521
8.   One drawback of longitudinal research is that subjects who are willing to be tested and retested often have lower-than-average IQs.

Ans: F, p. 522
9.   Schaie's studies of adult intellectual ability differed from earlier studies in that the earlier studies found no age-related declines.

Ans: T, p. 522
10.   Cohort differences are among the factors that account for inter-individual variation in adult intelligence.

Ans: T, p. 523
11.   Intellectual abilities sometimes rise, sometimes remain stable, and sometimes decline with age.

Ans: T, pp. 523-524
12. Abstract thinking and speed of processing are some of the mental abilities that make up fluid intelligence.

Ans: F, p. 524
13. Someone who has an extensive vocabulary and knows specific dates in history would rate high in fluid intelligence.

Ans: F, p. 524
14. For most people, both fluid and crystallized intelligence increase with age.

Ans: T, p. 524
15. In late adulthood, declines in fluid intelligence become so massive that crystallized intelligence is affected, and this is the point at which overall IQ begins to fall.

Ans: F, p. 525
16. Sternberg argues that there are eight intelligences that are closely related and interwoven.

Ans: T, p. 525
17. Over the long run, creativity is a better predictor of accomplishment than traditional measures of IQ.

Ans: T, p. 525
18. Analytic intelligence includes the mental processes that promote academic competence.

Ans: T, p. 525
19. Deciding on a plan for career advancement involves creative intelligence.

Ans: F, p. 525
20. Practical intelligence is best described as "book smarts."

Ans: F, p. 525
21. Practical intelligence seems to decline throughout most of adulthood, with some later-life increase.

Ans: F, p. 5260
22. Analytic intelligence is most useful in middle adulthood.

Ans: T, p. 526
23. Four of Schaie's five primary abilities increase from ages 20 to 50.

Ans: F, pp. 526-527
24. Studies on intelligence show that intellectual abilities follow distinct and predictable paths of development, regardless of life experience.

Ans: F, p. 527
25. The current cohort of young adults shows higher basic math skills than do older cohorts.

Ans: T, p. 528
26. Gardner believes that most people have the capacity to achieve at least minimal proficiency in all eight intelligences.

Ans: F, p. 528
27. Gardner's theory of eight intellectual abilities cannot explain why brain-damaged people can demonstrate remarkable capacity in the musical domain despite enormous deficits in language.

Ans: F, p. 529
28. Baltes believes that culture is significant during childhood and that biology becomes more important as adults grow older.

Ans: T, p. 529

29.   Although older adults tend to decline in the specific skills valued by psychometricians, they can learn these skills if the cultural setting encourages them.

Selective Gains and Losses

Ans: T, p. 530

30.   Many researchers believe that adults make choices about their intellectual development, quite separate from their culture and education.

Ans: T, p. 532

31.   Culture and context guide individuals in selecting areas of expertise.

Ans: F, p. 532

32.   Developmentalists use the term "expert" only for people who are extraordinarily gifted at a particular task.

Ans: F, p. 532

33.   Experts simply have more knowledge about a particular subject.

Ans: F, p. 532

34.   Compared to experts, novices generally rely more on the circumstances of the immediate context than on formal rules and procedures.

Ans: T, pp. 532-533

35.   Experts often cannot explain how they come to particular conclusions in their area of expertise.

Ans: F, p. 533

36.   Novices tend to be better than experts at developing strategies to accomplish a particular task.

Ans: T, p. 534

37.   Although novices show age-related deficits in many areas, experts of all ages are able to maintain their proficiency in many occupations.

Ans: F, p. 534

38.   Intellectual abilities are well established by middle adulthood and are not easily influenced by additional experience or education.

Ans: T, p. 535

39.   When common songs (such as "Happy Birthday") were played from midsong very slowly and gradually faster, speed of correct response correlated with level of musical expertise and not age.

Ans: T, p. 535

40.   Older employees are able to devise cognitive strategies to compensate for the decline of other job-related skills.

Ans: F, p. 536

41.   The amount of prior work experience is the most important factor in employee performance.

Ans: T, p. 536

42.   Doing paid work that is not intellectually challenging appears to decrease individuals' cognitive functioning.

Ans: F, p. 537

43.   Young college graduates are often more employable than older workers because of their age-related intelligence.

Ans: T, p. 537

44.   Successful bank employees scored high on a measure of practical intelligence of bank management, but not necessarily on a standard intelligence test.

Ans: F, p. 538

45.   People's thoughts about stressful events have little influence over whether the events become stressors.

Ans: T, p. 538

46.   Younger adults are more likely to attack a problem, and older adults are more likely to accept a problem.

FILL-IN-THE-BLANK QUESTIONS

Middle Adulthood: Cognitive Development

Ans: psychometric, p. 519

1.   The _____ approach to study intelligence involves the *measurement* of intelligence.

What Is Intelligence?

Ans: Spearman, p. 519

2.   According to _____, the *g* factor of intelligence can be inferred from various abilities, such as vocabulary, memory, and reasoning.

Ans: 18 and 21, p. 520

3.   Cross-sectional tests of adults in several New England villages indicated that intelligence peaked between the ages of _____.

Ans: cohort differences, p. 521

4.   It is impossible to select adults for study who are similar to each other in every aspect except age; for this reason, cross-sectional research can easily be distorted by _____.

Ans: Flynn effect, p. 521

5.   The rise in average IQ over generations is termed the _____.

Ans: cross-sectional; longitudinal, p. 522

6.   Schaie found that _____ research shows a gradual decline in intellectual ability, while _____ research, which may not be applicable to other cohorts, shows an increase in intellectual abilities throughout most of adulthood.

Ans: cross-sequential, p. 522

7.   To compensate for the effects of retesting in longitudinal research, Schaie developed a new research design called _____ research.

Ans: fluid, pp. 523-524

8.   A person who is quick at assembling puzzles and creative with words and numbers is someone with high _____ intelligence.

Ans: crystallized, p. 524

9.   The accumulation of facts and information that comes with experience and education is called _____ intelligence.

Ans: sensitive; resistant, p. 524
10.   Fluid intelligence is considered aging-_____, and crystallized intelligence is considered aging-
        _____.

Ans: analytic, p. 525
11.   According to Sternberg, _____ intelligence fosters efficient learning, remembering, and thinking.

Ans: creative, p. 525
12.   According to Sternberg, the _____ aspect of intelligence involves the capacity to be intellectually
        flexible and innovative.

Ans: practical, p. 525
13.   According to Sternberg, the intellectual skills used in everyday problem solving are part of _____
        intelligence.

Ans: cohort, p. 527
14.   Schaie's finding that successive generations increase in reasoning skills but decrease in number skills is
        an example of a _____ effect.

Ans: Gardner; brain, p. 528
15.   According to _____, each intellectual ability is based in a particular part of the _____, and thus all
        individuals have at least some capacity to obtain proficiency in each ability.

Selective Gains and Losses

Ans: optimization, p. 530
16.   The ability to strategically use one's intellectual strengths to compensate for declining capacities
        associated with age is called selective _____ with compensation.

Ans: expertise, p. 531
17.   Individuals develop _____ in one or a few areas that are personally meaningful, while paying less
        attention to other areas.

Ans: experts, p. 532
18.   When experts and novices are compared, psychologists find that _____ are more intuitive and less
        stereotyped in their performance.

Ans: automatic, p. 533
19.   The complex action and thought required for many elements of expert performance become _____
        and appear nonconscious.

Ans: strategies, p. 533
20.   As experts begin to lose fluid abilities, they are able to develop _____ to compensate for the loss.

Ans: 10, p. 534
21.   According to some researchers, _____ years of practice may be necessary in order to develop expertise.

Ans: complexity, p. 536
22.   The level of _____ in paid work is an important factor in the level of intellectual functioning of older
        workers.

Ans: Emotion, p. 538
23.   _____-focused coping involves attempting to change one's feelings about a problem.

ESSAY QUESTIONS

1. Choose an expert with whose work you are familiar—for example, an athlete or performer, a teacher, a businessperson, or a parent. Note the expert's age and experience, then describe the expert's performance in detail, emphasizing the ways in which the expert's performance differs from that of a novice in the same field. Identify any differences that seem to be age-related.

2. What is your age-group or cohort? Describe at least three factors or experiences that made your early education different from that of either your parents' generation or from that of the generation in elementary school today. You may choose to focus on technology, educational philosophy, subject matter, changes in the society that affect how afterschool hours are spent, and so forth. Use these examples to explain why researchers who study intelligence need to be conscious of cohort differences.

3. Design a research project for studying one aspect of intelligence in adulthood. Specify what aspect of intelligence you intend to study and exactly what you want to learn. Describe your research plan in detail, including testing procedures and selection of participants. How would you overcome the problems of cohort effects?

4. The textbook notes that many researchers feel that the important question is not, "What happens to intelligence in adulthood?" but rather, "What happens to intelligences in adulthood?" Do you agree or disagree? Explain why changing the question may also change the answer.

5. At a preretirement planning seminar, a woman expresses concern that her intellectual abilities will decrease after retirement. What would you say to her?

6. Describe three things you learned from this chapter about the development of intelligence in middle adulthood.

Answer guidelines to these essay questions can be found in the Appendix at the end of the Test Bank.

CHAPTER 22   Middle Adulthood: Psychosocial Development

MULTIPLE-CHOICE QUESTIONS

Middle Adulthood: Psychosocial Development

Middle Adulthood: Psychosocial Development, p. 543
Diff: E, Ans: e
1.   Which most accurately depicts middle age?
   a.   sandwich generation
   b.   midlife crisis
   c.   role overload
   d.   all of the above
   e.   none of the above

Personality Throughout Adulthood

Personality Throughout Adulthood, p. 543
Diff: M, Ans: b
2.   Throughout adulthood, the major source of an individual's developmental continuity is his or her:
   a.   career.
   b.   personality.
   c.   marriage.
   d.   family relationship.

Stable Traits: The Big Five, p. 544
Diff: E, Ans: b
3.   Which of the following is NOT one of the Big Five?
   a.   openness
   b.   generativity
   c.   extroversion
   d.   conscientiousness

Stable Traits: The Big Five, p. 544
Diff: M, Ans: d
4.   Sam is moody, anxious, and self-punishing. Sam is high in:
   a.   openness.
   b.   extroversion.
   c.   conscientiousness.
   d.   neuroticism.

Stable Traits: The Big Five, p. 594
Diff: E, Ans: b

5.   A person who has many of the personality traits associated with extroversion would most likely be described as:
       a.   depressed and anxious.
       b.   active and outgoing.
       c.   open and receptive.
       d.   creative and intelligent.

Stable Traits: The Big Five, p. 594
Diff: H, Ans: b

6.   A person who seems to thrive on changes in his or her work, lifestyle, and relationships would most likely be rated high on the personality dimension called:
       a.   extroversion.
       b.   openness.
       c.   neuroticism.
       d.   sociability.

Stable Traits: The Big Five, p. 544
Diff: M, Ans: a

7.   Matilda is usually a kind, helpful, and easygoing person. She is high on which of the Big Five traits?
       a.   agreeableness
       b.   neuroticism
       c.   openness
       d.   conscientiousness

Stable Traits: The Big Five, p. 544
Diff: M, Ans: c

8.   Davetta is very organized and tends to conform easily. She is high on which of the Big Five traits?
       a.   agreeableness
       b.   openness
       c.   conscientiousness
       d.   extroversion

Stable Traits: The Big Five, p. 544
Diff: E, Ans: a

9.   A particular lifestyle and social context that evokes and reinforces personality traits is called an:
       a.   ecological niche.
       b.   environmental fit.
       c.   adult community.
       d.   adaptable environment.

Stable Traits: The Big Five, p. 544
Diff: M, Ans: d

10.   Chris is high in extroversion and therefore will probably:
       a.   select an introverted mate as a balance for his personality.
       b.   have a life in constant flux.
       c.   become a librarian or safety inspector.
       d.   prefer to work with people and have a busy social life.

Stable Traits: The Big Five, p. 544
Diff: H, Ans: b

11. A man who changes jobs frequently, moves frequently, and always seems happier because of these changes is likely to be high in:
     a.   conscientiousness.
     b.   openness.
     c.   neuroticism.
     d.   extroversion.

Developmental Changes in Personality, p. 545
Diff: E, Ans: d

12. The Big Five personality traits:
     a.   are unstable throughout much of adulthood.
     b.   apply only to people living in North America.
     c.   include five unhealthy ways of functioning in midlife.
     d.   become quite stable by age 30.

Developmental Changes in Personality, p. 545
Diff: E, Ans: d

13. Who is likely to have the most stable personality?
     a.   a 5-year-old boy
     b.   a 14-year-old girl
     c.   a 23-year-old man
     d.   a 35-year-old woman

Developmental Changes in Personality, p. 545
Diff: M, Ans: c

14. Which of the following personality traits tends to increase with age?
     a.   extroversion
     b.   openness
     c.   agreeableness
     d.   neuroticism

Developmental Changes in Personality, p. 545
Diff: M, Ans: d

15. With age, extroversion tends to:
     a.   increase slightly.
     b.   increase sharply.
     c.   decrease.
     d.   remain stable.

Developmental Changes in Personality, p. 546
Diff: H, Ans: d

16. Which of the following is a true statement about the trait of generativity?
     a.   It is one of the "Big Five."
     b.   It decreases substantially with age, as people get more set in their ways.
     c.   It is part of openness and neuroticism.
     d.   It increases slightly from age 30 to age 65.

Developmental Changes in Personality, p. 546
Diff: E, Ans: b

17. Openness is viewed as a particularly positive personality trait in:
     a.   Italy.
     b.   the United States.
     c.   China.
     d.   Australia.

Gender Convergence, p. 546
Diff: E, Ans: b
18.   In some cultures, as they grow older, men find it easier to express emotions and women tend to:
      a.   remain traditional.
      b.   assert themselves.
      c.   become more sociable.
      d.   become less family-oriented.

Gender Convergence, p. 546
Diff: E, Ans: a
19.   The loosening of gender restrictions during middle age is most likely to lead to a gender:
      a.   convergence.
      b.   gap.
      c.   crossover.
      d.   disorder.

Gender Convergence, p. 546
Diff: M, Ans: d
20.   A biological explanation for gender convergence stresses:
      a.   midlife crises.
      b.   social obligations.
      c.   family responsibilities.
      d.   sex hormones.

Gender Convergence, p. 547
Diff: M, Ans: c
21.   The pushing of parents into roles they did not anticipate because of the demands of childrearing is referred to as the:
      a.   ecological niche.
      b.   gender convergence.
      c.   parental imperative.
      d.   crisis reaction.

Gender Convergence, p. 547
Diff: M, Ans: b
22.   Who believed that everyone has both a masculine and a feminine side?
      a.   Freud
      b.   Jung
      c.   Maslow
      d.   Erikson

Gender Convergence, p. 547
Diff: M, Ans: d
23.   The "shadow side" of personality is explored by men and women in middle age, according to:
      a.   Freud.
      b.   Levinson.
      c.   Sheehy.
      d.   Jung.

Gender Convergence, p. 547
Diff: M, Ans: a
24.   Longitudinal survey research suggests that gender convergence may be due to:
      a.   historical trends.
      b.   biological changes.
      c.   rigid sexism.
      d.   a patriarchal society.

The "Midlife Crisis," p. 548
Diff: E, Ans: b
25.   Our society recognizes a point called midlife which occurs at about age:
      a.   30.
      b.   40.
      c.   50.
      d.   60.

The "Midlife Crisis," p. 548
Diff: M, Ans: b
26.   Beginning with the "Big Four-O," birthdays are seen as:
      a.   time already lived.
      b.   time remaining to live.
      c.   too late to live it up.
      d.   hardly reason to live.

The "Midlife Crisis," p. 548
Diff: E, Ans: d
27.   Some people refer to a period of unusual anxiety, reexamination, and transformation during middle
      adulthood as a(n):
      a.   cohort bridge.
      b.   ecological niche.
      c.   gender trajectory.
      d.   midlife crisis.

The "Midlife Crisis," p. 548
Diff: M, Ans: c
28.   Which most accurately depicts middle age?
      a.   It is a time of severe emotional crisis.
      b.   There are very few changes at midlife.
      c.   Changes do not necessarily cluster around age 40.
      d.   It always begins at age 40.

The "Midlife Crisis," p. 548
Diff: M, Ans: a
29.   Which most accurately depicts researchers' current views on the midlife crisis?
      a.   Believing in its existence may help middle-aged adults cope with the changes that occur.
      b.   How people react to changes is directly tied to the calendar.
      c.   It exists for men but not for women.
      d.   It involves a multitude of changes that all happen around the same age.

Family Relationships in Midlife

Family Relationships in Midlife, p. 549
Diff: M, Ans: a
30.   Individuals who are accepted in a family that is not their legal or biological family are:
      a.   fictive kin.
      b.   kissing cousins.
      c.   social convoys.
      d.   generative allies.

Family Relationships in Midlife, p. 549
Diff: M, Ans: d
31.   A middle-aged adult who serves as a "cohort bridge" provides:
   a.   caregiving services.
   b.   an opportunity for parental pride in family accomplishments.
   c.   financial and emotional aid in an emergency.
   d.   the link across the generations.

Partners, p. 549
Diff: E, Ans: b
32.   Most middle-aged adults have their closest relationship with a:
   a.   cohabiting partner.
   b.   spouse.
   c.   friend.
   d.   grandchild.

Partners, p. 549
Diff: M, Ans: c
33.   The happiest middle-aged adults typically fulfill how many roles?
   a.   1
   b.   2
   c.   5
   d.   8

Partners, p. 550
Diff: M, Ans: b
34.   After the first ten years most married couples find:
   a.   financial problems are overwhelming.
   b.   tension decreases as children become more independent.
   c.   there are more fights over equity in domestic work.
   d.   job demands increase so less time is spent in shared activities.

Partners, p. 550
Diff: M, Ans: c
35.   After the children are grown, most married couples:
   a.   spend longer hours at work.
   b.   devote themselves to the marital relationship.
   c.   have adequate time for their relationship.
   d.   see little of each other.

Partners, p. 551
Diff: H, Ans: d
36.   Studies of long-term marriages:
   a.   have not been carried out for several decades.
   b.   show an increasing level of happiness for recent generations.
   c.   involve cross-sectional research.
   d.   involve a selected sample of couples who stay together.

Partners, p. 551
Diff: M, Ans: c
37.   A break-up would be most stressful for which of the following individuals?
   a.   Abby, who has just been married
   b.   Brenda, who has been married for five years
   c.   Carlene, who is in a long-term marriage
   d.   Dorothy, who is in a cohabiting relationship

Partners, p. 551
Diff: H, Ans: d
38.   Regarding remarriage in the United States:
    a.   most people remarry within two years of a divorce.
    b.   remarriage is more likely after 40.
    c.   about 25 percent of marriages are remarriages for one or both of the spouses.
    d.   men are more likely to remarry than are women.

Partners, p. 551
Diff: M, Ans: c
39.   After remarriage, women typically become more financially secure, and men:
    a.   work longer hours.
    b.   seek a close friendship with another female.
    c.   become healthier and more sociable.
    d.   become more interested in performing domestic chores.

Partners, p. 552
Diff: M, Ans: c
40.   Research indicates that remarried people:
    a.   are unlikely to get divorced.
    b.   report higher average happiness than those in first marriages.
    c.   have a higher chance of divorce than do people in first marriages.
    d.   are worse off financially than when they lived alone.

Partners, pp. 552-553
Diff: M, Ans: c
41.   Which of the following women is the least likely to find a marriage partner?
    a.   a 30-year-old European-American woman
    b.   a 55-year-old European-American woman
    c.   a 30-year-old African-American woman
    d.   a 55-year-old African-American woman

Partners, pp. 552-553
Diff: M, Ans: d
42.   The middle-aged woman who has the least chance of marrying is:
    a.   European American.
    b.   Asian American.
    c.   Native American.
    d.   African American.

Partners, pp. 552-553
Diff: H, Ans: a
43.   Which of the following does NOT contribute to African-American women's difficulty in finding a
        marriage partner?
    a.   males' higher immigration rates
    b.   males' greater tendency to marry outside their ethnic group
    c.   females' greater likelihood of obtaining a degree
    d.   none of the above

Partners, p. 553 (Table 22.2)
Diff: M, Ans: b

44.   Over the past several decades, the number of households that consist of a female sole head of
       household with children has:
       a.   decreased.
       b.   increased.
       c.   remained stable.
       d.   increased then decreased.

Partners, p. 553 (Table 22.2)
Diff: H, Ans: c

45.   In 1998, according to the data from the United States census, the group that had the lowest percentage
       of households headed by a woman was:
       a.   White.
       b.   Black.
       c.   Asian.
       d.   Hispanic

Other Relatives, p. 553 (Figure 22.3)
Diff: E, Ans: c

46.   Over the past several generations, the size of the U.S. household has:
       a.   increased dramatically.
       b.   increased slightly.
       c.   decreased.
       d.   remained stable.

Other Relatives, p. 553
Diff: E, Ans: b

47.   People who live together in the same dwelling are considered a:
       a.   kin group.
       b.   household.
       c.   generation.
       d.   family.

Other Relatives, p. 553
Diff: M, Ans: c

48.   The shift away from the extended family in the United States:
       a.   probably will not continue.
       b.   has affected only minority families.
       c.   has not eliminated family closeness, contact, and cooperation.
       d.   is the cause of the rising divorce rate.

Other Relatives, p. 553
Diff: E, Ans: a

49.   In a typical family, the "kinkeeper" is most likely to be:
       a.   a middle-aged mother.
       b.   a young adult son.
       c.   a middle-aged father.
       d.   the first grandchild.

Other Relatives, p. 553
Diff: E, Ans: a

50.   The person who is most likely to become a kinkeeper is a:
       a.   daughter.
       b.   son.
       c.   daughter-in-law.
       d.   granddaughter.

Other Relatives, pp. 553-554
Diff: M, Ans: a

51.   Who is most likely to feel burdened with elder care?
    a.   a daughter-in-law
    b.   a daughter
    c.   a son
    d.   a son-in-law

Other Relatives, p. 554
Diff: E, Ans: d

52.   Typically, the relationship between middle-aged adults and their parents:
    a.   stays about the same.
    b.   improves for men but not for women.
    c.   worsens with age.
    d.   improves with age.

Other Relatives, p. 554
Diff: M, Ans: d

53.   As Mark and Anne reach middle age, they will probably become:
    a.   less tolerant of their parents' aging problems.
    b.   more likely to blame their parents.
    c.   better able to see their parents' mistakes.
    d.   more accepting of their parents' limitations.

Other Relatives, p. 554
Diff: M, Ans: b

54.   A factor that contributes to good relationships between today's middle-aged adults and their parents is:
    a.   the tendency of older people to live with their middle-aged children.
    b.   the health and economic freedom that allow older adults to be independent.
    c.   that the older generation is giving up the old traditions.
    d.   that the elderly fear they may be abandoned by their children.

Other Relatives, p. 554
Diff: M, Ans: b

55.   Three-generation households are most common among which of the following ethnic groups?
    a.   Native Americans
    b.   Asian Americans
    c.   African Americans
    d.   European Americans

Other Relatives, p. 554
Diff: E, Ans: a

56.   In middle age a person's attitude toward his or her parents usually becomes more:
    a.   appreciative.
    b.   private.
    c.   ambivalent.
    d.   critical.

Other Relatives, p. 554
Diff: E, Ans: b

57.   The belief that family members should be close and supportive of one another even if it means sacrificing individual freedom and success is referred to as:
    a.   an extended family.
    b.   familism.
    c.   a closely knit family.
    d.   kinship.

Other Relatives, p. 555
Diff: M, Ans: a
58.   Closeness in the relationships between siblings over the years from childhood through late adulthood can be conceived of as a(n):
a.   hourglass.
b.   pyramid.
c.   sphere.
d.   rectangle.

Other Relatives, pp. 555-556
Diff: H, Ans: b
59.   Which of the following is NOT a true statement about sibling relationships in middle adulthood?
a.   They are greatly influenced by family values instilled in childhood.
b.   They are rarely a source of support for middle-aged adults.
c.   They can be strained when one sibling takes care of the parents.
d.   They can become closer when a parent dies.

Other Relatives, p. 556
Diff: M, Ans: b
60.   Mothers and daughters who had a stormy relationship during the daughter's adolescence generally _____ after the daughter leaves home.
a.   continue to have a stormy relationship
b.   have a close and friendly relationship
c.   have relatively little contact
d.   have difficulty mending the relationship

Other Relatives, pp. 556-557
Diff: E, Ans: c
61.   A seven-nation survey of thousands of middle-aged adults found that 75 percent communicated with their adult children:
a.   once a year or less.
b.   about once a month.
c.   several times a week.
d.   on a daily basis.

Other Relatives, pp. 557-558
Diff: M, Ans: d
62.   When adult children live with their parents:
a.   parents become dependent on their children.
b.   children take over the major chores of running the house.
c.   both see it as a rewarding relationship.
d.   both feel the loss of privacy.

Other Relatives, pp. 557-558
Diff: H, Ans: a
63.   Tom is 27 years old and lives with his middle-aged parents, Art and Edith. Which of the following is LEAST likely to be true for Tom and his parents?
a.   Tom pays most of the bills and does most of the housework.
b.   Tom and his parents live in what some call a swollen nest.
c.   Art and Edith are in good health.
d.   Tom is a single parent.

Grandchildren, p. 558
Diff: E, Ans: b
64.   Between age 40 and 65, what proportion of adults become grandparents?
a.   one-third
b.   two-thirds
c.   one-half
d.   three-quarters

Grandchildren, p. 558
Diff: M, Ans: d
65.   The most common reason that adults fail to become grandparents is that:
a.   their children remain childless.
b.   their daughters do not marry.
c.   their sons marry women who already have children.
d.   they have no children.

Grandchildren, p. 558
Diff: E, Ans: c
66.   Which of the following increases the likelihood of close grandparent-grandchild bonds?
a.   older grandchildren
b.   older grandparents
c.   the parent being the first sibling to have children
d.   all of the above

Grandchildren, p. 558
Diff: E, Ans: a
67.   Grandparents who are emotionally distant but who are honored, respected, and obeyed by grandchildren are considered to have which of the following grandparenting style?
a.   remote
b.   involved
c.   surrogate
d.   companionate

Grandchildren, p. 558
Diff: M, Ans: c
68.   Mildred and Louis are respected and obeyed by their grandchildren. They would be described as
_____ grandparents.
a.   involved
b.   companionate
c.   remote
d.   surrogate

Grandchildren, p. 558
Diff: M, Ans: b
69.   In the United States a century ago, the typical grandparent was:
a.   involved.
b.   remote.
c.   companionate.
d.   traditional.

Grandchildren, p. 601
Diff: M, Ans: c
70.   Mrs. Smith lives in the same house as her grandchildren and cares for them every day. Her grandparenting is:
      a.   surrogate.
      b.   remote.
      c.   involved.
      d.   companionate.

Grandchildren, p. 558
Diff: H, Ans: d
71.   Earl and Lynn enjoy babysitting their grandchild when their other commitments and their busy lifestyle give them time for it. Their grandparenting style is:
      a.   involved.
      b.   distant.
      c.   remote.
      d.   companionate.

Grandchildren, p. 558
Diff: E, Ans: c
72.   Companionate grandparents are:
      a.   emotionally distant elders.
      b.   active in the day-to-day life of their grandchildren.
      c.   independent and autonomous.
      d.   least likely to be close to their adult children.

Grandchildren, p. 558
Diff: H, Ans: a
73.   Companionate grandparents are more common today in part because of:
      a.   employment of most middle-aged grandmothers.
      b.   increased respect for the older generation.
      c.   less travel as airfare increases.
      d.   the need for child-rearing advice.

Grandchildren, p. 559
Diff: M, Ans: d
74.   Most contemporary grandparents in the United States prefer which role?
      a.   involved
      b.   remote
      c.   traditional
      d.   companionate

Grandchildren, p. 559
Diff: M, Ans: b
75.   The style of grandparenting that generally brings the most satisfaction to middle-aged individuals in the United States is the _____ role.
      a.   involved
      b.   companionate
      c.   remote
      d.   traditional

Grandchildren, p. 559
Diff: M, Ans: a
76.   U.S. grandparents born in which country are most likely to have grandchildren living with them?
    a.   Mexico
    b.   Canada
    c.   United States
    d.   Japan

Grandchildren, pp. 559-560
Diff: H, Ans: c
77.   Which of the following is a true statement about immigrant grandparents?
    a.   They are less likely than grandparents of the majority ethnicity to provide child care.
    b.   They are most likely to be companionate grandparents.
    c.   Their involvement can have positive and negative consequences.
    d.   Their role is determined more for cultural reasons than for practical reasons.

Grandchildren, p. 560
Diff: M, Ans: a
78.   Many teenage grandchildren of immigrants:
    a.   no longer obey their grandparents.
    b.   hold their grandparents in high esteem.
    c.   take on their grandparents' values, beliefs, and customs.
    d.   feel their grandparents have a lot to learn from them.

Grandchildren, p. 560
Diff: M, Ans: b
79.   Mrs. Williams's grandchildren live with her because their parents are both drug addicts. She is now considered a(n):
    a.   involved grandparent.
    b.   surrogate parent.
    c.   remote grandparent.
    d.   companionate parent.

Grandchildren, p. 560
Diff: M, Ans: b
80.   If the government pays the grandparent to provide for grandchildren because the parents have been judged neglectful or abusive, that is called:
    a.   full-time grandparenting.
    b.   kinship care.
    c.   limited parenting.
    d.   substitute grandparenting.

Grandchildren, p. 561
Diff: M, Ans: c
81.   Since 1970, every state has enacted laws that require continuation of a close grandparent/grandchild relationship following a divorce if the:
    a.   child is under the age of 5.
    b.   child or the grandparent request it.
    c.   child has lived with the grandparent.
    d.   custodial parent requests it.

The Myth of the Sandwich Generation, p. 563
Diff: E, Ans: d
82.   Because they are called on to help both older and younger generations of the family, middle-aged adults have been called the:
    a.   midlife generation.
    b.   family caregivers.
    c.   divided group.
    d.   sandwich generation.

The Myth of the Sandwich Generation, pp. 562-563
Diff: H, Ans: a
83.   Which of the following is a true statement regarding the middle generation as the sandwich generation?
    a.   Providing assistance to older and younger generations may be more a function of personality than of necessity.
    b.   Most middle-aged adults feel tremendous pressure because of their role as kinkeeper.
    c.   In the United States, middle-aged couples tend to have more contact with the husband's parents than with the wife's parents.
    d.   All of the above are true statements.

Work in Middle Adulthood

Overall Trends, p. 564
Diff: M, Ans: d
84.   During middle adulthood:
    a.   most adults seek a new job.
    b.   work attendance begins to lag.
    c.   job security increases.
    d.   many adults serve as mentors.

Balancing Work and Family, p. 565
Diff: M, Ans: b
85.   Men tend to rate being which of the following as the *least* important?
    a.   a loyal friend
    b.   a good worker
    c.   a loving spouse
    d.   a good parent

Balancing Work and Family, p. 566
Diff: E, Ans: a
86.   In an effort to balance work with family life, Kate and Henry have decided that they will only accept jobs that do not require weekend work or travel. They are adopting a strategy of:
    a.   scaling back.
    b.   accepting failure.
    c.   leveling off.
    d.   a child-centered family.

Retirement, p. 568
Diff: H, Ans: b
87.   Which of the following is a true statement about retirement in the United States?
    a.   Most retirees are pushed out by their employers or their failing health.
    b.   Many people underestimate the amount of savings they need for retirement because they misunderstand the average life span statistic.
    c.   Adults are retiring at older and older ages.
    d.   Retirees tend to be wealthier and healthier than their employed age-mates.

Retirement, p. 569 (Figure 22.6)
Diff: H, Ans: a
88.   The country with the smallest percentage of adults aged 55 to 64 who work full time is:
   a.   France.
   b.   The United States.
   c.   Germany.
   d.   Sweden.

TRUE-FALSE QUESTIONS

Middle Adulthood: Psychosocial Development

Ans: T, p. 543
1.   Few developmentalists today believe that the changes of middle age produce a midlife crisis.

Ans: F, p. 543
2.   Middle-aged women always feel burdened if they are simultaneously an employee, wife, mother of a child still in school, and daughter of a parent who needs assistance.

Personality Throughout Adulthood

Ans: F, p. 544
3.   The "Big Five" refers to the five years following the fortieth birthday.

Ans: F, p. 545
4.   Whether an individual ranks high or low in each of the Big Five personality traits depends solely on heredity.

Ans: T, p. 545
5.   A person who is anxious and depressed in young adulthood is likely to show the same traits in middle adulthood.

Ans: T, p. 545
6.   Changes in an individual's circumstances may lead to changes in personality.

Ans: F, p. 545 (Figure 22.1)
7.   Developmental changes in personality traits are quite different across different cultures.

Ans: T, p. 545
8.   When asked if their personalities had changed since young adulthood, middle-aged adults tend to say that it has changed, for the better.

Ans: T, p. 544
9.   In general, adults become a little less neurotic and open and a little more agreeable and conscientious with age.

Ans: T, p. 546
10.   Generativity tends to increase during middle adulthood.

Ans: F, p. 546
11.   In most cultures, gender-role demands become more rigid at midlife.

Ans: F, p. 547
12.   Gender convergence can change individuals' core personality.

Ans: F, p. 547

13.   Carl Jung believed that everyone has a masculine, feminine, and androgynous side.

Ans: T, p. 547

14.   The current cohort of adults has experienced less sharply-defined male and female roles than have previous generations.

Ans: F, p. 548

15.   For most people, a single biological event marks the transition from early to middle adulthood.

Ans: F, p. 548

16.   How people react to changes in middle adulthood is directly tied to calendar milestones.

Family Relationships in Midlife

Ans: T, p. 549

17.   The family is our most important individual support system.

Ans: F, p. 549

18.   In some cultures, families have been replaced by other social groups.

Ans: T, p. 549

19.   Fictive kin are particularly likely in African and African-American families.

Ans: F, p. 549

20.   A social convoy usually includes between three and five generations of family members.

Ans: F, p. 550

21.   The majority of middle-aged adults experience role overload.

Ans: T, p. 550

22.   People who stay married because the time is not right for divorce are generally simply postponing the inevitable.

Ans: T, p. 551

23.   Research on marital satisfaction in long-term marriages is based on selective samples since the unhappiest marriages have already ended.

Ans: F, p. 551

24.   Marriages of today are not as happy as marriages of previous generations.

Ans: T, p. 552

25.   Unmarried middle-aged woman are at a particular disadvantage regarding the chances of finding a marriage partner.

Ans: T, p. 551

26.   Divorce weakens a variety of family bonds beyond simply that of the husband-wife relationship.

Ans: T, p. 551

27.   After remarriage, men typically become happier and more sociable.

Ans: F, p. 552

28.   Remarriages are less likely to end in divorce than first marriages.

Ans: T, p. 553 (Figure 22.3)

29.   The number of people living alone or with only one other person has increased over the past 60 years.

Ans: F, p. 553

30.   Family ties have weakened over the past century.

Ans: F, p. 553

31.   In every nation that has been studied, relatives tend to have less closeness with other family members when they live far from each other.

Ans: T, p. 554

32.   The relationship between middle-aged adults and their parents tends to improve with time.

Ans: F, p. 554

33.   A strong marital relationship between elderly parents tends to disrupt the relationship between the parents and the middle-aged children.

Ans: T, p. 555

34.   Siblings who were not close in young adulthood may become confidants as late adulthood progresses.

Ans: T, p. 555

35.   During midlife, childhood sibling rivalries can reemerge.

Ans: F, pp. 556-557

36.   Most middle-aged adults rarely speak with their adult children.

Ans: F, p. 557

37.   Most middle-aged adults are dependent on their adult children for financial support.

Ans: T, p. 557

38.   Financial help and support services flow more freely from middle-aged parents to young adults than in the other direction.

Ans: T, p. 558

39.   In North America, neither parents nor adult children tend to be happy living in a swollen nest.

Ans: T, p. 558

40.   Grandparents tend to be closer to younger grandchildren than to adolescent ones.

Ans: F, p. 558

41.   Companionate grandparents tend to assume a large part of the child care of their grandchildren.

Ans: T, p. 559

42.   The role of immigrant grandparents may be determined to a large extent by practical considerations rather than simply cultural reasons.

Ans: T, p. 560

43.   About 20 percent of all grandparents in the United States spend at least some time providing a major portion of the care of at least one grandchild.

Ans: T, p. 562

44.   Because of their place in the generational structure, the middle-aged tend to be expected to help both older and younger generations of their family.

Work in Middle Adulthood

Ans: F, p. 564

45.   In general, most jobs are more a source of stress than of joy for middle-aged adults.

Ans: F, p. 564

46.   Employees in their early 50s are more likely to seek a new job than are employees in their early 30s.

Ans: T, p. 565

47.   Both men and women rate being a good parent and a loving spouse as more important than being a good worker.

Ans: T, p. 565

48.   The hours expected of employees by today's employers can contribute to "workaholism."

Ans: F, pp. 566-567

49.   Income is of less a concern for middle-aged adults than for younger adults, because their closeness to retirement means the beginning of Social Security payments.

Ans: T, p. 568

50.   Forced retirement is illegal in most jobs and in most countries.

FILL-IN-THE-BLANK QUESTIONS

Middle Adulthood: Psychosocial Development

Ans: generative, p. 543

1.   Often, the responsibilities of middle adulthood make adults _____ rather than stagnant.

Personality Throughout Adulthood

Ans: neuroticism, p. 544

2.   People who are anxious and moody are high in the personality dimension of _____.

Ans: extroversion, p. 544

3.   The personality dimension that is characterized by a tendency to be active, outgoing, and assertive is _____.

Ans: ecological, p. 544

4.   A particular lifestyle and social context that evoke and reinforce a person's personality needs and interests is a(n) _____ niche.

Ans: extroversion, p. 545

5.   Of the Big Five, the only trait that stays relatively stable from young adulthood to middle adulthood is _____.

Ans: convergence; crossover, p. 546

6.   A gender _____ occurs when males and females become more similar with age. A gender _____ would occur if the sexes switched roles and traits.

Ans: hormone, p. 546

7.   The greater passivity displayed by men and aggression displayed by women in middle age can be explained biologically by changes in _____ levels.

Ans: shadow side, p. 547
8.   Jung believed that middle-aged adults of both sexes explore their _____.

Ans: midlife crisis, p. 548
9.   The radical reexamination and sudden transformation that is widely believed to occur at age 40 is termed the _____.

Family Relationships in Midlife

Ans: convoy, p. 549
10.   Family members of the same generation who provide guidance and socialization to one another as they go through life are part of a social _____.

Ans: rise, p. 550
11.   The general trend in marriage is happiness at first, then a dip for a decade or so, then a gradual _____ over the years of middle adulthood.

Ans: five, p. 551
12.   On average, divorced men remarry within _____ years of being divorced.

Ans: more; more, p. 552
13.   The more times an individual has been married, the _____ likely it is that the current marriage will end in divorce and the _____ likely it is that the children will suffer academically and socially.

Ans: kinkeeper, p. 553
14.   A middle-aged woman who brings her adult children and their young children, as well as her mother, to her home for weekly family dinners is serving as a(n) _____.

Ans: kinkeeper; woman, p. 553
15.   In a family, the person who gathers the family together, and keeps in touch with relatives serves as a(n) _____; this person is most often a middle-aged _____.

Ans: familism, p. 554
16.   Ways are found to avoid living in a multi-generational household while still providing support when _____ is weak.

Ans: swollen, pp. 557-558
17.   A(n) _____ nest is a household in which an adult child lives with his or her parents.

Ans: Involved, p. 558
18.   _____ grandparents live in or near the grandchildren's household and see them daily.

Ans: companionate, p. 558
19.   Grandparents who maintain independence and autonomy and strive for love and friendship with their grandchildren have taken the _____ role of grandparent.

Ans: immigrant (or minority), p. 560
20.   Becoming an uninvolved grandparent with little generational continuity is especially unlikely for elders in _____ families.

Ans: surrogate, p. 560
21.   Grandparents who are the primary caregivers for their grandchildren are called _____ parents.

Ans: sandwich, p. 562
22.   Because they care for both older and younger generations, the middle-aged have been called the _____ generation.

Work in Middle Adulthood

Ans: mentor, p. 564
23.   Employees who achieve a certain status and expertise on the job are in a position to act as a _____ to an inexperienced employee.

Ans: scaling back, p. 566
24.   Deliberately putting less than full effort into employment is called _____.

Ans: less; more, p. 566
25.   When one person in a marriage designates their employment as a job to earn money, the other person is free to take on a career that pays _____ and is _____ fulfilling.

ESSAY QUESTIONS

1.   Do you believe in gender convergence? Think about middle-aged adults you have known for a long time, and use examples of them to support your position.

2.   For each of the personality traits of the Big Five, describe a person you know who has a high level of the trait. Describe specific behaviors the person exhibits that lead you to the belief that he or she has a high degree of the trait.

3.   A large corporation announces that it will be holding a workshop called "Caring for Your Older Parents: What Resources Are Available?" Why do you think corporations are beginning to be concerned with this issue? Which employees are most likely to attend the workshop?

4.   In recent years more young women with young dependent children are in the work force, and more men are involved in child care. What do you think the effects of these developments will be on these people as they reach middle age?

5.   Describe two things that could lead to personality change in adulthood. Explain your answers, showing how this would happen and how common it is.

6.   Describe two myths you learned about in this chapter, and provide evidence for the flawed nature of each.

7.   Evelyn and Barney are newly married. Barney is concerned about what their marriage will be like in middle adulthood. What are three things you could tell him about the marriages of middle-aged adults?

Answer guidelines to these essay questions can be found in the Appendix at the end of the Test Bank.

CHAPTER 23

Late Adulthood:
Biosocial Development

MULTIPLE-CHOICE QUESTIONS

Prejudice and Predictions

Prejudice and Predictions, p. 576
Diff: E, Ans: d

1. People of which of the following ages do NOT have prejudices about late adulthood?
    a. young adults
    b. middle-aged adults
    c. older adults
    d. none of the above

Ageism, p. 577
Diff: E, Ans: b

2. The term "ageism" refers to:
    a. the veneration of the elderly.
    b. judging people on the basis of chronological age.
    c. the view of society held by older people.
    d. the demographics of the population pyramid.

Ageism, p. 577
Diff: H, Ans: d

3. Which of the following is NOT an example of ageism?
    a. Neighbors of an elderly person assume he does not want to come to a neighborhood meeting.
    b. A restaurant has a policy that elderly individuals are not allowed to work in the kitchen.
    c. A city has a curfew for teenagers.
    d. All of the above *are* examples of ageism.

Ageism, p. 577
Diff: E, Ans: a

4. The multidisciplinary, scientific study of old age is called:
    a. gerontology.
    b. psychology.
    c. demography.
    d. geography.

Ageism, p. 577
Diff: E, Ans: b

5. Geriatrics refers to the:
    a. study of population numbers.
    b. medical specialty devoted to old age.
    c. study of prejudices.
    d. multidisciplinary, scientific study of old age.

Ageism, p. 577
Diff: M, Ans: b
6.   Which of the following is a true statement about gerontology and geriatrics?
      a.   They tend to view old age from similar perspectives.
      b.   Geriatrics, but not gerontology, is a medical specialty.
      c.   Gerontologists generally view aging as a necessary ill.
      d.   Geriatrics leads to the view of aging as a socially constructed problem.

Ageism, p. 578
Diff: E, Ans: c
7.   The study of population numbers is called:
      a.   gerontology.
      b.   psychology.
      c.   demography.
      d.   geography.

Ageism, p. 578
Diff: M, Ans: b
8.   What is the relationship between recent changes in demography and ageism?
      a.   Changes in demography have increased ageism.
      b.   Changes in demography have decreased ageism.
      c.   Changes in ageism have increased the importance of demography.
      d.   Changes in ageism have decreased the importance of demography.

Ageism, pp. 578-579
Diff: M, Ans: b
9.   When our present population is sorted according to age, the resulting graph is approaching a demographic:
      a.   pyramid.
      b.   square.
      c.   circle.
      d.   oval.

Ageism, p. 578
Diff: E, Ans: b
10.   What percent of the United States population is over age 65?
      a.   2
      b.   13
      c.   29
      d.   42

Ageism, p. 578
Diff: M, Ans: d
11.   The fastest-growing group in the population of the United States is those:
      a.   20-35.
      b.   35-65.
      c.   65-85.
      d.   over 100.

Ageism, p. 579
Diff: M, Ans: a
12.   Which nation has the lowest percentage of its population over age 65?
      a.   Syria
      b.   Spain
      c.   France
      d.   Japan

Dependents and Independence, p. 579
Diff: M, Ans: b
13.   A dependency ratio is calculated by comparing the number of _____ with the number of _____.
   a.   children; adults
   b.   dependents; self-supporting individuals
   c.   children; elderly
   d.   middle-aged adults; elderly

Dependents and Independence, p. 579
Diff: H, Ans: b
14.   The current dependency ratio is better than it has been for a century because:
   a.   nursing homes provide for the care of many elderly.
   b.   of the small size of the Depression-era cohort.
   c.   of the increasing birth rate since 1985.
   d.   many more elderly are putting off retirement to later ages.

Dependents and Independence, p. 580
Diff: E, Ans: d
15.   About one in _____ older adults in the United States is living in a hospital or nursing home.
   a.   three
   b.   five
   c.   ten
   d.   twenty

Dependents and Independence, p. 580
Diff: M, Ans: c
16.   In developed nations, which is the most common living arrangement for people over age 65?
   a.   living alone
   b.   living with adult children
   c.   living with a spouse
   d.   living with an unrelated age-mate

Dependents and Independence, pp. 580-581
Diff: H, Ans: a
17.   The main reason we may not notice the young-old is:
   a.   they do not fit our stereotypes of the elderly.
   b.   there are relatively few of them.
   c.   they are a problem-prone minority.
   d.   they are not integrated into the community.

Dependents and Independence, p. 581
Diff: M, Ans: c
18.   The term "successful aging" can be used to describe the:
   a.   middle-aged only.
   b.   optimal aging only.
   c.   optimal aging and usual aging only.
   d.   optimal aging, usual aging, and inspired aging.

Anti-Aging Measures, p. 581
Diff: M, Ans: a
19.   College students are *least* likely to stereotype people described as which of the following?
   a.   aged 70-85
   b.   old
   c.   elderly
   d.   oldest-old

Anti-Aging Measures, p. 581
Diff: M, Ans: a
20.   The chief reason the elderly have difficulty in getting enough nutrients is the:
        a.   reduced efficiency of the digestive system.
        b.   effects of arthritis.
        c.   use of vitamin supplements.
        d.   large number of calories they must consume.

Anti-Aging Measures, p. 581
Diff: M, Ans: b
21.   As people age, vitamin and mineral needs may increase because:
        a.   aging bodies use up the vitamins stored during younger years.
        b.   the body's ability to use nutrients is reduced.
        c.   breathing and heart rates increase, requiring more food.
        d.   food preferences change.

Anti-Aging Measures, p. 581
Diff: H, Ans: c
22.   Taking aspirin regularly, as many of the elderly do, increases the need for:
        a.   laxatives.
        b.   calcium.
        c.   vitamin C.
        d.   protein.

Anti-Aging Measures, pp. 581-582
Diff: H, Ans: b
23.   Which of the following is a true statement about calorie restriction?
        a.   Calorie restriction for humans is a practical solution to the problem of aging.
        b.   Daily caloric requirements decrease with age.
        c.   Mammals that eat a restricted number of calories tend to die younger.
        d.   The need for vitamins and minerals decreases with age.

Anti-Aging Measures, pp. 581-582
Diff: M, Ans: c
24.   An elderly person who begins taking large doses of vitamins:
        a.   will live longer.
        b.   need not worry about diet.
        c.   may upset natural nutritional balance.
        d.   can prevent cancer.

Anti-Aging Measures, p. 582
Diff: M, Ans: a
25.   The advice a doctor is most likely to give to an elderly patient is to:
        a.   consume a healthy diet.
        b.   take large doses of multivitamins.
        c.   eat anything you choose in any quantity you choose.
        d.   take vitamins E and C to slow the aging process.

Primary Aging in Late Adulthood

Primary Aging in Late Adulthood, p. 583
Diff: E, Ans: b
26.   The irreversible changes that naturally occur with time are called _____ aging.
   a.   normal
   b.   primary
   c.   secondary
   d.   geriatric

Primary Aging in Late Adulthood, p. 583
Diff: M, Ans: d
27.   The changes of primary aging are:
   a.   caused by disease.
   b.   reversible.
   c.   preventable.
   d.   universal.

Changes in Appearance, p. 583
Diff: M, Ans: d
28.   Will is 75 years old. He will probably:
   a.   feel as old as he looks.
   b.   be surprised at how young he still looks.
   c.   adjust quite easily to his aging.
   d.   be surprised at his aged appearance.

Changes in Appearance, p. 583
Diff: H, Ans: c
29.   Which of the following correlates most closely with chronological age?
   a.   blood pressure
   b.   skin changes
   c.   loss of hair pigment
   d.   hearing acuity

Changes in Appearance, p. 584
Diff: E, Ans: c
30.   In late adulthood, body fat is most likely to collect in the:
   a.   arms.
   b.   legs.
   c.   abdomen.
   d.   upper face.

Changes in Appearance, pp. 584-585
Diff: H, Ans: b
31.   Which of the following is a true statement about the muscles of older individuals?
   a.   A decrease in fat and an increase in muscle can cause weight loss.
   b.   Muscle loss around the vertebrate can cause lethal falls.
   c.   Although muscle strength decreases, muscle flexibility remains stable.
   d.   Muscle cannot be regained, even through strength training.

Dulling of the Senses, p. 585
Diff: E, Ans: d

32. Which senses become less sharp in late adulthood?
    a. smell and taste
    b. hearing and vision
    c. touch and smell
    d. all of the above

Dulling of the Senses, p. 585
Diff: M, Ans: d

33. Research in sensory functions in later adulthood indicates that:
    a. about 50 percent of adults have uncorrectable visual impairment.
    b. hearing remains virtually unchanged.
    c. hearing loss hampers one-word functioning.
    d. most visual and auditory losses can be compensated for.

Dulling of the Senses, p. 585
Diff: E, Ans: c

34. A thickening of the lens of the eye, causing vision to become cloudy, opaque, and distorted, is called:
    a. glaucoma.
    b. dry eye syndrome.
    c. cataracts.
    d. senile macular degeneration.

Dulling of the Senses, p. 585
Diff: M, Ans: d

35. Beatrice has vision problems due to a build-up of fluid within her eyes. She is suffering from:
    a. cataracts.
    b. nearsightedness.
    c. astigmatism.
    d. glaucoma.

Dulling of the Senses, p. 586
Diff: M, Ans: b

36. Which vision disorder is most difficult to treat?
    a. cataracts
    b. senile macular degeneration
    c. glaucoma
    d. senile farsightedness

Dulling of the Senses, p. 586
Diff: H, Ans: a

37. Sam is 70 years of age. He will probably:
    a. resist getting a hearing aid when he needs one.
    b. refuse to wear glasses, especially bifocals.
    c. be eager to get a hearing aid when his hearing begins to fail.
    d. view vision problems as more serious than hearing losses.

Dulling of the Senses, p. 586
Diff: M, Ans: c

38. Elderly people who are hard of hearing:
    a. are likely to get a hearing aid.
    b. compensate with extra social give-and-take.
    c. are often excluded from social give-and-take.
    d. suffer less from their impairment than those with poor vision.

Dulling of the Senses, p. 587
Diff: M, Ans: c

39.   Which of the following is crucial when older people have sensory loss?
   a.   acceptance
   b.   reduction in time spent out of the home
   c.   compensation
   d.   greater dependency

Dulling of the Senses, p. 588 (Figure 23.2)
Diff: E, Ans: d

40.   The age group *least* likely to be victimized by crime is aged:
   a.   20-24.
   b.   35-49.
   c.   50-64.
   d.   65 and older.

Dulling of the Senses, p. 588 (Figure 23.3)
Diff: M, Ans: d

41.   The age group *least* likely to be involved in motor vehicle accidents is aged:
   a.   25-34.
   b.   35-44.
   c.   45-54.
   d.   55-64.

Dulling of the Senses, p. 588
Diff: H, Ans: c

42.   Those speaking to the elderly need to:
   a.   speak in a higher register.
   b.   speak more rapidly and distinctly.
   c.   increase the logical pauses.
   d.   stretch out the words.

Major Body Systems, p. 589
Diff: E, Ans: a

43.   Primary and secondary aging combine to make major body systems:
   a.   slower.
   b.   more flexible.
   c.   more efficient.
   d.   function better under stress.

Major Body Systems, p. 589
Diff: E, Ans: a

44.   Which of the following describes the relationship of age and chronic disease?
   a.   Chronic disease increases with age.
   b.   Chronic disease decreases with age.
   c.   There is no relationship between chronic disease and age.
   d.   Chronic disease increases with age in men, but decreases with age in women.

Major Body Systems, p. 590
Diff: H, Ans: b

45.   Aging and disease are related in that the elderly:
   a.   never recover from their illnesses.
   b.   are more likely to die of a particular disease.
   c.   all suffer from several diseases.
   d.   are less susceptible to disease.

Major Body Systems, p. 590
Diff: E, Ans: d

46. Which type of cancer is in evidence in virtually every man who dies at age 80 or older, even when it is not the cause of death?
     a. lung
     b. skin
     c. liver
     d. prostate

Major Body Systems, p. 590
Diff: H, Ans: b

47. The reason for less aggressive treatments for cancer in older adults than in middle-aged adults is that older adults:
     a. are going to die soon anyway.
     b. have slower advances in disease.
     c. are more resistant to change.
     d. have diseases that respond less well to treatment.

Major Body Systems, p. 591
Diff: E, Ans: c

48. Compared to younger adults, older adults generally:
     a. spend more time in deep sleep.
     b. feel less drowsy in the daytime.
     c. take longer to fall asleep.
     d. spend less time in bed.

Major Body Systems, p. 591
Diff: M, Ans: d

49. Which of the following is the best treatment for insomnia in older adults?
     a. electrical stimulation of the brain
     b. narcotic drugs
     c. self-administration of alcohol
     d. accepting changes as normal

Major Body Systems, p. 591
Diff: E, Ans: a

50. Limiting the time a person spends being ill or infirm is referred to as:
     a. compression of morbidity.
     b. progeria.
     c. dependency ratio.
     d. senescence.

Theories of Aging

Wear and Tear, p. 593
Diff: E, Ans: a

51. The wear-and-tear theory of aging suggests that we:
     a. wear out our bodies by living our lives.
     b. are healthier if we remain active.
     c. can live to be over 100 if we take care of ourselves.
     d. must "use it or lose it."

Wear and Tear, p. 593
Diff: M, Ans: c
52.   The wear-and-tear theory of aging is weakened by the fact that:
        a.   the human body cannot repair itself.
        b.   many parts of the body wear out from use.
        c.   the human body is able to repair damaged areas.
        d.   machines cannot grow old.

Wear and Tear, pp. 593-594
Diff: H, Ans: b
53.   The wear-and-tear theory seems to be contradicted by the fact that:
        a.   repeated stress can damage joints.
        b.   the respiratory system benefits from exertion.
        c.   exposure to pollution is cumulative.
        d.   inadequate nutrition can cause problems in later life.

Genetic Aging, p. 594
Diff: E, Ans: d
54.   Maximum life span is defined as the:
        a.   number of years a newborn is likely to live.
        b.   risk of mortality.
        c.   average age at death.
        d.   upper limit to which members of a species can live.

Genetic Aging, p. 594
Diff: E, Ans: b
55.   The number of years an average newborn of a given species lives is the:
        a.   maximum life span.
        b.   average life expectancy.
        c.   species life expectancy.
        d.   minimum life span.

Genetic Aging, p. 595
Diff: M, Ans: a
56.   An important reason that average life expectancy over the past century has risen is that:
        a.   infant and child mortality rates have been reduced.
        b.   medical advances have extended the lives of the old.
        c.   people are marrying later in life.
        d.   couples are having fewer children.

Genetic Aging, p. 595
Diff: H, Ans: c
57.   Epigenetic theory tries to explain why:
        a.   many people die in middle adulthood.
        b.   evolution selected for people who lived to close to the maximum age expectancy.
        c.   many diseases that affect older adults have endured evolutionary change.
        d.   body parts wear out after years of use.

Genetic Aging, p. 595
Diff: M, Ans: b
58.   The theory that provides an explanation for aging that focuses on the importance of the reproduction of
        our species is:
        a.   the genetic clock theory.
        b.   the epigenetic theory.
        c.   the wear-and-tear theory.
        d.   cellular accidents theory.

Cellular Aging, p. 596
Diff: E, Ans: b

59.   The term "free radicals" refers to:
       a.   the idea that surgery can free the body of tumors.
       b.   electrons that are unattached to their nuclei.
       c.   the minority of the elderly who rebel against ageism.
       d.   cancer cells.

Cellular Aging, p. 596
Diff: H, Ans: c

60.   Which of the following is a true statement about free radicals?
       a.   Their association with the aging process is a myth.
       b.   Antioxidants have little effect on the damage that can be caused by free radicals.
       c.   Oxygen free radicals scramble DNA and produce errors in cell maintenance.
       d.   All of the above are true.

Cellular Aging, p. 596
Diff: E, Ans: d

61.   Vitamins A, C, and E are all:
       a.   free radicals.
       b.   oxygen by-products.
       c.   carcinogens.
       d.   antioxidants.

Cellular Aging, p. 596
Diff: E, Ans: b

62.   Antioxidants can be found in:
       a.   dairy products.
       b.   vitamins A, C, and E.
       c.   sea salt.
       d.   oil-based laxatives.

Cellular Aging, p. 597
Diff: M, Ans: c

63.   The concept of aging as a result of cellular duplication errors is based on the fact that the body's ability
       to make new cells that are exact copies of the original ones:
       a.   stops at about age 18.
       b.   stops at about age 80.
       c.   is altered by mutations as time goes on.
       d.   continues unchanged throughout life.

Cellular Aging, p. 597
Diff: H, Ans: b

64.   Which of the following is a true statement about cellular aging?
       a.   Cells can replicate indefinitely, but errors do occur.
       b.   Aging may be caused by the inevitable loss of the ability of cells to duplicate perfectly.
       c.   Damage is caused by free radicals that slow down the cell duplication process.
       d.   Cells from adults are able to duplicate more quickly and more times than are cells from embryos.

Cellular Aging, p. 597
Diff: M, Ans: c

65.   The theory that DNA regulates the aging process is called the:
       a.   cellular-accident theory.
       b.   error-catastrophe theory.
       c.   genetic-clock theory.
       d.   free-radical theory.

Cellular Aging, p. 597
Diff: H, Ans: d
66. Support for the theory that genes regulate aging is found in the:
 a.   number of people born with Down syndrome.
 b.   incidence of genetic diseases.
 c.   death rate from Down syndrome.
 d.   premature aging in Down syndrome individuals.

Cellular Aging, p. 597
Diff: M, Ans: a
67. When human cells are grown under laboratory conditions that encourage them to grow and divide, cells:
 a.   from human embryos stop dividing after about 50 divisions.
 b.   from children divide more quickly than those of adults.
 c.   lose their DNA.
 d.   continue to reproduce themselves forever.

Cellular Aging, p. 597
Diff: E, Ans: a
68. The Hayflick limit is a natural limit to the:
 a.   number of times cells can divide.
 b.   size of the population on earth.
 c.   number of children born to one set of parents.
 d.   life span of a victim of genetic disease.

Cellular Aging, p. 597
Diff: E, Ans: a
69. In the body's immune system, the attack cells, called B cells, are manufactured in the:
 a.   bone marrow.
 b.   thymus.
 c.   red blood cells.
 d.   white blood cells.

Cellular Aging, p. 597
Diff: M, Ans: c
70. B-cells defend the body against invaders by:
 a.   invading the bone marrow.
 b.   attacking cancer cells.
 c.   producing antibodies against bacteria and viruses.
 d.   making the circulatory system more efficient.

Cellular Aging, p. 598
Diff: M, Ans: c
71. Many illnesses are more likely to be fatal to the elderly because:
 a.   they are exposed to more risks.
 b.   they are less likely to take their medication.
 c.   their immune systems are less efficient.
 d.   their antibodies have been used up.

Cellular Aging, p. 598
Diff: H, Ans: b

72.   Which statement about the immune system is correct?
   a.   Males tend to have a stronger immune system than females.
   b.   The weakened cells of the older immune system may be the cause of aging.
   c.   The vulnerability of AIDS patients to diseases that are normally reserved for young children is evidence of the relation between a weakened immune system and aging.
   d.   The immune system gets stronger throughout life as people are exposed to more types of invaders.

Cellular Aging, p. 598
Diff: H, Ans: c

73.   The Smiths are an 80-year-old couple. Mrs. Smith:
   a.   is more likely to have a hearing problem.
   b.   probably goes to the doctor less often.
   c.   is more likely to suffer from rheumatoid arthritis.
   d.   is less likely to experience hemorrhoids and varicose veins.

Cellular Aging, p. 599
Diff: E, Ans: d

74.   In which of the following do people seem *least* interested?
   a.   preventing disease
   b.   treating disease
   c.   adding to the quality of life
   d.   postponing mortality

The Centenarians

The Centenarians, p. 600
Diff: E, Ans: a

75.   People who live to see their 100th birthday are referred to as:
   a.   centenarians.
   b.   centurians.
   c.   decadecadians.
   d.   the oldest-old.

Other Places, Other Stories, pp. 600-601
Diff: M, Ans: a

76.   The groups of people who, traditionally, live to advanced age usually:
   a.   work throughout life.
   b.   live in communities that provide superior medical care.
   c.   eat a very high-protein diet.
   d.   drink alcohol daily.

Other Places, Other Stories, p. 601
Diff: M, Ans: b

77.   A cultural factor that may increase longevity is:
   a.   polygamy.
   b.   being integrated into the community.
   c.   believing in life after death.
   d.   being segregated from the noise and activity of children.

Other Places, Other Stories, p. 601
Diff: M, Ans: d
78.   Parts of the Republic of Georgia, Pakistan, and Peru all have large numbers of people who enjoy
      unusual longevity. Which of the following do they also have in common?
      a.   a primarily urban civilization
      b.   large regions at or below sea level
      c.   high amounts of animal protein in diets
      d.   high respect for the aged

Other Places, Other Stories, p. 601
Diff: E, Ans: c
79.   A recent discovery about the long-lived residents of isolated areas in Russia, Pakistan, and Peru shows
      they:
      a.   have no children.
      b.   have different genetic clocks.
      c.   may be lying about their age.
      d.   have no maximum life span.

The Truth About Life After 100, p. 601
Diff: M, Ans: c
80.   Mrs. Calderi is 70 years old and, as a typical person in late adulthood, she:
      a.   is in the best of health with only minor aches and pains.
      b.   feels deserted by everyone and lonely most of the time.
      c.   is more satisfied with her life than are many young adults.
      d.   finds her daily activities to be severely limited.

The Truth About Life After 100, pp. 601-602
Diff: M, Ans: d
81.   For people who reach late adulthood in good health, the most important determinant of longevity may
      be:
      a.   medical care.
      b.   the climate in which they live.
      c.   the calorie content of their diet.
      d.   their activities and attitudes.

TRUE-FALSE QUESTIONS

Prejudice and Predictions

Ans: F, p. 577
1.   Ageism refers to prejudice against the elderly.

Ans: T, p. 577
2.   Ageism results in social isolation of older adults.

Ans: F, p. 577
3.   More and more people assume aging means disease and fragility.

Ans: T, p. 577
4.   The perspective on aging is different for specialists in gerontology and for specialists in geriatrics.

Ans: F, p. 577
5.   Professionals in gerontology contribute to strengthening of feelings of ageism.

Ans: T, p. 578
6.   Individuals over 100 constitute the fastest growing age group worldwide.

Ans: T, p. 579
7.   The poorest developing nations have a dependency ratio of approximately 1:1, while industrialized nations have a dependency ratio of approximately 1:2.

Ans: F, p. 580
8.   About one in three older adults in the United States is in a nursing home.

Ans: F, p. 581
9.   The ageist stereotype is based primarily on the old-old.

Primary Aging in Late Adulthood

Ans: F, p. 583
10.   Decreased testosterone levels are associated with baldness.

Ans: F, p. 584
11.   Weight loss in older people, similar to weight loss in younger people, is usually beneficial.

Ans: T, p. 585
12.   Weight training should be part of an elderly person's exercise program.

Ans: T, p. 585
13.   Without compensation for the loss of sharpness in their senses, social distancing of the elderly is inevitable.

Ans: T, p. 585
14.   At age 90, the average man is almost deaf.

Ans: F, p. 585
15.   About 50 percent of the elderly see well.

Ans: T, p. 586
16.   Senile macular degeneration can be compensated for by a computer that scans printed text and speaks the words.

Ans: F, p. 586
17.   Those with poor vision suffer more from their impairment than those who are hard of hearing.

Ans: T, p. 587
18.   Sensory loss can lead to depression in the elderly.

Ans: F, p. 587
19.   Even with technology and specialist care, most elderly individuals who have sensory loss function poorly.

Ans: F, p. 588
20.   The high rate of automobile accidents among older people is clear evidence that they do not recognize the sensory losses associated with aging.

Ans: F, p. 588
21.   Elderspeak is necessary to enable older people to comprehend speech.

Ans: T, pp. 589-590

22.   Older adults' difficulty in recovering from disease is the reason for the medical recommendation of flu shots for people over the age of 65.

Ans: T, p. 590

23.   Diseases progress more slowly in older adults than in younger people.

Ans: F, p. 590

24.   Prostate cancer causes death in virtually every man who dies at age 80 or older.

Ans: F, p. 591

25.   Prescribing narcotic drugs to aid sleep in the elderly is particularly beneficial.

Ans: F, pp. 591-592

26.   Identical twins who have the same genetic propensity for disease and who die at the same age always have the same compression of morbidity, even when they have different lifestyles.

Theories of Aging

Ans: F, p. 593

27.   The wear-and-tear theory proposes that we age because new cells are imperfect copies of old ones.

Ans: T, p. 593

28.   The fact that people in hospitals get sicker if they do not move is contrary to the wear-and-tear theory.

Ans: T, p. 595

29.   The maximum life span a millennium ago was probably the same as it is today.

Ans: T, p. 595

30.   Epigenetic theory tries to explain why people are more likely to die of genetic diseases in childhood and in later adulthood than during adolescence and young adulthood.

Ans: F, p. 596

31.   According to the wear-and-tear theory, normal cell duplication eventually allows aging, because minor mistakes accumulate.

Ans: T, p. 596

32.   Free radicals are capable of reacting violently with other molecules, sometimes tearing them apart.

Ans: T, p. 596

33.   There is evidence that consuming foods high in antioxidants reduces the number of free radicals in the body, thus slowing disease.

Ans: T, p. 596

34.   Errors in cell duplication are one part of the explanation for primary aging.

Ans: F, p. 597

35.   The existence of the Hayflick limit disproves the theory of the genetic clock.

Ans: T, p. 597

36.   According to one theory of aging, the genetic clock gradually switches off the genes that promote growth and switches on genes that promote aging.

Ans: F, p. 597

37.   Diseases such as progeria and Down Syndrome provide evidence against the theory that genes regulate aging.

Ans: F, p. 598

38.   Age does not weaken the effectiveness of T cells and B cells in defending the body against disease.

Ans: T, p. 598

39.   The decline in the immune system helps to explain why a disease like the flu can be fatal in late adulthood.

Ans: F, p. 599

40.   The prevention of aging is a top research priority.

Ans: T, p. 599

41.   Adults tend to be uninterested in extending life beyond what is considered normal.

The Centenarians

Ans: F, p. 601

42.   Most long-lived people live alone.

Ans: T, p. 601

43.   Most long-lived people include exercise as a part of their daily routine.

FILL-IN-THE-BLANK QUESTIONS

Prejudice and Predictions

Ans: ageism, p. 577

1.   Categorizing or judging people solely on the basis of their chronological age is referred to as _____.

Ans: gerontology, p. 577

2.   The scientific study of old age is called _____.

Ans: Demography, p. 578

3.   _____ is the study of population numbers.

Ans: pyramid, p. 578

4.   In the past, demographers portrayed the United States population in the shape of a demographic _____.

Ans: square (or rectangle), p. 579

5.   Because of falling birth rates and increased longevity, the shape of the population chart of age groups is becoming a _____.

Ans: dependency, p. 579

6.   The ratio of self-sufficient, productive adults to dependents is called the _____ ratio.

Ans: health; social, p. 580

7.   The distinction between the young-old and the old-old is based on characteristics related to _____ and _____ well-being.

Ans: digestive; nutrients, p. 581
8. One of the main problems that prevent the elderly from receiving adequate nutrition is the reduced efficiency of the _____ system, which makes the absorption of _____ more difficult.

Primary Aging in Late Adulthood

Ans: secondary, p. 583
9. Aging that is caused by diseases is referred to as _____ aging.

Ans: skin, p. 583
10. Evidence of primary aging first shows up in the _____.

Ans: falling, p. 584
11. The leading cause of death from injury after age 60 is _____.

Ans: senile macular degeneration, p. 586
12. The leading cause of legal blindness among the elderly is _____.

Ans: tinnitis, p. 586
13. An incurable buzzing or rhythmic ringing in the ears is called _____.

Ans: compensate, p. 587
14. Successful aging depends on a willingness to conquer and _____ for losses that primary aging brings.

Ans: elderspeak, p. 588
15. A way of speaking to the aged that uses short and simple sentences, exaggerated emphasis, slower speech, higher pitch, and repetition is called _____.

Ans: Prostate cancer, p. 590
16. _____ is evident upon autopsy in virtually every man who dies at age 80 or older.

Ans: compression; morbidity, p. 591
17. Researchers are trying to make more of the years of the life span good ones, a concept called _____ of _____.

Theories of Aging

Ans: wear-and-tear, p. 593
18. The oldest, most general theory of aging is the _____ theory, which likens human bodies to machines.

Ans: maximum life span, pp. 594-595
19. The number of years that a species is genetically programmed to live is called the _____.

Ans: free radicals, p. 596
20. Electrons that are unattached from their nuclei are called _____.

Ans: stops, p. 597
21. In Leonard Hayflick's experiments in culturing cells from human embryos, after about 50 cell divisions, the process of cell division _____.

Ans: Progeria, p. 597
22. _____ is a rare genetic disorder that produces accelerated aging, causing 5-year-old children to begin to lose their hair and develop wrinkles.

Ans: immune, p. 598

23.   T cells and B cells are part of the body's _____ system.

The Centenarians

Ans: centenarian, p. 599

24.   A _____ is a person still alive after his or her 100th birthday.

Ans: social (or family or community), pp. 600-601

25.   Four factors are typical of the long-lived people: moderate diet, lifelong work, _____ involvement, and a daily routine combining exercise and relaxation.

ESSAY QUESTIONS

1.   You have been hired by an organization that advocates for the elderly. They want you to outline steps that might be taken to lessen the problem of ageism. What would you suggest?

2.   You are a physician who has been asked by a senior citizen's group interested in "wellness care" to lecture on the type of medical attention and advice that helps people avoid illness and stay healthy. Describe three topics you would emphasize.

3.   Compare two theories of aging. Based on what you have observed of aging in relatives and people in your community, which theory do you think is most accurate? Support your answer with specific examples.

4.   Looking into your own future, what do you anticipate your physical condition will be when you are 80?

5.   What changes do you anticipate will occur in attitudes toward, and treatment of, the elderly between now and the time when you are 80 years old?

6.   You are assigned by the college newspaper to interview two centenarian alumni, a man and a woman. Describe the people you expect to find.

7.   What do you believe makes a person "old"?

8.   What are the four factors that are involved in older adults' compensation for sensory loss and aging organs? Provide an example of each.

Answer guidelines to these essay questions can be found in the Appendix at the end of the Test Bank.

CHAPTER **24**   **Late Adulthood:**
Cognitive Development

MULTIPLE-CHOICE QUESTIONS

Changes in Information Processing

Changes in Information Processing, p. 605
Diff: E, Ans: b
1. When Schaie tested adults on the five primary mental abilities, the average scores after age 60:
    a. declined in only one or two areas.
    b. declined in all areas.
    c. showed no change until age 75.
    d. remained the same as at age 50.

Changes in Information Processing, p. 605
Diff: M, Ans: c
2. In Schaie's Seattle Longitudinal Study, the cognitive decline of late adulthood was most evident in which of the following?
    a. fluid intelligence
    b. verbal meaning
    c. processing speed
    d. inductive reasoning

Changes in Information Processing, p. 605
Diff: E, Ans: c
3. For the average individual in late adulthood, traditional tests of intelligence demonstrate that:
    a. cognitive abilities remain stable.
    b. cognitive abilities continue to increase.
    c. cognitive abilities decline.
    d. some cognitive abilities increase and others decline.

Changes in Information Processing, pp. 605-606
Diff: M, Ans: a
4. The path of intellectual development over several years of adulthood for any particular individual is best described as:
    a. multidirectional.
    b. stable.
    c. quickly declining.
    d. slightly incremental.

Changes in Information Processing, p. 606
Diff: M, Ans: d

5.   People over age 80 who tested at a high level of intelligence in earlier years will surpass:
     a.   their peers.
     b.   many younger adults.
     c.   themselves.
     d.   a and b only
     e.   a, b, and c

Input: Sensing and Perceiving, p. 606
Diff: E, Ans: b

6.   The primary reason older people receive less input into their brains is that:
     a.   they are less interested in life.
     b.   their senses decline, reducing the sensory input.
     c.   their threshold increases.
     d.   they are not able to store information.

Input: Sensing and Perceiving, p. 606
Diff: M, Ans: a

7.   For most elderly people, the capacity of the sensory register:
     a.   shows minimal change.
     b.   declines markedly with age.
     c.   improves since middle age.
     d.   can no longer be measured accurately.

Input: Sensing and Perceiving, p. 606
Diff: H, Ans: c

8.   On average, if an older adult experiences a decrease of cognitive abilities, decreases in visual and auditory acuity account for what proportion?
     a.   one-tenth
     b.   one-quarter
     c.   one-third
     d.   one-half

Active Memory, pp. 606-607
Diff: M, Ans: b

9.   Older adults tend to _____ sensory deficits and _____ memory deficits.
     a.   be unaware of; underestimate
     b.   be unaware of; overestimate
     c.   overestimate; underestimate
     d.   overestimate; overestimate

Active Memory, p. 607
Diff: H, Ans: d

10. Loss of working memory is particularly likely to affect the ability to:
     a.   retain the image of a picture just seen.
     b.   remember public events of the past.
     c.   recognize friends on the street.
     d.   repeat a series of numbers just heard.

Active Memory, p. 607
Diff: E, Ans: a
11. One function of working memory is:
    a. temporary storage of information for conscious use.
    b. long-term storage of unconscious information.
    c. storage of visual and auditory afterimages.
    d. prevention of memory loss.

Active Memory, p. 607
Diff: E, Ans: b
12. Which component of memory shows the most substantial declines with age?
    a. explicit memory
    b. working memory
    c. knowledge store
    d. long-term memory

Active Memory, pp. 607-608
Diff: H, Ans: b
13. An older adult would probably be the *least* able to remember which of the following?
    a. the meaning and usage of the word "consternation"
    b. the facts surrounding the 1948 presidential election
    c. his feelings on his wedding day
    d. the rules of a game that he has played since childhood

Active Memory, p. 608
Diff: M, Ans: a
14. Which of the following types of events are remembered best by older adults?
    a. happy events that occurred between the ages of 10 and 30
    b. sad events that occurred between the ages of 10 and 30
    c. happy events that occurred between the ages of 50 and 70
    d. sad events that occurred between the ages of 50 and 70

Active Memory, p. 608
Diff: H, Ans: b
15. If an elderly person makes these four statements about an event that happened earlier, which one is most likely to be correct?
    a. "It happened in Pacolet, Nevada."
    b. "I was so thrilled."
    c. "It was right after Christmas of 1949."
    d. "And then he told me to hitch up both of the horses."

Active Memory, pp. 608-609
Diff: M, Ans: c
16. A study that compared adults' memory of a language they had learned in high school found that:
    a. older people remembered it better.
    b. memory dropped sharply after the age of 40.
    c. people who learned it best remembered it best.
    d. age had no effect on memory.

Control Processes, p. 609
Diff: E, Ans: d
17. Which component of the human information-processing system functions as executive?
    a. working memory
    b. knowledge base
    c. tertiary memory
    d. control processes

Control Processes, p. 609
Diff: E, Ans: c

18.   Storage mechanisms, retrieval strategies, selective attention, and logical analysis are all considered:
      a.   implicit memories.
      b.   explicit memories.
      c.   control processes.
      d.   unconscious processes.

Control Processes, p. 609
Diff: H, Ans: b

19.   An elderly man is diagnosed with a serious disease and the doctor recommends a treatment plan. Compared to a younger adult, the man is more likely to:
      a.   ask for a second opinion.
      b.   accept the doctor's recommendations.
      c.   read as much about the disease as he can.
      d.   analyze various treatment options.

Control Processes, p. 610
Diff: E, Ans: c

20.   Explicit memory:
      a.   includes habits, emotions, and routines.
      b.   is almost impossible to recall verbally.
      c.   involves words, data, and concepts.
      d.   is learned unconsciously.

Control Processes, p. 610
Diff: E, Ans: b

21.   Implicit memory:
      a.   is always conscious.
      b.   involves habits and routines.
      c.   is easy to recall verbally.
      d.   is impossible to measure.

Control Processes, p. 610
Diff: M, Ans: a

22.   Compared to implicit memory, older adults' explicit memory is:
      a.   worse.
      b.   better.
      c.   the same.
      d.   more unconscious.

Control Processes, p. 610
Diff: H, Ans: b

23.   Older adults most easily could:
      a.   describe the design on their kitchen floor.
      b.   prepare a complicated recipe from memory that they have made many times.
      c.   describe the steps involved in repairing something.
      d.   remember a list of vocabulary words.

Reasons for Age-Related Changes

Primary Aging, p. 611
Diff: E, Ans: c
24. What proportion of human genes is dedicated to the form and function of the brain?
    a. one-tenth
    b. one-quarter
    c. one-half
    d. all

Primary Aging: Thinking Like a Scientist: Neuroscience and Brain Activity, pp. 611-612
Diff: M, Ans: d
25. With age, what happens to the brain?
    a. Some parts shrink.
    b. Activity level sometimes increases, sometimes decreases, and sometimes stays the same.
    c. Using both hemispheres simultaneously becomes more likely.
    d. All of the above occur with age.

Primary Aging: Thinking Like a Scientist: Neuroscience and Brain Activity, pp. 611-612
Diff: M, Ans: c
26. Why have scientists recently begun to realize that some of their long-held beliefs about the aging brain were false?
    a. People are living longer.
    b. Older people have become more aware of their own brain functioning.
    c. Noninvasive imaging techniques that can be done on live brains have become available.
    d. More laboratory analyses of brains of deceased Alzheimer's patients have been conducted.

Primary Aging: Thinking Like a Scientist: Neuroscience and Brain Activity, pp. 611-612
Diff: H, Ans: b
27. Which of the following is an example of selective optimization with compensation in the older brain?
    a. Attention-deficit disorder is caused by an immature prefrontal cortex.
    b. Older brains naturally activate more neurons than they once did for a particular task.
    c. As the control processes become weaker, the brain more strongly differentiates which of its parts are involved in specific tasks.
    d. Inhibition fails and thoughts have a stronger tendency to wander when people are old.

Primary Aging, pp. 612-613
Diff: M, Ans: a
28. Which of the following is the main consequence of primary aging?
    a. a decrease in thought and response speed
    b. severely impaired judgment
    c. the inability to create new neurons and dendrites
    d. a decrease in accuracy

Primary Aging, p. 614
Diff: E, Ans: c
29. The overall slowdown in cognitive abilities in the days or months before death is referred to as:
    a. response drop.
    b. memory loop.
    c. terminal decline.
    d. deceleration.

Secondary Aging, p. 614
Diff: E, Ans: b

30. The effects of diseases, poor nutrition, and lack of exercise on brain function in older adults are examples of:
a. primary aging.
b. secondary aging.
c. tertiary aging.
d. ageism.

Secondary Aging, p. 614
Diff: E, Ans: d

31. What advice could you give a middle-aged adult who is concerned about the effects of secondary aging on brain function in old age?
a. exercise
b. try to avoid depression
c. eat healthy
d. all of the above

Ageism, p. 615
Diff: H, Ans: b

32. It is most likely that an older person's assessment of his or her memory skills in early adulthood is:
a. an underestimate.
b. an overestimate.
c. more accurate for implicit than explicit memory.
d. accurate overall.

Ageism, p. 615
Diff: H, Ans: d

33. Seeing which of the following words made older adults perform worse than younger age groups on cognitive tests?
a. wise
b. insightful
c. enlightened
d. senile

Ageism, p. 615
Diff: H, Ans: c

34. Which of the following is a true statement about the relation between ageism and the cognitive functioning of older adults?
a. Ageism is unrelated to cognitive functioning.
b. Ageism is the source of all differences between the cognitive functioning of younger and older adults.
c. Ageism causes some differences between the cognitive functioning of younger and older adults.
d. Poor cognitive functioning in older adults causes ageism cross-culturally.

Ageism, pp. 615-616
Diff: M, Ans: a

35. In a study by Levy & Langer (1994), who had the most negative views of aging?
a. hearing Americans
b. deaf Americans
c. older Chinese
d. younger Chinese

Ageism, p. 616
Diff: H, Ans: b

36.   Which of the following is true of laboratory tests of abstract memory that attempt to compare younger and older adults?
   a.   Older adults are more practiced at taking tests of memory.
   b.   Older adults may not try very hard if they expect to fail.
   c.   Younger adults are typically not able to use their larger knowledge base.
   d.   Older adults are more likely to be tested at the time of day that is ideal for them.

Ageism, pp. 616-617
Diff: M, Ans: a

37.   If asked about the effects of memory loss on their daily lives, most of the elderly would:
   a.   not consider memory loss to be a significant handicap.
   b.   consider memory loss to be a significant handicap.
   c.   believe that memory loss has interfered only with their problem-solving skills.
   d.   believe that memory loss has interfered with their ability to take care of themselves.

Ageism, pp. 616-617
Diff: M, Ans: d

38.   Which of the following is a true statement about testing the memories of older adults?
   a.   They tend to do *better* than younger adults in both laboratory experiments and in their daily lives.
   b.   They tend to do *worse* than younger adults in both laboratory experiments and in their daily lives.
   c.   They do *better* in laboratory experiments than they do in their daily lives.
   d.   They do *worse* in laboratory experiments than they do in their daily lives.

Ageism, p. 617
Diff: M, Ans: a

39.   When adults were tested on making a phone call every day at an appointed time:
   a.   older adults outperformed the younger ones.
   b.   most older adults forgot to call.
   c.   younger adults did better than older adults.
   d.   no age differences were found.

Ageism, p. 617
Diff: H, Ans: d

40.   In an experiment by Moscovitch (1982), when older and younger adults were asked to call an answering service once a week without using any reminders:
   a.   more younger than older adults made the call.
   b.   more older than younger adults made the call.
   c.   few adults of any age made the call.
   d.   some of the elderly used reminders anyway.

Dementia

Dementia, p. 618
Diff: E, Ans: d

41.   Dementia is:
   a.   benign forgetfulness.
   b.   a problem that affects *most* of the elderly.
   c.   a problem that affects *only* the elderly.
   d.   the pathological loss of brain functioning.

Alzheimer's Disease, p. 618
Diff: E, Ans: b

42. The most common cause of dementia is:
    a. normal aging.
    b. Alzheimer's disease.
    c. many strokes.
    d. Parkinson's disease.

Alzheimer's Disease, p. 618
Diff: M, Ans: a

43. Autopsies show the brains of Alzheimer's victims:
    a. have a proliferation of plaques and tangles.
    b. show damage from strokes.
    c. have shrunk to half of normal size.
    d. appear to be normal.

Alzheimer's Disease, p. 619
Diff: M, Ans: b

44. When Alzheimer's disease appears in middle age, it:
    a. is benign.
    b. progresses more rapidly.
    c. progresses more slowly.
    d. causes death within a year.

Alzheimer's Disease, p. 619
Diff: E, Ans: c

45. The biggest risk factor for Alzheimer's disease is being:
    a. female.
    b. of European descent.
    c. old.
    d. male.

Alzheimer's Disease, p. 619
Diff: M, Ans: b

46. The first stage of Alzheimer's disease is characterized by:
    a. deficits in concentration.
    b. absentmindedness about recent events.
    c. personality changes.
    d. generalized confusion.

Alzheimer's Disease, p. 620
Diff: H, Ans: a

47. In the second stage of Alzheimer's disease, a person:
    a. exhibits aimless and repetitious speech.
    b. has memory problems similar to normal forgetfulness.
    c. requires placement in a nursing home.
    d. can no longer manage his/her basic daily needs.

Alzheimer's Disease, p. 620
Diff: H, Ans: c

48. Going outside barefoot in winter, walking through the neighborhood naked, or forgetting about the lighted stove are behaviors often found in the _____ stage of Alzheimer's disease.
    a. first
    b. second
    c. third
    d. fourth

Alzheimer's Disease, p. 620
Diff: M, Ans: c
49.   In the final stage of Alzheimer's disease, patients:
        a.   may eat only a single food or forget to eat at all.
        b.   may have a firm belief that people are stealing from them.
        c.   no longer talk.
        d.   do all of the above.

Many Strokes, p. 621
Diff: M, Ans: c
50.   Vascular dementia is caused by:
        a.   Alzheimer's disease.
        b.   inadequate nutrition.
        c.   insufficient supply of blood to the brain.
        d.   environmental toxins.

Many Strokes, p. 621
Diff: E, Ans: d
51.   Vascular dementia:
        a.   is caused by strokes that destroy parts of the brain.
        b.   progresses in a step-like pattern.
        c.   often co-occurs with Alzheimer's disease.
        d.   can often be compensated for in its early stages.
        e.   is all of the above.

Many Strokes, p. 621
Diff: E, Ans: a
52.   Multi-infarct dementia may be prevented by:
        a.   regular physical exercise.
        b.   memory exercises.
        c.   vitamin C.
        d.   taking early retirement.

Subcortical Dementias, p. 622
Diff: M, Ans: d
53.   Which of the following is NOT a subcortical dementia?
        a.   Parkinson's disease
        b.   Huntington's disease
        c.   multiple sclerosis
        d.   Alzheimer's disease

Subcortical Dementias, p. 622
Diff: E, Ans: b
54.   Parkinson's disease produces dementia as well as:
        a.   flabbiness in the muscles.
        b.   rigidity in the muscles.
        c.   many little strokes.
        d.   high blood pressure.

Subcortical Dementias, p. 622
Diff: H, Ans: c
55.   Parkinson's disease is related to insufficient production of dopamine, which is an essential:
        a.   regulator of blood pressure.
        b.   defense against cancer.
        c.   neurotransmitter.
        d.   genetic regulator.

Subcortical Dementias, p. 622
Diff: E, Ans: b
56.   A disease that can produce dementia is:
        a.   tuberculosis.
        b.   AIDS.
        c.   sickle-cell anemia.
        d.   pneumonia.

Reversible Dementia, pp. 622-623
Diff: E, Ans: c
57.   The fact that many elderly people take five or six different medications means that:
        a.   they are less likely to have adverse reactions.
        b.   their dosages should be increased.
        c.   the drugs can interact and product adverse reactions.
        d.   they are especially aware of possible drug overdose.

Reversible Dementia, pp. 622-623
Diff: E, Ans: e
58.   Which of the following can cause reversible dementia?
        a.   overmedication
        b.   undernourishment
        c.   alcohol abuse
        d.   dehydration
        e.   all of the above

Reversible Dementia, p. 623
Diff: E, Ans: b
59.   Which produces symptoms that seem like dementia?
        a.   normal aging.
        b.   anxiety.
        c.   weight loss.
        d.   too much social interaction.

Reversible Dementia, p. 623
Diff: H, Ans: c
60.   An elderly person who expresses serious worry about losing his or her intellectual abilities is most
        likely suffering from:
        a.   a brain tumor.
        b.   Parkinson's disease.
        c.   depression.
        d.   Alzheimer's disease.

Reversible Dementia, p. 624
Diff: E, Ans: d
61.   Many elderly people suffering from depression do not receive treatment because:
        a.   there is no effective treatment for the elderly.
        b.   treatment is too dangerous to their health.
        c.   their depression will disappear in time.
        d.   their depression goes undiagnosed.

Reversible Dementia, p. 624
Diff: E, Ans: d
62. In the United States, the highest suicide rate is found in people aged:
    a. under 16.
    b. from 16 to 24.
    c. from 40 to 60.
    d. over 60.

The Current Outlook, p. 624
Diff: H, Ans: b
63. Which of the following is a true statement about dementia?
    a. Most individuals need nursing home or hospital care, starting at the earliest stages.
    b. Developmentalists are particularly concerned with the psychological health of dementia patients' caregivers.
    c. Scientists are close to a cure for many causes of dementia.
    d. All of the above are true statements.

New Cognitive Development in Later Life

New Cognitive Development in Later Life, p. 625
Diff: E, Ans: a
64. Abraham Maslow maintains that older adults are:
    a. *more* likely than younger people to reach self-actualization.
    b. *less* likely than younger people to reach self-actualization.
    c. *just as* likely as younger people to reach self-actualization.
    d. too emotionally impaired to reach self-actualization.

Aesthetic Sense and Creativity, pp. 625-626
Diff: M, Ans: b
65. The fact that many older people begin to demonstrate an interest in painting, music, or woodworking supports the idea that older people:
    a. find that boredom is a major problem.
    b. develop an appreciation for the aesthetic.
    c. still have a drive for power.
    d. become less interested in other people.

The Life Review, pp. 626-627
Diff: M, Ans: c
66. Audrey is 85 years old and has begun a life review. Her primary reason for doing this is probably to:
    a. entertain younger generations.
    b. embellish her past experiences.
    c. put her life into perspective.
    d. escape her present circumstances.

Wisdom, pp. 628-629
Diff: M, Ans: b
67. Which of the following is associated with wisdom?
    a. age
    b. social interactions
    c. gender
    d. intelligence

Wisdom, pp. 628-629
Diff: M, Ans: a
68.   Research on wisdom finds that:
        a.   a minority of adults are wise.
        b.   wisdom is more common at age 30 than age 70.
        c.   most of the elderly are wise.
        d.   wisdom is never found in adults younger than 50.

TRUE-FALSE QUESTIONS

Late Adulthood: Cognitive Development

Ans: T, p. 605
1.   Most older people are neither senile nor wise, but somewhere in between.

Changes in Information Processing

Ans: F, p. 606
2.   A younger person is always more intelligent than an older one.

Ans: F, p. 606
3.   All older adults experience age-related declines in cognitive ability the same way.

Ans: F, p. 606
4.   The sensory register declines rapidly in late adulthood, but sensory acuity remains strong.

Ans: F, p. 606
5.   It is always clear to elderly adults that they are experiencing problems with sensory input.

Ans: T, p. 607
6.   Working memory is also called short-term memory.

Ans: T, p. 607
7.   In both storage and processing functions, older adults have a decline in working-memory capacity.

Ans: F, p. 608
8.   Research proves that in late adulthood the long-term memories of most adults are extremely accurate.

Ans: T, p. 608
9.   Happy events that happened between ages 10 and 30 are remembered better than any other events which happened earlier or later.

Ans: F, p. 608
10.   Several objective test questions have been developed to compare the long-term memory of a 70-year-old with that of a 40-year-old.

Ans: T, p. 609
11.   Both short-term and long-term memory are somewhat reduced in older adults.

Ans: T, p. 609
12.   Inadequate control processes may explain many of the memory difficulties in the aged.

Ans: T, p. 609
13.   Older adults tend to use "top-down" problem-solving strategies.

Ans: F, p. 610
14.   Not knowing the capital of Bulgaria is an example of the tip-of-the-tongue phenomenon.

Ans: F, p. 610
15.   Implicit memory is consciously learned and easy to recall.

Ans: T, p. 610
16.   On some tests of implicit memory, older adults who are intellectually sharp show no evidence of decline.

Ans: F, p. 610
17.   Older adults are quick to use memory techniques (such as the method of loci) when taught to do so.

Ans: T, p. 610
18.   Some decline in control processes appears to be more a result of older adults' resistance to change than a direct result of aging.

Ans: T, p. 610
19.   Older adults have more problems with tip-of-the-tongue phenomena than do younger adults.

Ans: F, p. 610
20.   Explicit memory is more automatic than implicit memory.

Reasons for Age-Related Changes

Ans: F, p. 611
21.   It is clear that brain atrophy and cell loss contribute to the cognitive deficits of age.

Ans: T, p. 612
22.   Older brains may engage in both selective optimization with compensation and dedifferentiation.

Ans: F, p. 613
23.   Severely impaired judgment is the main consequence of primary aging.

Ans: T, p. 613
24.   A decrease in speed seems to be the crucial underlying explanation for many of the intellectual declines with age.

Ans: T, p. 613
25.   Older adults are slower at almost all measures of cognition, but they were not necessarily less accurate.

Ans: T, p. 614
26.   Many people demonstrate a marked loss of intellectual power and depression when death is near, even before a doctor notices a serious change in physical factors.

Ans: T, p. 614
27.   Feelings of depression and incompetence can cause a slowdown in brain functioning.

Ans: T, p. 615
28.   Elderly people often believe that their memory decline is greater than it actually is.

Ans: T, p. 615
29.   Negative stereotypes can interfere with the cognitive abilities of the elderly.

Ans: F, p. 616
30.   Older adults show greater motivation in laboratory tests of memory than do younger adults.

Ans: T, p. 617
31.   Older adults may remember some aspects of their daily lives even better than college students, because they have structured their lives with reminders.

Ans: T, p. 617
32.   Research has demonstrated that younger adults often put too much trust in their memories and thus sometimes have more problems with forgetting in daily life than do older adults.

Dementia

Ans: T, p. 618
33.   The term senile is ageist.

Ans: F, p. 618
34.   Diagnosing the particular cause of an individual's dementia is simple.

Ans: F, p. 619
35.   The biggest risk factor for Alzheimer's disease is being female.

Ans: T, p. 619
36.   The early-appearing form of Alzheimer's disease is inherited.

Ans: F, p. 620
37.   In the second stage of Alzheimer's disease, a person who was neat and tidy earlier in life would become particularly messy.

Ans: T, p. 620
38.   Typically, people die 10 to 15 years after the onset of the first stage of Alzheimer's disease.

Ans: T, p. 621
39.   Vascular dementia is caused by successive strokes that kill off parts of the brain.

Ans: F, p. 621 (Figure 24.2)
40.   Vascular dementia and Alzheimer's disease often co-occur and have similar patterns of progression.

Ans: F, p. 622
41.   Subcortical dementias initially affect the person's mental processes while leaving motor skills intact.

Ans: T, pp. 622-623
42.   Reversible conditions such as depression and drug interactions can cause the symptoms of dementia.

Ans: T, p. 623
43.   People with reversible dementia are often very upset by their memory loss, whereas people with cortical or subcortical dementia are often unaware of it.

Ans: F, p. 624
44.   Depression in late adulthood is very difficult to treat.

Ans: T, p. 624
45.   Misdiagnosis of the causes of dementia is a reason why some individuals do not get treated.

New Cognitive Development in Later Life

Ans: T, p. 625
46.   In late adulthood, many people seek to express and develop their creative impulses.

Ans: F, p. 626
47.   Although many artists continue their creative work into late adulthood, it tends to be of lower quality and creativity than their work at younger ages.

Ans: F, p. 626
48.   As people age, they become less reflective and philosophical.

Ans: F, p. 627
49.   The life review tends to be a solitary process, as people evaluate their successes and failures in life.

Ans: F, pp. 628-629
50.   Wisdom is related purely to age and intelligence.

FILL-IN-THE-BLANK QUESTIONS

Changes in Information Processing

Ans: sensory, p. 606
1.   The _____ register holds incoming sensory information for a split second after it is received.

Ans: sensory threshold, p. 606
2.   In order for information to register in memory, it must cross the _____.

Ans: sensory abilities, p. 606
3.   A significant reason for the overall variation in adult intelligence is due to the variation in _____.

Ans: working, p. 607
4.   The processing component through which current, conscious mental activity occurs is _____ memory.

Ans: knowledge, p. 607
5.   The _____ base is the storehouse for all information that was ever put into long-term memory.

Ans: source amnesia, p. 608
6.   Not remembering who or where a specific fact or idea came from is _____.

Ans: control, p. 609
7.   Storage mechanisms, retrieval strategies, selective attention, and logical analyses are _____ processes.

Ans: retrieval, p. 609
8.   Older adults' use of _____ strategies, such as running through an alphabetical mental checklist when trying to remember something, worsens with age.

Ans: Explicit, p. 610
9.   _____ memory involves words, data, and concepts that are consciously learned.

Reasons for Age-Related Changes

Ans: optimization, p. 612

10.   Recent advances in brain imaging have demonstrated that older brains may engage in selective _____ with compensation.

Ans: primary, p. 613

11.   Slower processing is the main result of _____ aging.

Ans: compensate, p. 613

12.   When older people find that their memory is declining, they structure their environment to _____ for the loss.

Ans: compensatory, pp. 613-614

13.   Using written reminders and mnemonic devices, repeating instructions, and focusing only on meaningful cognitive tasks are _____ methods that many older adults use to optimize their memory abilities.

Ans: overestimate, p. 615

14.   Studies find that people aged 50 to 70 tend to _____ the memory skills they had in young adulthood.

Dementia

Ans: dementia (NOT senility), p. 617

15.   Severely impaired judgment, memory, or problem-solving ability is referred to as _____.

Ans: plaques, p. 618

16.   A brain affected by Alzheimer's disease has _____ outside the brain cells and tangles of protein filaments.

Ans: short-term, p. 620

17.   The second stage of Alzheimer's disease includes noticeable deficits in concentration and _____ memory.

Ans: fifth, p. 620

18.   People become completely mute and fail to respond to any stimulus in the _____ stage of Alzheimer's disease.

Ans: strokes, p. 621

19.   Multi-infarct dementia (MID) is caused by a series of _____.

Ans: arteries, p. 621

20.   The underlying cause of the obstruction of blood to the brain in multi-infarct dementia is hardening of the _____.

Ans: subcortical, p. 622

21.   Huntington's disease and multiple sclerosis are _____ dementias.

Ans: Korsakoff's syndrome, p. 622

22.   Severe alcohol abuse can lead to loss of short-term memory due to lesions in the brain that result from a syndrome called _____.

Ans: depression, p. 623

23.   A symptom of _____ in late adulthood is exaggerated attention to small memory losses or refusal to answer any questions that measure cognition.

New Cognitive Development in Later Life

Ans: life review, pp. 626-627

24.   The examination of one's own past life that tends to be therapeutic is referred to as a(n) _____.

Ans: wisdom, p. 629

25.   Experience and practice in dealing with the problems of life tend to increase a person's _____, but sheer chronological age does not.

ESSAY QUESTIONS

1.   You have been asked to help design an intelligence test for the current cohort of adults over the age of 65. What characteristics of adult intelligence should be taken into account in the design of the test?

2.   An older relative is showing signs of dementia. He forgets things and he is disoriented, especially when he is riding in a car. How would you determine whether he is suffering from Alzheimer's disease rather than some other problem?

3.   You are the coordinator of a senior-citizens group. What activities would you plan to make use of the cognitive developments of later life?

4.   Review in your mind the abilities and needs that find expression in adulthood. Write a "life plan" of intellectual achievements you would like to make in early, middle, and late adulthood.

5.   Describe three ways the elderly can maintain cognitive functioning.

6.   Describe three things you learned from this chapter about interacting with elderly people.

Answer guidelines to these essay questions can be found in the Appendix at the end of the Test Bank.

CHAPTER 25 Late Adulthood: Psychosocial Development

MULTIPLE-CHOICE QUESTIONS

Theories of Late Adulthood

Self Theories, p. 634
Diff: E, Ans: c

1. Self theories emphasize:
    a. social forces.
    b. sexual or racial discrimination.
    c. human intentionality.
    d. circumscribed opportunities.

Self Theories, p. 634
Diff: E, Ans: a

2. Self-actualization refers to:
    a. reaching one's full potential.
    b. realizing all of the error one has made over the lifespan.
    c. recovering from a mental illness.
    d. preparing to die.

Self Theories, p. 634
Diff: E, Ans: c

3. Erikson called the final crisis of development:
    a. optimization versus compensation.
    b. generativity versus stagnation.
    c. integrity versus despair.
    d. activity versus disengagement.

Self Theories, p. 634
Diff: E, Ans: d

4. According to Erikson, integrity versus despair is the focus of:
    a. adolescence.
    b. early adulthood.
    c. middle adulthood.
    d. late adulthood.

Self Theories, p. 634
Diff: M, Ans: d

5. An elderly woman who seeks to integrate her unique personal experiences with the future of her community is in Erikson's stage of:
    a. generativity versus stagnation.
    b. optimization versus compensation.
    c. activity versus disengagement.
    d. integrity versus despair.

Self Theories, p. 635
Diff: M, Ans: c

6. Which of the following is a true statement about the self-esteem of older adults?
    a. It is high throughout the years of late adulthood.
    b. It is low throughout the years of late adulthood.
    c. It is high at the beginning of late adulthood and then decreases.
    d. It is low at the beginning of late adulthood and then increases.

Self Theories, p. 636
Diff: M, Ans: d

7. According to identity theory, the process of maintaining identity in late adulthood involves balancing:
    a. growth and change.
    b. optimization and compensation.
    c. identity and role confusion.
    d. assimilation and accommodation.

Self Theories, p. 636
Diff: H, Ans: b

8. Eighty-year-old Henry refuses to get a hearing aid even though he is nearly deaf. In fact, he becomes angry at the mere mention of it by his concerned relatives. According to identity theory, Henry has the strategy of identity:
    a. optimization.
    b. assimilation.
    c. compensation.
    d. accommodation.

Self Theories, p. 636
Diff: M, Ans: d

9. According to identity theory, the ideal way for older adults to cope with the effects of aging on their identity is to:
    a. fully assimilate the new experiences.
    b. fully accommodate their identities.
    c. resist both assimilation and accommodation.
    d. balance assimilation and accommodation.

Self Theories, p. 636
Diff: H, Ans: b

10. As he ages, a professional musician begins to limit his repertoire, practice more before concerts, and change the manner in which he plays. He is:
    a. giving in to the despair of the last stage of the life cycle.
    b. using selective optimization with compensation.
    c. becoming less ambitious and creative.
    d. showing the early signs of Alzheimer's disease.

Self Theories, pp. 636-637
Diff: M, Ans: a

11. Which of the following is true of selective optimization with compensation?
    a. It involves older adults figuring out how to accomplish what they want despite their limitations.
    b. Older adults who use it are those with poor self-efficacy.
    c. It was first emphasized by Freud and Erikson.
    d. It expects that older adults will attempt to continue to do everything they have always done.

Self Theories, p. 637
Diff: M, Ans: a
12. In recent years self theories have received substantial confirmation from:
    a. behavioral genetics.
    b. feminist theory.
    c. critical race theory.
    d. volunteer studies.

Self Theories, p. 637
Diff: H, Ans: b
13. Behavioral genetics has demonstrated that:
    a. personality traits remain essentially stable across the lifespan.
    b. people tend to become more truly themselves as their temperaments gain fee rein in late adulthood.
    c. life events, such as frequency of marriage, have no genetic component.
    d. all older people demonstrate the same changes in personality, regardless of environment.

Social Stratification Theories, p. 638
Diff: E, Ans: c
14. Which of the following theories claim that social forces limit individual choice and direct life, especially in late adulthood?
    a. dynamic theories
    b. self theories
    c. stratification theories
    d. behavioral theories

Social Stratification Theories, p. 638
Diff: E, Ans: a
15. The idea that opportunities and roles are determined based on age is referred to as:
    a. age stratification.
    b. selective optimization.
    c. self-actualization.
    d. social stagnation.

Stratification Theories, p. 638
Diff: M, Ans: b
16. The most controversial version of social stratification theory is:
    a. compensation.
    b. disengagement.
    c. optimization.
    d. activity.

Stratification Theories, p. 638
Diff: H, Ans: d
17. A man who is almost 65 years old develops a more passive style of interaction and withdraws from society. Which theory predicts this behavior?
    a. continuity
    b. self-actualization
    c. selective optimization
    d. disengagement

Stratification Theories, p. 638
Diff: E, Ans: c
18.   The antithesis of disengagement theory is:
       a.   epigenetic theory.
       b.   identity theory.
       c.   activity theory.
       d.   feminist theory.

Stratification Theories, p. 639
Diff: H, Ans: b
19.   The current view of stratification theorists is that:
       a.   elderly people need to remain active in a variety of social spheres and withdraw only because of
            ageism.
       b.   most older people become more selective in their social contacts and are happier as a result of it.
       c.   people's lives are constantly changing along with their social contexts.
       d.   aging makes a person's social sphere shrink, resulting in withdrawal and passivity.

Stratification Theories, pp. 639-640
Diff: E, Ans: a
20.   Which theory focuses on the gender divisions promoted by society?
       a.   feminist
       b.   continuity
       c.   disengagement
       d.   sexist

Stratification Theories, p. 640
Diff: E, Ans: c
21.   Currently in the United States, what percent of the population over age 65 is female?
       a.   20
       b.   50
       c.   60
       d.   80

Stratification Theories, p. 640
Diff: H, Ans: c
22.   Which of the following are of concern to feminist theorists?
       a.   the greater number of widows in comparison with widowers
       b.   the fact that medical insurance pays more for acute illness than for chronic illness
       c.   pension plans that are associated with a lifetime of continuous employment
       d.   all of the above

Stratification Theories, p. 640
Diff: M, Ans: c
23.   Critical race theory sees race as:
       a.   purely physiological.
       b.   no longer a barrier to success.
       c.   a social construct whose utility is determined by society.
       d.   a problem that disappears in old age.

Stratification Theories, pp. 640-641
Diff: E, Ans: d
24.   The notion that ethnic discrimination and racism shape experiences and attitudes is the view of which
       theory?
       a.   minority race theory
       b.   disengaged race theory
       c.   dynamic race theory
       d.   critical race theory

Stratification Theories, pp. 640-641
Diff: H, Ans: d
25. The fact that European-American elderly are more likely to own homes than are African-American elderly is of particular concern to which theory?
    a. minority race
    b. disengagement
    c. dynamic race
    d. critical race

Dynamic Theories, p. 643
Diff: M, Ans: b
26. Which theories state that each person's life is an active, ever-changing, largely self-propelled process, occurring within specific social contexts which are themselves constantly changing?
    a. self theories
    b. dynamic theories
    c. social-stratification theories
    d. identity theories

Dynamic Theories, p. 643
Diff: H, Ans: a
27. At age 65, Mrs. Walker reacted to her recent retirement in much the same way that she dealt with earlier life changes. This illustrates:
    a. continuity theory.
    b. activity theory.
    c. disengagement theory.
    d. diversity theory.

Dynamic Theories, p. 643
Diff: E, Ans: b
28. According to continuity theory, the Big Five personality traits:
    a. change in middle and late adulthood.
    b. are maintained throughout old age.
    c. suddenly change after age 60.
    d. follow no predictable pattern.

Dynamic Theories, p. 643
Diff: H, Ans: c
29. Continuity theory would argue that the reaction of a 70-year-old to the news that he has diabetes and must dramatically change his lifestyle is best predicted by the patient's:
    a. intelligence test scores.
    b. religious background.
    c. past coping patterns.
    d. diagnosis.

Dynamic Theories, p. 644
Diff: H, Ans: d
30. Self theories echo:
    a. social stratification theories.
    b. epigenetic systems theories.
    c. critical race theories.
    d. psychoanalytic theories.

Keeping Active

Chosen Activities, p. 645
Diff: E, Ans: a
31.   Which of the following is a program for continuing education for the elderly in the United States?
a.   Elderhostel
b.   Older Education
c.   Advanced Placement
d.   Senior Services

Chosen Activities, p. 645
Diff: H, Ans: a
32.   Mr. Inman is 71 years old and has just enrolled in a course at the local college. Which of the following is least likely to be his motivation?
a.   career advancement
b.   desire for social development
c.   developing a hobby
d.   the joy of learning

Chosen Activities, p. 646
Diff: M, Ans: b
33.   Much of the volunteer work undertaken by the elderly is:
a.   highly prestigious.
b.   informal.
c.   focused on the problems of young adults.
d.   unsatisfying.

Chosen Activities, p. 646
Diff: H, Ans: b
34.   The elderly benefit most from volunteering:
a.   for several different organizations.
b.   when they can become an integral part of the organization.
c.   if it doesn't interfere with their social lives.
d.   if they are encouraged to by concerned family members.

Chosen Activities, p. 646
Diff: H, Ans: a
35.   Which of the following statements about older people and religion is NOT true?
a.   Older people are more likely to attend weekly religious services than are younger people.
b.   Religious faith tends to foster health.
c.   Religious faith increases with age.
d.   Religious institutions are particularly important to older Americans who feel alienated from the larger society.

Chosen Activities, p. 647
Diff: E, Ans: d
36.   Individuals in which age group are most likely to vote?
a.   18-25
b.   25-45
c.   45-65
d.   65-85

Chosen Activities, p. 647
Diff: E, Ans: d
37. Which of the following is the largest organized interest group in the United States?
    a. NAACP
    b. NRA
    c. ACLU
    d. AARP

Chosen Activities, p. 647
Diff: E, Ans: b
38. The requirement for membership in AARP is that the person is:
    a. retired.
    b. over 50.
    c. over 70.
    d. collecting Social Security.

Home, Sweet Home, p. 648
Diff: M, Ans: a
39. When older Americans move, they are most likely to move:
    a. not far from their old residence.
    b. to a new community.
    c. to a different state.
    d. to a place where they can meet new friends.

Home, Sweet Home, p. 648
Diff: M, Ans: c
40. Where is an elderly person most likely to prefer to live?
    a. a planned retirement community
    b. in Florida
    c. his or her own home
    d. nursing homes

The Social Convoy

The Social Convoy, p. 649
Diff: M, Ans: c
41. The term "social convoy" refers to the truism that:
    a. he who travels fastest travels alone.
    b. it is not healthy to spend time alone.
    c. we travel through life in the company of others.
    d. we need a strong leader in times of conflict.

Long-Term Marriages, p. 649
Diff: M, Ans: a
42. Compared to single older adults, the married elderly tend to be:
    a. happier and wealthier.
    b. happier but poorer.
    c. poorer and less happy.
    d. similar with regard to happiness and wealth.

Long-Term Marriages, p. 649
Diff: H, Ans: b

43. Who is most likely to be the healthiest and happiest at age 70?
     a. Jan, who never married and lives alone
     b. Annette, who is living with her husband
     c. Carly, who is a widow and did not remarry
     d. Susan, who is divorced and lives with her grandchildren

Long-Term Marriages, pp. 649-650
Diff: M, Ans: b

44. Most studies of marriages of long duration find that compared to younger adults, the elderly are:
     a. more open to the possibility of divorcing.
     b. happier in their marriages.
     c. unhappy, but not inclined to divorce.
     d. less committed to marriage as an institution.

Long-Term Marriages, pp. 649-650
Diff: M, Ans: d

45. Compared to younger couples, older couples in long-term marriages:
     a. have more conflict.
     b. are less emotionally intense.
     c. have more frequent sex.
     d. are closer.

Long-Term Marriages, p. 650
Diff: H, Ans: c

46. When a man in a long-term marriage becomes ill and is cared for by his wife, the usual effect on the marriage is:
     a. divorce.
     b. significantly decreased marital satisfaction.
     c. increased closeness over the course of the illness.
     d. decrease in mutual support.

Losing a Spouse, p. 651
Diff: E, Ans: c

47. In the United States, women typically live _____ years longer than men.
     a. 1
     b. 3
     c. 6
     d. 10

Losing a Spouse, p. 651
Diff: M, Ans: c

48. In the United States, wives average _____ years of widowhood.
     a. 3
     b. 6
     c. 10
     d. 14

Losing a Spouse, p. 651
Diff: H, Ans: a

49. Mrs. Bronson has been recently widowed. Compared to a widower, she:
     a. probably anticipated her widowhood.
     b. can expect less help from friends.
     c. will have fewer financial problems.
     d. is less likely to ask for help.

Losing a Spouse, pp. 651-652

Diff: M, Ans: b

50. Elderly men may be more troubled by losing a spouse than elderly women are because men:
    a. need companionship more.
    b. are less likely to seek out comfort and help.
    c. are more likely to remain alone.
    d. have greater difficulty concealing their grief.

Losing a Spouse, p. 652

Diff: H, Ans: a

51. Which of the following older adults is likely to be most lonely?
    a. Barney, who has lost two wives in six years
    b. Fred, who lost his wife twelve years ago
    c. Wilma, who is in a long-term marriage
    d. Betty, who has lost two husbands in eight years

Friendship, p. 653

Diff: E, Ans: d

52. Today, most never married older adults are:
    a. pitied or ridiculed.
    b. immature or selfish.
    c. in need of supervision.
    d. happy and active.

Friendship, p. 653

Diff: M, Ans: b

53. Life satisfaction for the elderly correlates with:
    a. family more than friends.
    b. friends more than family.
    c. ethnic group more than religion.
    d. income more than social contact.

Friendship, p. 653

Diff: M, Ans: b

54. The most important buffer against the loss that comes from retirement and widowhood is having:
    a. several grandchildren.
    b. at least one close friend.
    c. children who live nearby.
    d. neighbors who live nearby.

Friendship, p. 653

Diff: H, Ans: d

55. During late adulthood, it is likely that:
    a. men have more friends than women.
    b. women have only relatives as closest friends.
    c. unmarried men have only male friends.
    d. unmarried women have only female friends.

Friendship, p. 653

Diff: M, Ans: c

56. When death or distance cuts off a close friend, an older adult is likely to:
    a. become physically ill.
    b. become depressed.
    c. make another friend.
    d. do none of the above.

Younger Generations, p. 654
Diff: E, Ans: a

57.   A family of many generations but only a few members of each generation is called the _____ family
      pattern.
      a.   beanpole
      b.   nuclear
      c.   stratified
      d.   collective

Younger Generations, p. 654
Diff: E, Ans: a

58.   The closest but most vulnerable family relationship when the parent is in late adulthood is the
      relationship between:
      a.   mother and daughter.
      b.   mother and son.
      c.   father and daughter.
      d.   father and son.

Younger Generations, p. 654
Diff: M, Ans: c

59.   Grown daughters often feel that their mothers:
      a.   defer to their wishes.
      b.   are too distant.
      c.   are intrusive.
      d.   need a lot of attention.

Younger Generations, p. 655
Diff: M, Ans: a

60.   With regard to their grown children, most elderly people:
      a.   are more likely to give financial support than to receive it.
      b.   try to control their children's lives.
      c.   lose interest in their children.
      d.   withdraw from family connections.

Younger Generations, p. 655
Diff: H, Ans: b

61.   Ed and Barbara are retired and in their 70s. We would expect their relationship with their children to
      include:
      a.   financial assistance from their children.
      b.   visits from their children on invitation.
      c.   children living with them.
      d.   frequent, spontaneous get-togethers.

The Frail Elderly

The Frail Elderly, p. 656
Diff: E, Ans: b

62.   The term "ADL" refers to
      a.   aged developmental limitations.
      b.   activities of daily life.
      c.   Alzheimer's disease.
      d.   association for disabled living.

The Frail Elderly, p. 656
Diff: E, Ans: a

63. Which of the following is one of the ADLs?
    a. bathing
    b. shopping
    c. paying bills
    d. phone calls

The Frail Elderly, p. 656
Diff: E, Ans: c

64. Which of the following is one of the IADLs?
    a. eating
    b. toileting
    c. grocery shopping
    d. dressing

The Frail Elderly, p. 656
Diff: M, Ans: d

65. The difference between ADLs and IADLs is that:
    a. ADLs are simple enough that even the frail elderly can do them independently.
    b. IADLs are the same across cultures.
    c. ADLs require professional training.
    d. IADLs require some intellectual competence.

Increasing Prevalence of Frailty, p. 657
Diff: M, Ans: b

66. Which of the following increases the number of frail elderly?
    a. People are dying of disease at younger ages.
    b. Hearing aids and hip replacements are less available to the poor.
    c. Doctors emphasize life enhancement rather than prolonging life.
    d. Morbidity is decreasing.

Increasing Prevalence of Frailty, p. 658
Diff: M, Ans: d

67. As the proportion of frail elderly _____ and the proportion of younger people _____, it will no longer be possible for the frail elderly to rely solely on the care of younger family members.
    a. decreases; increases
    b. decreases; decreases
    c. increases; increases
    d. increases; decreases

Age and Self-Efficacy, p. 659
Diff: M, Ans: a

68. Research on frailty in old age indicates that:
    a. self-efficacy and control are the best defense.
    b. upper body strength is a predictor of functional decline.
    c. low blood pressure, good vision, and high income are the best defense.
    d. there is no way to avoid frailty in late adulthood.

Age and Self-Efficacy, p. 659
Diff: H, Ans: b
69. Which of the following responses to weakening leg muscles in an older person is the best response in terms of maintaining self-efficacy?
    a. purchasing a walker
    b. beginning a strength training regimen
    c. becoming a chair-bound invalid
    d. adjust to staying only on the first floor of a home

Changing Policy: Between Fragile and Frail—Protective Buffers, pp. 660-661
Diff: H, Ans: d
70. Those concerned with the impact of social policy on keeping people from becoming frail focus most on which of the following?
    a. Social Security
    b. the availability of nursing homes
    c. family caretaking
    d. complex sets of regulations and assistance

Caring for the Elderly, p. 661
Diff: E, Ans: d
71. What percent of North American elders who need assistance are cared for by family and friends?
    a. 10
    b. 25
    c. 40
    d. 60

Caring for the Elderly, pp. 661-662
Diff: H, Ans: b
72. Which of the following is a true statement about family caregivers of the frail elderly?
    a. Daughters-in-law are often grateful that they can reciprocate for nurturing they once received.
    b. Dementia greatly increases the burden of caretaking.
    c. A majority eventually become clinically depressed.
    d. Public agencies frequently provide services to compensate for needs the caregiver is unable to fulfill.

Caring for the Elderly, pp. 662-663
Diff: M, Ans: d
73. Which of the following increases the likelihood of elder abuse?
    a. substance abuse by caregiver
    b. poverty
    c. frailty
    d. all of the above
    e. none of the above

Caring for the Elderly, p. 663
Diff: M, Ans: d
74. Most elder abuse is committed by:
    a. nursing home workers.
    b. health care providers.
    c. social workers.
    d. adult children.

Caring for the Elderly, p. 663
Diff: H, Ans: b
75.   Elder maltreatment is:
   a.   more likely to occur in a nursing home than at home.
   b.   likely to cause isolation, fear, and dependence.
   c.   always physical in nature.
   d.   usually at the hands of strangers.

Caring for the Elderly, p. 664
Diff: H, Ans: a
76.   All of the following are true statements about nursing homes EXCEPT:
   a.   the majority of elder abuse occurs in them.
   b.   good nursing home care is available for those who can afford it.
   c.   the abuses of the nursing-home industry in the United States in the 1950s have been greatly reduced.
   d.   good nursing home care involves providing privacy and independence for patients.

TRUE-FALSE QUESTIONS

Theories of Late Adulthood

Ans: F, p. 634
1.   Almost every older adult experiences depression and despair at the end of their lives.

Ans: T, p. 636
2.   In identity assimilation, new experiences are incorporated into the identity that was previously established.

Ans: F, p. 636
3.   Older people who rigidly holding on to their values and beliefs when faced with new experiences are adopting the strategy of identity accommodation.

Ans: F, pp. 636-637
4.   An older person's use of selective optimization with compensation is a sign that he or she is near death.

Ans: T, p. 637
5.   People with a strong sense of self-efficacy believe they can cope with the various events of aging.

Ans: T, p. 637
6.   Some inherited traits seem even more apparent in late adulthood, when people stop being constrained by family and work obligations.

Ans: F, p. 638
7.   Stratification theories maintain that social forces promote individual choice.

Ans: F, pp. 638-639
8.   Most developmentalists believe the elderly gain more satisfaction from disengagement.

Ans: T, p. 640
9.   Feminist theorists are especially concerned about late adulthood because women tend to live longer than men.

Ans: F, p. 640

10.   Feminist theorists contend that the medical insurance system is organized in such a way that it benefits older women more than older men.

Ans: T, p. 640

11.   Critical race theory is concerned that minority elderly are more likely to be poor and frail than are the elderly from the ethnic majority.

Ans: T, p. 641

12.   Because men are socialized to be self-sufficient, they are more vulnerable to loneliness and depression in late adulthood than women are.

Ans: T, pp. 641-642

13.   Some developmentalists believe that stratification theories are inaccurate and the lives of female elderly and minority elderly are evidence of human resilience.

Ans: T, pp. 643-644

14.   Continuity theory maintains that people maintain their core identity even while adjusting to changing circumstances.

Keeping Active

Ans: F, p. 645

15.   Older adults who take academic classes populated by mostly college students tend to do relatively poorly, as they are unable to compensate for declines in their reaction time and fluid intelligence.

Ans: T, p. 645

16.   "Universities of the Third Age" is a learning program for older people in Europe.

Ans: T, p. 645

17.   Older adult volunteers are particularly likely to volunteer to work with the very young, the very old, or the sick.

Ans: F, p. 645

18.   Older retirees are more likely to become involved in volunteer work than are recently retired individuals.

Ans: F, p. 646

19.   There is no evidence that the elderly benefit from volunteer work.

Ans: T, p. 646

20.   Prayer and other religious practices increase with age.

Ans: T, p. 647

21.   The elderly are more politically active than any other age group on nearly all measures of political activism.

Ans: T, p. 647

22.   In 2003, the AARP had more than 35 million members.

Ans: F, p. 648

23.   The amount of housework done by both men and women tends to decrease following retirement.

Ans: F, p. 648

24.   As Americans age, they commonly move to planned retirement communities.

The Social Convoy

Ans: F, pp. 649-650

25. Long-term marriages result in many serious disagreements during late adulthood.

Ans: F, p. 650

26. Most elderly spouses care for each other out of feelings of obligation.

Ans: F, p. 650

27. Passionate love is rarely, if ever, present in late life romances.

Ans: F, pp. 651-652

28. The emotional effects of losing a spouse are harder on women than on men.

Ans: F, pp. 651-652

29. After a spouse dies, women tend to have more social support than do men.

Ans: F, p. 652

30. Widows are more likely to remarry than are widowers.

Ans: T, p. 652

31. In the months following the death of their spouse, men are more often physically ill than their married contemporaries.

Ans: F, p. 652

32. The majority of elderly who were never married are unhappy.

Ans: T, p. 653

33. The quality of older peoples' friendships tends to improve to compensate for losses.

Ans: T, p. 654

34. Both family satisfaction and family resentment depend more on emotional ties than on the particulars of communication and help.

Ans: T, p. 655

35. The price of intergenerational harmony may be intergenerational distance because some families get along better when they do not live too close to each other.

Ans: T, p. 655

36. Assistance typically flows from members of the older generation to their children rather than vice versa.

The Frail Elderly

Ans: T, p. 656

37. For medical insurance and research on dependency, a person is usually considered frail if he or she is unable to perform three of the activities of daily living.

Ans: T, p. 656

38. The inability to perform IADLs can make a person frail and dependent on others.

Ans: F, p. 656

39. Frailty is defined by the combination of age and illness.

Ans: F, p. 656

40.   The majority of the elderly are frail.

Ans: T, p. 657

41.   The emphasis in medicine tends to be on prolonging life rather than enhancing life.

Ans: F, pp. 657-658

42.   An emphasis by the medical profession on prolonging life is decreasing the numbers of frail elderly.

Ans: F, p. 659

43.   Income and health are better predictors of future frailty, depression, and dependence than are any psychological measures.

Ans: T, pp. 660-661

44.   Social policy can make the difference between fragility and frailty in older adults.

Ans: F, pp. 661-662

45.   Care of elders with dementia is often less of a burden on family members than caring for other types of frail elders because the caretaker of a dementia patient can make all of the decisions regarding care.

Ans: F, p. 663

46.   Most elders and their relatives feel that nursing homes are a good option.

Ans: T, p. 663

47.   Elder abuse usually begins benignly and then becomes worse.

FILL-IN-THE-BLANK QUESTIONS

Theories of Late Adulthood

Ans: Self, p. 634

1.   _____ theories begin with the premise that adults make choices, confront problems, and interpret reality in such a way as to define and express themselves and achieve as fully as possible.

Ans: self-actualize, p. 634

2.   According to Abraham Maslow, people attempt to _____, that is, to achieve their full potential.

Ans: identity, p. 635

3.   The basic idea of _____ theory is that people of all ages need to know who they are even in the face of the inevitable experiences of aging.

Ans: accommodation, p. 636

4.   In identity _____, people adapt to new experiences by changing their self-concept, adjusting too much.

Ans: compensation, p. 636

5.   Paul and Margaret Baltes emphasize that people can choose to cope with physical and cognitive losses in late adulthood through selective optimization with _____.

Ans: more apparent (or stronger), p. 637

6.   Behavioral genetics has demonstrated that genetic influences on traits become _____ in late adulthood than earlier.

Ans: stratification, p. 638

7. When the oldest generations are given limited roles and circumscribed opportunities in society in order to make way for upcoming generations, the culture is practicing age _____.

Ans: Disengagement, p. 638

8. _____ theory states that aging makes a person's social sphere increasingly narrow, resulting in relinquishment of roles, withdrawal, and passivity.

Ans: Stratification, pp. 638-639

9. _____ theories focus on the ways in which people organize themselves and are organized by society according to their particular characteristics and circumstances.

Ans: continuity, pp. 643-644

10. According to _____ theory, each person copes with late adulthood in much the same way that he or she coped during earlier periods of life.

Keeping Active

Ans: Elderhostel, p. 645

11. _____ is a program in which older people live on college campuses and take special classes.

Ans: political, p. 647

12. The one aspect of _____ participation that the elderly are less likely to engage in is door-to-door campaigning.

Ans: AARP, p. 647

13. The major organization in the United States representing the elderly is the _____.

Ans: Social Security, p. 647

14. The elderly are very concerned with _____ and tend to vote against any reduction in it, which is why it is sometimes called "the third rail" of domestic politics.

Ans: equity, p. 648

15. Whether each generation contributes and receives their fair share of society's wealth is a question of generational _____.

The Social Convoy

Ans: social convoy, p. 649

16. The family members, friends, and peers who move through life together make up a _____.

Ans: spouse, p. 649

17. For many older people, a _____ is a buffer against many of the potential problems of old age.

Ans: older, p. 650

18. In comparing older to younger couples, domestic violence is less common among _____ couples.

Ans: females; females, p. 651

19. In comparing males to females, losing a spouse is more common for _____ and living without a spouse is somewhat easier for _____.

Ans: beanpole, p. 654

20. A _____ family consists of many generations but only a few members are in each generation.

Ans: obligation; affection, p. 655

21.   One difference between the sexes is that, when interacting with their older parents, sons feel stronger
        _____, and daughters feel stronger _____.

The Frail Elderly

Ans: frail, p. 656

22.   A person who needs assistance with only one ADL may be considered _____.

Ans: instrumental, p. 656

23.   Activities and actions that require some intellectual competence and forethought are referred to as
        _____ activities of daily living.

Ans: relatives, p. 661

24.   Today, most of the frail elderly are cared for by _____.

Ans: Respite care, p. 662

25.   _____ involves a professional caregiver temporarily providing care for an older person in order to
        give the family caregiver a break.

ESSAY QUESTIONS

1.   Which theory of late adulthood do you believe best explains the period? Discuss why and provide an
        example to support your position.

2.   What is selective optimization with compensation? Provide three examples of this notion.

3.   Outline a retirement-counseling program for middle-aged workers that would promote higher self-
        esteem for participants when they retire.

4.   You live in a newly created retirement community, and you have just been elected head of the social
        committee. What can you do to promote friendship and emotional well-being among residents?

5.   Your healthy 70-year-old uncle wants to marry a widow, just two years after his wife's death. What do
        you think your feelings would be? What do these feelings reveal about your stereotypes?

6.   You have just been hired as the activities' director for a nursing home. What activities would you select
        and why?

7.   Imagine you have unlimited financial resources. Design the "ideal" nursing-home facility, including
        physical plant, staff, programs, residents, and policies, explaining why as well as what.

8.   Describe three considerations a person must make when making the decision about whether to care for
        a frail elder by himself or herself at home or in a nursing home.

Answer guidelines to these essay questions can be found in the Appendix at the end of the Test Bank.

EPILOGUE **Death and Dying**

MULTIPLE-CHOICE QUESTIONS

Deciding How to Die

Medical Professionals, p. Ep-2
Diff: E, Ans: a
1. Slowly, the medical profession is becoming more concerned with:
    a. helping the dying achieve a good death.
    b. keeping the dying in hospitals.
    c. keeping information that death in imminent from the patient.
    d. prolonging life, regardless of its quality.

Medical Professionals, p. Ep-2
Diff: H, Ans: d
2. The medical profession may deprive the elderly of a good death by:
    a. giving in to death too quickly.
    b. providing frightening information about the patient's condition.
    c. not using the most effective life-support systems.
    d. trying to prolong life by extraordinary measures.

Medical Professionals, p. Ep-2
Diff: M, Ans: a
3. Laura has just entered a hospice. She can expect:
    a. pain-killing medication.
    b. artificial life-support systems.
    c. restricted visits from friends and family.
    d. a medical doctor as the only caregiver.

Medical Professionals, p. Ep-2
Diff: E, Ans: b
4. The function of the hospice is to:
    a. save the terminally ill.
    b. allow people to die in peace.
    c. segregate the dying from those who might recover.
    d. convince the dying to accept death.

Medical Professionals, p. Ep-2
Diff: E, Ans: c
5. The "unit of care" for the hospice is:
    a. the terminally ill person.
    b. a person who is willing to try experimental treatments.
    c. the dying person and his or her family.
    d. every patient in a particular area of the hospice.

Medical Professionals, p. Ep-3
Diff: M, Ans: b
6.   Which of the following is true regarding hospice care?
      a.   The person must have a reasonable chance for recovery.
      b.   A diagnosis of terminally ill must be made in order for insurance to pay.
      c.   Patients have generally not accepted the diagnosis of terminal illness.
      d.   Death for patients is anticipated within two years.

Medical Professionals, p. Ep-3
Diff: M, Ans: a
7.   Hospice care is expensive because:
      a.   it is labor-intensive.
      b.   of the high-technology equipment.
      c.   it requires elaborate facilities.
      d.   medication is very expensive.

Medical Professionals, p. Ep-3
Diff: E, Ans: d
8.   Palliative care:
      a.   is the legal term for a living will.
      b.   does not occur in a hospice setting.
      c.   is not acceptable to most religions.
      d.   provides relief from physical pain.

Medical Professionals, p. Ep-3
Diff: E, Ans: a
9.   The goal of palliative care is to:
      a.   relieve patients from pain and suffering.
      b.   treat terminal illnesses.
      c.   hasten death.
      d.   prepare families for the death of a loved one.

Medical Professionals, p. Ep-3
Diff: M, Ans: d
10.   Analgesic medications are under-prescribed for the terminally ill primarily because:
      a.   they are illegal.
      b.   they are expensive.
      c.   patients refuse them.
      d.   they are addictive.

Medical Professionals, p. Ep-3
Diff: E, Ans: a
11.   The phenomenon that medication relieving pain also hastens death is called:
      a.   double effect.
      b.   the "old man's friend."
      c.   terminal assistance.
      d.   palliative death.

Legal Preparations, p. Ep-4
Diff: E, Ans: b
12.   A seriously ill person is allowed to die naturally, without any medical intervention, via what is called:
      a.   assisted suicide.
      b.   passive euthanasia.
      c.   suicide.
      d.   active euthanasia.

Legal Preparations, p. Ep-5
Diff: H, Ans: d
13.   Which of the following is an example of passive euthanasia?
    a.   A doctor gives a patient a prescription for a lethal medication.
    b.   A husband injects his wife with an overdose of her medication, without her requesting this of him.
    c.   A patient asks his adult child to give him a lethal injection.
    d.   A doctor does not resuscitate a patient who stops breathing.

Medical Professionals, p. Ep-4
Diff: H, Ans: c
14.   An example of active euthanasia is:
    a.   not using a respirator.
    b.   withholding painkilling drugs.
    c.   injecting lethal drugs.
    d.   a patient's refusal to eat.

Legal Preparations, p. Ep-4
Diff: E, Ans: b
15.   A person whom a dying person designates to make his or her decisions is:
    a.   a spouse or child.
    b.   a health care proxy.
    c.   an attorney.
    d.   a hospice worker.

Legal Preparations, p. Ep-4
Diff: E, Ans: b
16.   A DNR order:
    a.   can be used only by hospice workers.
    b.   allows a natural death.
    c.   is not available to the terminally ill.
    d.   is a request to postpone death.

Legal Preparations, p. Ep-4
Diff: E, Ans: a
17.   A "living will" is written to:
    a.   specify how much medical intervention is to be given if the individual is unable to express his or her preferences.
    b.   divide property among the heirs.
    c.   prevent children from grieving over the death.
    d.   determine exactly how an individual would like to die.

Legal Preparations, p. Ep-4
Diff: H, Ans: d
18.   Which of the following is a true statement about living wills?
    a.   Living wills enable health care professionals to make decisions exactly as the patient would have expressed, with no uncertainty.
    b.   Family members may disagree about how much suffering is acceptable, even when a living will exists.
    c.   Low income and minority patients are especially likely to have a living will.
    d.   Even the most definitive living will cannot answer every question because terms like "extraordinary measures" mean different things to different people.

Legal Preparations, p. Ep-5
Diff: H, Ans: b

19. Which of the following is an example of voluntary euthanasia?
    a. A doctor gives a patient a prescription for a lethal medication.
    b. A patient asks his adult child to give him a lethal injection.
    c. A husband injects his wife with an overdose of her medication, without her asking this of him.
    d. A doctor does not resuscitate a patient who stops breathing.

Legal Preparations, p. Ep-5
Diff: H, Ans: a

20. Which of the following is an example of physician-assisted suicide?
    a. A doctor gives a patient a prescription for a lethal medication.
    b. A patient asks his adult child to give him a lethal injection.
    c. A husband injects his wife with an overdose of her medication, without her asking him to do this.
    d. A doctor does not resuscitate a patient who stops breathing.

Medical Professionals, p. Ep-4
Diff: H, Ans: b

21. George is terminally ill and in constant pain. He has asked his doctor for pain-killing medication that his doctor knows George will use to end his life. If the doctor gives the prescription and George uses it to die, it is considered:
    a. active euthanasia.
    b. assisted suicide.
    c. passive euthanasia.
    d. murder.

Legal Preparations, p. Ep-5
Diff: H, Ans: d

22. Which of the following is a requirement for legal physician-assisted suicide in Oregon?
    a. The patient is certified terminally ill by the doctor involved.
    b. The patient is mentally ill.
    c. The family doesn't object.
    d. The patient must wait 15 days between asking for the prescription and receiving it.

Legal Preparations, p. Ep-6 (Table Ep.1)
Diff: M, Ans: c

23. Which type of death was least common in the Netherlands in 2001?
    a. withholding medical treatment
    b. double effect
    c. assisted suicide
    d. voluntary euthanasia

Legal Preparations, p. Ep-7
Diff: M, Ans: a

24. In Oregon, physician-assisted suicide is highest among:
    a. younger and better-educated patients.
    b. African-American females.
    c. low-income males of all races.
    d. married patients.

Preparing for Death

Avoiding Despair, p. Ep-7
Diff: M, Ans: b
25. According to Kübler-Ross, the first stage of dying is:
   a. anger.
   b. denial.
   c. depression.
   d. bargaining.

Avoiding Despair, p. Ep-7
Diff: H, Ans: c
26. Mrs. Cannon has been diagnosed as terminally ill, but she insists she will recover because her laboratory results were mixed up with someone else's. Kübler-Ross would say that Mrs. Cannon is in the emotional stage of:
   a. acceptance.
   b. bargaining.
   c. denial.
   d. depression.

Avoiding Despair, pp. Ep-7 – Ep-8
Diff: M, Ans: a
27. Researchers who have subsequently investigated Kübler-Ross's stages have:
   a. rarely found the same stages occurring in sequence.
   b. found none of the stages she described.
   c. found only one of the stages she described.
   d. consistently found the same stages occurring in the same sequence.

Avoiding Despair, p. Ep-8
Diff: E, Ans: d
28. In Western cultures, which of the following is likely when death is near?
   a. planning for death
   b. distributing property
   c. seeking emotional closeness
   d. all of the above
   e. none of the above

Deciding How to Die, p. Ep-8
Diff: H, Ans: b
29. When merely imagining that they will die soon, adults of all ages seek:
   a. new experiences they have not gotten around to previously.
   b. emotional closeness and comfort.
   c. the help of a professional.
   d. any kind of activity that will provide excitement.

Cultural Variations, p. Ep-9
Diff: H, Ans: b
30. In most African traditions, death provides:
   a. a lower status for elders.
   b. an occasion for affirmation of the entire community.
   c. a community celebration of separation from its collective past.
   d. an affirmation of faith in Allah.

Cultural Variations, p. Ep-9
Diff: H, Ans: a
31.   Abdul lives in a Muslim culture. He is likely to view death as a(n):
   a.   holy reminder of his own mortality.
   b.   elevation of community elders to special status.
   c.   affirmation of life.
   d.   affirmation of connection with the past.

Cultural Variations, p. Ep-10
Diff: H, Ans: c
32.   Among Buddhists, death is believed to be:
   a.   an occasion for affirmation of the entire community.
   b.   a reminder of everyone's mortality.
   c.   one of the inevitable sufferings of life that may bring enlightenment.
   d.   something to hide away in hospitals and ignore, if possible.

Cultural Variations, p. Ep-10
Diff: H, Ans: a
33.   In Hinduism, death is:
   a.   welcomed if it is a holy death.
   b.   a reminder of one's own mortality.
   c.   an affirmation of community.
   d.   an elevation to the status of elders.

Cultural Variations, p. Ep-10
Diff: H, Ans: c
34.   For Native Americans, death is:
   a.   welcomed if it is a holy death.
   b.   a reminder of one's own mortality.
   c.   an affirmation of nature and of community values.
   d.   an elevation to the status of elders.

Cultural Variations, p. Ep-10
Diff: H, Ans: a
35.   In the Jewish tradition, death is dealt with by:
   a.   burying the deceased within a day after death.
   b.   making extensive preparations in advance.
   c.   leaving the dying person alone.
   d.   mourning in private with no open expressions of it.

Cultural Variations, p. Ep-10
Diff: H, Ans: d
36.   In Christianity, death is thought to be:
   a.   not an end but a beginning of eternity in heaven or hell.
   b.   an affirmation of connection with the past.
   c.   a reminder of one's own mortality.
   d.   an affirmation of nature and of community values.

Cultural Variations, p. Ep-10
Diff: E, Ans: b
37.   Which of the following seems the most influential source of variations in death practices?
   a.   gender
   b.   culture
   c.   the law
   d.   income

Coping with Bereavement

Coping with Bereavement (Table Ep.2), p. Ep-12
Diff: E, Ans: a
38.   Cremation following death is most common in:
   a.   Japan.
   b.   Australia.
   c.   China.
   d.   the Netherlands.

Bereavement, p. Ep-12
Diff: H, Ans: c
39.   Which of the following is a true statement about bereavement?
   a.   It is an abnormal response to death.
   b.   It does not occur when religion teaches that the dead person is being rewarded in an afterlife.
   c.   It can lead to a reaffirmation of life.
   d.   All of the above are true statements.

Bereavement, pp. Ep-12 – Ep-13
Diff: M, Ans: c
40.   In comparison with grief, mourning:
   a.   leads to less chance of reaffirmation.
   b.   occurs more frequently.
   c.   is more dependent on cultural practices.
   d.   is more likely to lead to depression.

Bereavement, pp. Ep-12 – Ep-13
Diff: E, Ans: a
41.   Reaffirmation refers to the search for:
   a.   meaning.
   b.   an explanation.
   c.   a solution.
   d.   comfort from others.

Bereavement, p. Ep-13
Diff: M, Ans: d
42.   Mourners are most likely to respond to death with shock and a search for meaning when the:
   a.   dead person is a relative they never liked.
   b.   dead person is a spouse.
   c.   death was long anticipated.
   d.   death was sudden and violent.

Contemporary Challenges, p. Ep-14
Diff: E, Ans: b
43.   In earlier times, when someone died:
   a.   mourning was a private affair.
   b.   there was a traditional mourning ceremony.
   c.   mourning ceremonies were less religious.
   d.   mourning was not very emotional.

Contemporary Challenges, p. Ep-14
Diff: H, Ans: a
44.   The person who copes best with death is someone who:
       a.   talks about experiences shared.
       b.   avoids gravesite visits.
       c.   gets rid of mementos and pictures.
       d.   puts life with the loved one out of mind.

Contemporary Challenges, p. Ep-14
Diff: M, Ans: d
45.   Which of the following is a concern for developmentalists?
       a.   the increase in the public nature of mourning
       b.   the lack of disenfranchised grief
       c.   the search for affirmation of life
       d.   the increased social isolation of the bereaved

Contemporary Challenges, pp. Ep-14 – Ep-15
Diff: M, Ans: d
46.   Which of the following may hinder the healing and affirmation of the bereaved?
       a.   autopsies
       b.   not having the deceased's body in a specific location
       c.   inadequate grief
       d.   all of the above

TRUE-FALSE QUESTIONS

Deciding How to Die

Ans: T, p. Ep-2
1.   During the twentieth century, when illness became the domain of medicine rather than the domain of religion, acceptance of death became elusive.

Ans: F, p. Ep-2
2.   Most medical textbooks discuss care for the dying patient.

Ans: F, p. Ep-2
3.   Hospices must often use death-defying interventions.

Ans: T, p. Ep-2
4.   Prolonging the lives of terminally ill people by extraordinary measures may deprive them of the opportunity of a good death.

Ans: T, p. Ep-3
5.   Almost no hospices serve children because parents and oncologists tend to be unwilling to accept that a child will soon die.

Ans: F, p. Ep-3
6.   Some pain medication can speed up death.

Ans: F, p. Ep-3
7.   The double effect is considered unethical and is illegal in the United States.

Ans: F, p. Ep-4
8.   Younger low-income patients are most likely to insist on signing a living will.

Ans: F, pp. Ep-4 – Ep-5

9.   Signing a living will and designating a proxy are two ways in which people can ensure that they die exactly as they wish.

Ans: F, p. Ep-5

10.   Medical directives in living wills are always followed by hospital staff.

Ans: T, p. Ep-5

11.   Physician-assisted suicide and voluntary euthanasia are two forms of active suicide.

Ans: F, p. Ep-5

12.   Voluntary euthanasia involves performing an act that ends one's own life.

Ans: F, p. Ep-5

13.   Although active euthanasia is illegal in most places in the world, it probably happens in most places in the world.

Ans: T, p. Ep-5

14.   In voluntary euthanasia, but not in physician-assisted suicide, the doctor may administer the lethal drug.

Ans: F, p. Ep-5

15.   In Oregon, a physician may assist a patient in dying without consulting another doctor if the patient requests it.

Ans: T, p. Ep-5

16.   Physician-assisted suicide is legal in Oregon.

Ans: F, p. Ep-6

17.   Physician-assisted suicide is used extensively in the Netherlands.

Preparing for Death

Ans: F, p. Ep-7

18.   According to Kübler-Ross, the final stage of dying is depression.

Ans: T, p. Ep-7

19.   Kübler-Ross's five stages make feelings about death seem much more predictable and universal than they actually are.

Ans: F, p. Ep-7

20.   Kübler-Ross found that most dying patients were apathetic about talking about their condition.

Ans: T, p. Ep-7

21.   In terms of its dealings with patients, the medical profession in the past attempted to deny death as a reality.

Ans: F, p. Ep-8

22.   It is impossible to maintain organ functioning in a person after brain death has occurred.

Ans: F, p. Ep-8

23.   Modern medicine has increased the likelihood of a "good death."

Ans: F, pp. Ep-9 - Ep-11

24.   The specific meanings attached to death are the same throughout the world.

Ans: F, p. Ep-10
25.   For Hindus, a holy death is one that is fast and unexpected.

Ans: T, p. Ep-10
26.   In Jewish tradition, a dying person should never be left alone.

Ans: F, p. Ep-11
27.   Open-ended interviews with severely ill people who had immigrated to Canada from India found that the longer they were in Canada, the less important India and Hinduism became as they thought about death.

Coping with Bereavement

Ans: F, p. Ep-12
28.   Mourning is more private than grief.

Ans: T, p. Ep-13
29.   Mourning customs are designed by various cultures to channel grief toward affirmation of life.

Ans: T, p. Ep-14
30.   Recent trends in dealing with grief privatize and mask its expression.

Ans: T, pp. Ep-14 - Ep-15
31.   Inadequate grief is thought to harm both the bereaved and the larger community.

Ans: F, p. Ep-15
32.   The best antidote for mourning is to force the person to get out of the house and get on with his or her life.

Ans: F, p. Ep-15
33.   Bereavement tends to be a short-term process.

Ans: T, p. Ep-15
34.   In some cases, it may be appropriate for the bereaved to refuse to visit the grave, light a candle, cherish a memento, pray, or sob.

Ans: T, p. Ep-16
35.   A bereaved person may develop a deeper appreciation of human relationships.

FILL-IN-THE-BLANK QUESTIONS

Deciding How to Die

Ans: Elisabeth Kübler-Ross, p. Ep-2
1.   A major factor in our changing attitudes toward death has been the pioneering studies of _____.

Ans: hospice, p. Ep-2
2.   The institution which provides palliative care to a dying individual is a(n) _____.

Ans: terminally ill, p. Ep-3
3.   To be accepted by a hospice, patients must be diagnosed as _____.

Ans: double effect, p. Ep-3
4.   The fact that some pain-relieving drugs speed up death is referred to as the _____.

Ans: medical interventions, p. Ep-4

5. Experiencing a natural death means the person will be given no _____.

Ans: resuscitate, p. Ep-4

6. The initials DNR on a patient's hospital chart mean "do not _____."

Ans: living will, p. Ep-4

7. A document that indicates what medical interventions an individual wants if he or she is incapable of expressing his or her wishes is a _____.

Ans: voluntary euthanasia, p. Ep-5

8. A doctor who administers a lethal injection to a dying patient who requested to be helped to die is practicing _____.

Ans: slippery slope, p. Ep-5

9. Some people believe that allowing physician-assisted suicide and euthanasia will lead to a(n) _____, in which more and more extensive practices of eliminating the elderly, the disabled, or the poor will occur.

Preparing for Death

Ans: five, p. Ep-7

10. Kübler-Ross proposed that the dying go through _____ emotional stages.

Ans: thanatology, p. Ep-7

11. The study of death is called _____.

Ans: spiritual enlightenment, p. Ep-10

12. According to Buddhism, the task of the dying individual is to gain _____ from the experience.

Coping with Bereavement

Ans: bereavement, p. Ep-12

13. The sense of loss following a death is referred to as _____.

Ans: mourning, p. Ep-12

14. Expressing grief over the death of a loved one in various ways designed by religions and cultures is called _____.

Ans: isolation, p. Ep-14

15. Research indicates an increasing tendency toward social _____ for those who have just lost a loved one.

ESSAY QUESTIONS

1. What kind of ceremony or mourning ritual do you think is the best for people with your religious beliefs or cultural values? Why?

2. Your 40-year-old friend has recently been widowed. List three things you should say or do or not say or do and explain why.

3. There has been a great deal of media coverage regarding physician-assisted suicide and voluntary euthanasia. Define both and state whether you think either is acceptable. Explain your reasoning and give specific examples to justify your answer.

4.   If you were hired to set up and administer a hospice program in your community, what type of program would you choose? Be specific and explain your choices.

5.   What is your opinion on whether to prolong life with medical interventions? Why?

6.   Describe two things you learned from reading the Epilogue that made you think differently about preparations for death in your own family.

Answer guidelines to these essay questions can be found in the Appendix at the end of the Test Bank.

Appendix Answer Guidelines to Test Bank Essay Questions

Chapter 1

1. Students should affirm that age matters in this case. Specific views will vary, but students should demonstrate an understanding of the importance of historical context. For instance, 70-year-olds grew up without computers, 30-year-olds grew up using computers for a much more limited number of tasks, and 12-year-olds have grown up using the computer as a means of communication.

2. Race is meant to be a biological categorization (e.g., hair and skin color), whereas ethnic group is meant to be a category based on national origin, religion, customs, and language. Social scientists prefer not to use race, because there are no clear-cut categories. SES refers to income, education, community, etc., and is related to ethnic group but is certainly not the same.

3. Development is not always linear. There are many directions in which development can occur. Examples will vary, but student should provide two examples and evidence to support their argument.

4. Answers will vary, but student should choose a social construction and sufficiently describe specific aspects of the historical contexts that would influence differences in ideas.

5. Researchers interested in human development study different cultures in order to allow them to notice when patterns are universal and to provide insights into the effects of various practices. Examples will vary, but students should provide an example that demonstrates one of these purposes.

6. The five main steps involved in the scientific method are: formulating a research question, developing a hypothesis, testing the hypothesis, drawing conclusions, and making your findings available.

7. Naturalistic observation involves watching people in their natural setting. Research questions will vary, but should not involve cause and effect, and should include variables that can be observed in a natural setting. Advantages of naturalistic observation include that it is unobtrusive and that people act naturally. Limitations include that the researcher has minimal control and that one cannot make claims about cause.

8. A correlation exists between two variables when one changes (increases or decreases) as the other changes. It is impossible to determine cause and effect from correlations because correlations indicate a connection between two variables, but cannot determine a reason for the connection.

9. The experiment is a research method in which a researcher manipulates one variable and then looks for and records any changes in some other variable. Sample research questions will vary, but should involve an independent variable that can be manipulated (i.e., not age, gender, race, intelligence, etc.) and a dependent variable that can change. Advantages include ability to determine cause and effect relations and ability to manipulate or control the environment. Limitations include that it is usually an artificial situation and participants usually know they are research participants, so we don't know how people behave in real-world situations.

10.   Answers will vary, but students should describe two reasons. For instance, people may try to make themselves look smart or nice, wording of questions may influence results, data may be incomplete if everyone doesn't respond, and people can be inaccurate reporters (e.g., memory difficulties).

11.   The case study is research focusing on one individual. Sample research questions will vary, but should involve gathering a great deal of information about a single person over a period of time. Advantages include the ability to gain a lot of detailed information and the ability to understand an individual more thoroughly. Also, it is a good starting point for other types of research. Limitations include the possibility that the qualitative data or interpretations of it are biased, and the fact that what holds true for one particular individual may not hold true for others.

12.   The students should state that they will find several groups of children ranging in age from 4 to 10. They will then evaluate each child's reading ability or ask parents or teachers to do so. Finally, they will compare the children of various ages and look for differences.

13.   Longitudinal research is research in which people of a given age are studied repeatedly over time to measure their stability and change over time. Cross-sectional research involves examining several groups of people of different ages at a single point in time in order to examine age differences on a particular variable. Longitudinal design uses a single group, whereas cross-sequential design uses multiple groups of different ages. Advantages of longitudinal design over cross-sequential design are that it is simpler to conduct and analyze. Advantages of cross-sectional design over longitudinal design include that it can differentiate between true developmental changes and effects due to cohort, or historical period.

14.   Students should show that they can form a hypothesis about a topic and use their knowledge of the chapter to create ways to test a hypothesis.

15.   Answers will vary, but students should be evaluated on how well they understand the scientific process, can form a hypothesis, and understand the purposes of the particular research methodologies that they choose.

16.   Answers should acknowledge that cross-sectional research is faster and less expensive than longitudinal research. Answers should also indicate that longitudinal research has its shortcomings. For instance, it is difficult to follow the same individuals for a long period of time, and it is hard to assess the impact of participation in the research on their development. Alert students may also point out that historical factors are always a potential source of error with both longitudinal and cross-sectional research; results that were true for a particular cohort in one historical period may not hold for other cohorts growing up earlier or later. For instance, some of the long-term results of child abuse may well depend on the attitude and actions of the community with regard to abuse and the ability of medical personnel to detect abuse—both of which have changed markedly during the past twenty years.

17.   The answer should incorporate an ecological approach to describe the effects of poverty on cognitive development. Answers will vary, but should include the relation between poverty and family interactions (e.g., parents' stress will decrease quality of parenting), school/peers (e.g., the condition of schools), neighborhood/community (e.g., may be unsafe neighborhood, causing children stress on the way to and from school), and cultural values/economic policies (e.g., Head Start program).

18.   When involving children in research, experimenters must ensure that the subjects are not harmed, participation is voluntary, children and parents are informed about what will occur, and all information is kept confidential.

19.   Answers will vary, but ethical experiments are ones that will ensure that the subjects will not be harmed by the research process and participation is voluntary and confidential. Unethical experiments would involve violation of any of these conditions. One that would be difficult to evaluate would be a study in which there is some potential for harm but that there are potential benefits as well (e.g., effects of particular medicines or therapies).

20. Answers will vary, but a clear understanding of the ethical issues regarding children in research should be addressed.

Chapter 2

1. Answers will vary but should include three of the following: (1) Theories help us understand the influences of human behavior; (2) they form the basis for testable hypotheses regarding behavior and development; (3) they help us summarize our knowledge sensibly; (4) they generate discoveries; (5) they offer insight and guidance for every day concerns.

2. Answers will vary, but may include two of the following: (1) Freud has fewer stages than Erikson, and his stages end at adolescence, whereas Erikson's continue through adulthood; (2) Freud was more concerned with sexual impulses, whereas Erikson was more concerned with family and social aspects; (3) Freud considered his stages a time of conflict, whereas Erikson describes his as challenges or crises.

3. Oral (birth to 1 year), anal (1 to 3 years), phallic (3 to 6 years), latency (6 to 11 years), and genital (adolescence). See page 37, Table 2.1, for a description of what occurs during each stage.

4. Answers will vary, but students should show a grasp of Freud's genital period and of Erikson's identity vs. role diffusion stage. Students should state an opinion about which theory might be more useful and provide support for the opinion. This should include an understanding that Erikson's stages take family and society into account.

5. The cat associates the can opener's sound with food. Initially, the cat did not respond to the can opener (neutral stimulus). However, because the sound of the can opener was repeatedly paired with food (meaningful stimulus), that excites the cat. The cat now gets excited every time it hears the sound of the can opener.

6. In classical conditioning, individuals learn to associate a neutral stimulus with a meaningful stimulus and come to respond in the same way to the neutral stimulus as they naturally responded to the meaningful stimulus. In operant conditioning, individuals increase their behavior when it is frequently paired with a reinforcer and decrease their behavior when it is frequently paired with a punishment. Examples will vary. Answers for the biggest difference will also vary, but may include the following: classical conditioning (CL) generally involves a naturally-occurring response, whereas operant conditioning (OP) involves a behavior that can generally be controlled; OP involves learning the consequences of a behavior, whereas CL involves learning the association between two stimuli.

7. Answers will vary, but student should demonstrate an understanding that one needs to reinforce the roommate whenever she does make her bed (or does any behavior that is in the direction of that end).

8. Social learning theory acknowledges that humans appreciate the touch, warmth, reassurance, and example of other humans. In addition to the classical and operant conditioning on which behaviorism focuses, social learning theory holds that social learning, or modeling, is a prime source of learning.

9. Sensorimotor (birth to 2 years), preoperational (2 to 6 years), concrete operational (6 to 11 years), and formal operational (12 years through adulthood). See page 44, Table 2.2, for a description of what occurs during each stage.

10. With assimilation, we interpret new experiences so that they fit in with our existing ideas. With accommodation, we have to change our old ideas as a result of new experiences. Answers will vary, but similarities include the fact that new information puts old ideas into disequilibrium and the goal is to return to equilibrium. Differences include that changing of old ideas is a necessity for accommodation but not assimilation.

11.   Answers will vary, but student must demonstrate an understanding that assimilation involves keeping one's old ideas, whereas accommodation involves changing them.

12.   Answers should describe the person's original way(s) of thinking, the use of assimilation, or, more likely, accommodation, to deal with the new experience that put the thinking into disequilibrium, and the establishment of equilibrium after the change.

13.   Answers should reflect knowledge of behaviorists' emphasis on behavior: what are the immediate causes and consequences of this problem? Students should point out that there must be reinforcement for the disruptive, aggressive behavior and suggest ways to use reinforcers for nonaggressive behavior.

14.   Included in responses should be differentiation of the three schools of thought. Psychoanalytic psychologists will stress underlying motivation, possible psychosexual explanations, and Dina's psychosocial stage; behaviorists will concentrate on her specific behaviors and ways to reinforce changes in it; cognitive psychologists will consider her thinking and her developmental stage.

15.   Answers will vary, but students should demonstrate an understanding of guided participation and zone of proximal development. The child is learning if he or she needs less and less support to succeed and avoids boredom or feelings of being overwhelmed.

16.   Answers will vary, but students should demonstrate an understanding of the interplay between genes and environment. For instance, only individuals with genes for high cognitive capacity who are stimulated with language and numbers at an early age will become geniuses.

17.   Most of the behaviors can be experienced from more than one theoretical perspective. What is most important is that students demonstrate an understanding of how specific elements of a theory can be used to explain a particular behavior. Most students will probably choose behaviorism to explain Randy's conditioned smoking, Anne's behavior in the supermarket and in the car; and Coco's ability to detect narcotics; psychoanalytic theory to explain Alec's fear, and cognitive theory to explain Debra's thinking about the stability of gender differences.

18.   Answers will vary, but students must demonstrate an understanding of the distinction between nature and nurture and of how they interact.

Chapter 3

1.   They are adenine (A), cytosine (C), thiamine (T), and guanine (G). The combinations are A-T, T-A, G-C, and C-G.

2.   Monozygotic twins are created when a zygote splits apart in the early stages of duplication and division. These twins are called identical because they have the same genetic instructions. Dizygotic twins develop when two ova are fertilized at about the same time, thus forming two separate zygotes. These twins are sometimes called fraternal and are no more alike than any two siblings. Dizygotic twins are more common.

3.   Answers should show an understanding of phenotypes and what they indicate about the underlying genotype. Students should show awareness that most of a person's characteristics are the result of both genetic and environmental influences.

4.   Additive genes relate in an additive fashion. All of the additive genes for a particular trait contribute fairly equally. Dominant-recessive genes relate in such a way that the phenotype reveals the dominant gene more than the recessive gene. Examples will vary, but should demonstrate students' knowledge that with additive genes, the resulting phenotype will be a combination of all alleles, and with dominant-recessive genes, the resulting phenotype will reflect the dominant gene (at least mostly).

5.   Answers will vary, but may include two of the following: (1) there are vast similarities among animals of different species; (2) the number of human genes is smaller than what had been thought; (3) the more closely related the organisms, the more genes they share; (4) we can use other animals to examine human diseases and treatments.

6.   Answers may vary, but should include three of the following: (1) availability of alcohol; (2) cultural values; (3) biochemical make-up (related to place of origin); (4) personality traits, such as having a quick temper, a readiness to take risks, and a high level of anxiety.

7.   There are more recessive abnormal genes (not necessarily known disorders) than dominant abnormal genes, because dominant disorders are generally not passed down as recessive genes are. This is because most dominant disorders are severely disabling and lead the affected individual to not reproduce.

8.   Most answers will note that increased testing and counseling will reduce the occurrence of defects, because parents will usually choose either not to risk pregnancy or to terminate an affected pregnancy. Testing will also result in a greater ability to treat problems early, even in utero, resulting in fewer affected individuals. However, it should be noted that prenatal testing and genetic counseling are not flawless.

9.   Students should note that testing will allow these parents to prepare for the birth of a child with special needs, or, if the child has an abnormality that can be treated early in development, to be prepared for that Some students may note that intrauterine treatment may be a possibility with some disabilities.

10.   Answers should demonstrate an awareness of the importance of learning about inherited disorders in order to prevent and/or treat them through genetic counseling, gene therapy, and various other techniques.

11.   This answer should include the various factors known to put a couple at risk for having a child with a genetic disorder: Older mothers and fathers, parents from the same ethnic group, parents related to each other, previous spontaneous abortions, or having had children with inherited disorders.

12.   Answers will vary. The guidelines should indicate an understanding that harm can come from uncontrolled distribution of genetic information. Individuals might be denied jobs, insurance policies, or access to services and education, based solely on their genetic background.

13.   Genetic counseling is recommended for individuals who have a parent, child, or sibling with a serious genetic condition; are women age 35 or above; are men age 40 or above. It is recommended for couples who have a history of spontaneous abortion, stillbirths, or infertility; or who are from the same ethnic group or subgroup.

14.   Answers should include the severity of the risk, the likelihood of the risk, whether prenatal diagnosis is possible, whether the condition is treatable at birth, and whether the couple would consider abortion.

Chapter 4

1.   Students will note that the earlier the age of viability, the earlier "preterm" becomes. An earlier age of viability therefore results in more immature infants being delivered, resulting in a need for more information about what is required to sustain their lives.

2. Students should mention that most abnormal embryos are aborted spontaneously, often before the woman knows that she is pregnant, and that the rate of failure of fertilized eggs to implant is very high. Abstinence or moderation of drug usage, as well as social support, during pregnancy, can reduce risk. Techniques such as more sophisticated prenatal testing and even surgery should enable potential parents to make informed decisions about aborting or continuing with pregnancies that are found to be defective.

3. Early knowledge of pregnancy allows a woman to change any habits that might be detrimental to the fetus in the earliest stages of development (such as alcohol ingestion), or to consider terminating an unwanted pregnancy. However, because the incidence of spontaneous abortion of early pregnancies is so high, early detection might result in more disappointment and a greater fear of "miscarriage."

4. Among the many possible questions students might suggest are: How old is the mother? When did her prenatal care begin? Does she use any drugs, smoke, or drink? Has she undergone any recommended prenatal tests, and what were the results? The answers will give the prospective parents some idea, though not complete certainty, about the chances that the infant will be normally developed and healthy.

5. Students should describe a woman of low socioeconomic status without access to good nutrition and prenatal care, who smokes, drinks, and has had a short interval between children. Risks can be reduced by avoidance of drugs, good nutrition, and good prenatal care beginning as soon as pregnancy is confirmed.

6. Most infants' prenatal senses are working well, especially toward the end of pregnancy. By 9 weeks, the fetus moves in response to the mother's movement. When amniotic fluid is sweeter, fetuses swallow more. Immediately after birth, the smell of amniotic fluid is more soothing than other smells. The fetus can perceive bright light by the 27th week. The fetus responds to the sound of music or slamming doors. Also, when read a book by the mother in the ninth month, infants prefer that book (and their mother's voice and language) after birth.

7. Students should cite specific teratogens in the areas of diseases, medicinal drugs, psychoactive drugs, and environmental hazards. Answers should be supported by the effects these teratogens have on biosocial, cognitive, and psychosocial development.

8. Answers will vary, but each should provide a coherent argument that supports the student's position.

9. Answers will vary, but the student may wish to discuss the effects that these drugs have, as well as freedom of choice and "protective custody."

10. Answers will vary, but students may wish to discuss the mother's safety, the notion of when an embryo or fetus becomes a person, and "protective custody."

11. Students should demonstrate an understanding of the chemicals that can cross the placenta and harm the prenatal child. Answers should deal primarily with the obligation, if any, that society has to the unborn child and also the rights of the mother to determine her own life.

12. The answers will vary but some may include genetic vulnerability, drug usage, low pregnancy weight, low body fat, low total weight gain, inadequate vitamins, and poor nutrition.

13. Students should mention that home birth does not provide for Cesarean birth in those cases where birth becomes too stressful for the mother or the infant, or for a respirator and other special equipment and treatment for a newborn who is preterm or whose Apgar score is low.

14. Most students will probably note that this information is the beginning of the child's health record. It also informs the child's caregivers about the parents' attitudes and abilities in caring for the child's health, and alerts them to potential early problems. Finally, the best answers will reflect that these are only some of the many circumstances that affect development.

15.   The baby's head is low in the mother's pelvic cavity and the uterine muscles contract, pushing the fetus downward. This puts pressure on the cervix, causing it to dilate to about 4 inches. This process typically lasts 6 hours for first births and 3 hours for subsequent births.

16.   The second stage of labor begins with the head "crowning" (becoming visible) at the opening of the vagina. The head, then the rest of the body, emerges. This whole process typically takes less than one hour.

17.   The Apgar scale is used at 1 and 5 minutes after birth to measure the newborn's body functioning. It measures skin color, heartbeat, reflex irritability, muscle tone, and respiratory effort. Each of these is measured with a score of 0, 1, or 2. Higher scores are better. A 5-minute score of 7 or greater means that there is no danger. If the total score is below 4, the baby is in critical condition.

18.   Medical attention makes delivery faster, easier, and safer for the mother and child. Further, most women prefer medical attention. Students may wish to describe some of these benefits in greater detail.

19.   Some utilized procedures are unnecessary. Medically aided childbirth costs more. It is often less comfortable than in other settings. It can affect the family relationships by providing reduced opportunities for immediate bonding. The use of medication can lead to a variety of negative effects. Cesarean sections also lead to longer recovery times and make it less likely that the mother will breast-feed. Further, medical interventions are more expensive.

20.   Research has found no long-term benefits to immediate bonding for humans. However, the concept of bonding has led many women to feel quite guilty or saddened when not given immediate opportunities to spend time with the newborn. That said, it has proven to be beneficial for first-time mothers who are young, poor, or otherwise stressed because providing opportunities for immediate bonding reduces risk of postpartum depression.

21.   Good essays will point out that the parent-infant bond is not dependent on contact immediately at birth. Humans are much more variable with regard to the age and circumstances of bonding.

Chapter 5

1.   A profile of an infant susceptible to SIDS would be a bottle-fed, 1- to 3-month-old male infant of African descent who is the later-born child of a mother at the poverty level. See Table 5.1 for additional risk factors. Preventative measures include encouraging the baby to sleep on his or her back, not wrapping babies so tightly that they are unable to move, and limiting sleep to short periods of time.

2.   The answers should address increased size, myelination, and transient exuberance. Additional topics may be included also.

3.   Students will probably point out that the bright lights, cameras, heat, and noise of a movie or television set would be difficult for a newborn to handle; newborns would not be expected to respond or behave appropriately. Also, the typical newborn is far less attractive than most people's idea of the adorable infant.

4.   The answer will vary, but students should demonstrate good understanding of infants' visual abilities. As for the environment, the student should mention that in order for things to be seen clearly by newborns, they should be close. Further, infants prefer new images, large, slow-moving, high-contrast objects with complex visual patterns, and contrast density.

5.   Students may suggest various techniques involving measuring variations in infants' physiological responses, such as heart rate, sucking response, and eye movements during the presentations of stimuli and during periods of habituation to stimuli.

6.   There are many, including shorter stature; stunted intellectual growth; differential treatment from parents; starved brain development; impaired neurological networks; lack of interest in sensory, intellectual, and social events; later crawling and walking; limited perceptual growth; increased fussiness; impaired learning; concentration difficulties; and impaired language skills.

7.   The advantages of breast-feeding include the release of hormones that reduce pain, encourage attachment, regulate various internal organs, determine the timing of sexual maturation, and provide immunities. Also, it's more digestible and contains more vitamins and minerals than cow's milk. Further, breast-fed babies have fewer allergies and stomach aches. The disadvantages include the potential to transmit teratogens that the mother might ingest, the family's inability to participate with the mother in the feeding, and the lack of convenience of feeding on demand, especially in a society that is not entirely comfortable with breast-feeding in public.

8.   Answers will vary, but students should mention that parents must be flexible and attentive. Further, becoming educated about children's nutritional needs and treating their own depression are good ideas, too.

9.   Answers should show an understanding of the extent of infant undernutrition and its consequences. The answer should be innovative, yet realistic. Administration, funding, and clientele should all be addressed.

Chapter 6

1.   Responses should show an understanding of the various areas of research on perception including affordances (Gibsons' view), graspability, inter-modal perception, and cross-modal perception. The student should also show an awareness that not all the research is perfect. The reliance on various types of infant reactions from which the researchers assume perception is occurring is always a problem. In addition, there has not been enough replication of this research. It would be expected that the student will find some areas of this research to be believable and some to be problematic.

2.   Affordances are all the different ways in which we can understand an object. By trying different affordances, we can understand what an object looks like, tastes like, smells like, etc. Further, we can find different ways to use or to interact with the object.

3.   To measure depth perception, Gibson & Walk placed babies on a surface that apparently ends with a sudden drop. Ten-month-olds fearfully refuse to cross over the "cliff" even when their mothers called them. The researchers felt that the stopping demonstrated that 10-month-olds had depth perception. However, research with 3-month-olds showed that they noticed the difference.

4.   Look for answers that describe a standard test (toy under blanket, dish behind furniture or testers' back) and note factors Piaget did not consider, such as the child's motivation to search, familiarity with the objects used. Mention might also be made of memory, a factor Piaget does not discuss.

5.   We see plenty of evidence of memory that lasts for a few minutes; for example, habituation studies, cross-modal perception, and object permanence. As for long-term memory, we know that young babies can remember given certain conditions. Students may discuss the research of Rovee-Collier featuring kicking movements and mobiles and also might mention Piaget's deferred imitation.

6.   Students creation of this scene should note variations in a particular behavior (filling a shovel, pail, sneakers with sand; digging with a shovel, fingers, and a stick); experimentation; trial and error; and pretending.

7.   Refer to Table 6.3 for a quick wrap-up.

8. The answers should stress involving the baby in social interaction, especially games that involve turn taking and babbling. The best answers will include the idea that the sitter should be sensitive to the infant's gestures and other signs indicating which activities are enjoyed.

9. All normal human infants are very similar in their capacity to perceive and respond to language. Baby talk all over the world has similar characteristics because it reflects language adaptations best suited for communication with infants.

10. The possible explanations should include normal lag between comprehension and articulation, as well as severe problems in hearing and/or mental development, with several explanations in between, such as the possibility that the child does not hear enough language spoken to him or her. Further, you may comfort your friend by pointing out that using and understanding any form of communication is more important than language usage, per se.

11. Answers should differentiate between Skinner's theory of reinforcement and conditioning and Chomsky's structuralist approach, based on the child's inborn predisposition to learn speech (LAD).

12. In the first two years, perceptual development involves learning the affordances of objects, the constancy of objects, depth perception, and inter-modal and cross-modal perceptual skills. Cognitive development includes the beginning of understanding of categories, object permanence, memory skills, and cause-and-effect reasoning. Language development includes babbling, holophrastic speech, two-word speech, and larger combinations of words.

13. The answer depends on whether (1) the child can understand what others are saying, (2) what culture the child is raised in, (3) the child is able to make her needs known in other ways, and (4) the child's hearing and ears have been tested. Children that are most adept at expressing emotions nonverbally tend to be slower to talk.

14. Also known as *child-directed speech*, *baby talk* is a high-pitched communication with any low-to-high fluctuations, simpler words, and shorter sentences. It is used universally when talking with infants.

15. The stages of sensorimotor intelligence are:
    Stage One: Reflexes. These include all of the reflex actions apparent at birth. The infant gains information about the world through the repeated exercise of these reflexes.
    Stage Two: The First Adaptations. These include primary circular reactions such as thumb-sucking, through which the infant learns the limits of his or her own body.
    Stage Three: An Awareness of Things. These include secondary circular reactions, such as banging on pots and pans, through which the infant learns about things in the environment.
    Stage Four: New Adaptation and Anticipation. These include goal-directed behavior, which stems from an enhanced awareness of causes and effects, and the emergence of the motor skills needed to achieve these goals.
    Stage Five: Experimentation. These include tertiary circular reactions and trial-and-error learning.
    Stage Six: Mental Combinations. In this stage, toddlers are able to try out various actions mentally without actually having to perform them.

Chapter 7

1. Diana should approach cautiously and watch the child carefully. She should also stay calm and at a distance. The child's response will depend not only on Diana, but on the child's temperament, the security of the mother-child relationship, how the mother responds, how near the mother is, and the child's current mood.

2. The answer should definitely mention something about social referencing and how the child's response will probably depend on the parent's response.

3.   Well-developed answers should show an understanding of the research on the roles mothers and fathers traditionally play in the area of child care. Differences and similarities should be mentioned, with appropriate criticisms and recommended changes, all with the well-being of the child kept uppermost.

4.   Answers will vary quite a bit, but the student should mention how each parent feels about this choice and how society might respond. The student should mention that Hugh will probably provide care that is just as good as Rebecca's would be. However, fathers tend to interact with their children in ways that are different from how mothers respond. The student should address some of these differences.

5.   Behaviorists believe that personality is almost entirely shaped by the parents who provide rewards and punishment for various behaviors.

6.   Freud believed feeding was important because it satisfies oral needs. Erikson believed it was important because it helps establish a sense of trust between child and parent.

7.   Look for evidence that the student realizes that both autonomy and shame are mixed blessings. Autonomy leads to strong self-confidence and independency, but might make the individual insensitive to the customs of society or the needs of others. Shame and doubt might produce the opposite— someone too concerned with others' opinions.

8.   Answers should indicate the adaptations that parents are required to make to an infant's particular physical, cognitive, and psychosocial needs. For example, parents must adjust their routines to accommodate a child who is particularly active, adventurous, or outgoing, just as adjustments must be made for those who are relatively inactive, disabled, or shy.

9.   Both behaviorists and psychoanalysts emphasized the importance of early experience and the influence of the mother, but the behaviorists emphasized conditioning, imitation, and observation as the primary means of acquiring various skills. Psychoanalysts emphasized stages linked to physical development that occur in all children without the influence of the environment.

10. The focus of cognitive theory is on the mental world of values, thoughts, opinions, etc., brought about through early family experiences. From these experiences, the infant attempts to generate a basic idea of what to expect from others around them, i.e. a "working model" of projected expectations of others. This becomes a (Piagetian) schema not focusing on the environmental experiences, but rather on the child's mental interpretations of these. Epigeneticists focus not on experiences, but on genetic predispositions. Temperament is therefore primarily a result of genetically-generated unique differences in emotions, activity level, and self-control factors. Epigeneticists speak of temperament as based on this genetic "constitution," not perceptual frames of references as haphazard as unique experiences tend to be.

11. Although there is a correlation of low socioeconomic status (SES) with low child intelligence, poverty does not have a direct influence on the infant, but rather an indirect one. As poor parents try to cope with the factors in their stressful existence, the stress itself may stress the infant in the form of undesirable actions and reactions on the parents' part such as that noticed by attachment researchers which create deleterious responses by the infant that may lead to disorganized attachment. The value system of low SES will have a cultural impact on the parental expectations and behaviors in the areas of breast-feeding, language-learning, object play, etc., as socioculturalists have noted.

12. Self-awareness is linked with self-concept. As toddlers become aware of what they are capable of and what they are not, pride develops as a result of matching their abilities and shame when they do less than what they are capable of. Pride appears to develop not from parental praise, but from personal assessment on the toddler themselves and cognitive recognition of how they are performing. Negative parental criticism does lead to increased shame, however, and neutrality on the parents' part in evaluating their children's behavior seems to guide children to do things on their own which enable the process of self-evaluation as an internal predetermining mechanism for the development of both pride and shame.

Chapter 8

1. Students should indicate that since children grow more slowly between the ages of 2 and 6 than they did in the first two years of life, their appetites are smaller. The most common nutritional problems of preschoolers are insufficient intake of iron, zinc, and calcium, all of which can be avoided with a proper diet.

2. Students should demonstrate a strong grasp of the patterns of physical development, particularly brain maturation, as well as preschool play activities and gross and fine motor skills. Students must take into consideration that the child is a girl.

3. An understanding of the material covered in the changing policy box on injury control, including the research on the effectiveness of various approaches to educating the public about safety measures, should be apparent in the answers. Students should also indicate those factors that make a child most susceptible to injury.

4. Answers should describe a preschool program that takes into consideration the changing needs of the child from 2 to 5 years of age. The program should include activities to enhance the development of gross motor skills and fine motor skills as well as an environment that takes into consideration children's play styles and playmate preferences.

5. Answers should mention some of the reasons why hazards are more prevalent, such as lower-income homes and environments being more hazardous.

6. Answers will vary, but they could include riding a tricycle, climbing a ladder, swinging, and throwing, kicking, and catching a ball.

7. Abuse is any action that is harmful to a child's well-being, whereas neglect involves inaction that leads to a failure to meet a person's basic needs.

8. There are many possible answers here, but answers should mention various cultural, familial, and economic factors. Social isolation and poverty are considered two of the most powerful predictors of maltreatment.

9. Students should mention both short-term and long-term consequences. In addition, they should note that the duration of the abuse and the age at which it began play a role in determining the consequences.

10. The state-funded project encourages high-risk families to voluntarily agree to have trained visitors come to the home during the child's first five years. The visitors provide emotional support, model positive parent-child interactions, and help the mother find health-care providers and other local agencies. Students can state their opinions regarding whether the program would work, but should demonstrate an understanding of the program and give specific reasons why they feel it would or would not succeed locally.

11. Answers will vary, but the student should show a good understanding of primary, secondary, and tertiary prevention.

12. Answers will vary, but the student should show a good understanding of the three types of prevention. Most should include that it would be wisest to prevent maltreatment before it ever occurs (primary prevention).

13. The acceptance of these terms has made it easier for American children to overeat, adding foods in-between meals. This is a contributing factor to obesity. More calories consumed without added exercise create fat storage.

14.   Child abuse is a deliberate action which harms the child, either physically, emotionally, or sexually. It includes sexual abuse as a sub-category. Child neglect is failure to take some action on behalf of the child so that their physical, educational, or emotional needs are met. Child neglect, therefore, cannot include sexual abuse as a sub-category.

15.   Myelination in neurons increases the speed of signals between neurons. It allows children to think and react much more quickly than toddlers can. It is helpful in recognition tasks, but invaluable in processing several thoughts in succession. Myelination is especially strong in the auditory and visual areas of the brain accompanying experience in these areas. The functions of memory and reflection are aided by myelination, as well.

16.   As infants lie in their cribs, they face toward one hand, primarily. Moving it as they watch, they gain dexterity, making that hand more dominant. It is in this way that experience influences hand preference.

17.   The right hemisphere basically controls the left side of the body and the functions of generalized emotional and creative impulses, including appreciation of most music, art, and poetry. The left hemisphere basically controls the right side of the body and the functions of specific logic, detailed analysis, and the basics of language. The left side notices details and the right side grasps the "big picture."

Chapter 9

1.   Conservation is the concept that the number or amount of something is the same, regardless of changes in appearance. Students can describe any two of the conservation tasks, but be sure they mention the initial presentation, the transformation that the child watches, and the question asked.

2.   Steps that contribute to effective scaffolding include:
    1. presenting challenges for new learning.
    2. offering assistance with tasks that may be too difficult.
    3. providing instruction.
    4. encouraging the child's interest and motivation.

3.   Vygotsky would say that the parents *definitely* should get involved. The parents can offer assistance by providing direct instruction, encouraging the child to try to do it, interacting with Francesca, gradually letting her do it more on her own, using directive comments, and helping her see her progress.

4.   He would say it plays a critical role, because the culture will determine what cognitive skills are valued. Students should provide an example of a particular cultural value.

5.   Answers should indicate an understanding of Piaget and Vygotsky, especially their disagreement about how learning occurs (genetically programmed as opposed to socially and culturally driven; individual as opposed to guided). It is important that students cite relevant examples from their own personal experience rather than rewording examples found in the book.

6.   Students should cite low teacher-student ratios, a wide variety of materials that help develop fine and gross motor skills and that challenge children intellectually, a curriculum that emphasizes cognitive goals rather than behavioral management, and teachers with training in early childhood education.

7.   This question allows a wide range of creativity in the answer. The most important thing is to be sure that students support any of their ideas with relevant research and/or experience. They must include consideration of the needs of families in which the parent or parents must work for the family to survive; the needs of preschool children from a biosocial, cognitive, and psychosocial perspectives; and the needs of society as a whole.

8. The word "selfish" describes a person who is well aware that others have needs of their own, yet they arbitrarily satisfy their own needs to the exclusion of others'. "Egocentric" describes one whose entire awareness is of themselves and their needs and wants, without any intention of denying others their own expression. One who is selfish is at the same time necessarily egocentric, but it is common to see young children being egocentric without being selfish.

9. It refers to the ability of children, beginning at around age 4, to comprehend that mental phenomena may not reflect reality. Theory of mind implies the recognition that there is an internal view of the world and its workings, yet understanding that it is still a version of reality and, as such, is subject to opinions and appearances. It is a major step forward in adaptation to life from being the impressionable child to becoming the reasoning adult.

10. The "critical period" is the only time which one may learn a particular aspect of language. Once that period has come and gone, no amount of training or exposure to the environment will modify the developing person so that they might advance. The "sensitive period" is not as rigid, and suggests that there are best or optimum times to learn the language component, but if that period passes, it will still be possible to learn the component later via training or new experiences.

11. "Fast mapping" involves the use of an interconnected set of categories for vocabulary-building which speeds the development of learning new words. It is imprecise in the sense that the new word is not necessarily accurately defined before it is assimilated and its meaning is grouped with a category or group of words that are used to discuss or think about a topic. The "logical extension" concept refers to the child's having learned a specific word, and then applying it to other, unnamed objects in the same category. Logical extension is similar to generalizing from a specific fact to a group of items. Both terms allow a terrific surge of perceptual interrelationships between words for the child.

12. Two views prevail in this issue. One indicates that learning one's native language first will allow the child to later add the second language. The other argues that such proficiency is not required in the native language before the second is attempted. That view recommends that very young children be exposed to both languages simultaneously in the home and, if possible, at school, later. The text indicates that the latter approach is more likely to be more effective, and is especially valuable in learning the nuances of that second language, such as subtle intonations, pauses, and gestures that accompany that language.

13. Every child is encouraged to master skills that are characteristic skills of a child of about 7. Artistic expression, exploration of the environment, and collaboration between parents and teachers is supported. This implies an infusion of experiences and the use of adults as enablers and teachers, with less focus on stages, such as those suggested by the Piagetians.

Chapter 10

1. Tell a story about how he can master the experience. For example, the story could involve confronting the bully or telling the teacher, who puts an end to the aggression.

2. During Erikson's initiative versus guilt stage, children try to prove what they can do. They attempt to master tasks by themselves. They express pride in their success and guilt about their failures. Their self-esteem is blossoming. They appraise their abilities and try to do what adults are doing.

3. Students should be aware that children with no siblings can benefit from play dates with other children, enrollment in nursery school, and visits with cousins or other family members of the same age. Such interactions will help children to develop an increased understanding of others their own age, modify aggressive behaviors, engage in various types of play, and develop better language skills.

4.   Rough-and-tumble play mimics aggression but it is purely for fun with no intent to harm. Boys engage in it more frequently than girls do. Sociodramatic play involves acting out specific roles. This type of play is more common among girls.

5.   The example must demonstrate that children are acting out specific roles. Sociodramatic play is important for children to explore social roles, test their ability to convince and explain their ideas, regulate their emotions, and examine their personal concerns in a nonthreatening manner.

6.   Students should write a clear statement that reflects the research on the influence of television cited in the chapter. They should address the issues of the number of hours spent viewing television and the content of the shows (especially violent content).

7.   The student must show that he/she understands what aggression is by providing an acceptable example and correctly identifying the type of aggression being demonstrated.

8.   Baumrind observed children in preschool activities, interviewed both parents, and observed parent-child interactions in both the laboratory and the home.

9.   Students should be able to summarize the parenting styles discussed in the text. It is important that they give examples from their own experience in order to bring together issues of family size, ethnicity, economic factors, and cultural context.

10. Obviously, answers will vary here, but the student should be able to provide a good understanding of the style(s) chosen and enough description that you can be certain that the selected style(s) matches the description. Students may tell you that their parents were different or that their parents' style changed over time.

11. There are many possible answers here. Some factors influencing parenting style include culture, religious beliefs, ethnicity, the parent's sex, the parent's upbringing, economic well-being, the parent's personality, family size, birth order, and the child's temperament.

12. Answers will vary depending on opinion here, but some of the advantages are that only-children receive more parental attention and are more verbal, more creative, more likely to attend college, and more intelligent. The only disadvantage seems to be social. However, given the availability of day care and preschool education, this may not be an issue. Further, students may mention their own experiences and how this decision might affect the parent.

13. Sex differences (such as anatomical differences) are determined by biology, whereas gender differences (such as toy preference) are due mainly to culture.

14. More students will probably note that this example illustrates cultural acceptance of less rigorously gender-stereotyped behavior (and more androgyny) but indicates the persistence of tendency, influenced perhaps by both biology and culture, toward aggression in boys.

15. There is an attraction to the opposite-sex parent and a rivalry with the same-sex parent. Boys also experience pleasure when touching their penis, whereas girls may experience penis envy. By the end of the phallic stage, identification (wanting to be like) with the same-sex parent should occur.

16. Freud (and the psychoanalytic theorists) claimed that during the phallic stage (ages 3 to 6) the young girl becomes jealous of boys because they have a penis. The girl blames her mother for this "incompleteness" and decides that the next best thing to having a penis is becoming sexually attractive so that someone with a penis (such as father) will love her. In other words, she will identify with women (such as mother) who father finds attractive. Many students will strongly disagree with (and perhaps even be offended by) this notion.

17.   Answers should present a clear assessment of the stereotypical roles assumed by men and women, and the influence these roles have on the developing child. Answers should take into account how the three theories—psychoanalytic, learning, and cognitive—explain gender-role development. Students should be able to point out positive and negative aspects of the current gender roles and provide some creative suggestions for improvement.

18.   Epigeneticists are interactionists at heart, focusing on the interplay between growth from the genetic blueprint and the early experiences of the child. They do not believe in the radical behaviorist's view, which is that experience is mainly responsible for how children develop. The student may relate the text example here, of the behavior of men and women being different in prehistoric times for the purpose of adaptation to a harsh world. In today's world, epigeneticists would believe that all sex and gender differences have a genetic origin, but society can enhance or redirect those differences.

Chapter 11

1.   Genetics, lack of exercise, television viewing, nutrition, cultural attitudes toward food, and precipitating traumatic events are the primary causes.

2.   The program that each student develops should incorporate each of the areas—heredity, exercise, television-viewing habits, attitude toward food, etc., discussed in the chapter.

3.   Answers should point to the importance of providing a variety of activities appropriate to the physical development, skills, and reaction times of children at various ages. The best answers will include discussion of sex differences and similarities in athletic skills and discussion of the needs of special children. Students should show a good understanding of motor abilities during these ages. Further, the students should stress making the activities exciting, not too competitive, and avoid comparisons between players.

4.   Students should be aware that the child's body is not mature enough to handle the rigors and strain of classical techniques. The teacher is putting into practice the general principle that children should not simply imitate adult athletic or physical abilities, but should participate in age- and ability-appropriate physical activities.

5.   Good answers will note that general knowledge, reasoning ability, mathematical skill, memory, and vocabulary skills are evaluated; that scores tend to predict school performance; and that, among other things, emotional stress, health, test-taking anxiety, and cultural differences can result in invalid test scores.

6.   The student should mention that both are common (aptitude) tests of intelligence. They both measure general knowledge, reasoning ability, mathematical ability, memory, vocabulary, and spatial perception.

7.   The student should mention that this score is just below the average range, on the high end of the classification for a slow learner. From here, answers will vary. Students may wish to mention the student's motivation and concentration abilities, the tester and the testing environment, the validity or appropriateness of the test, and the fact that it only measures certain types of intellectual abilities.

8.   In infancy, the child may appear to be normal, even unusually well behaved. Severe deficiencies in communication ability, social skills, and imaginative play emerge in early childhood. As the child gets older, the lack of social understanding becomes the worst problem and will probably be a lifelong experience. The symptoms also become more varied.

9.   The most important thing in this answer is that the student give an accurate assessment of what learning disabilities are and are not; in other words, dispel the myths about them. Well-developed answers will include the types, the frequencies, the reasons why some children are undiagnosed, the possible causes, and what help can be obtained (special tutoring and attention to social skills).

10. Answers should point out that the effects of ADHD can be abated through medication (drug therapy), psychological therapy, and restructuring the home and school environment. Further, students should discuss the possibilities of mainstreaming, integration, inclusion, and resource rooms. Students should specifically describe each of these treatments/responses.

11. The student ought to mention that the answer will depend on the type and the severity of the problem. Also, students should address how their answer as a parent may be very different from a teacher's response. The student should show a good understanding of the various possibilities (for example, mainstreaming, resource rooms, inclusion, and integration).

Chapter 12

1.   The sensory register momentarily stores information received by the senses; however, most of this information is discarded. The meaningful information then goes to working memory for processing. In long-term memory, information remains.

2.   Selective attention improves; children begin to use storage and retrieval strategies; their processing capacity expands, as working memory improves and mental activities become more automatic; their knowledge base expands and they become better able to recognize and use effective cognitive strategies. Sixth-grade teachers, therefore, should offer problems that demand more concentration, challenge the student to choose and use various cognitive strategies, enhance memory skills, and draw on the student's growing knowledge base and processing capacity. First-grade teachers should be aware of their students' cognitive limitations, encouraging intellectual curiosity and perseverance, coaching them in simple cognitive strategies, and exposing them to a variety of subject matter to help enlarge their knowledge base.

3.   Students should refer to improvements in selective attention, processing speed and capacity, the automatization of certain tasks, better storage and retrieval strategies, and metamemory.

4.   The basic story involves a man (Heinz) stealing medicine for his dying wife after the pharmacist had charged 10 times the drug's cost and refused to lower the price or let Heinz pay later. Students' answers about what Heinz should do will vary, but they should be sure to defend their position.

5.   The main criticisms presented by the text are that (1) the theory is too narrow and restrictive, because of its focus on reasoning, (2) it only reflects liberal Western values, and (3) it overlooks male-female differences. Students' opinions on these criticisms will vary, but students should be able to show that they understand Kohlberg's theory and its critics.

6.   Gilligan believed that women relied on a morality of care, which involves nurturance and compassion for others. She felt that men used a morality of justice, which is more abstract and based on rules. Students' attitudes toward this will vary.

7.   Reciprocity (or *inversion*) is the understanding that two things may change in opposite ways to balance each other out. Students should also point out that reciprocity is especially relevant to the development of math understanding where subtraction is the inverse of addition and multiplication the inverse of division.

8.   With immersion, the child's instruction occurs entirely in the second language. With English as a second language (ESL), children speak only English, but students work together toward the goal of learning English. With bilingual education, students are instructed in their native language and English.

9.   Answers will vary, but students should mention that immersion tends to fail when students feel shy, stupid, or socially isolated. Further, if the attitude of the school is that the child is deficient, immersion will tend to fail.

10.   Her teacher's attitude may have promoted achievement and learning, but it also may have damaged Nancy's self-esteem and pride, at least temporarily. The teacher could have encouraged her use of the second language by saying, "We speak English in class so that everyone can understand," which would have allowed Nancy to retain her informal ease with her friends.

11.   Students should mention learning the new language early in life, learning with peers, having adults provide encouragement, encouraging immigrants to learn the new language, and remembering that each child and family is different.

12.   The answer should include instruction in choice of formal or informal speech, preservation of the dignity of the first language, an early start in working with the second language, and the encouragement of communication in the new language among children. Students might also consider the merits and drawbacks of the various forms of bilingual education mentioned in the chapter.

13.   The established hierarchies involve the ability to deal with part-whole relationships, that is, the understanding that every category or group of things includes some elements and excludes others, and each is part of a hierarchy. Items at the bottom of a category hierarchy belong to every higher category but this process does not reverse. This means that inclusion operates in a one-way fashion that is helpful in understanding classes of things. Classification also involves the organization of things into part-whole relationships and uses the same inclusion and exclusion system of relationships.

Chapter 13

1.   The Freudian perspective places the school-age child in latency or in the stage of industry vs. inferiority (Erikson), with a focus on quiet emotional drives, submerged and unconscious conflicts, and mastering cultural values. The behaviorist, sociocultural, and social-cognitive perspectives emphasize respectively, acquisition of new skills, social awareness, and self-understanding. These perspectives share the view that children have more openness, insight, and confidence; distinct competencies unify; and new abilities to learn, analyze, and express emotions, and to make friends become more focused and consistent.

2.   Thoughtful students will consider whether "social cognition" is part of what we usually define as "intelligence," and may question whether understanding social interactions is as important as, for example, perceiving spatial relationships. The specific skills measured in such a section might include the ability to understand the motives and responses of others, to anticipate how personality characteristics might affect responses, and to differentiate between appropriate and offensive comments in a social conversation.

3.   Older children come to focus on motives, feelings, and the social consequences of behavior. They also understand motivation, can analyze the future impact of people's actions, and can use personality traits to predict behavior. Children come to understand that people can have several emotions simultaneously and that people sometimes disguise their true emotions.

4.   The peer group is defined by the text as: "a group of individuals of roughly the same age and social status who play, work, or learn together." The examples given will vary according to the time referent.

5.   Good responses will include descriptions of the popular child as: socially mature, understanding and helpful, having a pleasing appearance and a high level of academic achievement, and tending not to be physically aggressive. Rejected children may need assistance with personal grooming and/or academic skills, should seek out peers similar to themselves (in terms of sex, intellectual ability, etc.), and participate in activities and relationships that increase self-esteem and self-understanding. As they begin to derive confidence from their own strengths and interests, the number and quality of their friendships are likely to improve.

6.   You should be concerned as victims of bullying are anxious, depressed, and underachieving at the time, and may have low self-esteem and painful memories years later. You should get involved by teaching your child problem-solving skills, improving your child's academic skills, and changing your child's negative assumptions. Further, you might want to make the teachers aware of this situation. Teachers can discuss reasons to stop bullying and ways to successfully mediate peer conflicts. If the situation persists, the teacher can move the bully to a different class or discuss the situation with the parents.

7.   The five ways are: meeting basic needs (for food, clothes, and shelter), encouraging learning, developing self-esteem, nurturing peer friendship, and providing harmony and stability. Students should be able to give a good description of how their family succeeded or let them down.

8.   Students should mention that differences in age might be a factor; a child may be especially vulnerable if he or she is in a transitional phase, such as entering first grade or adolescence. Differences in sex have an effect (boys generally have a more difficult time adjusting), as does the magnitude of the change(s) required of the child, such as switching to a new school or taking on more responsibility for younger siblings. Persistent or long-term problems might be related to a specific handicap, making one child more vulnerable than another to the stresses associated with parental divorce.

9.   First, keep in mind that the child's life is currently in great turmoil. You should also consider that joint custody is difficult to carry out, especially when the parents are arguing. That said, the more competent and more involved parent should probably receive custody, regardless of whether that is the father or mother. You will want to keep in mind that the goal is for both parents to remain involved in the child's life and this is more likely to occur when the father receives custody. Other factors to consider would be income, the child's sex, the presence of a stepparent, and the parent's willingness to accept help.

10. Students' answers will vary, but Table 13.2 provides a quick overview. Some of the more salient factors include the parent's maturity and age, his or her income, the stability of the situation, and the parent's overall social situation. In and of itself, a single-parent household does not have to be a negative situation for the child.

11. Support groups for single parents provide emotional support and practical advice through contact with others in the same situation. A grandparent or other relative might help with child care and perhaps contribute financial support, while the child's teachers and school counselors can help with school-related problems and with the child's general adjustment. Friends and neighbors might volunteer to baby-sit, do the shopping, or help out with other errands.

12. The answer should begin with a description of a stress-resilient child that is based on research cited in the chapter. Suggestions for helping children become more invulnerable should include development of competencies, social support structures, and religious factors.

13. Students' answers should reflect a good understanding of the impact that parents, grandparents, and teachers (as well as others) can have on a child's development. Caring, attention, and keeping in mind the child's best interest should be foremost in students' responses. The answers may be on a one-to-one level or they may reflect changes that could be made within the community.

14.   Stability is the key factor. Children must be placed in a situation where they do not move, change schools, or suffer separation from caregivers. Ideally, the parents should be rehabilitated so that they provide a more stable home. If not, the children need to be placed with more stable adults. It is also important that this answer includes the understanding that younger children are usually homeless in that they live in temporary facilities with their parents; in contrast adolescents may literally not have a roof over their heads because they have become runaways or throwaways—usually victims of their highly dysfunctional families.

Chapter 14

1.   In both boys and girls, the changes of puberty are triggered by hormonal signals from the hypothalamus to the pituitary gland. Hormones from the pituitary trigger increased production of estrogen and progesterone in girls and testosterone in boys. See Table 14.1, textbook page 342, for sequence of physical changes. Answers should also include information about differences between early and late maturers.

2.   There is a more rapid arousal of emotions. Emotions quickly shift to extremes, too. Boys experience an increase in sexual thoughts and in masturbation. Girls experience mood changes as a result of the ebb and flow of hormones during the menstrual cycle.

3.   Answers should include a description of the positive and negative characteristics of adolescents in each of the four conditions. The advice should include the impact of family conditions, schooling, peer groups, and the macrosystem (in particular, the media). For instance, both early-maturing girls and late-maturing boys might experience greater amounts of stress than their "on-time" peers. Late-maturing boys may never entirely "outgrow" their problem, as evidenced by their lack of adult leadership positions. Both sexes may be helped by a stable family environment, sex education in the schools, and alternative sources of status.

4.   Physical development in adolescence is often uneven, with the nose, lips, and ears growing before the head itself reaches adult size and shape. Therefore, the surgeon prefers to wait until Joshua's ears and head have finished growing so that permanent proportionate results can be achieved. As he is typical of those in his age group, Joshua is already concerned about his appearance and will probably want to have the defect "fixed" earlier.

5.   The 18-year-old's superior performance is due to his or her faster reaction time, increased heart and lung capacity, increased physical endurance, reduced likelihood of asthma, and greater strength.

6.   A description of the sequence of pubertal events should be given, accompanied by an explanation that the timing of these events is highly individualistic. Answers should include mention that pregnancy is possible, even though first menstrual cycles tend to be anovulatory and sperm concentrations tend to be low.

7.   Answers should reflect ways in which the body becomes prepared for reproduction. Changes in the uterus, vagina, testes, and penis should be addressed. Students should also mention menarche and spermarche, as well as an increased risk of pregnancy.

8.   Answers should mention changes in hair, voice, and breasts.

9.   Physical factors include the adolescent's uneven growth that often results in temporary anomalies and clumsiness. Social factors include the importance of appearance in gaining approval from members of the opposite sex and the possible effect of variations in timing. Among the cultural factors, students should mention the unrealistic standards of appearance promoted by the culture, especially the media.

10.   There are many. Suicide, drug abuse, and running away from home are a few self-destructive acts that sexually abused teens may engage in. Further, some teens vandalize or act violently following sexual victimization. Drug and alcohol usage, earlier sexual activity, school suspension, and dropping out are also more common for children who have been sexually abused. Girls are at a higher risk of pregnancy; boys often feel ashamed of their perceived weakness and may worry that they are homosexuals.

11.   Answers will vary, but they should not simply state that all drug use is evil. Students should mention specific measures, such as ongoing education, law enforcement, increasing prices, or teaching parents how to talk with their children.

Chapter 15

1.   Teenagers refine their ability to construct a logical argument, to persuade effectively, and to use words to stand for abstract ideas. They can reason hypothetically and use more complicated figures of speech, such as analogies, to communicate their needs.

2.   The teenager should be able to make systematic calculations based on multiplying the weight times the distance from center. Younger children will do this randomly or by trial-and-error.

3.   Analytic thought is formal, logical, rational, hypothetical, and deductive. Examples will vary, but it should involve rational analysis of many factors, such as the scale-balancing problem. Intuitive thought starts with a prior belief or assumption and involves applying memories or feelings. Examples will vary. Adolescents use intuitive thinking to such a great extent because it is fast and powerful. Additionally, increased hormonal production brings emotion to the forefront of adolescents' thought processes.

4.   Answers will vary, but students should demonstrate that they understand one of the types of adolescent egocentrism (invincibility fable, personal fable, or imaginary audience) described in the text.

5.   Students can mention modeling, the invincibility fable, making decisions based on intuitive thinking, poor analysis of risks and benefits, the thrills of acting in this way, the increased social status, or not considering all alternatives or possible outcomes.

6.   Examples will vary, but should involve a decision about school, jobs, sex, or risk-taking behavior. Students may mention some rational thought processes, but should be sure to include a description of intuitive or emotional thinking or adolescent egocentrism.

7.   Answers will vary. Recommendations should include measures to decrease the "volatile mismatch" between adolescents and the traditional structure of high schools. Examples include increasing supportive interaction among students and between students and teachers, decreasing class size, decreasing intense competition, making behavioral demands less rigid, changing the schedule to make school begin later and/or to allow subjects to be less delineated (allowing for curiosity and formal operational thought), increasing personal involvement in extracurricular activities, and encouraging students and teachers to focus on effort as a source of learning.

8.   Students' opinions here will differ, but students should mention that some drawbacks are that grades will probably decline, the teen might find the job to be boring, and that the money earned will probably be spent frivolously. The teen will be at an increased risk of using drugs and becoming sexually active. It is unrealistic to believe a job could help the teen become more responsible or better at managing money or that the job would be good preparation for a career.

9.   The text mentions that the facts about the biology of sex and the likelihood of pregnancy learned in sex education classes provide teens with experience with formal operational thought. Giving students practice with emotional expression and social interaction, such as saying "no," provides experience in intuitive thinking.

10.   Students should definitely mention the invincibility fable. Beyond that, answers may differ, but they might include the immediate benefits of unsafe behavior, not thinking through all possible consequences, and not having practice in saying "no" to coercion.

11.   Answers will vary. The answer should include grade or age at which the program would start, topics aimed at the interests of the children or adolescents, and a format that encourages formal operational thinking (small classes, high teacher-student interaction, personal involvement) and practice with saying "no" to coercion.

12.   Each ethnic group has a different pattern of teen risk-taking behavior, but one cannot make very accurate predictions from culture and ethnicity alone. Knowledge of family factors is more accurate. Students can mention factors such as whether the teen lives with one or both parents, income level, or family, school, peer, or individual characteristics.

Chapter 16

1.   Erikson's choice of a name (Erik, son of Erik) reflects his forging of a new identity. He maintains continuity with his past by using Homberger as his middle name. His wandering can be seen as a period of moratorium, and his choice of a career and vocation as identity achievement.

2.   Answers will vary, but the student should be able to choose one of the four identity statuses (foreclosure, diffusion, moratorium, or achievement) and provide evidence for that choice.

3.   Identity achievement refers to the point at which an individual understands who he or she is as a unique individual. This status is characterized by questioning and commitment. Identity diffusion refers to a state in which an individual is apathetic about who they are. This status is characterized by not questioning and no commitment. Identity moratorium refers to a state in which an individual is taking a break from identity formation to explore alternatives. This status is characterized by questioning and no commitment. Identity foreclosure refers to a premature identity formation in which an adolescent adopts parents' or society's roles and values without questioning them. This status is characterized by not questioning and commitment.

4.   Answers will vary, but students should point out that the less flexible roles of the 1950s probably caused more foreclosure and perhaps less diffusion than now. Students should indicate that the change in levels of foreclosure is probably more pronounced for women than it is for men.

5.   Answers will vary. Drugs or alcohol might form part of a negative identity as a way of disobeying parents. They might be part of the aimless casting around characteristic of diffusion or the experimentation of the moratorium phase. This period may pass without incident.

6.   The general trend is for feelings of competence and self-esteem to decrease from childhood through adolescence. This pattern is similar across a wide variety of domains, and it is consistent across genders and cultures.

7.   There are numerous answers here. Parasuicide, suicidal ideation, and cluster suicide could be mentioned, as well as depression and frequent fits of rage. The following factors increase the likelihood that suicidal ideation will lead to a suicidal plan, parasuicide, or death: availability of lethal means (especially guns), lack of parental supervision, use of alcohol and other drugs, being male, and cultural attitudes.

8.　　The rates of suicidal ideation and parasuicide are higher for females than for males, but the rate of actual suicide is higher for males than for females. The higher rates of suicidal ideation and parasuicide for females stem from higher rates of depression for females. But, females also have a greater likelihood of seeking help or signaling distress and a lower likelihood of using immediately lethal means (such as guns), leading to a lower rate of actual suicides among females.

9.　　Incidence refers to how often adolescent crime occurs. The incidence tends to be high. Prevalence refers to how widespread adolescent crime is. The prevalence also tends to be high. This means that cracking down on a few repeat offenders will not bring the adolescent crime rate down much, since there are many offenders who commit only one crime.

10.　　Answers will vary, but students should demonstrate knowledge of the following two points. First, life-course-persistent offenders have a history. They are antisocial in preschool and elementary school, show signs of brain damage (hyperactivity, poor emotional control, being slow to express ideas in language), are the first of their cohort to have sex and use drugs, are least involved in school activities, and are most involved in hanging out with older, lawbreaking youths. Second, those with this childhood history who have some kind of support (exceptional school, cohesive neighborhood, supportive peers, or a stable family) are *less* likely to become life-course-persistent offenders. Grant money should focus on children with this history. Grant money could go toward taking these children out of the environment (as in foster care), providing parental training, or providing training for children on how to cope with their problems.

11.　　Students may mention the invincibility fable (see Chapter 15), lack of parental interest and supervision, problems in school achievement and social life, socioeconomic class, unemployment, and so on. Solutions should focus on effective ways to address these root causes.

12.　　Students should note that parents need to allow their children to stand on their own feet, fall over sometimes, and get back up again. Independence and autonomy are important topics at both developmental stages: verbal restraints are more likely to be placed on the teenager's independence as opposed to the physical limits placed on the toddler. At both stages, parents must loosen their hold over the young person's actions in an age-limited, responsible way, encouraging learning about the world, independence, and feelings of self-competence, while providing a base of love and support.

13.　　When an adolescent goes away to school, the mother is relieved of the role of "nagger." While at home, the mother usually has more conflict with the adolescent because she is the one to remind her child to do homework, to perform chores, and to keep on top of personal hygiene. With the child away at school, much of this becomes the responsibility of the child. The adolescent gains more independence, which may be more satisfying.

14.　　Parents should know where their children are and what they are doing. Effective parental monitoring helps to limit adolescent use of alcohol and drugs, as well as weapons. If parents are too interfering and exert too much control, however, it can lead to depression in the adolescent. The teen will not feel trusted, competent, or loved. This can lead to anxiety and rebellion.

15.　　(1) Adolescents do not simply fall in with the wrong crowd. They seek out peers who are similar to them in values and interests. (It is true, however, that negative peer influence can be stronger in times of uncertainty, as when a student is new to a school.) (2) It is true that adolescents behave in ways together that they would not do individually.

16.　　Answers will vary. Peers can support changes associated with adolescence, they can allow for experimentation with identity, they can be a sounding board, and they can help to negotiate conflicts at home or with one's culture. The student should provide specific examples of when the peer group did or did not live up to these functions.

17.　　(1) Groups of same-sex friends, (2) loose associations of girls' and boys' groups, with all interactions very public, (3) smaller, mixed-sex groups, formed from the more advanced members of the larger association, and (4) pairing off of heterosexual couples, with private intimacies.

Chapter 17

1.   Answers will vary. Students may point to (1) the greater percentage of violent deaths for young men (causes include testosterone, male gender roles, the explosive combination of high self-esteem and dashed expectations); (2) the increased rate of senescence for males (causes include the fact that men don't take care of themselves as well as women or themselves, biological factors such as estrogen, and psychological factors such as marriage, friendship, and help-seeking that are more prevalent among women); or (3) the earlier decrease in sexual responsiveness for males (causes include cultural conditioning and evolution).

2.   Answers will vary. Good news may include increased physical strength and that decreases in organ capacity and rate of homeostatic adjustments are rarely perceived. Bad news may include changes in skin tone, hair color and quantity, lung efficiency, and vision and hearing.

3.   Young adulthood is the most common period for drug use and drug abuse. Answers for contributing factors will vary. The stressful transitions of the early adult period (e.g., the need to establish a residence of one's own, make career decisions, achieve intimacy, etc.) are discussed in this chapter. Living away from home, frequenting bars and large parties, living in an urban area, not being religiously involved, failing to seek medical advice, and being single are among the factors that correlate with drug abuse in early adulthood.

4.   Answers will vary but should contain a discussion of the causes of infertility in both men and women. They should also include ideal reproductive ages for both the man and the woman. Treatments such as in vitro fertilization should be described.

5.   The factors include cultural pressure to be thin, a need to find a husband, conflict with parents, genetic influences, and pressure in the workplace to be more like men. Students should demonstrate an understanding of two of these factors and propose a solution.

6.   Answers will vary. Students should demonstrate an understanding of the factors involved. Due to genetics, lifestyle choices, or exercise, differences in fitness and physical abilities in work and leisure activities will occur. Differences in organ reserve and the effects of drug use may be included. Psychological satisfaction should be greater for the person who is fit and toned.

7.   The uncle has probably stopped playing on the softball team because he can no longer compete with younger players. He has gained weight over the years even though he has tried several diets but has been unable to keep off the weight. He probably did not start wearing corrective lenses until his 40s. He has noticed a gradual slowing down in all of his physical abilities over the past 30 years.

8.   Homeostasis is the body's attempt to maintain equilibrium. Examples could include the body's responses to hunger and thirst, regulation of the heart rate when exercising and at rest, perspiring to cool the body and shivering to warm it, and breathing deeply during periods of activity.

Chapter 18

1.   Answers will vary. Academic course work employs formal thinking; so might certain games and activities involving logical reasoning, and certain kinds of financial planning. Problems dealing with choices, compromises, and contradictions involving a large number of variables would probably benefit more from postformal thinking; among those are problems in relating to others.

2.   Answers will vary. Findings include: (1) adults are better than adolescents at seeing multiple perspectives; (2) adolescents are particularly bad at reasoning when emotions are involved; (3) adolescents strongly believe in either objective or subjective thought, whereas adults are better able to use both in combination; and (4) adults are better able to combine experience with knowledge.

3.   The possibility that one's appearance or behavior will be misused to confirm another person's oversimplified, prejudiced attitude is referred to as stereotype threat. Examples will vary. Answers will vary, but may include: (1) Women might not get involved in technological fields because they are afraid that they will do poorly and their performance will be evidence in support of the stereotype that women are not technologically savvy; (2) Women may come to believe the stereotype; or (3) Women may tell themselves that technological abilities are unimportant and thus devalue these skills.

4.   Dialectical thinking involves integrating an idea with its antithesis into a new idea. Examples will vary, but they should demonstrate an understanding of integrating an idea with its opposite. Dialectical thinking contributes to an evolving view of oneself or of the world because no answer is ever final. Ideas are constantly being synthesized with their opposites.

5.   The decisions that adults are forced to make require them to be flexible, reflective, and dialectical, stimulating moral growth. Students may point out that the decision-making process can lead adults to deeper convictions. Examples will vary but should demonstrate this claim.

6.   Answers will vary. The two examples should be appropriately labeled for the stages described. Students may point out that Fowler's theory is only the opinion of one person and not a given fact. Criticisms may include an understanding that various stages of faith may be more appropriate at different points in a person's development and for different situations and questions about why so few people advance to the final stages.

7.   Answers should include current demographics (e.g., more women, lower-income students, ethnic minorities), differences in patterns of education (e.g., more part-time students, more working students, more career-based curriculum, greater importance placed on financial benefits of getting a degree), and the differences in structure (e.g., higher enrollment in community colleges; more female and minority instructors). Students' opinions will vary, but may include that any collegiate education heightens cognitive skills regardless of where one goes to school; but factors like the form of instruction and the cultural life of the school probably affect cognitive growth.

8.   The postformal approach picks up where Piaget left off, emphasizing the possible emergence of a new stage of thinking and reasoning in adulthood. The psychometric approach uses IQ tests to analyze the components of intelligence. The information-processing approach studies the encoding, storage, and retrieval of information throughout life.

Chapter 19

1.   Maslow believed that adult needs are hierarchical; that basic needs, such as food and safety, need to be met before other needs can be addressed. Love and belonging come once the two levels of basic needs are met, and then success and esteem follow. Answers will vary, but students should provide a clear explanation for why they agree or disagree and offer an example that supports their argument.

2.   Answers will vary. Female friendships are more self-disclosing and more emotional, and females spend a great deal of time just talking. Male friendships are about sharing activities and interests. Intimacy is peripheral to these activities. Females are looking for an attentive and sympathetic ear from their friends, whereas males expect practical advice. Cross-sex friendships are particularly difficult because of the different needs and expectations of the two friends. In addition, sexual boundaries may be an issue.

3.   The answer should note that the social clock, which indicates that Frank is late, does allow for variations. Acceptable variations may include extended education, such as graduate school, family responsibilities, or volunteer service. A higher-level job would engender more consideration for the delay, and a higher SES individual would not be expected to conform as strictly to the early norms.

4.   The three dimensions of love are passion, intimacy, and commitment. Examples will vary. At the beginning of a relationship, liking, infatuation, and romantic love are probably common, whereas empty love, companionate love, and consummate love take time to develop. Students must specify whether each example does or does not have passion, does or does not have intimacy, and does or does not have commitment.

5.   Answers will vary, but students should give an example from each of the three categories delineated in Table 19.5 on page 472.

6.   Common couple violence refers to a form of abuse in which one or both partners engage in outbursts of verbal and physical attack. Intimate terrorism refers to a very controlling form of abuse in which one partner, usually the man, uses violent methods of accelerating intensity to isolate, degrade, and punish the other partner. Students' answers may vary, but they should provide support for their argument. The high level of control in intimate terrorism probably makes that type less likely to lead to divorce.

7.   Answers will vary but should include two negative aspects of both parents working such as workload problems, equity of household chores, child care responsibilities, and increased risk of divorce because of not spending adequate time together; positive impact might include the wife's greater satisfaction with her roles, extra money, more equity in roles, and child care responsibilities.

8.   Answers will vary but should be supported by the research discussed in the text.

9.   Answers will vary but may include changes in the type of work, who the workers are, the workplace itself, the schedule, and the teamwork involved. Answers should include a description of the effects of each of the three examples on individuals and/or families.

10.   A social clock is a timetable, based on social norms, for the "best" ages for particular events and endeavors, such as becoming independent from one's parents, finishing school, establishing a career, and having children. Examples will vary.

Chapter 20

1.   Answers will vary, but students should demonstrate an understanding of at least five changes that occur during the ages of 35 to 65.

2.   Describe the differences between primary and secondary aging, and give an example of each.

3.   Answers will vary. Students should develop five recommendations. Examples include avoiding smoking and drug and alcohol abuse, exercising regularly, decreasing stress, avoiding excessively loud noises, getting preventative medical care, and avoiding obesity.

4.   Answers should mention changes in appearance, which may be more difficult for women in our culture; greater hearing loss among men; higher incidence of chronic illnesses such as arthritis among women; and the special vulnerability of women to breast cancer and osteoporosis. Differences in the way men and women experience reproductive changes and express their sexuality should also be discussed.

5.   Students should define mortality, morbidity, disability, and vitality. Answers regarding the most important measure will vary, but should be supported with arguments.

6.   Answers will vary, but students should demonstrate an understanding that QALYs involve all four measures of health and that one QALY is given for each perfectly healthy year.

7.   Answers will vary, but may include differences in genes, access to and quality of health care, stress, nutrition, prejudice, pollution, crowding, drug use, and exercise.

Chapter 21

1.   Answers will vary and should identify qualitative differences between the expert and novice, such as more intuitive, more automatic, more strategic, and more flexible.

2.   Answers will vary. Students will probably mention computers and related technological changes as distinguishing features of their own experience and that of the upcoming generation. Other recent changes include wider availability of preschool and after-school programs, which add up to more time spent away from home, and the various toys and programs aimed at teaching infants. Examples chosen are less important than that students demonstrate an understanding of what constitutes a cohort difference and of how such differences might affect learning.

3.   Answers will vary. The best answers will describe a specific and measurable intelligence and a research design appropriate to studying it.

4.   Answers should focus on multidimensionality of intelligence and the evidence that supports it, the fact that different abilities have different patterns of development in adulthood, and that intelligence may be shaped by experience. Looking at the type of intelligence measured by standard IQ tests will reveal a different picture than looking at a variety of abilities.

5.   Answers will vary. The woman should work on emotional relationships, education, and financial security. Physical health is also a factor in intellectual functioning, so good health habits should be maintained. The woman will likely experience decline in some abilities more than others, but she should be able to maintain skills in her area(s) of expertise.

6.   Answers will vary, but may include the following: (1) In general, intellectual abilities increase slightly from the beginning of adulthood until midlife and then remain stable through middle adulthood; (2) Age-related declines in intellectual functioning are first noted in items that require quick thinking and speedy reaction time; (3) Intellectual functioning as measured by IQ tests is powerfully influenced by years of schooling in childhood, adolescence, and early adulthood, and some of a person's level of intellectual functioning throughout adulthood is a direct result of education received years earlier; (4) Especially during adulthood, intelligence follows many patterns of development; (5) Experts are able to keep their abilities at high levels in comparison with novices.

Chapter 22

1.   Answers will vary, but students should demonstrate an understanding of gender convergence.

2.   The answer should include a person who is representative of each of the categories: agreeableness, extroversion, openness, conscientiousness, and neuroticism. Specific behaviors should be included that support the choices of category for the person.

3.   Answers will vary, but students should point out that many middle-aged adults find themselves in the position of having to care for their aging parents at the same time that their grown children are turning to them for financial help and child care. This is a concern for employers who want a large number of work hours from their employees. Women are more likely to be kinkeepers and caretakers, especially daughters (more so than daughters-in-law). Adults who provide assistance probably have a generous personality.

4.   Answers will vary, but students should demonstrate that for both men and women, having multiple roles should protect them from the stresses of midlife and from strains in their careers.

5.   Answers will vary, but may include one's ecological niche which is influenced by such things as the death of a spouse, a new career, moving to a new cultural setting, taking mood-altering medications, and age.

6.   Answers will vary but will most likely include two of the following: midlife crisis, sandwich generation, or role overload.

7.   Answers will vary but may likely include two of the following: divorce rate, changes in marital happiness with age, retirement plans, or grandparenting.

Chapter 23

1.   Answers will vary but should include suggestions on ways to integrate the elderly back into the community and with their relatives instead of segregating them. Also, it might be suggested that researchers focus more on the young-old and less on the oldest-old.

2.   Answers should emphasize the importance of prevention, compensation, and remediation. For example, advice about exercise, diet, routine tests of vision and hearing, monitoring for the early stages of disease, compensating rather than passively accepting losses, and maintaining active interests and pleasure in life might all be included.

3.   Answers should acknowledge the fact that the body does not wear out like a machine but can repair itself and replace damaged cells. However, there is a slowdown of functions. The other theories deal with cellular accidents (free radicals), decline in the effectiveness of immune system, and genetic preprogramming (end of cell division).

4.   Answers will vary but may focus on several areas: the present physical condition of elderly relatives, health habits of the individual, and the potential for development of cures for illnesses such as arthritis, heart disease, and cancer.

5.   Answers will vary but should reflect that the increasing number of elderly in our society and the advance of gerontology will no doubt produce dramatic changes in attitudes toward the old and how they are treated.

6.   Students' responses should reflect an openness to finding individuals who are healthy, active (though probably limited in the physical activities they can pursue), interesting, and involved in life.

7.   There are many ways to define aging and the students' answers will be varied. The importance of both physical health and psychological attitude should be stressed.

8.   The four factors are technology, specialist care, personal determination, and personal and/or cultural accommodation. Students should provide an example of each.

Chapter 24

1.   Answers should note the difficulty older adults have in making fast responses, and therefore, should recommend an untimed test. An emphasis should be placed on real-life and adaptive problem-solving skills. And the test should be standardized on older adults.

2.   All answers should suggest that the relative be examined by a physician to rule out physical problems such as overmedication, undernourishment, and dehydration. Psychological problems should also be considered. The relative severity of the problem should be carefully evaluated and the progression of cognitive deficits should be analyzed. If the symptoms have been increasing steadily over a number of months or years, the problem may be Alzheimer's disease. If the problem appeared suddenly, the relative may be a victim of multi-infarct dementia. If the relative is bothered by problems, it is more likely to be due to depression or anxiety.

3.   The activities suggested should recognize the greater aesthetic sense and the increased philosophical approach. Answers will vary. These areas could be enhanced with programs in art and nature that allow the members to express their creativity in an individualistic way and discussions and debates on philosophical issues that require high levels of reflection and review.

4.   Although answers will be highly individualized, look for an appreciation of the skills characteristic of each age group.

5.   The elderly individual can be sure to get plenty of exercise and cognitive stimulation, and he or she should stay on a healthy diet and get plenty of vitamins C and E. There may be some benefit in taking some amounts of aspirin or Ibuprofen. Overmedication should be prevented, and mental health should be maintained.

6.   Answers will vary, but may include application of issues about ageism, sensory threshold problems, resistance, compensation, preventative measures, greater problems with explicit memory than with implicit memory, and the life review.

Chapter 25

1.   Answers will vary, but students should demonstrate an understanding of their chosen theory.

2.   Answers will vary, but students should demonstrate an understanding of the concept.

3.   Answers should recognize the importance of staying active and independent, involved with the community and family, and/or recognizing and compensating for limitations as they arise.

4.   Students' social plans should recognize the variety of individual interests and activities residents will enjoy and should allow for choice and control by residents.

5.   Positive responses should recognize that intimate relationships are important for the elderly person in terms of their caregiving and emotional well-being. Negative responses may include feelings of anger or betrayal or a failure to value the importance of late-adult relationships. Stereotypes that may be explored include the view that children and grandchildren can fulfill all the affiliation needs an older person might have and also a mistrust of decisions made by older people.

6.   Answers should reflect the needs of the elderly, especially those who are institutionalized. Suggestions should include a variety of interesting activities from which residents can choose, opportunities for residents to use their creative abilities, and social activities calling for cooperation among residents themselves and with the outside community.

7.   In addition to well-balanced meals and good medical care, designs should include attention to physical well-being, physical concerns such as handrails, tacked down carpeting, good lighting, and so forth. Equally important is an emphasis on privacy and the maintenance of residents' cognitive and psychosocial skills, which can be helped by encouraging residents to actively participate in their own care.

8.   Answers will vary but may include the emotional well-being of the proposed caregiver, whether the elderly person has dementia, financial concerns, and social support for the caregiver.

Epilogue

1.   While wide individual variation can be expected, students should demonstrate appreciation of the value of rituals to the bereavement process and the value of social support for family and close friends.

2.   Students answers will vary but they should demonstrate an understanding of the importance of grief and reaffirmation. For instance, as examples of what to say or do, one should not ignore the mourner's grief, or leave her alone without support (unless she requests to be alone), or tell her to move on with her life.

3.   The answer should include a brief explanation of the difference between voluntary euthanasia and assisted suicide. Specific examples should be used to justify whichever side of the issue is supported.

4.   Among the things considered, students should demonstrate an understanding of the goal of hospice care and what criteria should be used for admittance. Answers should attempt to address the criticisms of current hospice care.

5.   Answers will vary, but students should demonstrate an understanding of the desire of some to die naturally.

6.   Answers will vary, but students should demonstrate an understanding of living wills, health care proxies, and perhaps euthanasia.